THE CHURCH IN ENGLAND

Imprimatur
> JOANNES A. CHARLTON, C.SS.R.,
> *Prov. Sup. Ang.*

Nihil Obstat
> HENRICUS DAVIS, S.J.,
> *Censor Deputatus.*

Imprimatur
> EDM. CAN. SURMONT,
> *Vic. Gen.*

WESTMONASTERII,
27 *Januarii*, 1921.

THE CHURCH IN ENGLAND

BY
THE REV. GEORGE STEBBING, C.SS.R.

AUTHOR OF
"THE STORY OF THE CATHOLIC CHURCH"

WIPF & STOCK · Eugene, Oregon

Wipf and Stock Publishers
199 W 8th Ave, Suite 3
Eugene, OR 97401

The Church in England
By Stebbing, George, C. SS. R
ISBN 13: 978-1-60899-802-9
Publication date 7/30/2010
Previously published by Herder, 1921

PREFACE

THIS elementary book upon the fortunes of the Catholic Church in England is planned on somewhat similar lines to those which the present writer had in his mind some years ago in writing the *Story of the Catholic Church*. But, in the present case, he has been preceded by a greater number of able English writers than had gone before him in his former enterprise. Yet, once again, he would fain hope that his labour has not been in vain. At any rate, he believes that he has been able to gather into one continuous whole, reaching down to the present day, information not easily accessible to the general reader.

The chapters have been numbered in one unbroken succession, and hence not grouped into epochs or periods. Such divisions are often very arbitrary, though the present writer still thinks that the dividing line between the Middle Ages and Modern Times should be placed earlier than some historians place it. The gathering of the whole period from the break of Henry VIII. with the Church till the accession of Elizabeth into one chapter is meant to emphasise the fact that the mighty changes of those years all took place in a space of time only equal to the reign of Henry VII. or the Catholic part of the reign of Henry VIII.

The author feels that he need not apologise for the relatively large space taken up by the Tables, by the Chronological Index and by the General Index at the end. These things must add to the value of a book of this kind.

PREFACE

He further desires to return his heartfelt thanks for the self-sacrificing labours of Rev. Henry Davis, S.J., the Diocesan Censor, and for those onerous works of charity which Rev. Austin Clark, C.Ss.R., and Rev. Joseph Coyne, C.Ss.R., took upon themselves, the former in making the exceptionally full index, and the latter in revising the proofs.

THE AUTHOR.

CONTENTS

		PAGE
PREFACE		vii
I.	THE CHURCH IN ROMAN BRITAIN (A.D. 63-597)	1
II.	THE APOSTLES OF ENGLAND (597-625)	17
III.	EVANGELISATION OF THE HEPTARCHY (625-671)	27
IV.	THE ORGANISATION OF THE ANGLO-SAXON CHURCH (671-735)	43
V.	THE TRIPLE LEADERSHIP (735-800)	56
VI.	THE RISE OF WESSEX (800-871)	66
VII.	MAKERS OF ANGLO-SAXON MONARCHY (A) KING ALFRED THE GREAT (871-901) (B) EDWARD THE ELDER AND ATHELSTAN (901-940)	75 84
VIII.	THE ADMINISTRATION OF ST DUNSTAN (940-978)	90
IX.	THE DANISH CONQUEST OF ENGLAND (978-1042)	100
X.	REIGN OF ST EDWARD THE CONFESSOR (1042-1066)	112
XI.	THE LIFE OF THE ANGLO-SAXON CHURCH	123
XII.	THE NORMAN CONQUEST (1066-1087)	140
XIII.	ENGLAND UNDER THE CONQUEROR'S SONS (1087-1135)	152
XIV.	THE TRANSITION UNDER STEPHEN (1135-1154)	167
XV.	HENRY PLANTAGENET AND THE CHURCH (1154-1189)	178
XVI.	CŒUR DE LION AND LACKLAND (A) RICHARD I. (1189-1199) (B) THE REIGN OF KING JOHN (1199-1216)	196 203
XVII.	THE CHURCH UNDER HENRY III. (1216-1272)	212

CONTENTS

		PAGE
XVIII.	EDWARD I.—THE ENGLISH JUSTINIAN (1272-1307)	233
XIX.	THE DESCENDANTS OF EDWARD I.	
	(A) EDWARD II. (1307-1327)	245
	(B) EARLIER YEARS OF EDWARD III. (1327-1349)	252
XX.	THE DECLINE OF THE PLANTAGENETS	
	(A) LATER YEARS OF EDWARD III. (1349-1377)	260
	(B) THE REIGN OF RICHARD II. (1377-1399)	271
XXI.	THE CHURCH UNDER THE HOUSE OF LANCASTER	
	(A) HENRY IV. (1399-1413)	283
	(B) HENRY V. (1413-1422)	290
	(C) HENRY VI. UP TO THE WARS OF THE ROSES (1422-1455)	296
XXII.	THE EPOCH OF THE WARS OF THE ROSES (1455-1485)	305
XXIII.	CATHOLIC LIFE IN MEDIAEVAL ENGLAND (1066-1485)	315
XXIV.	THE HOUSE OF TUDOR AND THE RENAISSANCE (1485-1509)	336
XXV.	THE DEFENDER OF THE FAITH (1509-1534)	348
XXVI.	THE ROYAL SUPREMACY	
	(A) HENRY VIII. (1534-1547)	363
	(B) EDWARD VI. (1547-1553)	379
	(C) RESTORATION UNDER MARY (1553-1558)	386
XXVII.	THE ELIZABETHAN SETTLEMENT (1558-1603)	397
XXVIII.	CATHOLICS AND PURITANS	
	(A) JAMES I. (1603-1625)	418
	(B) CHARLES I. AND THE COMMONWEALTH (1625-1660)	429
XXIX.	CATHOLICS AND THE RESTORATION (1660-1689)	442

CONTENTS

		PAGE
XXX.	Catholics and the Revolution (1689-1745)	461
XXXI.	The Pressure of the Penal Laws (1745-1778)	472
XXXII.	The Early Relief Acts (1778-1803)	482
XXXIII.	Catholic Emancipation (1803-1829)	498
XXXIV.	The Restoration of the Hierarchy	
	(A) Catholic Revival before the Hierarchy (1830-1850)	515
	(B) Development under the Hierarchy (1850-1865)	531
XXXV.	The Battle for Catholic Education (1865-1892)	542
XXXVI.	The Dawn of the Twentieth Century (1892-1919)	557
XXXVII.	Catholic Life in Modern England	569

Leaders and Prelates 581
Chronological Index 593
General Index 599
List of Some Books of Reference 617

THE CHURCH IN ENGLAND

I.

THE CHURCH IN ROMAN BRITAIN.

(A.D. 63-597.)

HAD our eyes ranged over the surface of England as it was in the Middle Ages, they would certainly have been arrested on the southern slope of the hills in Somerset. For, somewhat raised above the level of the plain, which lies at the foot of the Mendip range, they would have been caught by a vision of beauty. There was to be seen a glorious minster stretching across the landscape; this was the Abbey Church of Glastonbury. And around it was clustered a noble pile of monastic buildings, and then, farther off, the churches, and towers, and cottages of Glastonbury village. Of all this religious splendour there now remain but scanty ruins—an arch here, an ancient chapel here, a crumbling wall there. It is true that with loving reverence the nation has purchased at a great price that shadow of departed glory. But it is vain to hope that it will ever rise again. All the more welcome therefore is it that on a neighbouring hillside, almost within sight, there are crystallising into shape the stately church and abbey of Downside: almost a challenge from the monks of to-day to the ancestors whose work and whose memory they keep alive! And there is much to remember at Glastonbury. It is the centre of those venerable legends which connect the beginnings of Christianity in our midst with the immediate disciples of Our Lord. Even if, as Professor

Glastonbury Abbey.

Freeman has said, we do not accept the Glastonbury legends as facts, that they have existed in the way they have is a great fact. It is for this reason, not from any desire to give to those traditions more than their just value, that the Story of the Catholic Church in England must start with these primitive times. It is for this reason also that the historical student must turn first to the scenes so long believed to be the place where the Faith was first planted in the land. Those traditions bring before us the legends of St Joseph of Arimathea. We cannot forget that on this legend hung in great part the importance of Glastonbury in Mediaeval England. This was the association which won for it the popular name of the English Jerusalem. What then was the popular belief about the place?

Legend of St Joseph of Arimathea.

William of Malmesbury, one of the most celebrated of the monastic chroniclers, relates that in the year A.D. 63 Joseph of Arimathea was sent into Britain with eleven companions by the Apostle St Philip, and that he, being hospitably welcomed by the king, Arviragus by name, was endowed by him with twelve hides of land in the Isle of Glass, sometimes called Avalon. Iniswytryn was the Celtic name of this place, and here these first missionaries, he tells us, built a wattled church of wood in honour of the Blessed Virgin; here also Joseph of Arimathea, when his earthly course was finished, laid his bones. The marshy streams from the Somersetshire moors flowing round Iniswytryn formed a boundary and a defence. Thither also came, according to the same chronicler, the missionaries sent by Pope St Eleutherius. Thither likewise, as he would have us believe, came St Patrick and Benignus his disciple. Thither also came St David the Patron of Wales. Later traditions added the history of the Glastonbury thorn, as being St Joseph's staff, struck into the ground, and blossoming miraculously at Christmastide. Thus it will be seen that the traditions of the church in Roman Britain circle to a large extent round Glastonbury. To our Catholic ancestors it was the starting point of their primitive Christianity. And this pride of place was allowed to prevail in practical life so far as to set the Abbot of this monastery in a place of pre-eminence among his brethren from elsewhere, and to make the Abbey a storehouse of pious offerings from all classes in the land, the highest as well as the lowest.

The legend of St Joseph of Arimathea is not the only one we can read of as to the beginnings of the Faith in Britain, but the next in order of time which needs to be mentioned carries us on into the next century. It would seem to have its origin in a single sentence of the old Book of the Popes or Liber Pontificalis, which is of the fifth century. It is there stated that the Pope St Eleutherius, who filled the Papal Chair approximately from A.D. 173 to 188, received a letter from Lucius, King of the Britons, asking for admission into the Christian Church. Venerable Bede, who copied this sentence into his "Ecclesiastical History," goes on to say that thenceforward the Britons remained in tranquil possession of the Faith which they had received until the persecution of Diocletian. Chronicles of the eleventh century add further details, the Book of Llandaff localising the place to which the Roman missionaries came as South Wales. Geoffrey of Monmouth gives their names as Faganus and Duvanus. William of Malmesbury makes them settle at Glastonbury, and there re-people the site already hallowed by St Joseph of Arimathea with twelve holy anchorites as before, the same twelve hides of land being once more occupied by them. It is a problem to the learned how much truth underlies this tradition. It is antecedently quite improbable, but there seems no adequate reason for its gratuitous insertion in the Liber Pontificalis. But, at any rate, we know enough of the Roman power and methods of conquest to feel sure that no independent king could have reigned over South Britain in the second century. At that we must leave it. Positive evidence is almost entirely wanting as to the progress of Christianity in that and in the following century. There is the *obiter dictum* of Tertullian that Britain and places untrod by the Romans already contained Christians in his day. No doubt here, as in the other Provinces of the Empire, the advance of the Faith was a very chequered and gradual process. Beginning with a convert here, and another there, these new disciples of Christ would usually practise their religion in secret for fear of persecution. There was constant intercourse between the various

Roman Provinces and the centre of the Empire. A few well-known names have been preserved and cherished, as being those of individuals who were Christians and Britons as well. Bran, the father of Caractacus, is reported to have become a Christian while kept as a hostage at Rome. Claudia, the wife of Pudens the Senator, mentioned by St Paul, is considered to have been a Briton, and the same thing is assumed, though on weaker authority, about Pomponia Græcina, wife of the Governor Aulus Plautius. Among the legionaries sent to Britain would certainly have been found a certain number of Christian soldiers, and this in increasing numbers as the years rolled on.

The material remains of the imperial dominion in the island are interesting enough. The arrangements made for administration differed and developed with the progress of the conquest. The most complete organisation of which we have any record counted the whole of Britain as the seventh Diocese of the whole Empire, placing it in the Prefecture of Gaul, under a vicar or legate of the Prefect of that quarter of the Roman world. It then comprised five or for a short period six provinces, namely, Britannia Prima, Britannia Secunda, Flavia Cæsariensis, Maxima Cæsariensis, and Valentia. The sites of the chief Roman cities have also been identified, and if there is any foundation for the statement of Geoffrey of Monmouth that the British Church contained three metropolitan and twenty-eight episcopal sees, these cities would suggest the position of most of them. But much controversy has taken place among antiquaries as to the relative position and importance of these towns. There would seem to have been six which enjoyed more municipal independence and privileges than the rest. These were St Albans (Verulam), York, Chester, Lincoln, Gloucester, and London. To these may be possibly added Caerleon or Usk. The names of some eighty others are known, in many cases occupying the sites of existing British towns. Some of the best known were Colchester, Cirencester, Wroxeter, Sarum, Leicester, Exeter, and Winchester. There were ports at Richborough, Dover, and other places. At Silchester, near Reading, the foundations of a complete Roman town have been excavated, with the ground plan of a small

Roman Remains.

Christian church or basilica: almost the only case where either of those two things has been done. Roman forts and villas continue to be disinterred from time to time. The ruins of two Roman walls, that of Hadrian from the Tyne to the Solway, and that of Antonine from the Forth to the Clyde, still exist in various places. The network of stone-paved roads is still traceable among the highways of the land with such names as Watling Street, Ermine Street, Stane Street, Akeman Street, the Fosse Way, and Iknield Way. In addition there have been found in plenty such things as coins, images, inscriptions, and pottery. But they are nearly all the traces of civilisation which was pagan, or at least not distinctly Christian in its character.

It is when we come to the Tenth Persecution, which began about the year A.D. 303, that we meet with something more definite and positive with regard to Christianity. To this period belongs the martyrdom of St Alban, who is called the Protomartyr of Britain. However, there is some difficulty in assigning the exact date to his death. Diocletian, who began his reign in 284, did not give rein to the persecutor's rage for nearly twenty years after this, namely, in 303, and about this time Constantius Chlorus was already Cæsar or secondary Emperor in Britain. As to place the information is more satisfactory. Moreover, there is the monumental evidence of the great Abbey of St Alban's still standing in its unrivalled length of six hundred feet: more fortunate in its preservation than Glastonbury has been. It is a silent witness to the tradition that St Alban suffered in the neighbourhood of the Roman *municipium* of Verulam. This was the first city of importance founded by the Romans in the island, and it always retained a privileged position throughout the four hundred years of their domination. St Bede tells us that during the persecution of Diocletian, a pagan of Verulam gave hospitality to a Christian priest, whose name, according to Geoffrey of Monmouth, was Amphibalus, sheltering him thus from the pursuit of his persecutors. This pagan was the Alban who afterwards was honoured as the Protomartyr. He noticed that his guest spent his time day and night in continual watching and prayer. Then, after some days had passed, a ray of Divine Light

St Alban the Protomartyr of Britain.

shone upon Alban, showing him that the religion which
led to such close union with God must be the true one.
He therefore asked the priest to instruct and baptise
him. Amphibalus did so, but it was not long before it
came to the ears of the pagans that a Christian lay
concealed in Alban's house, and in consequence a
search-party was sent to apprehend him. This gave his
host the immediate opportunity for an act of heroism.
When the soldiers drew near, in order to save his guest,
he clothed himself in the long robe of the priesthood
and was seized and led off to trial as though he himself
were the Christian priest. He was brought before the
judge at the very moment when the pagan magistrate
was sacrificing to the heathen gods. Alban was at once
interrogated, when he boldly confessed that he was a
Christian. He was straightway called upon to offer
sacrifice to the idols whom the judge was worshipping.
Then, on his refusal, he was scourged. But Alban
bore it all not only with courage, but even with joy. So,
seeing him unconquerable, the judge sentenced him to
death. Followed by a large concourse of people who
assembled to witness his fate, Alban was led out of
Verulam to a pleasant hill, says St Bede, some five
hundred paces distant, well suited to be the scene of a
martyr's triumph. It was green with verdure and radiant
with field flowers. Together with St Alban there
suffered also the executioner, Heraclius, who, marvelling
at the sight of the wonders which took place on the
occasion, refused to behead Alban and became Christian,
being baptised in his own blood. Some time later, it is
related, the priest, Amphibalus, died a martyr's death.
Many other Christians also suffered in the Tenth
General Persecution in England: the names of SS.
Aaron and Julius have been preserved, but Caerleon,
Chester, and Carlisle have all been assigned as the place
of their martyrdom.

The first gathering of the Church in Council after the
Edict of Milan gave it peace, and made such an assembly
possible for East and West, was that held at Nicæa in
325. This was the first Ecumenical Council. But
twelve years earlier, immediately after the granting of
toleration to Christianity, that is to say in 314, there
was an important Council at Arles, in Gaul, which
affected the whole of the Western Patriarchate. Just as

CHURCH IN ROMAN BRITAIN 7

Arius and his heresy gave occasion to the meeting at Nicæa, so did the schism of Donatus lead to the gathering at Arles. In the one case as in the other we find advantage taken of the Council thus convoked to pass canons of discipline for the general good of the Church. Further, in the one case as in the other, we find traces of British co-operation. **Britons at the Council of Arles (314).** In the list of the Fathers who met at Arles we meet the names of Eborius of York, Restitutus of London, and Adelphius of Lincoln. These three bishops signed the decrees of the Council. It is furthermore probable that the British bishops were at Nicæa, and at the Council of Rimini in 359. Saint Athanasius is quoted in support of this assertion, but the names are difficult to identify, and thus the matter is involved in some obscurity. But the state of the evidence is such that we may draw two deductions: the former of which is that the British Church appears as an organised body in the fourth century with bishops meeting on a footing of equality with those of the rest of Christendom; the latter is that they must have been in the same close union with the Holy See as the others who met under the legates of Rome at Nicæa, and whose decrees at Arles were signed and confirmed afterwards by the Roman Pontiff.

Constantius Chlorus was the father of Constantine the Great by his spouse, St Helena, who is thought by many to have been a British princess. He was Cæsar, or secondary Emperor, in the Prefecture of Gaul, according to the fourfold division of the Empire which had been inaugurated by Diocletian in 284. Constantius Chlorus was not a Christian, but, at any rate, we may be sure that he **The Roman Empire Christian.** was no persecutor, though he felt compelled to repudiate his Christian wife, St Helena, and to marry Theodora, the daughter of the Augustus Maximian, inasmuch as the former was of a social rank inferior to his own. His son, Constantine the Great, succeeded him, first in the subordinate position of Cæsar over the Western Provinces, and then at last as Augustus over the whole undivided Empire. He was the instrument chosen by Divine Providence to set on foot the great process of the public christianising of the Roman State. And, in fact, starting with him all the emperors with the one exception of Julian the Apostate were Christians, until at last the Empire fell under the attacks of its enemies. Consequently, for all the century which elapsed between the Edict of Milan in 313, and the summons to the legions in 411 to leave Britain and hasten to the defence of the provinces nearer home, we must suppose that the Roman districts or provinces in Britain were Christian much in the same sense as the rest of the Empire was, and shared in the general life of the Christian Church as it was led under the influence, partly protection, and partly interference, of the Christian Emperors. Christianity was the religion of the State, but here, as elsewhere, there remained an important minority or "residuum" of pagans.

Britain in the Christian Empire of Rome.

Among the officers sent to Britain in the period between the days of Constantine and the Fall of Rome, the most illustrious by far was the future Emperor, Theodosius the Great. The final catastrophe to Roman power in Britain, which resulted from the withdrawal of the legions, was led up to by many incursions of the barbarians of a more passing character. A more than usually severe inroad was made in the reign of Valentinian. Things were in a perilous state when this sovereign despatched the Spanish general, Theodosius, to Britain, to make headway if possible against the invaders. Theodosius landed at Richborough at the head of an army, and, attacking the barbarians, put them to flight. For a time at least tranquillity was restored to the unwarlike provincials. Theodosius is even thought to have been the first to name the northernmost district Valentia, in honour of his sovereign Valentinian. However, when his work in Britain was supposed to be done, Theodosius departed to do battle for the Empire in the East, and then the trouble began anew. And each time the resistance was feebler than before. At last when Rome itself fell into the hands of Alaric the Goth, a summons went forth that the legions still quartered in Britain should be withdrawn for the defence of Rome and its nearer possessions, and henceforth the Britons were left to their own resources. They had received some impress of the Latin civilisation, but they had not

Theodosius the Great in Britain.

Withdrawal of the Romans.

CHURCH IN ROMAN BRITAIN

been trained in the art of war well enough to defend themselves from those northern savages whom Rome herself had never tamed. Hence they soon fell a prey to their barbarian foes. Aëtius, the skilful general, who accomplished such feats in the effort to hold Gaul against the Huns and other fierce tribes, was appealed to for aid by the distressed Britons. But the appeal was in vain, as Aëtius had enough to do to hold his own in Gaul. The result was that Picts from the North and Scots from the West ravaged the land: and the natives had to seek for assistance from some other quarter. They found help of a kind from among the barbarians themselves: and they had not long to wait. Less than forty years elapsed between the first summons to the Roman legions to leave Britain, and the first landing of those hardy warriors who, under the name of Jutes, Saxons, and Angles were to make Britain the land of the English.

By a strange coincidence there was a spiritual invasion of Britain by heretics almost exactly at the same time as the Roman rule came to an end. For it was about the year 411 that the Briton Pelagius, or Morgan, either left Rome willingly or was driven forth on account of his heterodox opinions on grace and on original sin. It is not quite certain that he was a Briton, but this is the common belief, and in any case it was to Britain that he directed his steps when his teaching fell under censure at Rome, the centre of orthodoxy. Little is known of his history, but in conjunction with an Italian named Celestius, he developed erroneous teaching both as to grace and as to original sin. He asserted that man can be saved by his natural powers alone, without the aid of Divine Grace, and likewise that Adam's sin injured himself alone, not being transmitted to his descendants. The heresy spread into Africa, and was there controverted by St Augustine, Bishop of Hippo, while in 412 it was condemned by the Council of Carthage. However, it was not at once ended, for it extended itself into Gaul and Britain. It is quite possibly Pelagius himself who propagated it in both these countries after his departure from Rome. The evil in fact attained such formidable proportions that the British bishops, being, as we are told, unskilled themselves in theological controversy, applied for assistance to the hierarchy of Gaul. This

The Pelagian Heresy.

was the origin of the mission of St Germanus into Britain in 429.

The envoy sent to Gaul to ask for help appears to have met the Gallic bishops in a Council held at Troyes, where it was agreed to refer the matter to the Pope St Celestine. We know this from the testimony of St Prosper, who was a native of Gaul, and at that time was acting as secretary to the pontiff. He tells us that St Celestine sent Germanus, Bishop of Auxerre, into Britain, in his name, to assist the bishops against the heresy which was assailing their flock. With him went St Lupus, Bishop of Troyes, and also St Patrick, who a few years later was to begin his great career as Apostle of Ireland. "In this way," St Prosper concludes, "did the Holy Pontiff make the barbarian island Christian, whilst he endeavoured to keep the Christian island Catholic." The missionaries on reaching their destination preached throughout the land with power and unction. Nor were signs and wonders wanting to confirm their words. At last a conference was arranged with the Pelagians, which took place, as tradition asserts, at Verulam, not far from the tomb of St Alban. The result of the discussion was the complete discomfiture of the heretical teachers. St Prosper calls it the victory of faith over presumption, and of piety over pride. Meantime, the cure of a sick girl, who had applied to the heretics in vain, came as a divine testimony to the teaching of Germanus and of his companions. A public act of thanksgiving was made at the shrine of the Protomartyr. St Germanus next came to the aid of the British Christians in an affliction of another kind. The Picts of the North, unsubdued by the Romans, took advantage of their departure Romewards to harass and plunder the peaceful inhabitants of the provinces they had abandoned. These fierce invaders came down upon the assembled Christians in Lent, 430, just as they were preparing to keep the Easter Festivals. As soon as the religious rites were over, St Germanus agreed to lead the people out to meet their adversaries. We are told that he had them posted in separate bands among the encircling hills with instructions, as soon as the enemy was visible, to shout out the Easter cry of "Alleluia." The echoing voices of St Germanus' flock, rolling among the rocks in reverberating thunders of sound, struck terror

Mission of St Germanus.

CHURCH IN ROMAN BRITAIN 11

into the Picts. Thinking themselves outnumbered, they took refuge in flight, and this peaceful victory, which is known as the "Alleluia Victory," was the salvation of the Christian people from their savage foes.

After this double triumph over heresy and over barbarian invasion, St Germanus and his companions returned to Gaul. However, when in the course of years the same erroneous opinions as to grace and original sin began to show their heads once more, he was called to visit the island again, and responded to the invitation in the year 446, or 447, his companion this time being the disciple of St Lupus of Troyes, Severus of Treves. Once again the force of his arguments and the power of his preaching quelled the partisans of heresy; and he could go home rejoicing. The memory of St Germanus is kept alive amongst us by more than one tradition, going back to those early days. There is the ruin of St German's Church in the Isle of Man; there is the name of St German's, still given to the town in Cornwall which some believe to have been the see of the Cornish bishop. St German is also the title of dedication of many churches both in England and Wales. St Gerran's is a Cornish variation of the same name.

Soon after the final departure of St Germanus to Gaul came that new invasion of Britain which was to make the greater part the home of another race, and to give to the southern portion of the island the name of England. The Pictish raid which comes into the history of St Germanus was but one of many such which that warlike nation carried far south into the land of the Britons. There was much plunder to be won, and experience proved that the peaceful inhabitants of the land were not equal to the task of beating off their enemies. Embassies to Rome to ask for the return of some part at least of the Roman army met with no response, so that the distracted Britons thought of looking elsewhere for defenders. The skilful general Aëtius, who strove against heavy odds to hold Gaul for the Empire, could spare no troops, even though he had employed barbarian levies to stand at his side. But his conduct in enlisting the northern barbarians gave the Britons an example to follow. All unity of government had ceased since the Roman officials were gone, and authority

The landing of the Anglo-Saxons (449).

must have been split up among a number of petty kings. It was to one of the strongest of these, Vortigern, that the opportunity came. It came to his knowledge that Saxon rovers in three long keels, under the brothers Hengist and Horsa, were cruising in the Channel. Vortigern invited them to Kent to help him against the Picts and the Caledonians. His invitation was promptly accepted. The Saxon ships came to land at Ebbsfleet, and the Isle of Thanet became their camping ground. They were, of course, pagans, and bore a reputation for courage and for savage ferocity beyond their neighbours. For six years they served the Britons, and their valour was of the utmost assistance in putting to flight the invaders from the north. But after this a change took place. Progressive increase in the number of the Saxons at last made their demands for provisions and subsidy more burdensome, and when these were at last refused, open war was the result. The Battle of Aylesford, at the passage of the Medway, went in favour of the strangers, who followed this up by a still greater victory at Crayford. After a period of further desultory fighting Kent was given up to the Saxons, and at his death in 488 Hengist left a compact domain there to his son, Disc. Ella, another Saxon chief, had already landed in the Isle of Selsey, but it was not until the fortress of Anderida was taken in 490 that Ella's kingdom of the South Saxons, or Sussex, was firmly planted. Before long, Cerdic sailed up the Solent, but at first made little impression on the natives. Then two successive bodies of reinforcements enabled him to rout the Britons at Charford, and found the West Saxon realm in 519. Meanwhile, the news of these successes emboldened leaders of the neighbouring tribes called Angles, as well as other Saxon chiefs, to emulate these enterprises. In this way Erkenwin founded Essex in 527, and Uffa gained possession of the more extensive lands, called after his followers East Anglia. Then came a still more powerful expedition under Ida which drove the Britons from the broad lands between the Forth and Tees, while Ella in 560, conquered the land of the Deira, which we now call Yorkshire. Creoda planted the Kingdom of the Mercians among the Britons of the Midlands in 586, so that only Wales, Cornwall, and Strathclyde were left under the sway of the natives. Thus we may say, roughly speaking, that the conquest of the island by the Anglo-Saxons occupied about a century and a half.

On the other hand it must not be forgotten that the districts of Wales, Strathclyde, and Cornwall, embracing between them a considerable part of the whole island, had their native princes, and enjoyed independence, not only after the Saxon invasion, but even after the invaders themselves had yielded to the Dane and the Norman. Hence, during those centuries the British Christians went on leading their own life apart, and in spite of the immense difficulties, producing saints as well. Doubtless the consolations of their religion must have been an inspiration to the British warriors in their battles against the heathen. A tradition tells us that St Germanus while in Britain consecrated the far-famed St Dubritius as Bishop of Llandaff. From this venerable man starts a succession of Welsh or British saints whose deeds form a romantic and pathetic cycle in hagiography. Inasmuch as he at one time fixed his abode at Caerleon, he is represented with two crosiers to typify the two sees of Llandaff and Caerleon which he filled. King Arthur's kinsman, St Iltyd or Iltutus, being converted by St Cadoc, founder of the monastery of Llancarvan, came to Dubritius, under whom at first he served, and was then himself the the founder of a new monastery at Llan Twit in Glamorgan, where at different times he counted among his disciples St Samson, St Gildas, St Malo, and last but not least St David, who is called the Patron Saint of Wales. Into the hands of St David Dubritius, before his long life came to an end, resigned his pastoral charge. Caerleon is thought at this period to have held a kind of metropolitan rank among the British sees. The career of St David rivalled that of St Dubritius himself in length, while his great renown brought pious pilgrims from afar to learn holiness from his lips. He too, when death drew nigh, gave up Caerleon, and retired to Menevia, since called after him St David's. Another of the disciples of St Dubritius was St Daniel, who passed into North Wales and became the first Bishop of Bangor. St Asaph, bishop of the see named after him, was a disciple of St Mungo or Kentigern, Bishop of Glasgow. This latter saint, forced for a time by the outbreak of persecution to leave Strathclyde, founded in North Wales

Later British Saints.

the monastery of Llan Elwy, but later on, being enabled to return to the north, once more settled at Glasgow. He left his Welsh foundation in charge of his favourite disciple, Asaph, and the name of this latter saint was substituted for Llan Elwy as the name of the diocese.

Attempts have been made to trace a succession of bishops for the sees in Wales during the period of struggle between Britons and Saxons, but though a certain number of the names given are probably authentic, and we can make out without difficulty the diocese of Caerleon or Llandaff, of Bangor, of St Asaph's, and of Menevia or St David's, as well as St German's in Cornwall, this is almost all we can rely upon as trustworthy history. The organisation of the British Church as a whole is only matter of conjecture. If we can argue from what St Patrick did in Ireland, we shall conclude that this organisation was in the main monastic with a large number of clergy in bishop's orders, somewhat after the manner of those early Christian communities which were presided over each one by a bishop without any extensive territorial jurisdiction. The reputation of some of the more celebrated monasteries has survived. Among the greatest were the two Bangors, on the Dee and in Caernarvon respectively, Llan Carvan, Llan Twit, Llan Elwy, Glastonbury, and Menevia. But the immense numbers assigned to those religious houses, such as three thousand at Llan Twit and one thousand at Glastonbury, hardly deserve credit. Even outside the monasteries we may feel assured that the Cymri were in the mass a Christian nation. They were evidently in full communion both with Rome and with the neighbouring land of Gaul. In fact under the pressure of hostile invasion they crossed the sea thither in such numbers that as the result of their emigration the most westerly province of that country received and retains the name of Brittany. Several of the Breton saints, such as St Malo, St Brieuc, and St Samson, were emigrants who had come over the channel from Britain with their fellow-countrymen. Those who remained had vast difficulties to contend with; hence it is not to be wondered at if many of them fell below the standard of Christian practice. So far from being able to impress their Faith on their heathen enemies, they had as much as they could do to guard its precepts in their own hearts.

St David is still counted as the chief Patron of Wales, but there is a gracious female saint for whom a popular veneration is felt which is even more widely spread. This is the Virgin Martyr St Winefride, or as she is commonly named in the British equivalent of her name, Guinevere. Connected through her uncle, St Beuno, who was living a monastic life hard by, with other royal saints of Wales, she was passionately loved by the son of a local chieftain. Rejecting his advances for the sake of leading a virginal life, she turned his affection into hatred, so that overcome with ungovernable rage at her refusal, he struck off her head with one blow of his sword at the place now called Holywell. This name commemorates a spring of water which gushed miraculously from the soil on the very spot where her head first touched the ground. Her Acts go on to say that at the prayer of St Beuno her life was given back to her, so that she was able to live for eight years at the head of a community of nuns in a convent which had been built over the holy spring. When the torrent of Saxon conquest swept over the land, she retired to a remote valley near the source of the River Elwy, where at length she died, after an earthly existence made beautiful by prayer and miracles. Her relics were afterwards taken to Shrewsbury, where they were venerated in St Mary's Abbey. But Holywell has never ceased to be a place of pilgrimage and of heavenly favours granted through St Winefride's intercession. There are many at the present day, sceptical enough in general about the miracles related of the saints, who yet feel unable to gainsay the evidence in this case, and therefore make an exception for her who is sometimes called the Virgin Mary of Wales and of her wonderful well.

St Winefride V.M. (600-660).

Whatever mixture of legend is to be found amid the histories of the British saints is far surpassed by the fanciful and romantic tales which in great part make up the secular chronicles of the race. We are introduced to heroes whose marvellous deeds have come out of the fertile brains of poets and national bards. A few names indeed stand out as preserving the memory of the chief champions of the native Britons against their foes. *Aurelius Ambrosius* appears as the solitary Roman leader who remained to general and to advise the natives when the legions were gone. *Natanleod* is remembered even in the Saxon Chronicle as their great opponent in the struggle for Wessex. *Pendragon* stands forth both in legend and history as a leader against the Angles in the north. Lastly round the name of *King Arthur* has clustered a whole epic of romance and of warlike poetry. Tennyson has told us in the " Idylls of the King " how:

> " Arthur and his knighthood for a space
> Were all one will, and through that strength the King
> Drew in the petty princedoms under him,
> Fought and in twelve great battles overcame
> The heathen hordes, and made a realm, and reigned."

II.

THE APOSTLES OF ENGLAND.

(597-625.)

The inspiration to evangelise the heathen tribes of Jutes, Saxons, and Angles who had conquered Britain did not come from anyone within the shores of that country. By the end of the sixth century, as we have seen, after a century and a half of contest, their mastery was established over the natives, save in the north and west. But already with far-seeing zeal the Roman Pontiff, who had by that time succeeded to Peter's Chair, had conceived the wish to convert them, and had taken steps to accomplish his design. Long before he was called to the Pontificate, Gregory the Great cherished the idea of himself carrying the Gospel to those far-off pagans. He had met, we are told, young slaves of Angle race, put up for sale in the Roman forum amid the varied merchandise of that great market. Struck by their fair complexion and golden hair, he asked: " Of what nation are these fair children? " " Angles," was the answer. " Say rather Angels," said he. " And from what province do they come? " he continued. " They come from the Province of the Deira," rejoined the one whom he questioned. " Nay, but being heathens they must come away from the wrath of God " (*Dei ira*), replied the saint, with that love of a play upon words which dwelt in him in spite of his classical tastes. " Do you know the name of the king in their country? " was his next question. " Yes, he is called Ella," he was told. " Some day may they sing Alleluia," was his comment as he passed on his way. Did he buy the fair-haired strangers, as some have thought, or did he

St Gregory
the Great
(540-604).

18   THE CHURCH IN ENGLAND

walk on turning over in his mind plans for the conversion of their race? We know not. But, at any rate, he gained the consent later on of the reigning pontiff, Pelagius II., to issue forth as the first missioner to those heathen tribes. Gregory made his preparations with all secrecy and then set forth. But no sooner was it noised abroad that he was gone, than a deputation waited on Pelagius to plead for his recall on the ground that his loss would be irreparable for the Roman Church. The arguments seemed so weighty that Pelagius felt obliged to yield to them. Hence swift messengers were despatched in all haste, who soon overtook the northward bound missionary, and brought him back with them to the city of Rome.

Debarred henceforth by a voice, which he recognised as the sign of the Divine Will, from undertaking in person the Apostolate of the Angles, Gregory ever kept the project deep in his heart and mind. Still, years had to pass before any practical steps could be taken to realise it. It was in 595, five years after Gregory had been chosen pontiff, that he found himself in a position to send forth apostolic missionaries to accomplish in reality what he had so long and so ardently longed to set his hand to himself. In his monastery of St Andrew, on the Cœlian Hill, he had been gradually making ready the instruments for the work, and now the hour had struck. News had been brought him of the power of Ethelbert, King of Kent, who was Bretwalda, or chief ruler of the Heptarchy as the seven English kingdoms were called. But what touched him most was the information that this monarch had married a Catholic princess, though he was a pagan himself. This Christian lady was Bertha, daughter of the King of Paris. Moreover, he had learned from Gaul that the Angles were desirous to hear something of the doctrines of Christianity. The chosen leader for the mission of evangelisation was Augustine, prior of the monastery of St Andrew. But Gregory had no thought of sending him on his enterprise unprovided or alone. Like the true Roman that he was, he meant a regular *colonia* to go forth from his city, ready to settle down and lead the Roman life in monastic regularity, and drawing the rough barbarians to Christ as much by

St Augustine of Canterbury (550-604).

THE APOSTLES OF ENGLAND

example as by precept. Augustine was made Abbot, or Superior, of the new community.

The journey from Rome to Britain through Gaul was in those days a long and weary one. It is true that the Holy Pontiff had provided the travellers with letters of recommendation to the bishops in Gaul, in which he begged them to entertain these new Apostles of the Faith with kindly hospitality, and to speed them on their way. St Bede mentions among these prelates Etherius, Bishop of Lyons, and also refers to Queen Brunehild. Nevertheless, as they proceeded farther on their journey, the difficulties of their mission, the savage character reported of the Saxons, their own ignorance of the Saxon speech, and the doubtful prospect of success made so deep an impression on the little band that they fell into discouragement and prevailed upon Augustine to leave them in Gaul, while he returned to Rome with a view to persuade St Gregory to release them from the work he had entrusted to them. But the Pope had his enterprise too much at heart to allow of its frustration by imaginary ills, and after encouraging Augustine sent him back to his companions with a letter, exhorting them not to abandon the good work, but to trust in the Divine guidance and persevere in it under obedience to Augustine. He also sent back several new recruits to join the band which, thereupon, being encouraged by the Pontiff's exhortation, and also reinforced by the addition of several Gallic priests to act as interpreters, resumed its perilous journey. It by this time consisted in all of some forty individuals. Early in 597 the expedition set out from the coast of Gaul, and landed in due course **Landing of** at Ebbsfleet, a cove where the white cliffs **Augustine** part asunder and thus give easier access **in Kent** to the Isle of Thanet. Thanet was at this **(597).** period really an island, cut off from the main part of Kent by an encircling arm of the sea. It was not far from the ancient Roman port of Richborough, and was within the dominions of King Ethelbert, on whose alliance with the Christian Princess Bertha, and on whose position as Bretwalda they were relying to further their missionary enterprise. It was not long before the news of their arrival was carried to the king. Wherefore some days later Ethelbert himself came into Thanet to interview them. The monarch, under the influence of pagan superstition, sat in the open air to receive them, for it had been whispered to him that within the walls of a dwelling-house they might prevail over him unrighteously by means of magic arts. As soon as Augustine came to know that the king had arrived in the neighbourhood he formed his little colony into a procession, putting at their head a silver processional cross. And bearing a painting on wood, which represented Our Lord, thus marshalled they advanced chanting the Litany to meet the pagan king. Being seated at Ethelbert's command Augustine in the name of them all explained the cause of their coming, and preached to them the good tidings of salvation which he had brought. The pagan listened with attention to what he said, and then replied in words such as these: fit augury of the spirit in which his countrymen have over and over again listened to the words of strangers with caution, and yet with even-handed toleration: "Fair are your words and your promises, yet to me they are new and of uncertain import, so that I cannot accept them so far as to leave that which I have hitherto followed with all my people. But since you have come from so far, and as I feel sure with the desire to teach us what you hold to be true and good, we will not be hostile to you, but will entertain you and provide you with all that you need to live. Nor shall you be hindered from preaching and winning over to your religion as many as you are able."

With this Ethelbert departed, but he straightway assigned to Augustine and his companions a dwelling-place in his capital, which was Canterbury. **Foundation of Canterbury by Augustine.** Thither then before long they betook themselves in pilgrim wise, once more having at their head the silver cross and Our Saviour's image, chanting as they went, according to Venerable Bede: "We beseech Thee, O Lord, in Thy mercy to turn away Thy anger and Thy wrath from this city, and from Thy Holy House, for we have sinned. Alleluia." Outside the town stood the little Roman Church of St Martin, never destroyed, where Queen Bertha assisted at the Christian worship in safety, and where Mass was celebrated in her presence by Bishop Luidhard of Senlis. This for a time was the place

THE APOSTLES OF ENGLAND

assigned for the home of Augustine and the others. It was hard by this church that they began, as soon as possible that rule of monastic observance, and that assiduity in the celebration of the Church's services which they hoped would bring down the blessing of God upon their labours for souls. They carried with them to this place the books which Pope Gregory had sent from Rome as a beginning for their library: the Book of the Gospels, the Martyrology, the Psalter, and some Homilies on Holy Scripture.

It was not long before the attraction of the holy life they led and the fame of the miracles which accompanied their preaching told with marvellous effect upon the men of Kent. King Ethelbert, though he had cautiously abstained from committing himself at once to embrace Christianity, had not ceased to watch their proceedings and to listen to their words. At length, on Whitsunday, the 2nd of June, 597, he sought Baptism, and was followed by many thousands of his subjects. The Sacrament was administered at a ford of the River Stour at Canterbury; and that Pentecost Day with its crowds of Kentish men flocking into the fold of Christ was the greatest holiday which the Church had celebrated since the baptism of Clovis at Rheims a century before.

The Baptism of Ethelbert.

Now that the foundations of a new Christian nation had been thus auspiciously laid, it was necessary for the development and organisation of the flock that Augustine should be made bishop. He, therefore, repaired to Gaul, where he was consecrated by St. Virgilius of Arles, the papal legate in that country. And as he could be ill spared from his work in England, we may well believe that he returned as expeditiously as the length of the way permitted, and took up anew his labours. King Ethelbert before long handed over to him his palace at Canterbury, moving off himself to reside at Richborough or Rewlvers. Augustine transformed the royal gift into an abbey, restoring also an old ruined church of Roman times which stood alongside of it. This was the future Cathedral and Priory of Christchurch, the primatial see of England, where Augustine ruled his community of monks, and as Archbishop guided the progress of the Church in England. Moreover, eastward of the city, half-way to the old

Church of St Martin, King Ethelbert at the saint's suggestion began the Abbey of St Augustine, as it was afterwards called, which in interest and splendour rivalled the cathedral itself. This was to be the burying place of Augustine and his successors. It took seven years to build, so the holy Archbishop did not live to see its completion. It was solemnly dedicated by Laurentius, his successor, to the holy Apostles, SS. Peter and Paul, in the year 613.

After this it appears that Augustine was able to extend the field of his labours from time to time, and even to preach and evangelise the Saxon tribes as far as the confines of the still independent Britons. But he never lost touch with the saintly pontiff whose messenger in the first instance he was. A good deal of his correspondence with Gregory is still extant, so that we are able to appreciate both the difficulties with which the new enterprise was faced, and Augustine's careful reference of the greater questions to the Roman see. Moreover, they show us Gregory, the Great Doctor, still in heart and mind Apostle of England, encouraging, instructing, warning, guiding his disciple with a solicitude which ceased only with his death. At one time he warns him of the danger to his humility which might arise from the glory of the miracles he had been allowed to work. At another time he directs that the temples of the idols are not to be destroyed, but after the idols have been broken or burnt, the temples are to be blessed and used as Christian churches. At another time he answers in detail quite a number of questions submitted for decision in matters of discipline and government. With true Roman breadth of view as to discipline, Gregory writes: "My view is that if you have found anything in the Church of Rome, or in that of Gaul, or in any other, which you believe to be more pleasing to God, you select it with care, and give it a place in the new Church of the English. For customs are not to be loved because of the places whence they come, but rather places because of the good customs." The offerings of the faithful are to be shared in the traditional four portions by bishop, clergy, poor, and the Church. Augustine, as a monk, is to continue to lead a life in common with his clergy. The punish-

Letters of Gregory and Augustine.

ment of theft, even if sacrilegious, is to be tempered with mercy. The marriage laws are to be kept, as far as they are essential. Augustine has no authority over the Gallic bishops, nor they over him. He is to consecrate twelve bishops dependent on the See of Canterbury or London, and to send, moreover, a bishop to the See of York, who will henceforward likewise preside as metropolitan over twelve other bishops. Gregory sent Augustine at the same time the pallium of metropolitan, as well as sacred vessels for the altar, various ornaments for the churches, precious relics of the saints, and likewise many books. He, moreover, sent with these things a further reinforcement of missionaries, chief among whom were the Abbots Mellitus, Justus, Paulinus, and Rufinian.

All this gave St Augustine new opportunities of advancing the standard of the Kingdom of God, and he was zealously seconded in his enterprises by the pious Ethelbert, who had become such a thoroughly fervent Christian that he has deserved the revered name of saint. Ethelbert built a church at Rochester, and Augustine consecrated Justus as the first bishop of that see which was to comprise the western portion of the realm of Kent. Sebert, the King of the East Saxons, was nephew to Ethelbert, and that circumstance gave an entry into Essex to the Christian missionaries. To care for them, St Mellitus was sent forth from Canterbury, and eventually consecrated bishop, with his see fixed at London, which was then considered part of the East Saxon kingdom. Finally, in order to begin friendly relations with the clergy of the British, who were still in possession of the west, Ethelbert got a conference between him and them arranged through his influence. The meeting was at a spot, since called "*Augustine's Oak*," near the banks of the River Severn. Augustine began by a charitable exhortation that they would unite with him in preaching the Gospel to the pagan Saxons. He then discussed with them the traditions of discipline, which they held to, somewhat differing from the Roman use. Though, as St Bede tells us, St Augustine received an increase of authority for his contention, by the striking miracle he wrought, in giving

London and Rochester.

Discussion with the Britons.

sight to a blind man, the Britons pleaded for adjournment to another and greater conference. This took place, and was attended by seven British bishops and some of the most learned of the monks of Bangor. Unfortunately, before they started, they had taken advice from a certain hermit, who counselled them to be guided by the bearing of Augustine. "If," said he, "he rises up to meet you, he is a meek and humble servant of Christ; if he does not, but despises you by remaining seated, then do you, as being more in number, despise him." Consequently, when they reached the place of meeting and found Augustine seated, they at once charged him with haughtiness and want of respect for them. They were prepared to contradict all he said, but with that largeness of view which he had learned from Gregory, Augustine declared that all other differences being mutually tolerated, he only asked for three things: unity of date for keeping Easter, the Roman rite for the giving of Baptism, and co-operation in the evangelisation of the pagans. But they could not be prevailed upon to accept this minimum, and the conference was broken up. The sequel, as far as the monks of Bangor were concerned, was a tragic one. The Saxon chroniclers, perhaps with little reason, are led to see in this sequel a judgment of God upon the exclusiveness and want of charity of these monks. Anyhow, in 613 Ethelfrid, the pagan king of Northumbria, attacked North Wales with a mighty host, and defeated the Britons with great slaughter near Chester. On a hill hard by were gathered the monks of Bangor, not fighting, but like Moses praying for the success of their brethren in the fray. "What is that band of men on the hill doing?" said Ethelfrid. "They are not fighting, but praying for the victory of the Britons," he was told. "It is all one," he continued, "they are opposing us as well as those who fight. Kill them all." And so it was done; so that in the great battle which these Christians were fighting against the heathen for their homes and their land, not only the warriors fell or were put to flight, but one thousand two hundred monks and other non-combatants were slain by the savage enemy. So, at least, says the ancient chronicle.

Besides the suffragans for London and Rochester, Augustine, before he died, consecrated Lawrence, one of

THE APOSTLES OF ENGLAND 25

the monks out of the original band who landed at Ebbsfleet, and pointed him out as his successor, lest at his own departure the infant Church should have no one to stand at the helm. In this he is thought to have wished to imitate the action of St Peter, when he ordained St Linus and St Clement to provide for the Church of Rome after his martyrdom.

King Ethelbert was also to survive him, it is true, and he, with his wife St Bertha, ruled as a model Christian monarch. Gregory had written to him a letter full of admiration and warm exhortation, likening him to the great Constantine, who had made the Roman Empire Christian. And inspired by the spirit of the religion he had embraced Ethelbert became a legislator as well. The laws known as the Dooms of Ethelbert are still extant, and have been published under the direction of the Record Office among the Ancient Laws and Institutes of England.

Gregory and Augustine both departed from this mortal life about the same time: Gregory on the 12th of March, 604, and Augustine some two months later. The foundations of the Church of the Angles had been laid by these two men as God's instruments, though in a different way. The noble Pontiff who conceived the lofty idea had found with unerring instinct the loyal missioner and disciple to carry it out. He had kept the success of the English mission close to his heart until death came. The faithful prior of St Andrew's on the Cœlian knew how to unite with complete obedience to his master the unwearying zeal which made him what the Church calls him—and the title is a lofty one: to the one and to the other a grateful posterity gives the proud title of Apostle of England.

The second foundation at Canterbury was the abbey which Augustine and Ethelbert united to found in honour of SS. Peter and Paul. It was not so long before it became known as St Augustine's, and it subsisted through the Middle Ages as one of the greatest Benedictine abbeys in the land. It became the resting-place for the bones of both bishop and king, who had worked together for its establishment. Moreover, several of the successors, both of Augustine and of Ethelbert, found an honoured tomb within the same sacred walls. Its privileges gave it quite a special position among the religious houses of the country, while the benefactions of the Catholic people gradually raised it to a place of great opulence and extensive ownership of land.

A third Canterbury church of great interest and of even greater antiquity than either Christchurch Priory or St Augustine's Abbey is the venerable church called St Martin's. It can be traced back to the days of British Christianity before the coming of St Augustine or of the Anglo-Saxons. It is celebrated not only for its antiquity, but also for giving his title to the Bishop of St Martin's, who acted as suffragan or auxiliary to the Primates of Canterbury up to the days of the Norman Conquest. The title and office were then abolished, and henceforward the Bishop of Rochester acted as the chaplain or assistant by office to the Archbishop.

Summary. It may fairly be claimed that St Augustine in founding the See of Canterbury had already impressed upon it, at least in two outstanding points, the characteristics which we find constantly distinguishing it until the Reformation broke the succession, and blotted out those characteristics in heresy and schism: (1) St Augustine was not without influence in fixing the purely *Roman character* of the church in Kent, even though that point was almost decided by the lack of contact with the Celtic Christians; (2) even more remarkable was his influence in determining its *monastic character*, as contrasted with the closer union of other sees with a body of secular clergy. He made it grow up gradually out of the Christchurch Monastery, and the monks had a voice both in choosing the archbishop, and in administering the diocesan property. There was no other chapter but theirs. The mediaeval cathedral remains a venerable and fascinating pile, with its five towers, and its almost unique display of the development of Gothic styles. But the city has never recovered from the catastrophe which made the far-famed Pilgrims' Way purposeless, and trailed the glory of the Primate's dignity in the dust for tyrants and politicians to trample on.

III.

EVANGELISATION OF THE HEPTARCHY.

(625-671.)

ST LAWRENCE, the first successor of St Augustine, kept up the same cordial relations as he had done both with the Holy See and with Ethelbert the Kentish king. He also made another attempt to come to an understanding with the British Christians, but in vain.. In order to promote uniformity of practice with regard to the keeping of Easter and other matters of discipline, Lawrence wrote a joint letter with Mellitus and Justus to the Celtic bishops, and an Irish bishop named Fagan seems to have travelled as far as Canterbury to confer with him. But it appears that this envoy was so little contented with the reception which he met with that he declined even to take his meals with the clergy there. Meanwhile, Mellitus, the Bishop of London, proceeded to Rome to consult Pope Boniface IV. on the affairs of the Church of England, and, having taken his place in a synod held there before the Pope with the other clergy, returned home bearing papal letters for St Lawrence. In this way passed an interval of twelve years of progress after the death of St Augustine. But after the death of Ethelbert and of his nephew, Sebert of Essex, there began a storm of trial and pagan reaction which tried both pastors and flock to the utmost.

St Lawrence (604-619).

Kent fell to Eadbald, the eldest son of Ethelbert, and he refused to become a Christian. He was living in incest with his father's second wife, now a widow. At about the same time, Essex fell to the three pagan sons of Sebert, who openly professed idolatry, and strove to lead the people

Pagan Reaction.

back to their heathen worship. Being present one day at Mass, when St Mellitus was administering Communion, they demanded that they also should be given "that white bread" which their father used to partake of, and which many of the people still received. St Mellitus told them first to be washed in the saving waters of baptism, and then, said he, they might be admitted to the holy table. This condition they refused. Hence, on the holy bishop standing firm in his refusal of Communion, they banished him and his clergy from their kingdom. Mellitus betook himself to Canterbury to take counsel of Lawrence and Justus. But even here the prospect looked dark enough. If Mellitus was banished from his see, Lawrence and Justus were in the domains of a young prince who would not become a Christian, and by his conduct set even the law of nature at defiance. Moreover, this vicious young pagan was subject at times to fits of madness and demoniacal fury. The results of their united consultation was that they must leave England for a while, taking refuge on the continent of Europe till better times should dawn. In fact, Mellitus and Justus had already taken their departure, and Lawrence was preparing to follow them when he was startled by an apparition in his sleep of the Blessed Apostle Peter, who scourged him, and chid him for planning to abandon the flock which had been confided to his care. On the contrary, he ought to be ready to give his life for those sheep, even as Peter himself had done. St Bede tells us that when he awoke he found that the bruises of his scourging were real, and then bethought him of going to King Eadbald, and trying to move him to repentance by the recital of what he had suffered on account of him and his crimes. The pious historian goes on to tell that this appeal was happily successful. Eadbald, struck by the words and sufferings of Lawrence, begged him not to leave, but to recall Mellitus and Justus. He then turned from his idols of stone to embrace Christianity, he put away his unlawful partner, and even built another church at Canterbury. Thus was the pagan reaction stayed, and a new turn of the tide began.

Mellitus and Justus both returned, and Justus was able to occupy once more his see at Rochester. But, though this conversion of Eadbald appears to have been sincere, he was not possessed of the influence outside of Kent, which his father, the Bretwalda, had exerted. He was, therefore, unable to restore the Bishop of London to his diocese. Mellitus, therefore, continued to reside in Canterbury for the remainder of St Lawrence's lifetime. Then, when the latter died in 619, he was appointed to succeed him in the metropolitan see. Still, his tenure of this high office was but short, for twenty-four years of missionary toil had sufficed to wear out the zealous monk whom Gregory had selected as the leader of his second band of apostolic men, and in 625 he breathed his last. Justus still survived at Rochester, whence he was at once translated to Canterbury, but he likewise only held the archiepiscopal dignity for a short period. He died in 628. We may suppose that the reversion to Canterbury of one after the other of the bishops who had been sent farther afield was a symptom of delay in the progress of the evangelisation of the country. It is true that Justus lived to receive the pallium and a letter of encouragement from Pope Boniface IV., and to consecrate Romanus as successor to himself at Rochester. Yet it was not so much through keeping hold of Rochester as by consecrating Paulinus for the north that Justus was able to give an important impetus to a new advance in 625.

St Mellitus and St Justus.

Edwin, King of Northumbria, was looked upon as Bretwalda or chief ruler of the Heptarchy after the death of Redwald of East Anglia. Now it happened that he asked for Ethelburga, daughter of King Ethelbert of Kent, in marriage. The answer was given that such a union between a Catholic and a pagan was against the laws of the Church. However, Edwin persisted, urging that the princess would be left perfectly free to practise her religion, and further that if on examination by his wise men the faith of Christ proved better than his own, the king himself would be willing to accept it. This put a new light on the proposal, and Ethelburga was promised to him. It was settled that Paulinus, one of the Canterbury monastic community, should accompany the princess as her chaplain. Paulinus was therefore consecrated by Justus on the 21st of July, 625. The journey to the north was accomplished in safety, and Paulinus on arrival laboured much both

St Paulinus at York (625).

to retain those who were already Christians in their obedience to the Gospel, and to win over to the worship of Christ the pagans among whom his lot was now cast. The infant born to the royal pair in the following year was baptised under the name of Eanfleda with eleven others of her household. This was the firstfruits of the Apostolate of St Paulinus among the Northumbrians. Edwin gave thanks to his idols for the happy birth of his little daughter, though Paulinus assured him that it was to the God of the Christians that thanks were really due for this favour. The king listened, and at last said that if the God of the Christians gave him the victory in an expedition to avenge himself on the King of Wessex which he was then making ready for, he would leave his idols and worship Him. Meanwhile, Pope St Boniface IV., who knew of the expedition of St Paulinus, intervened with two letters, one to Ethelburga, exhorting her to prayer and to every zealous endeavour for her husband's conversion, the other to Edwin himself, calling upon him to desist from the worship of senseless idols, and to devote himself to the service of the true God, whose faith Paulinus preached. Edwin now departed on his warlike expedition to punish the King of Wessex, who had tried to have him assassinated, and having defeated the men of Wessex, came home victorious. Since his promise to the bishop he had adored his idols no longer, but he could not yet bring himself to accept with mind and heart the teaching of Christianity. A year passed in this state of conscientious deliberation, and then in 627, when the Witan or Council of Wise Men met, Edwin laid the case before them, and asked for their counsel upon it. Coifi, the pagan high priest, when his turn came to give his advice, said: "I verily declare to you, O king, that the religion we have hitherto professed has, as far as I can learn, no power in it. No one has applied himself more diligently to the worship of those gods than I; and yet there are many who receive greater favours, higher place, and more prosperity than I do. Now, if the gods had any power, they would surely further my interests, who have been more zealous for them. Consequently, if on examination we find these new doctrines better and more efficacious, let us at once turn to them and accept them." Then rose another of the king's chief men, and spoke after this fashion: "The present life of man, O king, seems to me like the swift flight of a sparrow through the hall, while you sit at supper in winter with your aldermen and thanes, and a good fire in the midst, whilst the storms of rain and snow are raging outside. The sparrow, flying in at one door and out at another, is safe, whilst he is within, from the storm of winter; but after a short rest he vanishes out of your sight into the darkness out of which he has come. So this life of man appears for a little while, but of what went before, or of what is to follow after, we know nothing. If, therefore, this new teaching tells aught of this, it seems right that we should follow it." Others went on to give advice in the same strain.

St Paulinus was now introduced, and at the desire of the Witan began to explain to them the Gospel of Jesus Christ. Thereupon the king gave him leave to preach to all, and declared that for his own part he was convinced, and would become a Christian. Coifi, the high priest, having borrowed the king's horse, rode up to the chief temple of the heathen gods, and flung his spear into it in derision, to signify to the rest that he gave up his former superstitious worship. Then they brought fire, and burnt the idols and demolished their temples. This happened at Goodmanham, some six miles east of York. And then on Easter Day, 627, all were full of festive gladness in the northern capital, for on that day Edwin was baptised with his nobles and a great company of his people. A wooden church had been already built by the king in preparation for this event, but soon afterwards another and nobler church was built of stone, enclosing the former wooden one. Moreover, on that site was later on erected the noble structure we know as York Minster. And though the heart is moved and every artistic feeling is stirred to admiration as the visitor of to-day gazes on that glorious fane, so splendid in its dimensions, so grandly simple in its plan, yet a deeper chord is touched when we go down into the crypt and there try to trace the still visible stones of Edwin's church, and the enclosure of the spring from which Paulinus baptised those early Northumbrian converts.

Baptism of Edwin (627).

Edwin's reign continued to be a victorious one for

several years after his baptism. He was easily the most powerful king in England. He has left his name on the most beautiful city in all Great Britain, for Edinburgh is really the burgh or city of Edwin the Northumbrian. And as long as he reigned Paulinus and his assistants were able to push on with their work of evangelisation. The holy bishop travelled into Mercia, and at Lincoln converted and baptised the chief man, Blacca, and many others. It was also while he was at Lincoln that Paulinus was able to consecrate a successor of St Justus of Canterbury who had just died (628). The new archbishop was Honorius, who was destined to rule in Canterbury almost as long as all his predecessors combined. But trouble was brewing in Northumbria, for though Edwin could easily overcome any one of his rivals singly, he was to fall a victim to an alliance between them. Cædwalla, the Christian king of North Wales, whose people longed to avenge the slaughter wrought by Ethelfrid at Chester, joined his forces with those of Penda, the still pagan king of the Mercians. Penda was a fierce warrior, full of hatred to Christianity. Edwin went forth to meet them at the head of his men, and at the battle of Heavenfield was defeated and slain. Confusion now reigned in all the kingdom of Northumbria. The family of Edwin fled; so did Paulinus and the clergy who were with him, and, for the present at least, the prospects of religion were blighted. It was a pagan reaction comparable to that in Kent twenty years before, when Ethelbert died. Paulinus betook himself to his former companion, Honorius, who now sat in Augustine's chair. It happened that through the death of Romanus the diocese of Rochester was then vacant, so Paulinus was installed there, and remained in charge of the see until his death in 644. It is to be noted that Paulinus, as Archbishop of York, according to St Gregory's original arrangement, and Honorius, as Archbishop of Canterbury, both received their pallium from the Pope Honorius, who also wrote to the Scots exhorting them to follow the Roman calculation for observing the Easter Festival.

Those of King Edwin's family whom the victorious Mercians were able to lay hands upon were ruthlessly slain by them, but Oswald, son of Ethelfrid, effected

Death of Edwin (633).

his escape to the country of the Scots. He was Edwin's nephew, and had always remained a faithful Christian. In the course of the following year he was able to collect a trusty body of troops, small but of tried valour, and having set up the Cross as a standard of victory, gave battle to his enemies at Heavenfield in 635. He was overwhelmingly successful, and the complete rout of the Mercians put Northumbria into Oswald's power. He was thus enabled to undertake its restoration both in church and state. When Paulinus and his band fled from York, there had remained behind the deacon, James, and this pious man carefully tended the embers of the faith, even when they seemed completely extinguished in the pagan deluge. Yet Oswald saw that more was wanted if religion was to be restored in his kingdom. In his youth he had been trained to Christianity by the Irish monks whom St Columba's zeal had brought to the Isle of Iona. It was to this sacred spot then that Oswald sent his appeal for assistance in the great work of making his dominions Christian.

St Oswald becomes king (635).

The appeal was at once responded to, though the first missionary sent from there met with but indifferent success in his mission. It was when this missionary returned to his brethren, and announced that the task was hopeless, so hard and savage were the pagan strangers, that Aidan stepped forward. He suggested that the cause of failure had been too great severity in dealing with the heathen. Before long he found himself entrusted with the task of trying the effect of the milder means and more gradual instruction which he recommended. Having received bishop's orders, Aidan fixed his see on the Isle of Lindisfarne, which is now known as Holy Island, and is sometimes called the English Iona. With its low-lying shores and group of ruined buildings Lindisfarne is still an object of interest to the traveller along the eastern coast of Northumberland, as it is seen across the narrow strait, which separates it from the mainland. From this centre Aidan went forth to evangelise Oswald's kingdom. He always travelled on foot, unless absolute necessity required that he should ride. And all his company, whether clerics or laymen, employed the time

Mission of St Aidan.

of the journey in reading the Scriptures, or reciting the Psalms by heart. Occasionally he would be asked to dine with the king, but even this feasting was spare enough, for after a quite moderate repast, he would rise from table, and go off to resume his prayers, or his reading and writing. Whatever money came to him in gifts he bestowed on the poor, or for the ransom of captives. On Wednesdays and Fridays he fasted until the ninth hour. On the rich or mighty he never bestowed gifts, save the food with which he sometimes entertained them. Hence his example told powerfully on a soul like Oswald's. For Aidan and Oswald were together at table on Easter Day when word was brought to the king that a multitude of beggars stood without, asking for alms. Oswald gave orders that whatever food was on the table should be immediately taken and distributed among the mendicants. Aidan, struck with admiration, seized the generous hand of the king and exclaimed: "May this hand never perish." And the legend is that it never did, even when the rest of Oswald's remains were all reduced to ashes.

St Oswald reigned over Northumbria for nine years, until at length he was killed in battle at Maserfield fighting against the same pagan, Penda, whose coming had been fatal to his kinsman, Edwin. His brother Oswin took up the inheritance, which was withal an unquiet and precarious one. Penda was never far distant with his marauding army, never happier than when he could inflict some mortal harm on the neighbouring Christian realm. Nevertheless, Oswin managed to keep some kind of sway over the kingdom for eight-and-twenty years.

Meanwhile, one of the greatest champions of the English Church had already begun to exercise influence upon public affairs. This was the dauntless St Wilfrid, who was destined to wage such long and hard-fought combats for Roman uses and Christian faith. He was born in 634 of the highest Northumbrian rank, and brought up under the care of King Edwin's daughter, Eanfleda, who had been St Paulinus' firstfruits at the baptismal font. Wilfrid then became a monk at Lindisfarne, which was still the centre of Northumbrian Christianity for many years after Oswald's death. St Aidan died at Bam-

St Wilfrid
(634-709).

borough, which was served from the island monastery, in 651, but his successor, St Finan, made every effort to carry on his work. In 652 St Wilfrid, in company with St Benet Biscop, determined to go to Rome, being the standard bearer of that long procession of Anglo-Saxon pilgrims, which visited the shrines of the Apostles during the succeeding ages. What he saw there made him an enthusiastic advocate of Roman rites and Roman customs. Hence, when he returned to England in 654 he undertook to propagate these things in Northumbria, supplanting the Celtic usages which had been learned from Lindisfarne. Alchfrid, Oswy's elder son, sent for Wilfrid, and between this prince and him there began a friendship which greatly strengthened the latter's position in the kingdom. Alchfrid had founded a monastery at Ripon, which had been colonised by a community from the Celtic monastery of Melrose, but now, under Wilfrid's influence, the prince required these monks to keep the Roman Easter and conform to the Roman rite. As they declined to do so, Eata, Cuthbert, and others went back to Melrose, and Wilfrid was installed as head of the community at Ripon. Battle was now fairly joined between the two sets of customs, and was carried on directly and indirectly for wellnigh fifty years. Men's minds were divided throughout Northumbria, some adhering to St Colman, Finan's successor at Lindisfarne, and others favouring the adoption of the distinctive Roman rites.

Oswy had hardly come to the middle of his reign when he was able to take vengeance on the Mercians at the Battle of Winwidfield, where Penda was slain (655), and the liberation of Northumbria from Mercian inroads was accomplished. Penda had remained a pagan to the end, but his two sons, Peada and Wulphere, who succeeded him in turn, became Christians. An entrance was now gained for the evangelisation of the Midlands. Among the disciples of St Aidan at Lindisfarne were four brothers of Angle race, Chad, Cedd, Cynegils, and Ceawlin. The first of these was to become the patron of the Mercian diocese. But much of the glory of the propagation of the Faith in Mercia belongs to the Irish monks at Lindisfarne, who had trained the instruments for the work. Diuma, Ceollach, Trumhere, and Jarman had all been

Christianity in Mercia.

consecrated by St Finan at Lindisfarne, and had passed on to lay the foundations of religion in the newly opened field. St Chad went from Lindisfarne to Ireland, and lived under St Egbert for a while at Mayo of the Saxons, as it was called. Then he came home to unite with his brother, St Cedd, in the foundation of a monastery at Lastingham in Yorkshire. Cedd joined him after still more extended travels, having co-operated with the King St Sigebert in the preaching of the Faith to the East Saxons. Cedd now remained at the head of the Lastingham Monastery until his death, when his brother, St Chad, became his successor. He was consecrated bishop after a while with a view to his becoming Bishop of York, but Prince Alchfrid opposed this, urging the prior claims of his friend, St Wilfrid, and Chad retired to Lastingham. Still, his retirement was but brief, for by this time King Wulphere had made much progress in the development of the Faith in Mercia, over which he now ruled, and, besides giving a liberal charter for a new abbey at Medehampstead, since called Peterborough, over which Sexwulf was set as first Abbot, began a generous foundation to establish a see at Lichfield. In 669 St Chad was called to become the first Bishop of Lichfield, and having built a church and monastery, he resided there until his death in 672. His bones rested in the Cathedral until the Reformation, when, unlike so many precious relics of the saints of old, they were fortunately removed before they could be desecrated. Long ages afterwards they were enshrined in the new Catholic Cathedral dedicated under his name at Birmingham.

The Apostolate of St Cedd had come to an end many years before that of his brother Chad. Cedd had been made a bishop much sooner, and then laboured with the support of the good King St Sigebert to restore the Faith in Essex, whence it had been banished by Sebert's sons, when they drove away St Mellitus. Cedd more than once came to visit his native Northumbria. It came to pass that he was there when Lastingham was founded, and he seems to have accepted the government of that house. At Lastingham pestilence proved fatal to him in 664. Thereupon, Wini, Bishop of Wessex, seems to have taken charge of the diocese of London until his

New Evangelisation of Essex.

HEPTARCHY EVANGELISATION

death in 675. St Theodore of Canterbury then consecrated St Erconwald to fill the vacant see.

Redwald, King of the East Anglians, became a Christian while in Kent in St Ethelbert's reign. He did not remain faithful to the doctrines which he had accepted. Hence but little progress was made in the conversion of East Anglia as long as he lived. Neither were things much brighter under his elder son and successor, Eorpwald. But his younger son, Sigebert, who had incurred his father's enmity, fled into Gaul, and was there baptised. Now, it came to pass that when Eorpwald was dead his inheritance fell to Sigebert, and he being a good and zealous Christian had nothing more at heart than the conversion of his subjects to Christianity. A Burgundian bishop named Felix was at that time staying with Honorius, Archbishop of Canterbury, to whom he expressed his longing to engage in evangelical labours for the conversion of some part of England which still remained pagan. To East Anglia then Honorius directed the zealous prelate, who received a cordial welcome from Sigebert, and was able to establish himself at Dunwich in Suffolk, which thus became the first episcopal see in East Anglia. Here St Felix lived as bishop for seventeen years, during which time he was able to plant the Faith firmly in the kingdom of Sigebert. When he died in 647, the same Honorius, who had directed him to East Anglia, consecrated a successor, Thomas, to fill his see. Dunwich has been swallowed up by the encroaching tide, but the seaside town of Felixstowe still bears the name of the Burgundian saint. There also came to East Anglia in Sigebert's reign the holy Irish monk, St Fursey, who built himself a monastery at Burgh Castle, and remained in the country for fifteen years, during which, as St Bede tells us, he was the divine instrument in the conversion of many souls. After this, Fursey passed into Gaul, where he presided over a noble monastery, and lived a most ascetic life.

St Felix and St Fursey in East Anglia (647).

To Wessex there came an apostolic missioner, Birinus, direct from Rome, sent by Pope Honorius, and consecrated by St Asterius at Genoa in 634. Landing in Hampshire in 635 he began to preach to King Kynegils and his people. His success was immediate. Kynegils was baptised, and it is noteworthy that St Oswald, who had come from the north for the hand of the king's daughter, stood as his godfather at the baptismal font. A joint arrangement made by Kynegils and Oswald secured the foundation of a bishop's see at Dorchester, near the Mercian border. There St Birinus established himself. Kenwalch, the son and successor of Kynegils, refused to become a Christian, but being expelled from his kingdom after a crushing defeat at the hands of the Mercian Penda, he took refuge with King Anna, who had succeeded Sigebert in East Anglia. Here, the example and exhortation of this pious prince induced him to embrace the Faith, and when he was later on enabled to return to his kingdom he did so as a Christian. He found St Birinus already dead in 650. But a French or Gaelic bishop named Egilbert, on his way from Ireland to his native land, visited at this time the court of Kenwalch, and by his piety and learning so impressed the King of Wessex, that the latter induced him to settle down and become bishop and teacher of his people. Egilbert, therefore, continued to reside for some years at Dorchester, thus becoming in an informal sort of way the successor of Birinus. Still, on further acquaintance, the foreign speech and manners of Egilbert so disappointed Kenwalch that the monarch resolved to persuade Wini, an Anglo-Saxon who had been consecrated in Gaul as a missionary to his fellow-countrymen, to stay with him. To provide a sphere of labour for both, Wini was installed at Winchester, of which city he is counted as the first bishop, while Egilbert continued to act as bishop for the northern part of the kingdom at Dorchester. It was a subsequent quarrel with the king which caused Wini to leave Wessex and undertake the government of the vacant see of London, where he remained until his death in 675. Egilbert remained in Dorchester for some time, and even took part in some of the Mercian and Northumbrian affairs, but eventually he decided to return to his own country He was begged to return, but did not see his way to comply with the request. However, he had his nephew, Eleutherius, consecrated, and sent him to England in his stead. This prelate played a considerable part in the ecclesiastical history of the next period.

St Birinus in Wessex (635).

HEPTARCHY EVANGELISATION

Amongst the various realms of the Heptarchy there now remained but one which had not received the good tidings of the Christian faith. It was the smallest of all, that of the South Saxons, a tribe cut off from all communication by land with its neighbours on account of the great forests of the Andred's Weald, which stretched along its whole northern border. Sussex had to wait for the coming as an exile of the indefatigable St Wilfrid in 681. But ere this happened, stirring events had changed the course of Church History in the northern parts of England.

In Northumbria there was rivalry and disunion both in calendar and customs, though we must be on our guard against imagining that this meant diversity of faith as well. Celt and Saxon strove with noble emulation to advance the kingdom of Christ. Monasteries were built and churches founded with equal zeal by the one party and the other.

St Hilda, Abbess of Whitby (680).

The first two Bishops of Lindisfarne, St Aidan and St Finan, also exerted themselves to extend the benefits of the monastic life to women as well. They found their chief instruments in effecting this in the royal sisters Hilda and Hereswitha, kinswomen of St Oswald and Oswy. They had both passed south from their northern home with the intention of taking the veil at the Abbey of Celles in Gaul, when Hilda was called back to Northumbria at the prayer of St Aidan, who offered her land for a house of religious women at Southwick-on-Wear. After spending some time in setting on foot a house for nuns on this spot, she was called to preside over an already existing convent at Hartlepool. Finally, after governing this establishment for some years, she quitted it, and under the guidance of St Finan, began a new abbey on the Yorkshire coast, choosing the lofty promontory of Strenshall, now called Whitby, for a site. St Finan, and after him St Colman, the third Bishop of Lindisfarne, continued to watch over this house, and St Hilda governed it so wisely and well that it became a centre of piety and sacred science. Out of that sacred retreat came forth no fewer than five bishops destined later on to play a great part in the affairs of the Church. These were Bosa, St John of Beverley, and St Wilfrid—all in turn occupants of the see of York, Hedda of Winchester, and Oftfor of

Worcester. Within the same peaceful home lived the chief Anglo-Saxon poet, Cædmon, who was a labourer employed in the simple agricultural labours of the monastery. Cædmon was thought to be quite unskilled in the arts of music and song on which his contemporaries set so much store. But, really, his incapacity was only that of being unable to bring down his genius to sing on the trifling themes which others sang of : on divine things he could make poetry as no one ever did in the Anglo-Saxon tongue either before or since. His great poem known as the " Creation " can be likened to nothing except Milton's " Paradise Lost," and is certainly the masterpiece of Anglo-Saxon literature.

Whitby being what it was, small wonder that when King Oswy, disturbed at the confusion caused even at the royal court, by some keeping Easter at one time, and others at another, suggested a conference to determine the points at dispute, this sanctuary of piety and learning should be chosen as the meeting-place for the Council. This is known as the Synod of Whitby. Egilbert, who had recently retired from the see of Dorchester, was there, and with him stood Wilfrid, both convinced champions of the Roman rite. On the other side was St Colman, Bishop of Lindisfarne, whose rites and customs naturally found favour with St Hilda and her community. So did then also with the Bishop St Cedd, who was there, while King Oswy and his son Alchfrid attended to hear what was to be said on both sides of the argument. Bishop Colman spoke first, defending the Easter observance of the Celtic Church by the authority of St John the Evangelist, and the Easter Cycle of Anatolius, urging also that their father, the wonder-working St Columba, had ever kept the same reckoning. Bishop Egilbert then directed Wilfrid to speak in his name in favour of the Roman observance of Easter. This he did, quoting the practice of the Holy Apostles Peter and Paul, and the general usage of the Catholic Church, approved by the decrees of St Peter's successors, and only dissented from by a comparatively insignificant minority. "As for Columba," he went on, "though he was a holy man and a worker of miracles, yet can he be preferred to the most blessed Prince of the Apostles to whom the Lord said: ' Thou art Peter, and upon this

Synod of Whitby (664).

rock I will build my church, and the gates of hell shall not prevail against it, and to thee will I give the keys of the Kingdom of Heaven?' Then said the king: 'Is it true, Colman, that these words were said to Peter by Our Lord?' 'It is true, O King,' he replied. Then said he: 'Can you show any such power given to your Columba?' Columba answered: 'None.' 'Then,' concluded the king: 'Since he is the doorkeeper I will not contradict him, lest when I come to heaven's gate there be none to open it to me, if he is my adversary.'"
The decision was a final one, and the cause of the Roman rite had triumphed. Colman left Northumbria, and returned to the land of the Scots. Cedd abandoned the Celtic custom and conformed to the Catholic observance. So did the abbey of Whitby, where St Hilda continued to rule until her death in 680. Tuda became Bishop of Lindisfarne, but only survived for a few years, when he was replaced by Eata, the Abbot of Melrose. But the Easter controversy was at an end as far as the Church in England was concerned.

No one exercised so great an influence in securing that the decision taken at Whitby should be finally accepted in Northumbria as the far-famed St Cuthbert. For, even if not a Celt himself, he was the most illustrious scholar of the Celtic monks of Melrose and Ripon. He was probably the son of a peasant, born near Melrose Abbey, and he had not advanced far along his way of life when his piety led him to put on the monastic habit at the Abbey, where at that time St Eata was abbot and St Boisil prior. When St Aidan made his second foundation at Ripon, before he fixed his see at Lindisfarne, St Eata, whom he transferred thither, took Cuthbert with him to join the new community. But when Eata was replaced by Wilfrid at Ripon, Cuthbert returned to Melrose with his Abbot, being chosen Prior at St Boisil's death in 664. After the Synod of Whitby held in that same year, Cuthbert was sent as prior to Lindisfarne with the express object of introducing the Roman Easter into that religious house, which by this time had surpassed Melrose in importance. He was eminently successful, but, after some years, through love of the contemplative life he retired from the monastery to an eremitical cell on the small island of Farne, which was nine miles distant.

St Cuthbert (635-687).

Once he went to Coquet Island to hold conference with St Elfleda, who succeeded St Hilda in 680 as Abbess of Whitby. Then came the synod on the banks of the Alne, held by St Theodore, where he was chosen Bishop of Lindisfarne, while St Eata was named for Hexham. His humble reluctance to accept the dignity being overcome, Cuthbert was consecrated at York in 685 by Archbishop Theodore. For two years he continued his labours, preaching and teaching with marvellous effect, but at the end of 686 he seems to have felt the approach of death, and resigning his see, once more retired to the solitude of Farne, where two months later he breathed his last. His remains, which were found incorrupt, were several time translated. They found at length a noble resting-place in the new cathedral at Durham, where they became the centre of widespread veneration which went so far as to enhance the whole dignity of the see, and to win for its County Palatine the title of the Patrimony of St Cuthbert. An unsettled controversy is waged over the question as to whether his bones still remain there, or were removed for safety at the time of the Reformation. His episcopal ring is kept at Ushaw College, and the copy of the Gospels found in his coffin, known as the " Book of St Cuthbert," is in the British Museum.

IV.
THE ORGANISATION OF THE ANGLO-SAXON CHURCH.

(671-735.)

AT the death of the Saxon, Frithona, better known by his Latin name, Deusdedit, who was Archbishop of Canterbury from 655 to 664, there was already a tendency to strengthen the organisation of the church by giving a fuller measure of metropolitan rights to the future occupant of that see. It was with this object in view, that Wighard was selected by the Bretwalda and the King of Kent to go to Rome, in order that being consecrated there, he might come back armed with full powers. Wighard, indeed, travelled to Rome, but took ill and died in that city in 667 before the rite of episcopal consecration was performed. Thus it became a pressing problem to choose someone to execute the great work which had been expected from him. It was unlikely that England, which had presumably sent her best, could provide another man fit for the great opportunity; and there was danger in delay. The eyes of the Pope and his advisers first fell upon the Abbot Adrian, an African, who was at that time head of a monastery near Naples. This humble religious, however, shrank from the honour, and being asked to point out another to take up the burden in his stead, named the Greek monk, Theodore of Tarsus, a man well versed in both Latin and Greek letters. It is true he was already more than sixty years of age, and though a monk had hitherto played not a small part in public affairs. Still, on condition that Adrian would accompany him, he accepted the weighty office, and neither his age nor his previous seclusion seemed to stand in the way of twenty-two years of most active and

St Theodore of Canterbury (671-693).

authoritative rule. Not being a priest as yet, he was ordained and consecrated; and then in 671 started for England with Adrian and Benet Biscop and quite a large band of helpers for his work. On his arrival in the country his first step was to appoint Benet Biscop Abbot of SS. Peter and Paul at Canterbury. However, a little later, when Adrian, who had been detained in Gaul, arrived, Benet gave up this charge to him, and set off on what was to him a fourth journey to Rome, to secure more helpers and more books for the work before him.

It was not very long before Archbishop Theodore set out to make a successive visitation of almost every part of England. During this round, full of organising energy, his constant adviser and companion was the Abbot Adrian. Where sees were vacant he filled them up, where things had fallen into confusion he made regulations for future good order, where lawful authority seemed doubtful he gave decisions which made for certainty. It was in this way that at last he reached York, where he found the bishop an exile, and Chad installed in his place. The result of his inquiries was to make it clear to him that St Wilfrid had been unjustly deprived. Hence he decreed that Wilfrid should assume once more the episcopal charge at York, and that St Chad should retire. The latter passed in the first instance to the monastery of Lastingham. There he remained until the munificence of King Wulphere made it possible to appoint him to the See of Lichfield, which that monarch had founded. Wilfrid, being thus reinstated at York, entered upon a period of almost unbounded influence in the Northumbrian kingdom. York was his, the capital of the kingdom and the cradle of Northern Christianity. Ripon was his: it was the monastic home of his youth. Hexham likewise was under his sway; and there were many who thought that its new and well-built minster rivalled the glories of either of the older churches.

Theodore's Visitation (671).

Having then, as he hoped, settled the possession of these northern bishoprics, and also filled the vacant sees, and paved the way for unity in the Easter question, Theodore thought the time had come for a National Synod. This council was held at Hertford in 673, and was attended by Theodore, Archbishop of Canterbury, and

Council of Hertford (673).

THE ANGLO-SAXON CHURCH 45

also in person or by proxy by Bisi, Bishop of the East Anglians, Wilfrid of York, Putta of Rochester, Winfrid of Lichfield, and Eleutherius of Dorchester. The canons of this Council, which are still extant, are of the highest interest, as being the earliest examples of conciliar legislation for the English Church possessed by us. It was laid down (1) that all shall keep Easter together on the Sunday after the fourteenth day of the moon of the first month; (2) that no bishop shall intrude into the diocese of another; (3) that no bishop shall interfere with consecrated monasteries or remove anything thence; (4) that monks shall not change their abode without the leave of their abbot; (5) that no cleric shall leave his own diocese, nor be received in another, without letters of recommendation from his bishop; (6) that bishops and priests shall not officiate outside of their own diocese without leave of the local ordinary; (7) that there shall be a yearly council at Cloveshoe; (8) that the bishops shall be contented with the precedence given them by the date of their consecration; (9) that additional bishops shall be appointed as the number of the faithful grows; (10) that marriages shall not be made within the forbidden degrees of kindred, nor broken by divorces, and separated persons not allowed to marry again. All then agreed to acknowledge Theodore as their sole metropolitan or primate, and the fathers separated to return home.

This Council comes down to us clothed with a double importance; for not only was it the exemplar and beginning of the numerous synods of the English Church in the centuries to come, but it also formed a pattern and motive for civil legislation as well. The Witenagemots of the Anglo-Saxons and the Parliaments of Norman England, if they are traced back to their origin, will be found in embryo in the primitive gathering over which Theodore presided at Hertford.

Although the Synod of Hertford in this way laid down the main lines on which the chief outstanding difficulties could be met, it was very far from solving them all at once. Theodore found resistance, **Theodore's** of what kind we know not, from Winfrid **Difficulties** at Lichfield, and thereupon deposed him in (678). favour of Sexwulf, the Abbot of Medehampstead. Putta also had withdrawn from Rochester, which had suffered severely in a Mercian inroad, and after the fruitless appointment of Chuichelm, it was only by the appointment of Gifmund that the see found stability in its pastor. And then there were still greater difficulties from Northumbria. St Wilfrid's prosperity in that kingdom was to be clouded over by ill-will. King Egfrid's second wife, Ermenburga, began to suspect the holy bishop of taking part in proceedings hostile to her and her friends, and proceeded to breathe her suspicions into the ear of the king. Finally, Egfrid seems to have been led to judge Wilfrid in an unfavourable manner, as being too powerful and imperious, and in order to get him deposed invited Theodore to the north. His case was put so well that Theodore deposed Wilfrid and divided the Northumbrian land into two dioceses, viz., that of York and that of Hexham, besides which, he named a bishop of Lindsey and another for the Picts. This appeared to Wilfrid like cutting his former jurisdiction into four parts, and he felt aggrieved and paralysed in his activity. But there is one refuge for the Catholic clergy, whether priest or bishop, in the hour of violence and abuse of jurisdiction: the See of Peter. To Rome then Wilfrid determined to appeal, and announced his intention of going there to plead his cause in person. And he was not the man to interpose delay between his projects and determined efforts to carry them through.

Travelling by way of Frisia, Wilfrid encountered a journey full of adventures and delays. The pagan Frisians, among whom he first landed, treated him with such hospitality that he made a stay of some months in their midst, repaying their generosity by preaching to them the Gospel. When one of the Frankish kings sent to demand that he should be given up as a captive, the Frisian prince absolutely refused. And the overtures of another Frankish prince that he would stay and accept the See of Strassburg were equally powerless to make him forget his goal in Rome. At Rome then at length he arrived, though of course he found the envoys of his opponents, who had travelled more directly, already beforehand with him. However, the Pope, St Agatho, got together a council of some fifty bishops, and St Wilfrid's appeal was gone into. The result of the inquiry was that the emptiness of the charges made against him by the ill-will of his enemies was established, while

Wilfrid in Rome.

in the division of his diocese, without his being consulted, it was ruled an uncanonical procedure had been used. Wilfrid declared he did not object to the appointment of a greater number of bishops, but only claimed that these new arrangements should be made after taking counsel with all the bishops. Consequently, he was pronounced clear of all the charges made against him, and sent back to his see, the bishops who had supplanted him being ordered to retire. He was to choose such episcopal helpers as were required by the state of the work and of the diocese.

After an interval spent in satisfying his piety by visits to the different Roman sanctuaries, Wilfrid started on his return journey to England. It is probable that he had as fellow-travellers St Benet Biscop and John the Precentor or Arch-cantor of St Peter's choir. *Wilfrid's Return.* The ostensible object of the latter's mission was to teach the Roman chant in St Benet's abbey at Wearmouth, but he is said to have been further commissioned by the Pope to inquire into the faith of the English Church, and to secure its explicit adhesion to the doctrines recently defined against the Monophysite and other Eastern heretics. It was no doubt part of the same design to assemble a synod of the chief bishops and clergy which met at Hatfield in 680 and drew up a Profession of Faith, extracts from which have been preserved in St Bede's "History." The Five General Councils are mentioned and accepted, as well as Pope Martin's Lateran Council of 649, which condemned the Monophysites and anathematised the celebrated Three Chapters of Ibas, Theodore, and Theodoret. The Abbot John seems to have signed the synodal decrees as delegate of the Holy See, but the disciplinary arrangements did not meet with the same unanimity as the dogmatic decrees. It is true that the archiepiscopal rights of York were admitted, and the charter of the new monasery of Medehampstead was signed, but the directions of the Holy See concerning the restoration of Wilfrid aroused violent opposition, especially on the part of the king and queen. Wilfrid was seized and shut up in the castle of Brunanburgh (or Bamburgh). His release was owing to the intervention of the Abbess of Coldingham, who represented the injustice of this persecution to the king with rare courage. Egfrid then gave the holy archbishop his liberty, and he retired into Mercia. However, it chanced that the Queen of Wessex was sister to the Northumbrian queen, Ethelburga, and hence he was ordered to leave the realm. The same thing happened in Wessex, and it was then that, chased from place to place, St Wilfrid passed over into the pagan kingdom of Sussex, and repaid their shelter by labouring for the conversion of both king and people as narrated above.

Meanwhile, Benet Biscop and the Abbot John had gone on to the Monkwearmouth monastery, which had suffered severely during the absence of its founder. The commencement of the monastery which Benet Biscop had built on the Wear goes back to 674, and since then he had journeyed to Rome repeatedly for its good. He had always returned laden with good things, both spiritual and temporal—books, vestments, relics, with workmen for the buildings, and now he had brought the Abbot John as an instructor to his community in all the intricacies of the Roman chant. King Egfrid had been generous in his grants of land to the new abbey: in fact its possessions reached, at any rate at one point, from the Wear to the Tyne; so when the number of the brethren allowed of it, Benet sent forth a colony, and at the northern extremity of the abbey lands built a second religious house at the place called Jarrow. Just as the former foundation had been in honour of the Apostle St Peter, so was this to bear the name of St Paul. This took place in 682, but for many years Benet continued to rule both houses, which were so closely united in harmony and love as to be as St Bede declares, "One single monastery built in two different places." Once again Benet went on pilgrimage to Rome, for the second monastery needed treasures of books and paintings and altar furniture no less than the first. But this time on his return he found that a fatal pestilence had carried off a great number of the monks, and desolation reigned in the once prosperous homes of prayer. Sigfrid had been chosen abbot at Wearmouth; at Jarrow only Ceolfrid and a little boy remained. Benet set himself to repair the losses as well as he could, though he himself was struck by illness for three years. Still, gradually the life of both monasteries revived, and when Benet and Sigfrid were dead, Ceolfrid became abbot of both the houses.

Monkwearmouth and Jarrow.

THE ANGLO-SAXON CHURCH 49

There are those who think that the little boy, who, together with Ceolfrid, was the surviving link between Benet's first and later community at Jarrow, was no other than the Venerable Bede, who was to be the glory of his house and his race. Born on the lands of St Benet's monastery, probably at Monkwearmouth, about the year 673, he himself tells us that he was placed at the age of seven under the care of St Benet at Wearmouth. Later on, when the Jarrow monastery had been founded, he was transferred thither under the care of Ceolfrid, its first abbot; and in this house he spent all the rest of his laborious life. He tells us that he was ordained deacon in the nineteenth, and priest in the thirtieth, year of his age, by St John of Beverley, at that time Bishop of Hexham. It is recorded of him that from time to time he took short and apparently unfrequent journeys to visit religious friends in various monasteries of the north. But, apart from this, his life was an unwearied round of monastic duties, turning from the direct service of God, to study, teaching, and writing, and then back again to psalmody or liturgical celebrations. His knowledge was, according to the measure of the time, quite encyclopædic; and he was ever most diligent to increase his stores. "*Semper aut discere aut docere aut scribere dulce habui*," was his motto, and to this he was faithful till old age came on and the lamp of life died down. His works, which fill several folio volumes, comprise almost every subject on which a scholar could write in those times. Geography, astronomy, chronology, history, biography, and above all the Holy Scriptures are to be found treated with an industry and moderation which stamps the author both as an Englishman and a Benedictine. But the judgment of the Holy Church has found higher qualities still. Using his homilies for a very large number of the lessons in the Breviary, she has in these latter days accorded him the honourable title, borne by barely a score of her luminaries, of *Doctor of the Church*. He was still occupied in his favourite studies when he died. He had all but finished his translation of St John's Gospel into Anglo-Saxon when his strength seemed to fail so completely that his power to dictate any further seemed gone. "Dearest master," said the scribe, "one sentence yet remains." "Write

The Venerable Bede (673-736.)

D

quickly," replied the dying saint. And he went on with his dictation till it was done. With the exclamation of the writer, " Now it is finished," he found strength to say : " You say truly it is finished. Now take my head in your arms and turn me towards the holy place where I have so often prayed." Then, lying on the floor of the cell, he intoned for the last time the Doxology : " Glory be to the Father and to the Son and to the Holy Ghost." As he pronounced the name of the Third Divine Person he gave up his soul. Peaceful and yet laborious end to the life of the true monk who had never spared himself in learning, teaching, and writing, and now solemnly ended by consecrating all to God !

But while Benet Biscop and Bede were engaged in such solid work for the religious life amongst men, others were labouring with equal devotion to provide havens of security for consecrated women. St Wilfrid in his early years had been familiar with the glories of Whitby under St Hilda ; some time later he was concerned with the still more romantic career of St Etheldreda, Abbess of Ely. She was the daughter of King Anna of East Anglia, and had been betrothed to a neighbouring prince named Tonbert, but had never lived with him. Tonbert's early death left her a period of five years to cherish the vocation to a religious life which had been given her. However, at the end of that time, Anna married her for political reasons to Egfrid, King of Northumbria. She was not a consenting party to the contract, but Egfrid applied to St Wilfrid to induce her to accept him as in very truth her husband. The saint, being put in possession of all the facts of the case, counselled delay. She was consequently allowed to go to the convent at Coldingham, which had been founded and was ruled by her aunt, St Ebba. There she remained for some time in peace, but when it became clear that Egfrid was still minded to carry her off by force, she fled with two companions to her native East Anglia. In this kingdom she owned an estate on the Isle of Ely, and, being assisted by her royal relatives, she succeeded in establishing in this place what afterwards became the renowned Abbey of Ely. Wilfrid, in the meantime, had gone to Rome again, and being in complete sympathy with her aspirations, busied himself whilst there in gain-

St Etheldreda at Ely (667).

THE ANGLO-SAXON CHURCH 51

ing approval and precious privileges for the new foundation from the Holy See. Yet these favours never reached her, for while St Wilfrid was still absent, she fell ill, and died of the plague in 679. Nevertheless, the house she had founded waxed strong, first under her sister, St Sexburga, and then under a line of holy abbesses, so that it became one of the chief abbeys of the land; in fact it was eventually the site of a powerful diocese. St Etheldreda's shrine was the centre of a quite extraordinary veneration in the magnificent church which afterwards replaced the original one. It is still a landmark as it stretches its graceful and noble length across the landscape of the Fen country. Among the Saxon saints it would be hard to find one more renowned among our forefathers, or more honoured to-day than St Etheldreda or St Audrey, as she is sometimes called. When the bishops of Ely became great prelates, and must have a London palace, the chapel they built to serve it was dedicated to St Etheldreda. This same elegant Gothic building, now restored to Catholic hands, forms one of the most touching links to be seen between modern London and the city of mediaeval days.

There was another foundation for religious women begun in this period, scarcely less interesting than Ely, which is more especially connected with the memory of Archbishop St Theodore: this was the abbey at Minster in Thanet. Its history takes us back to one of those families composed of saints, which were such an honour to the Anglo-Saxon Church. This was the household of Merewald, King of the Mercians, and his holy spouse, St Ermenburga. The Mercian princes, Ethelred and Ethelbert, had been murdered in Kent: hence it was agreed that by way of expiation a religious house should be built, and the place selected was Minster in Thanet. St Ermenburga travelled thither to arrange the necessary details, being either accompanied or followed by her daughter, Mildred. The latter then proceeded to the Abbey of Celles in Gaul, there to receive her training in the life of the cloister. She persevered in the austere life of that house for several years in the midst of various difficulties. Then she returned to Kent, where she found that the community at Minster, under the fostering care of St Ermenburga, and the protection of St Theodore, had grown to

St Mildred in Thanet.

the number of seventy persons. Mildred was solemnly received into the house by the holy archbishop, and not so long after chosen abbess. Mildred presided over the abbey for nearly thirty years, and when she died, was followed as abbess by another saint, who had been her disciple, St Edburga. The remains of St Mildred, after being interred at Minster, were translated to St Augustine's Abbey at Canterbury, where they were visited by many pilgrims and graced by many favours granted to her clients. One of St Mildred's sisters, St Milburga, founded a convent at Wenlock in Shropshire, while another, St Mildgyth, led a holy life in one of the religious houses of Northumbria.

Wulphere, King of Mercia, had been instrumental both in solidifying the Mercian power, and in propagating the Christian religion in his dominions. His influence was felt beyond the bounds of the former Mercian realm, as for instance in the establishment of Medehampstead, in the Fen country and in the annexation and evangelisation of the Isle of Wight. Eoppa was sent south to preach Christianity to the islanders. In fact, when Mercia could get no further north through the Northumbrian resistance ever steadily renewed, Wulphere seems to have turned his attention to the extension of his power at the expense of Wessex and Kent. Towards Sussex he was friendly, giving over the Isle of Wight to Edilwalch, the South Saxon king, on the day of the latter's baptism, the credit for which must be divided between Wulphere and the great Northumbrian exile, Wilfrid. But Wulphere's power melted away even before his death: both Northumbria and Wessex got under arms against him, and after his death Egfrid was able to ravage the northern part of his lands. On the other hand in Wessex there was a great revival under the warlike Cædwalla who, after being banished through a family feud, made friends with St Wilfrid, also in exile, and then came home to Wessex to ascend the throne with general favour. He made war in turn on Sussex, Kent, and the Isle of Wight, and reduced them all once more to dependence on Wessex. His friendship with St Wilfrid was followed by his conversion to Christianity by that saint. His baptism was, however, deferred, as he wished to receive it from the Sovereign Pontiff himself. To Rome then he travelled as a pilgrim and penitent, but after receiving the Sacrament of initiation into the Church on Easter Eve, 688, took ill, and died within the week, never having laid aside the white garments in which the newly baptised were clothed. Cædwalla was buried in St Peter's basilica.

The work of organising what Cædwalla had won fell to his kinsman, Ine, who was now chosen king. The Christian piety of Ine has won for him the appellation of saint. Having assembled his Witan, he drew up a code of laws in seventy-nine articles, which established a scale of compensation for injuries, checked feuds, and gave state protection to the subjugated Britons. His warlike enterprises were likewise many. He was able to make advance in the gradual progress of subduing the Britons of the West; he once more devastated Kent, and conquered Essex. His struggle with Mercia was sanguinary but only led to indecisive results. With the Weregild, which he exacted from Kent for the death of his kinsman, Mollo, whom the Kentish men had burnt to death, he was able to make pious foundations for their souls, and for the health of his own. The old sanctuary of Glastonbury was restored by him, this time as an Anglo-Saxon monastery. Malmesbury owed him much. Moreover, when Hedda, Bishop of Winchester, died in 705, Ine favoured the division of Wessex into two dioceses, and with his assistance a new bishopric was established at Sherborne, Hedda's successor, Daniel, being restricted to the eastern portion of the kingdom.

Ine, King of Wessex (688-725).

For the government of the new diocese Ine had the services of the pious scholar whose work threw an early morning light on Anglo-Saxon literature— his kinsman, St Aldhelm. Sprung like Ine of the royal house of Cerdic, most probably Aldhelm owed his early training to that Irish monk, Maildulf, who had already established a religious house at Malmesbury. But, besides this, he paid two visits to Canterbury, where he profited much by the lessons of the Abbot Adrian, whom he gratefully commemorates as his master and "the opener of his intelligence." At Canterbury he studied Holy Scripture and the classic languages to such effect that he easily surpassed all contemporaries in Britain in literary attainments. When his studies were over, Aldhelm returned to

St Aldhelm (639-709).

Malmesbury, where he succeeded Maildulf as abbot, and ruled the abbey for thirty years. Under the protection of King Ine the abbey grew so rapidly in numbers and importance that it became one of the first in the land, and Aldhelm may with reason be looked upon as its chief founder. The saint was over sixty years of age when Hedda died, and he was reluctantly obliged to accept the office of first Bishop of Sherborne. He survived but a few years, and did not during that period give up the abbacy of Malmesbury. In the year 709 St Aldhelm breathed his last. He is the earliest Anglo-Saxon author in prose, whose works are extant, though it must be confessed that they are all in Latin, unless it be true that the earlier portions of the Anglo-Saxon Chronicle, as some hold, are from his pen. His chief work is a treatise on the "Praise of Virginity." His Saxon verses are spoken of, but they have unfortunately perished. He also wrote a letter on the Paschal Question to the Western Britons, which is said to have brought many of them back to unity on this point.

The close of the life of King Ine was not unlike that of his predecessor, Cædwalla. Having done much for the furtherance of religion (for, besides the foundations already spoken of, he had built churches at Abingdon and Tisbury), when old age came on, and he found himself no longer equal to the cares of government, he summoned his counsellors around him in a Witan held in the year 728. He then voluntarily abdicated, and soon after set out for Rome in company with his consort, Queen Ermenburga. Arrived there, he sedulously visited the shrines of the Holy Apostles, and the other resorts of Christian piety. He lived in Rome for less than a year in retirement, clothed in plain clothes, and leading a simple workman's life. He died in 729 and was buried in the City of the Popes, probably in the porch of St Peter's Church. He was not long after followed to the grave by Queen Ermenburga. The establishment of the Anglo-Saxon hospice in Rome, under the name of *Schola Anglorum*, is attributed to him by Matthew Paris, though William of Malmesbury assigns it to King Offa. Probably Offa endowed or re-founded what Ine had begun. In the same way the establishment of the Rome-Scot of a silver denarius from each family is spoken of in the case both of Ine and of Offa, though its

THE ANGLO-SAXON CHURCH 55

connection with the maintenance of the *Schola Anglorum* at Sto. Spirito in Sassia is made clearer in the case of Ine. Great indeed must have been the devotion of this old Saxon warrior to the Universal Church whose centre is Rome, for not content with laying his bones at St Peter's feet, he did all that in him lay to secure by his pious foundation that the same spirit should be kept warm and lasting in the princes and people who were to come after him.

V.

THE TRIPLE LEADERSHIP.

(735-800.)

Northumbria, Mercia, and Wessex. WHATEVER external signs of equality might appear among the seven kingdoms of the Heptarchy from the fact that they all began independent of each other, these soon vanished. Kent and Sussex fell into a state of dependence upon Wessex; East Anglia and Essex began to suffer more and more from the inroads of the Northmen, and at last their separate existence was a very precarious one. There remained the more powerful kingdoms of Northumbria, Mercia, and Wessex. These three long contended for the mastery which remained doubtful among them. There were for all of them alternations of success and failure for nearly a century. Hence the period comprised in this chapter was above all one of intestine war between these three rivals. So persistent were the conflicts, and so baleful their effects, that the development of Christian civilisation was thereby woefully hindered. Amid lawlessness and disorder piety and the religious life were allowed to languish.

When King Ine resigned his crown in 728, he gave the Witan a recommendation to choose as his successor his brother-in-law, Ethelheard. Two rivals, Oswald and Cuthwin, started up to dispute the inheritance, but Ethelheard was able to overcome them, and then to reign over Ine's realm for the space of thirteen years. Still, he was unable to avoid an acknowledgment of the superiority of Ethelbald, King of Mercia (723-757), who in the course of a long reign attained a greater width of dominion than any of his Mercian predecessors had

THE TRIPLE LEADERSHIP

reached. Ethelbald's youth was stained with many vices, but, as he advanced in years, he appears to have reformed his conduct. Ethelbald was present at the Council held at Cloveshoe in 747, under the presidency of Cuthbert, Archbishop of Canterbury, for the rooting out of abuses and the good of morality. The Council of Hertford ordered annual synods, but this is the first after Hertford of which we have a reliable account. It was held in response to letters from Pope St Zachary, addressed to the whole English nation. Twelve bishops attended, including Cuthbert of Canterbury who presided, and, besides King Ethelbald, many of the clergy and laity were also there. The decrees throw some light upon the state of the Church in England at the time. They may be summarised as follows: The proceedings began with the reading and translation of the two papal letters, after which about thirty canons of discipline were drawn up, by which in the first place bishops are commanded to fulfil the duties of their charge with all solicitude, being careful, moreover, to keep unity and harmony with one another, however widely divided they may be by distance of place. The duty of canonical visitation is to be carefully discharged. The clergy must be examined before they are ordained. In the administration of the Sacraments, and in the celebration of Mass, as also in the recital of the Divine Office, the Roman rite is to be exclusively followed, as well as the uniform keeping of Feasts and Fasts according to the Roman calendar. The name of St Augustine is to be added after that of St Gregory in the Litanies, and the Feasts of both these apostles of the country are to be kept with solemnity. We also find words of exhortation to clerks, nuns, and monks to live apart from the laity, and to wear the dress of their own state in life. Public prayers are enjoined for kings and dukes and all Christian people.

The Council of Cloveshoe (747).

Archbishop Cuthbert lived for another ten years to rule Canterbury after the Council of Cloveshoe, dying only in 758, after an episcopate of twenty-two years. In the following year Bregwin, who came from the " old Saxon land," but had not so far held any high office, was chosen to succeed him on account of his merit and reputation for

Succession of Primates.

prudence. He filled the see from 759 to 765. He was then laid to rest beside his predecessor in the cathedral. However, the tradition is that Jaenbert, Abbot of St Augustine's, came with an armed force to remove the body to that abbey, but found the funeral already over. Of this he complained, and declared that he would appeal to the Pope. The appeal did not prevent him from making such a good impression upon the monks of Christchurch that they decided at once to end the dispute, and fill the vacant see by choosing Jaenbert for their archbishop. His conduct was assigned to zeal for the honour of his abbey, and taken as a good omen for what he would do as archbishop. He soon obtained the pallium from Pope Paul I., and as Primate gained a high character for energy and courage. He is the first Archbishop of Canterbury of whom we possess any silver coins. His protest was unavailing to prevent the limitation of his jurisdiction procured by the Mercian King Offa. He survived until 790, and at his death the see remained vacant for three years. Ethelheard, probably the Mercian Abbot of Louth, was then consecrated in 798, in spite of the opposition of some of the Kentish clergy. Higbert of Lichfield was the consecrator, and this fact did not make Ethelheard more acceptable to the West Saxons and the men of Kent. Ethelheard had to bide his time for the opposition to die out, but there is no evidence that he favoured the Mercian ascendency. Furthermore, in a few years' time, he was able to vindicate the rights of his see, and get back all the jurisdiction that Jaenbert had been deprived of. The first profession of obedience by a suffragan to the Archbishop of Canterbury, of which we have a record, is that made by Eadulf of Lindsey to Archbishop Ethelheard.

The eighth century had hardly begun when the power of Northumbria showed signs of declension. Osric, the

Northumbrian anarchy and St Ceolwulf. son of Alchfrid, was only eight years of age when, at the death of his father, he was called upon to ascend the throne. His reign was taken up with the struggle to maintain himself against usurpation on the part of his brothers, and domination on the part of his nobles. At his death the crown went to his uncle, Ceolwulf, the pious prince to whom St Bede dedicated his "Ecclesiastical History." He is commemorated in the

calendar as St Ceolwulf, but it may be doubted whether
in public affairs he showed the vigour needed for a ruler
in those days. After two years of reign he was shut up
in a monastery. It is true that he was able some time
later to escape from confinement and mount the throne
again. But eight years in all sufficed to lead him to an
act of voluntary abdication, when he took the religious
habit at Lindisfarne, lived there till his death, and was
buried hard by the tomb of St Cuthbert. The two saints'
bodies were afterwards brought to the mainland together
with all reverence by their community.

One notable thing which Ceolwulf did during his brief
span of power was to nominate his cousin, St Egbert, to
the See of York in 732. This meant much
for the northern metropolis, since Egbert   **St Egbert,**
may be looked upon as the second founder   **Archbishop**
of that archbishopric. Since the time of   **of York**
Paulinus the see had fallen in importance,   **(732-766).**
but once Egbert had been named for the office, he petitioned for the pallium, which was granted him by Pope
St Gregory III. He was then able to set his hand to
the reforms which the circumstances demanded, some of
which had been probably urged upon him by Venerable
Bede. It was his brother Eadbert who succeeded Ceolwulf as king, and this enhanced still more the position
of Egbert in Northumbria. He was keen upon the
importance of raising the standard of morality and of
discipline all through his diocese; and is also looked
upon as the first to introduce the parochial system into
the north of England. He was a great benefactor to the
Minster at York, and set up a mint in his episcopal city.
The School at York was his foundation, and chiefly for
its sake he gathered a library there, which was looked
upon as the best in the country. We are informed of
this by the learned Alcuin, Charlemagne's preceptor,
who calls St Egbert his master, and records for us his
order of the day. Having despatched all necessary business in the morning, he would sit on his couch and there
engage in teaching the young clerics of his school up to
noon, when it was his custom to celebrate Mass. Then,
as soon as his frugal repast was ended, he would somewhat relax as he listened to the younger clergy discussing
literary matters in his presence. In the evening after
Compline he would give a blessing to each in turn before

they retired to rest. *Egbert's Penitentiary* still exists, and gives us a good idea of the severity of the discipline of penance in his day.

Once we waive the question of how far St Paulinus exercised metropolitan rights during the few years of his tenure of the see of York, there is a true sense in which St Egbert may be considered the first archbishop of that see. As he was the brother of Eadbert, the Northumbrian king, no doubt his action in seeking the pallium from Rome was part of the struggle to assert the independence of Northumbria. When it was granted to him three suffragans were assigned to him. These were the Bishops of Hexham, Lindisfarne, and Whithern. The holy archbishop died in 766, and his successor is also counted as a saint. This was Albert or Ethelbert, who ruled the Church of York from 766 to 782. He had been first Egbert's pupil, and then his fellow-teacher in the York School, and hence at his death was unanimously chosen to succeed him as archbishop. He finished the buildings at the cathedral which Egbert had begun, and before his death was able to consecrate the sacred edifice.

But while Egbert thus succeeded in defending the metropolitan rights of the See of York, neither Eadbert nor his successor, Eldred, was able in the civil government of the kingdom to stand up against the growing power of their southern neighbours. King Ethelbald had already pushed forward the Mercian power further than any of the kings who reigned before him, and in 757 when the sceptre fell to Offa this predominance became still more marked. During this celebrated prince's reign of thirty-nine years he made Mercia the first of the Anglo-Saxon kingdoms. His earlier years were spent in consolidating his position at home. First of all he had a rival claimant to the throne to dispose of, and then he had the internal resources of Mercia to develop before he was in a position for a successful advance abroad. But once this due preparation was assured, he waged a series of victorious campaigns in turn against all his neighbours. He defeated the men of Kent at Otford, and then routed the King of Wessex at Bensington. He followed this up by an expedition against the Welsh. Here again he was victorious, and

Offa, King of Mercia (757-796).

THE TRIPLE LEADERSHIP 61

as a fruit of his victory proceeded to annex a considerable part of the territory which they had hitherto held. Furthermore, to ensure the permanency of the boundary which he then imposed upon them, he made the deep cutting known as *Offa's Dyke*, which still in a rough way marks the division between Wales and England. On the other hand, an arrangement was accepted by the feeble rulers of Northumbria, acknowledging in some fashion the overlordship of Offa and of Mercia. The frontier between Wessex and Mercia was now fixed at the Thames.

An additional step towards the leading position now assumed by Mercia was the foundation of a new ecclesiastical province with its metropolitan see at Lichfield. Very likely what St Egbert had accomplished at York may have suggested to Offa a similar achievement with regard to Lichfield. *Lichfield an Archbishopric.* But it was acknowledged that the consent of the Holy See was necessary, and therefore royal messengers were despatched to Rome to endeavour to obtain it. Pope Adrian X. responded by sending two legates, George and Theophylact, who were both bishops, to arrange the matter. And it was with this end in view that Offa, the two legates, and many of the bishops assembled in council at a place called indifferently Chelcuith, Chelsey, or Calcuith. After discussion Lichfield was raised to metropolitan rank, the dioceses between the Humber and the Thames being assigned to it as suffragan sees. Cut off for the time from the North and the Midlands, Canterbury had to be content with the South for its province. Egilbert of Lichfield became the first archbishop of the new province. His successor, Adolf, was also styled archbishop, but the arrangement did not last long, being reversed by the next Pope at the prayer of the Archbishop of Canterbury. Advantage was taken of the assembly at Calcuith to promulgate a code of disciplinary laws, made under the guidance of the papal legates and grounded in great part on Roman practice. These enactments are still extant. With regard to Holy Orders, there was to be a strict adherence to the ancient provisions of the Council of Nicæa. Baptism, except in case of necessity, was only to be conferred at Easter and Pentecost. Bishops must be faithful in visitation of their dioceses, and religious exact in the observance of their rule. Illegitimate children must be excluded from succession to the crown and from the inheritance of property. The clergy must not say Mass barefooted, nor with sacred vessels made of horn. The payment of tithes and the observance must be strictly maintained. The " heathenish " custom of tattooing or staining the body with dyes must be forbidden. The clergy must not take their meals alone, apart from the community to which they belong. Such prescriptions as these throw an interesting light upon the customs of the period. It is to be noted that at this Council, though it was held in Mercia, Jaenbert, Archbishop of Canterbury, and his suffragans were present. No doubt the presence of the legates lessened any difficulties about his position amongst the Midland bishops. On the other hand, there would seem to have been a separate council held for the northern province of York.

The chief blot upon the fair fame of King Offa comes from the probability that he was to some extent responsible for the assassination of Ethelbert, King of East Anglia, in 793. This prince was a suitor for the hand of Etheldrida, sister of the Queen of Wessex, and daughter to Offa. Yet, at the very court of Offa, which was then at Sutton near Hereford, Ethelbert was treacherously done to death, and it was whispered that Offa was privy to the bloody crime. Ethelbert was buried in Hereford Cathedral, which henceforward bore his name as a dedication title, for he was canonised in popular estimation under the style of St Ethelbert the Martyr. Offa made whatever reparation was in his power. He made a penitential pilgrimage to Rome, he promised a Rome Scot of 365 mancuses of gold each year for the poor and for the maintenance of lights at St Peter's tomb. He is also credited with making arrangements for rendering more lasting Ine's foundation of the *Schola Anglorum*. Whatever doubt be cast on the pilgrimage of Offa, the donation of Peter's Pence by him is an indubitable fact. Other religious foundations were also endowed by him, and he rebuilt the venerable Abbey Church of St Albans. Offa died in 796, and was buried near Bedford.

Offa's Penance and Death.

Offa's son, Egfirth, who had been already crowned at

THE TRIPLE LEADERSHIP 63

the Council of Calcuith, succeeded his father, but only survived for one year, when the crown went to Kenulf, descendant of the race of Penda but not of Offa's family. All that king's direct descendants were dead. Kenulf used his royal authority in several ways to promote peace in the troubled affairs of the Church in Mercia. **Kenulf and St Kenelm.** But his first intervention in civil government was with regard to the kingdom of Kent, where, the last scion of the house of Hengist being dead, the cleric, Eadbert, saw a chance of raising himself to the royal dignity. Ethelheard, Archbishop of Canterbury, refused to sanction this attempt or to yield him obedience, and an appeal was made to the pope, St Leo III., who excommunicated Eadbert, and called upon the neighbouring kings to eject him from his usurped position. This sentence was carried out in drastic and even barbarous fashion by Kenulf, who seized Eadbert, put out his eyes, cut off his hands, and then with great parade restored him to liberty at a great assembly of the realm which took place on the occasion of the dedication of Winchelcombe Abbey. As a step towards peace, Kenulf then yielded to the representations of Ethelheard with respect to the separation of the Mercian dioceses from the jurisdiction of Canterbury. He agreed to a letter being addressed to St Leo III. in his own name and in that of his counsellors, asking for a reversal of the decision given by his predecessor as to the see of Lichfield and the new province. Archbishop Ethelheard must have been only too desirous to carry this appeal to the Sovereign Pontiff. St Leo listened to Ethelheard when he presented the king's letter, dissolved the province of Lichfield, and gave back its territory to Canterbury. Kenulf reigned in considerable splendour for twenty-six years (796-821), and when he died was succeeded by his only son, Kenelm. This holy young prince in the course of a few months was betrayed to his death. He was led into the Forest of Clent at the instigation of his sister, who was ambitious to reign in his stead. There he was set upon and murdered, but his body was afterwards discovered, and removed for burial hard by his father in Winchelcombe Abbey. There his tomb was greatly venerated as that of a saint and martyr, and his relics became the centre of many pilgrimages. As to the regal power, his sister failed to retain the sceptre which she had grasped: it soon passed into other hands. Henceforth, the star of Mercia paled before the growing influence of the realm of Wessex.

Wessex takes the lead. At last after nearly a century of wearisome domestic strife the West Saxon kingdom began definitely to take the lead. After the resignation of Ine, Ethelheard, his brother-in-law, had agreed to share the royal power with Oswald, who was a collateral descendant of Ceawlin. But there was dissension between them up to the time of Oswald's death. The Britons took advantage of this to inflict several defeats upon the West Saxons. Moreover, Ethelbald of Mercia insisted upon his overlordship being acknowledged. Consequently, Ethelheard enjoyed but little peace or glory for the remainder of his reign. Cuthred, his successor, asserted his independence of the Mercians in 741, and also inflicted a crushing defeat on the Britons. After Cuthred's death there began the warfare of a disputed succession between Sigebert and Kynewulf, which was only terminated by the murder of the former prince. Henceforth Kynewulf was able to reign alone for thirty years (754-785). At the end of that period the vengeance of Sigebert's family at last reached Kynewulf. Sigebert's brother lay in wait for him when he went to visit his mistress in a forest between Winchester and Merton. Taken unawares, he seized his weapons and strove to defend himself, but was slain with all who were in his company. One day later a similar fate overtook the band of conspirators at the hands of Osrie, Ealdorman of Hampshire, who had pursued them post-haste with whatever forces he could gather. Thus was the rivalry of the two families extinguished in blood in a manner highly characteristic of the savage customs of the age. The thanes of Wessex exercised the powers of election which they always in theory claimed to possess, and chose as king, Brihtric, a prince who had married Eadburga, daughter of King Offa. The jealousy and wicked vengeance of this unprincipled woman ended by involving her husband in ruin. Envious of the favour shown by Brihtric to a young nobleman of his court, Eadburga resolved to make away with this unfortunate youth by poison. Through some mistake the king also drank of the same cup, and died as well as his young thane. Eadburga escaped to the continent of Europe,

THE TRIPLE LEADERSHIP

but so great was the abhorrence excited in England by her crimes that the Witan straightway made a law that for the future the consorts of their kings should never be put on the same level of royal dignity with their husbands. With the vacancy caused by the death of Brihtric, Egbert, another scion of the house of Cerdic, who had kept out of Brihtric's way at the court of Charlemagne, returned to England. He had served for several campaigns in the Frankish army, but now he was unanimously chosen to fill the throne of his ancestors. With the advent of Egbert to the West Saxon kingdom in 800, a new period began to open out for that power, and new developments took place, the narration of which will occupy us in the next chapter.

VI.

THE RISE OF WESSEX.

(800-871.)

Wessex takes the lead (800).
WESSEX had been, if anything, the weakest of the three Anglo-Saxon kingdoms which had been struggling for the first place in England during most of the eighth century. Yet, it was neither Mercia nor Northumberland, but Wessex, which was, after all, to prove the predominant and unifying force and to weld the independent kingdoms of the Heptarchy into a Monarchy. Cerdic had planted the West Saxons firmly on the banks of the Itchen and the Avon long before Ida or Ella had landed north of the Humber, or Creoda had pushed into the Midlands. But the advance of Wessex had been more chequered by repulses than that of her rivals had been. For, in her case, besides the rivalry common to all the kingdoms of her countrymen, there had been a stiffer conflict to wage against the Britons. It was only inch by inch that these latter were driven west into Cornwall. Hence, it was not until the ninth century had dawned that Wessex was free to move into the place left vacant by the waning power of her competitors.

Egbert (800-838).
King Egbert, who may be considered the founder of this lasting superiority, began his reign over his ancestral dominions in the year 800, just when Charlemagne had laid the foundations of mediaeval Christendom by restoring the Roman Empire of the West. Nevertheless, he cannot be considered as more than King of Wessex until 823. In that year the battle of Ellandune established his superiority over Beornwulf, King of Mercia. His

THE RISE OF WESSEX

subsequent victory over the King of Kent, and the acknowledgment of his overlordship by the East Angles and also by the men of Sussex and of Essex led to Egbert assuming in 828 the title of Bretwalda, which had been borne by seven of the earlier Anglo-Saxon kings, but had not been used, during a period of doubtful supremacy. It strengthened his position still more that a few years later he was able to lead a victorious expedition against the Northern Welsh, whose submission he then received. But, already, before he died, Egbert had to face the first onset of the coming invasion from Scandinavia. We are told that in 835 or 836 thirty-five ships laden with Danish warriors came to Charmouth, and after a bloody battle with Egbert remained in possession of the battle-field. The last ray of glory on his reign shone two years later, when the Danes, having come again, and made common cause with the Britons from Cornwall, Egbert was able to defeat their united forces at Kingston. In the next year (838) Egbert died.

Ethelwulf, Egbert's son, was at once acknowledged as king in his stead. Though his reputation for piety cannot be said to stand on the same level with that of his holy spouse, St Osburga, **Ethelwulf and his sons.** he was a man of true Christian principle, whose household was not unworthy of training a band of Christian champions for the war against the heathen Danes. Moreover, he was so much attached to studious pursuits that it has been held by some that he was even enrolled amongst the clergy, for in those days the clergy had an almost exclusive monopoly of learning and education. This is probably the only basis for the theory. The royal power in Kent and Sussex was made over by Ethelwulf to his eldest son, Ethelstan, but the inroads of the Danes went on increasing in frequency, and both father and son had as much as they could do to hold their own. They seem to have died much about the same time, and then Ethelbald, the second son, succeeded his father in Wessex, while Ethelbert, the third son, took up his elder brother's position as subordinate King of Kent and Sussex. Before his death Ethelwulf is known to have made the pilgrimage to Rome, where he stayed for some twelve months. His companion was his youngest son, Alfred, who was crowned by the Pope in his father's lifetime, and adopted as his godson in confirmation. Passing through the court of Charles the Bald in France on his way home, he gained that monarch's daughter, Judith, as his second wife, St Osburga being dead, and then came home with his new bride amid general rejoicing. Ethelwulf did not, however, survive his return from Rome longer than for about two years. Ethelbald had been already acting as king in Wessex during his father's absence, and in fact seems never to have handed back the government again. By an instrument popularly known as the *Donation of Ethelwulf*, he is credited with initiating both the system of tithes and the payment of Peter's Pence. If this is assuming too much, at the very least he may be believed to have thereby devoted the tenth part of his personal revenue to the service of the Church, and to have imposed on every ten hides of land the obligation of supporting one necessitous person.

The death of Ethelwulf in 858 left the chief claim to the succession in the hands of Ethelbald, while Ethelbert continued to hold a subordinate kingship over Kent and Sussex. But the former monarch had already lived most of his life, and done most of his warlike deeds, with his father still alive. He married his father's widow, Judith, and does not bear a good name in the history of the time. After a few short years he died, and was buried at Sherborne. Ethelbert now became king over the whole kingdom. His reign of five years was taken up in one incessant struggle with the Danes, who now began to winter in the land instead of returning to Scandinavia. First, they settled in the Isle of Sheppey, next in Thanet, and then on the mainland. They also captured Winchester, from which they could only be dislodged after an obstinate battle. When Ethelbert was laid by his brother's remains at Sherborne, Ethelred assumed the crown. His piety was not less lofty than his valour. Both shone out for example at the battle which he, in conjunction with his younger brother, Alfred, fought against the heathen at Ashdown in Berkshire. The invaders had divided their force into two armies, one led by their two vikings, and the other commanded by subordinate chiefs. To counter this

Three short reigns.

THE RISE OF WESSEX

arrangement the Saxon host was also divided, one part being under Ethelred himself, and the other under Alfred. After a day of inconclusive slaughter the Danes threw the whole weight of their attack on Alfred's division, which was so hard pressed that the prince sent a message to his brother to come to his relief. But Ethelred was hearing Mass in his tent, and sent back the message that he would not stir till the Mass was over. Then, strengthened by prayer, he issued forth bold as a lion, led a furious attack on the Danish army, and drove them in disorder from the field. Ethelred is said to have fought no fewer than nine battles against his heathen foes in the space of one year, and in most of them he was victorious. However, being defeated at Devizes in 871, he received a wound in the fray, from the effects of which he died, leaving the crown to his youngest brother, Alfred.

We must now retrace our steps to consider the changes which took place in distinctively ecclesiastical affairs during the period under review. The reversal by St Leo III. in 803 of Pope Adrian's creation of a new archiepiscopal see at Lichfield at the prayer of Ethelheard of Canterbury almost coincided with the beginning of Egbert's reign, and may be thought to typify in church government the end of the threefold equality of Northumbria, Mercia, and Wessex. Archbishop Ethelheard survived until this was accomplished, and died almost immediately after. Consequently, the Primate who was contemporary with Egbert was Wulfred, who was archbishop from 805 to 832. During that space of time he witnessed a complete renewal of the episcopate, and was able to consecrate a new incumbent for nearly every see as it fell vacant. He was also able to keep on good terms with Kenulf, king of the Mercians, as well as with Egbert, and the Midlands being less taken up with wars than Wessex was, Kenulf was in a position to pay more attention to law-making and organisation. At Calcuith in 816 there was held a council of all the bishops south of the Humber, while King Kenulf and his thanes were also present at the assembly. The canons of the Council are interesting enough, and characteristic of the period. There is a profession of the Catholic Faith. There is a canon that all churches are to be consecrated

Council at Calcuith (816).

by the bishop of the diocese. There is next an exhortation to unity and harmony, which are to be promoted by mutual prayer. There is a declaration that it is the bishop who has the right and the duty to decide on the fitness of those chosen to be abbots and abbesses. There is a prohibition against any Scot being employed in any priestly duty on account of the uncertainty of such a stranger's ordination. There is also a provision recorded that the rules made by former bishops or earlier synods are to be considered still in force, unless they have been expressly abrogated. There is a prohibition against alienating any ecclesiastical or monastic estates on the part of those who hold them as superiors for the time being. There is a rule against the suppression of any religious house which has once been canonically established. There is a rule forbidding any bishop from encroaching upon the rights of any other bishop. Baptism by immersion is enjoined. Lastly, it is laid down that at the death of a bishop the tenth part of his substance should be given in alms to the poor, while all his English slaves are to be set free, and suffrages are to be offered for his soul for thirty days, including seven "belts" of Paternosters—possibly an ancient form of our modern Rosary.

Archbishop Wulfred had sixteen years of his episcopal career still before him after the Council of Calcuith; but many of those who had sat there in synod with him passed away soon after. Ethelnoth of London cannot be traced beyond the year of the Council. The same remark applies to Wigbert of Sherborne. The next year witnessed the death of Herewin of Lichfield. Twice the archbishop had to consecrate an incumbent for this Midland see, and twice he had to provide a bishop to rule East Anglia from Elmham. On the other hand, Beormod, Bishop of Rochester, had not finished his forty years' tenancy of that diocese when Wulfred himself was carried to his grave in 832. The Saxon Chronicle tells that not only did he receive his pallium from Rome, but he also made a pilgrimage thither in time to get the blessing of the great Pontiff, St Leo III., before he died. At Wulfred's death the abbot, Feologild, was chosen as archbishop, but he died in less than three months after his appointment to the metropolitan see. Meanwhile,

Bishops of the ninth century.

THE RISE OF WESSEX

the northern archbishopric at York was either subject to repeated vacancies, or the names of the metropolitans have been lost, for during the whole of the ninth century we can only feel sure of the names and dates of two prelates in this see. These are Wigmund, who was consecrated in 837, and Wulfhere who seems to have occupied the throne of York from 854 up to about the year 900. Eardulf, the last Bishop of Lindisfarne, who was consecrated by Wulfhere in the year of his own accession, seems to have survived until about the same date as his metropolitan. The archiepiscopal see of Canterbury was held during the four reigns of Ethelwulf and his three sons by Kelnoth, or Ceolnoth, who was consecrated in 833, and survived until 870, the last year of Ethelred's reign. But the most renowned prelate of the period was undoubtedly St Swithin, Bishop of Winchester. It was Ceolnoth who consecrated him in 852, and he presided over what was, after all the West Saxon capital for ten years, dying in 862. But, according to the chronicles, for long years before he became bishop he had been one of the chief advisers of King Egbert. He was the counsellor of that monarch in spiritual affairs, while Eilstan, Bishop of Sherborne, advised the king in temporal matters. Very likely he had the chief part in the education of Ethelwulf. When he died in 862, his will was that he should be buried outside the north wall of his cathedral, where the people might pass over his tomb, and the raindrops from the eaves fall upon him. But a more glorious fate awaited his remains. They were translated to a costly shrine within the cathedral by his successor, Bishop Ethelwulf, in 981. And again, when the Norman bishop Walkelin built his new cathedral in the Conqueror's reign, St Swithin's relics were again moved to a still more splendid resting-place. Until the shrine was desecrated in 1538, St Swithin, at whose tomb numerous wonders had been wrought, was the chief patron of the Minster. But his biographers, who wrote centuries after his death, were more concerned to relate these miracles than to give a critical history of his life. Hence their writings are of little value for the history of the times.

St Swithin (862).

Although it is fair to say that the chief interest of history during this period is to be found in Wessex, there were some examples elsewhere of such attractive sanctity and piety that a history of the English Church cannot pass them over. The almost ceaseless incursions of the Scandinavian vikings, which made the reigns of Ethelwulf and his sons such a period of trouble and confusion, brought still greater ruin to the kingdom of East Anglia. The king whose lot it was to face them was St Edmund, who is stated by the old chronicler to have been of the race of the old Saxon kings. But we have little to rely on as to his genealogy. He reigned over the East Angles for some thirty years in righteousness, and with such mild charity that he knitted to himself the hearts of all his people. At length, in the year 870, the Danish army having wintered in York made a descent upon the eastern counties, and as they advanced, burned and slew wherever they were opposed. Their leaders were the brothers Inguar and Hubba, who were the sons of the viking, Ella. St Edmund, though he could only muster far inferior forces, resolved to do battle for country and Faith, and drew his brave men around him at Hoxne, on the borders of Norfolk and Suffolk. A fierce battle was fought in this place, and many of the invaders bit the dust. Nevertheless, at last their superior numbers prevailed, and the Saxons were driven back and scattered. Edmund himself was taken prisoner, and brought to Inguar. The heathen chief offered him his life if he would renounce Jesus Christ. But the noble king, of course, refused the offer with scorn, and thereupon was handed over to death. By the orders of the Danish leader he was fastened to a tree and shot to death with arrows. He was then beheaded, but his body was left behind with contempt by the invaders, as they swept along in their headlong course to other localities. But when they were gone, his faithful subjects sought out the sacred remains, and reverently bore them away as a precious treasure. They rested at various places in a sort of triumphal procession, until they were finally interred at Beodricsworth, which since has gained in his honour the new name of Bury St Edmund's. Round his tomb in this place there arose in later days the buildings of a Benedictine Abbey with one of the largest churches in England. The almost total destruction of this stately centre of religion and pilgrimage is one of the gravest

St Edmund the Martyr (870).

THE RISE OF WESSEX

losses which the dissolution of the religious houses in the reign of Henry VIII. inflicted upon the country. Strange it is that the little wooden church at Greensted in Essex, where the martyr's bones found a temporary resting-place, has survived the magnificent fane where they were once held in such high veneration. Until the Reformation there was also a monastic house at Hoxne, the scene of the holy king's martyrdom. We may consider St Edmund as the last independent Saxon King of East Anglia, for when Alfred's contest with the Danes was interrupted by the Peace of Wedmore, the terms of that treaty left East Anglia to the invaders. Guthrum, the Danish viking, ruled over it without any effective opposition on the part of the Saxons. For fifty years it was subject to the Danish domination. And when Edward the Elder brought it back to the Anglo-Saxon sceptre, it was not restored as a separate kingdom, but formed part of his gradually increasing realm.

In this savage fashion a great step was taken towards the establishment of the Danelagh, which gradually encroached on Saxondom until it comprised (1) Northumbria, (2) the Mercian lands which were grouped round the five boroughs of Derby, Nottingham, Leicester, Lincoln, and Stamford, and (3) East Anglia. It was an ominous advance, foreshadowing an eventual Danish conquest, and shaking the unity of the Anglo-Saxon rule over England in a way from which it never recovered. After the death of St Edmund the Danish tide of invasion swept on. Humbert, Bishop of Elmham, who had anointed and crowned St Edmund at Burva in 856, fell into the power of the Danes in the same year as his sovereign, and was put to death by them for the same glorious cause. The king's brother escaped, and wishing to lead a life of retirement and prayer, became a hermit at Cerne in Dorsetshire, and is known as St Edbold. East Anglia now became a Danish colony, and there is no record of any bishop succeeding to the see of Elmham until the latter part of the next century. It cannot be said that the other Saxon kingdoms died out, either through Danish invasion or through West Saxon predominance. But the first place obtained for Wessex by King Egbert was never again

The Danelagh.

Danes hold several kingdoms of the Heptarchy.

lost. On the other hand, it must not be forgotten that Northumbria as well as East Anglia became the seat of a long enduring Danish power. Doubtless, as they gradually settled down, and secured a rule of some degree of permanence over their Saxon neighbours, the Danes themselves embraced Christianity. We have no record of any later agreement with them comparable to Alfred's Peace of Wedmore. So the process must have been a slow and chequered one. But even this much is anticipating the events of the next age. Alfred had yet, in 870, to begin his fruitful reign, and until his day the Danes always came as marauders from without; they were looked upon as heathen savages, and were to be resisted with utmost effort as though in the best of holy wars for religion.

VII.

MAKERS OF ANGLO-SAXON MONARCHY.

(871-940.)

(A) KING ALFRED THE GREAT (871-901).

THE ravages of death and battle had nearly exhausted the line of West Saxon kings when Ethelred died in 871. But there still survived the youngest of the sons of Ethelwulf, Alfred, who was now called on to continue the struggle for civilisation and Christianity. During the thirty years of his reign over the kingdom this prince was destined to perform such deeds of military prowess and such acts of heroism that he has come to be regarded as the ideal Anglo-Saxon king. To call him the *Great* was not praise enough for his admiring countrymen: they must name him in affectionate remembrance *England's Darling.* He has only just missed the authoritative title of *Saint* as well. He was born at Wantage in Berkshire in 848 or 849. His parents rejoiced to see the docility of his young mind to assimilate whatever learning could be put within his reach. At Rome, whither he was taken by his father, Ethelwulf, St Leo III., in accordance with a custom not uncommon in those days, anointed him and crowned him king in his father's lifetime, and then adopted him as his godson. As soon as he was old enough to bear arms, his youth had to be one of constant warfare. He fought at his brothers' side in the battles which they, like a family of Machabees, had to fight in defence of the people of God. In Ethelred's last battle, where Alfred shared the command, he was less fortunate than Ethelred in his leadership, but he had survived the contest,

Alfred the Great (849-901).

whereas Ethelred had fallen, and the last hope of his family and his people now reposed upon him. He could hardly have been called upon to govern at a more critical moment, for Wessex was now fighting for her very life, and he would fain have escaped the task which was laid upon him. But he could not hold out against the imperative voice of duty. And, although it is true, Ethelred the King was dead; Ethelred the Archbishop was still alive. His honoured hands imposed the crown of Wessex upon the head of the young prince anew, almost unwilling though he was. He accepted the choice, which was thus ratified by the counsellor of the realm, and henceforward took up the burden of government.

He was only twenty-two years of age, and his first trial of arms as Saxon leader against the Danes met with but scanty success. As before, in his brother's time, he attacked with valour and impetuosity, but after a while the Northmen rallied their forces and returned to the attack with such determination that they drove back the Saxon bands in confusion. It was probably by negotiation, and perhaps by the payment of a ransom, that the invaders were prevailed upon to retire at least for the moment, and in this way a brief breathing space was obtained. The arrangement, nevertheless, was soon upset, either through the bad faith of those bands of barbarians who had agreed to it, or by the predatory habits of others who had not been parties to it. Hence it came to pass that the first seven years of Alfred's reign were spent in repeated warfare against the heathen. At length, wearied and exhausted, he had to take refuge in the morasses of Athelney in Somersetshire. Here he lay in retirement for some time. To this period is usually referred the simple story of his taking refuge in the neat-herd's hut and allowing the hearth-cakes to burn. At length, disguising himself, as the legend says, as a strolling minstrel, he made his musical skill serve him for an introduction to the Danish camp, where he was able to gain valuable information as to their number, and as to the carelessness which repeated success had engendered. Fortified with this knowledge, Alfred returned to his countrymen, once again assembled his scattered forces, and sallied forth to do battle for

Alfred's Wars against the Danes.

his country. The Danes, dispirited by the loss of their Standard of the Raven in a preliminary engagement in Devonshire, when King Alfred fell upon them at Ettsandune or Edington, they suffered so signal a defeat that they were forced to sue for peace. The alternative was offered to the vanquished army, either to embrace the Christian Faith or to quit England for good.

These conditions were ratified at the Peace of Wedmore, by which, with far-seeing policy, Alfred handed over to those who chose to remain and become Christians all the lands to the north and east of Watling Street, that thoroughfare being accepted as the boundary between Saxon and Dane. After this Guthrun, the Danish viking, with many of his leading men, received baptism at the hands of Archbishop Ethelred, Alfred himself standing as godfather to the new converts. Thus the foundations were laid of a peaceful settlement of both Danes and Saxons in the land. Those who refused this alternative left the country under the leadership of Hastings and sailed across the Channel to ravage France, where they at last got possession of Normandy. These were the ancestors of those Normans who were to come back two centuries later and impose their rule upon Saxon and Scandinavian alike. *Peace of Wedmore (878).*

King Alfred now turned his attention for the next fifteen years to the peaceful administration of his realm and the problems of reconstruction it must have presented. His diligent perseverance during that period enabled him to repair in some measure the ruin which had been wrought, and draw out the outline of a prosperous and contented kingdom. He enjoys a great reputation as a legislator, but no complete code of laws has come down to us under his name. Even of the provisions, the memory of which history has preserved, many were probably revivals of still more ancient legislation. The division of the land into counties, of the counties into hundreds, and of these into tithings, which has been attributed to him, may have been originally grounded upon the ancient one handed down from earlier times, but fallen into abeyance through the troubles of the times. For Alfred was as much concerned to restore the observance of the old laws as to make new ones.

King Alfred and the Church.

Religious matters always took their rightful primacy of place in King Alfred's mind. Hence he occupied himself to do his utmost to repair the ruin which the Danish invasion had wrought in the affairs of the Church. The monastic life had been almost destroyed, the laity had very little opportunity of practising their Christian duties, and it is a marvel how the bishops contrived in any way to keep up the succession of pastors in the different dioceses. Ethelred had been consecrated as metropolitan in 870, just before Alfred's accession, but he is also called Bishop of Wiltshire. Probably he took charge of the Wiltshire diocese, after the death of Heahstan in 871, for some time until a new bishop was appointed. However, once appointed to Canterbury, Ethelred seems to have faced the difficulties and consecrated bishops to the sees in his province with but little delay. It was thus Werefrith, who was to be one of the king's best helpers in his literary work, was made Bishop of Worcester in 873. Denewulf became Bishop of Winchester in 879, and held that see until 908, when Alfred and most of his contemporaries were dead. Ethelred himself only lived until 889, and in the following year the Abbot Plegmund became Archbishop of Canterbury. Asser, Alfred's friend and biographer, was made Bishop of Sherborne in 892, when Wulfsy was moved thence to London, or another of the same name appointed to that see. Alfred also set his hand to the difficult task of restoring the monastic and conventual life. He founded two monasteries for men, the one at Athelney in Somersetshire, where he made John, the old Saxon, abbot; the other at Winchester, which had been in existence before, but had fallen into the hands of seculars. Alfred found an abbot for this latter house in the person of the learned Grimbald, who had been sent to him from the household of Fulk, Archbishop of Rheims. For religious women the king founded a house at Shaftesbury, where his own daughter, Ethelgiva, took the veil and became abbess. To fill his religious houses he invited foreigners to join the ranks of his communities, while to provide for the future he gathered within their walls a certain number of carefully chosen children, who, when trained to the monastic life, would gradually take the places of those who fell out of the family through old age and death.

But Alfred was very far from contemplating the building up of a merely national Church divorced from Catholicism and eschewing all subjection to it. From earliest childhood he had been led to see in Rome the centre of Christianity. There he had been hallowed king, and during his reign he repeatedly sent envoys and money thither at the intervals which his difficulties at home allowed. Pope Marinus sent him as a present a large relic of the Holy Rood, or True Cross: an offering the most acceptable that could be to a king like Alfred. But he made his charity extend not only to the centre of Christendom, but also, if we may believe the Saxon Chronicle, to its circumference as well. He sent alms to the Patriarch of Jerusalem, and even to the Christians of St Thomas in distant India. His was a Christianity which embraced the whole Church, and yet never forgot the special claims upon him of his native land. For, we are told, he took a special interest in the English school at Rome, and won for it special privileges from the Pontiff Marinus.

Alfred's Embassies.

The greatness of King Alfred's character far exceeded the scale of the external achievements recorded of him. Of these some were not of the magnitude that makes things splendid, while others were doomed to failure. But we can look into his inner life as far as it has been recorded for us, and his intimate relations with others, and we shall find nothing to disappoint or repel us. His wife was named Elswitha, the daughter of Ethelred, a Lincolnshire alderman, and Edburga of the royal line of Mercia. He had two sons and three daughters. One of his sons, Edward, succeeded him as king, and the other, Ethelward, devoted himself to clerkly pursuits, and is thought by some to have been made a bishop many years later. Of his three daughters, one, Ethelfleda, was espoused to Ethelred, King of Mercia, Elfryth married the Count of Flanders, who was the ancestor of the Norman King Stephen, but the third daughter gave herself to the conventual life at Shaftesbury. The king took every care that his children should receive all the best training which it was in his power to procure for them. Learning by heart the Psalms and Saxon Song Books, reading both Latin and Saxon, writing also, and the exercise of such arts as the state of the country allowed were all

Alfred at home.

made use of that his offspring might not be unworthy of their royal descent when their turn came to play their part in life. But outside of his own family circle Alfred had attracted to his court every scholar that he could, both in order to improve his own education, and to become his companions in those literary labours which lay so near to his heart. Such was Werefrith, Bishop of Worcester, who translated for him the "Dialogues of St Gregory the Great." Such was Plegmund the Mercian, who was later raised to the see of Canterbury, but who in earlier years was sometimes called Alfred's Preceptor, because the king made such constant use of his superior knowledge to supplement what was lacking in himself. Such were his chaplains, Ethelstan and Werewulf. Such was the Abbot Grimbald, brought from Gaul to preside over the Winchester foundation on account of his learning and piety. Such was John, Abbot of Athelney, who had come from the still more distant region of continental Saxony. Such, lastly, was the Welshman, Asser, invited by the king to spend half the year with him if he could not be absent continuously from his native Wales, but who at last was won over by him to be his constant companion. Asser was later on Alfred's biographer, and in all probability Bishop of Sherborne for the last years of his life (892-900).

It was with the assistance of these men that the great king laboured perseveringly for the education of his countrymen. The earliest literary composition we hear of was the king's "Handbook" or "Enchiridion" which was a collection of choice extracts, of maxims, and of texts of Holy Scripture which Alfred kept constantly beside him, ready for immediate use. The manuscript which he meant to serve for the instruction of others as well as himself has unfortunately been lost. The first translation he made, with the assistance of his scholars, was "St Gregory's Pastoral" with a preface of his own. Then came an Anglo-Saxon translation of Venerable Bede's "Ecclesiastical History of the English," which, of course, only carries the reader down to a time more than a century earlier than Alfred's reign. He did not continue it in the same form, but took up the *Anglo-Saxon Chronicle* which already existed in rudimentary fashion, as first begun in all likelihood by St Swithin,

King Alfred and Literature.

and carried it on with such an extension as fitted it to be the beginning of a national history. He followed this up with a version of the "History of the World" by Orosius. Here he omitted what he thought was not useful for his own people, and subjoined the "Voyages of Othere and Wulfstan," to the White Sea and the Baltic. His last complete work was the version of Boethius on the "Consolation of Philosophy." At the very end of his life he determined that there should be an Anglo-Saxon translation of the Book of Psalms, and the work was taken up. King Alfred died before it was finished, but it is probable that a certain number of the Psalms, perhaps as many as fifty, are from his pen.

These peaceful labours, extending over a period of fourteen or fifteen years, were interrupted in rudest fashion in 893 by a fresh invasion of the marauding Northmen. Once more the king had to gird on his sword and become the champion of his people in their fight for their homes and their freedom. The invasion was begun at two points: at Appledore in Sussex, and at Milton in Kent. It would seem that being so far disappointed in their hopes of effecting a permanent conquest of Normandy, the Northmen deliberately decided to try and conquer England. The fact that they came with wives and children and horses would point to this being no mere raid but an effort of lasting conquest. The chief leader was the Hastings who had left rather than settle down peacefully after Edington in 878. But King Alfred was now better prepared to meet them than he had been before. He had his fyrd or national militia in order, he had a trained body of house thanes at his side, and, moreover, he had built warships longer and swifter than those of the Danes. Even so, it meant nearly four years of warfare, chasing the hostile bands nearly all over the country from post to post, before the invasion was finally beaten off. The Danes settled in East Anglia and Mercia in defiance of their treaties with Alfred, always took sides with their countrymen whenever they were able, and this made the task of conquering them much more difficult. At last, by dint of perseverance, showing meanwhile considerable military skill, Alfred was master in his own land once more, and the Northmen sailed away in 897.

New Invasion of the Danes.

King Alfred was now able once more to take up his labours for his people's good, his studies and his writing, his prayers and his works of charity. But he had nearly come to the end of his earthly pilgrimage. He had ever been dogged through life by pain and disease, and his life had been a hard and strenuous one. We may well believe that though not much over fifty years of age his frame was exhausted, and death was approaching. He had made the most of the years which had been granted him. Scarcely any division of the hours of the day is more celebrated, or more attractive in its simplicity and self-sacrifice than his. Eight hours were for reading, writing, and prayer, eight hours for carrying on the public duties of his office as king, and eight hours for sleep, recreation, and refreshment. His revenue was subjected first to a twofold division into equal parts: one half was given to God, and the other half was devoted to temporal purposes. The part which Asser tells us was given to God was subdivided so as to provide for four great good works: there were the poor to be helped, there were his two new monasteries to be supported, there was his palace school to be kept up, there were other servants of God to be embraced in his wide charity. His gifts went not only to the monasteries of England, but to Wales, Scotland, Ireland, and even further. Out of the second moiety of his means he provided for his thanes and soldiers, for his ministers, for the workmen whom he had collected for the public works he undertook, and for the strangers from foreign parts who came to him in considerable numbers and were assured of a truly royal welcome. In 900 or 901 King Alfred died, and was buried in the minster at Winchester.

The figure of King Alfred the Great still shines bright and heroic across the long centuries which have elapsed since his death. He was fortunate in his biographer, Asser. The faithful friend who shared his counsels and his studies has succeeded in presenting a lively and attractive portrait of his master, even though the compass of his work is so modest. The scale of the kingdom he ruled, of the events in which he took part, was limited enough; and he ruled in the midst of disaster, barely snatching the remnant of his race from imminent ruin. It is the genius and personality of the man which soars

over all these things, and makes him the greatest as
he is surely the most attractive of all our kings. And
the undying impress he has put on our history is also
a testimony to the power of literature. "Now," he says
in his preface to Boethius, "would I say briefly that I
have wished to live worthily while I have lived, and
after my death to leave to men who should come after
me my memory in good deeds." Thanks to his pen
and his scholar's habit he has done so, and speaks to
his countrymen still. And he did his work with a mind
fixed on God and eternity. "Lord God Almighty,
shaper and ruler of all creatures, I pray Thee for Thy
great mercy, and for the token of the Holy Rood, and
for the maidenhead of St Mary, and for the obedience of
St Michael, and for the love of Thy holy saints and
their worthiness that Thou guide me better than I have
towards Thee." These are the simple words of King
Alfred's prayer. The character of this great son of the
Church has so impressed the non-Catholic historian
Freeman that he pronounces this short but pregnant panegyric upon him: "Alfred, the unwilling author of these
great changes, is the most perfect character in history.
He is a singular instance of a prince, who has become
a hero of romance, who as such has had countless
imaginary exploits and imaginary institutions attributed
to him, but to whose character romance has done no more
than justice, and who appears in exactly the same light
in history and in fable. No other man on record has
ever so thoroughly united all the virtues, both of the
ruler and of the private man. . . . A saint without
superstition, a scholar without ostentation, a warrior all
whose wars were fought in defence of his country, a conqueror whose laurels were never stained with cruelty,
a prince never cast down by adversity, never lifted up to
insolence in the day of triumph" (Norman Conquest I.,
51). The historian of the Church can hardly praise him
more cordially than this outsider. In some of the old
martyrologies he is honoured with the title of blessed,
but this has not been authoritatively confirmed
by the Roman Church. At any rate, Christian hero,
scholar, warrior, legislator, model of his people, in
one of their darkest hours, his memory is one that
may well be cherished in state and in Church with equal
honour.

84 THE CHURCH IN ENGLAND

(B) EDWARD THE ELDER AND ATHELSTAN.

King Alfred had not a very long life, though indeed he just attained the years of Napoleon, Shakespeare, and others of the world's greatest geniuses. He had laid the foundations of national greatness, but the edifice had still to be raised. It is not saying too much for his son and successor, Edward the Elder, to claim for him that he added very materially both to the extent and to the solidity of his father's realm. He was crowned at Winchester by Archbishop Plegmund, and reigned for about four-and-twenty years. As a warrior he was scarcely inferior to Alfred, but he had not those varied titles to honour which adorned the character of the last monarch.

Edward the Elder (901-925).

The meaning of saying that Edward added to the solidity of the West Saxon sway over England may be illustrated from the case of Mercia, where Ethelfleda was queen. This notable personage was King Alfred's eldest child, who had been married during her father's lifetime to the Mercian King Ethelred, it being, of course, understood that this prince admitted a kind of overlordship in favour of Wessex. But Ethelred died soon after Alfred the Great, and Ethelfleda did not marry again, but ruled alone in Mercia. This meant that a West Saxon princess ruled this kingdom in her own name, no longer the consort of a Mercian prince. Henceforward brother and sister united their forces, so that Midlands and West were governed with one harmonious policy. Ethelfleda, who was undoubtedly a strong and high-spirited woman, is known in history as the Lady of Mercia.

Ethelfleda, Lady of Mercia.

As these first years of the tenth century rolled round, so many of the bishoprics had fallen vacant, whilst others had proved inconveniently large that the Pope wrote to Plegmund, Archbishop of Canterbury, in words which seemed to imply that he had not done all in his power to provide for the wants of the faithful, at least in this matter. The consequence was that a council was called by the joint efforts of the king and the Primate to deliberate upon what the Pontiff had written. Besides filling up the vacant sees, it was decided to establish

Archbishop Plegmund (890-914).

three new ones, namely at Wells, at Crediton in Devonshire, and at Ramsbury or Wilton. This came to pass in 909, and the Council may be looked on as a landmark in the history of the Anglo-Saxon Church. It came to pass that the archbishop on this occasion consecrated no fewer than seven bishops on the one day. Frithstan was consecrated for Winchester, and Ethelward, who was possibly a son of King Alfred the Great, was also appointed to Sherborne, which had been vacant since the death of Asser in 904. Bernige became Bishop of Selsey and Eadulf of Crediton. The remaining dioceses were filled by the appointment of Ceolwulf to Dorchester and Ethelstan to Ramsbury: for Wells, Athelm was raised to the episcopate. This prelate was later on to succeed Plegmund in the metropolitan See of Canterbury. In the course of his tenure of the primatial see, Plegmund made two journeys to Rome, the first time at the end of Alfred's reign, when Formosus was Pope, and the second time in 910, when it became known that the acts of Pope Formosus had been declared invalid by his successor. Possibly he may have had news in time to procure the papal confirmation of the arrangements he had made in the Council of the previous year. Plegmund died in extreme old age in the year 914. Then Athelm of Wells was translated to the see of Canterbury, and immediately consecrated a successor to himself at Wells in the person of Wulfhelm, who, in his turn, nine years later was to sit in the chair of St Augustine.

As the years went on, Edward's dogged warfare against the Danes began to yield fruit. The Welsh having made common cause with these invaders in the West, he led an expedition in that direction to punish them. And, when his sister, the Lady of Mercia, died, he was able definitely to join Mercia to his own patrimony. His progress was not merely the successful march of a victorious army. The five boroughs which were the chief stronghold of the Danish power in the north Midlands, Derby, Leicester, Nottingham, Stamford, and Toncaster (or Lincoln) were restored to Saxon sovereignty in the territories which he had won. This was a more lasting means of establishing a lasting dominion than any battle he could have fought, as these boroughs were fortified and in some cases walled. Moreover, besides these Edward built at intervals burghs or fortified places to secure the lasting possession of the districts he conquered in all directions; and as these parts of the country fell little by little into Anglo-Saxon hands, it would appear that the conversion of the Danish inhabitants to Christianity gradually went on. It is unfortunate that the details of this process are lacking. Ethelfleda died several years before her brother, but not before the Danes of Mercia had been in great part subdued. This illustrious English queen was buried in the Abbey of St Peter at Gloucester. For the last years of his reign we hear little of Edward, but when his earthly course was run his remains were laid beside those of his father at Winchester (924).

The work of establishing the West Saxon power over the whole land begun by Egbert, carried on by Alfred and Edward the Elder, never came nearer to completion than in the reign of the next king, Athelstan, who was Edward's son and successor. Athelstan was probably illegitimate, but he was the favourite of his grandfather, Alfred, and after his death was brought up at the court of his aunt, Ethelfleda of Mercia. Archbishop Athelm survived to crown and anoint him at Kingston, and died very soon after; when Wulfhelm became archbishop. One of Athelstan's first acts was to make a marriage treaty with Sihtric, the Scandinavian King of Northumbria, who in accordance with this became the husband of Athelstan's sister. The death of Sihtric in the following year gave the West Saxon monarch an opportunity of intervening more effectually than had hitherto been possible in the affairs of the Northumbrian kingdom. But Athelstan's ambition had a more far-reaching aim than this. When Guthfrith, the brother of Sihtric, refused to act in the submissive manner he demanded, he expelled him from his kingdom. After this, Athelstan met all the chief rulers of Britain at Dacre in Cumberland, and succeeded in gaining from them all an acknowledgment of his overlordship. There is a legend that he was rowed in his barge on the river by eight subordinate kings. These were Howell Dda of Wales, Owen of Cumberland, Constantine of Scotland, Eldred of Northumberland, and several Scandinavian chieftains. Athelstan now called himself king of all Britain: *Rex totius Brittaniæ*, being the first monarch to claim this high-sounding title. It

Athelstan (924-940).

ANGLO-SAXON MONARCHY

does not seem that, notwithstanding their submission, these subjects proved to be very peaceful vassals. For Athelstan invaded Scotland in 933, penetrating as far as Kincardineshire. Then he had another war with Wales in the following year. Lastly, in 937 he had to withstand a powerful alliance, whose members included the Scottish king as well as the King of Cumberland and two Danish chieftains from Ireland. This was the most formidable combination which the Anglo-Saxon monarch had been ever called upon to face, but he proved himself equal to the occasion. The armies met at Brunanburgh, and Athelstan's complete victory, which was celebrated in a battle poem which still remains, freed the kingdom from the gravest peril of overthrow which had confronted it for many years. This put the crown on the king's other successes, and was probably the greatest contributory cause to his title of Athelstan the Victorious.

Notwithstanding the disturbance caused by these frequent wars, several councils or synods were held in the course of Athelstan's reign. These assemblies form a good illustration of the way in which civil and religious legislation were interwoven in the Anglo-Saxon period. These assemblies dealt with both almost indifferently, looking upon them as quite inextricably connected together. The names of such councils held at Exeter, Faversham, Thunderfield, London, and at Greately in Hampshire have been preserved to us, as well as much of the lawmaking, especially what was enacted at the last named place. The council at Greately is assigned to 928, and was guided in its deliberations by Archbishop Wulfhelm. The payment of titles is insisted on. Each town is commanded every year to free one slave, and to maintain one poor man at the king's expense. A uniform currency is set up for the whole country. Fines are imposed for buying or selling on a Sunday. The *Weregild* or sum to be paid according to Saxon law for the slaying of any man was not settled by this council, but spoken of as a thing already arranged by custom. It ranged from two hundred shillings for the life of a peasant up to ten thousand for a king, and five thousand for an archbishop, while between these extremes there were many intermediate grades. To settle such a matter would hardly be the normal function of a synod. It was in the year

Synods and Councils.

940 that King Athelstan died. He was buried in the royal Abbey of Malmesbury. He had distinguished himself during his short reign of fifteen years by his warlike ability, but the chroniclers report him as equally distinguished by the attraction of his personal qualities. He is said to have been a great favourite with his grandfather, Alfred, who knighted him. Not long after the king the primate Wulfhelm breathed his last in 942, and then St Odo, who had been presented to the See of Ramsbury or Wilton by Athelstan, was asked to transfer himself to Canterbury. This he did, though very unwillingly, and lived to play a considerable part in the events of the following reigns.

Meanwhile the territory of the northern dioceses being in the hands of the Danes either by force of arms, or by means of such treaties as Edward the Elder and Athelstan were able to make with them, the Anglo-Saxon writers do not supply us with any very complete succession of bishops for these sees. Ethelbald and Rodewald are both mentioned as being in turn Archbishops of York in the tenth century, but in neither case do we know the date of their death. There may easily have been considerable vacancies during those years of strife and foreign invasion. Still, when we come to the latter part of Athelstan's reign, we are on firmer ground. We are told that Wolstan or Wulfstan, called Wolstan I. to distinguish him from the better known archbishop in the following century, was consecrated archbishop in 931, and did not die until 956; and he seems to have joined his efforts with those of the southern metropolitan to bring about peace between the Saxons and the Danes. From his time forward we are able to trace the dates of the regular succession of the see of York. With regard to the occupants of the northern suffragan sees during this period we are still more in the dark. Uhtred succeeded Wigred at Chester-le-Street in 944, but the date of the former's death is unknown. None of the bishops of Whithern at this time are known to us, though there may have been a regular succession of bishops there. Earnulf, Columban, Exbert, Edward, and Alfred were all probably suffragans of York during their reigns, but their sees and length of episcopate are merely conjectural.

The period embraced by the two reigns we have spoken

margin note: Province of York.

of all fell in the darkest part of that tenth century which is sometimes known as the Iron Age. The records are not abundant, for learning was at a very low ebb. Moreover, the standard of morality was not high, and although the Church of God is never without saints, this was an epoch in which we can find exceptionally few to point to as examples of light amid the darkness. There is one, however, whom we must not pass over, for he was the outstanding figure of Athelstan's reign. This was St Odo, afterwards Archbishop of Canterbury, but from 923 to 943 Bishop of Ramsbury or Wilton in Wessex. *St Odo of Canterbury.* He was probably of Danish extraction, and from the time when he was consecrated by Wulfhelm to the Wiltshire diocese was the trusted counsellor of King Athelstan. He was with his king at the battle of Brunanburgh, and legend tells that he miraculously restored that sovereign his lost sword in the midst of the battle. But he was not a combatant. In fact he seems to have been one of the chief workers who tried to secure a peaceful settlement between the Saxons and Danes. Just after the death of Athelstan, the archbishop also died, and then St Odo had another sixteen years of responsibility as metropolitan. These years belong to the next period, and during that time he had the powerful support of St Dunstan in his efforts to raise the level of morality in England. He was buried at Canterbury, and it is said that St Dunstan, who entertained the greatest veneration for his memory, never passed his grave without saying a prayer to invoke his assistance in the work that fell upon him as his successor.

VIII.

THE ADMINISTRATION OF ST DUNSTAN.

(940-978.)

THE illustrious name at the head of this chapter at once points out the personal influence which did more to give unity to the period than any of the short-lived kings who succeeded one another during those years. No Anglo-Saxon ever filled so high a place in Church and State at the same time as St Dunstan did, and it is the simple truth to say that very few ruled in either of these spheres with equal loftiness of aim. As King Athelstan left no children when he died in 940, the succession to the crown devolved upon his brother, Edmund, who was only eighteen years of age at the time. Edmund was crowned at Kingston, and was immediately afterwards called upon to deal with the menacing situation which had arisen in the north of England. The Danish viking, Olaf or Anlaf, King of Dublin, had crossed over from Ireland at the head of a hostile expedition with the intention of wresting Northumbria once more from the dominion of the Anglo-Saxons. Edmund attacked the Danes, but his success was only partial, and Olaf was able to push into Mercia, and unite with the Danes who had settled there. It was some time before the Saxons were able to gain the upper hand in a lasting way.

Edmund I. (940-946).

In 942 Wulfhelm, Archbishop of Canterbury, died. The vacancy was filled by the transfer of St Odo from the Diocese of Ramsbury, where he had been for seventeen years. He was in his humility most unwilling to be raised to the higher dignity, which indeed, at the time, brought more of anxiety than of glory or comfort to its

St Odo at Canterbury (942-959).

holder. When he was at length persuaded into acceptance, the best preparation he could think of to fit himself for the weighty office was to ask by letter for the boon of the religious habit from the Abbot of Fleurus in France. This prelate sent him the monastic habit, affiliated him to the monastery, and thus lessened to some extent his reluctance for his new pastoral charge. Anyhow, Odo bent his back to the burden and ruled the see of Canterbury for as long a period as he had spent at Ramsbury. He was of Danish extraction, and this made his assistance all the more influential when he accompanied King Edmund on his expedition to the North. When both parties grew tired of the prolonged desultory warfare which wore away their strength, St Odo, in conjunction with Wulfstan, Archbishop of York, was instrumental in negotiating the treaty by which Edmund and Olaf came to terms. Watling Street was again to become the boundary between the dominions of the two princes, while the survivor was to inherit both. This was, of course, the undoing for the moment of Athelstan's supremacy over the whole land. Yet Olaf was not to enjoy for long the lands which had thus been ceded to him. He died in the following year, and then Edmund at once reasserted his authority in accordance with the treaty. Olaf's two sons submitted, and also received baptism, Edmund becoming sponsor to Olaf, and receiving Ragnald into his household. But they were soon at the head of a new rebellion, when Wulfstan of York took the field against them with the Ealdorman of Mercia, and they were expelled from England.

King Edmund's next enterprise was the endowment of Glastonbury. The biographers of St Dunstan tell us that from the very beginning of Edmund's reign the youthful monk, Dunstan of Glastonbury, was an intimate counsellor of the young king. He was at once bidden to *Growing Influence of St Dunstan.* take up his residence at court, where he was employed in giving advice and in judging disputes in the royal name. He conducted himself with such exemplary prudence practising that faithful stewardship which he afterwards exercised on a much larger scale when he had been raised to the highest dignity in the English Church. But the voice of calumny, directed by those who were envious of his influence, so far prevailed with the young king that Dunstan was banished from the court in disgrace. The reparation came when the king and his court were at Cheddar in Somerset. It happened one day when the king was hunting that his horse, in pursuit of the game, was rushing at full speed to the edge of the cliffs which fall precipitately to the plain, and instant death seemed to face the monarch, when he remembered the wrong he had done to Dunstan. It was but the work of a moment to confess his fault, and for the horse's feet to be arrested on the very edge of the descent. Henceforward nothing was too much for Edmund to do to make amends. He handed over to Dunstan Glastonbury and its lands, and installed him there as perpetual abbot. This is an event which the most careful chronology places in the year 946. It cannot have been later, for in that year the short and disturbed reign of the young sovereign came to an end. He was keeping St Augustine's Feast at Pucklechurch in Gloucestershire, when Liofa, a well-known outlaw, intruded himself into the royal banqueting chamber. Being ordered to leave, he resisted, and the king himself rushed angrily to the spot. Liofa then drew a dagger from beneath his cloak, and stabbed him to the heart. Edmund expired on the floor of the hall, and Liofa was hewn in pieces by the enraged courtiers. At Glastonbury, which he had given new life to by his endowment under the rule of Dunstan, Edmund's body found its resting-place hard by the tombs of many royal princes of his race.

Edmund's sons, Edwy and Edgar, were mere children at the time, so the Witan, exercising its traditional power of modifying the succession, adjudged the crown to Edred, brother of the late king, and youngest son of King Edward the Elder. The usual coronation ceremony, which as in the preceding reign took place at Kingston, was performed by the archbishop St Odo. No sooner was it over than by common consent the North claimed the first attention of the king. The news had come that a new Scandinavian king had been set up there in the person of Eric, brother of the Norwegian king. Edred marched to York and thence into Northumberland, and after several campaigns was able to suppress the rising and return to the South, bringing with him many Norse

Edred (946-955).

captives, Edred was a noble young prince, but was dogged all his life through by painful and obstinate illness. St Dunstan was the trusted counsellor of Edred from first to last, and much of the burden of the government, as well as the success of his enterprises, may be ascribed to him. Moreover, Edred had another skilled adviser among the clergy in Turketul, his chancellor, who had been foremost likewise at the court of Athelstan and Edmund. He was entrusted by the king with securing the fidelity of Archbishop Wulfstan of York, who seems to have been inclined to favour the Danes. Wulfstan was put into captivity for a year, but was afterwards, restored to his diocese. It was on this journey that Turketul visited the monks of Croyland, now reduced to a scanty remnant of the once flourishing community. He felt a strong desire to remain with them, and to try and bring back the monastery to its former prosperity. It was only after repeated refusal that he at length obtained permission to leave the court and return to the solitude of Croyland. He then made all his arrangements, paid his debts, and endowed Croyland out of his ancestral estates. Moreover, Edred came to the rescue, and gave back to the monastery other lands which had fallen into the possession of the crown. Turketul became abbot, and obtained from the king a new charter for Croyland, confirming all its old privileges, with the exception of the right of sanctuary, which he declined as a dubious and onerous favour. Here he presided over the fortunes of the abbey for seven-and-twenty years, and when he died about 975, had the satisfaction of knowing that Croyland was once more a flourishing religious house, inhabited by a large body of monks. Edred could at last keep up the struggle against disease no longer and died in 955. He was interred in Winchester Cathedral.

Edwy, the young son of Edmund, had even now scarcely reached man's estate. Yet Odo, the archbishop, crowned him at Kingston, after he had been acknowledged by the Witan as lawful heir. But at the very outset he gave only too clear proof of the violence of his passions and the utter unworthiness of his conduct for the royal dignity. On his coronation day itself, he left the assembly of his thanes and prelates gathered to keep high festival on

Edwy (955-959).

the occasion, that he might visit two women, Ethelgifu and her daughter, Elgifu—the latter being his mistress, and might thus indulge himself in the dalliance of love. Though the scandal was great, none durst interfere but the Abbot Dunstan and his kinsman, Kinesige. These, at the request of Archbishop Odo, followed up the royal fugitive, and after a warm remonstrance to him, and sharp rebukes to the shameless women, brought him back to the noble gathering. But though Dunstan was successful for the moment, he was never forgiven, and very soon became the object of relentless hostility on the part of Ethelgifu and her friends. At first he fled to Glastonbury, and when this was no longer safe, then from one to another of the English monasteries. Nevertheless, the pursuit of him with the avowed object of putting out his eyes went on until at last he quitted the country, and fled to the court of Ernulf, Count of Flanders, who assigned him a monastery at Ghent to live in, where Dunstan remained in exile for a year (957-958). Meanwhile events moved rapidly at home.

Freed from the influence of Dunstan, Edwy gave himself up to his pleasures, neglecting the duties of his royal position, until the dissatisfaction with his rule grew deep and widespread. His attempted marriage with Elgifu was denounced by the archbishop as irregular. And at last the Mercian nobility broke out into open revolt, and chose Edgar, the king's brother, as King of Mercia. At first Edwy resisted this, but at last an arrangement was come to by which the Thames was to be the boundary, Edgar ruling Mercia and Edwy retaining Wessex. One of Edgar's first cares was to recall St Dunstan from Flanders, and the see of Worcester, which was in Edgar's dominions, falling vacant, Dunstan was persuaded, seeing the necessities of the time, to accept it, and was consecrated by Odo in 958. Not so long after this Odo died, and Elfsine, Bishop of Winchester, was chosen as his successor; but while he was on the journey to Rome to receive the pallium was frozen to death amidst the Alpine passes. As soon as this was known in England, Edwy indicated that he wished Brihthelm of Wells to be translated to Canterbury. We find several bishops of this name, almost contemporaries, one in London, one at Wells, and one at Winchester, and possibly they were all the same person

translated from see to see. Anyhow, St Dunstan
followed Brihthelm at London, holding, however, at
the same time his previous diocese of Worcester. And
it only needed the death of Edwy, which happened in
the same year (959), to make his advancement to the
metropolitan see a certainty.

Edgar was immediately and almost unanimously
accepted as king in Wessex as well as in Mercia, and
St Dunstan was already his chief and confidential adviser. One of his first acts was
to nullify the choice made of Bishop
Brihthelm for Canterbury, on the ground
that he was unequal to the responsibilities which he
already bore, and to nominate Dunstan to the primacy.
In the following year (960) Dunstan travelled to Rome
and obtained the pallium from Pope John XII., distinguishing himself as he went his way by his great charity
and the abundant alms he bestowed. As soon as he
returned, he took up the position of the virtual ruler of
England both in Church and State, as Edgar was a mere
youth, and was guided in all public affairs by his counsel.
Would he had been more faithful to his guidance in his
private life as well! This seems to have been free and
licentious enough, though some of the stories remembered
against him may be discredited. But though he did not
keep from sin we have a record of his doing penance,
notably the public one of having his coronation deferred
for seven years because he had committed the sin of
sacrilege with a nun of the abbey at Wilton.

Edgar the Peaceful (959-975).

St Dunstan was able, notwithstanding the king's
private misdeeds, to govern the kingdom in his name with
such prudence and wisdom that it enjoyed
a period of prosperity and peace, such as
had been long unknown to it. St Dunstan
was a true Reformer, both in Church and State, and
his opportunities were such as fall to the lot of few men.
He began by arranging for the filling up of the vacant
episcopal sees. For Worcester and London, which he of
course vacated, he recommended St Oswald, a nephew of
St Odo, and Elfstan respectively. Brihthelm seems to
have held Winchester, after being rejected for Canterbury, until his death in 963, and then St Ethelwold,
abbot of Abingdon, was appointed in his stead. It was
on the co-operation of these two holy men that Dunstan

Dunstan the Reformer.

relied more than on all others for the great work of the restoration of the monastic state in England to which he had put his hand. Oswald in Mercia, and Ethelwold in Wessex deserve a large share of the credit of this beneficent revival. St. Oswald, indeed, had other and higher offices to fill, for on the death of Oskytul, Archbishop of York in 971, he was named to succeed him in the charge of the northern archiepiscopate. And in 973 he was present with St Dunstan at the coronation of King Edgar. He seems also to have retained the administration of Worcester, for it was only at St Oswald's death in 992 that Aldulf was consecrated to succeed him as bishop of that see. Another Elfstan than the Bishop of London mentioned above was made Bishop of Rochester in 964, unless we suppose the two sees held by the same individual. But, notwithstanding all this, it was even more by the influence he exerted over the monastic and conventual life, than by the provision of good pastors for the vacant sees, that St Dunstan has a claim to be looked on as one of the Church's great reformers. His first enterprise of this kind, the restoration of Glastonbury, has been already spoken of in telling of the deeds of his early life. It only need be added that he continued to watch over the abbey, and did all in his power to secure the permanence of the new life, which he had infused into it. But when raised to the chief position in the Church in England he was able to labour for the same end in a more general way, and besides this, to enlist the services of more powerful co-operators.

King Edgar only survived his coronation, so long delayed as we have seen, for about two years, but they were years of peace and prosperity. He paid great attention to sea power, and is said to have reorganised the navy. It was in connection with this that the old chronicle records a remarkable pageant when eight kings rowed the king in his royal barge along the river Dee. At any rate the kings of Wales, Northumbria, and the other neighbouring lands must have acknowledged his overlordship, and this would be a way of showing it that must have appealed to the popular imagination. The only charge made against his public administration was a too great friendliness with the Danes of Northumbria, and his share in the appointment of St Oswald, a

Dane of this kind to the see of York, was put down to a policy of his, which after all must have been one of the means employed to win over these people to the acceptance of his supremacy. Edgar heartily supported St Dunstan and his fellow-workers in their work of reviving the monastic life, and before his reign was over some fifty abbeys had begun a new period of regularity and vigorous life.

When Edgar died in 975 both his sons were children, and so loose was the law of primogeniture that it seemed that the claims of Ethelred the younger against Edward might lead to civil war. However, St Dunstan called together the Witan, and convinced the counsellors who were there of Edward's superior right, and thereupon crowned him with the general consent of the nobles. **St Edward the Martyr (975-978).**
Still, Elfrida, the mother of Ethelred, did not abandon the project of setting her son, Ethelred, on the throne, and did not shrink from the crime of murder to achieve success. One morning Edward, while on a hunting expedition, drew up on horseback at Corfe Castle where Elfrida lived. A cup of mead was proffered to the unsuspecting young prince, and while he was in the act of drinking it, a treacherous hand stabbed him to death. He fell to the ground, and shortly after expired. All that Dunstan and the Earl of Mercia could do was to inter him with regal splendour at Shaftesbury Abbey near his royal ancestors. And, though never really canonised, popular affection, consecrated by the words of the Roman martyrology, has given him the title of St Edward the Martyr. He is regularly commemorated on the 18th of March.

St Dunstan had now finished his work as chief counsellor of the realm. He could have no share in the new regime, for he knew that the power had passed through crime into hands which he could not guide. It was above all in the reign of Edgar that he was able to accomplish so much, and he had worthy fellow-workers. As to the replacing of the secular canons by religious, the following are the chief restorations which were then effected: Benedictine monks were placed at Chertsey, Exeter, Milton Abbas, Ely, Peterborough or Medehampstead, and Thorney. Perhaps it was in Mercia more thoroughly than in Wessex that he was able to win his way. The fact seems to be that in the West Saxon lands the opposition both on the part of the secular clergy and of the nobles was more powerful. But after all it meant a beneficent movement in favour of regularity and of morality too, and that would be enough in itself, apart from his other claims to honour, to establish the fame of St Dunstan as one of the chief influences in the Catholic Church of his day.

St Dunstan now retired to Canterbury, where, having cast off the burden of secular cares, he spent ten fruitful years with his monks in the monastery occupied in the more immediate labours of his office. His manner of life is described for us in his biography, and forms a pleasing picture of the old age of a great servant of God. First and foremost in his mind ever came the various exercises of the direct worship of God. Now he was to be seen presiding over the public offices in his cathedral, or the daily round of psalmody of the monks. Now he was watching in prayer all alone through the night. Now again he used the early morning light in literary pursuits, composing or correcting the manuscripts of others, or patiently copying in the Scriptorium of Christchurch priory. At another time he would be engaged in what was always one of his favourite pursuits, teaching the young scholars who were preparing for the sacerdotal ministry. Sometimes, by way of relaxation from more intellectual pursuits, he was back again at the manual labours in which he had been so skilled in youth, the construction of musical instruments, or ornamental woodwork. But though secluded from the press of mundane affairs, he was able during these tranquil years to consecrate six or seven prelates for the various sees which fell vacant, three of whom in turn succeeded him in the archbishopric. These were Ethelgar, whom he consecrated for Selsey in 980, St Elphege, who was appointed to Winchester in 984, and lastly Siric, who filled the see of Ramsbury from 985 to 990. At length, as the Ascension Festival of 988 drew near, the end of his earthly pilgrimage was reached. On that holy day he preached twice in the cathedral with a force and energy far beyond anything he had hitherto attained. He was at the high altar celebrating Mass, and he not only gave the usual homily after the Gospel had been

St Dunstan in retirement.

ST DUNSTAN

sung, but also had burning words of exhortation to say at his blessing of the people after the chant of the Agnus Dei. He then proceeded to the refectory, where he shared with joy in the common meal of the Festival. Then he went as usual to take a short repose in his cell. There his last illness seized him. He had still strength, when the monks had assembled, to utter a few consoling words of farewell and encouragement. But his strength was ebbing away, and two days later he peacefully expired, namely, on Saturday, the 19th of May, 988. He was buried in the cathedral, where his tomb became a place of pilgrimage frequented by crowds of that Anglo-Saxon folk to whom he had been father and shepherd.

IX.

THE DANISH CONQUEST OF ENGLAND.

(978-1042.)

Ethelred II. (978-1016). THE accession of Edward's younger brother, Ethelred, styled the Redeless or Unready, in 978, marked the beginning of the Anglo-Saxon kingdom's fall. This prince had a reign of thirty-eight years in all, but he was of an unstable and careless disposition, given up in the main to his ease and his pleasures. Unfortunately for the Anglo-Saxon monarchy, it happened that this was the very period when the growing resources of Denmark rendered resistance to the attempts made thence to conquer England more difficult than it had ever been before. The invaders pushed on and on, until at length they had seated a Danish sovereign upon the Anglo-Saxon throne. Ethelred was crowned at Kingston by St Dunstan, in the presence of St Oswald of York and other bishops, and with all the usual ceremonies. There is still extant a promise made by the king, as also an exhortation delivered by the holy Primate on this occasion, which shows the latter still doing all in his power that the new ruler should begin his reign with the standard of Christian kingship clearly before his mind: " In the name of the Holy Trinity I promise the Christian folk three things: first that God's Church and all Christian folk of my realm have true peace; the other is that I forbid robbery and all unrighteous things to all ranks; the third is that I promise and bid righteousness in all dooms, and mildness of heart, so that the gracious and mild God through His mercy forgive us all, Who liveth and reigneth. The end."

This formula was, no doubt, substantially the same as

that used at the coronation of former kings. It is also noteworthy that it was again used as late as A.D. 1100 at the crowning of the Norman king Henry I. Its citation here will be a reminder that it was with a promise most solemnly taken amidst his nobles to reign well, and in the presence of saints that King Ethelred began his reign, pledged by sworn engagements to be a king in conduct as well as in name.

The withdrawal of St Dunstan from public affairs took away the intrepid champion who had so often intervened to steer the ship of state safely through the midst of perils. The new archbishop, Ethelgar, did his best to advise the king, but it seems clear that Ethelred went his wayward course almost unrestrained, just as the tide of circumstances or his caprices drove him. The result was a reign of great confusion and misery for the people. The chronicler, William of Malmesbury, says epigrammatically that it was "cruel in the beginning, wretched in the middle, and disgraceful at the end." The events of those years go far to justify his summing up. Ethelred was twice married: first to a Saxon lady, Elfleda, whose son later on became king, and is known as Edmund Ironside; the second time he espoused a Norman princess named Emma, daughter of Richard, Duke of Normandy, by whom he had two sons, Alfred and Edward. There was a suspicion that Ethelred had been privy to the assassination of his brother, Edward the Martyr. It is no more than an unproved assertion, but Ethelred founded at great expense a monastery at Celisige for the repose of Edward's soul, handing over the care of it to Germanus, Abbot of Winchelcombe. This is a sign of his faith, though not necessarily of his guilt. The real condemnation pronounced upon him comes from his conduct during the subsequent years. It was during these years that the fatal system was begun, either on the king's own responsibility, or, as some have thought, on the advice of Archbishop Ethelgar, of buying off the Danish marauders by money payments. An ill-omened precedent had been set in the case of the king himself in the early part of his reign. He had quarrelled with Elfstan, Bishop of Rochester, and to punish him marching against his episcopal city in hostile fashion, he laid siege to it. He would probably have

Ethelred and his family.

stormed and plundered the place, but, fortunately for Rochester, St Dunstan was still alive, and he came to the rescue as mediator. He bought off the king's hostility by the payment of one thousand marks. Yet, even while doing so, he could not forbear exclaiming against the meanness of a sovereign who could thus barter his favour towards his own bishops for money. It was not long after this when the Danish invaders recommenced their inroads with redoubled fury. Then it was that Ethelred employed the ruinous expedients of placating them by a money payment. The Danes at first took the money and retired, but this transaction only made them all the greedier for a second payment, and this for a third, until the tribute became regularised into an annual sum, which later on received the name of Danegeld or Dane money.

Still, year after year, new invaders came on, now landing on one coast, now on another, and though it is but fair to the Saxons to say that they sometimes met with a sharp repulse, yet the general effect of their incursions was to tighten their grip upon England, and to inflict untold misery on its wretched inhabitants. Hence it is evident that it was only after the provocation afforded by numberless outrages that the cruel and cowardly plot was hatched among the Saxons for a general massacre of all the Danes in the country on the same day. This bloody act of revenge was carried out on Saturday the 13th of November, 1002. It is known as the massacre of St Brice, because on this day is celebrated by the Church the memory of that saint. Ethelred is accused of complicity in the plans for this wholesale slaughter, and there is some likelihood that in one way or another he was concerned in it. With him, as with the people, the reputation which the Danes had earned for ferocity was no doubt an exciting cause, if not an excuse. The massacre was carried out with every aggravation which passion and national hatred could devise. In London, even those who had taken refuge in the churches were killed round the very altars. Gunhilda, sister to Sweyn, King of Denmark, was one of the most prominent victims. Hence, the next year (1003) had not gone very far in its course when that monarch was already at sea with a warlike expedition,

Massacre of St Brice (1002).

burning to avenge the death of his sister and of his fellow-countrymen. He first sailed to the West, where he gained possession of Exeter. Using this place as a stronghold and centre, his fierce soldiers ravaged the neighbouring counties far and wide, returning periodically to Exeter to store their plunder, and to rest from the battle. The same method of procedure henceforward began all over again each year as soon as spring appeared, and always with results more and more disastrous to the natives. They met indeed with a certain amount of resistance, but such was the savage valour of the invaders, and so skilful was Sweyn as a leader in warfare of this kind, that whenever the Saxons ventured to meet them in the field they were routed with great slaughter. It was not until 1007 that Sweyn felt he had wreaked adequate vengéance on the Saxons for the massacre of St Brice. At last he agreed to a truce on the payment of a large sum of money.

The Danes ravage the land.

The cessation of hostilities which had been thus purchased gave the Saxons a certain breathing space, so that when in the following year they found their enemies determined to give them but the alternative of another ransom, or a renewal of hostilities, the Witenagemot decided by common consent to strain every nerve for a strong and desperate attempt to bear off their foes. It was in accordance with this resolution that the strongest armament, we are told, which the country had ever raised was put on board the royal fleet at Sandwich, and Ethelred himself embarked to take the command. Yet, even now, dissension was at work, and treachery was suspected. Anyhow, Ethelred was not the man under those circumstances to lead his despairing country to victory or success. After an ineffectual cruise the king came to land again, and a Danish general named Turketul was able to attack and rout the Saxons in detail. He then proceeded to harry and plunder some thirteen counties.

In the midst of this general dislocation of the civil and domestic life of the country, it must have been a work of considerable difficulty for the pastors of the Church to tend their flocks, or even to keep up the succession of prelates in the various episcopal sees. Still, a more successful effort to provide for this last necessity was made than we should at the first glance think possible. Ethelgar, St Dunstan's immediate successor as primate, only lived until 989, when Siric, or Sigric, who had been consecrated Bishop of Ramsbury, was translated to Canterbury. Elfric, whom he had been followed by at Ramsbury, then became Primate, and presided over the archbishopric for ten years (995-1005). At the next vacancy, the holy bishop, St Elphege, who had already held the important see of Winchester for one-and-twenty years, was moved to Canterbury, and had to take up the burden of the archiepiscopal office at the very time when things were most desperate for the Saxons. St Elphege was able, during the few years that remained to him before his career came to an end in captivity and martyrdom, to provide a prelate to follow in his footsteps at Winchester, first in the person of Kenulf, and then, when he died in the following year, in Ethelwold II., who was still bishop there when St Elphege died. He also seems to have been able to consecrate five or six bishops for other English sees in the course of as many years. The ravages of the heathen came to a climax about the year 1011. Having devastated not only the southern counties, but a great part of East Anglia, and Mercia as well, they forced King Ethelred to sue for peace, promising them a large tribute of money. However, though the promise was made, the sum demanded, which seems to have been forty-eight thousand pounds, a very considerable one for those times, was not forthcoming. This disappointment was the signal for a fresh hostile attack on the part of the Danes, who before long laid siege to the city of Canterbury. Through treachery, or the attack made from outside, Canterbury was set on fire, and this made it easier for the Danes to storm it. They then put the inhabitants to the sword with every species of hideous torture. St Elphege, Godwin, Bishop of Rochester, the canons of the cathedral and many others were prisoners in their hands. The archbishop was kept in captivity for seven months in the hope that a large ransom would be paid for his release. On Easter Eve, 1012, the Danish leaders offered St Elphege life and liberty for a sum of three thousand pounds. However, the holy prelate positively refused to take any steps to induce his people to raise this money. He was then kept a prisoner in London

Martyrdom of St Elphege (1012).

for another week. Finally, on Easter Saturday, the 19th of April, the savage invaders being gradually worked up into a state of fury by his forbidding anyone to pay money for his ransom, they dragged him before their council. At the time they were exceedingly drunk with copious potations of wine, and starting up from their seats, they flung him down on to the ground and pelted him with stones and the bones of oxen. At length, a soldier, whom he had once befriended, moved with some sort of pity for his sufferings, ended them by splitting his skull with his axe. He died a martyr's death at the hands of a man whom he had blessed. First he was interred in St Paul's at London, but afterwards his relics were translated to his own cathedral. There he was duly honoured as the chief martyr of the place, until in later ages his fame was somewhat eclipsed by that of St Thomas. Still, St Elphege always remained a popular hero to our forefathers, and a considerable number of churches were dedicated in his honour.

Sweyn, who was just then in Denmark, soon had information of all these events. The successes won by Turketul showed him how feeble the resistance had become, while the terms agreed upon by him for a truce with the Saxons made him suspect the loyalty of that leader. *Sweyn conquers England.* He, accordingly, determined to put forth his whole strength to effect a complete conquest of England. In 1013 he left Denmark with a large and well-appointed armament, and landed at Sandwich. His plans were somewhat disarranged by his finding that the Danish army there was minded to keep the truce they had made with the Saxons. Sweyn, therefore, sailed north to the Humber, and gradually gained possession of Mercia, East Anglia, and Northumbria. After this, he again turned to the south, and attacked London. Resistance was made for some time, but then the city surrendered to the Dane, and he was near completing the conquest of the whole land. King Ethelred fled with a small guard of troops, first to the Isle of Wight, and then to Normandy, where Queen Emma's brother, Duke Richard, gave an asylum both to his sister and to her husband. Elfhun, Bishop of London, also took refuge on the continent, as also did Lyfing, the former Bishop of Wells, who had been translated to Canterbury in the year after the death of St Elphege. Ethelred may easily have expected a long exile in Normandy, but the unexpected death of Sweyn in February, 1014, gave him his opportunity. For, though the Danish army at once elected Canute as king in his father's room, this choice was not ratified by the Saxon Witan. They attempted once more to assert themselves, and sent to Ethelred, inviting him to return. Ethelred first sent his son, Prince Edward, to promise that henceforward he would reign according to the law, and would put away all the abuses of which they complained. This being accepted, and promises of loyalty having been given, Ethelred himself crossed the sea soon after, and was acknowledged as sole king by the Saxon nobles. They supported him so well that he was able to lead an army into East Anglia to meet the Danes. Canute found himself for the moment so unequal to the contest that he fled to Denmark, whereupon the Danish settlements in England were committed to the flames, and many of their inhabitants ruthlessly slain.

These bloody reprisals were an ill augury for the peace of the future, and the assassination of Sigferth and Morcar, the chief Danish jarls in the Five Boroughs, being attributed to Ethelred, he was still very far from enjoying the respect and confidence of his people. Even among his own kindred he could not count on submission. Edmund Ironside, his eldest son by the lady Elfleda, who had shared in the attack on the Danes of Mercia, demanded the possessions of the two murdered jarls for himself, and being refused, gathered an army in the North, and took forcible possession of them. In 1016 Canute felt ready to renew the conflict, and once more crossed the sea from Denmark. Ethelred retired into Wiltshire broken in spirit and worn out with disease, while Edmund Ironside put himself at the head of the Saxon troops. Coming to London in April to meet his son, Edmund, Ethelred died there on the 23rd of April, and was buried in St Paul's. The Witan, who were at London, acclaimed Edmund as king, and he made a brave effort to defend the kingdom which was entrusted to him. It was difficult enough to organise any united resistance to the Danes, but gradually Edmund's exploits and martial character encouraged a large part

Edmund Ironside (1016).

of the nation to rally round him. If any man could have turned back the tide of Danish conquest, Edmund would have done it. In the course of the year 1016, he fought five pitched battles, the details of which are in great part preserved for us in the Anglo-Saxon Chronicle. Still, the net result of it all was to plunge the whole realm into an intolerable welter of civil war. At last the two monarchs were forced to come to a compromise. They met at Olney, in Northamptonshire, and agreed that Canute should reign over Mercia and Northumbria, and Edmund over Wessex and the South. It was arranged that the Danegeld should be paid in both parts of the land. Edmund did not long survive this arrangement. He died on the 30th of November, 1016, not without the suspicion of foul play, and was buried by the side of his grandfather, King Edgar, in Glastonbury.

Edmund's unexpected death left Canute practically without a rival for the English crown, but he took two steps in the immediate future which still further strengthened his position. In 1017 he met the Anglo-Saxon Witan, and was formally elected king by the assembled nobles. And in the course of the same year he likewise married Ethelred's widow, Queen Emma, agreeing to the settlement that at his death the crown should pass to their offspring, to the exclusion of Harold and Sweyn, his sons by his former mistress, Elgifa. He seems henceforth to have done his best to act as a constitutional monarch, putting off the rôle of a foreign conqueror. In confirmation of this policy he admitted the Anglo-Saxons to a share in his counsels, and appointed them to positions of trust. Lyfing, the Archbishop of Canterbury, came back from his exile, and held the primatial see until his death in 1020. A like return was made by other prelates and clergy who had taken refuge from the storm by leaving the country. As to the administration of the realm, Canute's plan was to divide England into four great earldoms, of which he retained the immediate control of Wessex for himself, while he entrusted East Anglia to Turketul, Mercia to Edric, and Northumbria to Eric. These leaders were all Danes, or partisans of the Danish supremacy. Canute's legislation was rather a revival or enforcement of the older laws made under Edgar and Ethelred than a code of new

Canute the Great (1017-1036).

enactments, but there was now a king firm enough and strong enough to see to their observance. For the greater portion of his reign Canute attained to a nearer approach to the position of an international ruler, or Emperor, than any previous King of England had done, being sovereign not only of this country, but of Denmark, Norway, and part of Sweden as well. Yet the bond of union was too personal to be permanent, as indeed was recognised by the monarch himself, since on his deathbed he divided up his dominions among his heirs. His early life had been that of a rough and semi-barbarous viking, but he rose to his new station and well deserves the appellation of the "Great."

Canute became, in quite an unusual degree, the Protector of the Church all through his wide dominions.

Canute and the Church. When Archbishop Lyfing died, Ethelnoth, Prior of Christchurch at Canterbury, was chosen in his stead, and was consecrated by Wulfstan, Archbishop of York. The new primate made the journey to Rome in 1022 to ask for his pallium, and there Pope Benedict VIII. received him with high honour. He personally invested him with the pallium at High Mass in St Peter's, sung by the archbishop himself. There was then a banquet, at which Benedict and Ethelnoth were both present, and the latter was able to commence his homeward journey in all gladness. Ethelnoth was much trusted by Canute, and became one of his chief counsellors. To him belongs much of the credit of the administration of the English part of the sovereign's realm. He survived Canute, only coming to the end of his episcopate in 1038. Wulfstan only survived at York until 1023, when he was replaced by Elfric, or Alfric Puttoc, whom Ethelnoth consecrated at Canterbury. It is noteworthy that Alfric did as Ethelnoth had done, and made the journey to Rome to receive his pallium from Pope John XIX. Some have, without sufficient reason, identified the archbishop with the writer of "Alfric's Homilies." But it is more probable that the latter was another ecclesiastic of the same name. Canute gave a still further proof of the bonds which bound him to the Church and to the Holy See by making himself a pilgrimage to Rome in 1027. He visited the tombs of the Apostles with great devotion, offering splendid gifts on the occasion. He also paid considerable sums of money with the object of securing the exemption of both scholars and pilgrims from England, from the legal dues which had been exacted from them. Canute was present on Easter Day in St Peter's, when the Emperor Conrad and his wife, the Empress Gisela, were crowned by the Pope, and when the coronation ceremony was over escorted Conrad home to his palace.

The chief source of our information concerning the doings of Canute in the city of Rome is an excellent letter of his which we possess, addressed to the two archbishops, Ethelnoth and Alfric, to all the bishops and "to all English folk both of high and low degree." *Canute's letter from Rome.*
In this epistle he tells them how the object of his journey was to pray for the forgiveness of his sins, for the safety of his realm, and for all his people. He protests that he gives thanks to God for being allowed to accomplish this Roman journey successfully. It is because he knows that St Peter has received the power of binding and loosing and the keys of the kingdom of heaven that he has travelled so far. He then describes the coronation in a few words, going on to tell his people how he had protested against the excessive tolls and tributes levied upon them when they came to Rome, and especially the large sums which had to be offered at the bestowal of the pallium. Finally, he commands that all dues owing through ancient custom should be paid promptly before his return. He mentions in particular the plough scot, the tithes, the Peter's Pence, and the firstfruits. He has vowed, he says, henceforth to reform his whole life, and to govern his kingdoms in justice and equity, making amends for any wrong done to anyone in the past, either through carelessness or through the intemperance of youth. Such was the effect of a pilgrimage to Rome upon the great Canute.

It is remarkable that he calls himself king not only of England, Norway, and Denmark, but also of a part of Sweden. Yet his hold on the last named country must have been sufficiently precarious. The Swedes, in fact, seem to have worsted him in battle, but no doubt he kept up the conflict, and may have reduced to submission some part of the country. Of Norway he really got possession, as well as of Denmark. It was by way of Denmark that he made his return journey to England,

and afterwards undertook an expedition against Malcolm, King of Scotland. Malcolm appears to have agreed to accept his overlordship in some form or other, but neither Malcolm nor Canute was to reign for much longer. There were now a few years of comparative tranquillity for Canute, broken only by the death of several of his bishops. In those years died Elfsige of Winchester, Merewit of Wells, and Etheric of Dorchester, besides the King of Scots. In 1036 Canute himself breathed his last at Shaftesbury, and is certainly one of the most notable of the great personages interred in Winchester Cathedral.

Canute was hardly dead before the testamentary arrangements he had made for the succession were promptly disregarded. Harold Harefoot, Elgifa's son, was at hand, determined to claim the kingdom of England for himself.

Harold Harefoot (1036-1040).

The Danish influence in the land seems to have been exerted in Harold's favour, but Queen Emma, though Alfred, the son of Ethelred, landed expecting her to take his part, threw in her lot with Hardicanute, evidently preferring the children of her second marriage to those of her first. Alfred was seized, and his eyes put out with such brutality that soon after he died at Ely. His followers were either slain or reduced to slavery. Although Hardicanute was supported by Emma and the powerful Earl Godwin, he was not able to make good his claim to the whole kingdom. A Witan held at Oxford decided that Hardicanute should have Wessex, and Harold Mercia and Northumbria. But the former tarried in Denmark, so that before long Harold became king over the whole land. He summoned the good archbishop, Ethelnoth, to crown him, but the latter does not seem to have been by any means convinced that Harold was the rightful heir. He therefore laid the crown upon the altar, saying that he neither gave it nor refused it, but at the same time he strictly forbade any other bishop to usurp his right to crown the king. Later on he seems to have been prevailed upon to perform the rite with the usual solemnities. When Ethelnoth died in 1038 his auxiliary bishop at St Martin's, Eadsige, became primate in his place. Harold did not long enjoy the crown which had been placed upon his brow. In 1040 he died, and is said to have been buried at West-

THE DANISH CONQUEST 111

minster. His successor had his remains dug up and flung into the marsh, but later on he was again buried, this time at St Clement Danes', the usual burial place of his race.

Harold's death, in the flower of his age, left the field open for the accession of Hardicanute. He came to England with a Danish fleet, and was acknowledged both by Northmen and Saxons. Nevertheless, to the latter he bid fair to be a hard master, and in the few years of his reign the Danish domination came to its highest point of arrogance. The English were treated as an inferior race, and the monarch himself seemed to be purely a foreigner, who had only left his native land when the diadem of royalty was put at his feet. Yet he loved a life of joyous festivity, and could entertain his friends with profuse hospitality. Edward, the brother of the murdered Alfred, came to Hardicanute's court from Normandy the year before he died, and lived in the royal household. Archbishop Eadsige went to Rome for his pallium, but returned while Hardicanute was still alive. The end of his reign came with a terribly sudden death. While in the house of Osgod Clapa, and raising his glass to drink at a banquet, he had a sudden fit and expired before anything could be done to help him. He lies with his father, Canute, in Winchester.

Hardicanute (1040-1042).

X.

REIGN OF ST. EDWARD THE CONFESSOR.

(1042-1066.)

St Edward the Confessor (1042-1066).

THE years of comparative peace which England enjoyed under the sceptre of St Edward the Confessor may be looked on as a period of transition. The unusual tranquillity of the time is ascribed by the old chroniclers much more to the influence of the monarch's personal character than to any external circumstances. But there was transition also. Edward had been brought up on the continent of Europe amongst the Normans, whilst at that time the Danes were lording it over his native land. He had then become persuaded of the superiority of the civilisation to which Normandy had attained, and of the higher standard of learning and conduct reigning amongst its clergy. Hence, in his efforts to raise his own country to a higher level, he was drawn to make use of Norman churchmen, and, to some extent, of Norman officials as well. In fact, this was at the time a ground of complaint for the opponents of reform, and has been recorded as a mark against him even in our own days by writers who put the claims of nationality above those of general civilisation and of Christian morality.

St Edward was one of the sons of Ethelred the Redeless by Queen Emma, and hence was half-brother to Edmund Ironside, the son of Ethelred and Elfleda, as well as to Hardicanute, the son of Canute and Emma. His own brother, Alfred, was killed in 1035. But even while this prince was alive the claim of Edgar Etheling to the crown was paramount according to the

ST EDWARD THE CONFESSOR

strict law of primogeniture. But that prince was absent in Hungary, and the Witan in England had always claimed the right to choose among the members of the royal family without following too nicely the order of precedence. Moreover, at the moment the whole nation was sighing for a sovereign of Saxon race, so oppressive had the tyrannous domination of the Danes become. It was therefore determined by a majority of the nobles that Prince Edward should be proclaimed as king without further delay. Edward was then about forty years of age, and had been absent from the kingdom almost ever since the Danish supremacy began. Towards the end of Hardicanute's reign he had come back to England, and in the following year, 1043, was crowned at Winchester by Eadsige, Archbishop of Canterbury, who, as the Anglo-Saxon Chronicle tells us, " well instructed him" on the occasion and " well exhorted him for his own and all the people's need." The new king found the country, to a large extent, in the hands of the three powerful earls, Godwin of Kent, Leofric of Mercia, and Siward of Northumberland. Doubtless, the intervention of Earl Godwin, the mightiest of the three, went far to secure the crown for Edward. Hence, he seems to have let himself be persuaded to strengthen his throne all the more by a marriage with Godwin's daughter, Edith, in 1045. All these three earls were with Edward when he rode off to the residence of Queen Emma, and took possession of the large royal treasure which she held there. This was popularly believed to be beyond reckoning, and may have comprised the chief bulk of the movable possessions of the crown, which were usually kept at Winchester. Emma was not removed, but suffered to reside, as formerly, at the West Saxon capital.

Coronation of St Edward.

Archbishop Eadsige, the Primate, being aged and infirm, consented in 1044 to the appointment of a coadjutor to assist him, or perhaps to administer the archdiocese in his name. The prelate selected for this office was Siward, who had, up to this time, been Abbot of Abingdon. He was now consecrated, and received the curious title of Archbishop of Upsala in Sweden. But the arrangement did not last very long,

New Primates and Bishops.

H

for after four years Siward resigned his coadjutorship, and retired once more to his abbey at Abingdon, where he died. Eadsige once again was in sole charge of the see of Canterbury until his death in 1050, two years later. But before this, so many of the occupants of the English sees had paid the debt of nature, that the choice of a new primate may be considered as the completion of what was practically a new body of bishops. Lyfing, whom the Anglo-Saxon Chronicle designates "the eloquent bishop," was a relative of Wolstan, Archbishop of York. In 1027 he was consecrated for the Devonshire see of Crediton, and held the Cornish diocese in conjunction with it, and as if this were not responsibility enough, on the death of Brihteag in 1038, he was given charge of Worcester as well. However, Lyfing's career was nearly over at the time Edward became king, for he died in 1046. Thereupon the union of the three bishoprics under the same incumbent was broken by the appointment of Leofric to Crediton, while Aldred was made Bishop of Worcester. Brihtwold, Bishop of Sherborne, died about the same year, and in his stead, Hermann, a Lotharingian by birth, and one of King Edward's chaplains, received charge of the Wiltshire diocese. A vacancy at Winchester not long after gave an opportunity to the friends of the nationalist Saxon policy in Church government to advance their nominee, Stigand, from his East Anglian diocese to this important see. It was a thoroughly bad appointment, yet advantage was taken of it to name the Norman, Ulf, to Elmham, no doubt with the view of promoting reform in the east of England. Grimkytel, Bishop of Selsey, was dead likewise, but in this case another Saxon, named Hecca, was installed in his place. King Edward, convinced as he was of the superiority of the continental clergy to the native Saxons, both in life and knowledge, used all his influence to establish them in the offices where they would be able to advance the cause of ecclesiastical reform. He made this a matter of conscience, but it inevitably brought him into collision with the trend of national sentiment. It was also so pronounced an attack upon the vested interests of the powerful families round the throne that it led first to loud-voiced discontent and then to armed rebellion.

ST EDWARD THE CONFESSOR 115

The champion of the nobles, and, in fact, of the whole national party, was the mighty Earl Godwin. The storm centre around which the hottest conflict raged was the question of the succession to the see of Canterbury. **Stigand (1000-1074).** Robert Champart of Jumièges, one of the king's chaplains, had been nominated Bishop of London in 1044, and had held this see until 1050, when old Archbishop Eadsige died. The king now passed over Alfric, who had been elected by the monks of Canterbury, and was a kinsman of Earl Godwin, and wished that Robert of Jumièges should be translated from London to the archiepiscopal throne. But this was not acceptable to the popular party, hence every nerve was strained to secure that Stigand should be moved from Winchester to Canterbury. Stigand, who was both ambitious and avaricious, desired to win Canterbury without giving up his previous bishopric. However, Edward held firm, and Robert of Jumièges was able to retain possession of the archbishopric until the following year. No sooner was he established in his see than Sparhavoc, Abbot of Abingdon, whom King Edward had nominated to succeed to the diocese of London, came to Robert to ask for episcopal consecration. The archbishop refused, pleading the Pope's command. However, even without bishop's orders, Sparhavoc took possession of the temporalities of the diocese, and maintained himself in London until next year. Then he was ejected, and William, a Norman chaplain of the king, was made Bishop of London. He was to rule the diocese until far into the reign of William the Conqueror. In 1052 the outcry against Archbishop Robert and all foreigners became so menacing that this prelate fled to Normandy, taking with him William, Bishop of London, and Ulf, Bishop of Dorchester. Robert never regained possession of Canterbury, but retired to his monastery at Jumièges, where he died many years later. Yet Stigand's path was not clear before him. St Leo IX., at that time Pope, declined to confirm his appointment to Canterbury, and suspended him from all episcopal functions. Not to be worsted by this refusal, Stigand now applied to the anti-Pope Benedict X., who sent him the pallium, one usurper thus confirming the appointment of another. For some time the unworthy prelate struggled hard to keep possession not only of the two sees of Canterbury and Winchester, but likewise of the important abbeys of Glastonbury, St Albans, Ely, and St Augustine's at Canterbury. The abuse of pluralities could hardly go further. Yet he was able to count on the support of the leaders of the Anglo-Saxon party.

Such acute differences of view as these, together with the domestic contests between the family of Earl Godwin and their enemies, interfered greatly with the tranquillity which otherwise would have reigned during King Edward's earlier years. For they were free from external wars. But as these feuds do not directly belong to ecclesiastical history, what has been said of their effect upon the episcopate may suffice for our present purpose. But they hardly came to an end even with the death of Godwin himself in 1053. There had been very unfriendly relations between the king and Godwin's house. Things had even come to the verge of open war, and nearly all the chief men of the kingdom were enrolled on the one side or on the other. However, peacemakers, wisely intervened, and some kind of a reconciliation was effected. The story of Earl Godwin's end which the chroniclers relate is this. He was sitting at table with the king on Easter Day when a remark made by the monarch made him suspicious that he was still thought of as concerned in the death of Edward's brother, Alfred. Calling God to witness to the truth of what he affirmed, he imprecated on himself that he might not live to eat the next mouthful if he had any hand in the death of Alfred. He then, say the chroniclers, put a mouthful between his lips and fell down speechless. Lingard and others ascribe the whole story to the malice of the historians, who very likely copied the story from one another. At any rate, we may believe that Godwin was suddenly struck with mortal sickness while at the royal table and expired soon after. He was buried at Winchester.

Earl Godwin (1053).

The death of Earl Godwin may be looked upon as marking the line of division between the earlier and later portions of King Edward's reign. Henceforward the monarch was able to devote himself in the main to that work of restoring the observance of the ancient laws, and to those labours of piety, which were far more to his taste than warfare or political strife. Pestilence

ST EDWARD THE CONFESSOR 117

and famine in turn visited the kingdom, but these calamities only made the pious king redouble his efforts to succour the unfortunate or the plague-stricken. He was never so happy as when engaged on such works of truly royal charity. Earl Harold, Godwin's son, now came to the front in public affairs, and wielded considerable power during the second half of St Edward's reign. Godwin's earldom and other possessions fell to him. The possessions which Harold had received in his father's lifetime passed to Alfgar, son of Earl Leofric. All this time Stigand was hand and glove with Harold. Outwardly, at least, the general reconciliation endured, and St Edward took back to his favour Queen Edith, whose detention in Wherwell nunnery was attributed to the charge of complicity in the designs of her family to rule the land.

St Edward intervened in the affairs of the Scottish realm during the usurpation of Macbeth, and the assistance of an English army under Earl Siward of Northumberland counted for much in defeating the tyrant, and in securing the crown for Malcolm Caenmore. Very likely Siward undertook the campaign with his own forces, having secured little more than approbation from his sovereign. But he was a veteran soldier, and his campaign was brilliantly successful. He had to mourn the loss of his son, Osbern, who was slain in the battle, but it is said that asking how he met his death, and being told that his wounds were all in front, he spoke somewhat in the style which Shakespeare has attributed to him:

St Edward and St Margaret.

" Had I as many sons as I have hairs
I would not wish them to a fairer death."

Siward himself died in the following year. He had founded a monastery near York in honour of St Olaf, his countryman, for he was of Norse descent, and there he was laid to rest. A decade later the bonds between England and Scotland were knit still closer by the marriage between King Malcolm and Margaret, daughter of Edgar Etheling, St Edward's grand-niece. This amiable and pious princess won her way into the hearts of her Scottish subjects, and exerted great influence in tempering the impetuous and warlike character of Malcolm. As St Margaret of Scotland, she has ever held a place of high veneration and deep love as the Patroness and Protectress of that kingdom.

St Edward's reputation as a legislator rests as much on the popular tradition enshrined in the oft repeated cry of his countrymen: " Give us the laws of good King Edward," as on any original enactments which can be traced to him. For, although much of this legislation is extant, and is even cited under his name, it was in the main the precise restatement and equitable enforcement of already existing laws, more than the creation of any new system. St Edward had made a vow to go on pilgrimage to Rome to visit the tombs of the Apostles, but when he raised the subject in the Witenagemot, his counsellors protested against his leaving the kingdom, where they considered his constant presence to be necessary. The king bent to the views of the nobles, and consequently sent Eldred, Bishop of Worcester, as envoy to obtain from the Pope, St Leo IX., a commutation of his vow. Eldred sped well with his mission, and the commutation inspired by the Pontiff was that Edward should bestow in alms on the poor a sum equal to what he would have spent on his pilgrimage, and should moreover build or endow an abbey in honour of the Prince of the Apostles.

The Laws of good King Edward.

Eldred had other business on hand in Rome of a personal nature in addition to his mission on behalf of his sovereign. He had been elected to the see of York, but had been permitted to retain Worcester as well. It was quite in accordance with St Leo's rôle of reformer that when the archbishop elect applied for the pallium, the Pontiff declined to acquiesce in this plurality of benefices. However, when Eldred promised to resign the see of Worcester, he was granted the archiepiscopal pallium, and was thus free to go home as approved incumbent of the northern metropolis. Before returning, nevertheless, he made the further pilgrimage, rare in those days, to the holy places of Palestine. He was able to offer gifts of gold and silver at the Holy Sepulchre, and then, with the king's work and his own both satisfactorily accomplished, came home to his native land.

Eldred, Archbishop of York.

St Edward immediately set to work to perform the commutation which had been laid upon him. It was a

ST EDWARD THE CONFESSOR

work of love, readily undertaken, to distribute the large alms to the poor prescribed by the Holy Father. To bestow his treasure on the needy, and to give personal service to the wretched was his chief delight as king, so we may well believe that he opened his purse with no niggardly hand. But the building of an abbey had to be a work of time. Yet there was no delay in setting about this enterprise, and it was planned in quite royal fashion. The site selected was Thorney Island in the Thames, somewhat higher up the stream than the city of London. There had been a religious house in this place since the days of Sebert, King of Essex, and the tradition was that its modest church had been dedicated by St Peter himself. *Foundation of Westminster Abbey.* Probably it was St Edward's special devotion to the Prince of the Apostles which led the king to select an isle already sacred to him for his new foundation. Besides, it was in this place that Edward had braved the scoffs of his court in order to carry the poor cripple on his shoulders to the altar. And legend told that in the old church he had also been favoured with a vision of the Holy Child in the Blessed Sacrament. The new buildings soon gained the now illustrious name of Westminster, and became in more ways than one the venerated sanctuary of both St Peter and St Edward. For the remaining years of his life the progress of the work engrossed much of the monarch's attention, and formed his chief consolation amid his ailments. It marked a striking advance upon all previous churches built in England. It was on a scale of what was then looked on as unexampled magnificence. Moreover, it embodied a new architectural idea, which became the pattern for the churches that were raised up in the years to come. It is said to have been one of the first cruciform churches in England. It covered nearly as much ground as the now existing church. It had its towers, and its bells, and its scripture, and its stained glass, and its roof was covered with lead. The existing community of monks was then strengthened by a new colony from Exeter. King Edward meant that the number of monks should be seventy, though it does not seem that at any period of its history there were more than fifty. As the year 1065 wore on it became so far advanced that arrangements could be made for its dedication. But

Edward had already had his summons to exchange his earthly for a heavenly kingdom. This soon became known to the physicians through his increasing weakness. The pious legend tells how it came to the king himself through his patron, St John, the evangelist, who brought him back in wondrous wise the beautiful royal ring which he had once given in alms in the Beloved Disciple's name. On Christmas Day he appeared in state wearing his royal crown, but that very evening his strength gave way. On Holy Innocents' Day, three days later, already fixed for the ceremony, he was too ill to preside in person. Queen Edith was there, Duke Harold also, and the two archbishops, Stigand and Aldred, but the king lay sunk almost in a stupor like death in the neighbouring palace. Then there was a rally, and for some days he was able to converse with Queen Edith and the clergy who were around. He spoke of strange things to come upon the land, and then of a revival and new life for his country. It was once more to flourish like a tree, and bear fruit and flower. On the 5th of January, 1066, he gave up the ghost. There is something pathetic, if not tragic, in the coincidence between the crowning of his work at Westminster and the closing of his mortal career.

The king was buried in the minster which he had built, and on the 13th of October, 1163, when new and still more splendid buildings had replaced those which owed their origin to him, a solemn translation of his relics took place to the new tomb behind the high altar. St Thomas of Canterbury presided at the function, and nearly all the bishops of England were present, as well as many abbots, among whom was St Ached, the English St Bernard who preached the panegyric of the saint on the occasion. Another saint—St Gilbert of Sempringham—was also present. Moreover, Henry II. and a long array of barons and knights, as also a great throng of the faithful, gathered round these leaders of the Church. In 1269, when the restoration made by Henry III. was complete, there was another Translation Festival to the present shrine. There still lie the remains of England's royal saint, in the midst of his people, many of whom have well-nigh forgotten him, and with the external splendour of his tomb somewhat dimmed, but yet a place of pilgrimage to those who have not for-

ST EDWARD THE CONFESSOR

gotten, and an almost matchless centre of royalty and nobles, historical memories to the days in which we live.

St Edward was little skilled in state-craft or in that warlike ability which go far to make a sovereign seem great in the eyes of his contemporaries, but he conquered the hearts of his people by his transparent goodness and his love of the poor. No one was more generous in giving pecuniary aid, nor more self-sacrificing in doing personal service to the subjects whom he ruled. His hair and beard were snow-white, and his countenance mild and gracious. He was credited with miraculous powers, and the cures attributed to his holy hand were the origin of the custom of bringing people to be touched for scrofula, (hence called the king's evil), by the reigning sovereign of the day. With his consort, Edith, he lived in continence, and at his death bade farewell to her, still a virgin. She survived him until 1075, and cleared herself on oath of the charges which had been made against her chastity. *Character of St Edward.*

It is impossible in the light of much conflicting evidence to be sure who it was to whom St Edward meant to leave his crown, as far as it was his to dispose of. The Norman writers have, naturally enough, asserted that he bequeathed it to their Duke William, thus wishing to strengthen the case for his expedition and for the Norman Conquest. The Saxons just as naturally declared that he intended Harold to succeed him, and this is thought by Lingard to be the more likely theory. It is quite possible, however, that he meant to leave the throne to Edgar Etheling, the exiled son of his brother, the murdered Alfred, but this prince was never in a position successfully to assert his claim. It remains one of the unsolved problems of history. The march of events made the death of the Confessor one of the turning points in the development of the story of England. *St Edward's heir.*

Nevertheless, nearly a year of confusion and warfare was to intervene before William, the Norman, could be enthroned on St Edward's seat. On the very next day after the Confessor died, January 6th, Duke Harold was crowned at Westminster, or according to others, in St Paul's Cathedral. Archbishop Stigand, as we know from the *Harold (1066).*

Bayeux Tapestry, was there to fulfil his office, but it is said that at the appointed moment Harold put the crown on his own head. As soon as the news of the coronation reached Normandy, Duke William sent envoys to remind Harold of an oath which he had taken to him when a shipwreck on the coast of Normandy had put him into his power, and to declare that their master would, if necessary, prosecute his claim by force of arms. Harold's answer was a denial of his right, and practically a defiance. William at once began to prepare for invasion. It was Harold's fate to have to cope with two enemies at once, for Tostig, the exiled Earl of Northumberland, arranged common action with the Normans, and also enlisted in the cause of Harold Hardrade, King of Norway. Knowing that an attack from Normandy might be expected, King Harold had drawn up his army to resist it between Pevensey and Hastings, when news was brought that Tostig, Harold Hardrade, and the Norwegians had already landed in the North. He was therefore compelled to break up his camp in Sussex, and hasten to meet this, the more immediate peril. At the battle of Stamford Bridge, he almost annihilated the Norwegian army, Tostig and Hardrade both falling in the fray. Two days later William of Normandy, with his carefully prepared expedition, landed in Sussex. There was nothing for it then, but for Harold and his men to return south as fast as ever they could to meet this still greater danger. The armies met at Senlac, eleven miles north of Hastings, and the result was the defeat of the Anglo-Saxons with great slaughter. Harold himself was among the killed. William was victor at one blow in the struggle, and pushed on to Winchester, and thence to London. Thus the battle of Senlac or Hastings put an end for ever to the Anglo-Saxon monarchy, and opened the way to a new race of kings, and a new period in the history of the Church in England.

XI.
THE LIFE OF THE ANGLO-SAXON CHURCH.

BEFORE going on to sketch the fortunes of the Church in the great mediaeval period which began with the Norman Conquest, it will be as well to pause for a while, and note briefly some of the general characteristics of the Christian life which had developed in England as the centuries rolled by after St Augustine and the other apostles of the land had laid its foundations. In one short chapter it will not be possible to refer to everything. All that can be done is to draw attention to some of the more obvious points, which, all the same, have their value in enabling us to understand the narration of our ancestors' doings.

It goes without saying that the relations between Church and State were very close. The traditional conception of one corporate Christendom sank very deep into the minds of our countrymen. Anglo-Saxon society was a very simple thing, almost patriarchal in its elements. *Church and State in England.* There was the king with his ealdormen around him in his Witan or council, and then there was the *folk-mote* where the mass of *franklins* or freemen met to hear what had been decided by it, and to acclaim justice as it was dealt out to them. And our forefathers had gained too much from Christianity to exclude it from any department of their lives: they were Christians in everything. It had conducted them from barbarism to truth. It had given them whatever measure of knowledge and of the arts which they possessed. Its prelates were almost its only learned men. Its monks had been their instructors in agriculture, in reading and writing, in music, and in many of the mechanical arts as well. Hence it was quite natural that in all national assemblies, as much as in gatherings of a lesser character, bishops and abbots should fill a prominent, and sometimes a dominant part. No doubt there were synods of the clergy in which laymen took no part whatever, but at Witan, at *shire-mote*, and at *hundred-mote* the bishops and even the inferior ranks of churchmen were present as honoured assessors. This was so even when cases of crime or civil causes came up for discussion. In fact, we may say that there was no clear dividing line between ecclesiastical and civil courts during the Anglo-Saxon period.

The more we study the evidence at our command the more we shall be convinced how close were the bonds which bound the Anglo-Saxon Church to the centre of unity. From Rome their first apostles had set out, and to Rome they owed innumerable helps, keeping them to the high place they were to hold in the kingdom of God. As to doctrine, what they had been taught by Augustine and his companions had been faithfully handed down. It was in strict accord with that teaching that they were content to call the Roman Pontiff "the heir of St Peter's marvellous power" with Alcuin, "the illustrious head of the whole Church" with St Bede, "the wisdom of the bishops of the universe" with Eddius, and to treat him as such. It was for this reason that they loved to travel to Rome for his blessing, and bowed to his decisions as to those of an acknowledged chief and ruler. It was for this reason, also, that they were in the habit of applying for papal charters to confirm the privileges of their foundations and the stability of their vows.

Anglo-Saxons and Rome.

Moreover, it was to the Pope they looked to limit or to extend the jurisdiction of their metropolitans and their diocesan bishops. It was the archbishop, in fact, as Lingard truly says, who was the connecting link between the bishops of a province and the bishop of Rome. It was after seeking and obtaining the pallium from the Pope, either journeying for it in person, or asking to have it sent to England, that the archbishops proceeded to exercise their high functions. It was the Pope who enforced the observance of canonical discipline,

LIFE OF ANGLO-SAXON CHURCH

and caused synods to be assembled for this purpose, not seldom under papal legates appointed for the purpose. And then, when the decrees of these synods had been made, it was to the Pope they looked to confirm, alter, or suspend them.

The letters of St Gregory the Great show us clearly that the idea of the Holy Pontiff at first was that there should be twelve sees in the south of Britain under Augustine and his successors as metropolitans at London, and twelve others in the North under a metropolitan at York. St Gregory may have named the two cities of London and York for the archbishops' sees as though going back to the times of the Roman occupation of Britain. It will not be forgotten that these cities were two out of the three represented at the Council of Arles, and that they held a front rank in the Roman settlement of the country. The Archbishop of Arles was Papal Vicar in Gaul. However, under the pressure of circumstances this plan was never completely carried out. Paulinus was indeed sent to York as bishop in 626. But he only maintained himself there for about seven years, and passing south, was then content to occupy till his death the suffragan see of Rochester. Meanwhile, the evangelisation of the country was carried out under prelates who fixed their abode in the various kingdoms of the Heptarchy. Thus it was with St Birinus in Wessex, St Diuma in Mercia, and St Felix in East Anglia. These ruled over districts, vast in extent, and with little attempt at any boundaries more definite than those of the kingdoms in which they found themselves. The South Saxon kingdom had at first no see of its own, even after the date of its conversion to Christianity, but depended upon Winchester. Thus in all we find seven episcopal sees during the earlier epoch, or if we add the bishopric founded by the Irish monks at Lindisfarne, eight for the whole of England.

The bishoprics of the land.

The next plan of organisation was that which in the main owed its origin to the genius of Archbishop Theodore. This he obtained approval for in Rome. Fixing the number of dioceses at twelve with Canterbury as the metropolis of them all, he passed over the claims of York. Both Mercia and Northumbria were to be subdivided. Henceforward, the former kingdom was to contain the Sees of Lichfield, Dorchester, Worcester, and Hereford, whereas the latter was to comprise York, Hexham, Lindisfarne, and Whithern. It was this subdivision which brought Theodore into collision with St Wilfrid. But as a whole, his arrangements were upheld by the Holy See, and allowing for the irregularities caused by intestine dissension and warfare, no further serious attempt was made for a generation to disturb them. Nevertheless, in 735 Egbert of York successfully pleaded with Pope Gregory III. for metropolitan rights, and the grant of the pallium. Furthermore, this Northumbrian success seems to have led King Offa of Mercia some fifty years later to try and accomplish the same thing for his kingdom. His plan was ratified by the Pope, and the sees between the Humber and the Thames were put under Lichfield, which he made an archdiocese. Later on, Pope St Leo III. was induced to come back upon this, and Ethelheard of Canterbury secured the consent of Kenulf, Offa's successor, to this reversal, but the pallium was given as a personal honour to the actual Bishop of Lichfield. Archbishop Brihtwald (693-731) succeeded in adding two more sees in the South, namely: Sherborne in Wessex, and Selsey in Sussex. Finally, Archbishop Plegmund, at a council held in 909, raised the total number of dioceses to seventeen by founding three new ones in Wessex: Wells, Crediton, and Ramsbury, or Wilton. All were to be in the province of Canterbury with the exception of York, Hexham, Lindisfarne, and Whithern. And, of course, the last two were not Anglo-Saxon foundations at all.

Monasteries and convents. If ever there was a Christian country where monasticism and the religious life led according to a fixed rule played a large part in ordinary life, surely that country was England. Whatever may have been the status of those early Christians from Palestine or from Rome who brought the Faith to Britain first of all, what happened when the Faith was brought to the Anglo-Saxon invaders is beyond dispute. Augustine was a monk; Gregory who sent him was a monk; and the missionary band was composed of forty monks from the Roman monasteries. They came at a time when the monastic life, in the mediaeval sense of the word, was more or less a new thing, but it was a new thing, which, being suited to the needs and the spirit of the age, made rapid progress; and the progress it made in England was at least equal to, if not superior, to what it achieved on the continent of Europe. There was soon an abbey at Canterbury in addition to the community of monks which served the cathedral. And wherever the missionaries of the Gospel passed to evangelise the people, as a general rule it was not long before either the suggestions of these pious strangers or the devotion of the native leaders called into existence one or sometimes more of these homes of piety and learning. Nor was the religious life offered only to men: women also had their full share in the sacrifice and in the reward. The noblest and the most innocent in the land sought in abbeys shut off from the world a refuge from the brutality and license which sometimes reigned supreme among their half-civilised countrymen.

If we turn to the labours of the Irish missionaries from the North, the same is signally true, if possible, in a more exclusive degree. It was as a monk of the strictest austerity of life that St Aidan set out to preach; it was from a monastery—the celebrated Iona—that he came; and when he had settled down to his English sphere of labours, it was from the island monastery of Lindisfarne that he sallied forth, and thither he returned to refresh his spirit after his journeying.

Many of the abbeys which afterwards attained greater renown and were graced with more splendid buildings in Norman times trace their origin to the earliest Anglo-Saxon centuries. And many of them are connected with the memory of some saintly founder, or patron, who lived in their precincts and trained their communities to holiness. Thus it came to pass with St Wilfrid at Ripon, with St Benet and St Bede at Monkwearmouth and Jarrow respectively, with St Hilda at Whitby, St Ebba at Coldingham, St Etheldreda at Ely. Thus was it also, though in another way, with Glastonbury, St Albans, and St Edmundsbury. Other Saxon foundations bear witness to the piety and spirit of generosity which, in the midst of much that was imperfect and sinful, was shown by the best of their kings. It was in this way that Medehampstead and Croyland, Sherborne and Wilton, Reading and Osney, came into existence.

Although the religious houses of this period cannot rival either in number or splendour those that began after the period of the Norman Conquest, yet, allowing for the smaller population, and the less developed state of the country, they played quite as great a relative part in national life as those of the later ages did.

In England, as among all the nations of undivided Christendom, the centre of Divine Worship was the offering of Mass. And it would not be easy to find in any other nation of those early times more striking testimonies to the veneration in which the Holy Sacrifice was held.

Worship among the Anglo-Saxons.

While it is well to note as a special feature in the language, all grades of the clergy were called priests, those raised to the sacerdotal dignity were distinguished by the honorable title of Mass Priest, while the server at the altar was called the Mass Priest's priest. The rite used was the Roman rite of those days, at least in the main, brought as it was thence by the first missionaries from that city. The broad-minded St Gregory, however, as we learn from his correspondence with Augustine, was not averse to the use of minor differences from the Roman customs, where the missionaries found anything more acceptable to the people among whom they laboured. We know little concerning the rite employed by the disciples of St Columba in the North. It was in all probability the same as that used by St Patrick, but gradually it was supplanted by the Roman rite, with the minor differences spoken of above. In order to secure the attendance of the faithful on the Lord's Day, not a decree of any ecclesiastical council, but the civil law made by the Witan came into force, which prescribed that on the Lord's Day servile work should cease, and all the people go to the Mass service in their own church. But the Lord's Day or Sunday began, not as with us at midnight, but on the evening or afternoon before, when the people were expected to come to church, if possible, for the evening offices. Probably this is the origin of the Saturday half-holiday, so prized and so characteristic of modern England.

Mass being the centre, there was grouped around it a constant round of prayer and praise known as the Course or Order of the Canonical Hours. There were Night-Song and Uht-Song and Prime-Song and Undern-Song and Midday-Song and Noon-Song and Evensong. These formed the appointed devotions for the clergy at which even the laity, when they could, were encouraged to assist. And if they could not follow the Latin of the service they were directed to occupy themselves with the Lord's Prayer and with the recitation of the Creed. By the clergy the Latin Psalter was known by heart, but of course this could not be required of the laity. We must not suppose from the word *Song* that the Psalms and other prayers were always chanted. Such could not have been the ordinary custom. But still our ancestors did attach considerable importance to the ecclesiastical chant. We are told, for example, that St Benet Biscop procured in Rome the services of John the Cantor, Abbot of St Martin's on the Esquiline, and that this skilled musician spent twelve months in the monastery at Monkwearmouth training the monks in the singing of Mass and of the Divine Office.

The Divine Service or Office.

As to the administration of the Sacraments, Baptism was given by immersion, both for adults and for infants, either in a baptistery specially provided for the purpose, or where this could not be had, even in a river or running stream. At first it was confined to the eves of Easter and of Pentecost, but this yielded to a more indiscriminate fixing of hours, above all when the majority of baptisms became those of infants, on account of the danger of delay in their case. The infant which was commonly called a " heathen child " before baptism was called " God's bairn " afterwards. To similar causes we may trace the disappearance of the custom of giving Confirmation immediately after baptism: it was no longer practical. Holy Communion, which was administered to the faithful under both kinds, at least in Saxon times, bore right up to Shakespeare's day the name of Housel. It was given to infants also, but only under the species of wine. Later on this last practice was discontinued. For the forgiveness of sins committed after baptism there was a remedy provided in the Sacrament of Penance. This comprised not only sorrow but confession, and also penitential works of satisfaction. The confessor was told to hear the tale of sin with attention

The Ritual of the Sacraments.

I

in order that he might distinguish between the different degrees of guilt, and might deal with the penitent in accordance with this knowledge. For the lighter sins he might no doubt give absolution and restoration to the Church's Communion at once, but for more serious crimes a severe and sometimes lengthy course of penance was ordered before the sinner could return to be absolved and admitted to Communion. In many cases, especially in those of public crime, the penance also had to be a public one, thus to make reparation for the scandal which had been given. Collections of the penances to be given for various sins were written out and promulgated by the rulers of the Church. These are called Penitentiaries. Several of these lists or collections are still in existence: one early and very celebrated example is the Penitentiary of Egbert, the Archbishop of York.

In the writings of the authors of this period which have been preserved for us, we find many and laudatory allusions to the ecclesiastical buildings which were raised in England by the kings and prelates of the land, but few specimens have survived to enable us to check these notices by ocular inspection.

Architecture of their churches.

The original method of building practised by the Scots, both in Ireland and in the North, was to form the church walls of oak trunks sawn down the middle, and to use a reed thatch for the roof. One most curious specimen of this style of building, which goes to prove that the Anglo-Saxons imitated the Celts in this, is still standing in the parish church of Greensted near Ongar in Essex, which is said to have been the resting-place for some time of the body of St Edmund the Martyr. But before long there is overwhelming evidence that they began to build churches with stone, which was often in blocks of enormous size. The shape was the quadrangular form adapted from the Roman basilicas with an apse at one end for the altar and pillars, dividing the body of the building into nave and aisles. Externally there was usually a belfry, at first detached from the main building, and a porch or atrium. Occasionally, instead of the apse, the chancel consisted of a square elongation of the nave, from which it was divided by the chancel arch. The cruciform plan seems to have been not unknown, though somewhat rare. We are left in great part to the descriptions of churches

LIFE OF ANGLO-SAXON CHURCH 131

to be found in the ancient writings to judge of their proportions and character, for very few of the ecclesiastical buildings of that distant age remain. Besides Greensted church, there is a church at Bradford-on-Avon and a venerable tower at Earl's Barton, Northants. The crypts of Ripon and Hexham both go back to Anglo-Saxon times. But Norman architecture, under the influences at work in St Edward the Confessor's reign, began to be introduced into the country before the expedition of William the Conqueror. There is in several places mention made of an organ in the church to assist the singing, and of church bells to call the people to the services.

Ample provision seems to have been made in the legislation of the Witenagemot for the support of the clergy and the upkeep of Divine worship. The *church-shot*, whose payment was decreed by these councils of the wise men of the kingdom, probably consisted in the firstfruits of the corn harvest. But besides this, the faithful were bidden to pay their *soul-shot*, which was a form of dues to secure the right of internment in God's acre, as they named the churchyard. *Rome fee* or *Rome-shot* was the offering afterwards known as Peter's Pence, and at first was a voluntary donation. But later on it seems to have become an annual payment collected from the people, and then forwarded to the Holy See. There was also a general obligation of paying tithes distinct from the above mentioned special dues. Yet a great proportion of the wealth of the Church came from the possession of ecclesiastical landed property with which the various dioceses, abbeys, and parishes had either been endowed by their first founders, or enriched by later benefactors. An extensive employment of the system of pecuniary fines for breaches of the peace, and even for grave crimes, was a prominent feature in the Anglo-Saxon system of law. But the same wish to bring religion into everything, which showed itself in the common blending of ecclesiastical and civil courts, made our ancestors bring the judgment on innocence or guilt under the decision of signs from the unseen world. It was in this way that they clung obstinately to the custom of seeking a verdict on accused persons by means of the Trial by Ordeal. This consisted in invoking the Divine Judgment on the

Church Finance.

matter by means of subjecting the accused to one of
several severe and curious tests. Among the more celebrated ordeals were those by barley bread, by cold water,
by hot water, or by fire. If the individual came
uninjured out of his trial without being choked, or
drowned, or scalded, or burned, as the case might be,
his innocence was held to be established. These rash
proceedings were repeatedly condemned by the Holy See,
but in spite of every prohibition they managed to hold
their ground to some extent for the space of six hundred
years. Trial by battle was an institution of the Norman
period only.

The respect accorded to venerable places hallowed by
sacred rites, or honoured as the resting-places of the
bodies of saints, led to some of these spots
Rights of receiving the so-called Right of Sanctuary,
Sanctuary. whereby an accused or suspected person,
who took refuge at one of these places, acknowledged by
public custom to have the privilege, could not be there
apprehended by the officers of justice, or by an avenging
enemy. Such was the rudeness of the times that this
right was sometimes violated in the heat of passion, but
by common consent the individual who did so was
marked as guilty of an offence against the common good.
Of course, such a right, even when respected, was a
prerogative of not unmixed advantage. Sometimes, it
is to be feared, the right of sanctuary was abused by
criminals who had no just title to escape from justice.
But, in an age of primitive customs, it did interpose a
temporary barrier between those suspected of crime, and
the execution of a vengeance, which was only too ready
to condemn without trial, and then had to repent at
leisure of bloody deeds done in a moment of unreasoning
passion. In some cases, as at Hexham and Beverley, and
in the Broad Sanctuary at Westminster, the limits to
which the privileges extended were very wide; in other
cases there was a frith-stool in which the refugee had to
sit, or a ring or knocker at the door which he had to
hold. Some of these remain to this present day. Royal
charters were often granted to fortify the immunity, and
the number increased as the centuries rolled on. There
are traces of these grants in Anglo-Saxon times at Hexham, Beverley, Bury St Edmund's, and other places.
But it is not easy to distinguish those whose origin only

LIFE OF ANGLO-SAXON CHURCH 133

dates from days after the Norman Conquest, from the more ancient ones. Eventually, at least twenty-two churches enjoyed this right by Royal Charter before the Reformation. The last survival of anything of the kind was the Whitefriar's Sanctuary in London.

Notwithstanding the tincture of Roman culture which four centuries of occupation had bestowed upon Britain, learning and science were practically non-existent among our ancestors when the teachers from Pope Gregory arrived in their midst. And the culture they brought was that of the decadent Italy of the sixth century. {State of learning and the Arts.} To Rome again they applied, when there was question either of instruction by the oral teaching of masters, or of the lore contained in books. In every monastery, for outside of these there was but little study possible, a good proportion of the time of those monks who could write was devoted to the useful and laborious work of copying manuscripts. It was only in this way that anything like a library could be created. However, the beginning of the library at Canterbury was made by the books which St Gregory had sent. Theodore of Tarsus brought others. An account of these volumes has been preserved. In the same way the five journeys of St Benet Biscop had enabled him to bring home many volumes, which provided the sources for the work of his fellow-monk, the Venerable Bede. And the untiring industry of Bede contributed by himself alone no inconsiderable increase. Bede dwells with pride on the Wearmouth library. York had an even better collection.

Theology or, as they called it, Sacred Doctrine, filled the chief place in the curriculum of study. And it was the Positive Theology of the ages before Scholasticism, resting on Scripture and the words of the Fathers. And in order to understand either of these foundations, the preparation had to be, at least predominantly, the thorough acquisition of ecclesiastical Latin. As there were no printed books, and as the labour of copying by hand could not but limit the number of volumes available, the memory had to be trained to retain things that our age would easily find in some small handbook at each one's side. The whole Psalter had to be learned by heart.

Pilgrimages. As soon as we reflect on the extreme difficulty of making distant journeys in those early times, comparing it with the ease with which modern pilgrims pass from place to place, it must seem wonderful to find the Anglo-Saxons so keen on pilgrimages to far-off shrines. Still, it was not out of any mere spirit of adventure that these labours and perils were faced. These journeys were sacred journeys to visit those places which they looked upon as beyond others sacred and holy: a pious curiosity took them above all to Rome and to Jerusalem. The most ancient description of such a journey which is extant, with the sole exception of the "Pilgrimage of Etheria," is the "Itinerary of St Willibald," a Saxon who braved the dangers of sea and land to visit the tombs of the Apostles at Rome and the holy places in Palestine. It would appear to be only a journey to Rome which St Willibald undertook in 723 in company with his father and his brother. Then, his father having died while he was in Italy, and his devotion having been satisfied in the Eternal City, he conceived the further design of prolonging his travels to Palestine. He and his party were arrested by the Saracens, and kept in confinement for some time, but they succeeded ultimately in overcoming the suspicions of their captors, and were furnished with a written passport allowing them to visit the holy places. Thereupon they passed from one to another of these sacred shrines, and the document which has survived records in a detailed and most interesting fashion what they saw, until having traversed the land in every direction they started to return home. Willibald spent two years in Constantinople, whence he betook himself to the Benedictine monastery of Monte Cassino. There he became a monk, but later on St Gregory III. sought him out and despatched him into Germany, where he died as Bishop of Eichstädt in 786.

With regard especially to Rome as the goal of pilgrimage, St Benet Biscop measured the long journey no less than five times. St Wilfrid also travelled there several distinct times. And in both cases the achievement was a truly remarkable one when we bear in mind the absence of all conveyances to travel without fatigue, as well as the unavoidable dangers of the road. No

LIFE OF ANGLO-SAXON CHURCH 185

fewer than eight Anglo-Saxon kings went on pilgrimage to this centre of the Church. These were: Cædwalla, Ine, Offa, Coenred, Offa of Mercia, Siric, Ethelwulf and Canute. The archbishops of Canterbury regularly started as soon as they were elected or consecrated, in order there to receive the pallium from the Supreme Pontiff. Of these Wighard died there; Elfsine lost his life on the way, being frozen to death in the Alps. And if there were some out of the long line of primates who never made the journey they showed their submission by claiming the indulgence of the Holy See on account of the distance and the difficulties of the journey.

In comparing one epoch of the Church with another, and one land with another, we shall find great inequality in the zeal with which these different portions of it pursued the work of evangelising the heathen. There is but one city and one centre where this zeal has always burned brightly, and that is the city of the Popes. However, it is only fair to the Anglo-Saxon Church to say that whatever its shortcomings in other departments of Christian practice, it was beyond reproach in this. Scarcely had the Gospel been everywhere preached, and the Faith professed all over England when zealous missionaries arose, sons of the soil, to devote their lives to spreading the good tidings in lands less favoured than their own.

Foreign Missions.

The same dauntless spirit who was the first of his countrymen in so many fields of activity was first also among them to preach in Europe. This was St Wilfrid. It is true that he was an exile, and was rather following the command to flee into another city when persecuted in the first than choosing foreign lands spontaneously. But, so it happened, that escaping from his enemies, and deeming it safer to avoid the harbours of Gaul, he landed on the sand-dunes of Friesland. He was hospitably received by Adelgise, prince of that country, and took advantage of this cordial reception to announce the Gospel to this still pagan tribe. It is said that the conversion of several chieftains, with some thousands of their followers, was the reward of his efforts. When the Frankish king, in league with Wilfrid's enemies, demanded that he should be given up to him, the Frisian rejected this traitorous proposal with contempt, and when the winter was over Wilfrid was enabled to proceed on his journey to Rome.

It was in Ireland, already the mother of numerous foreign missioners of her own, that the first Anglo-Saxon who deliberately devoted himself to this enterprise was trained. St Egbert, a Northumbrian priest, was one of the many English scholars who crossed over to Ireland in the double pursuit of learning and sanctity. This was emphatically the period when Ireland earned the title of Isle of Saints and Doctors. Nor was St Egbert's visit merely a passing one, for he became abbot of the monastery called Mayo of the Saxons. And though Egbert himself never passed beyond the Western Isles, his abbey became a veritable seminary of missions. From it St Willibrord and a band of twelve Englishmen, in 690, sailed to the mouth of the Rhine. He, like his master, St Egbert,

St Willibrord in Friesland.

was a Northumbrian, and he, like him, had sought learning and monastic discipline in Ireland. He now led a devoted band to preach to the pagan Frisians. At first he laboured among the southern part of the nation. These had been brought under the sceptres of Pepin of Herstal, duke of the Franks, but he was prompted later on to pass on to the Northern Frisians, who were still independent. Amongst these he laboured for many years with such success that he has won the honourable title of Apostle of the Netherlands. He visited Pope Sergius in Rome in 692, and was consecrated bishop by him, receiving the pallium and the dignity of metropolitan. When he returned he resumed his labours, founding monasteries and establishing bishoprics, himself fixing the archiepiscopal see at Utrecht, which had been given him for the purpose by Charles Martel. About 740 he died in extreme old age at Echternach in Luxemburg, so that St Bede was able in his history to speak of him as a venerable contemporary. Two of his disciples, St Ewald the White and St Ewald the Black, who were brothers, went farther afield to preach in Old Saxony, and were privileged to give their blood for the Faith in 695. Among other Anglo-Saxon missionaries there have been preserved the names of SS. Saithbert, Adalbert, Werenfrid, Plechelm, and others who evangelised various Teutonic tribes.

But the fame of all these champions of the Church

LIFE OF ANGLO-SAXON CHURCH

has been eclipsed by that of St Boniface, "the Apostle of Germany." In fact, the completeness of his career, the vast scale of his enterprises, as well as the results which attended them, leave him with very few rivals, externally speaking, in the whole history of the kingdom of God. He was a West Saxon, born at Crediton in Devonshire in 680 or thereabouts. He was christened under the name of Winfrid. Even from his earliest years he was powerfully drawn towards the monastic vocation. The monks of Exeter trained him in his youth, and he was then transferred to another religious community at Nutshall. At the age of thirty he became a priest, and was sent as an envoy from the Witan of Wessex to consult Archbishop Brihtwald on some disputed point over which there was litigation. He in this acquitted himself so handsomely that high and honourable employment seem assured to him. But the call to the Foreign Missions was ringing in his heart, so in 716 he left all and sailed from London for the coast of Friesland. Yet, for the moment, as the times were evil he met with no success, and came back to England. Three years later, in 719, he again sallied forth, and this time betook himself to Rome. The Pontiff, St Gregory II., approved his zeal, but assigned Upper Germany, not Friesland, to be the sphere of his labours. He then sent him forth with his blessing. Arriving in Upper Germany he began to preach, and at first met with some success, but when some obstacles came to interrupt his further labours there, he went on to St Willibrord, whom he assisted in his work for three years. After this he again made the journey to Rome, where St Gregory II. now consecrated him bishop, and sent him with a letter of recommendation to Charles Martel. That prince welcomed him with all honour, doing what he could to aid him, so that St Boniface was enabled to settle down to his great work of the evangelisation of Germany. He took an honoured place at the National Councils of the Franks, and was able to exercise a great and beneficent influence therein. Moreover, the Pope strengthened his position by sending him the pallium, and by appointing him his legate for Germany. Boniface took advantage of the powers he had received to consecrate bishops to help him in his work, while he also founded religious houses to train a future supply

St Boniface.

of clergy for the land. He is the founder of the sees at Erfurt, Eichstädt, Wurtzburg, and Burnburg, himself taking Mayence for the see of the Primate where he established himself. At first, indeed, he fixed himself at Cologne, and it was from that city that he proceeded to the council at Soissons in 744, which confirmed the former conciliar decrees, and thus laid the foundation of that wise legislation in Church matters which will be always connected with the name of Boniface. But in 748 Mayence became his final choice, and all the other bishoprics of the Germanic race were made subject to it. When the great political crisis developed, which placed a new line of kings—the Carlovingian—on the throne of the Merovingian dynasty, Boniface crowned the mayor of the palace, Pepin, according to the suggestion and approval of Pope St Zachary.

After his great labours, and amid the failing energies and strength of advancing age, St Boniface got his disciple, Lullus, named as his coadjutor.

Martyrdom of St Boniface. He succeeded also in getting his favourite monastery at Fulda put on a firm foundation with many rights and privileges, and there he put his own abode, handing over most of the administration to his assistant. But it was not really done in order that he might enjoy ease: he went back to his former work of preaching to the infidels. He penetrated across the Rhine to the remote parts of East Friesland. A good number of the natives were brought over to the Faith, but while preparations were being made for a public ceremony of baptism on a large scale at Pentecost, 755, a band of pagan natives approached. Instead of trying to save himself by flight, St Boniface advanced to meet them. They made a fierce onslaught on the saint and his company, and thus Boniface gained the martyr's crown, and added the title of Martyr of Christ to those of Bishop, Apostle, and Legate of the Holy See.

The preachers from England took quite as prominent a part in spreading the Gospel in Scandinavia as they did in Germany. Sigfrid, a priest of York,

Evangelisation of Scandinavia. left his native land in the tenth century to preach to the Swedes. The victory, nevertheless, was not gained without a struggle, and three of Sigfrid's companions paid for their zeal with their lives. But at last victory came.

LIFE OF ANGLO-SAXON CHURCH

No less than five episcopal sees were established, with Upsala for the chief of them, so that Sigfrid could feel that the Gospel had been firmly rooted in the land. Sigfrid's death is placed in 1002. In Norway St Olaf was the first Christian king; and also deserves to be called the Apostle of his native land, but his chief instruments in the gradual process of christianising his people were the Anglo-Saxons: Grimkel, Bishop of Trondheim, Sigfrid, Rudolf, and Bernard. In Denmark there was early progress, then relapse, then progress again. Canute the Great sent missionaries from England, when he reigned over both countries, to complete the good work (1020). It remains just to be noted that somewhat later, when the Swedish king, St Eric, had brought Finland under his dominion, and introduced the Christian Faith into that country, St Henry, an Englishman, was the chief Apostle, and he became the first bishop and pastor of the flock in Finland.

Of course, to go on pilgrimage to distant shrines, or to follow the vocation of preaching the Gospel to heathen tribes, could only be the privilege of a few; but to employ the means of sanctity which the Catholic Church provided for the attainment of even heroic virtue was within the reach of multitudes. *An Island of Saints.* And it may be safely said that great indeed was the number of those Anglo-Saxon Christians, who used the discipline of the primitive surroundings in which they lived so well as to win the title of Saints. It was the virtues of these simple Children of the Church before the Norman Conquest, more than anything else which won for England the appellation of an Island of Saints. It is but just to say that this was not an exclusive name, it was shared in a pre-eminent degree by the land to the West which we call Ireland. But the Anglo-Saxon saints were a noble company. And they could be found adorning nearly every rank and every station of life. There were bishops: the see of Canterbury alone was filled during this period by at least fourteen incumbents who are venerated as saints. There were kings and queens. There were warriors and nobles, franklins and serfs, holy widows and simple maidens, all knitted together into one living unity in the one Church of Christ.

XII.

THE NORMAN CONQUEST.

(1066-1087.)

The Conqueror's claims.

VERY likely the historian who traces the mutual action of the various races of mankind will see in the Norman invasion of England mainly an instance of that marvellous outpouring of the Northmen under their sea kings, which did not cease until long after they had helped to plant the Cross at Jerusalem. But William of Normandy, when he started on his warlike expedition in 1066, claimed higher rights than this. (1) In his public declarations he affirmed that the English crown was his by the will of the Sainted Confessor. (2) He made much also of the oath of fealty which Harold had been made to swear when the storm cast him a shipwrecked traveller on the Norman coast. Moreover (3) he protested that he held the written approval of Pope Alexander II. for his enterprise. And he exhibited a consecrated banner, which, he said, the Pontiff had sent as a standard for his forces. Among the barons who assembled their troops, and furnished the ships for their transport, a very prominent place was filled by Odo, Bishop of Bayeux, William's half-brother. The Abbot of St Ouen was also there "with many vessels and knights," says the chronicler. And in the host there must have been many clerics; amongst whom was that kinsman of the duke, who was afterwards to be celebrated as St Osmund. Perhaps the announcement that this was a kind of holy war, blessed by the Pope to reform the standard of living among the degenerate Saxons, may have made these Norman clerics all the readier to be of the company.

After the battle at Senlac was won, the royal foundation of Battle Abbey served to perpetuate both the memory of the victory and services of intercession for the souls of the fallen. On the other hand, the body of King Harold, which was probably handed over without ransom to his mother, was interred in the Church of Holy Cross Abbey at Waltham, which he had himself begun, and which thus became the mausoleum and chantry of the last Saxon King of England. William soon received the submission of most of the surviving Saxon leaders, of the two archbishops, Stigand and Eldred, of Edgar Etheling, and of the great earls who met him at Winchester. He then passed on to be crowned at Westminster by Eldred, Archbishop of York: this Saxon prelate receiving his constitutional promise "to defend God's Holy Church, and to rule all the people subject to him with righteousness and royal providence." If it is not clear why Stigand, the primate, did not crown him rather than Eldred, the reason must be sought in the former's uncanonical position. He had been suspended by Pope Alexander, and this would be looked on as making any rite administered by him invalid, or at least doubtful. However, when William visited Normandy in the year following, Stigand was in his train. But this did not imply that he meant him to keep his archbishopric. In fact, there is every reason to think that William intended to co-operate to the best of his power in such a reform of the clergy in England as would raise the position of the Church in the land, and would tell in favour of the morality of the whole nation. But he knew that he, rough soldier as he was, must call in for this work an ecclesiastic who was both holy and experienced. And he believed that he had such a one in Lanfranc, abbot of St Stephen's at Caen.

William is crowned.

Lanfranc was no Norman; he was born at Pavia in Lombardy in or about 1005. He had come to Herluin's foundation of White Benedictines at Bec about 1040, and his talents as a teacher soon made the Abbey School famous; indeed, he even drew pupils away from the lectures of the celebrated Berengarius of Tours. Then, when this latter teacher fell into error on the doctrine of the Real Presence, it was Lanfranc who confuted him. His beautiful work on the Blessed Sacrament still survives. Lanfranc went to Rome with the "Apostolic Pilgrim," St Leo IX., in 1050, and in that city he took part in the synods held against the teaching of

142 THE CHURCH IN ENGLAND

Berengarius. Duke William of Normandy had espoused Matilda, the daughter of Baldwin of Flanders, in spite of an ecclesiastical impediment, and Lanfranc was the means of putting the marriage right. The penance enjoined on the duke was the foundation of the two celebrated abbeys at Caen, one for men and the other for women. What more natural then, than, when the buildings were completed, to seek out Lanfranc to preside over that for men, known as St Stephen's? Consequently, Lanfranc left Bec where he had been prior, and became abbot at Caen. William regarded him as his wisest counsellor, and as his spiritual father. On his advice he leaned when at home, and when he went abroad, he committed the realm to his experienced guardianship. He was now minded to have him at the head of that great movement of organisation and reform which he realised to be necessary in England.

At the Council of Winchester held in 1070, after William had returned from stern repression of a revolt in the North, Stigand was formally deposed from the archbishopric as a simoniac and intruder, and the king then nominated Lanfranc to fill the vacant see. This choice was approved of by the assembled clergy, while the papal legate, Ermenfrid, Bishop of Sion, likewise urged Lanfranc to accept the proffered dignity. But only when the Abbot Herluin, his former superior and father, joined his counsel to that of the rest did Lanfranc yield to the unanimous voice. He was then consecrated at Canterbury by William, Bishop of London, Eldred, Archbishop of York, having died some months before these events.

Lanfranc's tenure of the primacy from A.D. 1070 to 1089 marked a wonderful development in the Anglo-Norman Church. He was tenacious of the rights of his see with regard to the northern metropolitan at York, and defended them successfully both before the Pope and before the king. When Archbishop Eldred died, Thomas of Bayeux, one of the conqueror's chaplains, who had come to England in the train of Odo, Bishop of Bayeux, was named as his successor. But Lanfranc broke off the consecration service at Westminster, even after the assistants were robed, because Thomas refused to make the promise of canonical obedience to him as Primate. Eventually

Lanfranc as Primate.

THE NORMAN CONQUEST 143

Thomas submitted, and was consecrated, and in the following year both Lanfranc and Thomas proceeded to Rome to ask for their pallium, having as their companion, Remigius, Bishop of Dorchester, whose consecration by Stigand was objected to as uncanonical. Pope Alexander II., after hearing the objections raised both against the position of Remigius and that of Thomas of Bayeux, ended by committing both cases to the judgment of Lanfranc, who thereupon reinvested both of them with ring and crosier. He then came back to Canterbury, having his position greatly strengthened by what had happened at Rome.

The deposition of Stigand involved not only the vacancy of Canterbury, but that of Winchester as well, for that notorious pluralist had held the two dioceses simultaneously. The latter see was now bestowed upon the Norman Walkelin, said to be a kinsman of King William. *The Anglo-Saxon bishops.* During his tenure of the see, which lasted nearly thirty years (1070-1098), Walkelin was able to rebuild the cathedral in great part on the magnificent scale which still testifies to his lofty ideas of architectural greatness. It has been already told how the death of Archbishop Eldred in 1069 made it possible before long to establish a Norman at York. The same thing happened at Durham before the year 1070 had run its course. This see had been held by two Saxon brothers, Egelric and Egelwin, in turn. Egelric resigned and returned to his monastery at Peterborough, and Egelwin became involved in the suspicion of favouring the northern rebellion, which William had just repressed when the Council of Winchester was held. He was outlawed for this, and the way was thus clear for the appointment of a Norman bishop. Walcher, who was the first Norman Bishop of Durham, only held the see until 1080, when he was killed in a fierce riot which took place in his episcopal city. He was replaced by William of St Calais, or Carilef, one of the royal ministers. He it was who commenced the building of the great Norman cathedral, "half church, half fortress," which overhangs the river Wear. Two other Saxon bishops, Ethelmar of Elmham and Ethelric of Selsey, were deposed at the same time, the former as being Stigand's brother, and the latter as having been consecrated by him. Two other bishops consecrated by Stigand were allowed to retain their sees: Siward of Rochester, who only survived until 1075, and Remigius of Dorchester, who had his appointment ratified through his appeal to Rome. There only remained one other Anglo-Saxon prelate, and he had been consecrated by Eldred of York. This was St Wolstan, who had been appointed to Worcester, when Eldred was forced to relinquish this diocese after he became Archbishop of York. Whatever may be thought of the legend that he was called upon to resign, and then laid his crosier on St Edward's tomb, from which no one proved able to lift it, it is certain that he remained a trusted counsellor of the new primate, and was left in the undisturbed possession of his see, amid a new and foreign episcopate, for five-and-twenty years after these changes took place.

It must be remembered that the influence of St Edward the Confessor had led to several of the dioceses being in the hands of foreigners long before the invasion of William the Conqueror. Elfward, the last Saxon Bishop of London, had died as early as 1044. Robert Champart, afterwards made Primate, began the line of Norman occupants of this see. In like manner Walter of Hereford and Giso of Wells had been consecrated at Rome by Pope Nicholas III. in 1061. Hermann, a Fleming, one of King Edward's chaplains, had held sway in St Aldhelm's see at Sherborne since 1058, and only died in 1078. Then, in addition to those prelates who have been already mentioned, Lanfranc proceeded to install Osbern, the first Norman Bishop of Exeter, and Peter, Bishop of Lichfield. For Rochester, after Siward's death, he procured in turn the help of two members of his former community at Bec, Ernost, who died after a year of episcopate, and then Gundulf, the bosom friend of St Anselm. Gundulf strove hard to restore the fallen fortunes of his see, and rebuilt the cathedral. He is also credited with extensive works at the Tower of London. At last, when Lanfranc died, he seems to have done his best, during the vacancy at Canterbury, to care for the spiritual interests of the archdiocese, as well as those of his own small territory. By a curious coincidence, even if it is no more than that, the same year which saw Archbishop Stigand deposed from his high

The new episcopate.

place as metropolitan, likewise saw a Bishop Stigand installed at Selsey, in place of Ethelric, who, we have seen, was deposed at the same Council. This prelate five years later removed his see to Chichester, thus becoming the first bishop of the latter city. One would be almost tempted to hazard the conjecture that these two Stigands were one and the same person, but there does not seem any authority to support the idea. Anyhow, they were probably both Anglo-Saxons.

But it was not only as the reformer of the hierarchy, and as the counsellor, we might almost say, reformer of the Conqueror himself, that Lanfranc holds so high a place in our history; he was also a legislator—the great promoter of our national synods or councils of the clergy. When he became primate a long time had passed since such assemblies had taken place, and the work to be done could hardly have been accomplished in any other way. In the Council of Winchester of 1070, which has been already mentioned, the Roman legates, Ermenfrid, Bishop of Sion, and the two cardinals, John and Peter, presided, when, besides the deposition of Stigand, thirteen canons of discipline were enacted. William the Conqueror was present, and other prelates besides Stigand found themselves deprived of their benefices. King William again summoned the bishops to meet in synod at Winchester in 1072. It is noteworthy that after both these synods there were supplementary councils at Windsor, which from the time of St Edward the Confessor gradually became the chief royal residence. Lanfranc gathered thirteen bishops around him with twenty-one abbots at St Paul's in London in 1075, and an almost equally important gathering took place at Winchester in 1076. It is in these two last councils that we find most of the legislation which was to be the *norma* of Church discipline for many years to come. Lanfranc was labouring at that general moral reform which St Gregory VII. was, during those same years, making such heroic efforts to accomplish in the universal Church. In William of Normandy he had a monarch to deal with who, in his rough way, was much more loyal to Christendom and to the papacy than was the Emperor Henry IV. His general attitude towards the Holy See is not inaptly expressed in his celebrated

K

answer to the message from Rome requiring him to do homage to the Pope, and to send on the overdue Peter's Pence: "The one I admit; the other I do not admit; homage I will not do; for I neither promised it, nor do I understand that my predecessors did it to your predecessor; but the money . . . shall be sent. Pray for us and for the state of our kingdom, for we have loved your predecessors, and sincerely wish to love you before all men, and obediently to listen to you."

On the other hand, in the struggle against simony and concubinage, Lanfranc proceeded with somewhat milder and more tentative methods than those which were employed by Gregory. In the Council of London, besides the decree ordering that episcopal sees should be transferred from villages to walled towns, the boundaries of the province of York were fixed as being from the Humber to the northernmost parts of Scotland, and Thomas of York signed his canonical obedience professed to the see of Canterbury. Canons were then passed against simony and divination, and against the clergy taking any part in a legal sentence involving anyone in the loss of life or limb. Next year, at Winchester, it was decreed that married priests in the villages or country parts might keep their wives, but that those unmarried must remain so. At the same time bishops were forbidden to ordain either to the diaconate or priesthood any but those who promised to observe celibacy. In the earlier councils it had already been decreed that no bishop was to hold more than one see; that bishops should hold a diocesan synod every year; that altars must be made of stone; that chalices must not be made of wax or wood; that baptism should not be administered, unless in danger of death, outside of the Feasts of Easter and Pentecost; that the clergy who failed to observe the celibacy of their state should give up their benefice.

Points of Legislation.

Lanfranc likewise came to an agreement with the Conqueror henceforward to keep the episcopal court and the *hundred-mote* quite distinct, both in time of meeting and in function. Hitherto, under the Anglo-Saxon kings, the two had often coalesced, and had been even in danger of being confused with one another. Now civil and ecclesiastical cases began to be classified more dis-

Ecclesiastical and Civil Courts.

tinctly. For the administration of his own diocese, the
Primate had hitherto habitually used the assistance of
a bishop called the Bishop of St Martin's, Canterbury;
but Lanfranc decided to do without the services of an
auxiliary of this kind, and found other ways of getting
help, notably from the Bishop of Rochester. It was in
ways such as these that the great Norman prelate went
on with his work of organising the Church of mediaeval
England.

He was, moreover, a scholar as well as a statesman and
ecclesiastic, and the second aim of his life work was to
advance learning as a handmaid to devotion and the
observance of the Christian law. His chief work, " On
the Body and Blood of Jesus Christ in the Holy
Eucharist," belongs to the period of his controversy with
Berengarius, whose heretical opinions he refuted, bringing out the true Catholic doctrine as an antidote to
them. Other books of his are to be found in the library
of the Latin Fathers. But another work of his, whose
influence has been even greater with ordinary students,
is the *Correctorium* of the Bible, which we owe to him.
He kept up a friendly correspondence with his old
monastic home at Bec through the intermediary of the
saintly abbot, Anselm of Aosta; they met several times
at Canterbury. With King William he exercised
immense influence, again and again his wise counsels
prevailed to guide the stern warrior along the path of
loyalty to the Church, as far as his fierce nature allowed.
And it may be said that he attained a considerable
measure of success. As long as William lived there was
in the main peace between Church and State. Lanfranc
avoided every unnecessary collision with all the prudence
and dexterity of a statesman. And bearing in mind the
position of the Conqueror as a mighty reforming influence
for churchmen as well as for the country at large, there
was tacit acquiescence in his making the appointments,
at least to the chief offices held by ecclesiastics without
much attention to the right of free election. But it must
be admitted that the bishops whom he designated,
probably with Lanfranc's approval, to fill the English
sees, were not mere worldly lords, but in the main
scholars and men of piety. Still, this privilege of
selecting rulers for ecclesiastical benefices became later
on an intolerable abuse, when it fell into the hands

of the more unprincipled monarchs who were to follow him.

William I. died in 1087 through an accident, while riding over the smoking ruins of the town of Mantes, which in his anger he had burnt. Lanfranc was present at the final scene when the dying monarch made that unequal distribution among his sons which gave Normandy to Robert, England to William, and to Henry, for all present share, a monetary legacy. But there was more to be said for his decision than might at first appear, for England was won by the sword, and not part of his ancestral domains, and perhaps he suspected that Henry would survive his brothers. The Conqueror had been a loyal son to the Holy Church, and, moreover, a devoted husband to Matilda his queen. Yet as he lay on his death-bed, remorse and even contrition seem to have been borne in upon him at the remembrance of the deeds of blood and savagery which he had wrought, or suffered to be done in his name. He implored God's pardon with the spirit of faith and trust in his Redeemer's merits. Hearing the sound of a bell, he asked what it meant. He was told that it was ringing for Prime at St Mary's Church hard by. "Then," said he, "I commend my soul to my Lady, the Mother of God, that by her holy prayers she may reconcile me to her Son, my Lord Jesus Christ." Immediately after this he breathed his last. He was buried by Abbot Herluin in the Abbey of St Stephen at Caen, which he himself had founded.

Death of William the Conqueror.

Lanfranc survived the king for two years. But they were years of bitterness and disappointment, for the new king proved to be far inferior to the old one. The Primate could not but be apprehensive of the future, although he did not live to see things at their worst. He came to England with the new monarch after his father's interment, and, in fact, it was the influence of his authority which went further than that of any other to secure for the Red King what measure of peaceful acknowledgment he attained. But when the first risings against him were suppressed, and Rufus felt himself moderately secure, he began to show himself in his true light. When Lanfranc remonstrated against a flagrant breach of his plighted

Death of Lanfranc.

word, he was met with the angry answer: "Who can keep all his promises?" But in 1089, being far advanced in old age, Lanfranc sank into his grave, and the thankless office of Mentor to William Rufus was vacant. Among his other great works had been the rebuilding of Canterbury Cathedral, and in this church his remains were laid. He was a skilful churchman and a learned scholar. But besides these titles to fame, he was a man of great piety as well. Hence, though he was never canonised, he enjoys the title of the Blessed Lanfranc. To him must in all justice be assigned the foremost rank in the great work of reorganising the English Hierarchy.

But though never canonised himself Lanfranc had two saints, one a Saxon, and the other a Norman, among his contemporaries in the episcopate. The Saxon was St Wolstan, the holy Bishop of Worcester, whose long and upright career *St Wolstan (1013-1095).* may be called the last of the glories of the Anglo-Saxon Church. He personified what was holiest and most attractive in the piety of the race. Though born outside the bounds of the county, it was in Worcester that his training was begun and completed. It was in Worcester that his pious parents, by mutual consent, sought refuge from the world in neighbouring cloisters. It was as Prior of Worcester that Wolstan led that life of austerity and humility which prepared him, though he knew it not, to be the pastor of that ancient see. When Eldred was made to give up Worcester in order to win the pallium and the Northern archbishopric, Prior Wolstan was set in his place, unworthy as he deemed himself. Worcester was happy in having such a bishop for three-and-thirty years. Having survived the wholesale transfers of Lanfranc's synods, and having won that prelate's confidence so fully as to be entrusted with the visitation of the diocese of Chester as well as his own, Wolstan got ready for the last summons, and in 1095 was called to his reward. His shrine was for centuries after his canonisation the chief place of pilgrimage in the beautiful cathedral of his see.

The Norman contemporary of Lanfranc was a member of the family of William the Conqueror. Osmund was amongst those who accompanied the conquering expedition of 1066. After that, he served the king for some years in various useful ways, until Bishop Hermann, who had transferred the Wiltshire see from Sherborne to Old Sarum, died in 1078. Thereupon St Osmund was selected by William as his successor, and this choice was ratified by the Pope. He proved a great bishop in more than one sphere of activity. At Old Sarum he built a cathedral, and established a chapter of thirty-two secular canons to serve it. But he is still better known for his great work with regard to the Liturgy, which brought the Mass and Divine Offices into one uniform order under what is usually designated as the *Sarum Rite*. This rite was not an invention of St Osmund, but was rather a codification of existing customs, modified where necessary in order to secure uniformity. The event proved that the arrangement had been so well done that it became practically universal in England and Scotland from 1250 until the time of the Reformation. At that period, under the authority of Cardinal Pole, the Roman rite was substituted for it. But it remains extant in noble tomes, a work of absorbing interest, and it behoves us to remember that when we think of our Catholic ancestors saying Mass or officiating at other Church services in mediaeval times, we must consider them as using this *Sarum rite*, and not the modern Roman one, in their celebrations.

St Osmund at one time thought St Anselm, who was already in the midst of his contest with Rufus before the holy bishop died, too unyielding in his opposition to the king, and at the Council of Rockingham in 1097, ranged himself among that monarch's supporters. However, he realised later on that he had misjudged the conduct of the Primate. He, then, with the most edifying humility, publicly asked his pardon. He died in 1099 before either Rufus or Anselm were called to their account, and was buried at Old Sarum. Later, his remains were translated to a shrine in the Lady Chapel in the new cathedral at Salisbury. There they remained until the shrine was desecrated and plundered under Henry VIII. It was only three centuries after his death that St Osmund was canonised in 1457 by Pope Calixtus III.

A notable share is attributed to St Osmund in another compilation very different from the Sarum Ritual. This

St Osmund (1009-1099).

is the celebrated " Domesday Book." Of course it is not professedly ecclesiastical at all, but it has its importance in any judgment on the position of the "Domesday Church at the time when it was put together. Book." Its chief purpose was to furnish the king with an accurate computation of the resources of his kingdom for the feudal system of taxation, and of a military levy in arms. The order for its commencement is assigned by the Anglo-Saxon Chronicle to the year 1085, and at least a considerable portion of it may be assigned to 1086. In the following year King William died, and we do not know whether he had the satisfaction of seeing its approaching completeness. It has been printed in two folio volumes, and Sir Henry Ellis has written an extensive introduction to it. The return is such an elaborate one that it gives invaluable information in detail as to the state of England at the time. As regards the Church, it contains much as to the temporal possessions of benefices, parishes, and dioceses. Of course it is a work of reference, and in no sense a monument of literature. It is disappointing, on account of the trivial facts which are recorded, but in its own sphere it is perhaps without an equal in other European countries.

XIII.

ENGLAND UNDER THE CONQUEROR'S SONS.

(1087-1135.)

William Rufus. (1087-1100). THE Conqueror, by the terms of his will, had tried to provide, as well as he was able, for the future concord of his descendants. William, his second son, had been for years his companion and favourite; and him he was naturally disposed to favour the most. The ancestral dukedom of Normandy was allowed to go by right of primogeniture to Robert, the eldest son, but as to England, which he had won by the sword, the Conqueror did not consider himself so strictly bound. This was all the more so, because here ancient custom left a certain freedom of election among the members of the royal family. William, therefore, hastened to England, while his father still lay dying, and with him went a royal messenger to Lanfranc, recommending his second son as his successor. A council of prelates and barons was then assembled under the Primate's presidency for the purpose of a formal election. In response to the questions Lanfranc put to him, William made the most liberal promises that he would govern according to the laws and constitution, and do justice to all. This he confirmed with an oath, whereupon Lanfranc used all his influence in his favour. Consequently, all Robert's friends being absent, the election went without opposition in William's favour, and he was immediately crowned at Westminster. This was on the 27th of September, 1087.

Of course the partisans of Robert did not take this without a struggle, and raised the banner of rebellion in various parts of the country. Still, mainly by the aid of the native English levies, William was able, in the course of the following year, to subdue them all. It could not be said that the new king was faithful to the engagements he had taken; in fact, he told Lanfranc in reply to his remonstrances that no one could keep all his promises. For some time the aged Primate may have been able to exert some restraining influence over him, and he certainly did nothing which could lead to a breach between the king and the leaders of the Church. It was thus that he acquiesced in the arrest of William of St Calais, Bishop of Durham, whom Rufus accused of unfaithfulness very much as he had not protested against the arrest of Odo, Bishop of Bayeux, in the last reign, on the ground that these prelates were feudal tenants as well, and could be called to account as such by their feudal lord. But from 1089, when Lanfranc died, the conduct of William took a decided change for the worse. He began to intensify the stern sway which his father's government had begun to put into operation, and this in a way which set at naught both the rights of the Church and the lawful privileges of the barons. His ministers and advisers were not men of the stamp of Lanfranc. Chief among them, above all in his financial exactions, was the unscrupulous cleric, Ralph Flambard. He was a Norman from Caen, who seems to have been already in England in the days of St Edward. At one time, in the household of Maurice, Bishop of London, he was transferred to that of the Conqueror, and seems to have been employed in various clerkly occupations at the royal court. It is guessed that he had no less a share than St Osmund in the compilation of the "Domesday Survey," with, no doubt, a somewhat different object in view. Anyhow, at the accession of William Rufus, his financial ability brought him to the front, and he became in practice both justiciar and treasurer to that monarch. Probably he for some time held the Great Seal as well. He it was who either suggested, or at least developed, the system by which the king procured large sums to meet his needs out of the revenues of vacant benefices, which had to be paid into the chancery, and then were appropriated to the royal use. Another means by which he strove to fill the royal

Ralph Flambard (1040-1128).

coffers was by the feudal reliefs which were exacted upon succession both to ecclesiastical dignities and to lay fiefs. The king led a life of extravagant debauchery, and was always in want of money. It was then quite in accordance with the above-mentioned policy that after Lanfranc's death the see of Canterbury was kept vacant for nearly five years in order that the royal purse might profit by the archiepiscopal revenues.

Ralph Flambard was rewarded for his services by the appointment to the see of Durham in 1099, by which time he had enriched himself as well as his royal master. But his later life was more edifying than we should have expected. He fled to Normandy at the death of Rufus, and at first sided with the party of Duke Robert. Nevertheless, after paying a large fine, he made his peace with Henry, and was allowed to return to his diocese. Henry had found other ministers whom he trusted more to help him. So Flambard resided in his see, where he enjoyed the almost regal state of a prince-bishop, except in name, and ruled his County Palatine. He became a great builder, for the chief part of the noble Norman pile of Durham Cathedral, begun by William of St Calais, is due to him. He also fortified his episcopal city, and built Norham Castle against Scottish invasion. Out of his immense wealth, perhaps in reparation for the somewhat unscrupulous methods by which he was thought to have acquired it, he founded a new religious house at Mottisfont, besides adding a further foundation to the existing priory at Christchurch in Hants. By charters which are still extant, he restored to the monks of Durham all the goods he had taken from them, and then, having publicly confessed the oppressive acts he had been guilty of, he died a penitent in 1128.

With such ministers as Flambard to assist him in his extortion, Rufus pursued for some years untrammelled his wild course of debauchery and lavish expenditure. There were wars to be waged both in Normandy and in Scotland, but, though he began his reign well provided with means in the treasure his father had amassed, no wealth could stand expenditure such as his in peace and in war, and he was ever in want of money. But in 1093 he fell dangerously ill at Gloucester, and the threatening shadow of death stirred him to remorse, hence, in a fit of repentance, he was moved to try and make some restitution for the wrongs he had wrought. Anselm, the holy abbot of Bec, who happened to be in England, was called to the sick monarch's bedside, and consulted by him as to what means he had to take to make his peace with God. He was immediately brought face to face with his injustice to the Church, and his tyrannical oppression of his people. He had said that as long as he lived he would never give up the revenues of Canterbury. But Anselm boldly told him that he must fill up the primacy and the other vacant sees, and promise to govern the nation justly according to the laws. These were the conditions of his forgiveness. The holy monk had done his duty in exacting these promises. But he was at once filled with terror and dismay by what followed. For William, declaring that no one was so worthy to be archbishop as the monk who had tended his soul, sent again for Anselm, who had withdrawn when his office of confessor was fulfilled. He was given to understand what the Red King wanted, but not all the arguments of those around him could convince him that God's Will was thereby shown. However, almost by force, he was drawn once more to the sick monarch's couch, and the pastoral staff thrust into his hand. Finally, in the midst of entreaties from the bishops, the royal invalid, pleading that his peace of soul depended on his acceptance, the shrinking monk resigned himself to the burden as to the Will of God.

Anselm, Abbot of Bec, visits William Rufus.

Anselm was consecrated at Canterbury by the Archbishop of York, in the presence of St Osmund, of Gundulf, his lifelong friend at Bec, now Bishop of Rochester, and of seven other bishops (4th December, 1093). As he had foreseen, he was plunged at once into the storms of strife and contention. Rufus, as though he had done him a favour, demanded at once a large sum of money for his expedition into Normandy then pending, and when Anselm freely offered him five hundred pounds he refused the sum as an insult, and at once king and primate were no longer friends. Moreover, he was soon met by much opposition from his fellow-bishops. Maurice, of London, succeeded in frustrating his first attempt at a metropolitan function, when he went to consecrate

St Anselm becomes Primate.

Harrow church. Still, notwithstanding his break with
the king, Anselm went to Hastings, to dedicate Battle
Abbey, and at the same time to bless the royal voyage
to Normandy. While at Battle he consecrated Robert
Bloët as Bishop of Lincoln. Bloët had been a royal
chaplain who had deserved the royal favour, so it is
likely that this nomination on the part of the king was
not made so purely at the call of conscience as that of
Anselm had been. William then crossed the sea, but
sent an embassy to the Pope to ask that the pallium
might be sent to Anselm, as it was not convenient just
then for him to seek it in Rome. Urban II. complied
with this request, and in 1095 Cardinal Walter, Bishop
of Albano, arrived in England as papal legate, bringing with him the prized emblem of the archbishop's
authority, which he took from the altar in the cathedral
at Canterbury in the presence of the legate and of the
English episcopate. There now came to the Primate a
period of comparative tranquillity, for the Red King was
absent on his wars, and the administration of the diocese
engrossed Anselm's care. Gundulf of Rochester was his
bosom friend, and the bonds between the two sees had
never been closer, but the calm was not to endure for
long. The king had already other grievances against
him, the chief of which was his acknowledgment of
Urban II. as lawful Pope, as against the anti-Pope
Clement, before the king had acknowledged him himself.
This he forbade, and told the archbishop to choose
between obedience to him and obedience to Urban. Of
course he did not for one moment hesitate. He had
already, earlier in the same year, declared his mind on
the subject at the Council of Rockingham, where he
clearly stated the position of the Pope in Christendom in
a magnificent address, which it was beyond the power
of any of the assembled bishops to refute, though some
of them were frightened by the king into the renunciation of obedience to the archbishop. But Anselm now
judged that the state of affairs in England was so serious
that it was his duty to consult the Pope in person, and
therefore he applied to Rufus for leave to set out to
Rome. This he at first refused, but afterwards sent an
ungracious message directing him to be ready to start
in eight days' time. Yet, although this permission was
so unwillingly granted, when the meeting of farewell

THE CONQUEROR'S SONS 157

took place. William did not refuse to bend for the Primate's blessing.

The succeeding years, until there was a new king on the English throne, were spent by Anselm out of the country. He went to Cluny, and thence to Lyons, for the archbishop was an intimate friend of his. From Lyons he proceeded to Rome, where he met the Sovereign Pontiff, and exposed to him the situation of affairs in the Church in England. Urban received him with much honour, greeting him as the "Apostolicus and Patriarch of another world;" and wrote to William a letter of remonstrance. Anselm then retired to the Abbey of Schiavi where he spent the autumn, elaborating his treatise *Cur Deus Homo* on the reasons for the Incarnation of Our Lord. Next year he was present at the Council of Bari (1098) which had been called to promote the cause of reunion with the Greek Church in the East. In that august assembly which took place in the great basilica which is the shrine of St Nicholas, it was his clear, acute, theological exposition of the Catholic doctrine which went further than anything else to establish the truth of the Procession of the Holy Ghost from both Father and Son. At first it was intended to excommunicate Rufus at this Council, but eventually a period of grace was given him until another council which Urban summoned to meet at the Lateran in Rome in the following April. Anselm would have left Rome on his return journey at once, but Urban retained him for this Council, which without censuring the Red King by name, pronounced an anathema on all who should become the vassals of a layman or accept investiture of an ecclesiastical benefice from his hands. After this, Anselm moved north into France, where he again sojourned for a while near his friend, the Archbishop of Lyons.

Anselm with the Pope.

Meanwhile, William Rufus was persisting in his career of unbridled licentiousness and of practical irreligion which was thought by some to amount to absolute infidelity. For the moment he seemed to prosper. He had the proud satisfaction of having the sword of state carried before him in solemn state procession at Westminster. With that taste for building which he shared with his age, he had completed Westminster

Death of William Rufus.

Hall, rebuilt London Bridge, and erected the ramparts round the Tower of London. Gundulf, the good Bishop of Rochester, had taken advantage of a terrifying dream which he had to warn him before it was too late to cease from persecuting the Church. "Do not go to the chase to-day," said the bishop. In consequence of what he had said, William stayed at home during the morning. But after dinner he ordered his horses and dogs and rode off to hunt in the New Forest. That same evening he was found lying dead in the Forest, pierced to the heart by an arrow, discharged at him by design, or perhaps flying at random. They buried the Red King in Winchester Cathedral, but the clergy refused to perform the funeral rites over his remains.

Henry, the third son of William I., was near at hand when the news of his brother's tragic death became known, whereas Duke Robert was far away from the kingdom. The few barons who were in the neighbourhood went through the form of electing Henry as king, and the royal treasure at Winchester was seized on his behalf. The see of that city, which chanced to be vacant, was immediately given to William Giffard, who was to be Henry's chief adviser instead of the Bishop of Durham. Henry was crowned, but it was in the absence of Anselm, whose right it was to perform the ceremony. But Henry wrote to the Primate at once to explain the reason of what had been done, and to invite him to return to England. In the course of his letter to Anselm he made the following solemn profession to the saint: "I confide myself and the people of the whole realm of England to your counsel, and that of those whose office it is to join with you in advising me." This promise was repeated publicly in the document called the Charter of Henry I., in which the king renewed also the customary undertaking to give freedom to the Church and to the whole nation peace and redress of grievances. This was done after the formula already cited as used at the coronation of King Ethelred.

Henry I.
(1100-1135).

Anselm, who had learned the death of William Rufus while at the monastery of Chaise Dieu, now came home in triumph. But the friendly dispositions of King Henry in his regard soon underwent a change. He plainly demanded of the Primate that the royal right to invest the bishops in his realm with ring and crosier should be admitted in spite of the Roman Decree which forbade this. Anselm at once refused, and Pope Paschal being appealed to, upheld the decision given by the archbishop. Meanwhile, Anselm had been able to adjudicate upon a matter which interested the king, in the king's favour, by pronouncing that life in a convent without taking the vows of religion, though the community life were shared, would not debar a woman from coming out and getting married. The case was that of Edith, or Matilda, as she was afterwards called, daughter of St Margaret, whom the king wished to marry. The marriage ceremony took place on the archbishop's authority. Even before this Anselm's influence had done much to paralyse the efforts made by Duke Robert of Normandy to gather a powerful party in support of his claim to the throne. King Henry was then enabled to carry the contest into Normandy, and having defeated Robert at Tenchebrai, was further in a position to bring the whole duchy under his sway; it required several campaigns fully to accomplish this, but at last the thing was done, and Henry was *de facto* Duke of Normandy as well as King of England. Henceforth it was against the French that he would have to hold his continental possessions. *Return of St Anselm.*

The controversy between Anselm and the king on the investiture question was still far from settled. Henry demanded that he should apply to be invested again by him, and the saint steadily refused. The king then sent envoys to Rome to gain the papal consent to royal investiture with ring and crosier, but though they declared at their return that Paschal II. had given a verbal consent, this was not borne out by the papal letters when they arrived, for they insisted on adherence to the previous legislation of the Church on this subject. During the interval, Anselm held a council at Westminster which passed various useful canons of discipline. But when he was called upon to consecrate the new bishops, Roger of Salisbury, William Giffard of Winchester, and Reinelm of Hereford, he steadily refused to do so, unless they handed back the crosier with which they had been invested by the king. Gerard, Archbishop of York, at first agreed to consecrate them, but before *Investiture Settlement (1107).*

the actual rite had been performed his courage failed him, and they remained unconsecrated. It was Henry himself who suggested that Anselm should proceed again to Rome to consult the Pope on the whole investiture question, and the saint set out once more, and found the Supreme Pontiff still decided not to grant what the English monarch demanded. He then prepared to come back to England, but in revenge for his failure Henry sent to forbid the Archbishop to land in England unless he was prepared to submit to him. However, it chanced that Anselm had turned aside from his road through Normandy to visit Adela, Countess of Blois, the king's sister, who was lying sick at the time. This lady now intervened, and brought about a meeting between her brother, the king, and the archbishop. A reconciliation took place, and Henry seems to have admitted to himself that he was beaten. At a council (1107) held in London in Westminster Hall, at which the terms of settlement were agreed upon, investiture, with ring and crosier, were given up by the king, while the Church on the other hand allowed him to receive from the prelates feudal homage for their temporal possessions. This arrangement was the exemplar which was afterwards followed in the Concordat of Worms, and the Ecumenical Council of the Lateran which followed it (1123). Anselm then consecrated the new bishops, Roger, Reinelm, William Giffard, and William Warelwast, the last named being made Bishop of Exeter. For the two remaining years of his life, St Anselm enjoyed comparative tranquillity, and was able to occupy himself in his pastoral duties, and in the more congenial employments of study and prayer. But his strength was nearly at an end, and in 1109 he died, going forth as from a land of exile and weariness to the everlasting feast of his true country.

But it is not only as the champion of the cause of the rights of the Church that St Anselm has impressed **St Anselm's Works.** the mark of his genius on his age; he was a great thinker and writer as well. It is true that the greater part of his immortal works were written in the cloister before the turmoil of the world was able to touch him. Yet the same lofty genius remained with him to the end. He saw clearly the final outcome of the investiture struggle with the same penetrating intellect which had plunged into the depths of the doctrine of the Incarnation, and foreshadowed the scholastic method. His recognition as Doctor of the Universal Church is an authentic testimony to his position in Christian thought. He was, indeed, rather a pioneer of the scholastics than a master of their fully developed system. Yet it may be doubted whether a loftier intelligence was ever employed in theological speculation. The argument for the existence of God embodied in the *Proslogion* has appealed to a number of minds who remain unmoved by the fivefold proof of St Thomas in his *Summa*. The contribution made in *Cur Deus Homo* to the Theology of the Incarnation is still enshrined in Manuals of Dogma. The *Monologion* still keeps its place. The refutation of the Byzantine errors is still valid and valuable. The warm words of devotion in the writings on the Blessed Virgin still fire the piety of her clients. The *Mariale* is still a household word among her hymns. His *Prayers* and *Meditations* still bring spiritual consolation to pious souls. Take him for all in all he is in the company of St Thomas, St Bonaventure, and St Athanasius among Catholic teachers, while as a captain in the army of the Church he stands scarcely lower than St Thomas Becket, Hildebrand, or Innocent.

In spite of the investiture settlement, King Henry was not above taking any minor advantage he could of ecclesiastical temporalities being unemployed, and thus the see of Canterbury remained unfilled for five years. But, even had he been zealous to promote the appointment of a good pastor, his attention was still much taken up with his continental dominions, and he was rarely in England. His brother, Robert, was in prison, but he had a son named William still at large, and the King of France supported his claims to the duchy of Normandy. It was still more important from the English national point of view that those claims found a sympathetic hearing with Pope Calixtus II. Baldwin of Flanders also joined the French king in opposition to Henry. Henry had a darling son also named William, to whom he made his barons do homage in advance. Yet, seeing the array of enemies against him, there seemed every prospect of a lengthy war. At length the Supreme Pontiff stepped in as mediator, visiting King

L

Henry at Gisors. The English monarch defended himself before the Pope with much skill, both with regard to his treatment of his brother, Robert, and with regard to Robert's son. Finally, Henry having protested that he was animated by the most peaceful intentions in both respects, Pope Calixtus successfully accomplished the task of making peace, which left him in possession of Normandy for which his son, William, did homage to the French king. Thus in 1120 King Henry was able to arrange his return voyage to England with every hope that he had secured peace and the claims of his beloved heir. But alas! for the accidents of human affairs, the young prince was wrecked in the *White Ship* on this very journey, and perished in the waves. The clouds of grief and disappointment which settled upon Henry were never removed.

Meanwhile, Ralph d'Escures, who had been consecrated by St Anselm as Bishop of Rochester, had been administering the archdiocese after the saint's death. At length, in 1114, the pious Ernulf, Abbot of Peterborough, being promoted to Rochester, he was elected archbishop, and was a strong supporter of King Henry, who in his turn seems henceforth to have steadily supported the rights of Canterbury. Almost at once after his appointment he was involved in a lengthy dispute with the northern metropolitan. Thomas II., archbishop of that see (1109-14), the son of Samson of Worcester, and nephew of the former archbishop, Thomas of Bayeux, had only made profession of obedience to the Primate at the king's command, and when he died in 1114, and Thurstan, King Henry's secretary, was elected to succeed, the dispute was renewed. Ralph refused to consecrate him without it, and eventually he was only consecrated by the Pope himself five years later. Urging the maxim "One primate, one king," Ralph enlisted Henry strongly on his side, but though consecrated, was not able to take possession of his see until 1120.

Ralph d'Escures (1114-1122).

But there was another prelate among those consecrated by St Anselm whose influence over the king and whose services to him far surpassed those of Archbishop Ralph, and lasted far longer. This was Roger, Bishop of Salisbury, who is sometimes called Roger the Great. He had been made bishop in 1102, but the royal dispute with

St Anselm had delayed his consecration. He filled, in turn, the offices of chancellor and justiciar, and remodelled a great part of the civil administration of the realm. His wealth was considerable, and he used it like a true Norman in the erection of buildings both secular and religious. Salisbury Cathedral was partly rebuilt by him, and on a scale of unsurpassed magnificence, while the castles at Devizes and other places in the diocese were entirely his work. He was riding with the king and Robert Bloët, Bishop of Lincoln, when the latter called out, "I am dying," and soon after expired in the king's arms. His influence was able to secure the see of Lincoln for his nephew, Alexander, in 1123. Furthermore, about the same time his sway over the king secured the bishops' nominee, the secular clerk, William de Corbeil, the succession of Canterbury in spite of the opposition of the monks, and the dislike of the Holy See to set a secular over the Canterbury monks. The height of his power was reached when, Henry having to pass the greater part of the years 1123 and 1124 in Normandy, Roger was made regent of the kingdom. He maintained the peace of the country in such seeming perfection that he is called in his Epitaph "the Sword of Righteousness." But some of his punishments seem to have been severe to the verge of cruelty. However, he had a very difficult office to hold, and the verdict of posterity has been in his favour. The testimony of William of Malmesbury may be taxed with partiality, but he declares that amid all his secular business his Church duties were not neglected but performed in the morning early. Anyhow, he seems entitled to the honourable appellation of Roger the Great.

Roger the Great (1107-1138).

It would appear to be beyond dispute that the latter part of the reign of Henry I. brought great progress in general civilisation and ordered government to England. The king himself was absent much of the time in Normany. But he had the faculty of choosing able ministers, and things prospered in their hands. In order to secure a male heir he married a second time, his choice being Adela, daughter of the Count of Louvain, but the marriage proved childless. By his various mistresses he had several illegitimate children of whom Robert, Earl of Gloucester, is the most celebrated.

He was the only one of all these children present at his father's death, and the dying monarch having declared that the succession and all his goods were to go to his daughter, the Empress Matilda, Robert of Gloucester constituted himself the champion of his half-sister's claims (1135).

If we want proof of the ordered state of the country, especially in Church matters, perhaps we may find it in the legatine visit of Cardinal John of Crema in 1125. After visiting King Henry in Normandy, he came to England, and was received at Canterbury by the archbishop, and sang High Mass in the cathedral on Easter Day. The old chronicle then goes on to tell us how he went all over England to all the bishoprics and abbeys, and everywhere was received with great honour, "and all gave him great and noble gifts." There was a council in the summer at Westminster, at which both archbishops and their respective suffragans were present, as well as many abbots and inferior clergy. The legate took precedence of both archbishops, and promulgated anew the legislation which St Anselm had collected. When he returned to Rome in the autumn, Archbishop William, as well as Thurstan of York, accompanied him thither, together with Alexander of Lincoln, and they were received by Honorius II. with great honour. The English prelates did not come home until the spring. The Archbishop of Canterbury was concerned to protest against the appointment of a legate other than himself as derogatory of the traditional rights of his see. And before he left he got himself named Legate of the Holy See in England.

Another proof of the efforts being made for the advance of learning may, perhaps, be found in the appointment of Gilbert the Universal to the see of London on the death of Bishop Richard in 1127. He got his surname from the encyclopædic character of his attainments, and was found by King Henry teaching with great éclat at Angers. Several of his works exist in manuscript, but he only survived till 1134, and did not distinguish himself as an administrator as his reputation would have led men to expect.

King Henry's foundation of Reading Abbey, which he enriched with a noble endowment, is to be referred to the same period. The abbey maintained a great

THE CONQUEROR'S SONS

reputation for piety and hospitality. After the king's death his body was brought from Gisors and interred in the abbey church.

The foundation of a school at Cottenham under the auspices of Geoffrid, Abbot of Croyland, with regular courses of grammar, logic, rhetoric, and Holy Scripture, which rapidly attracted crowds of scholars both there and later on in the neighbouring town of Cambridge, may be the true origin of that celebrated University. Possibly Gilbert the Universal was one of the professors.

King Henry and his elder brother, Robert, died much about the same time (1134-5). According to the king's own account he had kept Robert in honourable and comfortable quarters; according to his enemies he had guarded him in close imprisonment, first in the Tower of London, and then in Cardiff Castle. Robert was at any rate a dangerous rival in a disputed succession, and he survived to a great old age.

We must also refer to this reign the founding of two of the English episcopal sees: that of Ely and that of Carlisle. The former was begun in 1109, and first filled by Hervey, Bishop of Bangor, who, being expelled from his see by the Welsh, was living as a guest in Ely Monastery. The latter was not commenced until the year 1133 when Adelulf, a Canon Regular of the house in that town, was made bishop, the see being erected at the instance of Thurstan of York, who consecrated the new bishop for Cumberland and Westmoreland. Practically likewise the see of Norwich began about this time, for Herbert de Losinga, who had been consecrated Bishop of Thetford in 1091, having purchased his elevation by simony, received as part penance from the Pope the building of a new cathedral. This he decided to fix at Norwich, and thereupon transferred his see to that city in 1094, and his successors abode by this arrangement. He and his successor between them completed the magnificent Norman church, and the secular canons were replaced by monks. When Hervey, the first Bishop of Ely, died, Roger of Salisbury had another nephew to replace him, Bishop Nigel of Ely, who became treasurer to King Henry II. for a considerable part of his long episcopate (1133-1169). He in his turn passed on the office to Ralph Fitznigel, a son who was born to him before he became bishop. Fitznigel became Bishop of

London, but he is more celebrated as treasurer than as a diocesan bishop. His Book of the Accounts of the Royal Treasury, called "Dialogus de Scaccario," is still extant, and furnishes a most interesting record of the state of the country from a financial point of view during the reign of Henry II. and that of his successor, Richard I.

XIV.

THE TRANSITION UNDER STEPHEN.

(1135-1154.)

At King Henry's death there were two sons of his sister, Adela, and of the Count of Blois, in England or near it. The younger, Henry, was a churchman, who, after being made Abbot of Glastonbury, was also appointed Bishop of Winchester in 1129. The elder, Stephen, a brave soldier, had been marked out by the late king as a main support for the throne of Matilda. But this was not to be. Stephen claimed the throne for himself, and proceeding to London, was acclaimed king by the citizens. Thenceforward he advanced very much on the lines which thirty-five years before had secured the disputed inheritance for Henry himself. He betook himself to Winchester, where he found three powerful bishops to support him, Roger of Salisbury, with his nephew, Nigel, Bishop of Ely, and as an influential third, his own brother, Henry of Winchester. He persuaded Roger, who was justiciar, to hand over to him the very considerable royal treasure which was there, and then returned to Westminster for his coronation. William of Corbeil, the Primate, had taken the oath of allegiance to Matilda, but was prevailed upon to crown Stephen, though, as the chronicles relate, " in much perturbation of mind and body." The Bishops of Salisbury and Winchester were the only others present of episcopal rank, nor was the attendance of the lower ranks more than scanty. Stephen, in a quite short formula, promised to confirm the laws and privileges both of his uncle and of " good King Edward," and that was all.

Stephen (1135-1154).

Meanwhile, Normandy likewise seems to have accepted Stephen as its ruler, in spite of several attempts at rebellion. Robert, Earl of Gloucester, also gave an external acquiescence, and King David of Scotland, though wishing to take up his niece's cause, was at least temporarily bought off by the surrender of Carlisle. To strengthen himself still further, Stephen signed a second *Charter of Rights* in the very first assembly of the prelates and nobles which could meet after he assumed the crown. This took place at Oxford, after the interment of the late king in Reading Abbey in January, 1136. This Charter, which was apparently granted twice—once before Stephen had had his succession confirmed by Innocent II., and then again when he was able to show a papal letter to that effect—is sometimes called the second of all the chief royal charters which we possess. It is mostly concerned with the rights and privileges of the Church. Simony is forbidden, and all keeping of the revenues of vacant benefices on the part of the crown is abjured. Likewise, all interference with the testamentary provisions of bishops, abbots, and others is disclaimed, while all the privileges and customs admitted in former reigns are confirmed. Liberty to hunt on his own lands is granted to everyone: the forests made for the crown by Henry I. are given up. In fine all the good ancient laws are to be kept. This Charter is attested by the Primate and thirteen other bishops, as well as by the leading barons and officials at the royal court. Probably Stephen made the grant in such ample terms in order to secure the allegiance of the clergy, for this was tendered to him conditionally upon his adherence to what had been therein laid down. It was, moreover, a great point for him to obtain papal confirmation of his election, so, doubtless, the promises he made went far towards gaining this. But Stephen did not, and perhaps could not, keep all these promises. He was a brave soldier and a faithful friend, but he has small claim to be looked upon either as a skilful general or a capable ruler of the kingdom. It may be admitted that the two first years of his reign were years of peace and prosperity: they were thus brought into sharp contrast with the very wretched time of disorder which the country passed through as the years advanced. Indirectly, of course, the power both of the Church in general, and of the Holy See in particular, was increased

Stephen's Charter of Rights.

by Stephen's efforts to secure their assistance. In fact, there has scarcely been a reign during which the ecclesiastical elements in the life of the nation have been more prominent. This is almost the sole redeeming feature in what was otherwise a period of constant warfare and feudal anarchy.

Quite early in the reign, a report got abroad that Stephen was dead, and this provoked an unprepared rising, which the king was able to suppress with the promptitude and valour of a good soldier such as he was. But this rising led him on to become suspicious of the loyalty both of the barons and of the clergy. He singled out as objects of special distrust, Roger the Great, Bishop of Salisbury, and his two episcopal nephews, Nigel of Ely, and Alexander of Lincoln. Roger had built himself strong castles at Devizes and Malmesbury, and was surrounded by all the splendour of a princely court. Moreover, he was justiciar of the realm. It was this last circumstance which gave all the greater character of unconstitutional action to the sudden stroke by which Stephen had uncle and nephews arrested, and put into prison. He, in fact, seized justiciar, chancellor, and treasurer at one blow, for the two latter offices were then held by the Bishops of Lincoln and Ely respectively. This was naked tyranny, and was resented as such by the clergy, who met in Council at Winchester, and there made a strong remonstrance against the arrest of the bishops. This Council of Winchester was quite an event of national importance. Aubrey de Vere, the royal lawyer, attended the Council as the king's advocate, and charged the bishops with disloyalty and seditious conduct. Henry, Bishop of Winchester, demanded a fair trial for Roger and his nephews, and the restitution to them of their castles, at least until their guilt was proved. At the next session, Hugh, the Archbishop of Rouen, spoke in the king's favour, claiming that the bishops as churchmen had no right to the possession of fortified castles. Aubrey de Vere then in the king's name threatened an appeal to the Pope, and there was a half-hidden attempt to use violence on the part of some knights of the king's party. Bishop Henry, therefore, acting probably as legate of the Pope, dissolved the synod, and its members went

Stephen and the family of Roger the Great.

their way. Still, before himself leaving, he made a final effort for peace by going to the king in company with Theobald, the new Archbishop of Canterbury. They both knelt at Stephen's feet, begging him to liberate the bishops, and to restore their castles. But they found him fixed in his hostile intentions. Henceforth the king himself was to be the sport of misfortune, captivity, and the changing fortune of war.

Of the two prelates who thus knelt to Stephen in vain, Henry of Winchester, as being legate and the king's own brother, was at that time the more influential, but now, for the first time, the other, just made Archbishop of Canterbury, came into prominence as a real leader for the Church and for the people as well.

Archbishop Theobald. Theobald, who was to hold the primatial see for twenty-five years, had been Abbot of Bec. His reputation stood high, when after the death of William de Corbeil in 1136, the monks of Canterbury elected him as archbishop. Thus, for the third time, that illustrious Monastery of Bec gave an incumbent to the see of St Augustine. Theobald was consecrated at the beginning of 1139 by Alberic, Bishop of Ostia, at Canterbury in the presence of most of the bishops of the province. Alberic was at that time legate at the Holy See in England. Theobald and the legate left England together with several of the bishops, for the new primate had to petition at Rome for his pallium. Theobald was present at the Second Ecumenical Council of the Lateran held in that year (1139), as were also the Bishops of Worcester, Coventry, and Exeter. Theobald, of course, obtained the pallium, but the office of legate was bestowed upon Henry, Bishop of Winchester, the king's brother. This was, no doubt, a disappointment to the archbishop, and greatly hampered him in the exercise of his leadership of the Church in England.

It was, in fact, upon the power and skill of his episcopal brother that Stephen's chief hopes reposed for securing the support of the hierarchy of his realm. Henry had already played a considerable part in affairs in the preceding reign, for he had come to England in the train of his cousin, Henry I. The accession of Stephen did but enhance his lofty position. In 1126 he had been made titular Abbot of Glastonbury,

Henry of Blois, Bishop of Winchester.

TRANSITION UNDER STEPHEN

and when he was elected to the see of Winchester, three years later, he retained his former benefice *in commendam* as it was usually expressed. His royal brother had tried to secure that he should be made Archbishop of Canterbury instead of Theobald, but in this he failed. However, the next best thing for the king was that he should be papal legate, and this he obtained. During the greater part of Stephen's reign Bishop Henry came nearer to being virtual ruler of the land than any man alive, and to mark his sense of his influence is styled by the old chronicler "Lord of England." He was a man of high principle, and had no mind to be a mere catspaw in his brother's hands. Yet his general support enabled Stephen at first to carry on his contest with Bishop Roger and his family with some measure of success. When at length Devizes Castle fell into the king's hands, Roger seems to have abandoned all hope of retaining his power or his possessions. He handed over all that he could to his see, in order to save it from falling into the royal grasp, but he never recovered from the blow. He was, indeed, already an old man, yet it is likely that it was more from a broken heart than from old age that he died before the end of the same year. Bishop Nigel of Ely effected his escape from the realm until the general pacification made it safe for him to return.

But, while Stephen was contending with the men whom he looked on as his enemies in the South, equally powerful foes had taken the field against him in the North. David, King of Scotland, who had been induced to refrain from espousing the cause of Matilda in arms in the first year of the reign, did not remain friendly for long. In 1138 he invaded England at the head of a powerful army, and penetrated as far as the town of Northallerton. The English king found a doughty champion in Thurstan, Archbishop of York. He was an

The Archbishop of York and the Scots

aged man, and had held the see for nineteen years, having been consecrated in 1119 by the Cistercian Pope, Calixtus II.; for the Archbishop of Canterbury refused to consecrate him, and he had appealed to Rome. Returning to England with his pallium, it needed the threat of an interdict to induce Henry I. to acknowledge him. But the threat did its work, and Thurstan went on to York in triumph. But, though broken with age, his spirit was as active as ever, and he was the soul of the resistance which was organised against the Scottish invasion. As he could not be on the field in person, the Bishop of Orkney was there in his name, to bless and absolve the levies which Thurstan's efforts had collected: He had ordered the Sacred Host to be raised on high encircled with banners as a standard, or rallying point, for the English host. Hence the decisive victory which routed King David and his men is known as the *Battle of the Standard.* Thurstan was a firm friend to the Cistercians of Fountains Abbey, whose abbot, Henry Murdach, became his successor. At the last he had time to put all his affairs in order, and he then retired to the Cluniac house at Pontefract, where he died in 1140. The election of Henry Murdach to the vacant see was not accepted by the king without a struggle; it was seven years before he could receive episcopal consecration.

St William Fitzherbert (1154). Stephen's support was given to St William Fitzherbert, his kinsman, who was chosen by a party in opposition to Murdach, and made bishop at Winchester by Henry of Blois in 1143. The inevitable result was an appeal to the Holy See, when Eugenius III. decided in favour of Henry Murdach, whom he personally consecrated in 1147, deposing St William from his office. St William then retired to Winchester, where he lived under the protection of Bishop Henry, his uncle, until the death of Henry Murdach and of Pope Eugenius, both of which events happened in the year 1153. He was then suffered to take possession of his cathedral. He remained in full exercise of his rights as archbishop until his death, which happened rather suddenly, and not without the suspicion of poison in 1154. He made friends with the Cistercians of Fountains, who were thought to have opposed him, but would not countenance the succession of Hugh de Pudsey to the see of Durham. His remains were solemnly translated to a shrine at the back of the high altar in York Minster in the presence of King Edward I., and the popular veneration for his memory was confirmed through his formal canonisation by Martin IV. in 1282.

Under the double influence of Stephen's want of adherence to his constitutional promises, and the pressure of the partisans of Matilda from without, the king's supporters fell away from him one by one, and within a month after the council at Winchester, which united the clergy in opposition, Matilda landed in the kingdom. Robert of Gloucester, an illegitimate son of Henry I., and one of the most powerful nobles in England, took up arms to support her. Moreover, Stephen's own brother, the Bishop of Winchester, thorough churchman that he was when he saw that Stephen had abandoned the cause of the Church's freedom, went over to the party of the empress. London was taken, and for a while the case of Stephen seemed desperate. But Matilda was an unsatisfactory sovereign to serve. She soon disgusted many who would otherwise have fought for her by her haughty and arbitrary conduct. The first false step was taken at London, where the citizens in receiving her asked for the reinstatement in full of the "laws of good King Edward." This request was quite scornfully rejected, in fact instead of this a heavy fine was imposed on the city as a punishment for its former acceptance of Stephen. This at once stirred up the Londoners to resentment, in fact they never forgot the proud imperiousness of the royal lady, who by this time, through her marriage with Geoffrey of Anjou, after the emperor's death, had become the mother of Henry, the future king. Still, for the time, she was able to keep hold of London, and most of the nobles and clergy being on her side, Stephen's authority was reduced to narrow limits. At Lincoln he was defeated and taken prisoner, though he fought bravely enough in the fray. He was taken to Bristol, where he was incarcerated and treated with great severity. But the fortune of war was soon to change. Matilda found London too hostile for a capital, and betook herself to Winchester, which she attacked and in part took possession of, but her opponents were reinforced from London and elsewhere, Stephen's queen having raised a force to effect her husband's release from prison. Hence it was hard to say who were the besiegers and who the besieged, until at last between the contending armies the city was set on fire, and much of it destroyed. Matilda and her troops now endeavoured to retreat, but they were overtaken, and most of them killed or captured, among the latter being the Earl of Gloucester. Matilda

Civil war and anarchy.

herself reached Gloucester Castle almost alone and in disguise. Negotiations were now opened, which began with the exchanges of the two prisoners, Stephen and Robert of Gloucester, and were followed up in a council which met at Westminster in the following December (1141). A letter from the Pope was first read, recommending the legate-bishop to do all in his power to free his brother from his enemies. Stephen, who was also present, then spoke, complaining of the want of fidelity shown by his subjects. This led the bishop to speak in justification of the part he had played, while on the other hand an advocate of Matilda held a discourse, in which he laid the whole blame of the dissensions upon the Bishop of Winchester.

No further result seems to have been attained by this conference, so that in the following year hostilities began anew, and were conducted with varying alternations of success and failure on the one side and on the other. These years of desultory warfare brought dire distress upon the country before anything like a permanent peace could be arranged. But the prelates of the Church made untiring and praiseworthy efforts to mitigate its horrors, while it lasted, and to bring it as soon as possible to a final conclusion. It was with this double object in view that a council was summoned in London, in 1143, by the Bishop of Winchester as legate, which published the sentence of excommunication lately decreed by the Second Lateran Council against those who should strike or wound a member of the clergy. It also enforced the observance of the *Truce of God* which forbade hostilities from the Saturday to the Monday of each week, and protected the husbandman and his plough from being attacked or interfered with by the warring soldiery.

Council of London (1143).

As time went on the predominant position held by the Bishop of Winchester somewhat declined. He was high in the good graces of Innocent II., and is thought to have planned using that influence to secure the pallium for himself and metropolitan rank for the see of Winchester. But, when that Pontiff died in 1143, he fell into disfavour with the Roman court, for he was credited with trying to prevent Archbishop Theobald from attending a council held by the Pope at Rheims. He threatened him, in the king's name, with the forfeiture of his goods and outlawry should he set out. But Theobald preferred to have Stephen's anger rather than disobey the papal summons, and crossed to France in an open boat. But neither Stephen nor his brother were to gain anything from this contest. Eugenius III. revoked the legatine office to the see of Canterbury, and for the time likewise, even suspended the Bishop of Winchester from his episcopal functions. When Theobald returned to England after the council, he was ill received by the king, and then banished from the kingdom. But he was now legate as well as primate, and was thus able to assume the position of leader of the Church in the land. He soon retaliated upon Stephen by laying all those districts which were in the latter's power under an interdict. This forced the monarch to effect a reconciliation, and the interdict was only removed when peace had been made between the king and the archbishop. Henceforth Theobald was able to act for the Church and the land with the untrammelled influence of his office, and he was a leader well worthy of his high station. A scholar himself, he was the patron of men whose learning became far more celebrated than his own. He had gathered around him in his household so much of the rising talent of his day that it has been compared to a miniature university. Prominent among these younger men was his successor, the martyr, St Thomas Becket. His own brother, Walter, was to be the future Bishop of Rochester. It was under his auspices, too, that Roger Vacarius founded at Canterbury the first school of civil law of which England could boast. As a monk full of energy and zeal, Theobald must have been deeply interested in the great development of the Cluniac and Cistercian Orders which took place in this reign despite the disturbance of the civil wars. He survived King Stephen long enough to be the chief spokesman of the clergy in the early years of the following reign. With the court of Henry II. he was always able to maintain harmonious relations.

The Office of Papal Legate.

The provisions made in the Council of London (1143) had availed to alleviate the horrors of the civil war, for they were observed even in the thick of the conflict, but they did not succeed in restoring peace for several years to come. In 1147 Matilda retired to the continent, but next year she sent her son, Henry, to carry on the war in her name. But in spite of the latter's energy he was too young and inexperienced to be a match for Stephen, and had to return whence he came. Stephen, having come to terms with Theobald, and thus recovered the favour of the Roman see, endeavoured to secure the papal approval for the coronation of his son, Eustace of Boulogne, in order thus to pave the way for his succession to the throne. This was refused by the Supreme Pontiff, and Matilda's son, Henry, once more landed in England. It was at this juncture that Archbishop Theobald and Henry of Winchester united their efforts to bring about a meeting between Stephen and the young prince, Henry. This took place at Wallingford in 1153,

Treaty of Wallingford (1153).
and resulted in a compromise, which was afterwards ratified at Westminster, but is usually known as the Treaty of Wallingford. The sudden death of Prince Eustace, Stephen's eldest son, at about the same time, made the monarch less anxious about the succession, and thus indirectly contributed to a peaceful settlement. The main provisions of the Treaty of Wallingford were: (1) that Stephen should retain the crown for his lifetime, but (2) that at his death it should pass to Henry and his heirs, while (3) the partisans of both gave security that they would abide by these dispositions, and (4) the bishops and abbots engaged to enforce them if necessary by ecclesiastical censures. The treaty was the work of Theobald more than of anyone else, and proved to be an abiding arrangement. Stephen and Henry made progresses in company with one another to the chief cities of England, and after some months the latter returned to Normandy. Thus the main part of the task of seeing that the treaty was duly acted upon fell to Stephen. But he did not live long to enjoy the crown which it had secured to him. His stormy career soon came to an end, for he died at Canterbury on the 25th of October, 1154, and his remains found their resting-place beside his queen in Faversham Abbey, which he had himself founded.

Bishop Henry of Winchester had a career which was protracted far into the following reign. At first he retired to the abbey of Cluny, of which he was already an *alumnus*, and of which he became one of the chief benefactors. Yet, after the lapse of some years, he was allowed to return to England, when he took up his residence in his see, devoting himself to diocesan labours, to alms-deeds, to penance, and to prayer. He was also a great builder; both Farnham Castle and Holy Cross Abbey may be looked upon as chiefly his foundations. He did not approve of St Thomas Becket taking up such a bold and uncompromising attitude towards the king and his demands, but later on in 1170, when martyrdom had put the seal upon that saint's struggles for the rights of the Church, he had the courage to rebuke Henry for his share in causing the Primate's death. In the following year (1171) Henry died himself, and tradition says that he was buried before the high altar in his own cathedral.

Full of trouble and bloodshed as the reign of Stephen undoubtedly was, there were compensations in several important developments of the religious life which sprung up in the midst of its strife and confusion. St Gilbert of Sempringham was able to labour at the establishment of the only English Order which the Middle Ages produced. *Religious Life of the Reign.* Though the first informal communities of Gilbertines belong to the reign of Henry I., the establishment of a definite and distinct religious order is to be referred to 1148. In like manner the Golden Age of the Cistercians has its commencement at about the same year as that in which Stephen began his reign, and before 1153 there were more than fifty Cistercian houses in England. The chief growth of the Cluniac reform also falls within this period. Hermits likewise, such as St Ulfric in Somersetshire, were able to lead lives of solitary contemplation, undisturbed by the warfare which was in great part carried on by mercenary bands, and left the cloister untouched. To Stephen's reign we must also refer the far-famed legend of the martyrdom of St William of Norwich, who is said to have been kidnapped and crucified by the Jews in that city. The character of transition which marked Stephen's reign, stormy as it was, made it, through the religious influences which were at work amidst the chaos, the passage to a higher plane of civilisation and religious progress.

M

XV.

HENRY PLANTAGENET AND THE CHURCH.

(1154-1189.)

Henry II. (1154). THE Treaty of Wallingford, which had been concluded mainly by the instrumentality of such churchmen as Archbishop Theobald and Henry, Bishop of Winchester, gave the crown after Stephen's death to Henry, son of the Empress Matilda. Theobald was on the watch to forestall any opposition, so that there was no one to whom the new monarch was under stricter obligations of gratitude. Henry of Winchester had also been a party to the settlement, but he seems to have felt that his own part in public affairs was well-nigh over. Being alarmed at the destruction of his castles, which was carried out by the young king's order, he at first retired to Cluny, but afterwards returned to England, and spent what time remained to him in the administration of his diocese. Besides Theobald, Henry had amongst his counsellors the treasurer, Nigel, Bishop of Ely, and Thomas Becket, who, after being brought up in Theobald's household, had been introduced by him to the king's notice and favour. Becket sped so well in his career that in the following year (1155) he was made Lord Chancellor at the age of thirty-eight. Thenceforward he became a much more intimate friend to Henry than either of the older churchmen. In fact, Theobald was falling into old age, and felt that his strength was failing. The queen-mother, Matilda, was likewise in retirement, though she indirectly exercised no small influence over the earlier years of her son's reign.

Several of the bishoprics were vacant, and the aged

HENRY PLANTAGENET

Primate was desirous to make provision for them while he was still able to advise and approve. Richard Peche, who had been nominated for Lichfield and Coventry, was consecrated in Theobald's name by his brother, Walter, Bishop of Rochester. For Exeter, when Robert Warelwast died after a few years' tenure of the see, he furthered the appointment of Bartholomew, who was to rule the see for over twenty years, but there was much delay before he could get permission for his consecration. The ceremony was again performed by Bishop Walter of Rochester, but by this time, the primate, was already dead. There had been a project to translate Gilbert Folliott, who was considered the most learned of the bishops, and withal, one zealous for the rights of the Roman see, from Hereford to London. But Gilbert would have none of it. And strangely enough, to those who study his later history, his refusal was based upon the injustice of the demands made upon him to grant part of the revenue to the king. In 1161 Theobald sank into the tomb.

Meanwhile, those years from 1155 to 1161 had been years of successful negotiation and warfare for Henry, especially in the affairs of his continental dominions, and he had been so ably seconded by his chancellor that many authorities give all the credit of the success to his zeal in the king's service and his outstanding ability. He was Archdeacon of Canterbury still, but he did not scruple to lead the royal forces against the French in person, and it was his military prowess which won colours and laid the foundation for the subsequent honourable arrangement made between the kings of France and England. He was a cleric, and never disgraced his order by immorality, lying, or plunder, but he certainly went as far as his conscience would allow to do the king's work. When he travelled through France, or marched forward at the head of his army, it was done with a display of magnificence which enhanced his master's prestige indeed, but did not accord too well with the character of a minister of the Church of the Prince of Peace. He was too powerful and too straightforward in his conduct and language not to make many enemies, especially when it was patent that he stood foremost in the king's good graces. Foremost among these

St Thomas Becket as Chancellor.

was his old rival, Roger de Pont l'Eveque, since 1154 Archbishop of York.

For the intervening year, 1161-2, while the see was vacant, the temporalities of Canterbury were administered by the chancellor. It created little surprise when it became known that the king wished him, his chief favourite, to fill the office of Primate. The election held by the monks of Christchurch took place in May, 1162, and a royal messenger brought them the royal views with regard to the candidate to be chosen. The monks protested that the election must be a free one, but all the same they voted for the royal nominee, whereupon the result was announced to the bishops of the province.

<small>St. Thomas elected as Archbishop.</small> Folliott, Bishop of Hereford, was at first inclined to protest, but then, finding himself alone in this, he changed his tone, and became loud in Becket's praise.
At Whitsuntide the new Primate was made a priest by his old friend, Walter of Rochester, but for the episcopal consecration there were rival claims. At last it was decided that Henry, the aged Bishop of Winchester, should perform the rite, which he did at Canterbury on Trinity Sunday. Nearly all the bishops of the province were there. Thomas now sent envoys to Montpellier, where Pope Alexander III. then was, to ask for the pallium, which was readily granted. The Martyr Primate of the Church's independence was thus armed with full powers of sacrament and jurisdiction to face his weighty task. He had already warned the king that he would no longer find him the assiduous servant of the royal will. As Tennyson tersely puts it:

"I served our Theobald well when I was with him,
I served King Henry well as chancellor:
I am his no more, and I must serve the Church."

In token of this he resigned the chancellorship, though much against Henry's inclination. It was not long before he found himself forced into the forefront of that struggle which Theobald had foreseen, and as far as he could, deprecated. With his dying breath the old archbishop had recommended to the king respect for the liberties of the Church.

The meeting between the king and the new archbishop was of a very cordial character. The saint had just

HENRY PLANTAGENET

come home from an important mission in France. The first ecclesiastical business taken up was the filling up of the vacant See of London. The Pope, the king, and the primate, were unanimous in their selection of a candidate, who was Gilbert Folliott, Bishop of Hereford. His reputation for learning and for austerity stood high, and hitherto he had taken a strong line in support of the interests of the Church and the papal authority. There was nothing to suggest the part he was hereafter to play, and little to show that Henry had cast him for that part. All seemed serene, so that the Primate, with nearly all the English bishops, was able to attend a large council held by the Pope at Tours in 1163. Later on in the same year, St Thomas consecrated Reading Abbey, Henry's royal foundation, and then on the 13th of October, presided at the translation of St Edward's relics in Westminster Abbey, which has been described above. The next year witnessed the bursting of the storm.

The first collision was one touching the rights of the ecclesiastical courts. The Archbishop of Canterbury had always exercised the right to present to any benefice belonging to his own manors or to those of his barons. Such a one was Eynsford, to which, in accordance with this custom, St Thomas presented a certain priest named Lawrence. Upon this the lord of the manor expelled Lawrence's people who had come to take possession. He at once found himself excommunicated for having done so. Of this he complained to the king, whereupon Henry wrote to St Thomas, directing him to absolve the lord of the manor in question. He hesitated, but eventually yielded, after a strong declaration that the case was for him, not the king, to decide.

The written draft being then produced, Henry demanded that to avoid later contention, the Primate and bishops should affix their names and seals to the document. This St Thomas positively refused to do; though there are some, whose account is accepted in Tennyson's drama, who say that he signed without examining the provisions, but on reflection refused to seal. In either case the refusal to seal was taken as sufficient sign of dissent. He then left the court, and towards evening rode to Winchester, sad at heart that he had promised in a general way to keep the royal customs, but glad that he had refused to sign and seal the provisions of the written document.

Henry persisted in the attempt to force the submission on which he had set his heart. He first sent an embassy to Rome, asking that Roger of York should be made legate instead of St Thomas, and this was granted after much negotiation. But the conditions appended to this grant made it practically useless, and the brief was returned to the Pope. But two cases of appeal were decided in the papal court against St Thomas, viz., that of the Abbot of St Augustine's that the archbishop should install him in his own abbey and not elsewhere, and that of Folliott, Bishop of London, that he need not take a second oath of obedience to the archbishop on his translation from Hereford. But when St Thomas sent the Constitutions of Clarendon to Pope Alexander for approval, this was refused, and King Henry held him responsible for the refusal.

Progress of the dispute.

The contest was carried further at a council held at Westminster in October, 1163, where the king met all the bishops as well as the Primate. The first object of the assembly was to vindicate the rights of Canterbury against the claims of Roger, Archbishop of York, who demanded to be treated as a Primate, and in token thereof to bear his cross on high even in the Canterbury province. Against this assumption St Thomas was supported by his suffragans, who, when Roger appealed to Rome, sent an envoy to represent him before the papal court. Still, this dispute was thrown into the background by the claim of the king that all the bishops should promise to observe the royal customs—"*avitae consuetudines*" as he called them. The reply of St Thomas was that he would observe them "saving his order." This reply was in turn made by the rest of the bishops, except by Hilary of Chichester, who said instead "in good faith." After receiving this almost unanimous reply, Henry left in high anger, leaving the bishops very apprehensive of what the consequences might be. Some of them remonstrated with the Primate, urging him to withdraw the obnoxious limitation, but in vain. It was only when letters came from the Pope in which he counselled moderation and all possible concession that he consented to withdraw the words.

The next development in the battle was at the Council

of Clarendon in January, 1164. The royal lawyers had drawn up a body of constitutions, sixteen in number, embodying the so-called royal customs. The justiciar, Richard de Lucy, is looked on as the official who had the chief part in drafting them, and this was the reason why he was afterwards excommunicated by St Thomas. Without enumerating them all in order, they may be easily summarised as follows:

Constitutions of Clarendon.

(1) All suits concerning presentations to benefices, or debts made on oath or promise, or concerning clergy accused of any crime to be prosecuted in the civil courts.
(2) No clergyman to leave the country without the king's leave.
(3) No tenant *in capite* of the crown, nor anyone residing on crown lands, to be excommunicated without notice to the royal officers.
(4) Prelates of the Church to be regarded as barons of the realm, and to be bound to serve the king as such.
(5) The revenues of all greater benefices to belong to the king during their vacancy, and the election to be made in the chapel royal with the king's consent (*congé d'élire*).
(6) No appeal to be allowed beyond the archbishop's court without the royal leave.

The joint effect of these provisions, and of the minor ones not here mentioned, would be greatly to strengthen the royal power over the Church, and hamper the independence needed for its freely discharging its divine mission. St Thomas was then approached by the bishops and others to persuade him to agree to the Constitutions. In sober fact all the surroundings, the armed guards, the presence of the king and of his cringing officials, and the fixed mind of the king to enforce submission had a very terrifying effect. But St Thomas was not terrified. Yet, being moved by the protests and prayers of those around him, he went to Henry, and gave his promise to keep them " in good faith and in the word of truth." All the time assurances were redoubled that the king meant to make no innovations, and only wanted to be saved from the disgrace of being worsted in a contest of this kind. To the first demand that he should pay a fine of five hundred pounds of silver for not answering the king's summons to appear in an appeal from him to the royal court, he consented for peace's sake, all the bishops advising him to do so. But, when this was followed by a series of other demands, the last and greatest of which was that he should account for the revenues of all the bishops and abbacies vacant during his chancellorship, it was clear that the king was determined to go to all lengths. Henry, Bishop of Winchester, reminded him how Henry, through his son, had freed him, when he was made archbishop, from all previous secular obligations. He demurred to this demand, but offered Henry two thousand marks as a peace offering on his own behalf. This was refused, and Hilary of Chichester told him that nothing would satisfy the king but his resignation of his see.

The next scene in the struggle took place at the Council of Northampton in October, 1164. This assembly had been called by the king expressly to bring matters to a head. St Thomas was not formally summoned, probably as a studied insult, but he went to the Council, and immediately sought an interview with Henry. The meeting took place, but was not a success, the king showing unmistakable signs of resentment. On the next day, the 8th, the Council held its first session, who ought to be excommunicated that the king was angered beyond measure. Then came the question of the revived danegeld of two shillings on every hide to be paid to the sheriffs. St Thomas declared that this should be a voluntary aid paid to the sheriffs so long as they did their duty, and not into the royal treasure. King Henry swore with his usual oath, "By the eyes of God," that he would have it, but the Primate's oath that he should not seems to have prevailed, though the king can scarcely be said to have forgiven this defeat.

After one day spent in prayer and consideration, and another under the pain of a sharp attack of illness, **Climax of the struggle.** St Thomas came to the climax of the fight on the 13th of October. He first met the bishops, and ordered them, if any violence were offered to him, to pronounce the censures of the Church against all who might take part in it. Folliott protested, and all the bishops left him except Henry of Winchester and Jocelyn of Salisbury. He then prepared himself for the battle by saying Mass, and then, throwing a cloak over his vestments, and carrying the Blessed Sacrament concealed, proceeded to the hall. When he arrived, he grasped his Primate's Cross. Folliott again protested, but he heeded him not, and passed in procession with the other bishops to the inner room where the king was. Henry cried out that he was coming against him as against an enemy, and the courtiers took it up with a volley of abuse, but after a long altercation St Thomas ended a dignified address by appealing to the Pope:

> "I refuse to stand
> By the king's censure, make my cry to the Pope,
> By whom I will be judged; refer myself,
> The king, these customs, all the Church to him,
> And under his authority—I depart."

He then left the hall and rode back to his lodgings. He next dined, and then rising from the table got the three bishops who were most friendly to him to go to the king for permission for him to leave the country. Henry replied that he would answer on the morrow. But the archbishop's friends fearing a plan to seize him, he fled during the night in disguise by circuitous roads to Sandwich. Thence he crossed the sea to Gravelines. He was warmly received by King Louis VIII., and going on to Sens, threw himself at the Pope's feet. He was cordially greeted, and his offer to resign was declined, though some of the cardinals thought this would give a good chance of making peace with Henry. At first Alexander spoke with some severity of his momentary compliance at Clarendon, but then hearing the whole story of his contests and sufferings, he commended him, and said there was none so worthy to be Primate.

It was necessary to choose a home for the exile, and the place selected was the Cistercian Abbey of Pontigny, where he and his train were most hospitably entertained for about two years (1164-6). **St Thomas in exile.** He devoted himself to prayer and study, finding in these pursuits balm after his warfare. King Henry showed his revenge by banishing his relatives and dependents, obliging them to swear that they would

present themselves before the Archbishop of Pontigny.
Some got a lawful dispensation from their oath, but
enough came before their spiritual father in his exile
to wring his noble heart with grief. He did his best to
relieve their wants, giving some of them letters to powerful friends, consoling others, and spurring himself on
to renewed austerity in his own life. Prudence suggested
that time should be allowed for the king's anger to cool.
But, when Alexander had greatly strengthened St
Thomas's position by once more making him his legate,
both Pontiff and Primate wrote to the king in order to
try and bring him to a reasonable frame of mind. But
all was in vain. Henry wrote back to the Pope, appealing against the archbishop, whom he accused of arrogance and of breaking the ancient customs of the realm.
He also threatened vengeance on the Cistercians for
their entertainment of the offending prelate. St Thomas,
as soon as he realised that he was drawing the Cistercians
into trouble, left Pontigny, and went first to Soissons
and then to Vezelay. From the latter place he issued
excommunications against all who should injure the See
of Canterbury, naming certain notable opponents of his.
He likewise specified and condemned some articles of the
Constitutions of Clarendon, absolving the bishops from
their oath to observe them. Those concerned at once
appealed to the Pope, but he confirmed the sentence
passed by St Thomas. At Sens he was again entertained by Louis VIII., and met the Pope, in whose
company he went to Bourges, and then leaving him,
went back to Sens. King Henry now asked for two
legates to judge the dispute in the Pope's name. The
royal envoy, John of Oxford, succeeded, in spite of St
Thomas's protest, in getting two cardinals appointed,
William of Pavia and Otho, with authority to adjudicate
on the question and to absolve those whom the Primate
had excommunicated. Further representations, however, caused the Pope to write to them that their commission was limited to acting as mediator between King
Henry and the Archbishop of Canterbury. It was in
consequence of these instructions that the two cardinals
held lengthy conferences, first with St Thomas, and then
with the court of King Henry in November, 1167. The
result was a recommendation that for the sake of peace
St Thomas should be translated from Canterbury to

HENRY PLANTAGENET

some other see. Pope Alexander in the meantime had passed out of France, and was residing at Benevento. He was soon besieged there by envoys from King Henry. The pressure which they were able to use won letters from the Holy Father, suspending St Thomas from the exercise of his powers until a reconciliation should be effected. This was a hard blow for the saint, and he addressed a dignified yet respectful expostulation to the Pontiff on the subject.

Meanwhile Henry tried every means in his power to detach the archbishop's friends from him, and also had an interview with the King of France, which resulted in the latter's withdrawing his favour from the saint at least for a while. St Thomas was invited to this conference, and, when he came into the presence of the two kings, threw himself at his sovereign's feet. But this did not mean that he meant to yield up the rights of the Church to him, and Henry would have peace on no other terms. Still, the worst was over, for the Pope wrote again, explaining that at the time of his former letter he had expected a speedy arrangement, and this not having been attained, he would restore his faculties to him. Moreover, the King of France before long once more showed himself as friendly as ever.

St Thomas made use of his restored faculties to excommunicate the Bishop of London and others at Clairvaux on Palm Sunday, 1169. The list included also the Bishop of Salisbury, the Earl of Norfolk, and Ralph and Robert de Broke. Though the sentence was in general disregarded at court, two courageous messengers managed to secure its publication at St Paul's in London on Ascension Day. On the following Trinity Sunday the bishops met at Northampton to deliberate upon a new appeal to Rome against the Primate. But it soon appeared that nothing like united action could be expected. *The last appeals.* Meanwhile, further censures threatened by the saint at Clairvaux had been added to those pronounced by him at that time: his own archdeacon, Richard of Ilchester, Richard de Lucy, and William Giffard, were now added to the list. King Henry was full of anger when he heard of these sentences, but it gradually became clear to him that he could no longer count on the support of the bishops. It is true he had his son, Prince Henry, crowned by Roger, Archbishop of York, in defiance of the Primate's rights. But when St Thomas threatened to put England under an interdict, he found that many of the bishops intended to observe it in case it should be published. However, the Pope and the King of France and many others were working to effect an arrangement between king and Primate. At last they were successful. The first meeting at Montmartre in Paris failed, as Henry still refused to give the archbishop the kiss of peace. But on the 22nd of July, 1170, at a second meeting held at Fréteval, better results were attained. Henry hastened to salute the saint, embraced him, and spent the greater part of the day in his company. There was a suspicion of hollowness about the whole transaction, but outwardly the archbishop had triumphed, and on the 2nd of December he landed at Sandwich, where he was received by thronging crowds with enthusiastic greetings. Within less than a month he was to give his life for those liberties for which he had so dauntlessly contended. From Sandwich to Canterbury is only six miles, and it was a triumphant procession the whole way. The three bishops whom he had excommunicated came to him instant for absolution, but as they would not fulfil the conditions which he laid down, he declined to have anything to do with them. Roger of York, with the Bishops of London and Salisbury, for these were the three under censure, then betook themselves to King Henry at his palace near Bayeux in Normandy. Henry burst out into one of his fits of anger and exclaimed: "What wretches I have brought up, who have no more loyalty to their king than to suffer him to be mocked by this low-born clerk." Four knights, FitzUrse, De Tracy, De Morville, and Brito, overhearing this, started for England at once, and travelling by different routes reached Saltwood Castle on the 28th of December.

Return of St Thomas.

On Christmas night St Thomas sang High Mass, and before doing so again in the morning preached a beautiful sermon on the Feast. He then kept the day in joyous wise with the monks. During the next few days he got several messages warning him of his impending fate. After passing the night of the 28th at Saltwood, the four conspirators rode off to Canterbury early on

Martyrdom of St Thomas.

the morning of the 29th. It was about four in the afternoon when, in company with about a dozen men at arms, they arrived at the archiepiscopal palace. The saint had assisted at Mass in the cathedral, and then visited in turn, as it was his custom, the various altars and shrines. He then spent some time in spiritual conversation with a number of the monks in the chapterhouse. He next went to Confession and took the discipline. At three he dined in the refectory with the monks, and being congratulated on his cheerful mien he answered: " A man must be cheerful who is going to his Master." After grace he went to his private room to discourse with his friends. While he was there, he was told that four knights were asking to speak with him, and he gave orders that they should be admitted. They thereupon came into his presence, but after an insulting volley of charges and threats they left with great noise, frightening the domestics and the crowd of people who had gathered. St Thomas then decided to go to the church, where Vespers were being sung. He went in procession, his cross being borne before him. But by this time the noise of the armed men at hand and the entrance of the archbishop seems to have stopped the Vespers, though St Thomas ordered them to continue the service. He refused to allow the church to be barred, and soon after the knights in armour, followed by soldiers, burst into the building. St Thomas was urged to fly but refused, and hearing his name called said: " Here I am; no traitor but the archbishop." The knights then attacked him, and struck repeatedly with their swords. His last words were: " For the name of Jesus and the defence of the Church I am ready to die." Having assured themselves that he was dead, the conspirators rushed from the church shouting: " King's men!"

Thus was the sacrifice of the " holy blissful martyr" of the rights of the Church completed. As soon as the monks and people had recovered from their panic, the holy body was deposited in the crypt, and the doors securely fastened. The news of the crime soon spread, and became known all through the country. It reached Prince Henry at Winton; it became known to the king at Bayeux; it reached the Holy Father himself at Frascati. There was a universal cry of sorrow and execration. Henry at once sent envoys to the Pope, and they with remarkable audacity tried to lay the blame on the archbishop himself. Still, when they found that the Pontiff was preparing to excommunicate the king, they swore in his name that he would in all things obey the papal commands. The Pope then only excommunicated in general the murderers of St Thomas and all who had abetted them. The continental dominions of Henry were laid under an interdict. At last, after earnest petitions, for the king was now full of remorse, he received the papal absolution in the cathedral of Avranches on the 22nd of May, 1172, taking an oath never to leave the obedience of Pope Alexander, to take the cross for three years, and to give up all customs against the liberties of the Church. Two years later, on the 12th of July, 1174, Henry went on a penitential pilgrimage to the tomb of the Holy Martyr, walking part of the way barefooted. Arrived at the tomb, he ordered a public act of regret to be made in his name by the Bishop of London. He then made an offering for the shrine, and promised to build a monastery in honour of St Thomas, who by this time had been canonised by the Pope. He then bared his shoulders, and received three strokes of the scourge from each monk. The penance was accomplished, and the king had hardly performed it when good news came to cheer his broken spirit.

The Penance and Absolution.

Faulty as Henry II. undoubtedly was, both in his private life and in his conduct towards the Church, it can hardly be doubted that he was one of the ablest as well as one of the most powerful of the English kings. As for his domestic affairs, it was only the *diriment impediment* between his queen, Eleanor of Aquitaine, and her former spouse, King Louis of France, which enabled him to marry her himself. The union was not a happy one, and during the latter half of his reign he found Queen Eleanor arrayed with his sons in a series of revolts against his government. No English monarch had up to this held possessions so extensive on the mainland of Europe as Henry did. Half of modern France was his: a territory larger than either England or the France of those days. But the best part of it had come to him as Eleanor's inheritance, and gave him

Character of the Government of Henry II.

much trouble to rule. Still, he made very determined
struggles to do so effectively. Perhaps he even thought
it the more important half of his dominions; he spent
more than half his time during the later years of his
reign out of England. The Archbishop of Rouen was
almost as great a prelate in his eyes as the Primate at
Canterbury, and he was not much more of an Englishman
than the preceding Norman kings had been. Yet
his reign saw the blending of Norman and Saxon take
place more rapidly than ever before. It remains true
that it is not always recognised to what an extent
Henry II. was a continental monarch. Once he left
the shores of Europe England was not enough for him;
he had designs upon Wales, upon Ireland, and he meant
Scotland to be at least tributary to his throne. These
later years were years of suffering and remorse, but there
is reason to hope that he took the troubles which came
upon him in penitential dispositions, whilst he tried to
be an industrious administrator of the vast domains
which he claimed as his own.

The martyrdom which made of Canterbury Cathedral
one of the chief shrines of the land had taken place before
Henry II. had come to the middle of his reign. But if
we except the penance done by the remorseful monarch,
and the amends which he strove to make to the injured
Church by religious foundations, and in other ways, the
second half of the reign contains less to engage the
Church historian than the preceding years. After his
return from Ireland, which he had visited rather to
escape papal censures than from any plan to conquer
the country, Henry's years were much occupied with the
rebellions of his sons and undutiful nobles. He had not
been a faithful husband to Queen Eleanor; and she
encouraged her sons in their attempts to gain some share
in their father's power. As we have seen, he had had
the eldest crowned, and had given high titles to the
others, but all real power he kept in his own hands.
William the Lion, King of Scotland, and Louis, King of
France, joined the young princes in what became a
regular conspiracy. And in addition to this, there was
a large proportion of the feudal nobility ready for revolt
against the king's projects to limit their power and
to extend the administration of the royal law courts.
The majority of the commons, whose interests were

bound up with the royal legislation, and also nearly all the bishops and great churchmen, held to the king. It must be confessed that Henry dealt with the crisis in an exceedingly able and energetic manner. He drove the King of France out of Normandy, and crushed the revolt in Brittany, and then came over to England to deal with the barons and the Scots. His son, Geoffrey Plantagenet, and the loyal barons, rallied the forces of the king in the North, and on the very morrow of his penance at St Thomas's tomb, he got the good news that William the Lion was a prisoner in his hands. The King of Scots was sent to Normandy, and Henry's sons made some sort of submission. Yet there was no lasting peace between them and their father. Neither did they remain at peace with one another. John was his father's favourite, but though not so openly hostile, in heart he was as rebellious as any. Henry, who had been crowned king, died of fever, asking forgiveness for his misdeeds, in 1183. Geoffrey, who had married Constance, Duchess of Brittany, also died some years before his father.

It was with chastened dispositions, at any rate for a while after the death of St Thomas, that Henry II. dealt with the affairs of the Church. The vacancy in Canterbury was not filled up for nearly four years, but in 1174 Richard, the Prior of Dover, was consecrated as Primate by the reigning Pontiff, Alexander III., at Anagni, and later on is the year the other vacant sees were filled by the consecration of Richard Toclive for Winchester, for Henry of Blois had died soon after St Thomas, of Robert Folliott for Hereford, and of new incumbents for Ely and Chichester. The Constitutions of Clarendon had not been repealed, but in the awe which followed the archbishop's martyrdom they had not been acted on. Then in 1176 Cardinal Hugo came to England as legate to effect a settlement, and being both friend and relative to Henry, was well qualified to make a satisfactory one. In a council at Northampton in the January following these four points were conceded by the king: (1) No clergy should be brought before a lay judge save regarding the forest laws or a lay fief; (2) no see or abbacy should be kept in the king's hands when vacant for more than a year; (3) those guilty of the murder of clerics should suffer, besides capital punishment, the forfeiture of their goods; (4) clergy were to be exempt from the "wager of battle." The king then notified the Pope of the arrangement which he had come to with the legate, and congratulated himself on having, on the whole, retained very substantial privileges in ecclesiastical affairs.

With that abounding energy which kept him up even in the midst of multiplied troubles, Henry now devoted himself to the organisation of the legal system of the country, and made regulations at Northampton, and in a whole series of councils, which have left their mark upon England. *Henry's Legislation.* In order that it might be possible to obtain legal justice without its being necessary to approach the royal court, where the great legal officers such as the justiciar and chancellor were to be found, he divided the country into six circuits, within each of which itinerant justices were to make a progress, trying cases in convenient centres, as occasion allowed. Among the justices sent on each circuit was in every case a bishop, as the king did not intend that they should merely adjudicate upon outstanding cases, but should make a general inquiry into the position both in Church and State within the limits assigned to them. It would be easy to extend the narration of Henry's doings in the sphere of legislation by describing his regulations as to the "Assize of Arms," the "wager of battle" and the forest laws, but this is hardly the place to dilate on such things. Suffice it to say that Henry's achievements were considerable in the department of law-making, and that in all his later arrangements the rights of the clergy and of the Church always counted for much.

When Richard of Dover, the Primate, died in 1184, Baldwin, whom he had consecrated in 1180 as Bishop of Worcester, was chosen as his successor without much delay. It was a case of mutual agreement between the bishops and the king, and though met by the Canterbury monks with an appeal to Rome, was afterwards acquiesced in by them with the formality of an election, and was then confirmed by the Pope. In the same year Gilbert Glanville became Bishop of Rochester, while in the following year it became Baldwin's privilege to consecrate as Bishop of Lincoln, when Walter of Coutances was dead, the saintly Hugh of Avalon, Prior of the Carthusian Monastery at Witham. By this time nearly all the bishops who had been the contemporaries of St Thomas were dead. Roger of Pont l'Eveque, who had played so equivocal a part in the controversy over the Constitutions of Clarendon, died in 1181, and a period of ten years elapsed before Geoffrey Plantagenet was consecrated as his successor. Bartholomew of Exeter was also dead, and Gilbert Folliott, the learned but temporising Bishop of London, died shortly after. Hence Archbishop Baldwin had quite a new bench of bishops surrounding him for the five years during which he presided over the see of Canterbury.

In order to please his favourite son, John, King Henry had estranged Richard, and now discovered that John was himself at the head of the rebels, and that he had brought so much trouble on himself for the sake of a traitor. The death stroke came soon after Henry fell into a fever and invoked the curse of God upon his ungrateful sons. He was at Chinon, and the only one of his children at his bedside was Geoffrey, possibly the offspring of the fair Rosamond. He was in the ranks of the clergy, and was destined by his father for the See of York. Henry then asked for the last Sacraments, which were administered to him; he was then carried into the church, wishing to die there in the guise of a penitent. Geoffrey waited on his father's dying hours with pious assiduity, and the old king expressed to the clergy around the wish that the vacant see of York might be his.

Though he was illegitimate, Geoffrey's royal descent seemed to mark him out for a notable career long before the scene at his father's death-bed. He had been early enrolled in the ranks of the clergy. Then when the see of Lincoln fell vacant by the death of Bishop Alexander, and remained empty for four years, a good opportunity occurred of providing for Geoffrey, albeit at that time he was as yet only a deacon. Thereupon he took possession of that extensive diocese. Nevertheless, though he was in receipt of the revenues, and exercised the customary jurisdiction, he took no steps to get himself ordained. At first the Pope confirmed the election, but later on, when five years had elapsed and Geoffrey was a deacon still, the Holy Father insisted that he should either be consecrated or resign the see of Lincoln. He chose the

Geoffrey
Plantagenet
(1150-1212).

latter alternative, and was succeeded by Walter of Coutances (1181-3).

Geoffrey, notwithstanding his resignation, continued to keep his other benefices; he considered himself a churchman still, and all through the rebellion of Henry's others sons remained faithful to the old king, leading an army against the Scottish invaders, and then being entrusted by his father with the chancellorship of the realm. In deference to his father's dying wish, the new king, Richard, gained the votes of a majority of the Chapter of York in his favour. On the other hand, a minority held firm in resistance to the appointment, and before his confirmation came from Rome a long delay intervened. Geoffrey took advantage of the delay to be ordained, and to proceed to York. Here there was much disturbance, and even positive riot. Though confirmed by the Pope, he had to purchase the king's help by large pecuniary payments, and even then in face of the hostile Canons his tenure of power was precarious and fluctuating. At last he was forced to take refuge in Normandy, where he died in 1212.

Henry was buried in the Abbey of Fontevrault, and by his will made liberal provision for alms and for Masses for his soul. The mediaeval chronicler expresses the belief that God sent him abundant crosses and troubles towards the end of his life upon earth in order to spare him in the life to come.

XVI.

CŒUR DE LION AND LACKLAND.

(1189-1216.)

(A) RICHARD I. (1189-1199).

Richard I. (1189-1199). A FEW weeks after the tragic scene at Chinon, when Henry II. breathed his last, his eldest surviving son, Richard, came to England. His first act was to free Queen Eleanor from captivity, and she went her way with all the dignity of a queen, affirming that Richard was now the lawful heir, and also scattering abundant alms for her late husband's soul. The formality of an election having been gone through at Winchester, the court passed to Westminster for the coronation. Richard was crowned by Baldwin, Archbishop of Canterbury, with a magnificence of pageantry whose record still forms a picturesque page in history. And outwardly all seemed to promise a glorious and successful reign. However, these high hopes were not to be realised. Richard had already taken the cross for the Crusade before his father died, and was bent on hurrying at once to the career of heroism and victory which he thought awaited him. Eventually he only spent six months out of his ten years' reign in England. Before leaving the country, however, several appointments, chiefly of churchmen, were made to provide for the government of the realm. William Longchamp, Bishop of Ely, was made chancellor, Hugh Pudsey, Bishop of Durham, became justiciar; the diocese of London and the treasury fell to Richard FitzNigel. The sees of Salisbury and Winchester were bestowed on Hubert FitzWalter and Godfrey de Lucy, soon of Richard de Lucy, the former justiciar.

FitzNigel proved an able financier, and his account-books are still extant. The Bishop of Durham purchased the earldom of Northumberland for ten thousand pounds. Geoffrey Plantagenet, the king's half-brother, was able by the payment of three thousand pounds to maintain himself in the royal favour as Archbishop of York. In 1191 he was consecrated by the papal order at Tours, and he thus complied with what had been required of him on the part of the Church. Besides this, many other offices were sold to ambitious applicants. Thus was Richard able by various expedients to supplement the royal treasure, which was insufficient for his great enterprise. Hugh of Lincoln, the noble Carthusian saint, held the largest diocese in the country, and was looked upon with feelings of veneration by the monarch. But he was too unworldly to play a leading part in the rough politics of the day; and absolutely fearless in speaking out against tyranny and oppression of the poor. Hence, we do not find him in any of the commissions appointed to carry on the government of the country during the Crusade. Yet the king trusted him. His great qualities also won for him the confidence of the Holy See, and he twice was appointed, with legatine powers, to decide difficult questions in dispute among the clergy.

St Hugh, that noble and gentle glory of King Richard's reign, was not a native of the country whose hierarchy he was to adorn. We shall have to seek his birthplace under the shelter of the Western Alps in Dauphiny. He first of all devoted himself to the religious life amongst the Canons Regular of Villard Benoît. But the austere life of the monks of the Grande Chartreuse won his heart, and he passed into their community while as yet only a deacon. In that home of religious perfection he passed ten years of peaceful seclusion, in the course of which he was ordained priest. He then was made procurator of the monastery, and held this office for seven years. It happened that while Hugh was an inhabitant of the Grande Chartreuse Henry II. of England undertook the foundation of the religious houses which was to constitute part of his penance for the treatment he had meted out to St Thomas Becket. One of these new monasteries was to be the first Carthusian house in England. It was established at Witham in Somerset

St Hugh of Lincoln (1140-1200).

in the year 1180, after two years of ineffectual attempts to make a stable foundation elsewhere. St Hugh was chosen to be the first prior, and left his native land for England. The six years which he spent at Witham sufficed both to set a high standard of sanctity for those who came after to aspire to, and to complete a new church and monastery for their use. But in 1186 the Canons of Lincoln were summoned to elect a bishop for that important see, which had been without a pastor for many years. They were unable to agree on any one candidate, for the office was considered an eligible one. However, a choice had already been made, though in an informal way, by the king and the Primate, who were gathered with the bishops at Eynsham Abbey. Henry, who by this time was sincerely anxious to remedy the evils of the past, proposed the holy Carthusian prior, and Archbishop Baldwin, himself a monk of Citeaux, cordially fell in with the suggestion. Consequently, when the Canons failed to elect anyone, Hugh was proposed for their approval. There was some demur at first, but they gradually came to look upon him as the best possible candidate, and he was at last formally chosen by them. In spite of the opposition caused by his humble reluctance, he had to accept, and was consecrated by Archbishop Baldwin in Westminster Abbey. At the same time William of Northall was consecrated for Worcester. St Hugh now set out for his diocese. His first care was to surround himself with worthy assistants in the great work of reconstruction and reform to which he had put his hand. They came in response to his appeal, not only from England, but even from distant foreign parts. One great enterprise, the success of which we can appreciate even to this day, was the restoration or almost rebuilding of the great cathedral which the first two bishops of the see had erected. The magnificent fane which St Hugh caused to rise in Our Lady's honour on the hill at Lincoln may be held to have been the exemplar of the new style of architecture which afterwards gained such celebrity as the Early English Style. But his care for spiritual things was greater far. None was more assiduous in the visitation of the vast diocese committed to him; none more zealous in providing the Sacraments and other spiritual ministrations of religion for his flock. It must be admitted also that none at least of his contemporaries was so utterly uncompromising in resistance to the encroachments of the king, whether on the Church or on his people. Yet he succeeded in retaining the veneration both of King Henry and of Richard.

At first the chief power at home during the absence of both king and Primate was in the hands of Longchamp, Bishop of Ely, the chancellor, and the administration of this prelate proved to be singularly harsh and unpopular. One of his chief employments seems to have been to wring out all the money he could both from clergy and laity to meet the very considerable expenses of the Crusade. Moreover, he took advantage of the opportunities he possessed to live in great splendour, enriching both himself and his relatives by many expedients. The loyalty of the king's brother, Prince John, was under suspicion from the very beginning of the reign. Longchamp, faithful to his sovereign's interests, successfully frustrated for a time all efforts made by John's friends to take the lead. But he had other enemies such as Hugh Pudsey, Bishop of Durham, the Percys of Northumberland, and De Lucy, Bishop of Winchester; and, to hasten his fall, when he arrested Geoffrey Plantagenet, Archbishop of York, he committed an error which united all his enemies against him. Being summoned to a council of barons and bishops, he failed to appear, and was excommunicated. He fled to the Tower of London, but was besieged there and forced to surrender, engaging to resign his offices and to leave the country. Later on, still faithful to his royal master, he visited him when he was in captivity. This was not forgotten after the king's return, and at Richard's second coronation at Winchester, he once more walked by his side as chancellor of the realm.

Longchamp, the Chancellor.

There is no reign in English history in which the Crusades fill so large a space as in that of Richard. He was more than ever enthusiastic to go on the Holy War, as soon as his accession to the throne made it depend still more upon him. Having summoned his subjects to prepare to follow him, or else to pay a pecuniary equivalent if they remained at home, he added still more to his resources by selling or pledging crown lands on a large scale. He

The Third Crusade.

hastily called a meeting of the clergy at Pipewell Abbey to arrange as far as possible for the filling up of vacant sees and benefices, and then passed into Normandy. At Rheims he met the French king, Philip Augustus, who was to be his chief ally in the Crusade. He then set sail from Marseilles, and coasting along the Italian shore, landed in Sicily. Here, delay followed on delay, and there were quarrels in plenty besides. Still, as soon as these allowed it, a great part of the Crusaders from England arrived in Palestine long before their sovereign. They were put under the command of Baldwin, Archbishop of Canterbury. This prelate, however, died at Acre, and then Hubert FitzWalter, Bishop of Salisbury, took charge of the English host temporarily until the arrival of King Richard. It was June, 1191, before that monarch arrived in Palestine, though he had left England in 1189. His career on the Crusade was that of a hero, but during the four years he remained out of England it cannot be said that he attained the great object for which he had gone. Cyprus was taken, so was Jaffa, and Acre likewise fell. Then Richard, dealing vigorous blows at the Saracens, was able to lead his Crusaders as far as Bethany, and even within sight of the Holy City. But dissensions were all this time undermining the unity of the Christian host, and when it became clear that nothing like general consent could be had for an attack on Jerusalem, a three years' truce was concluded with Saladin, the Saracen leader, in October, 1192, by which the Christians gained free access to Jerusalem in return for the dismantling of Ascalon and the retirement of the army. Richard took his homeward journey overland, leaving the bulk of his troops to be transported by sea. In Austria he was taken prisoner by the duke of that country, and held in captivity until he could be ransomed with a large sum of money which had to be collected for that purpose. The sum demanded was one hundred thousand pounds, or about twice the crown revenue for a year. Clergy as well as laity were forced to give up their treasures and their plate in order to make up the amount. In the end, the main part of the sum was paid, and the king was set free on the 4th of February, 1194. He made the best of his way through Cologne to Antwerp, and thence to Sandwich, where he was received with joyful acclamations by his people.

As successor to Baldwin in the primacy, after his death became known at home, Reginald FitzJocelyn, Bishop of Bath, had been elected in 1191, but he did not live to take possession of the archbishopric. The Archbishop of Rouen was then made justiciar of England in the room of Longchamp, and for two years maintained some kind of government. The great strain of those days was to find the king's ransom. When a large sum had been collected, the Archbishop of Rouen betook himself to Germany, resigning the justiciarship into the hands of Hubert FitzWalter, who had been made Archbishop of Canterbury after the death of FitzJocelyn. It was Hubert who led home the crusading army during the king's journey and captivity in Germany. He had helped greatly in the raising of the ransom. It was, therefore, in the spirit both of trust in his fidelity and of gratitude for his services that Richard had nominated him for the archiepiscopal see. For the rest of the reign the predominant part in ruling England fell to him. He was made papal legate at the king's request, and retained the office of justiciar also till 1198. Though he had not shown the same indomitable front against the king's exactions as St Hugh of Lincoln and a few others had, he at last drew the line, and ranged himself with St Hugh and with Herbert Poore, Bishop of Sarum, in a regular constitutional opposition to the king's tyrannical imposts.

Hubert FitzWalter (1191-1205).

King Richard's short visit to England in 1194 was mainly taken up with various efforts to raise money. To his other expensive calls now came the need to find the rest of his ransom. His second coronation was not much more than a solemn protest of his sovereignty after the homage which had been forced from him by the emperor. He demanded from a great council that Prince John should be outlawed, but in the end generously forgave him. His mind was still set upon another crusade, but the opposition of the emperor, and the hostile action of Philip Augustus of France, frustrated his plans. Philip had invaded the duchy of Normandy. So, leaving England before the end of 1194, he attacked the forces of the French king at Gisors with considerable success. Philip Augustus himself was in considerable danger of death by drowning before he could get away in headlong flight. It must have been a lively satisfaction to Cœur de Lion to have put to flight in this fashion the rival who had done so much to spoil his career in Palestine. Nevertheless, the operations of war did not all go in favour of the English. There were four years of exhausting and desultory warfare without any lasting result on either side, first between the forces of the two monarchs of France and England, and then between Richard and his insubordinate vassals. Meanwhile, England itself, though free from the disturbance of any war at home, was oppressed by heavy taxation to pay for the king's foreign campaigns. Archbishop Hubert FitzWalter, who acted in the double capacity of justiciar from 1194 to 1198, and likewise of papal legate in 1195, was practically the governor of England for half the reign. He was a conscientious man, who strove to strike the mean between an excessive severity in exacting from the people what the king demanded and unreasonable resistance to his will. He succeeded in pleasing neither monarch nor subjects. At the Council of Oxford in 1198 he presented a demand for a levy of three hundred knights with the money needed to maintain them for a campaign in France. This was resisted by St Hugh of Lincoln and Bishop Herbert Poore of Sarum, who made him eventually withdraw the demand. Soon after he resigned the justiciarship, and was succeeded by Earl Geoffrey FitzPeter. The financial pressure continued, as did the consequent discontent, when early next year came the unexpected news that Richard had perished in an attempt to storm the Castle of Châluz, where he believed that one of his vassals had secreted a treasure which, he held, was his by right. He was shot from the walls by an archer, and his wound was unskilfully treated, so it was said, by the surgeon. Symptoms that his wound was mortifying, warned the king of the approach of death. He sent for his confessor, received the Sacraments in the most penitent disposition, and calling for the archer whose bolt had stricken him to death, forgave him, and, further, gave him his liberty.. It is said that Richard's mercenary soldiers set upon the man secretly in spite of this, and had him flayed alive. Richard was buried in the Abbey Church of Fontevrault at the feet

Richard I. in France.

of the father whom he had formerly treated so undutifully. But his heart, the Lion Heart which gave him his surname, was sent to Rouen to mark his sense of that city's loyalty to him.

(B) THE REIGN OF KING JOHN (1199-1216).

Richard left no legitimate children, so that his crown, according to the strict laws of hereditary descent, would fall to Arthur, son of his elder brother, Geoffrey, who had married Constance of Brittany. But Constance had unwisely alienated the goodwill of Richard, and old Queen Eleanor was urgent in pressing the claims of her younger son, John. John found those who were around him at the death-bed of Richard hostile to his claims. Nevertheless, having first of all secured whatever royal treasure he could at Chinon, he passed on to Rouen, where he got himself acknowledged by the archbishop and barons as Duke of Normandy. Then he crossed over into England. Fortunately for his success, Archbishop Hubert took up his cause and gathered a council at Northampton, where the assembled nobles elected him as rightful heir to the crown. He then proceeded to Westminster, and in the abbey church the archbishop crowned him with the similar rites and pomp to what had been used in the case of Richard. Hubert on this occasion made a remarkable speech, in which he declared that the election of the nation, after the grace of the Holy Ghost had been invoked, conferred the right to reign. John then took the usual oath to govern well, respecting the liberties both of the Church and of the people. Hubert was once more made Lord Chancellor, and it seemed, at first as if the Primate would be able to keep up that honest administration of the realm, which he had carried on in the latter part of the preceding reign. But, in reality, things were very much changed. John was a man of very different stamp from his brother. Moreover, though there was no open breach between him and the archbishop, it was remembered that they had strongly opposed one another in policy; and John was not likely to forget this.

King John (1199-1216).

The attention of King John was absorbed for the first years of his reign by the state of affairs in his continental dominions, which had been left by his brother in a very unsettled state. The change of monarchs in England meant a resumption of hostilities on the part of the King of France. He was encouraged to this not only because he had no longer to deal with such an experienced soldier as Richard, but also by the opportunity afforded him of embracing the cause of Prince Arthur of Brittany, whose claims to the English crown had not been abandoned. From 1200 until 1206 there was a series of campaigns in Normandy and in Poitou. John won some partial successes and captured Prince Arthur, who was first imprisoned in Rouen Castle, and then put to death. It is to be feared that this cruel execution was carried out either by John's orders or with his connivance. But the end of the contest meant disaster to the English king. Up to 1206, it is true, he struggled fitfully to maintain his hold, but at that date when his levies would not embark from England to his assistance, and the armies of the French king pressed on, he was obliged to listen to the voice of the Pope, who had been striving for years to mediate between Philip Augustus and John. In 1203 Innocent III. sent the Abbot of Casamari to France to decide the dispute between the rival sovereigns. Philip at first declined to negotiate, and the abbot passed into England, where he met the clergy at a council held in London in 1204. He was able to take back with him certain definite proposals for peace. But Philip would not wait, and it was only when the whole of Normandy and Anjou had fallen into his hands that the war was brought to a standstill. On the 13th of October, 1206, a truce for two years was concluded, which was nearly all in favour of the French. These adversities seem to have embittered and worsened John's character to a considerable degree. Henceforward he had to be contented with England alone as his sphere, unless his somewhat shadowy hold on Scotland or Ireland could be claimed as any extension of his power. The result was to bring him face to face with the nation as a whole, represented by its prelates and its barons. This was so to an extent that had never been experienced by his predecessors. Thus the way was prepared for the great constitutional struggle, which ended in the concession

Loss of the Duchy of Normandy.

of Magna Charta, and in a great limitation of the royal power.

The brightest light in the Church in England was extinguished in the year after John's accession through the death of St Hugh of Lincoln. The general veneration in which he was held obliged even John to treat him with respect. How far these outward signs of honour corresponded with his inner feelings is not so easy to determine. Anyhow, the king sent for him to be present at the Peace of Les Andelys, which put an end, at least temporarily, to the war between him and the French monarch. Hugh took advantage of this royal summons to visit once again the Grande Chartreuse, as well as the two great abbeys of Cluny and Citeaux. He then set out to go home to his diocese, and the journey became almost like a regal progress, so great were the testimonies of popular love and esteem which were thrown at his feet. He never reached Lincoln alive, for he took ill at his house, known as Lincoln House, near Lincoln's Inn Fields, in London, and there he expired on the 16th of November, 1200. His remains were carried in procession to his cathedral church, and there buried in a noble tomb. But the shrine was rifled at the Reformation, and all efforts to trace his relics have been fruitless.

Death of St Hugh of Lincoln (1200).

Hubert FitzWalter, the Primate, survived for a few years longer, and in the very year in which St Hugh died held a National Council at Lambeth, nothwithstanding the opposition of Earl FitzPeter, the justiciar. Besides the promulgation for England of legislation of the Universal Church passed in councils held on the continent, decrees were made upon the manner of decorously conducting the Divine offices, upon the marriage laws, and forbidding priests to say Mass more than once a day. The archbishop presided at a second coronation of the king together with his queen, Isabella, in 1201, and after the rite was over, he entertained the royal pair in high state at Lambeth Palace, which he had fought hard to make a centre of ecclesiastical life and government. Hubert was a skilful counsellor for the realm, deeply versed in its laws and customs. His long career was brought to an end in

Death of Archbishop Hubert (1205).

1205, when he died. At West Dereham in Norfolk, his birthplace, he founded a house of Premonstratensian Canons, and likewise began a Cistercian foundation at Wolverhampton. The work of bringing the Thames waters round the Tower of London by deepening the moat is also ascribed to him.

The Christchurch monks had their choice of a successor to Hubert already made before the Primate was buried. Their selection was Reginald, sub-prior of their house, and they strove to manage the affair so secretly that they would have him confirmed by the Pope before either king or bishops could interfere. But John had his own candidate. This was Bishop John de Grey of Norwich, whom he now wished to translate to Canterbury. The matter was therefore referred to Pope Innocent III., who, after hearing both sides in the matter, set aside both the candidates, and recommended the election of Stephen Langton, who was already a cardinal, and one of the chief scholars in the Papal Curia. This recommendation was acted on by the monastic chapter at Canterbury, and the Pope himself consecrated Langton at Viterbo on the 16th of May, 1207.

Cardinal Stephen Langton, Primate.

In this way Innocent joined issue with the king, and in the end proved himself more than a match for the English monarch, whose conduct was partly weakness and partly arbitrary violence. Of course, John refused to receive Langton as Primate, and practically dared the Pontiff to do his worst. Further, as an earnest of the lengths to which he was prepared to go, he sent an armed force to drive out the monks of Christchurch from their house. He seized their possessions, and the community had to take refuge beyond the seas. The Pontiff now commissioned the three Bishops of London, Ely, and Worcester to seek an interview with the king, and endeavour to bring him to terms. Failing in this, they were to publish an interdict over the whole country in the Pope's name. They were badly received by John, who refused all accommodation. The consequence was that in Lent, 1208, they put the kingdom under interdict, and forthwith departed from the country. For the most part, the interdict was observed; but there was a minority of whom the most celebrated was De Grey, Bishop of Norwich, who disregarded it. John himself was enraged beyond measure, and retaliated by a general seizure of all the goods of the clergy he could lay hands upon. In the following year Innocent followed up his previous blow by a sentence of excommunication against King John, which he ordered to be published in every cathedral and monastery of the land. Hampered by the interdict, and harassed by the officers of the crown, many of the clergy left England, and the general discontent grew apace. Moreover, the Pope had still another weapon in his armoury for use in the struggle. In 1211 he proclaimed that unless the king submitted he would absolve his subjects from their allegiance, depose him, and commit the execution of the sentence to Philip Augustus, King of France. This brought the disaffection to a head, and thoroughly frightened John. He was reminded how his nephew, the Emperor Otho, had gone down before the Pontifical authority in somewhat similar circumstances; he learnt that Philip Augustus was preparing an army to carry out the papal commission; and he could not count on the support of his subjects: he therefore decided upon complete submission, at least in outward seeming. Then, having made up his mind to this, he acted at once. He begged that a papal envoy might be sent to him. Pandolf, a subdeacon of the Roman Church, was despatched to England, and at Dover on the 13th of May, 1213, the king and the nuncio met. John made his submission to the Pope, resigning the crowns of England and Ireland into the hands of his envoy, afterwards receiving them back as a vassal, taking at the same time an oath of fealty to the Sovereign Pontiff. He likewise agreed to accept Langton as Primate, and to take back the bishops and clergy who had fled from the kingdom. All this was consigned to writing in a document sealed with the Great Seal, which Pandolf took with him when he started on his return journey.

But John had still his barons to deal with. They had been fairly passive amid the spoliation of the goods of the Church, but they felt their own turn would come; in fact the hand of the oppressor had begun to touch their possessions already. Over and over again exorbitant taxation had been levied upon them in spite of their protests, which had been strongly voiced, especially by Geoffrey Plantagenet, Archbishop of York, some time before his death. During these years they had been fined for not going to war, while the king had taken money from his enemies to keep the peace.

Hence, when John, having settled with Rome, prepared for a military expedition on a large scale into France, the barons refused to accompany him. They would serve in England; their feudal duty did not oblige them to do so beyond the seas. Filled with indignation, the monarch made ready to take summary vengeance on the malcontents; but, whether the means to execute his threats failed at the last moment, or he was persuaded by his advisers to bide his time, the year 1213 came to an end before his plans were in any way advanced. Meanwhile, the Primate and the chief barons held a series of meetings or councils to consult on what could be done to keep the king within the limits of the Constitution. The first of these meetings took place at St Albans on the 4th of August, 1213, and a supplementary gathering was held in St Paul's at London on the 25th following. Earl FitzPeter, the justiciar, who had hitherto been the leader of the barons, just as Langton had led the clergy, died at this juncture, and the king's action in consequence of this angered his opponents exceedingly. He made Peter des Roches, a foreign ecclesiastic, who as Bishop of Winchester had supported John in his resistance to the interdict, justiciar in room of FitzPeter, and there was no chance that he, like FitzPeter, would be at the head of any movement for constitutional liberty. King John moved towards the North to punish those tenants who had refused to follow him to the war in Flanders. But he again found himself face to face with Langton, who boldly stated the barons' case, and threatened that he would excommunicate him if he took hostile action against them against the laws and customs of the realm. John turned back upon this, and having now made peace with Rome, once again doing homage to the papal legate, Nicholas of Tusculum, believed he could safely proceed to the Continent to conduct the warlike operations he had planned in Flanders. This was in 1214, the year when, in the course of an unsuccessful campaign, he lost the battle of Bouvines. After this, through the intervention of the papal envoy, an Englishman, Cardinal Curzon, an accommodation was come to, between King John and the French monarch.

At home in England John so far had not really settled with the barons at all. They continued a series of meetings, at which they gradually elaborated the conditions they looked upon as necessary for securing the peace of the kingdom and the observance of the laws. When they met at Bury St Edmunds they came to the decision, which was a long step towards civil war, to maintain a sufficient armed force to back up their demands until they obtained redress. John strove by various expedients to sow dissension in their ranks. To detach the clergy from the rest, he published a charter granting them freedom of election to all benefices. He also took a vow to go on the Crusade, that it might thus become a sacrilege to attack him in arms. But, just then, clergy and barons could not be divided: they held together, and furthermore won for their policy the valuable support of London, and even of some members of the royal court. Yielding then at last to the inevitable, the king met barons and clergy at Runnymede near Windsor on the 15th of June, 1215, and there publicly signed and sealed that long enumeration of liberties and of privileges which we know as *Magna Charta*. The freedom of the Church was put in the forefront of its provisions, the king engaging to respect the liberty of election to benefices, especially to bishoprics, as well as all the customary privileges which the clergy enjoyed. **Magna Charta (1215).** Then, following up this commencement, the charter embraced the rights of all orders in the nation, in whose name the bishops and the barons were acting. It provided for the consent of the estates being given for the levying of taxation, at the same time defining and limiting the feudal aids which the monarch could claim. It asserted the right of all to a fair trial, not at the king's court, but in a "fixed place." It reiterated the great principle: "No free man shall be taken or imprisoned, or disseised, or outlawed, or exiled, or any wise destroyed; nor will we go upon him, nor send upon him, but by the lawful judgment of his peers, or by the law of the land. We will sell, deny, or delay to no man right or justice." As a matter of fact the Magna Charta, based in the main on the Charter of Henry I., was not a code of new laws, but a confirmation and pretty complete statement of the old ones. On the one side stood Cardinal Langton, Robert FitzWalter, William Marshall, and most of the bishops and barons; with the king were the officials of the court, many of them foreigners, Pandolf, the papal nuncio, Simon of Apulia; lately made Bishop of Exeter, and Peter des Roches; Walter de Grey, Bishop of Worcester, and a few others seem to have tried to hold a middle position.

Unfortunately, it soon became evident that John had no intention of keeping to the engagements which he had taken. He appealed to the Pope against the barons. At first, Innocent III. having been given to understand by him that the concessions had been extorted by violence, found fault with what had been done, and wrote, exhorting the Primate to try and lead back the barons into the path of obedience to their sovereign. A letter of excommunication was entrusted to Pandolf, with whom were associated the Bishop of Winchester and the Abbot of Reading, which was to affect all those who should refuse to make peace with the king or who should disturb the peace of the nation. When all efforts to promote an arrangement had failed, though Langton had tried to act as peacemaker ever since the Charter was signed, the three prelates, acting on the Pope's instructions, published the excommunication. Langton had striven to prevent this sentence from being promulgated, but Pandolf took it on himself to suspend the archbishop, and soon after left England to attend the Fourth Ecumenical Council of the Lateran. To this Council the barons now appealed. However, before anything could come of this, war broke out in England, and John took full advantage of the division in the ranks of his opponents to which the excommunication had given rise; the bishops could no longer take an active part against him, and even some of the barons wavered. John's military measures were well planned and carried out with energy; so that the leaders of the baronial party were almost reduced to despair.

Struggles after the Charter.

The tyranny and infamous behaviour of the king must have sunk deep into the minds of the barons to lead them to do what they now did. This was to cast off their allegiance to him, and to offer the crown of England to Louis, son of Philip Augustus, King of France. Gualo, the papal legate in that country, did his uttermost to dissuade the French court from listening to the proposal. It was all the same accepted by them, and Louis landed in England on the 21st of May, 1216. He was soon able to put himself at the head of a considerable army, and the tide of war began to turn against John. Louis took possession of London, and then in succession went on to establish himself in the South, the East, and the North. Little beyond the Western counties remained to the English monarch. Still, he doubled on his enemies with a kind of desperation, and was able to push forward into Lincolnshire. From there he led his army across the borders of the Wash, but at Sleaford took ill, and had to halt. Hearing that Pope Innocent III. was dead, he wrote to his successor, Honorius III., recommending his children to the papal protection. Then, when he made an effort to advance again, at Newark he felt that his end was approaching. He sent for a Confessor, and also made a short will, in which he appointed his son, Henry, to be king after him, and ordered his body to be buried in Worcester Cathedral, hard by St Wolstan's shrine. On the 19th of October he breathed his last, leaving the reputation of being the worst king who had hitherto sat on the throne of England.

Death of King John (1216).

XVII.

THE CHURCH UNDER HENRY III.

(1216-1272.)

HENRY III., son and heir of John Lackland, was a child of barely ten years of age when the news of that monarch's death became known. He was crowned at Gloucester with a plain circlet of gold, the regalia having perished in the Wash. Gualo, who was now papal legate, officiated, and the Bishops of Winchester, Exeter, and Bath and Wells assisted at the rite. The young boy was made to take the usual constitutional oath and to do homage to the Pope. William Marshall, Earl of Pembroke, was entrusted with the guardianship of both king and kingdom. Langton, of course, was out of the country, and somewhat under a cloud. A large portion of England was to all appearance under the power of the French prince, Louis; but before very long the foreign aspirant was shaken off, and the throne secured for young Henry. For the effect of the letter which John had written to beg the protection of Honorius III. for his children was that the legate felt empowered consistently to support his claims.

Accession of Henry III.

It did not take Gualo more than about three weeks to gather together a council at Bristol, which was attended by eleven bishops as well as by a large number of lesser prelates and barons. Here the oath of allegiance was exacted from both clergy and laity, fealty was sworn, and a revised edition of the Magna Charta solemnly ratified. Furthermore, an excommunication was launched against all who should continue to support Louis. As soon as a reply could be given from Rome,

The legate intervenes for Henry.

CHURCH UNDER HENRY III. 213

Pope Honorius wrote, encouraging Gualo to work in Henry's interest, and strengthening him with the fullest powers for that purpose. He also condemned the oath of allegiance to Louis which many had already taken. These measures, which meant a practical assumption of control on the part of the Holy See over the affairs of the kingdom, ended by bringing over many waverers to Henry's side. Furthermore, the death of John, making an end of his intolerable despotism, allowed the memory of his evil reign to become fainter. Nor were there wanting grounds of national offence occasioned by the behaviour of Louis's French followers. Though it looked at first as if England would have to pass through a period of divided allegiance to two sovereigns, in reality this was not of long duration. After William Marshall had defeated the French in the battle called the Fair of Lincoln in 1217, and Hubert de Burgh had beaten their fleet at sea, Louis was glad to sign the Treaty of Lambeth, which pledged him to retire from the contest. After this Gualo absolved him from the excommunication which he had incurred, and Louis quitted England for ever.

Cardinal Langton was absent from the country until 1218. He had gone to Rome to ask for the removal of the suspension which the legate had subjected him to. Nor was there any other representative of the English episcopate who could in any way compete with the papal envoy in his influence on public affairs. The see of York had just fallen to Walter de Grey, who had been one of John's chief supporters both at Runnymede and elsewhere. He swayed the destinies of the metropolitan see of the North for forty years (1215-1255). His suffragan at Durham was the learned Richard Marsh, who was also an earnest reformer of abuses. But he only lived until the year 1226. He was then replaced in St Cuthbert's chair by Richard Poore, his friend, the most distinguished member of a great episcopal family. It will be remembered that Richard of Ilchester, who had been in the front rank of the legal counsellors, conspicuous on the king's side in the early years of Henry II., was made Bishop of Winchester in 1174. He was there for fourteen years until his death, which happened in 1188. It is remarkable that two of his sons eventually became bishops. Richard was then dead, but probably

214   THE CHURCH IN ENGLAND

An episcopal family. his powerful influence had been used to procure for them some of their earlier benefices. Herbert Poore, the elder of the two, was consecrated as Bishop of Old Sarum in 1194, and held this see until 1217. Before he died he had begun to arrange for the transfer of the diocese from Old Sarum, where there was a royal fortress to New Sarum or Salisbury, but he did not survive to carry out the contemplated changes. This was accomplished by his younger brother and successor, Richard. It had been proposed to choose Richard for the still more important diocese of Winchester. But adverse influences had prevailed, and Innocent III. had himself confirmed the election of Peter des Roches, an Angevin, who, being consecrated by the Pope, held the diocese of Winchester for forty years. During this time he was the main support of the foreign party whose policy was so bitterly opposed by Hubert de Burgh and the other national leaders. Instead of Winchester, Richard Poore was given Chichester, until in 1217 he was translated to the see of his deceased brother, Herbert, at Old Sarum. A new site having been selected, Bishop Richard proceeded to undertake one of the greatest architectural feats of his own or of any other age in the erection of the present magnificent cathedral of Salisbury. He lived to see the dedication of the Lady Chapel, but not the completion of the whole church. Yet the plan which was carried out was undoubtedly his, so that he has provided an almost unique example of a great Gothic minster all built in one and the same style. In another sphere we probably owe to Richard Poore a monument of mediaeval life in England almost as well known. This is the *Ancren Riwle*, or rule, for female recluses, which is one of the best examples of the English language of the period which we possess. Richard passed to the see of Durham for the last eight years of his life, and died in 1237.

Pandolf as legate. In 1218 the legate, Gualo, was replaced by Pandolf, who had been the Pope's envoy, though with more limited powers, in John's time. He now came with full faculties, of a *legatus a latere*, and with instructions to do all that was possible to effect a full settlement of the outstanding questions in Church and State. It happened that the great Earl of Pembroke, the king's guardian, died in 1219, the year after Pandolf's arrival, and thus it came to pass that Pandolf had to take the lead in secular affairs as well as in those directly affecting the Church. He had to endeavour to keep the balance between two statesmen who represented rival parties now brought into violent opposition. One of these was Peter des Roches, Bishop of Winchester, who had identified himself with the continental interests of the monarchy; the other was Hubert de Burgh, who made himself the champion of English interests as paramount, and resisted any attempt to subordinate them to a policy dictated from Anjou or from any other part of Europe. From this time until his recall in 1221, it is scarcely an exaggeration to say that Pandolf was the real ruler of England. The proofs that he acted in this way with a generally admitted supreme authority, as legate in an acknowledged fief of the Holy See, are overwhelming. The Earl of Pembroke had in dying handed over his trust as guardian of the kingdom, though not of the king, to him; and he was able to assert his superiority over both the rivals, Des Roches and De Burgh.

An influence which was adverse to the long continuance of Pandolf's government of the country on these lines appeared when Cardinal Langton, no longer in disfavour at Rome, returned from his exile in 1220. Pandolf had been appointed Bishop of Norwich, which was a suffragan see of Canterbury, and, though not yet consecrated, acted as bishop of the diocese in everything in which orders were not required. But he hardly treated Langton as his metropolitan. He was present, as well as the archbishop, at the second coronation of the king in 1220, and there is no doubt that Langton felt his being in England as legate as a derogation from his own unimpeded exercise of the customary powers of Primate. Immediately after the coronation Langton once more set out for Rome, and the object of his journey was apparent, when at his coming to England in the following year, loaded with privileges from the Holy See, Pandolf was called back to Rome, and no other legate was sent in Langton's time. Pandolf was consecrated by the Pope himself as Bishop of Norwich, after he had reached the papal court, where the rest of his life was spent. After his death, however, his remains were brought back to England and interred in Norwich Cathedral.

Council of Osney (1222). Delivered from the presence of the legate, Langton was able to preside in the traditional manner of his predecessors over the assemblies of the clergy, and in 1222 held a Provincial Council at Osney Abbey near Oxford, which for importance in Church affairs has been sometimes compared to that of the meeting at Runnymede in the general history of the constitution. It produced, in fact, quite a code of ecclesiastical legislation; all classes of the Church's children are dealt with. Bishops have their duties pointed out to them; they must be charitable to their flock, reside in their sees, be present at the offices in their cathedral on Feasts, and even spare time for the hearing of confessions. The parochial clergy are urged to feed their flock with the Word of God, to visit the sick, and to have everything in good order in their churches. None are to have the care of parishes but such as will reside in their cures. Secular pomp, incontinence, and a worldly way of life must be carefully avoided. The Sacraments must be administered with care, and those who have not been confirmed must take the best opportunity that offers of receiving the holy unction. Special laws are issued to secure regular observance by those who live in the religious state. In applying these statutes to their own dioceses some zealous bishops, such as Richard Poore of Salisbury, made additions, but the hope of Cardinal Langton and his suffragans was that faithful adherence to this legislation made in common would lead to a high and uniform standard of discipline in the whole province.

Policy of Hubert de Burgh. For the remaining six years of his life Langton was able to wield a preponderating influence in the affairs of the Church, and to some extent in those of the State as well. Peter des Roches and Hubert de Burgh were still contending for the mastery over the royal policy. At last Hubert was able effectively to paralyse the party of which his rival was the head, and the bishop under the pretext of going on the Crusade left England. De Burgh was now for several years supreme in the government of the kingdom. Aided at first by the general support which

CHURCH UNDER HENRY III. 217

Cardinal Langton gave him, he tried to steer a middle course between the despotic views of the extreme royalists, and the opposed feudal theories of the barons. He managed to keep the peace with France, and at the same time to uphold the efforts of the national party to exclude foreigners from dominating affairs at home. The same moderation was seen in the distinction he observed between paying no regard to the representatives of the Pope, and yielding without protest to all their demands for money and temporal benefits, which now began to be unpleasantly exacting. Even when death deprived him of the prudent co-operation of Langton in 1228, he was still able to retain the management of public affairs for a few years more.

The patriotic and high-souled Primate, who had made his brother, Simon, Archdeacon of Canterbury, and in the last years of his life had been greatly aided by him in his work, had deserved well both of Canterbury and of England. He was a scholar as well, and the familiar division of the Bible into chapters is ascribed to him. He died at his manor of Slindon, but his remains were brought to his cathedral for interment. There was to all intents and purposes a somewhat lengthy interval before there was a Primate ready to take up the high duties of the archbishopric. The nominee of the monks of Christchurch was not accepted by the king or the bishops, and when the matter was referred to Pope Gregory IX. it is said that a theological examination proved the unfitness of the candidate. Richard Grant, Chancellor of Lincoln, was then proposed by the royal envoys instead. No exception could be taken to him on personal grounds, and the Pontiff accepted this choice. Richard was consecrated at Canterbury by Henry Sandford, Bishop of Rochester, in the presence of the king and a great assembly, but having gone to Rome to defend the rights of his see, he took ill and died on the return journey in 1231. Thereupon the dispute as to the right of election was enkindled anew between the monks, the bishops, and the crown. Several candidates were offered, one after the other for papal approval, the most celebrated of whom was Ralph Neville, Bishop of Chichester. These were all rejected in turn, Simon Langton being at this time the principal adviser of the Pope in English affairs.

After these repeated failures the Pontiff determined to take the matter into his own hands, and having made careful inquiries, recommended Edmund Rich, treasurer of the diocese of Salisbury. In 1233 he was proposed to the chapter, accepted by them and confirmed by the Pope. In the following year he was consecrated by Roger Niger, Bishop of London, in the presence of the king and thirteen bishops. The pallium was at once sent from Rome.

The pious cleric, who was thus installed in the great primatial see, was he whom all Catholic England now looks on as one of its national saints and patrons under the name of St Edmund of Canterbury. He was the son of poor townspeople at Abingdon, and from his earliest infancy had been trained in piety by his excellent mother, Mabel. When his childhood passed into youth, he was sent to pursue his studies at Oxford and then at Paris. Long years were spent in the will to "scorn delights and live laborious days" at these two homes of learning. Edmund was a thorough scholastic, and once his own brilliant course of learning was completed, he was chosen to lecture on Aristotle at Oxford, being, it is said, the first to explain the Greek philosopher's writings in that university. He also accepted a canonry in Bishop Poore's new Chapter at Salisbury, but it is not at all certain that this meant the cessation of his work as a teacher, for dispensations, if necessary, from constant residence were frequently obtained for such reasons. But some time later the office of treasurer of Salisbury was also conferred on him. This he held until messengers came to seek him out in his prebend at Colne with the overwhelming news that he was chosen to fill the great see over which St Augustine and St Thomas Becket had presided. It was rather with fear and trepidation than with joy that he bowed to the Divine Will.

St Edmund of Canterbury.

It was not for nothing that St Edmund had been raised to high station. A leader was badly needed both for the clergy and for the nation, torn as it was with the quarrels of contending factions; he felt bound to put himself at the head of the popular party. In 1232 Peter des Roches, by making himself the champion both of the royal

Policy of St Edmund.

CHURCH UNDER HENRY III. 219

authority and the more extreme papal claims in the matter of taxation, had accomplished his rival's downfall. Hubert de Burgh was dismissed and then put into prison. But a Nemesis was at hand, which in a few years reached Des Roches and hurled him from his pinnacle. Richard Marshall, son of the great Earl of Pembroke, took the lead in a large assembly of the barons, and St Edmund with other bishops undertook to support them. St Edmund in particular used the influence he enjoyed as Primate to admonish the king that there could be no tranquillity until Des Roches and the foreign counsellors were dismissed. For the time his advice was disregarded, with the result that civil war broke out. Richard Marshall was killed, but the strength of the opposition was by no means broken. Edmund now returned to the charge with the king, and finally won his way. Peter des Roches was sent home to his diocese, Hubert de Burgh was restored to liberty and to his estates, and the king announced that he would take the government into his own hands.

There was now a short breathing-space in public affairs which enabled St Edmund to devote his attention to the administration of his diocese. In 1234 he undertook a systematic and careful visitation of it all. Wherever he went he was accompanied by his brother and faithful companion, Robert Rich, by his chaplain and biographer, Eustace, by his chancellor, the saintly Richard de la Wych, and by several Dominican friars. Yet he did not commit to these attendants all personal audiences with his flock, but was accessible to all and always. Then he was able on several occasions to provide the vacant dioceses of England with new pastors. It must have been a singular consolation to him to consecrate such a worthy bishop as his friend, Robert Grosseteste for Lincoln, the richest and most populous of all the land. The rite was performed at Reading Abbey on the 17th of June, 1235. Walter de Cantelupe had been consecrated by Pope Gregory himself, but it was St Edmund's privilege to enthrone him in Worcester Cathedral. Then, on the 14th of January, 1236, the routine of his ordinary work was broken by the splendid function of the marriage of King Henry with Eleanor of Provence, which he solemnised at Canterbury. He also officiated when the

St Edmund as Pastor.

queen was crowned at Westminster a week later amid scenes of unusual magnificence.

Close upon these festivities followed a great council of the realm held at Merton Abbey in Surrey, where the Archbishop met not only his episcopal brethren, but also King Henry and the barons. Several statutes were passed, but St Edmund's attempt to bring English law into harmony with that of the Church and the empire, in allowing subsequent marriage to make legitimate any children born to the parties before they were married, failed before the opposition of the barons, who then for the first time proclaimed the celebrated dictum: *Nolumus leges Angliæ mutari*. Turning his attention then to purely ecclesiastical legislation, St Edmund published in the course of the same year a body of forty-one Provincial Constitutions which by their practical character bear witness to his zeal in striving to find a remedy for the prevailing abuses of his day. They order that every care should be taken for the careful administration of the Sacraments, that the clergy should avoid drinking bouts and every kind of bad example, that every precaution should be taken to guard the lives of babes and young children, that all should go to Confession and Communion at Easter, and should have the opportunity of doing so at Christmas and Pentecost as well. Fortune-tellers, freebooters, and those who abuse the Sacraments are to be excommunicated. All wills are to be made in presence of the parish priest. All who live in any community or public institution must do so under an approved rule. The exemption of church property from the exactions of lay officials is once more affirmed. These are some of the leading prescriptions of a striking collection of decrees for the guidance of the clergy.

Council of Merton (1236).

The quiet persistency of the Archbishop in resisting any royal action which was not constitutional, and in voicing the reasonable complaints of the barons was by no means pleasing to King Henry. As a counterpoise, he took the expedient of asking the Pope to send a legate into the country. Gregory IX. at once acceded to the king's request, and Cardinal Otho landed in England in that capacity in July, 1237. He

The Legation of Cardinal Otho.

was an experienced diplomatist, and seems to have acted with moderation, but his presence was a source of great embarrassment to Edmund, especially as Otho acquired considerable influence over the king, and was successful in showing the need the Holy See had for financial assistance from England. When Otho thought he had made some progress towards a general pacification, he called a great council of the realm which met in St Paul's at London on the 19th of November, 1237. However, the Council had not proceeded far before strong opposition made itself felt. The legate had put forward the decree of the Lateran Council against the holding of several benefices by the same person when Walter de Cantelupe, Bishop of Worcester, who was the foremost prelate in the national party, rose and defended the plurality of benefices by all the arguments in his power. He foretold general resistance to the enforcement of the decree, and asked that the matter should be specially referred to the Pope. Otho seems to have yielded to this, and received later on a letter from Rome, counselling him to proceed in this matter with the greatest caution. When this difficulty had been put aside the rest of the business of the Council went on more smoothly, and a set of decrees was enacted which in importance may be fitly compared with the Constitutions of St Edmund. On the whole they refer more particularly to clerical discipline than those made by St Edmund, urging such matters as the duty of having churches, of keeping a register of ordinations, of examination for the clergy, while the Eves of Easter and Pentecost are pointed out as the fittest times for receiving the Sacrament of Baptism. Regulations are promised for the good order of religious houses. These last were given at a meeting of abbots which the legate convened in 1239.

The Archbishops of Canterbury and York were both present at the Council of London, but before 1237 was ended St Edmund had started for Rome to plead his cause in three different controversies in which, by this time, he had become involved. The first of these was his claim to certain rights over the possessions of Christchurch Abbey at Canterbury, which that community contended were exempt from the archiepiscopal jurisdiction. The second was his endeavour to use the right of visitation at the Abbey of Westminster. The third was occasioned by his claim that he and not the monks of Rochester had the right to choose the bishop of that see. Early in 1238 both the Archbishop and his adversaries had an opportunity of arguing their case before the Pontiff. However, it so turned out that St Edmund failed to gain a favourable reply to his representations. The case at Rochester was decided against him, as was also the exemption of the monks of Westminster from his visitation, while the decision in the long-drawn-out dispute with the Christchurch monks was again deferred. It is probable that St Edmund asked for the recall of Otho. But this recall only took place in 1241. Meanwhile, the saint, after a final and fruitless interview with Gregory IX., returned to England. As might have been expected, he went home to the turmoil of controversy and of preparation for civil war. For a while there was a lull in the dispute with the monks, but it was soon renewed upon another ground. St Edmund had gained leave from the Pope to make a new foundation for secular canons at Maidstone, meaning to build a new church and make a fitting endowment for it. But, here again the monks of Christchurch appealed, and the saint had to argue the point at length before the Holy See. In this case he was successful, and the Pope decided in his favour. The monks then had recourse to the king, and in this way were able to paralyse the Archbishop's action. He showed his ready acceptance of the papal decision by consecrating the monk's choice, Richard of Wendover, as Bishop of Rochester. It must have been with feelings of more intimate cordiality that he in 1239 consecrated his old friend, William Raleigh, for Norwich. There were intrigues and disputes over the other vacant sees of Lichfield and Hereford. But eventually for Lichfield the Archbishop agreed to consecrate Hugh Pateshull in 1240: Hereford had no bishop until after his death. The papal needs were increasing and the consequent demands for financial aid towards meeting them were growing also. Although St Edmund was not so outspoken in his opposition as was Grosseteste, he felt the burden of trying to meet these calls most acutely, and when to all this was added the civil discord provoked by the king's arbitrary conduct, he seems to have given up the contest against evil in despair as beyond his strength in his difficult position as Primate. About September, 1240, he left England secretly, and took refuge in the Abbey of Pontigny. There he remained until he fell into bad health, and it was hoped that a change of climate would benefit him. Under advice he now moved to Soissy, a dependency of the Abbey of Provins. But instead of rallying, his ebbing strength soon showed that his end was approaching. Sitting in a chair, not lying on a bed like other people, he prepared with a calm and joyful spirit for his last passage, receiving the Sacraments with devotion, and bequeathing what keepsakes he could to those who were dear to him. On his seal he had engraved " *Edmundum doceat, Mors mea ne timeat* " round the representation of the martyrdom of St Thomas. And indeed his end was without fear or pain. He expired on the 16th of November, 1240. His relics remain the most striking treasure of the abbey church at Pontigny. Besides his *Provincial Constitutions*, we owe to him an ascetical treatise called *Speculum Ecclesiæ*. {Death of St Edmund (1240).}

It is hard to disjoin from St Edmund's history that of his friend and chancellor, St Richard de la Wych, although to relate it means to anticipate a few years. By itself it would form a romantic but somewhat detached episode. Born in Droitwich about 1197, he pursued his studies at Oxford and Paris in the midst of such poverty that he and his companions had but one cloak between them, which they used for alternate attendance at the public lectures. Yet Richard gained his university degrees with honour, and was early marked out by the observant eye of his master, Edmund Rich, as a young man of high promise. Later on, when the primate's throne was filled by the same saintly professor, he was chosen by him as chancellor of the diocese. An equally tempting offer was made to him by the great Grosseteste, but Richard preferred the household of Edmund. Henceforth they went side by side both at home and abroad. Richard took Edmund as the model of his life, and was in attendance at his saintly death. He then retired to prepare himself for the priesthood, and once ordained, came home to England, where in succession he filled the {St Richard of Chichester (1199-1253).}

offices of Vicar of Deal and Rector of Charing in Kent.
For a while he was persuaded to take up again the duties
of Chancellor of Canterbury. Then in 1244, when Ralph
Neville, Bishop of Chichester, died, the Primate recommended Richard to the Chapter of that see. Henry III.
had his candidate, Hugh Passelaw, and being vexed that
he should be passed over, deprived Richard for two years
of the revenues of the see. But Richard appealed to the
Pope, Innocent IV., who threatened the king with an
interdict if he should fail to yield the bishop his rights.
This was effectual, and Richard was able to take possession. His remaining years were spent in the most exemplary discharge of his duties in the government of his
diocese. He published many excellent rules for the good
order of Divine Worship, and other equally salutary ones
for the moral good of his flock. He was able, besides this,
to carry out various improvements in the fabric of
Chichester Cathedral. His part was an important one
in the labour of establishing the Dominican friars in
England, and like St Edmund he willingly consorted with
them. Still his life as a bishop was all too short.
Though in bad health in 1253, it came to pass that
being invited to dedicate a new church in honour of
his hero, St Edmund of Canterbury, he could not be
persuaded to refuse a request so dear to his heart. But
the effort was beyond his strength, and on the very next
day he died. He was buried in Chichester Cathedral,
where his elegant shrine and effigy are still to be seen.
He was canonised by Urban IV. in 1261.

The death of St Edmund left a great void in the
primacy, which was only tardily and imperfectly filled
by the election of his successor. The
B. Boniface of Savoy. opportunity seemed to Henry III. to offer
itself for recommending to the electors
Boniface of Savoy, the uncle of Queen Isabella. The
Pope needed the king's help and was disposed to agree,
though the monks at Canterbury knew nothing of him
except his royal lineage. But, in truth, his past history
had been an edifying one; he had joined the Order of
St Bruno at the Grande Chartreuse in his youth, and
then had been appointed Bishop of Belley, but not consecrated. He reached England for the first time in 1244,
and soon left again to be present at the Council of
Lyons in 1245. Here he was consecrated by Innocent IV.

CHURCH UNDER HENRY III. 225

in person, as was St Richard a few months later. But it was 1249 before he again set foot in England, and many struggles had taken place in the meantime under other leaders. In fact, Bishop Boniface was ill-qualified to be the champion of the Church in the country, being a foreigner and one so closely allied with the royal family. It was not merely a difference of birthplace: it meant divergence of policy and outlook. The papal demands for financial assistance had become still more pressing, and they were ill received by the clergy already heavily taxed for the needs of the king. A further burden was imposed as soon as Boniface took possession of his see, for he found that during the long interval the revenues had been seized and the buildings had become dilapidated. He at once set to work with vigour to repair all this and to pay off the debts of the diocese. He obtained from Innocent IV. a grant of the revenues of all vacant benefices in the diocese for some years for this purpose. The result was that he paid off twenty-two thousand marks, besides building the Great Hall at Lambeth Palace. Being a zealous promoter of discipline, he proceeded to make a canonical visitation of the whole province. The Canons of St Paul's refused any visitation save that of the Bishop of London, while at St Bartholomew's, Smithfield, things were carried further still. The community met him at the door, and a heated dispute took place. The legend is that the Archbishop struck the sub-prior to the ground, and being then set upon himself, only escaped with torn robes and ruffled dignity. Both parties appealed to the Pope as to the right of visitation, and after some time the archbishop again left the country. Naturally he was on the king's side in the Barons' War, but hardly filled a place in affairs commensurate with the traditions of his office. He died in Savoy in 1270 on his way to the Crusade of Edward I., and his *cultus* as Blessed was approved of by Gregory XVI. at the prayer of his kinsman, Charles Albert, King of Sardinia.

Walter Cantelupe, Bishop of Worcester from 1236 to 1266, was the most constant supporter of the popular or baronial party all through their struggle with the absolutism of Henry III., which culminated in the Barons' War. He was the counsellor who never failed them and never lost courage in the time of political

P

crisis. But in the ecclesiastical sphere the leader of the clergy both in their contests with the crown and in their protests against abuses in papal exactions was a still greater man. This was Robert Grosseteste, Bishop of Lincoln. From his lowly boyhood at the Suffolk village of Stradbroke, up through the various posts he held as professor and then chancellor at Oxford, as archdeacon and then as prebendary at Lincoln, he had always led a life of study. His reputation was that of being the most original thinker and foremost scientific writer of his day. His works attest the wide range of his acquirements. He was no mere commentator on the works of Aristotle, though he was evidently familiar with the works of that philosopher, neither was he a patient compiler of "Sentences of the Fathers." Nothing less than an encyclopædic grasp of the sum total of human knowledge could satisfy his capacious intellect. He essayed to classify all this in his work called *Compendium Scientiæ*, and wrote a great number of books on theology and other branches of science as contributions towards filling up this general plan. A small work on the difference between a regular monarchy and a tyranny furnished a theory and an inspiration to Simon de Montfort in his constitutional campaign. As Grosseteste approached old age his health began to fail, so that he resigned almost all his preferments, and devoted himself from 1232 to 1235 almost exclusively to study and religious occupations. Then in 1235, at the age of sixty, he suddenly emerged into the press of public life again by accepting the bishopric of Lincoln, which was by far the largest in England; and it was St Edmund whose hands consecrated him. After a few years, when that saint had passed out of this world, Grosseteste came to the front, and was seen in all his grandeur as the virtual leader of the English bishops in their public action. He had to fight for England, and he had to fight for the Church.

It would be a mistake to suppose that the appointment of foreigners to benefices in England came exclusively from the action of the Roman Curia. Henry III. was just as anxious to find livings for his relations and dependents from Anjou and Poitou as Innocent IV. was for Italians. This was resisted by Grosseteste and the

Robert Grosseteste, Bishop of Lincoln (1175-1253).

English clergy. The appointment of Boniface of Savoy made a beginning, but in the case of Winchester, William of Valence was rejected both by the Chapter and by the Holy See, and William de Raleigh was moved from Norwich instead. Another of Grosseteste's friends, St Richard, was made Bishop of Chichester in face of the royal nominee and of the royal opposition. King Henry was at war with St Louis, King of France, in Gascony and elsewhere, and his foreign expeditions ran him into debt, but when he summoned Parliament to furnish him with an aid in 1242, and again in 1244, he found the peers reluctant to incur further taxation. He went to the war indeed, leaving Walter de Grey, Archbishop of York, in charge of the kingdom. Still, his necessities soon forced him to come to terms with the bishops and the barons. A committee of twelve was appointed by the Parliament of 1244, including Boniface of Savoy, Cantelupe, and Grosseteste, besides Simon de Montfort and other leading barons, who drew up demands for a new charter, for a new ministry, and for the redress of other grievances as the price of new taxation. The discussion ended in a compromise, but the way had been prepared for more definite demands and a more determined struggle. While this was pending, came a nuncio from the Pope, who presented a most pressing demand for taxation to enable the Holy See to carry on its contest against the emperor, Frederic II. The insistence used by the nuncio, and the extent of the help asked for, seems to have greatly displeased Grosseteste and the rest of the clergy, already heavily taxed for the wars of the king. He was also involved in a dispute with his own dean and chapter, who disallowed his right of visitation. These reasons, no doubt, combined to make him set off for Lyons, where a council had been summoned for the following year, as early as November, 1244. His companion was his lifelong friend and former pupil, the learned Franciscan, Adam Marsh. The case against the chapter was soon won, the Pope giving him a bull which affirmed his right. But once in Lyons, Grosseteste remained for the Ecumenical Council of 1245. This great assembly was also attended by Boniface of Canterbury, by the Bishops of Worcester, Chichester, and Lichfield (the two last being consecrated at Lyons by the

Grosseteste's twofold contest.

Pope himself), and by a certain number of the inferior prelates from England. A solemn statement of grievances was made before the Fathers of the Council on the part of an English representative, in which above all the two points of excessive tribute to the Holy See and the provision of foreigners to English benefices were dwelt upon. Some impression was made by this both on Innocent IV., and on the Fathers of the Council, and vague promises were made that these things should be modified. It is to be feared, however, that they were not clear and thorough-going enough to content Grosseteste and those who agreed with him. He was thoroughly loyal to the authority of the Holy See, and could be no party to extremes, but he came home disappointed, albeit much impressed with the greatness and power of the Roman Church.

Grosseteste travelled a second time to Lyons in 1250 on other urgent business. He was an indefatigable visitor of his vast diocese, and out of this arose his perception of the need for the erection of an increased number of vicarages to care for the souls of the country-people who were far removed from the towns and monasteries. But his action in forming these new centres of spiritual life seems to have been opposed by the religious whose care these districts had hitherto been. The bishop wished to appeal to the Pope in order to carry his point. He had also been in collision with the rights assumed by Archbishop Boniface, and had in general a vivid sense of the evils from which the Church was suffering. He delivered a vigorous discourse on these matters before the Pontifical Court, but adverse influences seem to have prevented him from getting the satisfaction which he sought. When he came home he took up his battle against abuses with his old vigour, though with failing strength; he even refused to act upon a provision made by the Pope to a vacant canonry at Lincoln in favour of his nephew, Frederic 'de Lavagna. Even here he must not be regarded as an opponent of the lawful Papal Supremacy. He was clear-sighted enough to distinguish between the supreme power of the Pontiff at the head of Christendom and the incidental abuses of that power. What was left to him of life and strength he devoted to the care of his diocese, and in 1253 died and was buried in his cathedral church. When the coffin was opened in 1782, his crosier, paten, and chalice were found with his dust. Repeated efforts have been made to obtain his formal canonisation, but they have ended in failure. Yet, in popular language, and even in the writings of mediaeval scholars, he receives the appellation of St Robert of Lincoln.

By the time that Grosseteste had gone to his grave the celebrated popular champion, Simon de Montfort, had stepped into the front rank of political life. He had been for many years one of the greatest lords in England, but it was only in the latter stages of the struggle with Henry III. that he attained the full height of the leadership connected with his name. *Simon de Montfort.* He was the son of the great Catholic general in the Crusade against the Albigenses. He inherited the Earldom of Leicester, which his father had never been able to take possession of. He also inherited the ardent piety of his father, as well as, it must be allowed, his abilities, his ambition, and his spirit of adventure. Though under the disadvantage of being looked upon as a foreigner, he was able by the sheer force of his genius to lead the nation in its struggle for freedom against the absolutist government of the king. Henry had negotiated a marriage between him and his royal sister, Eleanor, the widow of William Marshall; and for a time he enjoyed the royal favour. At Rome he obtained a dispensation to make this marriage lawful, notwithstanding his bride's life in a convent, and in Palestine he took part in the Crusade of 1240. Returning to England, he was entrusted with the difficult task of governing Gascony, and in spite of the efforts of St Louis and the want of support at home, succeeded in keeping it for Henry. The final conflict between Henry and his barons was precipitated by the part the former took in the battle between the papacy and the empire. In order to have a counterbalancing force against the descendants of Frederic II., Pope Innocent IV. offered the crown of Sicily, which was a fief of the Holy See, to the English king. Henry accepted it for his second son, Edmund, but it was weighted with heavy conditions of pecuniary aid to the Pope. Hence, when the king put the case before Parliament with a demand for fresh and extravagant taxation, the whole scheme was disavowed, and he failed to obtain the large sums he asked for.

Discontent was growing apace, and next year (1258) a Parliament met at Oxford, called by the king's friends the *Mad Parliament*, which gave a commission of twenty-four prelates and barons the task of drawing up a scheme of reform known as the *Provisions of Oxford*. The share of De Montfort in this was a great one; three annual Parliaments were to meet, and a permanent council was to sit, by whose advice the king was to appoint his ministers and govern the kingdom. After much hesitation Henry consented to abide by the Provisions of Oxford, and the new system of administration lasted from 1258 until 1263. Still, there were elements at work which prevented it from being a permanent settlement.

It is evident that the new administration was rather of an aristocratic than of a popular character; its primary object was to check the misgovernment of the king. There was much dissension among the barons themselves. This led especially to keen rivalry between De Montfort and the powerful Earl of Gloucester. Moreover, the young Prince Edward now began to take part in public affairs, and at first threw in his lot with the barons against his father, the king. At last, in 1263, Gloucester being dead, and his son having gone over to the party of De Montfort, King Henry became reconciled with Prince Edward, and proposed that the barons should take an oath of allegiance to him. This was refused, and civil war broke out. Yet even then there were many, especially among the clergy, who strained every nerve to prevent actual hostilities. It was proposed to refer the questions at issue to the arbitration of St Louis, King of France. In deference to a very general wish, St Louis consented to mediate. His decision, given in the presence of King Henry and at least some of the barons, is known as the *Mise of Amiens*. It was mainly in Henry's favour, annulling the Provisions of Oxford, but declaring that all the previous charters must be maintained, and all present feuds given up. This was by no means satisfactory to the baronial leaders who knew their monarch better than St Louis did. They continued secretly to prepare for war. Actual hostilities began under the pretext of a war against the Welsh, but it is very hard to justify the conduct which disregarded the compromise arrived at, and strove to gain its ends by force of arms.

The Barons' War.

CHURCH UNDER HENRY III. 231

Yet the cause of the barons was popular, and they had a skilful military leader in De Montfort. On the 14th of May, 1264, at the battle of Lewes the royal army was defeated, both Henry and his son, Prince Edward, falling into the victor's hands. There was now further conference between the two sides, and by the *Mise of Lewes* the king recovered his liberty on the condition of accepting the Provisions of Oxford and abiding by the advice of his counsellors. Prince Edward was retained in captivity as a hostage for the king's fidelity to his promises. The chief counsellors appointed were De Montfort, the Earl of Gloucester and Berkstead, Bishop of Chichester. Hugh le Despenser became justiciar, and the saintly Thomas Cantelupe was made chancellor. They had at once to meet danger from abroad, where Queen Eleanor, with Earl de Warenne, Archbishop Boniface, and others, was preparing to invade England. The papal legate also threatened the barons with excommunication, and Simon Cantelupe and the other bishops had to appeal to the Pope against this formidable menace.

Meanwhile, under Simon de Montfort's influence, the celebrated Parliament of 1265 met at Westminster, where it held session for a considerable time in order to arrange for making permanent the engagements taken at the Mise of Lewes. **Simon De Montfort's Parliament.** Yet it is rather from its composition, representatives being summoned from the shires, cities, and boroughs as well as the peers, than from any lasting legislation, that this assembly has become so famous. In May, 1265, Prince Edward escaped from captivity, and in the rapidity with which he attacked the barons' forces in detail gave an earnest of his military talents. Finally, at the battle of Evesham in August of the same year he defeated Simon, who perished on the battlefield. Henry was now free from the barons' control, and proceeded to take vengeance on them by a general decree disinheriting all who had fought on their side. London and the Cinque Ports, which had been main supports of the barons, now submitted to the king. Still, the so-called *Disinherited* were prepared to offer the most desperate resistance. Their chief stronghold was Kenilworth Castle, an almost impregnable fortress to which the king had to lay siege. After six months of fruitless combat there was talk of a compromise. Three bishops and three barons were chosen to nominate as many more to act with them as arbitrators. Eventually their efforts resulted in an agreement known as the *Dictum of Kenilworth*, which affirmed the unlimited power of the king and the nullity of De Montfort's arrangements, but at the same time proclaimed the binding force of the charters, the freedom of the Church from the royal pretensions, and the means to be taken to remedy the real abuses spoken of in the Provisions of Oxford. One curious religious article was that which forbade men to venerate Simon de Montfort as a saint. Somewhat better terms still were granted in the Parliament held at Marlborough in the following year, and the *Disinherited* were relieved from their penalties on the payment of a fine. In this way the Barons' War came to an end, Henry III. henceforth reverting to a conciliatory and constitutional policy.

In 1270 Prince Edward started on a Crusade, and simultaneously there was an interval of peace in England. The restoration of Westminster Abbey was celebrated by an imposing function for the second translation of the relics of St Edward. All the bishops, many abbots, and a great gathering of earls and barons took part in the solemnity. This may be looked on as the national seal put upon the peace which had now been made between Henry and his rebellious subjects. Henry himself wished to go on the Crusade, for with all his faults he was a deeply religious man, and led a moral and Christian life. But when the question came up for discussion, Parliament intervened on the ground that his absence might endanger the peace so recently restored. The pilgrimage to the shrine of St Edmund the Martyr at Bury was a far safer enterprise. Apparently it was here that Henry III. breathed his last on the 16th of November, 1272. His body was borne thence for interment in the abbey he had restored at Westminster.

Death of Henry III.

XVIII.
EDWARD I.—THE ENGLISH JUSTINIAN.
(1272-1307.)

AT the moment of his father's death Edward, the eldest son, surnamed Longshanks, was still on his Crusade. The news of his succession to the English crown had been brought to the army not so long after the announcement that the papal legate, Theobald, Archdeacon of Liège, was elected Pope. But that zealous prelate had already gone to take up the burden of the papacy under the name of Gregory X. When Edward started homeward he had with him some of his best and bravest knights. He passed through Italy and France as in a triumphal procession, spent two days in Rome and then went on to Orvieto, where he was affectionately greeted by Gregory X. Everywhere he was acclaimed as a Christian hero and soldier of the Cross. Including a stay of some weeks at the papal court, and a still longer delay in France, it took him nearly two years to reach England, where he landed on the 2nd of August, 1274. He was crowned a fortnight later at Westminster with his Queen Eleanor, and immediately after the coronation called a Parliament together to deliberate upon the affairs demanding settlement in Wales, and upon other pressing business. He began his reign in the maturity of early middle life, having been born in 1239, and he was to rule England for thirty-five years, attaining an age which no subsequent English king did until the days of the Hanoverian Georges. He was well fitted to be leader and law-giver for the land which he ruled, being completely in sympathy with much of the temper and aspirations of the nation. His lapses from this attitude whether with regard to the Church or the State were but

Edward I. (1272-1307).

the temporary ebullitions of his masterful character for which he tried afterwards to make atonement.

He found the primacy in new hands, for Blessed Boniface of Savoy getting into bad odour with Henry III., and yet not being very acceptable to the nation at large, had once more retired to the Continent, where he died as stated above in 1270. The monks of Christchurch at once proceeded to elect their Prior Chittenden, but the choice was not ratified by the Pope. He appointed instead Robert Kilwardby, Provincial of the Dominicans, an eminent doctor of Paris and Oxford, whose works are still to be found in the great libraries in manuscript. Being allowed to choose his consecrator, he chose William Button, the saintly Bishop of Bath and Wells. Kilwardby attended the Council of Lyons in 1274, but returned home in time to crown the king. He then laboured conscientiously at his work as Primate, and gained a high reputation both for learning and for sanctity and love of the poor. He gave the Dominicans the convent at Baynard's Castle in London, since known as Blackfriars, but he did not take much part in the legislation of King Edward, who had other legal advisers more to his mind. In 1278 Nicholas III. made him Cardinal Bishop of Porto in the Papal Curia, and he left the country, taking with him curiously enough the Canterbury registers which have never been recovered. But he was too old to bear up against the change of climate, and died in the following year.

Cardinal Kilwardby (1273-9).

The Great Seal, held at Henry's death by John Kirkby, afterwards Bishop of Ely, was taken from him, and given to the Oxford scholar, Walter de Merton, even before Edward's return. But he only held it until the king was able to name as chancellor his chosen minister, Bishop Burnell. It is rather in the annals of education that in those of statesmanship that this learned man holds a notable place. He laboured long and well to promote the cause of education. As early as 1261 he set aside two manses at Merton in Surrey for the support of scholars in residence at the schools. In 1264 he drew up a set of statutes for the guidance of the pupils, and in 1274 transferred them from Merton to Oxford, where he established a college and endowed it for them under the name of Merton College.

Walter de Merton.

This is the earliest example of a strictly collegiate establishment in the University. Its foundation undoubtedly gives Walter a title to honourable mention in the history of the Catholic Church in England. Walter de Merton was made Bishop of Rochester, but died after three years of episcopate in 1277 from the effects of an accidental fall from his horse.

While Bishop Walter de Merton was shedding the light of his zeal for scholarship upon Oxford and its educational facilities, the See of Hereford was graced by the virtues of the noble prelate who may perhaps be called the Last of the English Saints. This was St Thomas Cantelupe, usually called after his diocese, St Thomas of Hereford. He was a kinsman of the chancellor, Simon Cantelupe, and a nephew of Walter Cantelupe, Bishop of Worcester, in the last reign. **St Thomas of Hereford (1219-1282).** He was brought up under his uncle's care, and had the great Dominican, Kilwardby, as his master at Oxford. After the end of the Barons' War he acted as chancellor for some time, but then resigned the charge, and returned to his studies at Paris and Oxford. But he never ceased to be a representative member of the English clergy, and assisted at the two Councils of Lyons in 1245 and in 1274. It was only in 1275, after his return from the latter, that he was chosen to succeed John Bredon as Bishop of Hereford. He held the see for seven years until his death in 1282. Mild and gentle as he was in his private life, the English bishops thought him a doughty champion enough to proceed in their name to Rome with their appeal against what they considered to be an unjustifiable interference with their rights on the part of the Archbishop of Canterbury, John Peckham. He pleaded their cause so successfully with the Sovereign Pontiff that a decision was given in their favour and against the archbishop. But the journey cost him his life, for he took ill on his return at Montefiescone, where he had gone to wait for a final decree. His body was brought to England and interred in Hereford Cathedral, where the shrine is still to be seen, though no longer decorated with precious offerings. It is somewhat doubtful whether the remains of the saint remain in their tomb. St Thomas was canonised by Pope John XXII. in 1320.

The earlier half of King Edward's reign, up to the year 1292, was chiefly a period of legislation, but there was one notable exception. The wars against the Welsh were undertaken almost as soon as Edward had taken up the reins of government. In fact Edward's general theory of his position was that he was to be Lord Paramount of the whole of Britain, including both Wales and Scotland, and the struggle for independence on the part of the former country was the nearest and most offensive obstacle that he encountered. Llewellyn, the native prince who fostered a considerable national revival in Wales, had achieved a position of practical independence from whatever subjection the Norman kings had reduced his predecessors to, and although he had in some fashion done homage to Henry III. at the end of the Barons' Wars, declined to repeat this in favour of his son and successor. Twice he was summoned in vain, so that the very first question brought up in the Parliament which Edward called after his coronation regarded the measures to be taken to enforce the submission of Llewellyn. There had been very frequent hostilities between English and Welsh on the marches or borders, but no very decisive result was attained. Now, however, the king determined to subjugate Wales completely, and gathered a large army for that purpose. Unfortunately for himself, Llewellyn had quarrelled with his own brother, David, with the result that this prince accompanied King Edward on his march. Llewellyn was overthrown, and David appointed as vassal Prince of Wales in his place. After the death of Llewellyn, David found the English monarch an exacting master, and led a new rising against the victorious army. He had promised to go on the Crusades, and more for this than for his resistance to Edward was excommunicated by the Archbishop of Canterbury. In 1283 he was captured, and tried as a traitor; he was then executed, and, by the so-called Statutes of Rhuddlan or Wales, that country was declared incorporated with England, and was to be governed by English law. Edward's son, born at Carnarvon in 1284, was set before the assembled Welsh leaders as the first Prince of Wales of the new order of things. It must be admitted that much of all this was destined to become almost a dead letter.

Wars in Wales.

Notwithstanding that the king was pretty fully occupied with the affairs of Wales even up to the end of 1284, he was very far from postponing his legislative schemes until he should have time to give them undivided attention. He took advantage of his very first Parliament, which met at Westminster in 1275, to commence earning that title of legislator which posterity has bestowed upon him. The gathering was an imposing and remarkable one, for it included not only the bishops and abbots and among the laity the peers of the realm, but "the community of the land," so that the king could claim that he was law-making with the advice of his counsellors and the common consent of those who had been summoned. The Statute of Westminster (the First) was the extensive work accomplished before the session was ended. It was rather a code of legislation than any isolated enactment, and comprised no fewer than fifty-one articles, covering almost the whole field in which there was room for the promulgation of laws.

The English Justinian.

The chief adviser of the king in his work of legislating for the good order of his kingdom was Robert Burnell, who had been made chancellor instead of Walter de Merton in 1274, and in the following year was raised to the see of Bath and Wells. It was not unnatural that when Kilwardby, being made cardinal, went to reside at the papal court, Edward should recommend the Bishop of Bath and Wells as his successor. However, the Pope declined to ratify this choice, as he did also his nomination at a later date to the important see of Winchester. But Burnell continued to be chancellor, and likewise retained the diocese of Bath and Wells for the rest of his life. He remained Edward's chief counsellor in all his earlier contests both with the clergy and with the barons, and may have been a party to the sudden unconstitutional expedients taken by the king to meet his financial needs. For his own part, he seems to have led a life of ambition and of grasping acquisition of wealth, so that at last he owned no fewer than eighty-two manors in nineteen different counties. He built the Episcopal Palace at Wells, probably one of the most attractive in the country, and also gained many privileges for his see. He died in 1292.

Bishop Burnell.

It is outside the purpose of this book to attempt a full account of the laws made either in the Parliament of 1275, or in the subsequent assemblies of the reign. These are details which must be left to the secular or constitutional historian. Yet some sketch must find a place here. The principle that the affairs of the Church must take a most prominent place in the matters dealt with at these time renders a short summary needful, so as to show in general how the clergy and their flocks were affected by parliamentary enactments which thus became law.

Probably the act which touched the status of the clergy in the most practical way was the Statute of Mortmain (1275). Up to the date of Edward I.'s accession all corporations in England, whether ecclesiastical or civil, had not been discriminated against as to the right of holding property in land and other possessions. The Mortmain Acts modified these rights on the ground that the grasp of a corporation on these things was that of a *morte main* or dead hand which was never released. The Mortmain Act which was passed in 1279, usually called the *Statute de Religiosis*, passing on from the general modifications already made to deal with the special cases of religious orders, enacted that land acquired by a religious corporation was to be forfeited to the immediate lord of the fief, or failing him, to his next superior, or finally to the crown. Edward and his Parliament followed this up in 1285 with a statute limiting the jurisdiction of the ecclesiastical courts to places and causes, such as churches, tithes, mortuaries, injuries to clerics, perjury and defamation, as Dr Stubbs explains. All this time Archbishop Peckham was fighting the battle for the privileges of the Church with courageous pertinacity, and inasmuch as Edward was not a lawless tyrant, with considerable success. In fact Edward's laws were not strictly anti-clerical. These statutes had their counterpart in those called respectively *Quo Warranto and Quia Emptores*, the former of which directed commissioners to proceed to inquire by what warrant the various franchises held by the barons existed; while the latter directs that in future transfers of land the purchaser should not continue to hold it of the feudal tenant who sold it to him, but of his feudal

(sidenote: Legislation concerning the Church.)

lord. In other words it forbade what was called subinfeudation. Between these acts come the twin statutes called respectively the Second Statute of Westminster (1285) and the Statute of Winchester (1285), which defined respectively the royal jurisdiction and the limits as well as the binding force of the ancient popular law. In 1292 Edward lost his chief legal advisers, but by that time the greater part of his legislation had been completed. Though there were constitutional struggles enough in the latter part of his reign there was but little law-making.

Archbishop Peckham has left a monument both of his zeal and of his wisdom in the numerous decrees made by him in the councils he held and in his visitations of the various parts of his province. He had had a distinguished career in his order before he went to Canterbury, having taught both in Paris and Oxford, and having been Provincial of the Grey Friars in England. Many of his scientific and theological writings are extant in manuscript in the various libraries of Europe, as well as many hymns and sacred songs, some of which found their way into the Divine Office. When the Pope decided to reject Burnell as Primate, himself consecrated Peckham in person at Rome, and his enthronement at Canterbury next year is admitted to mark an epoch in the development of the position of the English Primate. Being made papal legate as well, he was able to wield tremendous power in the work of raising the standard of discipline. Canonical visitations throughout his province were the chief instrument he used for this purpose. So uncompromising was he in the thoroughness with which he carried this out that he provoked much opposition from the other bishops, who appealed against him, sending St Thomas Cantelupe, Bishop of Hereford, as their mouthpiece to present their case to the Pope. Peckham also held important Provincial Councils at Reading in 1279, and at Lambeth in 1281. The chief decrees made were against the holding of several benfices by the same cleric, against non-residence, and against laxity in monastic observance. By ordering a copy of Magna Charta to be hung up in all cathedral and collegiate churches he gave the king the idea that he was opposed to the regal power; and he championed the

240 THE CHURCH IN ENGLAND

rights of the people with true Franciscan sympathy. But Edward really appreciated his single-minded devotion to duty, and often was on a very cordial footing with him. He employed him among other things in the endeavour to effect a peaceful settlement of Welsh affairs. The archbishop endeavoured to enter into negotiations with Llewellyn, the Welsh prince, but the latter declined the proffered arrangement. Peckham thereupon issued an excommunication against Llewellyn, retired from the Welsh marches, and the matter was left to the arbitrament of war. But, in spite of this participation in secular affairs, and similar ones, there is no doubt that ecclesiastical affairs held the first place in Peckham's mind. He was an ascetic friar, and an enthusiast for Church discipline to the last. He died in 1292, the year we have indicated as completing the civil legislation of Edward I., and was buried at Canterbury. His heart was nevertheless, as a sign that he was a Franciscan still, taken to the Grey Friars Church in London.

There was little delay about appointing a successor to Peckham, though on account of the vacancy in the papacy he was not consecrated until 1294, when the Cardinal of Sabina performed the rite at Aquileia. The archbishop-elect who thus received the fullness of the priesthood was Robert Winchelsea, a secular priest of the London diocese who, after a brilliant course at Canterbury School and the two Universities of Paris and Oxford, became a prebendary and preacher at St Paul's Cathedral.

Archbishop Winchelsea (1293-1313).

He made such a favourable impression on the Pope when he went to him for confirmation of the monk's election that he wished to keep him as a cardinal in Curia, but Winchelsea pleaded to be allowed to go to Canterbury, and the Pontiff gave way. He was almost immediately plunged in the stormy political events of the time. He gained the favour of Edward I. by renewing the excommunication against Llewellyn, but nearly lost it in the following year by publishing the Bull of Boniface VIII. "*Clericis laicos*," which forbade under pain of excommunication the taxation of the clergy by the laity, as well as a decree of the Council of Lyons to the same effect. However, there was no immediate quarrel, and the king contented himself for the moment with a mandate to the Provincial Council called by the Primate in the same year that they should pass no canon infringing on the royal prerogatives. Still, the day of combat was only postponed. Next year when it became evident that the clergy would not pay the levy of taxation which had been put upon them in spite of the papal prohibition, the king declared them all outlawed, and proceeded to seize the temporalities of the Church. Very great alarm and distress ensuing, an appeal was made to the Holy See as to what they were to do, and Boniface, having declared, in answer to the questions of the timorous, that he did not intend to forbid benevolences or voluntary offerings made by the clergy for the aid of the king in his necessities, many took advantage of this to pay. Winchelsea, nevertheless, personally refused to be any party to such an arrangement, and girded himself for resistance to the last. And by this time, under the pressure of the great expenses involved in expeditions into Flanders and Scotland, Edward's demands had grown to such an alarming extent as to provoke dissatisfaction which was not confined to the clergy. Winchelsea and the barons saw their advantage, and were not slow to face the king with a demand for a solemn Confirmation of the Charters before any supplies should be voted. The strong monarch burst into tears when he found himself confronted with such determined opposition on the part of the people he loved, and of the archbishop whom he could not help respecting. He promised that he would do what they required from him on his return from the expedition on which he was setting out. Winchelsea and the other leaders, though equally affected at the interview, kept him to his word. Consequently, a whole series of enactments known as the Confirmation of the Charters (1297) owes its origin to the last years of Edward I. It is well said that our gratitude to Winchelsea and to the Earls of Norfolk and Hereford ought not to be less than that we owe to Langton and the barons who won Magna Charta.

Meanwhile, John Balliol, King of Scotland, had renounced his allegiance to the English crown, and Edward was obliged to engage in another Scottish war. The Scots had further strengthened their position morally by claiming the protection of the Pope on the ground that Scotland was a fief of the Holy See. Thereupon Boniface VIII. wrote to Winchelsea directing him to seek out King Edward and command him in the Pope's name to abstain from any act of aggression against Scotland. The archbishop, after considerable delay, found the king at Carlisle, when he delivered to him the papal message. It was so far successful in arresting his progress that an armistice was arranged with the Scots, and Edward accompanied the Primate south, declaring that he must consult with his advisers and his Parliament before giving a final answer to the Pontiff. Some time later, in accordance with this, Edward called a council at Lincoln, and there protested that in a temporal matter, such as his rights over the Scottish crown, he did not acknowledge that he was bound to submit to the Pope's ruling: all the more that he did not admit the truth of the fact alleged that Scotland was a fief of the Roman See.

Later Scottish Wars.

It is not likely that Edward took kindly the vigorous action of Archbishop Winchelsea either with regard to the papal claims on Scotland, or with respect to his leadership of the barons in their constitutional opposition to his demands. Henceforth his chief clerical adviser was Walter Langton, who had lately been made Bishop of Lichfield. But Langton also had his enemies, and he was accused to the Pope of murder, adultery, and simony. The Pontiff committed the trial of the case to Winchelsea, and it is creditable to the latter that though Langton was undoubtedly his enemy, he gave him a fair trial, and honourably acquitted him of all the charges. Meantime, a change in the Roman Pontificate through the election of Clement V., a former friend of the king, gave Edward a chance of striking a blow at Winchelsea. Envoys were sent to the papal court with Bishop Langton at their head to lay before the Pope the royal charges and complaints against the archbishop. It does not appear that Winchelsea was charged with any fault reflecting on his moral character, but he had opposed the king, and so he had to suffer. He was known to be a saintly and most austere churchman. But, after appearing before Clement V., hostile influences were so strong that he was suspended from the exercise

Winchelsea and Walter Langton.

of his faculties. Langton remained triumphant until the king's death and in high honour with him. But with the new king his enemies came into power, and he was arrested. Once again Winchelsea nobly intervened, so that he was liberated and allowed to reside in his diocese. There he lived and ruled for another space of nine years, dying at Lichfield in 1321. His tomb is in his elegant cathedral, which he had adorned with a unique and beautiful Lady Chapel and other stately buildings.

The armistice with the Scots was suffered to run its course. Edward then once more collected his army and set out on a further martial expedition into Scotland. It was hopeless to contend with the experienced warrior and his powerful forces, so that he conquered wherever he went. In the course of a prolonged stay he not only subdued the land; passing north as far as Elgin, and even to remote Caithness; but spent the winter in the royal burgh of Dunfermline. He there endeavoured to organise the future administration of the country, but six months sufficed to destroy what it had taken him years to accomplish. Yet another rising was announced to him almost before he had settled at home in England, more formidable than any of the preceding ones. As Wallace had been the heroic leader of the Scots in their former battles for independence, so now a very capable champion came to the fore in Robert Bruce. Edward's lieutenants were driven from one position to another. The indomitable old king, now in failing health and approaching his seventieth year, no sooner heard this than he turned once more northwards to conduct a new attempt to conquer Scotland. But his strength soon failed him, and he died at Burgh-on-Sands before he could cross the border. He wished that his bones should be carried with the English army on their coming campaign, but this injunction was disregarded. He was interred hard by the shrine of his namesake, the Holy Confessor, in Westminster Abbey, beneath an austerely simple slab of black marble with the inscription, made or remade by Abbot Feckenham: "Edwardus Primus, Scottorum malleus hic est. Pactum Serva."

Death of Edward I. (1307).

The administration of Archbishop Peckham, and after

him that of Winchelsea, organised the Church in England with a success not inferior to that of Edward I. in civil government. Never again did the power and prosperity of mediaeval Catholicism shine over the land as in this reign. There were greater scholars later on perhaps, but never greater rulers, nor, it must be confessed, a better specimen of an English king, at once strong on his own rights, and yet not unmindful of the claims of the Church and of the people. The last of the English saints, St Thomas of Hereford, was indeed dead before Edward had reached the middle of his reign, but there were noble ecclesiastics left to carry on the great tradition. Besides those already mentioned, a place of honour is due to Anthony Beck, Bishop of Durham from 1284 to 1311, who was found worthy to be appointed Patriarch of Jerusalem in 1306. And we also find among the bishops, besides the royal minister, Walter Langton, mentioned above, another of the same name, John Langton of Chichester, towards the end of the reign, as well as Richard Gravesend of London, and Roger Walpole of Norwich, and Henry Woodlock of Winchester, all filled a great space in the history of the country. The Franciscans had about this time their Adam Marsh, their Duns Scotus, their Roger Bacon. The Dominicans could boast of their cardinal, Thomas Joyce, who after being confessor to the king and Provincial of his Order, was sent by Edward I. as envoy to the papal court, and when admitted to the Sacred College by Clement V., remained in the Curia. He died at Grenoble in 1310. Already during this reign there had been one Dominican cardinal from England in the person of Friar Winterbourne, who had in his turn been confessor to the king. But he was already dead before Joyce was made cardinal, having died at Genoa in 1304 before the seventy years of absence of the Popes from Rome had begun. Even had these personalities been less notable than they were, their appointment one after another kept up the representation of England in the counsels of the head of the Church, and in this way helped to knit the country still more closely to the centre of Christendom.

Summary.

XIX.

THE DESCENDANTS OF EDWARD I.

(1307-1349.)

(A) EDWARD II. (1307-1327).

As soon as his father was dead (3rd July, 1307) the first English Prince of Wales received the homage of the English lords at Carlisle, and of the Scottish at Dumfries. He then met his Parliament at Northampton, and passed on to Westminster for the solemn interment of the late monarch and for his own coronation. Application was at once made to Pope Clement V. for the absolution of the suspended Primate, Archbishop Winchelsea, but without waiting for this he asked to be crowned by the Archbishop of York. As there was some delay, Winchelsea was no sooner reinstated than he claimed his right to crown the king. Before the day arrived he became too ill to perform the ceremony, but his claim was admitted, and Bishop Woodlock of Winchester, who officiated, did so as the Primate's delegate. Edward II. was the first English king to be crowned on the traditional coronation stone, which had been brought by his father from Scone in Scotland.

Edward II. (1307-1327).

The young king began his reign fortified by the strong position which his father had won, but from the first there were signs of that unhappy reliance on favourite courtiers which at last led to his ruin. Many of these courtiers were foreigners from Gascony and elsewhere, and the leaders of the nation would have none of them. The general resentment centred on a certain Piers Gaveston, who had been brought up with Edward in

the royal household. At last the discontent nearly broke
out into open rebellion, or at any rate armed resistance,
but not until repeated efforts had been made to get rid
of the favourite without attacking the king. Twice was
Gaveston banished, and twice under one pretext or
another was he brought back to England under the royal
protection, and restored to his position. However, a
council was held at Westminster in March, 1310,
attended by the barons armed as for war, and then the
king surrendered at discretion. In order to obtain the
redress of a whole series of grievances already tabulated,
the chief of which was the favour shown to Gaveston,
a committee of lords styled Ordainers was
chosen to draw up a set of ordinances for the
better ruling of the kingdom. Foremost
amongst the "Ordainers," both in dignity
and by character, stood Archbishop Winchelsea, and it
is significant of the great part given to the clergy in
State affairs at the time that amongst the remaining
twenty no fewer than six were bishops. Langton of
Chichester was one, Baldock of London was another,
but in general it would seem to be their official standing
rather than any personal reasons that led to their being
chosen. The chief Ordainers among the laity were
Thomas, Earl of Lancaster, cousin of the king, Henry
de Lacy, Earl of Lincoln, and Aymer de Valence.
When at the next Parliament, held in 1311, these
Ordainers proceeded with their work of framing the
regulations, they drew up quite an extensive array of
enactments. It was stipulated that Gaveston should be
banished; that for the future the great offices of State
should only be filled up by the king with the consent of
the barons; that the king should neither levy war nor
depart out of the kingdom without the advice of his
council. We see the weight of the episcopal influence in
the provision that the Church courts should be left free
from royal interference. It was prescribed that henceforward one fixed system of coinage should be established.
The king fought hardest against the decree of banishment for Gaveston, but even in this he was forced to
yield, and the ordinances were at last accepted. Then,
when in spite of all that had passed, Gaveston was once
more recalled in the following year, 1312, he was seized
by the Earls of Warwick and Lancaster, and beheaded

The Church and the Ordainers.

DESCENDANTS OF EDWARD I.

without any form of trial at Blackloe Hill, Lancaster. Pope Clement V. now endeavoured to mediate between Edward and the discontented barons, while the bishops exerted themselves also to prevent actual hostilities. For the time they were successful, and in 1313 a general pardon was issued to all who had risen against the royal authority.

The independent and patriotic Archbishop Winchelsea died in 1313 at Oxford, and was buried in his cathedral. But though miracles were reported at his tomb, the efforts to obtain his canonisation proved unavailing. Still he was distinguished not only by the public spirit of which mention has been made, but by learning, by piety in his private life, and by generosity in giving alms to the poor. The royal influence was now exerted to install in St Augustine's chair Walter Reynolds, who had been King Edward's tutor, and then was made Bishop of Worcester and entrusted with the Great Seal. *Archbishop Reynolds (1313-1327).* He was not the choice of the Canterbury monks, who unanimously elected Thomas de Cobham, Dean of Salisbury, a very learned and exemplary man, but the king persuaded Clement V. to set aside this election and appoint Reynolds, who belonged to that circle of royal favourites amongst whom Gaveston and the Despensers earned such an unpopular place. Cobham, however, went to the papal court at Avignon, where he was detained for some years, but four years later, when Reynolds' successor at Worcester, Walter de Maidstone, died, he was there consecrated for that see, and held it for ten years. At the same time and in the same place, Adam Orlton, who was to play such a great part in subsequent political events in England, was likewise consecrated in the first instance for Hereford, though he was twice afterwards translated to greater sees. The two bishops came back to England to take up their respective duties. William de Melton, who had been made Archbishop of York only two months later by John XXII., had not been home from the Avignon court very long before he came into collision with Reynolds on account of his having had his archbishop's cross carried before him in the streets of London, which was, of course, outside his province. Reynolds put the city of London under an interdict, which was only removed when the point in dispute had been arranged. Reynolds may not have been a man of very strong or consistent character, but this incident, as well as what we are going to relate of his intervention in the case of Bishop Orlton, shows that he was not a mere puppet in the king's hands, but that he could stand up for the right of his see and of the clergy when occasion demanded. Yet, bearing in mind his position in the household of Edward I., and his personal relations with his successor, it was quite natural that he should support the royal interests wherever his conscience would permit.

The war in Scotland was renewed in 1314, and Edward, who inherited the instincts of a soldier, though not the genius of his father, took the command in person. But by this time the whole of Scotland had been roused to a final stand for national independence, and the English king with his powerful army was decisively beaten at the field of Bannockburn in 1314. Efforts were made by the papal legates to reach an accommodation in this case also, and a truce was proclaimed by them in London, but Robert Bruce refused to acknowledge it on the ground that the envoys of the Pope had not addressed him as Scottish king, although he had been already chosen by the nation as their sovereign. He held that this was to prejudge the case against him. He was thereupon excommunicated by John XXII. At Bannockburn he had practically won the liberation of his country, and was by no means anxious to forfeit his gains. Nevertheless, it is likely that the sentence of excommunication made him more desirous than he would otherwise have been of coming to an arrangement. In fact, at last he made his peace with Rome, being then acknowledged as King of Scotland, and engaging to go on a Crusade to the Holy Land. Still, he did not live long to enjoy the triumph he had won, and hence could not go personally to the Holy War. But he commissioned Douglas to take his heart with him when he should set out for the sacred expedition in token of his loyalty to his promise. The heart was afterwards treasured in the abbey at Melrose. Edward tried later on to renew the war in Scotland, but was so unsuccessful that he had to agree to a truce of thirteen years with the Scots.

Battle of Bannockburn (1314).

DESCENDANTS OF EDWARD I. 249

Edward II. seemed unable to live for any length of time without falling into the hands of unworthy favourites. The place once held by Piers Gaveston was taken in the later part of his reign by the two Hugh Despensers, father and son, of whom the former was made Earl of Winchester, and the latter Earl of Gloucester. The influence gained by these two men over the royal counsels was as much resented by the barons as that of Gaveston had been, and the State was once more plunged into angry strife. After several years of tumultuous discussion marked by dissension among the barons themselves, the Parliament of 1321 formulated several distinct charges against the two Despensers as evil counsellors of the king and impediments to harmony between monarch and people. Sentence was passed against both of them that they should forfeit their goods and be banished from the realm until recalled in a full assembly of the estates. Both parties endeavoured to gain the support of the Church and of the bishops, who were far from unanimous. Two months after the sentence passed by the Parliament, Edward, having got an opinion from Convocation that the proceedings then taken were illegal, summoned the royal forces and marched northwards with his levies against the opposing barons. At Boroughbridge the Earl of Lancaster was defeated and taken prisoner. He was then tried at Pomfret before the king and a Council of Peers, and being condemned as a rebel taken in arms, was beheaded (1321). Edward now proceeded to take vengeance on his enemies, some of whom were executed and others banished. Then, acting on the advice of the Despensers and other members of the court party, he went on to undo a good deal of the work arranged by the Ordainers. Nevertheless, Roger Mortimer, the most dangerous of the Earl of Lancaster's party, was allowed to escape from England. Queen Isabella, Edward's consort, proved faithless to her husband, and being bitterly opposed to the influence of the Despensers, fled to France, where, in conjunction with Mortimer, and with other leaders of the discontented people, she formed a conspiracy for the invasion of the country, and the forcible removal of the Despensers from power.

Although Edward had gained the opinion of the Houses of Convocation that the action taken against his

The Despensers.

favourites was illegal, it is certain that several of the bishops were on the barons' side. Henry Burghersh had been nominated by the king for the see of Winchester, but when the Pope refused the nomination, and appointed his legate, Reginald Asser, instead, he was asked to appoint Burghersh to Lincoln. This he eventually did, and Burghersh was strongly on the side of the barons. Adam Orlton, the Bishop of Hereford, was believed to have gone further still in the direction of rebellion, and was prosecuted before king and peers for high treason. This was the first case in English history of a bishop being tried for high treason before a lay tribunal. It is to the credit of Archbishop Reynolds that, much as he was attached to the king's party, he put himself at the head of the bishops to protest against this. Then, following up the protest, the three metropolitans of Canterbury, York, and Dublin came to the trial with their crosses raised aloft, and carried off Orlton from the court. Judgment was notwithstanding given against him, and the temporalities of his diocese were confiscated. It needed all the dexterity of Reynolds to make peace, but at last he was successful in doing so, and Adam Orlton had still a great part to play at the end of this reign and the beginning of the next one.

Conspiracy and Invasion. In fact, while Isabella and Mortimer, with their friends, were preparing an invasion from France, Adam Orlton was the moving spirit of the conspiracy in England itself. With him were Burghersh, Bishop of Lincoln, and John Drokensford, Bishop of Bath and Wells. Thus it came to pass that when Queen Isabella landed in 1326, Edward scarcely knew whom to trust, while his forces gradually slipped away from him. The general unwillingness to take up his cause is at least some *prima facie* argument for the reality of the misgovernment with which he was charged. In order to get assistance from the Church he turned to Archbishop Reynolds, but the help afforded him by the Primate was of the feeblest. Stapledon, Bishop of Exeter, who tried to hold London for the king, was murdered by the enraged populace as soon as Edward had left the capital. With him fell his brother, Sir Richard Stapledon, equally with him a victim to his loyalty towards his sovereign and the Constitution of the realm. The bishop was a great loss to the English

DESCENDANTS OF EDWARD I.

Church, for, besides his munificence in the city of Exeter, he had founded and endowed Exeter College, Oxford. He held the see from 1308 until his death in 1327. Already the king with his remaining adherents had retired before the advancing army of Isabella into Wales. The elder Despenser was taken at Bristol, and executed without any trial. The younger one suffered a like fate with his father, being hanged at Hereford on a gibbet fifty feet high. The pursuit of the king was kept up until he fell into the hands of the Earl of Lancaster, who conveyed him to Kenilworth Castle. The queen, being now victorious, turned back from the West, and entered London in triumph, accompanied by her son, Prince Edward, and many of her leading supporters.

The favourable reception accorded to Isabella in the capital emboldened her friends to call a Parliament, though a somewhat informal one, at Westminster, which deposed the king and elected his son to succeed him. To this the clergy, including Archbishop Reynolds, gave a passive consent. In fact, the Primate went so far as to deliver a discourse to the people based upon the text, "*Vox populi, vox Dei*," in which he elaborated the thesis on which he seems to have based his own action, and exhorted the assembly to fidelity to the young prince who had been elected. It was thought necessary to take steps to gain the consent of the old king to what had been done, and a commission was sent to wait upon him, asking him to resign the crown. The leading spokesmen in this were the three Bishops of Winchester, Lincoln, and Hereford, with a number of barons in their company. Edward had not much choice left to him, and made a formal resignation of the crown. Thereupon Prince Edward was proclaimed in the usual fashion, and crowned by the Primate in Westminster Abbey. His father survived for eight months, but it was clear that unscrupulous enemies would have every reason for putting an end to his life. On the 21st of September, 1327, he was secretly assassinated in Berkeley Castle.

Deposition and death of Edward II.

252   THE CHURCH IN ENGLAND

(B) EARLIER YEARS OF EDWARD III. (1327-1349).

There is a real continuity in the state of parties and the trend of their policies between the reign of Edward II.

Edward III. (1327-1377). and the early years of his son and successor. For a space of nearly four years (1327-1330) young Edward was not much more than the figurehead for the domination of the queen-mother, Isabella, and of her paramour, Mortimer, Earl of March. Under these actual rulers the ministers who carried on the public affairs of the kingdom were the same who had been the leaders of the faction at the end of the preceding reign. Adam Orlton, now translated from the See of Hereford to Worcester, may be considered the leading spirit among them. First he was treasurer, and then continued to exercise much influence as a diplomatist and statesman. Bishop Henry Burghersh of Lincoln had preceded him at the treasury, which he then gave up to become Lord Chancellor. He also was fully committed to the queen's party, and this is no doubt why the attempt was made, when Archbishop Reynolds died two months after Edward II., to get him named for the primacy. It was only at the end of 1330, when the young king, leading a party of armed men, seized Mortimer at Nottingham Castle, and had him executed in London, that the real reign of Edward III. began.

Already the Holy See and the monks of Christchurch had asserted their independence of the dominant faction.

Archbishop Meopham (1327-1333). Simon Meopham, a pious Canon of Chichester, was the choice of the Chapter for the vacant archbishopric, and they succeeded in carrying their point, for Meopham was confirmed by the Pope, and consecrated at Avignon. In this way they had a Primate, who did not suffer himself to be absorbed in the affairs of State, but devoted himself to the government of his Church and province. He it was who crowned King Edward's consort, Philippa of Hainault, but Bishop Burghersh was still chancellor, and being still in favour in 1330, christened the new Prince of Wales, Edward the Black Prince. At the same ceremony in Avignon, at which Meopham was consecrated, John Grandison was also consecrated for Exeter, and Thomas Charlton for Hereford. The former of these two prelates, who has left his mark on his episcopal city by his elegant buildings in the cathedral, became the most determined opponent of the Primate. Archbishop Meopham decided to carry out a visitation of his whole province, but when the turn of Exeter came Grandison appealed to the Pope to delay the visitation, and met the Primate at the frontier of the diocese in order to turn him back. The king intervened, and Meopham did not persist in his attempt to proceed farther. Soon after this the archbishop died, but not before he had held two Provincial Councils which made the " Immaculate Conception Feast " a holiday, and drew up a list of the holidays to be observed in England, directing the people to fast on their vigils, to come to all the church services, and to abstain from servile work on all these days.

Although the short episcopate of Archbishop Meopham was but little concerned with affairs of State, young King Edward did not lack solid support from other constitutional advisers, enemies of the court party, as soon as he had cast off the moral fetters in which that party had tried to bind him. The chief place among them is occupied by John Stratford, at the beginning of the reign, Bishop of Winchester, and then at Meopham's death in 1333 translated to Canterbury. He had already been chancellor once, while he held the see of Winchester, and occupied the office with a break until 1340, when he finally gave it up. From 1330 to 1340 he was the chief counsellor of the king, whose policy was guided by him both abroad and at home. From 1340 his relations with Edward III. were strained, and the king tried to fix upon him the responsibility for the ill success which attended his first campaigns in Flanders, but the archbishop was able to clear himself before public opinion, if not before the king, and became the champion of the cause of government by responsible ministers. His brother, Robert Stratford, Bishop of Chichester, had charge of the exchequer for a while, and when the Primate resigned the office of chancellor in 1337, stepped into his place for a period, but in the main supported the same line of policy. Another Stratford, whose name was Ralph, occupied the see of London from 1340 to 1355; his

The Stratfords and other ministers.

relationship to the Primate and his brother is not clearly established. William Melton continued to hold the metropolitan see of York until his death in 1340, and well deserves honourable mention among the prelates of his day. He gave his clergy and his people a lofty example both of regularity in his public duties, and of piety in his private life. Of course he was called upon to pay his meed of political service in the affairs of the whole country as well. At the end of the preceding reign he had been High Commissioner of the North, and in that capacity had been defeated by the Scots in battle. Still, he did not lose his credit thereby, for when Parliament met at York in 1332 he was called on to preside at the opening session. Like the other bishops just spoken of, he had to take his turn at the chancery, and at the treasury likewise, but was not betrayed into neglect of his important diocese.

Melton's chief suffragan has left a still more celebrated name on account of the appeal it makes to the lovers of literature and learning. This was Richard Aungerville de Bury, Bishop of Durham from 1333 to 1345. The annals of the Church in England do not show us any personality more enthusiastically devoted to books and to the cause of erudition than this mature and pious mediaeval scholar. He had been tutor to King Edward III. in that prince's youth, and hence rapidly came into favour when his pupil became king in 1327. When the see of Durham fell vacant by the death of De Beaumont in 1333, Richard was named to rule the County Palatine as bishop. Nor did that high office exhaust the responsibilities which were laid upon him. In 1334 the king entrusted to his old tutor the office of Lord Chancellor, and when this was handed back to Stratford in the following year, he went not into disgrace, but to the charge of the treasury. Moreover, he was several times the trusted royal envoy to Pope John XXII. at Avignon. Yet amid all the distractions of these weighty employments he was ever faithful to books and the love of literature. It must have been a keen pleasure to him to meet at Avignon the poet, Petrarch, as well as many of the most distinguished scholars of the time. But before and beyond all he was what we should now style a bibliophile, ready to spend

Richard Aungerville de Bury (1286-1345).

both his energy and all the material means at his command in collecting books and in having them transcribed. He kept a whole staff of copyists, illuminators, and correctors constantly employed, and in this way was able to supply himself with a library of exceptional extent wherever he lived. He was also himself the author of several works, the best known of which, the "*Philobiblon*," has been repeatedly translated into English. He takes occasion, in this book, to vindicate himself from the charge of spending too much money on his library, and glories in the immense pains he had been at to collect manuscripts to enrich it. Moreover, it would not be fair to consider him merely as a collector of books, for he was really a munificent patron of learning. The foundation of Durham College, Oxford, is owing to his liberality, and to the library of this institution he bequeathed many of the volumes which he had amassed in his lifetime. At the end of the "Philobiblon" he gives us an edifying glimpse of his humility and piety; he stands revealed as the true Catholic scholar, full of zeal for learning, and yet measuring all by standards which are not of this world. In 1345 he died at the episcopal manor of Bishop-Auckland, and was interred at Durham. Though no monument marks his resting-place, he may well be regarded as one of the glories of St Cuthbert's Patrimony.

But besides these notable ecclesiastics, Edward III. had also the services of several capable servants among the lay barons and knights, whom he employed in State business both in peace and war. Such was Simon, Lord Montacute, who had been at his side when he first threw off the yoke of Isabella and Mortimer. Such again was Robert Bourchier, who is the first layman of whom we hear as Lord Chancellor. Edward was much occupied in the first part of his reign in the Scottish wars, championing the claims of Edward Balliol to the throne. He twice supported him when he was driven into exile by his rivals, and twice restored him to his kingdom. In 1333 he won the battle of Halidon Hill against the troops of Douglas, the Scottish Regent, and instead of using his victory with moderation, insisted on a treaty by which all the Lowlands east of a line from Dumfries to Linlithgow were to be annexed to the English realm. Such an arrangement could not

War with Scotland.

256 THE CHURCH IN ENGLAND

be permanent. As long as Edward was at hand to uphold him with English forces Balliol managed to keep some semblance of authority, but as soon as the English king became occupied with his claim to the crown of France his cause languished. The adherents of David Bruce won stronghold after stronghold, and Balliol became a fugitive from Scotland. He was employed in the defence of the northern counties of England from the Scots. The fratricidal contest went on in a desultory way for many years, but the days of the successful expeditions from England into Scotland were passed away, at least for centuries, and the national independence had practically been won.

But the general character of the earlier part of the reign of Edward III. was an absorption of the king and many of the people in the war with France, to which they had been gradually committed by the adventurous mind of the young monarch and his love for display and military glory. He began by making an alliance with the cities of Flanders, and it was first of all to allay their objection to fighting against their suzerain—the French king—that Edward took the title of King of France and formulated his claim. In pursuance of this policy it was from Flanders that the first campaigns were fought from 1338 to 1340, but though much money was spent there was very little progress to show for it. However, in 1340 the navy won the battle of Sluys, which in great part ruined the French naval force, and made a direct descent upon France all the easier.

Beginning of the Hundred Years' War. Still things did not go well on land for the English monarch, and before the end of 1340 he suddenly appeared at the Tower of London, and made Archbishop Stratford give up the Great Seal, and Bishop Roger Northburgh the treasury: in fact all his chief judges and officials were removed. The Primate fled to Canterbury to be out of the way. He could not, however, avoid a lengthened quarrel with the king. Edward summoned him to court, and he excused himself. He then preached a set of sermons in Canterbury Cathedral, comparing the treatment given to him with that inflicted on St Thomas Becket by Henry II. Forgetting his dignity, Edward replied in an abusive and violent circular to the clergy known in history as the *Libellus*

Famosus, in which he charged the Archbishop with having failed to provide him with funds in the war for which he declared the prelate was answerable. Stratford replied by letter that he was not in office when the expedition was decided on, and was neither answerable for it, nor for the lavish expenditure by which the king had beggared himself. He ended by demanding to be tried by his peers. Edward answered by repeating the same charges in a weak and ineffectual way. Parliament met on St George's Day, and Stratford came ready to plead before the full assembly, but the king evaded meeting him. And whenever he appeared among the bishops, summoned to Parliament the king retired. The Archbishop had the sympathy of the bishops and lords with him, and Edward felt he had lost. Stratford had won a personal triumph, but he had also brought out the fact that ministers had to answer not to the king only, but to the full Parliament of the estates of the realm.

The king now got grants of money both from the clergy and the laity, and in 1344 renewed the war with France. He had several years of considerable success, winning the battle of Crécy in 1346, and taking the town of Calais after a prolonged blockade in 1347. In the same year he came back to England covered with military glory. This and the following year may be looked on as the brightest of his reign. To put the coping-stone on the court of romantic chivalry, which he desired his circle to be, he founded the Order of the Garter in 1348, having already spent large sums in building Windsor Castle, which he meant to be another Camelot with his Garter Knights as a revival of King Arthur's Knights of the Round Table. But the prosperity and glamour of the exterior covered much discontent and widespread financial exhaustion. Moreover, the counsellors and leading spirits of the kingdom were much changed since the early years of his reign. Henry of Lancaster was dead, so was Adam Orlton, and in 1348, Archbishop Stratford died. John Ufford, Dean of Lincoln, became chancellor, and William Edington, treasurer, the latter being made Bishop of Winchester also in 1346. During the years that followed there was luxury and extravagance, notably in dress, beyond all former bounds, but

Military successes of Edward III.

real prosperity was on the wane, and decay had really set in. At last, towards the end of 1348, an extraordinary visitation fell upon the country which produced far-reaching effects. This was the Great Plague known as the Black Death which had ravaged Italy as early as 1340, and being first seen in England in the middle of 1348, became an epidemic in London in November, and went on increasing till the early months of 1349. It did not cease its ravages until near the end of that year.

Mediation attempted by the Holy See. It would not be fair to the Holy See to omit the repeated and persevering efforts made by successive Pontiffs to prevent the outbreak of the fratricidal struggle between England and France, and afterwards to end it or at least limit it as far as possible. There seems to have been no matter of public policy nearer to the heart of the Pontiffs of those days. In fact, they put it forward as sufficient reason for prolonging their stay at Avignon. As early as 1339, as soon as it became evident that a serious attempt was being made by Edward III. to carry into effect the very ambitious design which he had formed in 1338 of appealing to arms to vindicate his claim to the French throne, Pope Benedict XII. repeatedly sent legates to the English court to try and dissuade him from the enterprise. But Edward was determined upon war, and evaded coming to terms. He protested indeed that he wished to reconcile with the Pope, Louis of Bavaria, who was supporting him against the French, but at the same time he assumed the style of King of France and quartered the arms of France with those of England on his shield. Benedict XII. died in 1342 without having been able to avert the coming conflict. Undeterred by this, or rather acting on the sublime instinct which impelled the Popes of those times to act as the peacemakers of Christendom, Clement VI. sent two cardinals to the rival courts, who succeeded in negotiating an armistice for three years (1343-6). But the conditions of the armistice were not really observed, and in 1346 King Edward undertook the campaign which was marked by the victory of Crécy. In 1347, after the fall of Calais, the papal envoys thought they saw an opportunity of renewing their instances for peace, and by repeated negotiation concluded an armistice which

only expired after an interval of six years (1347-53).
England was exhausted by the struggle, and France still
more so. And then there came down upon Europe the
scourge of the Great Pestilence before hostilities could
be renewed once more.

XX.

THE DECLINE OF THE PLANTAGENETS.
(1349-1399.)
(A) LATER YEARS OF EDWARD III. (1349-1377).

THE period of two centuries and a half, during which England was governed by the Plantagenet kings, embraced most of what was best in its mediaeval history both in Church and in State. But as that dynasty came near to the end of its tenure of authority, especially for the last half-century of its rule, it shared in the general decay of vigour which is noted by historians as a characteristic of the times in Europe at large. Perhaps Edward I. may be considered to have touched the highest level reached by his race. His son, Edward II., was but a degenerate son of such a father, and it is a remarkable fact that the chief personalities of his reign seem to have been as inferior to those of the preceding reign as he was to Edward I. It is true that Edward III. brought back again, at least for the earlier part of his reign, something of the vigorous life of his grandsire's days, besides displaying an external splendour and refinement which that stern warrior never had, and perhaps never aimed at. Yet in the later years of this monarch, when the glamour of his former achievements had somewhat faded away, the reaction set in afresh, and there were manifest signs of corruption and decay.

It can be asserted without any doubt that the continental wars engaged in by Edward III. to support his claim to the crown of France led to a great exhaustion of the resources of England. Many of the evils which they brought in their train were foreseen by the Roman Pontiffs, who, as we have seen, strove to mediate between the English and French monarchs. But both were in their own way set in their purposes,

Bad effects of the Hundred Years' War.

DECLINE OF PLANTAGENETS

and what is known as the Hundred Years' War was the result. The early successes at Sluys in 1340, at Crécy in 1346, and at Calais in 1347, only confirmed the English sovereign in his determination. But as time went on, after Edward returned to his own kingdom, things did not go on so well. Through the valour of his son, the Black Prince, a gleam of glory illuminated the field of Poictiers, but these successes were not maintained, and when at last peace was made at Bretigny in 1360, very little was left of the extensive conquests of the early years of the war. Moreover, the need of depending upon military services, which lasted longer than the old feudal system of the sovereign, led to the creation of a class of professional soldiers, whose life was warfare, who sometimes became mere mercenaries, and who were often a danger to the State at home and abroad.

Another potent agent of declension appeared in the epidemic pestilence which under the name of the Black Death raged over nearly the whole of Europe, and did not spare England in its oft-repeated visitations. The first and most terrible outbreak was from the end of 1348, until the middle of 1349, but it must not be supposed that it was the calamity of merely one year. It came back again and again, though with diminishing violence, and each of the years, 1361, 1362, 1369, has to record the raging of one or other of these attacks. As to the proportion of the inhabitants of the country that perished, opinions are conflicting, but the evidence is overwhelming that the effects produced in the country were various and far-reaching. In the Church it led to innumerable vacancies in benefices, and the consequent filling of these benefices by youthful or unsuitable incumbents. It meant also the depopulation of the monasteries to such an extent that it may even be questioned whether they ever recovered their former numbers even during the two centuries which elapsed before the suppression under Henry VIII. In agriculture the Plague produced a revolution in the manner of cultivating the land. And it is also held by historical authorities to have led to that social movement of the labourers which came to a head in the insurrection of Wat Tyler at the beginning of the reign of Richard II. As a result of the visitation, prices and wages had to be doubled. As to morality, the common

The Black Death.

observation no doubt held true that a pestilence does not as a rule lead to any amendment of the lives of the people, but rather to a desperate loosening of all the conventional bonds of discipline.

Archbishop Stratford died, leaving the see of Canterbury vacant, in 1348, and the king wrote to the Pope asking for a provision in favour of John Ufford, who had risen from one position to another until he was made Lord Chancellor, but who had never been made bishop so far. Ufford received the desired provisor, as it was called, but he did not live to enjoy it, for the Plague was now at its height. As early as June, 1349, before he could be consecrated, he caught the infection, and died of it. By common consent of king, chapter, and Pontiff the primatial dignity was now bestowed upon the brilliant Franciscan scholastic, Thomas Bradwardine, who was known in the universities as " Doctor Resolutissimus." Bradwardine, who had been confessor to King Edward, was consecrated at Avignon, and coming to England took possession of his see. However, whether he too contracted the fatal epidemic or not, certain it is that a few weeks later he breathed his last; and the hopes grounded upon his abilities and reputation were doomed to failure. The monks of Canterbury now selected Simon Islip for the archiepiscopal chair, and he was consecrated at St Paul's by Ralph Stratford, Bishop of London. He had already shown administrative ability in various charges both in Church and State, and he entered upon the duties of his new office with the greatest energy. His first labour was to make a canonical visitation in order to provide for the vacancies, and to regulate the disorganisation which had been the well-nigh inevitable results of the Plague. Islip had the reputation of being somewhat severe in his administration, and was complained of by some on that account. But he certainly strove manfully to remedy the evils which the Pestilence had left in its train, while his own life was austere and unostentatious.

For two years, namely from 1349 to 1351, as has been hinted by the chronology adopted above, there had been a cessation of public business; it was as though the national life had stopped dead, struck by the poisonous breath of the Black Death. However, in 1351, Parlia-

Rapid succession in the Primacy.

DECLINE OF PLANTAGENETS

ment met again, and began to legislate in a sense which at first is not easy to comprehend with regard to the affairs of the Church. It was in this year that the first Statute of Provisors was passed. By a provision was meant a papal brief instituting a cleric to a bishopric or lesser benefice, independent of an election by chapter or presentation by a patron. The practice of granting these briefs was an outcome of the residence of the Roman Pontiffs away from Rome at other Italian cities, and finally at Avignon. The ordinary revenues of the Roman see ceasing to come in as in the times when the Popes were the greatest landed proprietors in Italy, an elaborate system grew up to find the means of supplying the Pontifical necessities by means of firstfruits and fees for briefs of provision to benefices, both of which sources were used to supplement the Peter's Pence which had been contributed to Rome by England and other countries from almost immemorial usage. And, of course, though there was no question of the Pope's supreme jurisdiction, the exacting of these fees was felt as an abuse by the English clergy and to some extent by the laity as well. The kings were less opposed to the practice, as they found in it a means by arrangement with the Curia of over-riding popular election. So when the Parliament of 1351 met it passed an act which decreed that ecclesiastical elections should be free, and the rights of patrons kept, and that if by a papal provision either were disturbed, the appointment should fall to the king in defect of any other patron, while the provisor became liable to fine and imprisonment. The working out of this statute did not please the clergy, for the clauses relating to the royal claim to present had more influence in interfering with the freedom of the clergy than the more intermittent papal provisions had, and hence under the influence of Islip and the higher clergy it was amended in 1353.

Statute of Provisors (1351).

The Parliament of 1353 and subsequent Parliaments further proceeded to enact the celebrated laws which are usually spoken of as the Statutes of Premunire. These enactments brought upon all those who should procure in foreign courts (including the Papal Curia) any provision to an ecclesiastical benefice within the realm, together with their agents and assistants, outlawry

Statute of Premunire (1353).

from the king's protection, with forfeiture of their goods and chattels, and imprisonment until they had ransomed themselves with a suitable fine. The prelates, however, were not in any way more satisfied with this than with the original Statute of Provisors, and only assented with the condition that they did not mean to assent to anything against the prejudice of their dignity or estate. When the pressure of these laws began to make itself felt at the court of Avignon, the Pope wrote to Archbishop Islip to influence the king in the direction of their modification. This Islip seems to have done, for, after much negotiation, a working arrangement appears to have been come to which made them in practice less troublesome to the Pontiffs.

Meanwhile, the Primate's activities were extended to other fields more closely connected with his spiritual duties. When King Edward, as soon as war broke out anew, once more conducted a military expedition against France, Islip issued a mandate, directing prayers to be said for his success, and took advantage of the occasion to urge the better observance of Sunday by abstention from secular pursuits and attendance at the offices of the Church. He effected likewise a working compromise which settled the long-standing dispute with the see of York as to the right of the Northern metropolitan to bear his archiepiscopal cross before him outside of his own province. By this arrangement this right was conceded on the condition of a prescribed offering in gold being made at St Thomas's shrine in Canterbury. Thoroughly alive to promote the interests of learning among the clergy, Islip was likewise instrumental in the foundation of Canterbury Hall at Oxford, which was afterwards absorbed by Wolsey in the larger establishment of Cardinal College or Christchurch.

Cardinal Langham (1368). When Simon Islip died in 1366, the choice of the Canterbury monks fell upon Edington, Bishop of Winchester, but he was unwilling to be translated, and therefore the election was allowed to lapse, and King Edward petitioned the Pope to transfer Simon Langham, Bishop of Ely, from that diocese to the primacy. The request was granted, and the pallium sent, but it was not until Lady Day in the following year that Langham was solemnly enthroned in his cathedral. The new

DECLINE OF PLANTAGENETS 265

archbishop was a Benedictine monk who had ruled the Abbey of Westminster as abbot for twelve years, and had then been made Bishop of Ely and Lord Chancellor. In all these offices he had gained the reputation of being a capable and exact administrator, and thus it might have been thought that he would have had a career of high usefulness at Canterbury as well. The result turned out quite otherwise, for in the very next year the Pope named him cardinal without consulting the king, thereby causing considerable irritation. Langham had to resign the see of Canterbury, and went to live at Oxford. Eventually he got permission to proceed to Avignon, where he spent the remaining years of life. Instead of Canterbury the Pontiff bestowed upon him the suburban see of Palestrina. In the interval he made more than one attempt to return to England, and was once more elected for Canterbury. But the Pontiff protested that he could not spare him from his court; so at Avignon he remained. After his death his remains were brought home, and interred in the abbey at Westminster, where his heart had ever been, and where his last will bestowed all his remaining goods.

But, without waiting for Langham's death, the Pope had filled up Canterbury by translating William Whittlesey from London. He was a nephew of Archbishop Islip, whose Vicar-General he had been. He then filled in succession the sees of Rochester and London. There is not much to record of his six years' tenure of the archbishopric (1368-74), and possibly he may have been in failing health for much of the time. At any rate, when he died in 1374, and there was no chance of the return of Langham, the Chapter at Canterbury fixed their choice upon Adam Easton, a Benedictine monk of Norwich, who had probably accompanied Langham to Avignon, and received a post in the Curia. But it was no easier to get this choice confirmed than that of Langham. The Pope again intervened, and with the royal approval translated Simon Sudbury from London. As to Adam Easton, he had to accept the cardinal's hat from Urban V. in 1381, but afterwards became involved in the charge of conspiracy against that Pope at Nocera, and was imprisoned. He is said to have been liberated at the request of Richard II.

Archbishop Whittlesey.

Simon Sudbury at Canterbury was to have a harder fate even than incarceration. At first he seems to have sided with the party of John of Gaunt, but he later on incurred much unpopularity by the line he took in opposition to popular aspirations and sentiments. At Canterbury he spoke against the unreasoning reliance on indulgences, which might lead the ignorant to trust in them more than in a good life; but the sermon was an unpopular one and raised a tumult. He founded a college at Sudbury, and undertook the rebuilding of the nave of his cathedral. His tragic fate in the rebellion of Wat Tyler left the see vacant again in the year 1381.

Archbishop Sudbury.

A minister whose tastes were more congenial to the taste of Edward III. for refinement and magnificence was already deep in the royal counsels in the person of William of Wykeham, who was born in the Hampshire village of that name in the year 1324. At the age of twenty-three he was introduced to the notice of the king by his bishop, Edington, and was first employed as architect and surveyor in the king's vast building enterprises at Windsor Castle and elsewhere. Several ecclesiastical benefices were bestowed upon him as a layman. It was only in 1362 that he was ordained priest by Bishop Edington. He now became more and more indispensable to the king, who entrusted him with the Privy Seal, and consulted him on almost everything. At the death of Edington in 1366 Edward recommended Wykeham to the Chapter as his successor at Winchester. He was elected, and being approved of by the Pope, was consecrated next year. His public action, however, was now less successful in the State than it had been, and though made chancellor in 1367, he was only able to keep that high office until 1372, when there was an outcry against him, and he resigned. Henceforward he devoted himself to his diocese and became a really great bishop. He made a thorough visitation of his large diocese, and undertook, though he could not complete, the rebuilding of the cathedral nave, somewhat as Sudbury was doing at Canterbury. But his noblest work was what he accomplished for education. He established and endowed New College at Oxford, and got a royal charter for its government in 1379, and not contented with that,

William of Wykeham (1324-1404).

DECLINE OF PLANTAGENETS

devoted his energies to the foundation of a Grammar School of seventy-four scholars at Winchester, who might there prepare to carry on their higher studies at the college he had begun in Oxford. This is the still flourishing Winchester School. Wykeham spent his last years in still more fervent piety, his last days in devotion, and died at New Waltham in 1404. He was buried in the noble chantry, which he had himself founded on the south side of the nave at Winchester. There his effigy is still to be seen.

The Great Plague left as a legacy of its devastating passage over the country the seeds of a momentous social revolution, such as had some counterpart in almost all the countries of Europe. The Church, which entered into every department of the national life, had to intervene in this also, and exercised at least a moderating influence on the forces of disorder which such a vast public change must needs bring to the front. Even before the last outbreak of the Plague was over, it was clear that for many years to come there would be an immense scarcity of labour, and that in consequence much land would fall out of cultivation. A great rise in wages and in prices was the inevitable accompaniment of this. The results were so serious that the matter became one of the chief preoccupations of Parliament. A Statute of Labourers was passed as early as 1351, which attempted to fix the rate of wages by positive legislation. Then, as these provisions were not very effectual, repeated laws were passed in subsequent years to make them operative. At length, in 1376 the "Good Parliament" grappled with the whole question of the national poverty and needs in a far more fundamental way. Sir Peter de la Mere, elected speaker, laid before the Council a demand for the full publication of the royal accounts, and declared that the greatest cause of the prevailing distress came from the frauds practised in the markets; from the loans raised at usurious rates by the king; and from the plunder of the royal treasure at the bidding of evil counsellors. The chief offenders were imprisoned; and on the death of the Black Prince, which happened while a Parliament was in session, a standing Council was chosen to administer the affairs of the kingdom. The Archbishop of Canterbury and the Bishops of London and Winchester were among these counsellors. Finally, after making a great number of enactments to try and secure popular rights and to curb abuses the "Good Parliament" separated on the 6th of July, 1376, after sitting longer than any previous assembly of the kind had done. But from the very first the Duke of Lancaster and his friends openly declared that they did not intend to be bound by the decisions which the Parliament had taken. Sir Peter de la Mere was imprisoned at the instance of this party, while Wykeham, Bishop of Winchester, was impeached for misuse of State funds and misgovernment, and the temporalities of his bishopric were seized. Precautions were also taken to secure that the next Parliament should be of a different kind. In a few years the discontent broke out into open rebellion.

Alongside of this social revolution, and strangely connected with it in such a way that each reacted on the other, there arose about this time the religious movement which is usually known as Lollardy. The author of this new system, as far as it was due to any personal agency, was the well-known John Wycliffe, whose views, at first philosophical, and then dogmatic, became at last flagrantly heretical. Wycliffe's studies had been made at Oxford, where he became a teacher of great influence, and master of the new Balliol College. His university reputation became so widespread that it led to various benefices being conferred upon him, which he held simultaneously. But the incumbency of one or even more parishes did not imply that he ceased to reside in the university. It was not an uncommon thing to grant learned men a dispensation from the obligations of residing in their cures in order in this way to provide them with the means and leisure to prosecute their higher studies. The mastership of Balliol, indeed, was held by him for only a brief period, but it is not to be supposed that he resigned his other preferments so long as they did not interfere with his professorial occupations. There is a commonly held view that he was the Warden of Canterbury Hall, who was displaced to make room for the Benedictine Simon Langham, but there may have been two John Wycliffes at Oxford, in which case the warden and the heresiarch might not be the same person. At any rate, in 1374 he was presented by the crown to

Wycliffe and the Lollards.

the wealthy living of Lutterworth, which he continued to hold for the rest of his life. In 1374 also he was sent to Bruges as member of an English commission appointed to discuss various points in dispute between the Pope and king. But, though the success of this embassy was not great, the appointment to Lutterworth may have been an acknowledgment of his services on the occasion. He continued to visit Oxford from time to time as well as London. In the former place his academic ability, and in the latter his fame as a preacher, grew apace.

From this period his attacks on the clergy gradually developed from sharp criticism of the abuses of the day into a systematic onslaught on the holiest doctrines of the Faith. His treatise on Temporal Ownership, supporting the views of the extremists on the necessity of evangelical poverty for the clergy, had even before this recommended him to the notice of the political party who were pressing those opinions. John of Gaunt, Duke of Lancaster, had put himself at the head of this faction, and thus an alliance took place for a while between the Duke and Wycliffe. The Black Prince and his friends in the "Good Parliament" of 1376 drove the Lancastrian party from power. But the death of the Black Prince soon after enabled John of Gaunt once more to assume the ascendancy. Wycliffe, in theory, was inclined to go further even than those who attacked the special immunities of the clergy in Parliament, but he did not pass on to apply his doctrine about the reality of ownership being dependent on goodness in the individual owner either to clergy or laity. Mere academic theories had little effect on the multitude, and hence it is not probable that his writings directly influenced the Peasants' Revolt of 1381; but the doctrine was in the air, and it was easy for the intelligent to connect the two together.

When Wycliffe developed his dogmatic theories, denying the right of those in sin to any temporal ownership, he was summoned before Archbishop Sudbury and Courtenay, bishop of the diocese, in London. He appeared surrounded by his powerful friends, foremost among whom came the Duke of Lancaster. A hot quarrel took place between the Bishop of London and the earl. The Londoners thereupon took their bishop's part and chased away Lancaster and his armed men. Yet, all that was done was to impose silence on Wycliffe, and to appeal to the Holy See to condemn his teaching. A papal bull in condemnation of his errors was issued to the University of Oxford, and two others were despatched to the Primate and the Bishop of London, exhorting them to vigilance in checking the spread of doctrine which would be dangerous both to Church and State.

About the year 1381 a considerable development in Wycliffe's teaching took place. Twenty-four articles taken from his works were examined and condemned, and an inspection of these articles shows that by this time he denied Transubstantiation, the Real Presence, calling the Sacred Host an effectual sign, the lawfulness of the clergy holding temporal property, the need of the papal authority over the whole Church, while he asserted that all right to hold property is extinguished if a man is in sin, and that any excommunication by such a man is null and void—together with many other wild and false opinions. Some of the articles were censured as heretical, others only as erroneous, and the condemnation was signed by the Primate, by six bishops, and by a long list of Doctors in Law and Divinity. Whether Wycliffe appeared personally before the archbishop is not quite certain. At any rate he does not seem to have been molested by the authorities, and soon after the beginning of the new reign died in 1384. The fortunes of his leading followers must be briefly referred to in connection with the events of the reign of Richard II.

King Edward III. lost his consort, Philippa of Hainault, by death in 1369, and the remaining years of his life were years of weakness on his part, both in their moral and their physical aspect. He fell entirely under the domination of an ambitious mistress named Alice Perrers, whose influence seems to have been a public scandal among his subjects. While his sons, Edward the Black Prince and John of Gaunt, were contending for the upper hand in public affairs, the king himself seems to have slipped down into the helplessness of senility with scarcely an effort to recover himself. Yet he had been in his day the most brilliant sovereign in Christendom. He had not the military ability of his grandfather, but he was the pink of chivalry, and an accomplished knight versed in all its rules. Moreover, he was both kindly and

Last years of Edward III.

DECLINE OF PLANTAGENETS 271

affable in his intercourse with his people: always the gentleman in manner and in feeling. Nor would it be fair to omit all reference to the religious foundations which bore witness to his faith and his reliance on the power of prayer. Eastminster, though never so famous as Westminster, may be looked on as the chief of these. It was a Cistercian Abbey, built on Tower Hill, on the site of the present Mint, and was the fulfilment of a vow made to Our Lady of Grace for the king's safety from danger of shipwreck. But this was not his only pious foundation. He built a nunnery at Deptford, a hall at Oxford called King's Hall, while both St Stephen's Chapel at Westminster and St George's Chapel at Windsor owed much to his munificence. At last in his retirement at Shene he appears to have been deserted by all his family, and even by the dependants who had lived at his expense. One priest drew near, and was in time to administer to him the last rites of the Church. He died on the 21st of June, 1377, having reigned just over fifty years. His body was brought to the abbey at Westminster, and buried in the tomb we can still admire, next to Queen Philippa, and forming part of the imposing array which surrounds the shrine of the Holy Confessor. The king had twelve children: statuettes of all of them formerly surrounded the recumbent effigy of their father.

(B) THE REIGN OF RICHARD II. (1377-1399).

Richard of Bordeaux, son of the Black Prince, was only in his eleventh year when his grandfather, Edward III., died, leaving him undoubted heir to the throne. In spite of his peaceful character he had to reap the whirlwind of trouble which had been sown by the military adventures and the extravagance of the last reign. He was at once brought from Shene to the Tower of London, and proclaimed king. Then three weeks were spent in the elaborate funeral rites and "Requiem" Masses which were celebrated for the deceased monarch. At length on the 16th of July, Richard was crowned at Westminster by Simon Sudbury, the Primate, with all the magnificent ceremonial and the lavish expenditure on festivity in which that epoch

Richard II. (1377-1399).

delighted. High Mass and the Communion of the young king formed part of the elaborate function. Later on in the day Richard had to attend a crowded State banquet in Westminster Hall. As one day would not suffice, for all the public spectacles considered becoming, it was only on the morrow that the young sovereign passed in solemn procession through the city dressed in his coronation robes. On this occasion Thomas Brinton, the learned Bishop of Rochester, delivered a weighty discourse, in which he exhorted all parties in the State to lay aside their quarrels and unite to secure a happy reign for the new monarch. It made a considerable impression at the time, but alas! was all too soon forgotten. Earthly happiness was scarcely to be Richard's portion in life. He had inherited too many abiding evils in the State for this to be possible. There was, it is true, an effort at general reconciliation. William of Wykeham was received back into favour at court, and Peter de la Mere was freed from prison. John of Gaunt professed a desire for an understanding, and thus, immediately after the coronation, a Council of State was chosen, which embraced members of both the contending parties. But the discontent and unrest in the country was too deep to be dissipated by this compromise. First of all, there was a war with France actually going on, and this was a constant drain upon the resources of the country. Taxation was high, and would have to be higher, for supplies were urgently needed.

Parliament met on the 13th of October, and the situation of public affairs was explained by Sudbury, the Primate, in his opening speech. The Commons, all the same, were evidently in an independent and critical temper. They appointed Peter de la Mere Speaker, and two London citizens, William Walworth and John Philpot, treasurers, to superintend the spending of the liberal grant of money which they made. Alice Perrers had to submit to the punishment of banishment and forfeiture of all her goods. John of Gaunt, Duke of Lancaster, after a stormy scene in the hall, temporised for the present, but was thought to be still aiming at the control of the government of the country. He filled the largest place in the eyes of his contemporaries, and in the following year (1378) his feud with the citizens of London took on a more formidable character. At the

Parliament which met at Gloucester, he endeavoured to take the management of the treasury out of the hands of Walworth and Philpot. The clergy for their part were on no better terms with him than were the Commons. Bishop Courtenay seems to have thought that it was owing to Gaunt that the renewed proceedings against Wycliffe had come to nought. Further, he charged the Duke with abetting the breaches of the right of sanctuary which had been recently committed, and opposing the rights and privileges of the clergy. The Parliament had passed an act in favour of the clergy, enacting that no prelate or judge in the Church courts could be indicted for trying cases of tithes or concerning clerical rights according to old custom. But the outstanding difficulty was that neither this Parliament (1378) nor those held in the two succeeding years produced supplies at all adequate to the needs of the State. It was the last of these Parliaments which imposed a graduated Poll Tax, and thus led to the Rising of the Commons of 1381.

It was in Essex that the first resistance to the commissioners of the tax was met with, and several of the officials lost their lives in the rioting. When the disturbances became general in the county a disgraced priest, named Jack Straw, was put at the head of the movement. In Kent, soon after, and for similar causes, the peasantry rose under Wat the Tyler and an excommunicated preacher named John Ball. From these counties the movement was spread over the rest of the country, and before long there was rioting and rebellion in nearly every part of England. The king had been moved by his counsellors at the approach of danger to the Tower, where he was joined by his mother, by Archbishop Sudbury, and others. The rioters flocked to London, both from Essex and Kent, and poured into the city, committing great depredations on property, and summarily killing obnoxious inhabitants. Newgate was burnt, so was the Savoy Palace, the Duke of Lancaster's residence. It was resolved in Council to try the effect of conciliation and the granting of concessions. King Richard met a vast concourse of rebels at Mile End, and by the grant of charters, which confirmed the four points asked for, viz., the abolition of slavery, the reduction of rent to fourpence an acre, free markets, and a general pardon, persuaded the

Revolt of the Labourers.

assembled crowd to retire. But in the meantime, under Wat Tyler and Jack Straw, another body of insurgents had assailed the Tower of London, where they met with no resistance from the king's archers. Many prisoners were taken by the mob. Archbishop Sudbury, Sir Robert Hales, Master of the Knights of St John, who was royal treasurer, as well as Friar Appledore, the king's confessor, and several revenue officers, were led out to immediate execution on Tower Hill. The Archbishop, who had spent the night in prayer and had just finished Mass, met his fate with the calm courage of a martyr, and his skull was exposed from the Gate House of London Bridge. On the morrow the king, riding through Smithfield with a few horsemen, met Tyler at the head of a mob of twenty thousand men. There was a parley, and William Walworth, the Lord Mayor, interpreting a gesture of Tyler's as a threat to the king, plunged his sword into the rebel's throat. He fell, and was despatched by a royal squire. It was a moment of extreme danger for Richard, but he was equal to it. Riding up to the crowd, he cried, "Tyler was a traitor, my lieges. Come with me, and I will be your leader." They followed him, and then falling into the power of a strong force of royal cavalry, fell on their knees crying for mercy. For the moment, Richard resisted any attempt to take vengeance on the crowd, and commanded every man to depart to his home. Later on, however, bloody reprisals were indulged in by the landowners and royal officers; it is computed that in all seven thousand people lost their lives in combat, or through the subsequent executions. John Ball and Jack Straw were among those who suffered the death-penalty. But at the moment the only one in authority in the provinces who acted with decision was Henry Despenser, the young and warlike Bishop of Norwich, who at the head of a small force met the Norfolk insurgents, and thoroughly discomfited them. It was said of him that he first led his men to battle in complete armour, then tried the culprits as judge, and lastly, as pastor, himself gave them the consolations of religion before they suffered. The same prelate shortly after, being made papal legate in the Low Countries, led an army against the French to force them to abandon the cause of the anti-Pope, Clement VII. This expedition which thus became dignified with the appellation of a crusade, Despenser having taken the Cross with solemnity in London at departure, was at least as unsuccessful as any of those earlier Sacred Wars, and Despenser had to return to England.

When Parliament met, Richard gained its consent to the revocation of the charters he had under the pressure of necessity granted to the rebels. In fact both Lords and Commons were at least as anxious as the youthful sovereign that they should be revoked. A general pardon was given, and supplies were voted under a promise that the revenue officials should be kept back from rapacity and extortion. And though the revolt did not mean the end of villainage or slavery it certainly did mean that the labouring classes had begun to exert greater influence on the government of the country than ever before. The way was paved to still greater changes.

The chancellorship fell to William Courtenay, who had been Bishop of London since 1375, and who now both by the election of the monks of Canterbury and by the papal choice succeeded to the primacy. The first ecclesiastical business of importance which he had to deal with was the further examination of John Wycliffe and some of his followers. A synod met in May, 1382, which proceeded to pass judgment on twenty-four opinions taken from their writings. This synod is known as the "Council of the Earthquake," on account of its first session having been disturbed by this natural but alarming phenomenon. Parliament, which was sitting at the time, followed up the condemnation of the Wycliffite propositions by passing an act which provided for commissions to be sent into the different countries to arrest itinerant preachers, who wandered about without licence, preaching heresies and errors to the peril of souls and of the whole realm. Commissions were issued under the Great Seal, and action taken in accordance with this statute.

Archbishop Courtenay (1381-1396).

But while synod and Parliament were thus joined in taking action in London, there was considerable disturbance at Oxford through the teaching of Lollard professors and preachers in the University there. Nicholas of Hereford, a master in theology, had gone so far in defending Wycliffe's opinions as to say that Archbishop Sudbury

End of Wycliffe.

had been righteously slain, because he had opposed the truth of these opinions. And another doctor of the University, Philip Repingdon, had declared that he would defend all Wycliffe's moral teaching. Friar Stokes, a Carmelite, who had been preaching in Oxford against Wycliffe, was now ordered by the Primate to publish the condemnation decreed by the recent synod in London, and the chancellor of the University was summoned to answer for allowing these doctrines to be preached. The chancellor was made to ask pardon on his knees before the Archbishop, and sent back with orders to publish the condemnation. Hereford, Repingdon, and a certain theologian named Ashton were called on to sign the condemnation. The first two asked for time, and Ashton refused. Nevertheless, the Archbishop held firm, and under threat of excommunication Repingdon, and later on Ashton, abjured their errors and were restored, while Hereford pursued an appeal to the Holy See at Rome, and was there imprisoned. In the same way, and by similar means William Swynderby of Leicester was made to recant by the Bishop of Lincoln. Wycliffe himself appealed from the judgment of the bishops to that of the Parliament. But his friend, the Duke of Lancaster, came to him at Oxford and persuaded him to submit. In consequence of this he probably, though not certainly, read an orthodox profession of faith in the presence of Archbishop Courtenay and six other bishops, and was then allowed to retire to the rectory of Lutterworth, which he held in contradiction to his former teaching of the unlawfulness of benefices. Here he lived undisturbed for two years, and being struck with apoplexy while hearing Mass towards the end of 1384, expired two days later (December 29th to December 31st).

The death of Wycliffe in his obscure retirement was far from marking the end of the prevalence of his opinions. Lollardy continued to exert great influence, the measures of repression being for the time inadequate; it is only in the reign of Henry VII. that the best authorities find that the heresy was effectively extinguished. In fact the partisans of this sect used the ten years after their leader's death in organising a true conspiracy against both the doctrines and the discipline of the Church. The Great Schism was paralysing the strength

DECLINE OF PLANTAGENETS 277

of Church government; the bishops seemed unwilling to drive the sectaries to extremities. Eventually, these latter took the offensive and thus forced a decision. In 1395 libellous writings, both against the articles of the Faith and against the lives of the clergy, were posted by the Lollards at St Paul's Cathedral and at Westminster Abbey. There is little doubt that they were supported in this by high court influence, as well as by a section of the common people. This was followed up by a remonstrance addressed to the Parliament then sitting, comprised in twelve articles which are nearly all contradictory of one or other tenets of the Catholic Faith. Then at last the English hierarchy was driven to take action. A synod was held in London in the following year (1396) under presidency of the Archbishop of Canterbury, at which eighteen articles taken from a work of Wycliffe's called the "Trialogus" were condemned. The condemnation was reinforced by the framing of an oath which was tendered to leading men suspected of Lollardy, and the Archbishop at his visitation of the province, which followed immediately after, made diligent inquiry into the teaching of those under suspicion. At Oxford considerable opposition was offered to this visitation, presumably under Lollard influence. But at length the Archbishop succeeded in vindicating his right to visit the University.

The primacy was by this time in the hands of Thomas Fitzalan (or Arundel), brother of Richard, Earl of Arundel. Archbishop Courtenay died in 1396 at Maidstone, where he had founded a college for secular priests. Both these prelates were members of the nobility, for Courtenay was son of the Earl of Devon. But neither his high birth nor his dignity as Primate and chancellor had spoilt the noble humility of his heart. His direction for his funeral was that he should be buried in Maidstone Churchyard as unworthy to find a place in the cathedral. Thomas Fitzalan had spent fourteen years in the see of Ely, and eight in that of York before he was translated by papal provision to Canterbury. He received the pallium at the hands of Bishop William of Wykeham. He was a friend of the family of the Duke of Lancaster, and lived to be the chief instrument in bringing about the revolution which set Henry of Bolingbroke on the

Archbishop Arundel.

throne. But he had to pass through many storms before this result was obtained.

The greater part of King Richard's reign was taken up with the struggles of the national leaders and the royal favourites to obtain or keep the real government of the realm, nominally ruled by a youthful and inconstant sovereign. The chief favourites and ministers chosen by the king himself were Michael de la Pole, created Earl of Suffolk, and Robert de Vere, Earl of Oxford. But the king's uncles, and especially Lancaster, would not yield the first place in the royal counsels to these men, and their cause was in the main that of the Parliament and of popular liberty as far as it was then understood. In 1386 the king had been forced to put the administration into the hands of eleven Lords Commissioners, including Courtenay, the Primate, Alexander Neville, Archbishop of York, William of Wykeham, the Dukes of York and Gloucester, Richard, Earl of Arundel, and others. The Great Seal was taken from De la Pole and given to Thomas Arundel, then Bishop of Ely. Richard, nevertheless, made a fitful effort to stop the commission in the following year with the result that Gloucester and Arundel, with the Earl of Warwick, marched to London at the head of an army, and demanded the punishment of those who had advised the king against the legality of the continuance of the Commissioners' power. The five lords chiefly held responsible were impeached, one of these being, strangely enough, Alexander Neville, Archbishop of York. Courtenay, with his suffragans, protested that, saving their rights as peers, the bishops could have no hand in capital charges against the lives of those impeached. All the five were condemned to death, except Neville, but were mercifully let off the death penalty at the intercession of the bishops. As to Neville, in order to save the privileges of his order, the sentence was banishment, so Pope Urban translated him to the vacant see of St Andrew's. But, as the Scots, being on the side of the Avignon anti-Pope, would not receive him, he was obliged to accept a living at Louvain, where he died in 1391. Thomas Arundel was moved from Ely to York in his place.

The Parliament which had thus confirmed the power of the Commissioners is sometimes called the "Wonderful Parliament"; it went on before it separated to earn the

less desirable surname of the "Merciless Parliament."
Probably it did so at the instigation of the Duke of
Gloucester. Four knights, held to be friends of the king,
were appealed against or really impeached by the Lords
and Commons, and a long trial took place. But the issue
was prejudged, and the four, whose names were Burleigh,
Beauchamp, Berners, and Salisbury, were led to execution. The king was made to renew his coronation oath,
and for the whole of the next year was entirely in the
hands of the commission. Then, in 1389, by one of those
sudden strokes which show that though deficient in constancy he was not in vigour, Richard freed himself. He
asked his uncle in council to tell him his age, which was
twenty-one, then thanking the Lords for their former
services, he said he required them no longer. He
followed this up by taking the Great Seal from Arundel
and the key of the treasury from the Bishop of Hereford.
He was now his own master, and enjoyed a period of
comparative peace and prosperity until 1394. Parliaments met regularly, and enactments were passed renewing the Statutes of Provisors and Premunire in a revised
form, and also forbidding that aliens should take the
temporal fruits of any benefices in the kingdom to which
they might be appointed. Though these provisions were
protested against by the papal court, they greatly limited
an acknowledged abuse. The only way in which the
statutes could be evaded was by an amicable arrangement
between the Pope and the king, which henceforward
enabled now one, now the other, to carry his candidate
after a merely nominal form of election had been gone
through by the Chapter.

In 1394 King Richard went over to Ireland at the head
of an imposing array, as he had been given to understand
that the moment was favourable for the pacification of
Ireland, and for the establishment of the royal power in
the country. He passed from place to place with much
parade, and began to go into the question of reforming
abuses, when he was recalled to England at the request
of the bishops on account of the Lollard conspiracy already
spoken of. It was not long, however, before attention
was diverted from the Lollards by a new crisis in political
affairs.

The four or five years of power which King Richard
had enjoyed by 1394 seem either to have changed his

character, or at the least brought to light a phase hitherto
unknown. The death of his amiable queen, Anne of
Bohemia, in 1394, was the loss of one good influence,
and his marriage with Isabella of Valois, daughter of
the French king, seems to have stirred ambitions for an
absolute monarchy, which up to this had at least lain
dormant. His uncle, the Duke of Gloucester, was the
one who now more than any other crossed his designs
in this direction. He soon affected to believe that
Gloucester, with the Earl of Warwick and the two
Arundels, Earl and Archbishop, had formed a plot to
seize and imprison him. To be beforehand with them
he had them all apprehended and put in prison. Then,
when the Parliament met two months later, they were
impeached for treasonable practices by the Commons at
the king's direction. The Earl of Arundel was found
guilty, and beheaded at the Tower. Both Warwick and
Gloucester were also declared guilty and banished, the
former to the Isle of Man, and the latter to France.
Soon after it was given out that Gloucester was dead,
and it was not without suspicion of foul play on the
part of his guards. As to the Archbishop, under pretext
of respect for his office, he was not allowed to plead, but
treated as guilty, was banished from the kingdom.
Archbishop Arundel betook himself to the Pope, but
was followed up by letters from the king praying the
Pontiff to remove him from the primacy, and appoint a
successor. Boniface IX. gave way to the insistence of
the English monarch, translated Arundel to St Andrew's,
as Neville had been translated before, and gave a papal
provision to Roger Walden, Dean of York, the royal
treasurer. The king now conferred dignities and offices
on his chief supporters, and carefully organised the
elections for a Parliament which met at Shrewsbury in
1398. This assembly proved quite subservient to the
king's policy, granted him supplies for life, and finally
delegated its authority to a committee which was in the
main favourable to the royal theory of absolute monarchy.
The acts of the Merciless Parliament were rescinded, and
restitution ordered to be made to those who had suffered
or to their families. The triumph of the king seemed
now to be attained, but in reality he was very near his
fall. He was soon in new difficulties through sharp
accusations of treachery made against one another by

DECLINE OF PLANTAGENETS 281

Henry Bolingbroke, Duke of Hereford, and Bigod, Duke of Norfolk. It was agreed that they should clear themselves by wager of battle, or single combat, but at the last moment Richard stopped the duel, and banished Hereford for ten years and Norfolk for life. He then proceeded to rule by means of the powers which the Parliament had made over to him at Shrewsbury in every respect like an absolute monarch. Moreover, even advice from those who wished him well was ill taken or disregarded. It was thus that, paying no attention to the fact that his enemies were determined on revenge, and that the mass of the nation was estranged by his arbitrary behaviour, he again passed into Ireland in 1399 to punish those who had slain his cousin and heir, the Earl of March, who was ruling that country as Lord Deputy.

Hereford was an exile in France, similarly Archbishop Arundel was at Cologne. They met at Paris, and determined to return to England during Richard's absence. Three small vessels were hired, and with a few soldiers and some servants the duke and the Primate set sail and landed at Ravenspur in Yorkshire. Being joined by the Earls of Northumberland and Westmoreland with their retainers, Bolingbroke swore that he came merely to recover his estates, and that he would not advance any claim to the throne. The Duke of York, who was regent in the king's absence, gathered the royal army at St Albans. Yet, when Bolingbroke advanced to meet him at the head of an ever-increasing army, he retired towards the west, under pretext of meeting the king who was hastening back from Ireland. Henry therefore proceeded to London where he was welcomed by the population with loud acclamations. Thence with a great array he proceeded to Chester, a stronghold of those faithful to the king. Richard, meantime, having landed at Milford also turned north. The king and duke met at Flint Castle. Amongst the array which surrounded Henry was Archbishop Arundel; in the king's suite was Marks, Bishop of Carlisle. After an interview, resistance being impossible, possession was taken of the king and his followers, and he was brought to London, where he was secured in the Tower. It was decided by Henry that he would proceed by way of the double act of resignation on

Landing and Accession of Henry Bolingbroke (1399).

the part of Richard, and deposition on the part of the Parliament. Therefore Richard was persuaded to resign the crown, and as soon as this had been obtained thirty-three articles of impeachment against him were laid before Lords and Commons. Some of these were frivolous enough, but Richard was deservedly unpopular, and Parliament went on to depose him. Thereupon, Henry, in the presence of the whole assembly in Westminster Hall, claimed the inheritance in right of his descent from Henry III., combined with the right of conquest and the need for the common good of repairing the misgovernment of the late king. The claim was admitted by both houses, and Archbishop Arundel led the successful Lancastrian to the empty throne. He immediately summoned Parliament to meet again six days later, and then retired in royal state.

XXI.

THE CHURCH UNDER THE HOUSE OF LANCASTER.

(1399-1455.)

(A) HENRY IV. (1399-1413).

WHEN Henry Bolingbroke mounted the throne in 1399 after the deposition and resignation of Richard II., it made a change of dynasty, the results of which were far-reaching. The part of the English prelates, led by Archbishop Arundel, in effecting this change had been a very important one. Scarcely any had so large a part as Arundel in securing that Henry's claim should be acknowledged, and then in ratifying it in the name of the Church. It was, of course, Arundel who crowned Henry in Westminster Abbey on the 13th of October, 1399, and who counted upon his grateful co-operation in promoting the welfare of both priests and people. It was an outward sign of close union that at the coronation banquet Henry had the Archbishop of Canterbury on his right and the Archbishop of York on his left; and the other bishops were all seated at the king's table. The Houses of Parliament were already holding their first session of the new reign when Henry was crowned, and the Primate in his opening address was able to proclaim that the new king was resolved to maintain the liberties of the Church and to govern his subjects according to law.

Meantime, the clergy had already met in council or Convocation, and Arundel was able to show letters from the Holy See, cancelling his appointment to St Andrew's, and further declaring Walden to be a usurper, and confirming Arundel himself in the primatial see. Walden was for the time imprisoned, but later on set at

Henry IV. (1399-1413).

liberty. Furthermore, instead of showing himself hostile, Arundel used his influence to get him appointed Bishop of London in 1405. This was a peaceful settlement of the difference between them, but Roger Walden only survived until the following year. Thus in 1406 London was again vacant.

But Arundel does not seem to have waited for this restoration to his former archbishopric to take his seat in Parliament. Once more feeling himself secure in his position as Primate, he proceeded to publish a series of enactments which make this meeting of Convocation quite an historical event. Henry IV. had sent a message to the clergy which was in sharp contrast to the exacting demands of some of his predecessors, namely, that he did not ask for their money but for their prayers; he also promised to do his best for the repression of heresy. Arundel acted on the hint; no grant was made, but constitutions were drawn up against the Lollards, and a circular was put out by the Archbishop, and spread abroad amongst the clergy. This perhaps was a formal acknowledgment of Henry's request for prayers. Thomas Arundel then, like the devout prelate he was, goes on to say: "The contemplation of the great mystery of the Incarnation has drawn all Christian nations to venerate her from whom came the first beginnings of our Redemption. But, we English, as being the special servants of her inheritance, and her own Dowry, as we are commonly called, ought to surpass others in the fervour of our praises and devotions." He then proceeded to direct the ringing of the Angelus Bell, not only in the evening at curfew, but also early in the morning throughout the province of Canterbury. This is perhaps the first really official mention of England as the Dowry of Mary, but at the same time the archbishop expressly bears witness to the popularity of the title in ordinary parlance, thus claiming not to introduce any new form of language, but merely to adopt what had come down in the mouth of the faithful from bygone ages.

Arundel in Convocation.

The question had of necessity to be raised in Parliament as to what should be done with the late king so as to secure the permanency of the new regime. Thereupon, Thomas Marks, Bishop of Carlisle, with quite remarkable courage, rose and delivered an elaborate speech in defence of Richard, denouncing any unjust treatment of him in the future, and treating the new succession as a usurpation. The sensation created by this speech must have been very great, but Marks was straightway placed in confinement in the Tower of London, or at St Albans. Furthermore, the Lords having decided that Richard must be kept in close confinement, he was removed to Pontefract Castle. It was not very long before a conspiracy was set on foot to liberate him, and to seize on the person of Henry. However, the plot being discovered in time, its only effect was to hasten Richard's end. In this plot it was discovered that Bishop Marks, who had been freed from imprisonment, had been involved. He was thereupon apprehended, tried for his life, and sentenced to death. Even now Henry spared the bishop's life, and in order to get him out of the way the Pope translated him to a remote see in the Greek Island of Samos. Marks, in the end, contrived to maintain himself in England, a bishop without a bishopric, and then, having been pardoned by Henry, and magnanimously treated by Arundel, died in 1409 as Rector of Todenham. In 1400 William Strickland had already been appointed to Carlisle. Richard II. soon came to the end of his troubled career, though the manner of his death will always remain a mystery. It was affirmed by the Lancastrians that he starved himself to death out of grief at the fate of his friends and the failure of his plans. The more probable accounts, embodied in Shakespeare's play, declare that he was violently assaulted, and done to death in the castle at Pontefract. Henry IV. attended the public funeral at King's Langley.

Fate of Richard II.

Early next year (1400) Parliament undertook to legislate in several matters connected with the welfare of the Church. Penalties were decreed against all those who should avoid the payment of tithes, or who should fail in obedience to their lawful superiors. But a far more famous provision was that which was enacted against the Lollards. The bishops were authorised, each in his own diocese, to apprehend and imprison all persons suspected of heresy. These were then to be brought before the diocesan court, and if found guilty, handed over to the secular power, after all reasonable

Legislation against heresy.

effort had been made by exhortation and by imprisonment to secure their abjuration. Those who were obstinate and refused to recant were to be burnt in the presence of the mayor and sheriffs and before all the people, in virtue of a royal writ called "*De haeretico comburendo.*" In common parlance this title is transferred from the writ, ordering the individual execution to the entire act of Parliament, though, of course, this is not strictly accurate. William Sawtré, Rector of St Osyth's in London, was the first to suffer on account of this statute in the March of 1401. It must be confessed, however, that his execution had little effect in preventing the growth of the Lollard doctrines, especially of such as had a marked anti-clerical tone. Under the influence of these views attempts were made in the House of Commons to decree the confiscation of some part at least of the property of the Church, and thus lessen the burden of taxation on the laity. Archbishop Arundel defended the clergy with vigour, and going to the king begged on his knees the royal protection for them. Henry assured him that nothing should be done against the rights of the Church, and then the affair dropped. In fact, after some time the Commons asked the Archbishop's pardon for having made the proposal, acknowledging its injustice. In 1407 a Lollard priest, William Thorpe, was tried before Arundel and convicted out of his own writings, especially from one called "Thorpe's Testament," which was a violent attack on the hierarchy. Thorpe was imprisoned, and in the following year the Archbishop held a Provincial Council at Oxford to endeavour to check the growth of anti-clerical teaching such as Thorpe's, especially in the University. Decrees were made that henceforward examination and the licence of the bishop are necessary for all preachers. "The Approbation of the Church" is declared to be requisite for any translation of the Holy Scripture—evidently in opposition to Wycliffe's version. Wycliffe's works are furthermore condemned. All needful measures are ordered to be taken to extirpate Lollard teaching from the University of Oxford.

Although Bishop Marks escaped with his life from the entanglements arising out of his opposition to the Lancastrian line, his metropolitan, Archbishop Scrope of York,

Anti-clerical influences.

THE HOUSE OF LANCASTER 287

was not so successful. The Scropes of Bolton had been devoted to the interests of the late king, and Richard, who had been raised to the see of York in 1398, was no exception to the rest of his family. His brother, the Earl of Wiltshire, had been executed at Bristol for his share in the plots to bring back Richard II. in the very first year of the new reign. It seems that the Archbishop himself had acquiesced in the change of dynasty. Moreover, he was a man of blameless, and even saintly life, too much absorbed in the spiritual charge of his diocese to become the leader of any political movement. Yet, when the Percys rose against King Henry in the rebellion of 1405, he became involved in the attempt, which soon resulted in failure. Scrope was treacherously inveigled into a conference with the Earl of Westmoreland; he was seized on a charge of treason, and brought before the celebrated judge, Sir William Gascoigne. The latter boldly refused to try his prisoner, on the ground that a lay court had no authority to try an archbishop, who should be charged before his peers. But, notwithstanding this brave protest, another judge, more compliant than he, was found in Justice Fulthorpe, and Scrope was found guilty. He was sentenced to death, and at once executed, being the first bishop ever sentenced to death in England by a layman. The good Archbishop won an extraordinary reputation for holiness among the people in the north of England, being popularly known as St Richard Scrope. Percy, Earl of Northumberland, was likewise executed after a last futile rising in 1408, and both Archbishop and Earl found a grave in York Minster. The tomb of the former became a shrine at which rich offerings were laid, and to which men travelled from afar on pilgrimage. Henry IV. certainly lapsed from his better judgment and usual moderation in allowing the execution to proceed, and his subsequent ailments were ascribed by the people to the divine vengeance on him for the murder of a saint.

Archbishop Scrope (1405).

In the course of the year 1409 a special meeting of Convocation was summoned to choose representatives of the English clergy who might attend the Council of Pisa, which met later in the same year. The Great Schism was going on; and efforts had been made to induce the rival Pontiffs, Gregory XII. and Benedict XIII., to resign in order to allow of the election of a Pope who might be accepted both at Rome and at Avignon.

English Clergy at the Council of Pisa. When these attempts led to no result, the cardinals who were no longer with either Gregory or Benedict drew up an encyclical summoning a General Council to meet at Pisa with the object of putting an end to the schism. Among the representatives chosen by Convocation in London were Henry Chichele, Bishop of St David's, Langley, Bishop of Durham, and the celebrated Carmelite theologian, Thomas Netter, known as Waldensis. Robert Hallam (or Allen), Bishop of Salisbury, also went to the Council, and though the Council of Pisa only resulted in adding a third to the two previous claimants to the papacy, through its election of Alexander V., he remained for some time on the Continent, striving to promote the union of the different "obediences" as they were called. In his creation of new cardinals in 1411, John XXIII. named both Robert Hallam and Thomas Langley, but as this would have meant in the Pontiff's intention their residing in the Curia, and resigning Salisbury and Durham respectively, Henry IV. wrote to the Pope, begging him to excuse them from accepting the dignity. Langley then returned to England, but Hallam remained abroad until the Council of Constance, at which he was one of the leading spirits until his death in 1417. Henry Beaufort then stepped into his place as the chief spokesman of the English nation in that historic assembly.

Cardinal Beaufort (1367-1447). Henry Beaufort had already held the see of Winchester since 1405, and was to preside over that great diocese for another thirty years before he sank into his grave as an octogenarian in 1447. Nor was his election to Winchester the beginning of his public career; for he had already been Bishop of Lincoln for seven years when the death of William of Wykeham gave the opportunity for his translation to the old West Saxon capital. He was the illegitimate son of John of Gaunt by Catherine Swinford, and therefore brother to John Beaufort, Earl of Somerset, and half-brother to King Henry IV. Both he and his brother had been legitimatised by Richard II., but in such limited fashion as not to admit that they had any claim of succession to the throne. Even so,

THE HOUSE OF LANCASTER 289

there was dangerous rivalry between the two families descended from John of Gaunt, and grave dissension was the almost inevitable result. Beaufort became the chief adviser of Henry, Prince of Wales, and this helped to throw him into opposition to the king's brothers, the Dukes of Bedford and Gloucester, and to Archbishop Arundel. For two years, from 1410 to 1412, he was Lord Chancellor, and his policy, which favoured the assumption of almost the power of regent by the Prince of Wales, was in the ascendant; but at the latter date he was obliged to resign the Great Seal, and Arundel and the king's brothers returned to power. In 1417 he proceeded to the Council of Constance, Hallam dying in that year. Here his part was a very prominent one. His was the determining voice which decided the Fathers to give the election of a new Pontiff the precedence over the Decrees of Reform for which the Emperor Sigismund was pressing. It is interesting to note that together with Beaufort the six electors from England for the papal election were the Bishops of London, Norwich, Lichfield, and Bath and Wells, the Abbot of Bury St Edmunds, and the Dean of York. Eighteen others from the other nations were also joined with the cardinals to form the conclave. It was Richard Clifford, Bishop of London, who proposed Cardinal Colonna, who then became Pope Martin V.; and thus the schism was ended. Martin soon offered Beaufort the cardinal's hat in reward for his services, but the English king protested, and it was only much later that he did accept the dignity together with that of legate, while the royal acquiescence is only to be gathered from the absence of further protest.

But, long before these things happened, King Henry IV. had breathed his last. Though he was only forty-five years of age, the signs of premature old age were manifest, and the inroads of disease exhausted his strength. His confessor had been instrumental in leading him to penance for his share in the deeds of blood which had accompanied his establishment on the throne, and especially for whatever share he had had in the death of Richard II. and in that of Archbishop Scrope. Early in 1413 he was seized with a fit whilst at his devotions before the shrine of St Edward in Westminster Abbey. He was, therefore, carried from the church into what was called the Jerusalem Chamber in the abbot's apart-

T

ments. There he lingered for some days, though evidently in a dying condition; there also he breathed his last on the 19th of March. His body was taken to Canterbury Cathedral and interred in the chancel, outside the chantry known as the Chantry of Henry IV. His bones were laid close by the remains of that great warrior, who, had he survived, would have probably saved the nation the long-drawn-out rivalry of Yorkist and Lancastrian and the Wars of the Roses—the redoubtable Edward the Black Prince.

(B) HENRY V. (1413-1422).

Henry V. (1413-1422). The eldest son of the late monarch, known as Henry of Monmouth, had been so long before the public eye as Prince of Wales and as the acknowledged heir to the throne that his succession took place as a matter of course. Popular report had it that even while his father lay dying he had put the crown on his own head, and thus claimed it in the life-time of its actual owner. He was also credited with a career of youthful levity, of dissipation, and almost of lawlessness. But the same chroniclers who record these things speak likewise of a sudden and salutary change as soon as he became king. Immediately after his father's death he shut himself up in his chamber, and spent the day in solitary thought and prayer. Then he betook himself to a far-famed anchorite, Father John, who lived in a hermitage at Westminster, and made a general confession of his whole life. Nor was this merely an outburst of passing sentiment, for the resolutions of amendment which it is presumed he then made were translated into action without delay. His former bosom companions were sent away; the wisest and most experienced counsellors whom he could find were invited to his side: even those who had found fault with the follies of his youth were treated with respect and consideration. Furthermore, with rare directness and courage he at once reversed some of the more severe and repressive actions of the last reign. As an example of this policy, the Earl of March, who by the strict rule of descent was the lawful heir to the crown, was liberated from the imprisonment in which he had been kept, and the

THE HOUSE OF LANCASTER 291

remains of Richard II. were transferred with solemn funeral rites from King's Langley to Westminster. The Percys were restored to their estates, and Archbishop Arundel, that uncompromising Lancastrian and enemy of the Plantagenet regime, had once more to yield up the chancellorship which was before long bestowed on Bishop Henry Beaufort, the king's uncle. These measures taken together meant a bold effort to conciliate all classes of his accession, and it was in great part successful. Henry V. became the national hero and the leader of the whole people, seated on a throne too secure to be shaken by conspiracy or party intrigue. The preservation of England in undivided unity in the religion of their fathers was undoubtedly the prime object of his policy, and when his efforts in this direction and in the suppression of civil discord seemed to have borne fruit, he was able to turn to foreign affairs. Here his intervention was so potent that before his death he had become the mightiest prince in Christendom.

Archbishop Arundel lived long enough to see the Lancastrian dynasty, of which he had been on the whole the foremost supporter, firmly planted on the throne before he died in 1414. But it must have been a mortification to him to witness his policy of determined hostility to the House of Plantagenet considerably modified. He was the chief counsellor and statesman of Henry IV., but Henry V. relied more on the advice of Beaufort and of Chichele. During the last year of his life the Primate turned more completely from affairs of State to the religious situation in the country. He had to deal with one of the dangerous outbreaks of Lollardy of which we know. This was the conspiracy of Sir John Oldcastle. This notorious disturber of the national tranquillity had been one of the circle of companions who surrounded Henry V. in the days of his frivolous youth. But while the royal prince had turned from his pleasures to wisdom and piety, Oldcastle had turned aside in the opposite direction, to become an abettor of sedition and of heretical teaching. Convocation instead of summoning him to appear in the court, had denounced him to the king as a supporter of heresy. Henry then had a personal interview with his former companion endeavouring to win him over from his errors, but the effort

Arundel and the Lollards.

was made in vain. Oldcastle fled from the royal court to his country house, but Archbishop Arundel, having found that the king now committed the case entirely to the bishops, had the delinquent seized and committed to the Tower of London. He refused to appear before the episcopal court, strangely enough, appealing to the Holy See. However, he was twice brought forward, cross-examined, and then excommunicated. In the end, as he still held to his Lollard opinions, affirming that the Pope was Antichrist, and that prelates should only be obeyed so far as their lives were holy, he was declared to be an obstinate heretic, and was handed over to the civil power for punishment as such. But neither the King nor the Archbishop were desirous that he should be executed. Hence Arundel petitioned the crown for a respite of forty days in the hope that he might recant. Instead of this, he managed to effect his escape from the Tower, and joining his friends, formed a plot to seize the king at Eltham during the Christmas-tide. Henry got news of the plan in good time, so suddenly moving his court from Eltham to Westminster, he met the Lollards, who by this time had assembled in London in force, with such overwhelming preparations that the leaders were some of them seized and others scattered in different directions. Many of the conspirators were executed, though Oldcastle himself once more got away. It was only in 1417 that, taking part in another conspiracy against the king's authority, he was seized near the Welsh border, brought to London, and there executed on the 14th of December in St Giles' Fields. He was hanged, and his body afterwards burnt together with the gallows.

The long and stormy career of Archbishop Arundel came to an end in 1414. After the triumph of his policy in the change of dynasty, he had been for many years the most influential personality in England, and although he had been much engrossed in his work as a statesman, he was a true ecclesiastic as well. He was keen upon the reform of clerical abuses as well as those of the laity. He had made himself the inflexible champion of orthodox doctrine against the Lollard heresies, and he was a promoter of devotion to the Blessed Virgin Mary. In fact, it may be well said of him that he combined the double office of Lord Chancellor and

Death of Archbishop Arundel (1414).

Primate with remarkable success. He was buried in his own cathedral, but he has no tomb or monument there save it be the architectural features which owe their origin to his munificence.

The Canterbury monks elected Henry Chichele, Bishop of St David's, to the vacant archbishopric, but, when the papal confirmation was applied for, Martin V. wrote that he had meant to dispose of the see by papal provision, but that in order to avoid any dispute, he would provide in the case in favour of the same candidate whom the monks had elected. Chichele therefore was put in possession of the temporalities of the see, took his oath of obedience to the Pope, and duly received his pallium without having to go to Rome to ask for it. He already enjoyed a high reputation for learning and also for skill in administration, and at once came into the inner counsels of King Henry V. He held the primacy for nearly thirty years, but was not successful in retaining the favour of the Pope, who thought that the time was ripe for a strong protest against the Statutes of Premunire and of Provisors which had been passed in the Parliaments of earlier reigns. When he did not take such a strong line in this matter as the Pontiff wished, the Pope showed resentment by studiously passing him over, and by conferring the office of legate in England on Henry Beaufort, Bishop of Winchester. This prelate, as well as Archbishop Kemp of York, was raised to the Sacred College, but the cardinal's hat was not sent to Chichele. Still, it is a gross perversion of fact to represent him as a disobedient or lukewarm Catholic. He fully admitted the papal authority over the whole Church. It was from the papal provision that he had himself obtained the numerous benefices which he had held from the early years of his priesthood right up to his promotion to the primacy. Chichele was a very noble patron of learning. In Higham Ferrers, his birthplace, he founded a grammar school, which he endowed with revenues for the good of his soul. At Oxford his educational projects were even more extensive, and of course are far more renowned. His foundation of St Bernard's College was for the Cistercian students, and when it was replaced by the later establishment of St John's College, the statue of St Bernard was still left standing as Patron and Father

Archbishop Chichele (1414-1443).

over the chief doorway. Chichele's second Oxford college, All Souls, still subsists. It was on a munificent scale, and provided for more than forty members who were to pray for the souls of Kings Henry V. and VI., and of the English warriors who had fallen in the French war. "Chichele's Chest" offered funds to the poor Oxford scholars of any college who might be in need, and New College, where the Primate had studied, benefited by a similar sum allocated to its needs. The Professor of Modern History even to-day is known as the Chichele professor, and thus the memory of the great archbishop, who did so much for the well-being of the University, can scarcely die out in the place where he spent a great portion of his declining years.

It is not easy to feel sure what motives led Henry V. to revive the claim to the French crown which had been pushed with such disastrous results by Edward III. The theory that this war was undertaken to distract the minds of his people from domestic trouble is untenable. Henry V. was a conscientious Christian ruler, but he was also a mediaeval knight of chivalry, framing his ideals on the romantic models of King Arthur and the Crusaders. Possibly he held himself in duty bound, once peace was secure at home, to prosecute what he considered his rights on the Continent of Europe. Anyhow, no sooner was he free from disturbance at home than the claim was made, with more than all its original dubiousness of foundation, and when all discussion of it was indignantly rejected by the French, he prepared for war. In the following year the king landed in France at the head of a powerful army, and having taken Harfleur at the cost of immense loss both of time and men, inflicted on the French the signal defeat of Agincourt. All Henry's plans were laid with a combination of military skill and of statesmanship which displayed his eminent ability. In 1416 he returned to England in triumph, and endeavoured to strengthen his position by an alliance with the Emperor Sigismund and with the Duke of Burgundy. Sigismund visited England in the course of that year, and was received in state, while Henry, never losing sight of the interests of the Church, endeavoured to co-operate with him in the effort to put an end of the Great Schism of the West. In 1417 he resumed his military operations

Henry V. and France.

THE HOUSE OF LANCASTER 295

in France, devoting himself in the first instance to the Conquest of Normandy. Caen was taken by storm, and then began the difficult and protracted siege of Rouen, the capital. Finally, in January, 1419, Rouen fell, and the road to Paris was open before the English king. Attacked both by the English army and by the Burgundians, who were in alliance with them, the cause of the French, whose chief leader was the Dauphin, son of the feeble Charles VI., seemed desperate. At length the Treaty of Troyes (1420) was signed, by which it was agreed that Henry should be Regent of France as long as Charles VI. survived, and king after his death, marrying by virtue of the same Treaty Catherine, daughter of the French monarch. The Dauphin was thus to be excluded from the inheritance, and Henry was to unite the two crowns in his person. Soon after the Treaty had been concluded, Henry and Catherine were married at Troyes, and then made their state entry into Paris. From Paris Henry passed to the siege of Montereau and to that of Melan, both of which places were taken.

In 1421 the king thought he could take his new queen home to England. With ceremonial of great magnificence she was crowned at Westminster, and thence accompanied her husband in a triumphal progress through the kingdom, which extended as far as York. There the news of the defeat of the Duke of Clarence at Beaujé was a trumpet-note calling Henry to return to the war. Landing at Calais with nearly thirty thousand men he captured Meaux, and then went to Paris, where he was joined by his queen: and Whitsuntide was kept with high festive rejoicings. But before long an insidious malady, brought on, it is thought, by the hardships of camp life, put his life in danger, and but a few months elapsed before he died on the 31st of August at the Bois de Vincennes. As he lay dying *Henry V. dies.* he expressed his longing desire, now to be for ever unfulfilled, of going on the Crusade to win back the Holy Places of Palestine from the infidel. At any rate, from the time he mounted the throne he had striven to be a model Christian king; devoted to Holy Church and an enemy to her enemies; the determined opponent of drunkenness, of swearing, and of licence in his armies; and in his own life faithful to his marriage vows and to his friends. Nor must it be forgotten that he was almost as skilful a statesman as he was a great military captain. Had he lived longer things might have gone far otherwise than they did both in England and in Christendom:

"King Henry the Fifth, too famous to live long!
England ne'er lost a king of so great worth,"

so sings Shakespeare.

His remains were brought home to his native land, and laid in a splendid chantry at the end of St Edward's Chapel in Westminster Abbey. Its position between the mediaeval shrine of St Edward and the gorgeous Tudor chapel of Henry VII. fitly symbolises his position in history. James I. of Scotland, who had followed his army in France as a volunteer, now followed his corpse as the chief mourner: while immense throngs of his own countrymen were present at the procession and at the funeral rites, which were performed both in St Paul's and in the abbey. The stately chantry, which had been fitted with an Altar of the Annunciation, still remains. There it is to be believed that a great number of the twelve thousand Masses, which his will directed to be offered for his soul, were celebrated. But, beyond this, he had bedesmen to pray for his soul at the Charterhouse of Shene, and bedeswomen at the Briggitine convent of Sion House, Isleworth, for both these celebrated foundations owed their origin to Henry's liberality.

(c) HENRY VI. UP TO THE WARS OF THE ROSES (1422-1455).

The infant son of the deceased monarch and of Catherine of France was at once proclaimed without opposition under the title of Henry VI. A Council of Regency was appointed with Humphrey, Duke of Gloucester, one of the king's uncles, at its head to govern in his name. The Duke of Bedford, also his uncle, was made Regent of France. Beauchamp, Earl of Warwick, was named governor to attend to the king's education. At the age of eight Henry was crowned King of England at Westminster in 1429, and King of France at Paris in 1431: in each case many of the rites had to be omitted or curtailed. Before his death in 1471 he was destined

Henry VI. (1421-1471).

THE HOUSE OF LANCASTER

to lose the possession of both these kingdoms in turn. So great had been the personal ascendancy of Henry V. that his inheritance in England seemed at the first glance secure enough, but the hold of his race upon the French throne was clearly precarious even from the first. Charles the Dauphin was in possession of a considerable part of France, and Rheims being in the hands of the English, was crowned at Chartres. However, Bedford, the Regent, conducted the military operations with skill and determination. The battle of Verneuil was a heavy blow to the French hopes in 1424, and for five years, though no further conquests were made by him, he remained master of the Northern provinces, and even strengthened his grasp upon them. However, in 1428 he considered that the hour had arrived when he could safely advance southwards. The Loire had hitherto been, roughly speaking, the line of division between French and English. The river was now crossed by Bedford's orders, and siege laid to the important city of Orleans. It was at this place that the tide was definitely turned against the English invaders, though not without the intervention of a power beyond that of natural prowess.

The prolonged contest of the Hundred Years' War and the English domination in France, in which it culminated under Henry V., were brought to an end by a distinctly spiritual agency. The appearance in this political struggle of the Maid of Orleans is probably the clearest case which the History of the Church shows of supernatural power altering the course of natural events. The wonderful Christian maiden known as Joan of Arc, La Pucelle, or the Maid of Orleans, is the noblest heroine which French annals have to boast. Moreover, though this is a lofty claim, it is virtually admitted both in England and France. Joan was born at Domrémy in Champagne probably in 1412. Her youth was that of a simple country girl, full of piety and devotion. But before she was fourteen she became conscious of supernatural voices speaking to her within, not so much of her own interior life as of a mission entrusted to her for France and Christendom. She only realised this gradually, yet by May, 1428, she knew that she had to go to the French king, Charles VII., and rouse him up to the work of the liberation of the country. Her first

St Joan of Arc (1412-1431).

attempts to speak with him failed, through the incredulity of those around him. But, gaining credit through the fulfilment of her prophecy of the English victory called the Battle of the Herrings, she was suffered to have an interview with Charles in March, 1429. All that passed is not known, but she prophesied that she would relieve Orleans then besieged by the English, and that Charles would be crowned at Rheims in the following summer. In April she effected an entry into Orleans, and in the following month, putting herself in complete armour at the head of the French troops, drove the English in headlong flight from the city. This was followed by a series of victories until, on Sunday, July the 17th, Charles VII. was solemnly crowned in Rheims Cathedral, the Maid with war standard in hand attending at the throne. Six weeks later she was wounded in an unsuccessful attack near Paris. The Burgundians and even many inhabitants of the kingdom of France, as it then was, took the English side in the war, and divided counsels led to a truce for the winter. When the war was resumed in the following spring, Joan was taken prisoner by the Burgundians during an attempt to hold Compiègne against them, and afterwards sold to the English for a large sum of money. No serious attempt was made by Charles or the French to effect her release, while the English, filled with superstitious dread of her powers, had resolved upon her death.

St Joan's trial and death (1431). Application was made to Cauchon, Bishop of Beauvais, to try her as a witch and heretic, and this prelate made himself the tool of their fears and their vengeance. He presided over a court which was composed in the main of theologians of Paris University with an assessor to represent the Inquisition. This grossly partial tribunal examined the Maid from the 21st of February to the 17th of March. The official record of the trial is still extant. At the end of this ordeal, although she had appealed to the Holy See from the local tribunal, she was condemned to be burnt by the secular arm to which the ecclesiastical court handed her over. Some form of retractation had been extorted, but her subsequent conduct was judged as a withdrawal of this, and she was thereupon condemned as a relapsed heretic. The sentence was carried out in the Market Place at Rouen on the

THE HOUSE OF LANCASTER

30th of May, 1431, in circumstances of pathetic tragedy. The verdict was afterwards reversed by a court which met in Paris with the consent of the Holy See in 1457. In spite of the incredulity of rationalist historians, St Joan has ever been recognised as the ideal standard-bearer of Christian patriotism; English writers have vied with French in a chorus of praise and veneration.

Though the cause of the English supremacy in France never recovered from the blow which the achievements of the Maid of Orleans inflicted on it, it would be a mistake to suppose that the invaders straightway retired from the contest, and that henceforth all was peace. There were twelve years of desultory warfare, on the whole unfavourable to the English, before Maine was lost and a two years' truce declared. There were ten years more before the loss of Normandy in 1451 and of Guienne in 1453 reduced the English empire in France to a mere shadow. Meanwhile, at home the rivalry of the Duke of Gloucester with the Duke of Bedford and others kept politics in a state of ferment. With regard to France, Gloucester and Bedford were in favour of a determined prosecution of the war, whereas the party which was led by Cardinal Beaufort were disposed to attempt a conclusion of the war and peace with France. The Holy See again, as in Edward III.'s reign, made repeated efforts to end the war and induce the combatants to lay aside their arms. The young king took quite a precocious interest in public affairs, so much so that the Council made bold to warn him that his intervention would be inopportune and useless. *Henry and his uncles.* He tried to mediate between his uncles of Gloucester and Bedford, but as he grew older he gradually identified himself with Cardinal Beaufort's policy and the party of peace. The hostile faction could not touch the king personally, but they could strike at his policy through Beaufort, who at one time was obliged to leave England. There was still trouble with the Lollards, but the consistent and determined action of the bishops and the penalties invoked against those who were convicted of heresy seem by this time to have broken the strength of the movement. The Church was strong and influential, and efforts were even made to obtain the repeal of the Acts of Provisors and of Premunire which had been enacted in the reign of Edward III. The attempt failed, but explanations were asked and given, which resulted in a kind of compromise which often modified the working of the Acts.

The influence of Cardinal Beaufort continued to be very great up to the end of his long life. He was sent by Martin V. as papal legate both into Germany and into Bohemia in order to try and heal the last scars of the schism which he had already done so much to end. His last years were devoted to his diocese of Winchester, and to the noble cathedral which he was able to do much towards completing as we now see it. At the near approach of death he had a solemn Requiem Mass sung in his presence: a Memento Mori worthy of the imitation of Charles V.: then in the Chapter House his will was read. He then took leave of all, and was carried back to his chamber, where he died on the 11th of April, 1447. He was buried in an elaborate tomb behind the high altar of the cathedral.

Last years of Cardinal Beaufort.

At the back of famous prelates, such as Arundel, Beaufort, and Chichele, in their legislation against seditions and heretical innovators, stood a great ecclesiastical lawyer. This was William Lyndwood, pre-eminent as a canonist, even in that age of Canon Law, but scarcely recognised at his full stature in a glance over the mere surface of history. Lyndwood was not only the right hand man of authority in the various proceedings taken against the Lollards, but he was matched against the leading canonists of the Continent when sent as King's Proctor to the Council of Basle in 1433. His chief work was the *Provinciale* or collection of all the synods of the province of Canterbury down to his own time, and his writings may be looked on as an irrefutable proof of the full extent to which the Roman Canon Law was admitted and acted upon in England. This is acknowledged by such a recent authority as Lord Halsbury, and likewise, though grudgingly, by Bishop Stubbs, who naturally makes the most of the royal privileges as limiting it. From the year 1426 Lyndwood held the office of Dean of the Court of Arches, as well as several other benefices and places of preferment. It was not until nearly the end of his life that he was raised to the see of St David's, being recommended to the Holy

William Lyndwood (1375-1446).

THE HOUSE OF LANCASTER 301

See by the king himself. He was consecrated bishop in St Stephen's Chapel at Westminister, in which same historic place he was laid to rest four years later. In 1852 his tomb was opened, and his remains were found almost incorrupt.

But, though the legislation of the English Church Courts of the period doubtless owed much of its inspiration to Lyndwood, we must turn to one of his contemporaries to find the chief theological opponent of the heterodox teachers. This was the celebrated Carmelite, Doctor Thomas Netter of Walden, usually spoken of as an authority under the name of Waldensis. Though born about the same year as Lyndwood, he had a much shorter life, for he scarcely surpassed the half-century given to St Thomas or St Bonaventure. He was sent as one of the English theologians to the Council of Pisa in 1409, and probably the distinctive ability he showed while there formed one of the reasons which led to his being put forward as a champion of orthodoxy in the later stages of the Wycliffite controversy. Since the Duke of Lancaster's partisans had already turned strongly against the Lollards, even before the change in the royal succession, this was no obstacle to Netter's being royal confessor after that event. But the truth is that Carmelites were chosen one after another as confessors to the Lancastrian kings. When one of these, Stephen Patrington, was made Bishop of St David's in 1414, Netter took up the office as well as that of provincial of his Order. Henry V. had him with him in his French war, and he stood as a consoler and spiritual guide by that monarch's death-bed. He was then tutor to Henry VI., under Warwick's superintendence, and the king's piety did credit to the good friar's training. He was present at least at some of the sessions of the Council of Constance, where he devoted himself zealously to the cause of reform. With mingled zeal and charity he was equally earnest for the same high object in his own Order. It was while he was with the young king at Rouen that he died in 1430, in the odour of sanctity. Even recently the cause of approval in his cult as a "Beatus" has been before the Congregation of Rites. His works, though too voluminous and too topical for general use at present, have been a storehouse of learning and of argument for later writers.

Waldensis (1375-1430).

A great lawyer and diplomatist, who had been deep in the policy and confidence of King Henry V., passed from this mortal scene when Henry Chichele, Archbishop of Canterbury, died in 1443, after having held the primatial see for thirty years. At the age of eighty Chichele sent his resignation of Canterbury to the Holy See, but, before any notice could be taken of this, he died, and was buried in a handsome tomb surmounted by his effigy in Canterbury Cathedral. His last years were chiefly spent at Oxford, superintending the work on his princely foundations, and his name is kept alive in scholastic memory by the Chichele Chair of Modern History, still in existence in the University. His former Vicar-General, John Stafford, son of the Earl of Stafford, who had held the see of Bath and Wells for twenty years, was translated by Eugenius IV., without delay, to Canterbury. He was a learned ecclesiastic, and a reliable administrator, and may have owed his elevation in part to the commendation bestowed upon him by his predecessor. He was essentially a moderate and cautious statesman, and hence, in some respects, fell into the background at a time when parties in the State were contending so violently for the mastery. Neutrality in a churchman of his position was hard to maintain, and little appreciated. There was a prelate of more pronounced views long installed in the Northern archbishopric, and in many matters he seems to have taken the lead. This was John Kemp, who was a thorough-going supporter of Beaufort and the party who favoured peace with France, and was opposed to the policy of the Dukes of Gloucester and Bedford. He was the greatest example we have in English history of the translation of a prelate from one see to another until at last he became Primate. Kemp held five dioceses in succession. These were Rochester (1419-21), Chichester (1421), London (1421-6), York (1426-52), and Canterbury (1452-4). He was made chancellor in 1426, and had been created cardinal in 1439 in despite of Archbishop Chichele. He supported the papal efforts to bring about peace between France and England at the Congress of Arras and elsewere, but the proposals were not accepted, and the war went on. But, while the Pope's intervention failed to

Archbishop Stafford (1443-1454).

Cardinal Kemp (1452-1454).

THE HOUSE OF LANCASTER

bring peace, a temporary cessation of hostilities was brought about through the marriage of the king with Margaret of Anjou in 1445. This match was arranged through the diplomacy of De la Pole, Earl of Suffolk, who was practically Henry's chief minister from 1445 to 1450. But the policy of the peace party, marriage and all, was far from being popular in England. The war was badly conducted by Edmund Beaufort, nephew of the cardinal, who betrayed want of skill, and gradually lost ground. Gloucester and the cardinal both died in 1447, and Suffolk was murdered in 1450.

Fomented by the influence of Richard, Duke of York, the next heir to the throne, and exhausted by the continuance of the unsuccessful war in France, the nation began to lose whatever loyalty it ever had towards the House of Lancaster. In 1450 the popular discontent broke out into open rebellion in Kent, under the leadership of Jack Cade. The insurgents marched upon London, demanding the redress of grievances and the removal of all evil counsellors of the king. King Henry at first collected an army and marched against the rebels, but one band of his forces having been defeated, and signs of mutiny appearing among others, he altered his mind and retired to Kenilworth Castle. The Archbishops of Canterbury and York, with Waynflete, Bishop of Winchester, shut themselves up in the Tower of London, and from there it was left to them to deal with the insurgents. Cade entered London, and some rioting took place, but eventually Kemp of York, the chancellor, who seems to have taken the lead, partly overcame the rising through a repulse inflicted upon the Kentish men at London Bridge, at the same time promising the rebellious crowd the redress of grievances. But it is significant of the general state of unrest throughout the country that in the course of the same year (1450) two of the English bishops met with a violent death at the hands of the mob: John Ayscough, Bishop of Salisbury, in Wiltshire, and Adam Moleyns of Chichester at Portsmouth.

The Rebellion of Jack Cade (1450).

It was the weakness of King Henry's government, when face to face with these and similar disturbances, which gave the capable and popular Richard, Duke of York, his chance. When the king fell into bad health, and the state of his mind became so deranged that it was necessary to appoint a regent, the choice lay between the Duke and the king's consort, Queen Margaret of Anjou. In spite of the opposition of the friends of the queen, Richard of York was named Protector in 1454, but at the end of that year the king recovered, and there was a temporary reaction against the power of York. However, when Waynflete and the leaders favourable to Margaret and her son, the young Prince Edward, seemed to be rapidly regaining the upper hand, York, with the Earl of Warwick and the Nevilles, took decisive action. They flew to arms and marched towards London. Henry, with the Duke of Somerset and other leaders of the opposite faction, advanced to arrest their progress, and the two armies met at St Albans on the 22nd of May, 1455. The result of the battle was that Somerset was killed, and King Henry found himself in the hands of the victorious Yorkists. The battle of St Albans is generally looked upon as the beginning of the Wars of the Roses. The contest was to last for thirty years, and only ended with the defeat of Richard III. at Bosworth Field. This period, though not very rich in ecclesiastical events, demands a chapter to itself.

XXII.

THE EPOCH OF THE WARS OF THE ROSES.

(1455-1485.)

Character of the Wars of the Roses.
ANOTHER change in the constitution of mediaeval England was marked, and in great part caused, by the Wars of the Roses, which filled up the public history of the generation living between the battle of St Albans in 1455 and that of Bosworth in 1485. This long period of warfare may be looked at from more points of view than one. It may be considered as (1) a dynastic dispute between the rival Houses of York and Lancaster; or (2) as a popular protest against the breaches of the Constitution which the reigning house had given way to; or (3) as a faction fight between groups of great nobles; or (4), lastly, as a period of lawless domination over the land exercised by armies of professional soldiers, whose presence was a legacy of the Hundred Years' War. Still, there is no doubt but that the general result of these thirty years of anarchy was to weaken the position of the Church in England, at least indirectly. At the same time the Wars of the Roses were responsible for the destruction of a large proportion of the ancient noble families. In this way the road was paved for the absolute monarchy of the Tudors, as well as for the gaining of more power by the mercantile class and the landless man. A detailed narration of the military events of the period would be out of place here. The contest swayed to and fro with so many alternations of success and defeat that the dividing line between Lancastrian and Yorkist supremacy is not easy to draw. It was only in 1471 that Henry VI. was killed, yet it is usual to commence the reign of Edward IV. with his Coronation and subsequent acceptance by Parliament in

1461. In any case, the dates chosen above mark the beginning and the effective end of actual hostilities.

When Richard, Duke of York, took up arms in 1455, his cause was supported by many of the leaders of the party opposed to the French marriage, and above all by Richard Neville, the new Earl of Warwick. Much of the credit of winning the First Battle of St Albans was due to this last nobleman, who is popularly known as the Kingmaker. The political results of the victory were that York became Protector for a second time, and that Margaret of Anjou became the virtual head of his opponents. King Henry and Bourchier, by this time Primate, both strove hard to effect a pacification, and for a while with some measure of external success. A great ceremony of reconciliation took place in St Paul's at London on Lady Day, 1458. Still, the outbreak of renewed hostilities was not very long delayed. Armies were called into being the next year both by Warwick and by the supporters of the queen. The Yorkists won at Bloreheath in 1459, and at Northampton in 1460, where Henry VI. fell into the hands of the victorious Earl of Warwick. An arrangement was now made with the king that the Duke of York should be acknowledged as heir to the crown. But Queen Margaret, who was no party to this arrangement, attacked and defeated York at Wakefield at the end of the same year. The Duke fell, fighting to the last. The Lancastrians also won the Second Battle of St Albans, but lost that of Mortimer's Cross in 1461, after which Edward, son of Richard of York, proclaimed himself king. The sanguinary battle of Towton, later in the same year, completed the overthrow of the Lancastrians, and Edward was acknowledged as king and crowned at Westminster. Yet, Henry VI., inspired by his courageous queen, kept up the struggle for another ten years, with the aid of Warwick, who had gone over to the Lancastrian side. But in 1471 Warwick was defeated and slain at the battle of Barnet, while at Tewkesbury in the same year Margaret of Anjou was captured after an unsuccessful battle by Edward IV. Her son, also named Edward, was killed on the battlefield, and her hapless husband probably met the same fate in the Tower of London soon after the battle. Thus the supremacy of the House of York was assured as long

The Protector and the Kingmaker.

THE WARS OF THE ROSES 307

as Edward IV. lived, but there was to be yet another conflict, and the defeat of Richard III. by Henry Tudor at Bosworth Field in 1485 ended the rule of the House of York.

Amid all this welter of contending factions it remained true that the Church in England went on leading its life, hampered indeed by the political unrest, but at the same time deeply influencing the mass of the nation, and helping multitudes of souls, comparatively untouched by the vicissitudes of public affairs, to lead quiet Christian lives. No doubt it was partly due to the fact that the campaigns were not carried on by a levy *en masse* of the whole people, but by bands of professional soldiers, whose exploits loom large on the surface of history, but were far from exhausting the activity of the nation as a whole. During the whole of the period covered by this chapter, the Primate's chair was filled by Thomas Bourchier, brother of the Earl of Essex, and also connected with the Earl of Suffolk and with many of the great families of the Yorkist party. **Cardinal Bourchier (1404-1486).** He was already Bishop of Worcester in 1435, and was translated to Durham in 1443. His promotion to Canterbury came eleven years later in 1454, after the death of Archbishop Kemp. He survived until 1486, when Henry VII. was already in possession of the crown. Thus his career as a bishop extended for over half a century. He received the cardinal's hat from Sixtus IV. in 1475. For a brief period he was Lord Chancellor as well. This he owed to the personal favour of King Henry VI., for though so closely allied to the chief Yorkist nobles, he was never what could be called a violent party politician. He was essentially a peacemaker, and when the leaders of the Lancastrian party most hostile to York came into power, he resigned this last appointment. In collaboration with Waynflete of Winchester he tried to effect a reconciliation between the rival houses. After this attempt failed he attached himself to the rising fortunes of the House of York. He it was who crowned Edward IV., and later on Richard III. also. True, however, to his conciliatory disposition, he was one of the arbitrators selected to arrange peace between England and France. He it was, again, who crowned Henry VII. after Bosworth Field, and solemnised his marriage with Elizabeth of

York. In his old age he had the services of a coadjutor to aid him in administering his diocese, for he lived to the age of eighty. Near Sevenoaks there is a beautiful manor called Knowle, which he had acquired for his see, and there he breathed his last in 1486.

William of Waynflete. William Waynflete had a still longer career at Winchester than Bourchier had at Canterbury, and he has left a still more celebrated and honoured name. His real name was William Patten or Patyn, and Waynflete in Lincolnshire was his birthplace. He was born in 1395, and was educated at Oxford, though the details of this sojourn are uncertain. Anyhow, we find him after his ordination acting as head master of William of Wykeham's college at Winchester (1430-41). When Henry VI. visited this college in 1441, he was so struck with him that he made him provost of the new scholastic establishment he had founded at Eton. Here he remained until the death of Cardinal Beaufort in 1447. He then became the king's nominee for Winchester, and being duly elected, was consecrated at Eton. As bishop he played a very prominent part in the political vicissitudes of the times, being at first all in favour of his royal patron, Henry VI. He was Lord Chancellor after Bourchier, and in his turn tried to negotiate a compromise between York and Lancaster. But he made many enemies, and in 1451 appealed to the Pope against them. When the House of York came into power he had to give up the Great Seal, but was even then hardly looked on by the White Rose as an enemy. In fact he had been in favour of Richard of York being made regent for the period of King Henry's malady. It is a marvellous thing that amid all the strife of the Wars of the Roses he was able to proceed with the building of the magnificent chapel at Eton, and to advance with the foundation of Magdalen College at Oxford. This latter place justly claims him as its founder and chief benefactor. It is said that in order to secure his pardon from Edward IV. he had to oblige that king with a loan equal to forty thousand pounds of our money. But, in spite of this, he was able to add to the endowments of Magdalen College as time went on. He had his own favourite residence at Bishop's Waltham, where he breathed his last in the same year as Cardinal Bourchier. His effigy in the stately Waynflete Chantry in Winchester Cathedral, which he had built for himself in his lifetime, preserves his features for us. Here he was laid to rest.

If we now pass on to consider who were the other leaders of the clergy during the period of Yorkist sway, we shall give the first place to George Neville, brother of Warwick, the King-maker. His high birth and attainments early marked him out for ecclesiastical dignity, and he was some years after his university course chosen Chancellor of Oxford. When the see of Exeter fell vacant in 1455 he was elected to fill it, and consecrated in 1458 by Archbishop Bourchier. A Yorkist by family, he kept free from the rebellion of the following year, and, when Richard of York became Protector in 1460, was made Lord Chancellor. He it was who opened the first Parliament of Edward IV., and the triumph of the Yorkists in the North led to his installation as Archbishop of York when William Booth died in 1464. His taking possession of his cathedral was made the occasion of a sumptuous public display. He also retained the chancellorship for some time, but as the reign advanced the influence of the Nevilles in the royal council was overshadowed by that of the Woodvilles and other connections of the queen. Archbishop Neville then joined with his brother in the rising for the restoration of Henry VI. (1470-71), and for the brief epoch of success was chancellor to Henry, but after the battle of Barnet, where the King-maker was slain, he surrendered together with Henry VI. to the victorious Edward. He was imprisoned for two months in the Tower, and for a longer period in France, while his goods became forfeit to the crown. He died in exile in 1476 without ever being allowed to return to his see. Lawrence Booth, half-brother to William, who had been the predecessor of Archbishop Neville, was then transferred from Durham to the archiepiscopal see.

Archbishop Neville (1433-1476).

When these three eminent leaders of the Church during the Wars of the Roses have been spoken of, little remains to be said of the others. In general it was a period when frequent translation of incumbents from the less important to the greater sees was common, and yet we find some remarkably long tenures of office in the same bishopric. Thus Richard Beauchamp held the see of Salisbury for nearly the whole period, namely from 1450 to 1480; and Thomas Kemp was Bishop of London from 1450 to 1489. In some cases the influence of the royal family and of the Yorkist nobles was manifest in the promotion of scions of their race to episcopal rank. Traces of this are discoverable in the names of those prelates who were consecrated during this period. Thus, besides the appointment of George Neville to York, we find Lionel Woodville, the brother of Elizabeth Woodville, Edward's queen, made Bishop of Salisbury in 1482. William Grey was consecrated for Ely in 1454. Peter Courtenay, grand-nephew of Richard Courtenay, Bishop of Norwich (1413), and great-grand-nephew of the Primate, William Courtenay, became Bishop of Exeter in 1478, and was translated to Winchester in 1487 at the death of Waynflete. Although the powerful Courtenay family had been mainly on the Lancastrian side, the branch to which Peter belonged was Yorkist; it is in this way that we must explain his elevation to the episcopate in the reign of Edward IV.

An unfortunate fate was that of an eminent scholar of the period, Reginald Peacock (1395-1460). He was a native of North Wales, where he eventually became Bishop of St Asaph's, but long before this had become prominent in the controversy against Wycliffe and the Lollards. His most celebrated work was entitled the "Repressor of Overmuch Blaming of the Clergy," and in this he defended the bishops and clergy in general against the charges then levelled against them of luxury, fondness for money, and neglect of preaching. But in doing so he attacked so many powerful interests that he gave an opportunity for counter-charges against his own orthodoxy. Further, his friendship with the leaders of the Lancastrian party, to whose favour he owed his translation in 1450 from St Asaph's to Chichester, made him obnoxious to the friends of the White Rose. Almost as soon as the House of York was in the ascendant he was accused of heresy, and his writings examined by the Yorkist, Archbishop Bourchier, and by other prelates. He was condemned on several points, and ordered to retract under the threat of death.

Bishop Peacock (1460).

It is very easily conceivable that he fell into error in the midst of his general *apologia* for the clergy, but he certainly had no wish to teach anything against the Catholic Faith. He retracted what was erroneous, but also appealed to the Pope. It was represented at Rome that he had voluntarily resigned his see, and Pope Pius II. seems to have accepted this statement as true. But it is not a trustworthy assertion, and his enemies confined him in Thorney Abbey, where he was only allowed to hear Mass, but few books and no writing materials being allowed him. Here he died in 1460. Even if some of the heated expressions in his controversial works cannot be squared with dogmatic theology, there can be no doubt that his intentions were upright and zealous. The accusation of heresy was at that time a powerful weapon to accomplish the ruin of a public man. In modern times it is of course the very opposite, and though Peacock warmly opposed the Lollards, the very fact of his being under a charge of heresy has recommended him to the sympathy of Protestant writers. In reality, however, he may be regarded as a victim to partisan intolerance and the desire to be revenged on a political adversary of remarkable ability and power. It is sad to think that just when the advance of learning had come to encourage writers of the vigour shown by the author of the "Repressor," that writer himself should have had to go down in tragic obscurity through the violent passions excited by the disputes of the royal succession.

But while contending factions were thus struggling for the mastery in politics, a group of industrious and enterprising scholars were firmly establishing in England an invention destined to become the potent instrument of the coming Revival of Letters; this was the art of printing. The first English printer was William Caxton (1422-91) who learnt the art while resident in Germany in 1471. He there held the office of Governor of the English Merchants in the Low Countries. But, being something of a literary man as well as a craftsman, he worked himself at the translation of the "History of Troy" and "The Game and Play of Chess," which he got printed on the Continent at Bruges or Cologne. He and his art seem to have attracted the attention of the great Cardinal Bourchier, and we owe it to him that Caxton was asked to return to England, where in 1476 he set up his press at

Invention of printing.

the sign of the Red Pale in Westminster. He then enjoyed the patronage of Edward IV., himself the most accomplished prince of his time, and from 1477 to 1491 produced no fewer than ninety-six separate works, of which the "Dicts and Sayings of the Philosophers" by Lord Rivers was the first. Caxton was an industrious and scholarly man, and the favour bestowed upon him by Edward IV. was continued by Richard III., and by Henry VII. Not only was the first impulse to his establishment given by an enlightened churchman, but the early productions of his press were in great measure books of piety and devotion, which furnish a strong proof of what a large place religion held in the life of the period. The examples which survive of the works which Caxton produced bear evidence of a considerable degree of skill and of much patient labour on the part of the first English printer and his associates, and although his invention was to make an end of the art which enabled the caligraphist and the illuminator to write out the beautiful manuscript volumes of the Middle Ages, it cannot be denied that these were replaced by printed volumes executed and illustrated with the very highest degree of care and labour.

The last act of the drama of the Wars of the Roses was the bloodstained, though short, episode which we call

Richard III. the Reign of Richard III. When Edward
(1483-1485). IV. died the young Edward, his son, was
at Ludlow with the Council his father had assigned to him. Lord Rivers, Caxton's patron, was his governor, and Bishop Alcock of Worcester was at the head of his household. But there was at once a struggle for the guardianship of the king between the queen, his mother, and Richard, Duke of Gloucester, his uncle. The rapid and decisive measures taken by the latter soon settled this question in his favour. The queen fled into sanctuary, Lord Rivers was arrested, and the young king fell into the hands of Gloucester and his confederate, the Duke of Buckingham. Richard was proclaimed Protector, Russell, Bishop of Lincoln, chancellor, and both the coronation and the meeting of Parliament deferred. This delay was in order to give Gloucester time to mature his plans for claiming the crown for himself. In carrying out these plans he once more had the aid of the Duke of Buckingham. Archbishop Bourchier remained

passive, the strongest opponents among the Bishops, Rotherham and Morton, were thrown into the Tower, and a certain doctor was made to preach at Paul's Cross, setting forth the claim of the Duke of Gloucester to the throne. A petition was engineered and signed by the Protector's friends among the Lords of Parliament, inviting him to accept the crown, alleging the illegitimacy of Edward's children, the want of freedom from attainder on the part of Clarence's, and moreover his own fitness for the dignity. His hypocrisy over this was at least equalled by the way in which, though seeming to hesitate, Richard soon consented, and then proceeding to Westminster Hall, claimed the crown as his right. Edward V. and his brother, the Duke of York, disappeared from the scene, and according to the popular belief, were murdered in the Tower of London by their uncle's orders; Lord Rivers and Sir Richard Grey were executed at Pontefract only a few days after the usurpation, and other executions followed. Buckingham, after being Richard's tool, conspired with the queen's friends—the Woodvilles—against him. But the rising was easily suppressed by Richard's energy, and Buckingham, with many of his adherents, paid the penalty of their attempt by death. But the three bishops who had favoured this rising, Woodville of Salisbury, Morton of Ely, and Courtenay of Exeter, escaped to the Continent, and did not return till Richard was no more. Meanwhile, he had been crowned by Bourchier at Westminster with his queen, Anne Neville, and the Archbishop of York had also made his peace with him. John Howard was made Duke of Norfolk, the first duke of that family, and became his foremost supporter. Six months later, Richard met his Parliament. Bishop Russell of Lincoln, the chancellor, preached at the opening in the king's favour, and Richard did all in his power to conciliate all ranks of society to the acceptance of his title and the peaceful continuance of his rule. The clergy had their privileges confirmed to them by charter; the merchants were gratified by rules drawn up to favour trade and commerce; all were glad to have the granting of so-called "benevolences" declared unconstitutional. And yet all the rest of Richard's reign was given up to expedients of one kind or another to thwart conspiracies, to ward off dangers to the royal family, and to secure the permanence of the usurpation. Though at first he met with some measure of success, his enemies were numerous and very persistent, while his unscrupulous policy at home had the result of constantly adding to their number. At length on the 7th of August, 1485, Henry, Earl of Richmond, the son of Edmund Tudor and Margaret, the late king's widow, landed at Milford Haven with a military force, and, being joined by considerable numbers of Welshmen and some English, advanced into the Midlands. Richard marched against him with all the forces he could muster, but when the armies met at Bosworth, the powerful Stanleys with their levies went over to Henry, and though Richard fought with the courage of despair, he was defeated and slain. The crown of England was the prize of the conqueror.

The mediaeval history of England may be held to reach its end with the battle of Bosworth Field. Henceforth the nation was to live under new influences in great part, whilst the old ones acted in a greatly modified form. But as far as the Faith and religious practice of the nation was concerned, there was no break at all. The wave of heretical opinion expressed by the Lollards instead of being an advancing was a receding one. However much bishops and prelates might differ as to the merits of the Red Rose and the White Rose, they were all agreed as to the need of making war on the sectaries whose tenets meant anarchy both in Church and State. It is the matured opinion of the best historians of the time that they were successful, and by an admixture of severity and moderation had practically extinguished the movement long before that greater religious revolt known as the Reformation had gained any hold upon England.

XXIII.

CATHOLIC LIFE IN MEDIAEVAL ENGLAND.

(1066-1485.)

ADMITTING that the number of Normans who followed Duke William in his victorious expedition of 1066 was small in comparison with the total population of England, yet the changes his victory led to both directly and indirectly were great. It was not that the Conqueror, who claimed the throne likewise as the appointed heir of St Edward, wished to make any sweeping revolution at the moment. On the contrary, there was then no general dividing up of the land among his followers, though later on he was able both to confiscate and bestow on a larger scale. Moreover, the old Anglo-Saxon institutions such as the Witenagemot, the Fyrd or National Levy in arms, the system of fines for crime, the Wite and Were, and the Frankpledge were not abolished. At the very outset William had taken an oath to govern according to law, and to his people the law meant the laws of good King Edward, or rather the accumulated legislation of their ancient kings. It was only gradually that feudalism, or land tenure dependent on military services to the crown, became the dominant system. The confiscation of lands, not taken at the Conquest, but seized after the various rebellions, the deposition of unworthy Saxon prelates, the continued emigration from the Continent—all told in the same direction.

Gradual effect of Norman Conquest.

One result was that England was knitted closer to that great organic whole known—undivided in the Middle Ages—as Christendom. The idea that all the nations of Western Europe were members of one great federation or society was a noble and inspiring one.

The belief in the supreme position of the Pope in the Universal Church formed one corner-stone in the building of this idea. At the same time it harmonised with, if it did not suggest, the theory of a temporal head, elected by due authority, having his exceptional position consecrated through the blessing and approval of the spiritual head. This was the idea of the Holy Roman Empire. There is abundant evidence that the English of the Middle Ages accepted without question the Catholic tradition of organised unity, as far as the Church was concerned, with the Roman Pontiff as its ruler.

If we pass from dogmatic belief to practice in the exercise of that authority from Rome, we can be at no loss for examples. We find both the despatch of missioners and the sending of apostolic legates and nuncios usual and recognised things. We find the Archbishops of Canterbury claiming as one of their proudest titles that of legate *ex officio* of the Holy See. We find these same archbishops invariably applying to the Pope for the pallium as the sign of their jurisdiction. We find the Roman See receiving and pronouncing upon appeals, both from one bishop to another, and from regular against secular clergy, and the reverse. We find the limiting of boundaries, such as would be involved in the founding of new sees, settled in accordance with the decisions of the Holy See. We see canonical pains and penalties, such as excommunication, suspension, and interdict employed, often without protest, to enforce those Roman decisions. It is to the credit of the bishops of England that from the Conquest to the Reformation but few cases occurred where the deposition of a bishop for his unworthiness became necessary, but when it did, it was the Roman See which took up the matter: the unworthy prelate was ousted by its administrative authority. This was the case with the Saxon prelates deprived in the reign of William the Conqueror. Similar cases are recorded once at Norwich, and once at Chichester, in the twelfth century. Notorious immorality seems to have been very rare, at least in the case of the higher clergy.

The episcopal hierarchy in England continued to follow the arrangement made at the councils held under

Practical authority of Rome.

Lanfranc, with little further change up to the time of the Reformation. But two new sees were added by way of exception. These were Ely in 1109, and Carlisle in 1133. And though the accession of some of the bishops to newly chosen cathedral cities was somewhat later than the days of Lanfranc, these changes were merely transfers in accordance with the policy laid down by him once for all namely, that the titles of sees should be taken not from villages or ancient decayed towns, but from the centres of population and of national life. On the whole York kept its separate metropolitan rights, so that there was still both a Southern and a Northern province. Still, York had but few suffragans, at least in England. South of the Tweed, Durham and Carlisle were all that it could claim. Beyond the border to the north there was the ever renewed and ever disputed claim to jurisdiction over the Scottish sees, none of which was an archbishopric.

The English hierarchy.

Nothing of all this affected the overwhelming importance which the See of Canterbury held in the whole life of England. This aptly typifies the place of the Church in the scheme of national existence as it was then seen. The Primate certainly came next to the king in dignity. It was his privilege, jealously vindicated, to crown each new monarch. He was the first official counsellor of the king when once he had crowned him, and in the case of his absence was very often the viceroy to whom he entrusted the chief place in governing the realm. His right it was also to consecrate all the bishops of the Southern province, as well as the metropolitan of the Northern one, who consecrated his own suffragans. Very often he likewise held the office of Lord Chancellor of the realm; not seldom he was also a cardinal of the Holy Roman Church. He was styled *Legatus Natus*, that is by virtue of his being Primate, of the Holy See in England. From the Pope he was ever most careful to ask for the sacred pallium before he entered upon the duties attached to his see. The grant of the pallium typified the papal approval of his appointment, and required as its accompaniment an oath of canonical obedience to the Pope. By a strange retribution the occupant of the see of Canterbury has

Importance of Canterbury.

never since the Reformation been so powerful as in those Catholic days when he was proud to claim as his own special position the place at the Pope's right foot. It was a papal voice which called him "*alterius orbis apostolicus.*" It was to him that the bishops of the province took their oath of canonical obedience, as he himself had taken it to the Supreme Pontiff. He thus became in a very special way the intermediary between the Pope and his own suffragan bishops.

Much of the same theory held true, allowance being made for the smaller importance of the Northern province, for York and the suffragans of that see. The general doctrine was that for episcopal appointments the selection of candidates might be in various hands, but the final institution, appointment, or confirmation, as it was called, devolved upon the Supreme Pontiff.

Episcopal appointments.

The link between Pope and bishop was the metropolitan, who was to consecrate the prelate, and to whom the latter swore canonical obedience. For the most part, the election was made by the cathedral chapter, whether that body consisted of a college of secular canons, or of the members of a religious community. But presentations or nominations of individuals were often made on the part of the king with such force as practically to overrule the freedom of the chapter. Moreover, in numerous cases, the Pope of the day, setting aside both the royal nomination and the voting of the chapter, indicated a candidate of his own choice, instituted him out of the plenitude of his power, and thus kept the whole appointment in his own hands. This was the case, to give an illustrious example, with the celebrated Stephen Langton. Sometimes there was a petition from the king to the Pope, to provide for a vacant benefice over the heads of those who would otherwise have the choice. Sometimes the authority of the Roman See was invoked to vindicate the freedom of election against royal interference. In the matter of lesser benefices, such as parishes, there was usually no collegiate body to elect, such as a chapter would be. The nomination would therefore either rest with the bishop or with some patron, lay or clerical, always saving the right of the bishop to pronounce on the fitness of the candidate who was nominated.

MEDIAEVAL ENGLAND

The close of the Middle Ages was marked all over Europe by an extension of the exercise of papal power to appoint incumbents to vacant benefices. As time went on this became felt also in England. This right was claimed more especially in the case of the translation or promotion of an incumbent from one benefice to another. This claim, when exercised on a large scale, came to be regarded by the English clergy as a substantial grievance, especially when it was used to provide for aliens out of the revenues belonging to sees or benefices in this country. The practice even led to legislation, sometimes thought wrongly to be anti-papal, but which really only aimed at the accidental abuses of the Roman Curia. The Statute of Provisors was passed in 1351, expressly in order to limit the extent to which the Popes named to vacant benefices: and imprisonment was decreed against those who broke this law. But, as time went on, a compromise was effected by which the king sent out a letter directing those who had rights to choose, after indicating the person he wished to have elected. Then a letter was sent to the Pope, asking for the confirmation, which was in most cases granted. But the right to provide in the case of translation was customarily used by the Roman See, and numerous cases existed of reservation, that is to say of the Pontiff during the lifetime of a prelate reserving to himself the next appointment to that particular office. An abuse that resulted from this was the filling of numerous English benefices by foreign ecclesiastics. What has been said of bishoprics and other secular benefices also holds good of the appointments to the abbacies, whose claims were often pushed in the case of the greater ones, such as had seats in Parliament, or were mitred, and ranked as great prelates.

The English sees were of very unequal sizes, by far the largest being Lincoln, while Rochester was much the smallest. Canterbury was comparatively small, while York was large, though a good deal of the country now in the Northern counties was included in the diocese of Lichfield. It naturally followed from this that there was at least a parallel diversity in the number of parishes and chapels. If we comprise all those which were attached to the abbeys and priories, and also the quite small

Size of dioceses.

parishes which existed in populous towns, we shall find that at the end of the Middle Ages there were about nine thousand four hundred. This, of course, only gives an average area of about two miles square, which is a small average in comparison with the sizes of parishes in other Catholic countries. It is evident that if we add to the parish clergy, chantry-priests and religious, the spiritual wants of the faithful were abundantly provided for.

The best example of a great prelate whose position was akin to the prince bishops of the Holy Roman Empire was afforded in England by the Bishop of Durham. Walcher or Walker, the first Norman bishop, is said to have purchased the earldom of Durham from William the Conqueror. Then, when he had been named bishop over the same territory, and consecrated, as he was at Winchester, by Thomas, Archbishop of York, a great step had been taken towards making the episcopal chair and the feudal earldom one and the same dignity. It had both the special character derived from its being the borderland to be held against the inroads of the Scots, and the sacred prestige which came to it from its being held up before the world as the Patrimony of St Cuthbert. Ralph Flambard came to take possession of it in 1103, already a rich man, through his share in the plunder of vacant sees and abbeys. Doubtless, during the twenty-five years for which he administered Durham, he must have added considerably to the episcopal power. Eventually, Durham became a County Palatine like Chester, only that in this case the bishop, and not the crown, was at the head of it. It had its own courts, its own ten or twelve tenants in capite, or chief barons; even it had its own coinage. Consequently, after the two sees of the archbishops, Durham was the most important in the land. An incumbent was sometimes translated to it even from London or Winchester, and the bishop's revenues were very ample.

The See of the County Palatine.

The number of dioceses into which the country was divided was really small in comparison with lands nearer the centre of Christendom. Though not equal to the huge territorial limits of the German sees, they were larger than those of most other kingdoms, and few, indeed,

when compared with France or Italy. Hence, as
the work of the Church grew, it became evident
that these few prelates, often reduced still more in
numbers and efficiency by vacancies, and by being
employed in affairs of State, could not cope adequately
with the routine of the administration of their dioceses.
No doubt it was the recognition of this fact which
led to the additional dioceses, which had been formed
by Henry VIII. at Chester, Oxford, Peterborough,
Gloucester, and Bristol, being allowed to stand under
the Catholic revival of Philip and Mary. But other
means were in use long before to meet the constantly
recurring need. First of all there was a close tie
between Canterbury and Rochester. They
were not held by the same person, but the **Position of Rochester.**
see of Rochester, being a small and poor
one, the bishop of that diocese was able to assist the
Primate in the administration of his far larger care.
And this was done so habitually that the Bishop of
Rochester is sometimes called the Chaplain of the Archbishop of Canterbury. Moreover, bishops were often
consecrated to so-called sees *in partibus infidelium*,
with the express intention of aiding one or other of
the diocesan bishops in his work. Quite a long list of
names of bishops thus appointed in the
England of the Middle Ages has been **Auxiliary bishops.**
preserved. Sometimes titles were taken
not *in partibus infidelium* at all, but in places far
removed from what was to be the scene of their labours.
A similar practice was that of consecrating bishops to
sees in Ireland, not in order that they should proceed
to their dioceses, but that they might act as assistants
to English bishops. Such bishops as those of the classes
mentioned are often called suffragans by Protestant
writers, but they really held the place of those who in
the modern Church are known as auxiliary bishops.

It would be hard to find a country better suited than
England to exemplify the position which the great
monastic orders filled in the Church of the
Middle Ages. In the beginning monks **The Religious Orders.**
had ventured forth from their retreats to
bring it to Christianity, and they always counted for
much in its science, its arts, its piety, and even in its
National Councils. Alongside of the bishops who sat

in Parliament were also to be found no fewer than twenty-six mitred abbots, and exactly half the chapters of the cathedrals were Benedictine priories. The pious generosity of successive generations had built up these foundations until the abbeys and priories and other religious houses became great owners of land as well as centres of devotion, and thus also great dispensers of public charity. Various attempts have repeatedly been made to summarise the records which speak of these establishments, so that we may feel sure a fairly accurate reckoning of them has been made. But it must always be borne in mind that in speaking of money and wealth in pre-Reformation days we have to multiply the figures many times if we would find its equivalent in modern currency. In the same way also ought we to act in estimating the number of houses of monks or friars relatively to the nation at large. They dwelt in a land containing at most four or five millions of inhabitants, not a nation of more than thirty such as we have to-day.

The primacy of place among the orders belongs of right to the Benedictines, which also was the earliest of the various monastic institutes to settle in the land. There were, up to the time of the dissolution of the monasteries under Henry VIII., one hundred and three Benedictine foundations in England, although the Cistercians, with no less than seventy-five, do not follow so far behind.

Statistics of Religious Bodies.

Then to go back to the most austere of all monastic rules, that of the Carthusians, whose priories were in England given the name of Charterhouses, we find that they numbered nine in all. If we pass to the Canons Regular, no less than one hundred and seventy houses followed the rule of the Black Canons, and were known as Austin Canons; while the White Canons of St Norbert, who were called Premonstratensians, counted some thirty-five foundations. It is among the Canons Regular also that we find the only religious order that existed of purely English origin, that of the Gilbertines, founded by St Gilbert of Sempringham, which enjoyed a high measure of royal favour, partly, no doubt, because it was in no way dependent on alien superiors. There were in all twenty-five Gilbertine houses, many of them double, both for men and women.

With regard to the Mendicant Friars, the Dominicans had fifty-six houses before the Reformation, the Franciscans sixty, the Carmelites forty, the Austin Friars thirty-four. These were known respectively as Black, Grey, White, and Austin Friars. The Trinitarians had about eleven houses, and the Crutched Friars six or seven, while several minor bodies of friars had one house apiece. But we have yet to count the preceptories or houses of Templars and Knights of St John or Hospitallers, which were at least forty in number. Moreover, there were a number of cells or dependencies of the larger continental abbeys, known as "Alien Priories." The number of these is estimated by Cardinal Gasquet at somewhat over one hundred.

It is in sharp contrast with modern times that the conventual life for women was not developed to anything like the same extent as that for men. The universal rule of enclosure, the Nunneries. exclusion of religious women from good works outside their own walls, such as teaching in public schools, or nursing the sick in hospitals, may have been partly responsible for the limitation in their number. We can all the same identify about one hundred and thirty-three nunneries in the Middle Ages in England. Many of these had enjoyed an honoured existence for many centuries before their suppression, and some of them were amongst the earliest religious houses of which the country could boast. Such were the abbeys of Whitby, Shaftesbury, Ely, and Coldingham, and the celebrated abbey of Saxon nuns at Winchester. Hence we find Benedictines, Minoresses, Gilbertines, Canonesses of St Augustine, and others as familiar figures in mediaeval history. To sum up the statistics, then, which have been given, and counting religious houses of all kinds, abbeys, priories, alien cells, hospitals, preceptories or temples, as well as nunneries, we find a total of some nine hundred or more establishments for the practice of some form of that life of perfection known in Catholic history as the Religious Life.

The Church in England, at least in the Middle Ages, can only boast of a single religious founder, the St Gilbert of Sempringham, whose name has been mentioned above; although a position only second to that of founder can be claimed by St Stephen Harding (1066-

1134) among the Cistercians, and by St Simon Stock (1165-1265) among the Carmelites. St Gilbert is called by the name of the little village in the Lincolnshire Fens, which was the place of his birth. There his father, a Norman knight, held lands and a feudal residence. Gilbert's frail constitution forbade him the career of chivalry which his father had followed, and he was early marked out for the clerical state. After a course of studies both at home and abroad, he was presented by his father to the united benefices of Sempringham and Tirington. He did not, however, at once begin to reside in his parish, but attached himself to the household of his bishop, Robert Bloët of Lincoln. Neither did he at once take priest's orders, but in 1130, Bishop Alexander, Bloët's successor, promoted him to the priesthood in spite of his humble resistance. At the death of his father in 1131 he returned to Sempringham, where not only his benefice, but the lordship of the manor thus fell to his inheritance. He took up the duties and responsibilities which thus became his, and proceeded to use his wealth for the poor, and for the advancement of the religious life. He made a beginning of his Order some time in the same year (1131), starting not with men but with seven pious maidens, for whom he built a convent adjoining the parish church of Sempringham. As time went on he gradually added to this house of enclosed nuns, first a community of lay sisters, then another of lay brothers for the external manual labours, and then also a body of Canons Regular, whom he put under the rule of St Augustine. He journeyed to Citeaux in 1148, and while there, besides meeting the Pope and the great St Bernard, he vainly tried to induce the Cistercian superiors to accept the charge of the communities he had formed, by adopting them into their own Order. He was persuaded to abandon the attempt, and then established his disciples as quite a separate Order, adding further constitutions to the Augustinian rule. All through his life he continued to make new foundations, more or less after the example of Sempringham. In most cases these monasteries were double, containing a building for men and another for women. He had as many as thirteen before his long life came to an end. Accused by the royal

St Gilbert of Sempringham (1089-1189).

officials of lending help to St Thomas Becket at the time of his exile, he denied it, but refused to be sworn to it, lest he should seem hostile to the cause of the Church. He lived for almost a hundred years, and though a religious founder, only made religious profession himself in extreme old age.

Though not himself a founder, there is something of the splendour of the founder round the memory of the great Cistercian, St Aelred. He is sometimes called the English St Bernard, and certainly filled a somewhat similar place in the annals of the monastic revival due to the White Monks of Citeaux in England to the one occupied by the great doctor in his Order on the Continent. He was born at Hexham, and in his youth was a member of the household of St Margaret's son, the Scottish King David. If David had had his way St Aelred would never have left Scotland. He would have been one of the chief leaders in the ecclesiastical reform of the kingdom. But Aelred felt drawn to the cloister, and became a monk in the new Cistercian house of Rievaulx in Yorkshire. After a period spent there as Novice Master, he was sent into Lincolnshire to preside over a fresh foundation at Revesby. It was while there that he became knit in the bonds of a holy friendship with St Gilbert of Sempringham, who, we know, felt a powerful attraction towards the Cistercian Order. But Aelred was chosen Abbot of Rievaulx in 1146, and found himself at the head of what was now a large community of three hundred monks. Meanwhile, in addition to this, he was called upon to exercise the function of an Abbot Visitor to all the houses of his Order in England. He even visited Scottish houses, and thus was once more able to meet King David before that monarch's pious death. Henry II. also seems to have held him in high favour in the earlier part of his reign, and he was present with St Thomas of Canterbury at the lofty function of the translation of St Edward's relics in Westminster Abbey on the 13th of October, 1163. His panegyric on the occasion seems to have been practically the basis of his "Life of St Edward." Many other *sermons*, as well as various *ascetical* and *historical opuscula* likewise remain from his pen. But a full and complete edition of his works does not exist. Before

St Aelred (1109-1166).

the contest between Henry II. and the Holy Martyr of Canterbury had reached its climax, St Aelred had been already gathered to his fathers. He died in 1166 or 1167.

St Simon Stock (1165-1265). The position held in the Carmelite Order by the English General, St Simon Stock, was no wise inferior to that filled by St Aelred among the Cistercians. In fact it was an influence of an international character, inasmuch as he became the head of the White Friars for the whole Church. It was under his auspices that the venerable eremitical formation of Palestine developed into a world-wide institution of Mendicant Friars. For he it was who obtained the letter from Pope Innocent IV., which regularised the position of the Carmelites as no longer hermits, but preaching friars. St Simon was born in Kent, and in his youth lived as a hermit, but, later on, he was attracted to the Carmelites, and joined their ranks. Anyone who has seen the ruins of their first English house at Hulne, in Alnwick Park, will see that here indeed was an ideal place for a desert convent, an English Mount Carmel, in fact. Both Hulne and Aylesford were anterior to St Simon's generalate, which began with the Chapter of Aylesford in 1245. And when he was in office he quite accepted the missionary view of the vocation of his brethren, and fostered the attendance of the friars at Oxford and Cambridge Universities. There is a tradition that he, like St Gilbert, lived to be a centenarian. The most celebrated phase in his career is his connection with the now almost universal devotion to the Blessed Virgin, known as the Brown Scapular.

Anchorites and Anchoresses. But if the Carmelites did not restrain themselves within the narrow limits of the eremitical life, that life always had its devotees in Catholic England, and their writings and doings fill quite a notable place in the story of the Church. It was not a method of life which began with the coming of the Normans; we can see it already in existence among the Anglo-Saxons. The island in Derwentwater known as St Herbert's Isle keeps alive the memory of one of the earliest of these mortified servants of God. St Herbert was the disciple and devoted admirer of St Cuthbert, and under his direction lived a life of solitude on the Cumberland lake we have just named. At length, when near his end, he heard that St Cuthbert had come on his travels as far as Carlisle. The longing came to him once more to meet his beloved friend and spiritual father. So to Carlisle he betook himself. When they had conferred in pious conversation as long as they would, St Herbert returned to his lonely hermitage. It then came to pass that these two saints died on the same day. May we not say that it is with a sublime fitness, which we find not seldom in the Church's arrangements, that the same date, the 22nd of March, is graced with the memory of both these saints. Another celebrated hermit was St Godric of Finchale (1170) in the County of Durham. To him St Cuthbert was not an earthly friend, but a patron looking down upon him from heaven, and watching over his life. It was St Cuthbert, he believed, who appeared to him, and pointed out Finchale in the Weardale as the place for his life of solitude and prayer. There it was that he lived, visited and fortified by the Sacraments through a priest from Durham Priory, sent to him from time to time by the prior. Here too he died, and a priory was afterwards built in his honour on the spot.

The most celebrated ascetical writer of England was Walter Hilton, the Augustinian Prior of Thurgarton, near Newark. His work styled the "Scale of Perfection" was easily the best known ascetical work of the Middle Ages in England, and the reputation he acquired by it has even lead to his being considered by some as the author of the "Imitation of Christ." He lived in close touch with the Carthusian fathers of Val Grace in Nottinghamshire, but though he imbibed much of their spirit, he never jointed their ranks. We possess quite a number of mystic and contemplative works from the pen of Richard Rolle, a hermit who lived at Hampole, near Doncaster, the most considerable of which bears the title of the "Ayenbite of Inwit," that is to say the "Prick of Conscience." He was the director of the anchoress, or female anchorite, named Mother Margaret Kirkby, but does not seem to have been the author of the famous "Ancren Riwle," or "Rule for Anchoresses," which has been repeatedly edited as one of the standard works for the study of English literature before the Reformation. Though this work is anonymous, there seems some probability of its constituting one of the claims to immortal remembrance of the great builder of Salisbury Cathedral, Bishop Richard Poore. These hermits, or anchors and anchoresses, as they were called, often lived in a walled-up chamber, opening on to the parish church, and could communicate with the external world only through a small window in the wall. There they lived and prayed, taking a constant part in all the public offices of the church into which they had an aperture or window. Vestiges of these anchorages are to be found occasionally among the remains of Catholic England. The most famous of the female hermits was Mother Juliana of Norwich, who lived somewhat after this fashion at Costessy, and whose "Revelations of Divine Love" form a well-known book of devotion to the present day.

As the Middle Ages advanced, the learning of the time became centred more and more in the twin Universities of Oxford and Cambridge. In the earlier years the chief homes of the scholarship of the period had been the monastic schools; several of the first monks who took the lead in fostering study had come from the Benedictine School of Bec. Such was Lanfranc; such too was St Anselm and his bosom friend, the Bishop of Rochester, Gundulf. And not a few of the Benedictine Abbeys of England had in their turn gained a wide renown as seats of learning, and had produced scholars of worldwide reputation. Yet, as time went on and the universities grew, they absorbed into themselves more and more both of all the available teaching power, and also of the scholars who were attracted by the reputation of far-famed professors to leave home or monastery and sit at their feet. At first they probably, like St Edmund, had to lodge in private houses, but the Benedictine Abbey soon felt the need of having cells or hostels for the comfort of their members. And when, in the thirteenth century, the Mendicant Friars plunged into the stream of university life, and established themselves both at Oxford and at Cambridge, another great step forward had been taken towards making the universities supreme in matters of learning. With the fourteenth and fifteenth centuries came the systematic foundation of colleges of residence, leading up to the

University Studies.

ideal of a central teaching body, surrounded by an indefinite number of corporate residential bodies on their own premises, bound together by their own rules, and leading more or less a life in common. In this last sense the universities are more the creation of the decline of the Middle Ages than of their earlier and more vigorous prime. It would probably surprise anyone who has not gone into the matter to find how few of the colleges either at Oxford or at Cambridge were founded before those dates which are commonly assigned as the commencement of the period of decline.

Scarcely less in importance to the foundation of the colleges in the universities stands the foundation of grammar schools and public schools, either in the chief monasteries or in other chosen sites scattered over the counties of England. The founding of Winchester School in 1378 by William of Wykeham, bishop of that see, is one of his fairest titles to fame. It was founded to consist of a warden and seventy scholars to live in common, studying grammar " to the honour and glory of God and Our Lady," as he puts it. Henry VI. made this noble establishment the model, forty years later, for his royal foundation at Eton, where a provost, ten priests, twenty-five scholars, and twenty-five poor bedesmen were to be gathered in collegiate fashion alongside the parish church, which was made over to them. Wykeham's statutes were adopted almost without change, and the king sent an agent to Rome to secure the papal confirmation of what he had done. Whittington College, London, was founded in 1434 by the Lord Mayor of that name. Even in the case of later schools such as St Paul's, begun by the Dean, Dr Colet, in 1512, the Charterhouse, and the Blue Coat School, founded on the sites of the suppressed Carthusian and Franciscan houses respectively, it is not unfair to claim that inspiration and guidance was given by the older schools spoken of above. Nay, these early public schools of Winchester and Eton, as well as the grammar schools in less celebrated places too numerous to mention, pointed the way to Harrow, Rugby, and Westminster, as well as to the numerous smaller schools of modern times.

One great feature of the lives of our ancestors which

Old English Guilds.

was characteristic of them, and at the same time not without its lessons for us, was the vigorous growth of the associations which they called guilds. They were always combining in guilds, now for social purposes, now for trade and commerce, now to safeguard the interests of those engaged in some particular trade or avocation. There were guilds with a purely spiritual object, binding the members to some definite act of piety or charity. But their chief temporal value was the co-operation they secured in the various industrial and social works of the body of the people, and in that they foreshadow a possible remedy for the unlimited competition and the class warfare of our own days. They also bear witness to the extent to which even the secular life of the nation in mediaeval times was impregnated with the religious practices and the Christian belief of the Catholic Church. The City of London Companies of the present day, though very much changed by the circumstances of the times from their original purpose, form an interesting survival of those ancient institutions. Although we must not suppose that guild life was equally developed all over the country, the London guilds show us how in an important centre every trade and walk in life had its guilds with its own rules, its own corporate existence, and its own revenues. Some of these rules strangely foreshadow those made by the modern trades' unions, of which to a certain extent they formed the counterpart, always, however, keeping religion and piety in the forefront of their programme.

Miracle plays and moralities.

As our ancestors had their guilds to regulate their work, so did they make use of the drama, which is perhaps the most far-reaching of the Fine Arts, to enliven their holidays. Here again religion and the supernatural life abundantly held their own. The oldest English miracle play is the short one known as the "Harrowing of Hell," but there are four extensive cycles of such dramas in existence, going through the various Christian mysteries, and known respectively as the Towneley, Chester, York, and Coventry Plays. The number of plays is in all one hundred and forty-four. The transition between the miracle plays and the Elizabethan drama is furnished by the moralities, where the virtues and vices are personified and introduced as the characters of the piece. There is a real connection between the plays and the guilds, inasmuch as to meet expenses and provide for the performances, the plays were distributed among the guilds of the locality for them to exhibit in turn.

If we have to name one art by which our ancestors expressed above all their consecration of external things to the glory of God, we cannot hesitate for long. We shall find that it was into architecture that they put their souls, with a fullness which seems unattainable now, even by those who share their faith, and is unapproachable by those who do not believe as they believed. The various monuments of this which we still have with us in the cathedrals and parish churches of our land are a standing witness to the truth of it. The Catholic dioceses in England at the Reformation, as we have already seen, numbered seventeen, and the cathedrals of all but one are still standing to-day, and in use for the same number of Anglican sees. St Paul's in London is the one that has perished. The same number of new sees has been since erected by the Anglican Church, making a total of thirty-four, and it is interesting to note how their cathedrals have been provided. Six great abbey churches have been taken, and of course in this way saved from destruction. Eight priories or conventual churches of Catholic days serve for eight others. There remains but three or, counting St Paul's, London, four, which have been built by the Anglicans for themselves. Of the abbeys other than those converted into cathedrals a few are still standing of which the most notable are Westminster, Waltham, Tewkesbury, Selby; while we shall find the stones of others incorporated in the noble mansions of Woburn, Welbeck, Belvoir, Tavistock, and others. One is being restored from its foundations by the Benedictines at Buckfast. And quite a considerable number of priories and lesser religious houses have been made to serve as parish churches. But the rest have perished, or lie in ruins, as at Tintern, Fountains, Rievaulx, and a long list of other places. It is when we come to the parish churches of the Middle Ages, and see them studded over the face of the country in thousands, so that in some counties the modern building

Architectural monuments.

is the exception, and the ancient survival the rule, that we realise what incomparable builders were our Catholic ancestors; not wearying of the work, but renewing these edifices with more studied splendour, just on the eve of the great catastrophe. In the half-century of peace, which is comprised between the accession of Henry VII. and the Act of Supremacy in the last part of Henry VIII.'s reign, there was a great movement to rebuild the churches and to renovate the cathedrals all over the land. This is the explanation of those richly adorned specimens of Perpendicular Gothic which we can still admire from one end of the land to the other. Even where the solid masonry of Norman buildings still defied the hand of time after ages had passed over them, the taste for ornament and magnificence would sometimes lead men to case the stern strength of earlier days in elaborate Gothic such as that of the nave at Winchester.

The æsthetic taste of the Church in the Middle Ages expressed itself above all in architecture. But it would be an error to suppose that the other fine arts were ignored. They were all in their own way yoked to the car of religion, and made to serve her. Our ancestors did not leave their churches the sober masses of grey stone which we are accustomed to gaze upon, often almost unfurnished. But they made them real homes of faith and devotion; they painted and they gilded within until the place was warm with colour. They carved their roodscreens, they coloured their window-glass with hues that put to shame the glaziers of to-day. Their brasses were far more abundant than we are used to on wall and pillar and grave. Even their tiles partook of the warm colours they loved. And for all these things they employed a patient, loving craftsman's art, which loved good work and spared no toil.

Another art which was carried to a very high pitch of excellence was that of transcribing and illuminating manuscripts. The invention of printing not having been as yet achieved, the making of copies of even the most important books depended upon the labours of the transcriber. And it was in the *Scriptoria*, as the places provided for this work were called, of the great monasteries of the land that the bulk of this was done. And it certainly was done with marvellous devotion to the cause of literature and learning, and with a remarkable degree of finished workmanship. Caligraphy is almost a lost art in the cycle of modern education if we compare ourselves with the writers of those days. And they could find heart to tarry over their page to ornament it, or, if need were, to illuminate it in gold and bright colours. Our museums and libraries still possess among their chief treasures many magnificent folios, entirely written out by hand on the finest vellum and adorned with the most brilliant wealth of illumination, of the chief works which the mediaeval scholars wished to preserve. And they considered it a labour of love to reproduce them in a style which speaks eloquently of the esteem in which they held their text. Often these volumes are missals or service books or song books for the Divine Office, or else Prayer Books for private devotion. Sometimes they are portions of the Holy Scripture. But not seldom there are books of a more secular character. Without the labours of the monastic copyists the masterpieces of classic literature, orators, poets, historians, would inevitably all have perished. And they were willing to lavish such minute care upon the transcription of even a primer or a book of devotion that these things became heirlooms to be mentioned in their wills, and it is not too much to say that they were worthy of such a remembrance.

With regard to painting it is of course beyond dispute that correct outline and proportion were absolutely beyond the reach of the artists of the Middle Ages. However, both they and the people for whom they painted were keenly appreciative of bright and beautiful colours. These gave a warmth and animation to the solemn minsters and cathedrals which would otherwise have been wanting. We are accustomed to see these buildings in the sombre tints which their antiquity and modern taste have given them. But it would be a great mistake to think that our Catholic ancestors were contented with anything so subdued and neutral. The evidence at our command shows a preference for glowing colours and brightest hues, whether in pictures, or tombs, or shrines, or painted windows. Indeed the preparation of such strong and lasting tints as they employed seems almost a lost art.

They loved to employ the precious metals to make

altar plate, or to ornament the shrines of the saints.
But, it is, unfortunately, above all from the inventory of
such things made to serve the plundering hands of
Henry VIII. that we can form the best idea of the
scale on which gold and silver and precious stones were
thus dedicated to what is really their noblest use—the
public service of God. We have only to run our eyes
over these records of rifled sanctuaries to understand
what fine art meant in the ceremonies of the Church
in the days when England was Catholic. Their minsters
were decked both inside and outside with statuary. A
few sculptured west fronts, such as Wells and Exeter,
and a few magnificent specimens of the reredos, such
as Winchester or St Albans, have either survived or
been restored as hallowed memorials of those bygone
days. There were figures on the rood-screen, effigies on
the tombs, grotesque gargoyles on the roofs, which unite
to suggest an enterprising love of sculpture which out-
ran the power of execution.

As for the art of music, our ancestors were restricted
almost exclusively to the simple and devout melodies
of the Gregorian Chant. The few
examples we have of anything beyond this
seem to bear a very rudimentary character.
But as civilisation advanced more attention was paid
to the using of whatever means were at command to
render these austere tones correctly and worthily. There
is evidence that they called in the assistance of the
organ to steady and guide the singers. The young
pupils in the monastery schools were taught betimes to
take part in the church services, thus gaining from their
early years a familiarity both with her music and her
language. Slightly to anticipate we may remark that
in the age of the Renaissance, which immediately preceded the Protestant Reformation, this art took on a new
development in what is known as the contrapuntal or
polyphonic style. In this new departure English
musicians bore an important part. In fact it may be
claimed that they even took the lead. John Dunstable
(1453), whose reputation as a musician spread over the
Continent, is acknowledged by some writers as the real
founder of the new polyphonic style. In Thomas Tallis
(1584) and William Byrd (1623), the former of whom
was in time earlier than Palestrina, while the latter

Church music.

was his contemporary, we have two Catholic musicians who still further developed the same style which the Italian composer just mentioned carried to its perfection.

In the ways we have indicated and in others which cannot find a place here, our Catholic forefathers showed how they allowed the spirit of Christianity to penetrate the whole life of their country. **Summary.** Linked to the centre of unity in Rome by the threefold bond of doctrine, of worship, and of hierarchy, they brought their Faith into every region of existence, and even when they failed to act up to its requirements in their daily life, they tacitly admitted its theoretical supremacy. The whole structure of society was based on this. When the Christian of those days came to himself in repentance, he was prepared to do penance with a severity which seems to have almost passed from the world. To shorten his purgation he did all in his power to provide for his soul by Masses and the foundation of charitable and pious institutions, and he looked forward to another life as the reality for which this one was only a preparation, with a vivid realisation that modern ways of thought can hardly hope to rival.

XXIV.

THE HOUSE OF TUDOR AND THE RENAISSANCE.

(1485-1509.)

WHEN England accepted Henry Tudor for its monarch after the death of Richard III. at Bosworth, it meant a real settlement of the government of the land. This prince became ruler of the country in a fashion which his immediate predecessors had never reached. The way in which the nobility and gentry had been thinned out by the Wars of the Roses removed the strongest of his opponents out of his path. Moreover, the cautious calculating disposition of the new sovereign helped to consolidate the royal power. He was not the man to keep alive the unrest of the preceding reigns by engaging in such foreign expeditions as the Hundred Years' War. He meant indeed to be master in his own house, but England was house enough for him. In this line of policy he in the main succeeded, in spite of several abortive insurrections. Thus his reign became an epoch of progress in civilisation, of reconstruction, and of growing prosperity. The literary Renaissance, after coming to maturity in Italy, now began to tell upon life and upon education in England. This also told in the same direction. Henry had fought a pitched battle against a determined foe in order to win his crown, but he was not a warrior in the sense in which former kings had been. He was a diplomatist, a financier, a plotting schemer, if you will, but he was a man of peace. He was pious also, and devout in his own way. He went on pilgrimage to Walsingham before marching against

Reign of Henry VII. (1485-1509).

his rebels. He was a patron of learning, of the arts, and above all, of architecture.

He had first to reward those whose military prowess had helped to set him on the throne. Such was his uncle, Jasper, who became Duke of Bedford. Such also was Lord Stanley, now made Earl of Derby, and Sir Edward Stanley, now created Earl of Devon. He then proceeded to choose counsellors to assist him in governing. The chief of these were churchmen, foremost among whom were John Morton and Richard Fox. The former of these great men had been an adherent of the Lancastrian party, but had made his submission to Edward IV., and in 1478 was raised to the see of Ely. Richard III. had thrown him into prison, but he escaped to Flanders, where he remained until after the battle of Bosworth. He was then recalled by the victorious Henry, and, Cardinal Bourchier having died soon after presiding at the coronation, he was nominated to the primacy in 1486. Six months later he was made Lord Chancellor, while in 1493 the Pope made him a cardinal. He was, moreover, a man of considerable literary and scientific gifts. Blessed Thomas More, who was brought up in his household, draws a lively picture of him as he lived in his great circle of scholars and dependants. He was probably the author of the "*History of Richard III.*," attributed by some to More. His politics remained strongly Lancastrian.

Cardinal John Morton (1420-1500).

Richard Fox became Bishop of Exeter in 1487, and was at the same time appointed secretary to the king. In the course of his long career he was successively translated to the sees of Bath (1492), Durham (1494), and Winchester (1501). Besides his secretarial duties near the king's person, he was sent abroad on several occasions on various diplomatic missions. Being younger than Morton, he survived both Primate and King, and his wisdom made him one of the most trusted advisers of Henry VIII. in that monarch's earlier years.

Bishop Richard Fox (1448-1528).

Henry VII. was eminently filled by character to take advantage of the peace which settled down on the land, both to strengthen regal power at home, and to form foreign alliances. In the former undertaking he was aided not only by large-minded prelates like Morton and Fox, but also by officials of a meaner stamp, who were none too scrupulous in the means they used to further their master's interests and to fill his purse. The two who are best known, and are still held up to popular execration, bore the names of Empson and Dudley. By straining every bond which the law gave them for drawing fines from the gentry, and by exacting forced loans from those who possessed any money, these men inflicted considerable hardships on the people, and ended by making the king's rule very distasteful and harsh to the country.

Cardinal Morton was made visitor for the reform of such abuses as had crept into the monasteries: for example, the great Abbey of St Albans. He also legislated in synod against heretics. And both these efforts were so successful that, as Dr Gairdner says: "We cannot deny that very much of a beginning had been made in the correction of clerical abuses," while, as the same author observes, with regard to heretics in the reign of Henry VII.: "There were very many recantations and very few burnings." Morton deserves high praise as a moderate and at the same time efficient ecclesiastical reformer.

The tyrannical character of Richard III. and his consequent unpopularity had much lightened the task of supplanting him, but Henry VII. felt the need of strengthening his position by all the best means at his command. He therefore arranged to marry Elizabeth, the Yorkist heiress, daughter of Edward IV. This marriage was celebrated with the necessary dispensations at the end of 1485. But Henry applied to the Pope Innocent VIII. for a confirmation of this dispensation, craftily meaning to gain in this way the papal approbation of the settlement of the crown upon his heirs. In the following March he was in possession of the rescript from Rome, by which, after confirming the dispensation for the marriage between relatives, the Pope goes on to rehearse one by one Henry's titles to the throne.

Henry's titles. He was made to claim it (1) by right of conquest, (2) by right of inheritance, (3) by election of the estates of the realm, and (4) by Act of Parliament. He then for a fifth title (5) confirms by papal authority the settlement of the crown, already agreed to in Parliament, interpreting

THE HOUSE OF TUDOR

it to mean that in case of failure of issue by Princess Elizabeth of York it should devolve on Henry's children by any subsequent marriage. The Pontiff concluded by excommunicating all who should disturb the settlement thus made. The king had thus a summary of all his claims in a nutshell. We find that he set such store by this that in his progress through the chief towns of the land, when he attended the church services in state, as was his custom, the papal letter was read aloud, and one of the bishops explained it to the people.

Nevertheless, the reign did not pass without several attempts being made to oust the Tudor line. The details of these events do not belong to Church history, but to the general annals of the time. Two of these insurrections strove to overthrow the Tudors under the banner of pretenders, claiming to be Yorkist princes. Lambert Simnel was given out as Edward, Earl of Warwick, son of the Duke of Clarence, whom Henry had shut up in the Tower of London for his greater security. The second of these pretenders, Perkin Warbeck, claimed to be Richard, Duke of York, thought to have been murdered in the Tower with his brother, Edward V. Simnel and his supporters were routed by the king at Stoke-on-Trent. Warbeck gave more trouble, but was eventually taken and beheaded, as were several of the leading supporters of both pretenders. The real Edward, Earl of Warwick, was also executed, but Simnel was pardoned, and held up to public contempt as a menial in the royal household. Besides these risings, there was another in Yorkshire provoked by the king's harsh levies of taxation, and later on one in Cornwall. Though not Yorkist in origin, they were secretly favoured by that party. Moreover, the somewhat meagre annals of the reign give us indirect evidence of other lesser revolts and troubles scarcely mentioned in the ordinary histories. In general these risings were followed by some executions, and by many confiscations. In fact it was chiefly through fines and pecuniary exactions that Henry punished his traitors and disarmed his more powerful enemies. He continued to make these disturbances turn to the profit of the royal purse. In fact this was the oppressive side of his government. It was a yoke under which the people

Rebellions and risings.

groaned, but it did not interfere with his gaining the reputation of being the wisest, the most moderate, and the most pious prince of his time. For, though he amassed treasure, he was able to point to the expenditure of considerable sums upon religious undertakings. Moreover, though averse to wars against Christian princes, when Alexander VI. asked for a subsidy for a new Crusade, Henry replied that he would do more; he would lead the English Crusaders in person, and there seems some reason to suppose that he meant what he said. He made this the reason for characteristically excusing himself from any subsidy of foreign Crusades. Later on, the Roman Pontiff succeeded in getting a royal agreement to a moderate levy on the English clergy for this purpose. But none of the Catholic princes on the Continent would rally to any enterprise such as was proposed, so that Henry's promised Crusade also came to nothing. In the reign of the following Pontiff, Julius II., the Wars of the Holy League in Italy quite put any foreign expedition out of court in the near future. And if Henry was not too anxious to go to war for the Holy Places, still less would he plunge into martial adventure for any lesser cause. The popular epigram gives, after all, not too exaggerated an account of his political action when it says that he first obtained money from his subjects to enable him to make war on foreign princes, and then received more money from these foreign princes to induce him not to make war upon them. In this way the king's treasure grew until it reached to millions; and the peace was preserved.

But, although the king was unresting in his efforts to amass a fortune, he could spend with magnificence when he saw cause to do so. It was out of the treasures he had saved that he found means to build his splendid new palace at Richmond, as well as for the gorgeous chapel at Westminster Abbey, which he built both as a Lady Chapel to testify his devotion to the Blessed Virgin, and also as a mausoleum for himself and his race. Henry VII.'s chapel shows the highest elaboration of the Perpendicular Style of Gothic of which England can boast. But this did not exhaust his munificence in building, for, besides three royal monastic foundations, he put the finishing touch to King Henry VI.'s Chapel at King's College, Cambridge.

THE HOUSE OF TUDOR

It needs but a slight glance at the events of the reign to remark a great difference between its former and its latter half. So far is this the case that some recent writers, such as Professor Oman, contend that it is more reasonable to extend the period of the Wars of the Roses up to 1497, the year when Henry was at length victorious over the rebels, and able henceforth to reign in security. The reign is thus divided at 1497 into two equal parts of twelve years each. The latter period was one of great prosperity. It was then that Henry could add to his treasures, and it was then that he could raise the architectural piles which stand to his credit. On the other hand the evidence is strong that moral progress did not go hand in hand with material advancement. In other words there was more of decay and corruption in the various departments both of Church and State than there had been in earlier and rougher times. Before Henry himself fell under the dart of death, most of the leading men who had been prominent at the time of his accession had passed away. Cardinal Morton, of course, was dead, so was Thomas Rotherham, who had held York for twenty years (1480-1500). *Churchmen of the later years of the reign.* Neither did Rotherham's successor, Thomas Savage, who had reached the metropolitan see through Rochester and London in turn, survive the king. Henry Dean only held Canterbury for two years (1501-3). Thus there was need of new leaders to guide the ship of the Church in England. The most eminent of these was Thomas Warham, whose promotion to Canterbury after only one year as Bishop of London was rapid indeed. He then became chancellor also, and for the thirty years he presided in the Primate's chair was on several counts the first churchman in the land. York was left vacant for several years, until, just before the end of the reign, it was filled by the translation of Christopher Bainbridge from Durham. Richard Fox, already in the earlier part of the reign one of the chief royal advisers, passed in turn from Exeter to Bath and Durham, and thence to Winchester, where he was bishop from 1501 to 1528. His whole time of episcopacy extended for more than forty years. He divided with Warham the honour of being the chief statesman of his day. Richard Nykke held the see of Norwich for thirty-five years

(1501-36), until extreme old age exempted him from taking part on one side or the other in the catastrophic change brought about by Henry VIII. two years before. John Arundel held Lichfield and Exeter in turn. John Alcock, a notable scholar and patron of learning, became Bishop of Ely, having been translated there after some years' tenure of Rochester, and then of Worcester. It was as Bishop of Ely that he became the founder of Jesus College at Cambridge. Another eminent supporter of the revival of learning was Thomas Langton, Bishop first of St David's, then of Salisbury, and lastly of Winchester. Worcester was successively in the hands of two Italian brothers, who were the papal collectors in England, John and Sylvester de Gigli. Another celebrated Italian humanist, Adrian di Castelli, who was envoy from the Pope to the King of Scotland, gained the favour of Henry VII., and remained in England. He also for a time collected the papal revenue, and was made Bishop of Hereford, and then of Bath. He was then made English ambassador to the Holy See, and performed the duties of collector through a deputy, the celebrated Polydore Virgil. At Rome Adrian was made cardinal, but became involved in the Petrucci conspiracy against Leo X. Thereupon he was deprived both of his collectorship and of the diocese of Bath, nor did the intercession of Henry VII. avail to save him. He was a polished humanist, and the writer of elegant Latin poems. As for Polydore Virgil, being invited to write the history of England, he undertook this task, and went on with it, but incurred the enmity of Wolsey, and was incarcerated for a time. Richard Fitzjames, the Bishop of Rochester, being translated to London in 1504, was succeeded at Rochester by the learned and saintly John Fisher, later on cardinal, and martyr in 1534. None of his contemporaries in England had such a great reputation either for scholarship or for holiness.

It was surrounded by such men as these that King Henry VII. took ill in 1509, and was before long found to be in a dying condition. His conduct on his deathbed was that of a fervent penitent. He had the Mary Mass celebrated before him the very day on which he died. He made ample provision in his will for alms for his soul, as well as the perpetual chantry in the

THE HOUSE OF TUDOR

chapel he had built at Westminster. All who had received wrong at his hands were to be recompensed, and it was at the Blessed Virgin's feet that he wished to be buried. His consort, Elizabeth, had already been interred with sumptuous ceremonial in the still unfinished chapel. From Shene, called Richmond after him, where he died, the funeral procession passed to St Paul's Cathedral, where, after the Requiem, Bishop Fisher delivered a funeral sermon. Then the march was resumed to Westminster, the like rites were repeated, and Fitzjames, Bishop of London, delivered a sermon from the words of Job: "Have pity on me, at least you my friends, for the hand of the Lord hath touched me." A few weeks more and the Lady Margaret, Countess of Richmond, was laid to rest near her son, whose succession and whose prosperity she had done not a little to secure. Bishop Fisher was again the chosen preacher, and he was able to bear testimony both to her piety and to the many notable works she had taken part in for the good of religion and the advancement of learning. Fisher had been her director, or " ghostly father," as they then put it. He it was who had urged her on to the foundation of St John's College at Cambridge. In fact, as she died before the foundation had been completed, the whole burden fell upon him, and the title of founder is none too high for what he accomplished in this way. Through the Lady Chapel at Westminster being the burial-place of these three illustrious royal personages, it has become inextricably associated both with their line and their time. It is part of the abbey, and yet distinct from it, with a striking break at the noble porch. Perhaps, as the historian of the place suggests, it is a fitting symbol of the reign of Henry VII., connected with what belongs to the Middle Ages, and yet marked off from them by characteristics which belong to what we know as Modern Times.

The Renaissance in England.

The reign of Henry VII. witnessed the development in England of that intellectual movement which had taken firm hold of the educated classes on the Continent, and more especially in Italy, some fifty or sixty years earlier. It is a mistake, probably arising from religious prejudice, which represents this new impetus

to study as arriving in England with the Protestant
Reformation. Quite the contrary. It was in full
vigour before there had been any disturbance of Catholic
unity in the land. The real effect of the Reformation
had been, in the main, to retard and warp it. In
England it was just as much anterior to the religious
changes as it was in any of the countries of continental
Europe. The fall of Constantinople in 1453 was the
chief fostering cause of the revival of Greek studies,
and these studies may be rightly taken as the most
characteristic note of the new departure.

It was in the year 1464 that William Selling, monk
of Canterbury, got leave from his prior to go with
William Hadley to study abroad, and it
is to his studies in Greek during his sojourn
on the Continent that Cardinal Gasquet
attributes the first beginnings of the
revival of the cultivation of that tongue in England.
Selling became later on Prior of Christchurch, Canterbury, and devoted himself during the twenty years for
which he held that office to the work of establishing
on a firm basis the culture of the Renaissance in that
great monastic centre. His best known pupil was
Thomas Linacre (1460-1524), who cultivated both
medicine and Greek literature with equal ardour. He
passed from Canterbury to Oxford, and thence again to
the continental cities. After his return to England he
was made one of the royal physicians, when he had
nearly all the most distinguished men of the day as his
patients. He was the chief instrument in the foundation of the College of Physicians. But he continued to
make translations from the Greek authors, and composed
a Latin grammar for the Princess Mary, whose Latin
tutor he became in 1523. Linacre's studies in Italy
were shared by William Grocyn (1448-1519), who likewise came back to England at the same time that he
did, but whose subsequent career was of a different
character. Grocyn was appointed to lecture at Oxford,
and among his pupils in Greek he counted More
and Erasmus. Colet, Dean of St Paul's, got him to
lecture in the school he had founded, and eventually
Archbishop Warham named him as a master of the
collegiate school and church which he had established
at Maidstone.

English humanists and scholars.

John Colet (1467-1519) takes by right one of the highest places among the English humanists. He was son of the Lord Mayor of London, who was knighted by King Henry VII., and this distinguished ancestry early put him into the simultaneous possession of several benefices. However, he succeeded in getting sufficient freedom to enable him to travel for purposes of study in Italy and elsewhere, instead of residing in his parishes, and then on his return he lectured on the New Testament at Oxford. He was only ordained priest in 1498. The last fifteen years of his life were spent as Dean of St Paul's Cathedral in London. Soon after his appointment to this office he inherited his father's fortune, and was thus enabled to carry out his plan for the foundation of St Paul's School. He found a suitable head master for the institution in the humanist layman, William Lilly, but he retained himself a general supervision over the school, and even collaborated with Lilly in the composition of the celebrated Latin Grammar, which is the parent of the Eton and other public school grammars. Lilly's son, George, became a priest, and was afterwards made chaplain to Cardinal Pole. Colet was considered by many, including the members of his own chapter, to be anti-scholastic, and Bishop Fitzjames of London sided with his opponents. But on an appeal to the Primate, Warham, that great man warmly espoused his cause, and his enemies were discomfited. It is an outstanding fact that the support given to the efforts of the humanists by the highest and noblest ecclesiastics in the land is written large in the history of the Renaissance in England. It was not from Warham only, but equally warm encouragement was forthcoming from the saintly Fisher, from Langton, Bishop of Winchester, and from others. Yet, high as are the claims of the scholars already mentioned, the first place of all amongst the leaders of the Renaissance belongs to Desiderius Erasmus, the Dutchman, who may indeed be looked upon as a citizen of the world, but who was nowhere more at home than in England. Erasmus writes of Warham as his chief patron, and to him his unstinted admiration was given, but the close relations in which he lived with Sir Thomas More and his strongly humanistic household are well known. The closeness of

John Colet and others.

his intimacy with Fisher is scarcely acknowledged so generally, yet it is undeniable. His chief literary enemy was Edward Lee, afterwards Archbishop of York. He, with a certain number of monks and friars, survivors of the mediaeval schoolmen, vehemently accused Erasmus of unorthodox teaching. Yet when the probation came, Fisher, Erasmus himself, and many a prominent humanist remained faithful to the Church and the Pope, while Lee and not a few of the violent antagonists of these men abjured their faith in Christian unity at the bidding of a tyrannical king.

The position of More is a somewhat exceptional one. He remained a layman, but he was conversant with most of the matters debated in his day both in Church and State. The son of a judge of the King's Bench, he had been brought up in the household of Cardinal Morton, and passing thence to Oxford and Lincoln's Inn in turn, had spent his youth amongst the most learned and intellectual men of the day. When he rose to office and dignity as judge and as speaker of the House of Commons, his house at Chelsea became a sort of rendezvous for the humanist scholars whose aspirations he shared, and whose studies prompted him to a noble emulation. He was to seal his faith with his life's blood, as heroically as Fisher or any of the "spirituality," when the catastrophe of the next reign fell upon the land; but in his earlier years he was the ideal English scholar, inferior perhaps to Erasmus and others in classical knowledge, but amply compensating for this by his services to his native tongue. He is the best representative of English literature in the Renaissance period. His "*History of Richard III.*" is the first historical work in modern English of which our literature can boast. His "*Utopia*," though written in Latin, has an esteemed place in translations in the same roll of honour. And taking his other English works as they stand, nothing but religious bigotry can question his title to be looked upon as the foremost author of his time as far as his native land is concerned. It is probably due to the subsequent revulsion caused by the Reformation that they scarcely have attained the popularity which has been accorded to far inferior works which happened to be written on the Protestant side.

Blessed Thomas More (1478-1535).

THE HOUSE OF TUDOR 347

For a Catholic the case is otherwise, yet even for such a one the glory which belongs to him from the brightness of his literary gifts and of his legal attainments becomes overshadowed by the halo which spoke of another world, when he had sacrificed all that made this life dear to the claims of conscience and Catholicity.

XXV.

THE DEFENDER OF THE FAITH.

(1509-1534.)

Henry VIII. (1509-1547). RARELY, indeed, has a prince mounted the English throne with brighter promise of a reign of prosperity than Henry VIII. enjoyed. When his father breathed his last, he was at once peacefully proclaimed as king. England was waxing strong, and the new breath of life which had stirred the Continent had reached this country as well. It is clear that it had been taken advantage of to the full in the growth of trade, the restoration of old or obsolete buildings, and the general advance of civilisation. Moreover, the land was at peace. The policy of the late king, even if it seemed selfish and tortuous, had secured this at least; and the royal coffers were full of a treasure, accumulated as the reward of this peace, and also a security against war. There had been extortion, it is true, but when popular feeling had been appeased by the punishment of Empson and Dudley even the memory of this grew fainter. So the earliest years of the new monarch were devoted to the happy enjoyment of the rich inheritance which had fallen to him.

England in the Holy League. It was therefore an exuberance both of energy and of resources which led Henry VIII. before long to desire to play a leading part in the general drama of European politics. Pope Julius II. was nothing loath to encourage him in this. He had formed the Holy League to drive the French out of Italy, and there was a place for the King of England in its councils if he would but fill it. Christopher Bainbridge, who had been made Bishop of Durham late in the preceding reign, and was soon after translated to York, was sent to Rome as the king's ambassador in this matter. He received a warm welcome, was created cardinal at the next consistory, and eventually was appointed captain-general of the papal army. It was without doubt partly through his action and the Pope's insistence that Henry joined the League on the 13th of November, 1512, and England was committed to war against France. Bainbridge remained in the Papal Curia, though he still charged himself with the interests of his sovereign; but he only survived until 1514, when he died in Rome, being poisoned by an Italian domestic. His noble monument, to-day in the church of the English College, helps to keep alive the memory of this warlike prince of the Church.

Meanwhile, the English nation had engaged in a war for which they were hardly prepared, and it was some time before they were able to take part in it with any honour to themselves. But they were encouraged to proceed, and Leo X. despatched an envoy to confer with much ceremony a cap and sword of state upon the English king. There was not much progress made in hostilities against the French, and by this time Henry had the services of a statesman who extricated him from these difficulties with masterly skill, though not to the advantage of the enemies of France. This was Thomas Wolsey, who first appears as a member of the Privy Council in 1511, and from that time rose rapidly to the highest pitch of influence and royal favour. This great statesman was born at Ipswich in 1471 or thereabouts, and his father, a man of substance, is said on the strength of a somewhat doubtful tradition to have been a butcher. At Magdalen College, Oxford, he took his degree at the age of fifteen, hence gaining the sobriquet of the "boy bachelor." He then became fellow and tutor in the college for many years, thus having every opportunity of employing his transcendent abilities in the acquisition of learning. It was not till 1500 that he was presented to the living of Limington in Dorset two years after his ordination. He then became chaplain to Archbishop Dean, Henry VII., and Henry VIII., in turn, and received several benefices in addition to what he before enjoyed. He already began to be employed about the royal affairs, and the accession of Henry VIII. found him Dean of Lincoln. As Master of the Rolls he had

Thomas Wolsey comes into power.

ere this made his mark in legal business. He was soon
made Lord Almoner, Registrar of the Order of the Garter,
and further enriched by other benefices. By this time the
king had come to place the utmost confidence in his
counsels, and undertook little of public concern without
his co-operation. Warham and Fox, the old and trusty
councillors of Henry VII., the latter of whom had introduced Wolsey at court, gradually relinquished their
grasp of public affairs, and Thomas Wolsey stepped into
their places. The chief aim of his policy was to dis-
engage England from the ties of the Holy League, and
to come to an understanding with France. He was
Henry's ambassador to arrange the match between Louis
XII. and Mary Tudor, the king's sister. In this way the
road was paved for peace, and Wolsey had not long to
wait for his reward. In February, 1514, he was confirmed by the Pope as Bishop of Lincoln, and, Cardinal
Bainbridge dying in the same year, was translated to York
in September. It was entirely due to the exertion of all
the king's influence at Rome that next year Wolsey was
created Cardinal of St Cecilia. De Gigli, Bishop of
Worcester, who was now Henry's agent with the Holy
See, had promised in his name a tenth of the goods of
the clergy in support of the war against the Turks.
Wolsey received the hat in Westminster Abbey at a
function of almost unrivalled splendour, graced by the
presence of Warham and most of the bishops. And a
great banquet at York House in the evening was attended
by the king and queen in state. A month later Wolsey
succeeded Warham as Lord Chancellor, and this marked
the full attainment of the highest dignities by him, as
well as the final retirement of the older statesmen from
the management of affairs (1515).

There were two occasions in the course of the next few
years when Wolsey was almost the leading figure in
events which were marked by scenes of magnificence
characteristic of the period and of the personalities concerned. The former of these took place in 1518. The
Pope desired to send a legate to England to proclaim the
Crusade against the Turks, and though objection was
raised by Henry against a foreign cardinal coming as
legate to England, he waived the point on condition that
Wolsey should be associated with him in the office.
Wolsey thus added the dignity of legate to his

"blushing honours" at least for the time. The Italian legate, Cardinal Campeggio, was received with every demonstration of honour, and this ceremony was but the first of a series which reached its climax when in the presence of the two legates, of the king and of all his court in St Paul's Cathedral, the solemn betrothal of the Dauphin to the Princess Mary, Henry's infant daughter, was celebrated, together with the swearing of a treaty between France and England amid splendours which are pronounced by eye-witnesses to baffle description. But in the midst of Church functions and banquets, the original object of the legation was lost sight of, and after Campeggio's departure Wolsey managed to secure from the Holy See an extension of his own legatine powers for a term of three years.

Wolsey as Papal Legate.

The other occasion which afforded both Henry VIII. and Wolsey an opportunity of gratifying their somewhat extravagant taste for external magnificence and display was the meeting of the English and French kings to celebrate the restoration of friendly relations between them. This unique pageant, which is known in history as the Field of the Cloth of Gold, was a triumph of Wolsey's power and love of the picturesque working together. It was planned and carried out by him, and it was meant to symbolise the policy of an understanding with France for which he had been working during a considerable period. But in this latter respect it failed to produce any lasting result. Wolsey was overruled, and the march of events forced England and France again asunder.

Field of the Cloth of Gold.

Up to this time there was very little open heresy in England, for the prosecutions of the preceding reigns had been successful, and what heretical feeling remained in England was under the surface; nor is there anything to show, as Dr Gairdner admits, that the few heretical partisans who were in the country were enlightened or educated men. Of course there was a distinguished band of humanists in England, but the humanists were not necessarily irreligious, and the disciples of the Renaissance in England would compare in this respect very favourably with what we know of their fellow-scholars in Italy and elsewhere. But the relaxed state of so

352 THE CHURCH IN ENGLAND

many of the prominent churchmen both in Italy and in Germany was well known in England, and both sarcasm and serious condemnation were rife. Moreover, Italian ecclesiastics had been provided with benefices in the country, even bishoprics, and this was not acceptable to the native clergy. Two brothers, Giovanni and Sylvester de Gigli, in succession held the see of Worcester, and then it was given to Giulio dei Medici, afterwards Clement VII., and he in turn was succeeded by Ghinucci. It is true there was this special circumstance about Worcester, that its incumbent was supposed to act as royal agent at the court of Rome, but this was not all. Bath and Wells was given to Cardinal Adrian Castelli, and later on Salisbury was held by Campeggio from 1524 to 1535. Consequently, when Martin Luther's ninety-five theses against indulgences appeared at Wittenberg in 1517, it was looked upon much more as a protest against administrative abuses than as the proclamation of a new heretical campaign. The upshot of the discussions in Germany was that Luther took up a more definitely anti-Catholic position in his book on the "Babylonish Captivity," published in 1520, and the book created a great sensation. Copies were in England early in 1521, and in April King Henry himself had read it.

It was one of the ambitions of the English king to win a reputation for scholarship, as well as for splendour and power, and no sooner had he read the work of the German reformer than he determined himself to compose an answer. He must have set to work immediately with a debatable amount of assistance from Fisher, More, and the theologians whom he loved to join in their discussions. For Leo X. was informed that the book was to be dedicated to him, and pressed to acknowledge the compliment by conferring the title of *Fidei Defensor* on the royal author. Long before this De Gigli, Bishop of Worcester, the English agent, had been asking for a title which might be a set off to those of most Christian and Catholic borne by European monarchs. Difficulties were made at Rome, but in due time the book was presented, and Clerk, the new agent, was importunate for the reward. At last, some weeks before his death, Leo X. issued the bull

Assertio Septem Sacramentorum (1521).

DEFENDER OF THE FAITH

conferring the title *Fidei Defensor*. Numerous editions appeared, the work being translated from Latin into English and German. Of course, Luther rejoined, ascribing the book to Edward Lee, but, nevertheless, attacking the king in terms which made up in picturesque vituperation for any lack of solid argument. The irony of the position was that Henry defended expressly several of those points of Catholic Faith and practice which he was afterwards so shamefully to fling away, thus inviting us in Dryden's words to "confront but Henry's words with Henry's deeds." He made himself not only the champion of the Papal Supremacy and of the monastic life, but also of the sanctity of the marriage bond as against divorce and incontinency. It only needed the lapse of a few years for him to decree as far as in him lay the abolition of all Papal Supremacy in England, and likewise to violate repeatedly those marriage laws which he had defended. But the title which he had won he kept, and when another Pope withdrew it, it was confirmed to the monarch by Parliament, and has ever since been one of the stateliest appellations of Henry's successors.

The six years from 1521 to 1527 produced very little change in the outward aspect of things in England. Wolsey was ruling the country with considerable statesmanship, and Henry was leading a life of unrestrained pleasure under the veil of unwonted regal magnificence. **Wolsey the statesman.** Still other preferments were conferred upon the now all-powerful minister. The Abbey of St Albans was granted to him to hold *in commendam*, as it was called, and when Bath was taken from Castelli for his complicity in the Petrucci plot, it was given to Wolsey. However, he soon exchanged Bath for Durham, as soon as the latter see fell vacant, and six years later gave up Durham for Winchester. This latter move gave occasion to the translation of Tunstall from London to Durham. Cuthbert Tunstall was the only new bishop consecrated for England during these years, except that Clerk, the king's agent, was consecrated in Rome for Bath and Wells. It would be beside the aim of this book to follow the diplomacy of Wolsey in detail during this period; in the main he favoured an alliance with France, and was opposed to the claims of the empire. Twice he was put forward as a candidate for the papacy, but apparently outwitted by the imperial party. It is, however, but fair to say that his solemn protest that he himself did not covet the supreme dignity is believed by many leading historians. Neither is it fair to pass over Wolsey's lofty designs for the promotion of learning and education. He founded a college at Ipswich, his native town, and another still more important one at Oxford, which was then called Cardinal College, and is now known as Christ Church. In order to procure funds for these foundations he obtained a bull from Clement VII. in 1524, suppressing twenty-nine of the smaller monasteries in England, the best known of which was the Austin Priory of St Frideswide at Oxford. It may be allowed that the existence of some of these minor houses was hardly necessary, but a precedent was, in some sort, set for what afterwards became wholesale destruction.

Meanwhile, Henry was proceeding on a downward grade as far as morality was concerned. Whether he was a faithful husband in the first years of his married life is impossible to determine, but ten years after his marriage he had an illegitimate son by Elizabeth Blount, whom at the age of six (1525) he created Duke of Richmond. He had also entered into criminal relations with Mary Boleyn, daughter of Sir Thomas Boleyn; Viscount Rochford, when he transferred his passion to her sister Anne, who was one of the maids of honour in the suite of Queen Catherine. Had Anne been content to become his mistress the king would have been content; not from virtue, but more probably from ambition, she held out against his advances, requiring pledges as to her future position as queen, which he could not give. However, Henry was not to be baulked of the gratification of his passion, and began to cast about for the means of success. He thought of bigamy, and he thought of divorce, while the fact that a papal dispensation had been obtained for his marriage with Catherine, who had been previously espoused to his brother, Arthur, pointed out the expedient of throwing doubt on the validity of this dispensation. He opened his mind, at least ostensibly, to Wolsey on the subject, and prompted him to hold, in conjunction with Archbishop Warham, a private inquiry on the subject of the validity of his marriage. Though the inquiry led

Divorce proceedings.

to nothing final, Henry took advantage of it to inform Catherine that he had been advised by learned men that he had been married to her invalidly on account of the affinity due to her being his brother's widow. This drew from the queen the solemn declaration, amid a storm of tears, that the marriage with Prince Arthur had never been consummated. Henry now fell back on the impediment of "public honesty" due to the espousals with Arthur, which was not expressly mentioned in the dispensing bull. And Wolsey was despatched to France to collect theological opinions in favour of the divorce. But though he travelled in state as the acknowledged envoy of the king, Wolsey soon had evidence that Henry had other and more confidential agents. William Knight, the royal secretary, was sent straight to Clement VII., who had fled from Rome to Orvieto after the sack of Rome, to ask for a dispensation to be granted, together with a commission to Wolsey empowering him to try the case. Knight only succeeded in obtaining a conditional dispensation, to take effect if the commission proved the invalidity of his present marriage. But this was, of course, insufficient, and Henry now had recourse to Wolsey. Probably the divorce was against Wolsey's better judgment, but in the spirit of a courtier he used his utmost endeavour to secure what the king demanded. Stephen Gardiner and Edward Fox were therefore sent to Orvieto to ask for a *decretal commission*. After scenes of importunate insolence towards the Pope on the part of Gardiner and his companion, Clement at last yielded so far as to concede a secret commission in the form of a decretorial letter to Cardinal Wolsey and to Cardinal Campeggio, the legate, to try the case. Deciding the points of law in advance, it only left the question of fact to be judged. 'As the commission has never been found its exact wording is not known, but from drafts and other accounts preserved, it may be supposed that it pronounced the dispensation granted by Julius invalid, if the commissioners found that the motives alleged were contrary to the facts.' At any rate it satisfied the English envoys, and was entrusted to Campeggio with instructions to read it to the king, but not under any circumstances to part with it. To grant it under such pressure was no doubt an act of weakness on the part of Clement, but, if Campeggio kept to its instructions, it was altogether illusory.

Campeggio travelled to England in September, 1528, and arriving in October, produced before Henry his regular commission, and also the secret decretorial one which he read to the king, but when Henry asked for it, he protested that he could not part with it, and probably burnt it, as it has never been discovered. He then had private conferences both with Henry, whom the Pope had directed him to try and dissuade from the divorce, and also with Catherine, whom he was told to sound as to a voluntary retirement into a convent. But neither of these efforts led to any results, and before long Catherine produced a second dispensation in the form of a brief from Julius II., declaring that the previous dispensation for the marriage between Catherine and Henry was confirmed even in the case that the marriage with Prince Arthur had been consummated. This introduced a new element into the case, putting it outside the limits of the commission, and though the legates opened their court at Blackfriars on the 31st of May, 1529, and pleadings were taken up to the 23rd of June, Bishop Fisher and Standish, with Dr Ligham, supporting the queen's case, very little progress was made. Catherine made a formal appeal against the jurisdiction of the court, but this was overruled. Meantime, it was clear that Campeggio was protracting the proceedings as far as he could. At the end of June he adjourned the sittings over the usual Roman vacation. Finally, under pressure from the emperor, the cause was revoked to Rome; Campeggio declared that his commission was at an end, and then prepared to leave the country. On his journey his luggage was audaciously searched at Dover, but nothing was found that could help the king.

As soon as Henry realised how all these negotiations had collapsed, the full weight of his indignation fell on Wolsey. He had failed to effect the king's purpose for him, and it could be felt that the plan did not commend itself to his judgment. It is clear also that Anne Boleyn used her great influence to fan the flame of anger against the chancellor in Henry's breast. In October he was indicted for infringing the Statute of *Premunire*, and the penalties began to be inflicted. The office of chancellor was taken from him, and put into the all-unwilling hands of Sir Thomas More.

Fall of Wolsey (1530).

Wolsey was directed to repair to his diocese of York, and seeing that his career at court was ended, he had no choice but to obey. Meanwhile, he was stripped of his vast possessions, which one after the other were seized in the king's name. Henry had already appropriated the elegant Gothic pile he had built at Hampton Court, then came the demand for the surrender of York Place, Whitehall, and a few months later he resigned the diocese of Winchester and the Abbey of St Albans for a certain pecuniary compensation. On his way north he delayed for some time at Southwell Palace, a manor of his see, being evidently in failing health. Here came the news that Henry had resolved on the suppression of his colleges at Oxford and Ipswich. He was proceeding further north when he was arrested on the charge of high treason by the Earl of Northumberland. Well hated as he was by good and bad alike at court, in his diocese he gained general popularity and love, and seemed anxious at the eleventh hour to do all the good he could, and perform every act of kindness in his power. At Sheffield he was met by the Constable of the Tower, whose coming brought visions of the scaffold and the traitor's death. But by this time he was so ill that he could scarcely travel. Still, in a few days he managed to reach Leicester Abbey, to the community of which he had been affiliated some time before. "Father Abbot," he said, "I come to leave my bones among you." Kingston, the Constable of the Tower, was still near him, telling him that things were not so bad with him as he imagined. "Master Kingston," he replied, "if I had served my God as faithfully as I have done the king, He would not have given me over in my grey hairs." He lingered in life for nearly three days, but on the 29th of November passed away, and was buried in the abbey.

Even before the final crash of Wolsey's fortune came, there was at hand an ambitious and able politician, who at once stepped into his shoes, and became Henry's chief minister, and his tool in the career of lawlessness to which he was now committed. This was Thomas Cromwell. His career up to this point had not been a very lofty one, and certainly not an honourable one either. In his youth he had fled from England to Italy in

Thomas Cromwell (1485-1540).

disgrace, and there, probably at Florence, had become imbued with the unscrupulous political philosophy of Machiavelli. And when he came back to England his occupations were money-lending, legal practice, and the trade of dressing cloth. However, he soon found employment in the service of Wolsey as collector of the revenues of the see of York. In time he found his way into Parliament, and being named by Wolsey as one of the commission of inquiry into the state of the lesser monasteries, bore himself harshly, and acted arbitrarily in that office. Wolsey placed in his hands all the financial side of his beloved foundations at Oxford and Ipswich, and Cromwell found the money required. It is perhaps to his credit that when Wolsey was assailed in the House of Commons in 1529, Cromwell successfully defended his patron, but final success in this was beyond his power, and when Wolsey fell he was already deep in the king's counsels. In fact he is thought to have been the first to suggest the royal supremacy over the Church as the means which would secure the divorce he was bent on, as well as his absolute power as monarch. In 1531 he became a Privy Councillor. Then he was given charge of the crown jewels. In 1533 he became Chancellor of the Exchequer, and in the following year king's secretary. In fact, from this time until his disgrace and execution in 1540, he was in the forefront of all the royal proceedings, inspiring some of them, and the subservient instrument of the king's will in all matters entrusted to his charge.

The death of Archbishop Warham in 1532, at the age of more than eighty, opened the way to another of the king's servants. Warham had resigned the chancellorship long before in Wolsey's favour, and had abstained as far as he could from taking any part in the divorce proceedings. He had written to the Pope, advising him, if possible, to annul the marriage of Queen Catherine, and had been suggested by Henry as a suitable judge for the trial. This, however, he succeeded in avoiding, and just before his death made a solemn protest in Parliament against all the legislation of the last three years against the papal authority. But, now that the cautious and scholarly old prelate was dead, the king must have an archbishop who would actively promote his divorce, and he found one in Thomas

Cranmer. His record had been as discreditable a one as that of the lay minister, Thomas Cromwell, albeit that his sins were those of a timid man, not of a bold one. While at the University of Cambridge he had forfeited his fellowship by a secret marriage. His wife had died a
year or two later, and Cranmer was able to resume his university career as Professor of Scripture. On the Continent he nevertheless became acquainted with the German reformers, and falling in love with the niece of Osiander, married her in spite of the canonical impediment caused by his previous reception of orders. When Warham died, he was English ambassador at the imperial court, but Henry had not forgotten his previously expressed opinions on the divorce, and determined that he should fill the Primate's chair. Protests were made, but in vain, for Cranmer was summoned to England, and a successor appointed to him as ambassador. His marriage with the German lady had put him at a great disadvantage with regard to the primacy, but he came, and then was duly presented to Clement VII. for confirmation. The Pope made no difficulty about this. He had seen Cranmer as a subordinate member of the mission sent to him at Orvieto, and he contrasted the mild-mannered Cranmer with the rude and blustering Gardiner and Fox. But he little knew the future. Cranmer was consecrated by John Longland, Bishop of Lincoln, in St Stephen's Chapel at Westminster on the 30th of March, 1533, and Henry had an archbishop according to his mind.

Thomas Cranmer (1485-1556).

But he could not wait for this to bring his matrimonial case to a head. Pope Clement had once more written to Henry, admonishing him to put away Anne Boleyn and take back Queen Catherine under pain of excommunication, but the king was too far gone on the downward path to pay any attention to this. On the contrary, on or about the 25th of January, 1533, he was privately married to Anne by Dr George Brown, later on Archbishop of Dublin, or, as likely, by Rowland Lee, who was afterwards, probably in reward for his services, made Bishop of Chester. Anne was already with child, and it was in this way that Henry redeemed the promises he had made her. For the time the fact of the marriage was studiously concealed, but in March the king had the question of his divorce brought before Convocation. Such was the pressure of the king's insistence that Bishop Fisher was the only member of the Upper House to offer any serious resistance. He thus became henceforward the king's chief enemy. In the Lower House, too, the royal will worked its way, while the House of Commons, after some ineffectual protests against the abolition of papal appeals, passed the bill which abolished them. Cranmer, a few days after his consecration, asked permission to set up a court to try the divorce case anew, and received a royal commission to do so. This court met at Dunstable in May, and Queen Catherine was cited to appear before it. This she of course refused to do, whereupon the Archbishop pronounced her contumacious. On the 23rd of the month Cranmer proclaimed his decision that the king's marriage was invalid. He followed this up with a secret inquiry, held at Lambeth, as to the marriage between Henry and Anne Boleyn. The declaration he made as a result of this that it was a true and lawful marriage was a foregone conclusion.

Four days later Anne Boleyn was crowned with much gorgeous ceremonial, but at the same time amid the scarcely veiled vituperation of the populace as she passed along her way to Westminster Abbey. This took place on the 1st of June, 1533, and may be said to have precipitated the final breach with Rome. Only about six weeks were allowed to elapse before the Pope issued a bull, excommunicating Henry and pronouncing the divorce from Catherine and the marriage with Anne both null and void. However, by the terms of this document the king was given until the end of September to put away Anne and to restore Catherine to her rights. At the expiration of the interval the sentence was to take effect. Bishop Bonner managed to notify to the Pope, who was then at Marseilles on a visit to the French monarch, that his sovereign appealed from the Pope to the future General Council, but this was really only empty rhetoric. Yet the triumph of Anne Boleyn was but of short duration. Her daughter, the Princess Elizabeth, was born on the 7th of September, but already she had reason to be jealous of the king's gallantries with others. When she protested, she was

Triumph of Anne Boleyn.

rudely told to shut her eyes and bear it as her betters had done, and with this she had to be content. Only a few years were to pass before she was to expiate on the scaffold, her share in the great crime of the divorce.

Henry was greatly disappointed that the child Anne had borne him was a daughter, and not a son. He never really recovered from the shock this gave to his cherished hopes, and when, more than two years later, Anne was delivered of a still-born son, this feeling of his was only intensified. Moreover, there was a rival already far advanced in the king's good graces. This was Jane Seymour, daughter of Sir John Seymour of Wolfhall in Wiltshire. Egged on by her own family as well as by the numerous enemies of Anne Boleyn, this lady wormed herself into Henry's favour with such effect that all his efforts became bent upon getting rid of Anne, and marrying her. When a plan which the imperial envoy, Chapuys, and Thomas Cromwell, the royal secretary, had laid to bring the king back to union with the Pope and recognition of the rights of Princess Mary failed, Cromwell seems to have urged Henry to dispose of Anne by executing her for adultery. He seems to have thought that the expedient of a second divorce was, **Fate of Anne Boleyn.** taken by itself, too insecure and contradictory. Henry listened to the charges of adultery with four persons brought against Anne, and in consequence she, as well as these four, was arrested and committed to the Tower. The chancellor, Audley, presided at the trial of the four commoners, and they were all pronounced guilty and executed as traitors. Anne was tried by a court of peers, presided over by the Duke of Norfolk. Her brother, Lord Rochford, was also tried by the same tribunal. It was a notoriously hostile court, and both were found guilty of high treason. Lord Rochford and the other four were all beheaded on the day after the verdict against Anne, but in her case there was delay, as Henry wished to have Elizabeth declared illegitimate in order that she might not stand in the way of the heir he was hoping for. Cranmer presided over a court to try Anne's marriage once more. It must have been an unwelcome task, but he dared not refuse. The inquiry was held with closed doors, that the evidence might not become public. What was deposed has never been brought to light. Some hold that a pre-contract of marriage with the Earl of Northumberland was proved, but others hold that the " diriment impediment of affinity " on account of the relations of Henry with Anne's sister, Mary, was shown to exist. In any case, on the secret evidence, Cranmer pronounced the marriage invalid, and Elizabeth was thus illegitimate. After this there was no reason for putting off the execution. Two days later Anne Boleyn was beheaded at the Tower. She had been to confession, received Communion, and asked to have the Blessed Sacrament exposed in her cell, all according to the Catholic rite. Cranmer must have been the confessor, but no other was provided for the martyr Bishop John Fisher. She protested her innocence of the crimes against the king with which she was charged, and spent much of the time before her execution in prayer. At her own request she was beheaded with a sword and not with an axe. Kingston, Constable of the Tower, Audley, the chancellor, Thomas Cromwell, the Lord Mayor, and a considerable gathering were present at her death. Her remains were deposited in the Tower Chapel; but few showed any grief at her fate. King Henry married Lady Jane Seymour only eleven days later. Even her own daughter, Queen Elizabeth, never seems to have shown the least sign of affection for her mother's memory. But the Catholic poet, Aubrey de Vere, apostrophises her in words of pity and restraint:

" Death sentenced queen! was this the girl that prayed
Before Our Lady's shrine unmoved for hours?
I judge her not. The night before her death
She prayed her childhood's prayers—with tranquil breath."

XXVI.

THE ROYAL SUPREMACY.

(A) HENRY VIII. (1534-1547).

KING HENRY had been cut off from the communion of the Universal Church by the papal sentence pronounced on the 11th of July, 1533, but it was the legislation of the Parliament which met in January, 1534, which gave full form and effect to the new order of things in England. The most important of the acts passed by this assembly was the Act of Royal Supremacy, but though the whole legislation was directed towards securing this, the Act itself was not passed until November. A commencement was made by three Acts abolishing annates, or the payments of a year's value of a benefice made to Rome by the new incumbent, abolishing Peter's Pence and similar offerings, and abrogating appeals to Rome respectively. Then the Heresy Acts of Henry IV. which empowered bishops to summon those charged with heresy before them were repealed. Then came the Act of Succession, which entailed the succession to the crown on the king's children by Anne Boleyn. After this there was a long prorogation until the 3rd of November. It was at this latter date that quite a short Act declared the king to be the "supreme head under God of the Church of England," and made this one of the royal titles for all future time. It was followed by an Act of Treasons, making it treason to impugn the legality of the royal marriage with Anne Boleyn, who was then still in favour, and this by another which transferred to the crown the tithes and firstfruits which had been taken from the Holy See. Finally, Acts of Attainder were passed against those who refused to swear to the royal succession as settled by Parliament. With this, the work which had been imposed upon a subservient legislature with regard to the change of religion was fairly complete, but in the course of the year, while these things were doing in Parliament, many events of vital importance had taken place in the country at large, which we must now turn to relate.

On the 23rd of March, 1534, after many delays, judgment was pronounced at Rome by the Pope, declaring the marriage between Henry and Catherine to be valid, but it had the effect of making the king more desperate and headstrong in the course he had entered upon. The Act of Succession had exacted an oath to the succession from all of lawful age to whom it might be tendered, and the members of both Houses took it before the prorogation at the end of March. Outside of Parliament it began to be tendered to persons of note, some of whom took it without restriction, while others, like Margaret Roper, Sir Thomas More's daughter, took it " as far as it would stand with the law of God." More himself was the first to refuse, alleging that the words of the preamble, which denied the papal dispensing power in impediments to marriage, made it impossible. John Fisher, Bishop of Rochester, also refused. But after a few days both More and Fisher were arrested, and lodged in the Tower of London. Cranmer, meanwhile, made a visitation of the province of Canterbury, and presented to the clergy generally for signature declarations against the jurisdiction of the Holy See and in favour of the Royal Supremacy. The Archbishop of York acted in similar fashion in the Northern province. At the same time royal commissioners visited the universities and the religious houses to obtain the like declarations on oath from these establishments. George Browne, an Augustinian prior, and Hilsey, Provincial of the Dominicans, accepted the office of royal commissioners for the monasteries, and the process of visitation was not completed before the end of the year 1534.

Enforcement of the Oath of Succession (1534).

There were three stages, as Father Bridgett remarks, in the fall of the English clergy, the first was subserviency, the second schism, and the third heresy. And though as yet the second and third stages were not reached, a considerable distance had been travelled along the first stage, and the submission to the demands of the commissioners was very general. Two outstand-

THE ROYAL SUPREMACY 365

ing examples of noble exception to this were furnished by the Franciscan Observants and by the Carthusians. In the former case the demands of the visitors were firmly refused, whereupon the Observant friars were incarcerated in houses belonging to conventual friars of their own order, and the whole province of Observants was suppressed. In the case of the Carthusians, when John Houghton, the prior, was summoned, he declared that he could not take the oath, and was promptly sent to the Tower, together with the procurator of the house, Humphrey Middlemore. After a month, Stokesley, Bishop of London, and Archbishop Lee advised them that they might safely take the oath with the restriction "as far as was lawful." This they did, and being liberated from prison, went back to their monastery and persuaded the brethren to do likewise. Their arguments were reinforced by the arrival of Bishop Rowland Lee and a body of armed men. After this they enjoyed an interval of tranquillity, but were persuaded that this would not last, but that heavier trials were to come.

And so indeed it proved. As soon as the style of supreme head had been incorporated in the royal title in January, 1535, various measures were taken to enforce the compliance of those who had shown their hostility to the new Acts of Succession and Supremacy. A commission was issued in the same month for a general visitation of churches, clergy, and monasteries, and a reign of terror began which caused something like a panic in the general body of churchmen, and wide discontent in the ranks of the people at large. In April orders were sent out to arrest all those who continued to uphold the papal jurisdiction, and it was on the Carthusians and a few of their immediate friends that the storm first fell. John Houghton, the prior, was seized and put into the Tower on the charge of treason, and with him were also incarcerated Augustine Webster, Prior of the Charterhouse at Axholme, and Robert Lawrence, Prior of the House at Beauvale, who had both come to London to confer with the fathers in the capital. Richard Reynolds, a Brigittine monk of Sion House, and John Hale, Vicar of Isleworth, were also apprehended on the same charges. After fruitless efforts had been made to gain their submission, they were formally

The London Charterhouses.

tried for treason on the 28th of April, and the verdict of guilty having been obtained by the most barefaced intimidation of the jury, on the 4th of May all five were executed at Tyburn in the barbarous manner then prescribed for the crime of treason. Circumstances of brutality even beyond the letter of the law were in this case added to the sentence, and a vast gathering of lords and courtiers were present at the execution. It was hoped that the fate of the priors would frighten the rest of the Carthusians into compliance. It was not to be so, however, and on the 25th of May the procurator, F. Middlemore, Sebastian Newdigate, and William Exmew were arraigned. They followed their quondam superiors along the same bloody path of martyrdom on the 19th following. The remainder of the community were put under watch and ward, at first in their own monastery, and then in the Tower and Newgate, and as time went on the sufferings of their hard imprisonment increased. Chained in a filthy dungeon, they were left to die one by one as their tortures and lack of food overcame them. It was a long story, and was brightened by the heroism of Margaret Clement, afterwards head of the Convent of the Augustinian Nuns at Louvain, who bribed the jailers to allow her to visit his captives, and do what she could to relieve their pains. But in a short time they died in their prison, smothered with the stink and exhausted by want of food, with the exception of Brother William Horne, who lingered until the 4th of August, 1540, when he was hanged at Tyburn. Thus, although only a minority ever came to the scaffold, the whole community may be considered as the standard-bearers of the numerous and noble army of martyrs who died in the reign of Henry VIII. for conscience' sake and in witness for the authority of the See of Rome.

But long before the Carthusian company in London was thus gloriously extinguished in blood, the royal tyrant had already marked down still more illustrious victims. On the 11th of June, 1535, Bishop Fisher of Rochester was indicted for having said that the king was not the supreme head on earth of the Church of England, having been already attainted by Act of Parliament at the beginning of the year, and shut up in the Tower of London, as was also Sir Thomas

Blessed John Fisher and Blessed Thomas More.

More. He was tried before a jury on the 17th of June on the same charge. It should be noted that the Act of Supremacy did not require an oath, but the Act of Succession did, and the acceptance of the supremacy was indirectly included as being in the preamble to the Oath of Succession. Of course there was no attempt at a real inquiry as to the guilt or innocence of the bishop of the charge of treason. The jury were brow-beaten by the solicitor-general, Sir R. Rich, and given to understand that they were expected to bring in a verdict of guilty. This they did, and Bishop John Fisher was sentenced to death. Pope Paul III. had held a consistory, in which he had named Fisher cardinal, together with nine other notable churchmen. But Henry had sworn that if the Pope sent him the cardinal's hat he would take care that he had not a head to wear it on. The completion of this judicial murder was on the 22nd of June, when the illustrious cardinal was led out to execution. He was decapitated on Tower Hill in the presence of a numerous crowd of spectators. His body was interred in the church of All Hallow's, Barking, but was afterwards removed to that of St Peter ad Vincula within the precincts of the Tower. His head was set upon a pole and exposed on the gatehouse of London Bridge, but afterwards thrown into the river to put a stop to the crowds which were always to be found gathered to look with veneration upon this relic of the blessed martyr. The death of the Bishop of Rochester, who was known throughout Christendom as the most learned and ascetic of the English bishops, awakened a thrill of horror all over the Continent when it became known.

The noble chancellor had not long to wait before he had to tread the same path as his fellow-prisoner in the Tower. No doubt it was hoped that the news of Fisher's fate and that of the Carthusian fathers would have the effect of making him more submissive to the royal requirements. But this was very far from being the case. He had spent his time in prison in composing his "*Dialogue of Comfort against Tribulation*," and in cheery converse with those of his family who were allowed to visit him. Moreover, he had to stand repeated interrogations from the king's agents, undertaken with the object of making him waver in his opposition, but it was all in vain. At length, on the 1st of July, he was brought to trial. He defended himself with all a skilled lawyer's caution and ability, but without compromising the great principles for which he was prepared to die. The main questions put to him turned, as in Fisher's case, on the king's supremacy, and on the succession to the crown. The result of the trial was, of course, a foregone conclusion. The saying of Macaulay about the State trials of the time that they were " murder preceded by mummery " applies *par excellence* to the case of More, and the sentence was that he should die a traitor's death at Tyburn. However, shame caused the king to commute the sentence into that of beheading on Tower Hill. Here it was carried out on the 6th of July. Having prepared himself with an elaboration of meditative prayers and of long familiarity with the thought of death during his year of imprisonment, and having also, as is probable, been to confession, he walked to the scaffold with joy and with merry jests upon his lips. He protested that he died for the Catholic Faith, a true servant of the king, but above all a servant of God. When beheaded, his body was first laid in the Chapel of St Peter ad Vincula, and afterwards buried either beneath the belfry of that building or in Chelsea Church. The head was exposed on London Bridge, but its subsequent fate is unknown.

King Henry now launched forth into persecution of a far more general character than was implied either in the brutal massacre of the Carthusians or in the legal murder of his two chief opponents, Fisher and More. Thomas Cromwell had received a commission on the 21st of January, 1535, for a general visitation of all the churches and monasteries of England. Cromwell was already Secretary and Master of the Rolls, but to strengthen his hand still more he was appointed King's Vicar-General or Vicegerent in spiritual things, thus as a layman holding a position something akin to that of the Procurator of the Holy Synod under the Russian autocracy. But no steps were taken to carry out the work until the summer was far advanced. A beginning was then made with the Southern monasteries by Richard Layton, a clerk of the council, and Dr Thomas Leigh, both acting under Cromwell's orders. Moreover, in some cases Cromwell conducted the visitation in person. Having thus divided the work in the South between them,

Visitation of the Monasteries.

as soon as it was accomplished the commissioners met at Lichfield, and then proceeded to visit the Northern houses. They professed to embody the results of their investigations in a series of reports which are known as the " Comperta," and certain wholesale charges of laxity and even of gross immorality against the inhabitants of the monasteries and convents, suggesting at the same time that things were much worse in the smaller houses than in the greater ones. But these reports were really an unreliable special plea composed by the king's agents for a definite purpose, and are admitted even by Protestant historians to be full of gross exaggerations. The calumnious and prejudiced character of these " Comperta " has been established once for all by Cardinal Gasquet in his *Henry VIII. and the English Monasteries*." Not very long after the course of events showed the motive of the visitation and of the reports which were elaborated as a result of it.

The labours of Layton and Leigh came to an end early in 1536. A new Parliament, which quickly followed the one then dissolved, had already commenced its first session. As a chief legislative measure a bill was introduced to suppress all the lesser monasteries, that is to say, all those whose annual revenues had been found to amount to less than two hundred pounds a year. The " Comperta " were laid before the Houses of Parliament, and heavy pressure and threats were employed by the king's agents to force the bill through the legislature. These were successful, and in the course of the year 1536 no fewer than two hundred and fifteen religious houses of men and one hundred and three of women were forcibly suppressed by the Act of Parliament, which soon obtained the royal assent when it had passed both Houses. After completing other legislative business the Houses proceeded, before separating, to constitute what was called the Court of Augmentations, a board to receive and account to the king for all the wealth which came from the rents, tithes, and other revenues of the monasteries, as well as from the sales of their goods whether movable or immovable. The elaborate constitution of this court seems to indicate that Henry was already preparing for still more extensive confiscation than the goods of the lesser monasteries

Suppression of the smaller monasteries.

2A

involved. Yet, even this was considerable enough, if we compare it with the general scale of wealth in England at the time. It is a remarkable fact that no sooner had the king got the grant of these religious houses than he proceeded to refound a certain number of them with a new charter. It is true that they were also eventually suppressed, but in this way more than fifty gained a respite. Thus, though the total number affected was not far short of four hundred, the number actually at the time may be taken to be approximately what is stated above. The annual value of the lands which thus fell into the king's hands has been estimated at about thirty thousand pounds, and the number of monks dispossessed at about two thousand, while, if we allow for dependants and others, we shall find that probably some ten thousand persons were more or less cast adrift. The Superior was the only one in each case who could apply for a pension to the Court of Augmentations, and though some effort may have been made to provide situations for those who returned to the world, the distress was deep and wide-spread. The work was in a fair way of being finished by Michaelmas, 1536.

There were cases in which a violent but ineffectual resistance was made to the expulsion, but before long the general discontent led to armed rebellion on quite a large scale. The first rising was in Lincolnshire, where no fewer than thirty-seven of these suppressed houses were situated. This outbreak began at Louth, and soon spread over the whole country. The insurgents demanded the restoration of the monasteries, and the dismissal of civil counsellors and heretical bishops. The Lincolnshire rising was soon followed by the still more formidable rebellion in Yorkshire known as the *Pilgrimage of Grace*. This broke out in October, 1536, under the leadership of one, Robert Aske. It was essentially a religious movement, and those who took part in it were animated not by revolutionary instincts, but by the desire to retain what was dearer to them than life. York was easily taken by the insurgents, while Lee, the Archbishop, fled to Pomfret, which held out for some time, but was then in its turn taken, and the pilgrim host still grew. The Duke of Norfolk was sent by Henry to collect what help he could and attack the rebels, but when he reached

Pilgrimage of Grace

THE ROYAL SUPREMACY

Doncaster he found their numbers so formidable that he thought it best to parley with them. He offered a pardon in the king's name if they would disband, while deputies could go and present their demands to the king. Sir Ralph Ellerker and Robert Bowes were despatched to the royal presence, and after a delay of some two months returned to the North, bearing an answer from Henry which was deliberately ambiguous and suited to gain time. Two meetings were then held to consider the king's reply, one of the clergy and commons at Pomfret, and another of the nobles at Doncaster. The chief things which were complained of by the leaders of the rising were the Act of Royal Supremacy and the Dissolution of the Monasteries. The Duke of Norfolk felt himself obliged again to temporise: he promised in the king's name a free Parliament and the support of all those who belonged to the suppressed religious houses. With these promises most of the insurgents were satisfied, and they began to disperse. However, when it became apparent that the promises made by Norfolk were not to be kept, disturbances broke out afresh, and attempts were made to seize Hull, Scarborough, and Carlisle. When these failed the spirit of the rising began to be broken, and while wholesale surrenders to the royal mercy took place, bloody executions visited the king's vengeance on the leaders and on a vast number of others as well. It was by martial law that seventy-four rebels were hanged in one place; it was by forced convictions that sentence of death was pronounced and carried out against Aske, the chief leader, against Lord Darcy and Hussey, against Sir Thomas Percy, against the Abbots of Whalley, Sawley, Jervaulx, Fountains, and Woburn. It was only by terror and the unscrupulous rain of blood that quiet was at last restored (1537).

It is possible that at first the king and his ministers had intended to be content with the surrender of the smaller monasteries, leaving the larger ones to submit at the royal pleasure, but they were on a slippery path, and it was not long before the suppression of the larger religious houses was commenced. Pretexts were soon found in one way or in another. The regulations made by the royal visitors made life in these houses harder and harder. It was to the interest of the visitors to find or

Suppression of the greater Monasteries (1538-1540).

exaggerate abuses, and it was to the interest of the king's purse to believe what was reported. The final stage in the destruction of the religious life in England was reached by the suppression of the large monasteries, but before that was reached, several very important stages had been reached which led up to the consummation of the ruin. One of these was the Fall of the Friars, brought about in the year 1538. Their houses, which were very numerous, amounting to over two hundred, were for the most part small, but for one cause or another they had not been included in the bill for the suppression of the smaller religious houses, and at the beginning of 1538 were still intact. The friars were popular, while on the other hand their general poverty made them a less tempting spoil to the plunderer: no doubt both these facts delayed their fate. But they had ample ground for dreading the worst, and in expectation of this it is probable that they took advantage of their wide relations with foreign provinces of their own order to escape from the kingdom in considerable numbers. Another rising in the Eastern counties was made the pretext, and gradually one after another the friaries were surrendered into the king's hands, the communities dispersing. In some cases Bills of Attainder were drawn up against the priors and other heads of houses, in other cases unproved charges were made the excuse for seizing the property and getting rid of the friars. Small pensions were promised to the ejected religious: the movable property was appropriated to the royal treasury, while the sites and buildings were sold. The pensions were only granted to quite a few, and though the valuables were not great, the crown gained greater profit by the sale of the buildings and lands. By the end of 1538 the mendicant orders were fairly ruined.

Another step in the same process was taken by the suppression, or surrender of the nunneries, or religious houses of women, which are considered to have numbered about one hundred and forty. Even the calumnious reports of the royal commissioners have comparatively little to say against the character of the pious inhabitants, and of course as they could not be accused of political crimes they could not very well be proceeded against by way of attainder. Yet their fate was sealed. About a hundred

The convents of nuns.

THE ROYAL SUPREMACY

were suppressed under the authority of the Act of Parliament of 1536, and the rest were surrendered between 1537 and 1540.

There remained some one hundred and fifty-eight so-called greater monasteries, and these between the years 1537 and 1540 gradually fell into the king's hands. Twelve were suppressed by attainder after the Northern Rising, but the rest were gradually surrendered under the pressure of royal visitations and of the intimidation which the king's officers used. The same thing applies to the establishments, nearly fifty in number, which belonged to the Knights of St John. The last house surrendered, in 1540, was Waltham Abbey in Essex.

But before this was all accomplished much innocent blood had been shed at the king's behest, both from among the clergy and the laity. It is only possible in a short account such as this to mention some of the more celebrated of these martyrs for Catholic Faith and Papal Supremacy. And while the noblest and most courageous were carried off to execution, the most celebrated shrines in England were despoiled and wrecked. It was so with Our Lady of Walsingham; it was so with St Anne's Baths at Buxton. It was so again with the costly shrine of St Thomas at Canterbury, with that of St Edmund at Bury, and with the treasury of precious objects of devotion at Glastonbury, and in fact wherever they could be found.

Meanwhile the king soon got to know that his course of action had led him into difficulties which might even prove dangerous to his throne. He had used the German Protestants against the Pope, but he had no mind that their opinions should prevail in England. Moreover, the friendly terms on which the Emperor and the King of France now were, through the papal mediation, made him fear they might unite against him on behalf of the Holy See. He determined therefore to enforce a strict conformity with the chief points of Catholic doctrines, and even entertained the idea of coming to terms with Rome. It was with this in view that the celebrated Act of Six Articles was passed through the Parliament which met in 1539. Denial of transubstantiation was made to involve the penalties of heresy, while teaching against Communion under one kind, private Masses, auricular confession,

The Six Articles.

celibacy of the clergy, or the breach of a religious vow, was made a felony punishable by death. Commissions were sent into the various counties to enforce the provisions of the act. It was in this period that people could be seen sentenced to be burnt as heretics, while others were being hanged for denial of the Royal Supremacy. Both Catholics and Protestants suffered; but the scourge fell more heavily on the former. The Protestants for the most part were frightened, and kept quiet as to their beliefs.

By this time the suppression of the monasteries had proceeded so far that only a few of the greater ones remained. An Act of Attainder was passed against the Abbots of Glastonbury, Reading, and Colchester, who had so far refused to surrender their houses. Abbot Richard Whiting was hanged, drawn, and quartered on the Tor Hill at Glastonbury on the 15th of November, with two monks of his community. Hugh Farringdon suffered at Reading with two other priests on the very same day. Thomas Beche, Abbot of Colchester, suffered on the 1st of December. These examples were meant to accelerate the progress of the surrender. In 1539 or 1540, Westminster Abbey was given up, and the last to give up was Waltham, which was handed over on the 23rd of March, 1540. All the above are enrolled in the ranks of the English Martyrs, as well as Blessed Adrian Fortescue, Knight of St John, who suffered on Tower Hill about the same time.

The Three Benedictine Abbots (1539).

In England Henry was now unresisted, but he had an influential opponent who was out of his reach. This was Reginald Pole, his cousin, the son of Margaret Plantagenet, Countess of Salisbury. He had spent his youth on the Continent of Europe, and had early risen in the service of the Holy See, until after the execution of Bishop John Fisher he had been made cardinal, and had filled more than one important legation for the Pope. He had strenuously opposed the divorce, in spite of Henry's efforts to win him over. Moreover, he had written an exceedingly able treatise in Latin, "*De Unitate Ecclesiæ,*" attacking the tyranny and schism of the king in the strongest language. This book he had himself sent to Henry. Irritated beyond measure, the monarch had tried both by open means and by foul treachery to get him into his power or destroy him. But it was in vain.

But the royal tyrant was not to be baulked of his revenge. As he could not wreak on the cardinal himself the wrath he felt, his aged mother, the Countess of Salisbury, became the victim of his fury. Margaret Plantagenet was the daughter of George, Duke of Clarence, brother to Edward IV., and had been married to Sir Richard Pole, in whose veins, as in her own, ran the blood of the royal family. She had been chosen as godmother and the governess to Princess Mary, over whose court she presided at New Hall and other places. She was looked upon as, in the highest sense, one of the first and noblest ladies in the land. Her firm adherence to the Catholic cause and to Catherine of Aragon provoked the king's displeasure. But his pursuit of her until death must above all be put down to revenge for Reginald's opposition to the divorce and the schism. A Bill of Attainder was brought into the Lords against her and fifteen other persons, including Adrian Fortescue and Lord Montague, her eldest son, and rapidly passed a servile House and an equally servile House of Commons, almost without opposition on the 28th of June, 1539, and Margaret was at once removed from Cowdray, where she was then, to the Tower of London. In this gloomy prison she was kept in confinement without the sentence of death being executed for nearly two years. And during this time several other martyrs of note had to mount the scaffold. There suffered at Smithfield (July 30th, 1539) B. Thomas Abel, a Doctor of Oxford, who had written against the royal divorce, together with B. Richard Powell, the Vicar of St Mary Redcliffe at Bristol, who had given offence both by his book against Luther and by his sermons at Bristol in answer to Latimer, and also B. Richard Fetherston, who had been Latin tutor to the Princess Mary. All these were secular priests, and with impartial tyranny, at the same hour and place, where these Catholic martyrs were hanged as traitors, three Calvinist heretics, also apostate priests, Drs Barnes, Garrett, and Jerome, suffered death by burning at the stake. It was a new rebellion begun in Yorkshire under Sir John Neville in 1541, which furnished the pretext for carrying out the sentence

B. Margaret Pole is martyred (1541).

implied in the Act of Attainder on Margaret Pole. On the 27th of May she was told that she had to die that very day, and astonished as she was, summoned strength to walk from the Tower with a firm step to the place of execution, which was Smithfield Green. The Lord Mayor and a few others were present when she laid her head on the block. But, the regular executioner being absent, an unskilled youth was put in his place, and he only separated her head from her body after hacking her shoulders in the most brutal and blundering way. This it was which gave rise to the badly substantiated legend of her having run about the scaffold followed by the executioner, striking at her repeatedly. She had got ready a beautiful chantry in Christchurch Priory as her final resting-place, and this elegant chapel still remains. But her bones never occupied it: she was buried in the Church of St Peter ad Vincula at the Tower, by the side of Anne Boleyn, Catherine Howard, and other victims of the Tudor king.

Henry's arbitrary tyranny had now reached its highest point. It had for the most part been exercised with Thomas Cromwell as the instrument, and in many cases the moving spirit in what had been done. The unscrupulous minister was to meet his fate in another field. Jane Seymour, Henry's third queen, the mother of his son and successor, Edward, died immediately after the birth of this child (24th October, 1537). It was with

Fall of Cromwell (1540).
a view to strengthen the Protestant interests that Cromwell arranged in 1539 a marriage between his master and Anne, daughter of the Duke of Cleves, one of the leading Lutheran princes in Germany. The marriage, which was a political expedient, took place at the beginning of 1540, but Henry could never overcome his aversion to his new bride, whom he had not seen before the contract was made. As soon then as the advantage of being on friendly terms with the German Protestants no longer equalled Henry's wish to be on good terms with the empire, he determined to put away Anne of Cleves, to sacrifice Cromwell, and to change all his policy. Cromwell was arrested and sent to the Tower, where he was made to furnish evidence on the strength of which a commission appointed for the purpose decided that Henry's marriage was null, and that he was free to

THE ROYAL SUPREMACY 877

marry again. This was on July the 9th, and on August the 8th, to give further emphasis to the reaction in Henry's policy towards the empire and Catholicism, he married Catherine Howard, niece of the Duke of Norfolk. But ten days earlier Thomas Cromwell suffered the traitor's death on Tower Hill, having protested his grief for the part he had played, and having received the Sacraments as a Catholic.

Neither the alliance with the empire nor the marriage with Catherine Howard, which marked its culmination, was destined to be of long duration. As to the latter, in 1542 the enemies of the queen reported to him rumours of her unfaithfulness and adultery, as well as others charging her with an immoral life before Henry married her. There was probably much truth in these sinister stories. In any case they were enough to bring her to the block, together with her friend, Lady Rochford, in February, 1542, after an Act of Attainder had been passed. The influence of the house of Norfolk was eclipsed for the time. Having used the power of the empire against France, Henry also attempted in the same way to coerce Scotland, but though he won the Battle of Solway Firth in 1542, he was overreached by Charles V., and it cannot be said that his attempts to establish a suzerainty in Scotland were successful. At the death of James V., Mary, his daughter, became queen, and remained independent. **Henry's Foreign Policy.** Meantime the emperor made peace with France, and the King of England had to face France alone. It was in consequence of this that the friendship with Germany was dropped, and there was a reaction in favour of France and the German Lutherans. The change in foreign policy was reflected in domestic affairs at once. Under the influence of Cranmer a new exposition of doctrine known first as the Bishop's Book and afterwards, after receiving the royal assent, as the King's Book, was put forth in 1543, which though not meeting the views of the continental Protestants, modified and obscured Catholic doctrine on many points. Moreover, when in 1543 Henry married for the sixth and last time, his choice was Catherine Parr, who was favourable to the partisans of the reform in religion, and had been already twice married.

The opposition to the Protestant party was led in a

timid but not unskilful way by Gardiner, Bishop of Winchester, and Bonner, Bishop of London, and the remaining years of Henry's reign were a zigzag of advance and reaction between these contending forces. Henry himself fell sometimes under the influence of Cranmer, and sometimes his old Catholic traditions would reassert themselves. But he was failing in health, and before the end of 1546 fell into a mortal illness. The same uncertainty as to his religious position appeared again at his death-bed. Cranmer was there and seemed to get approval for his anti-Catholic views, but in the end old custom prevailed; Henry received Communion according to Catholic rites, and in his will left ample provision for Masses for his soul. He had plundered the chantries and seized innumerable foundations made for the benefit of the souls of others. His own directions were no better regarded than he had regarded the testamentary provision of others, and his Requiems were no better observed than theirs had been. But the other parts of his will fared better than his dispositions for prayers for his soul. He settled the succession in favour of Prince Edward, and failing him, of the Princesses Mary and Elizabeth in turn. The third part of his will appointed the executors of what he had laid down. Gardiner and the Duke of Norfolk, as well as Thirlby, Bishop of Westminster, were excluded, but the names of most of the other members of the Royal Council were included, and Somerset was entitled Protector.

There is a story that Catherine Parr, against whom a charge of heresy had been brought, only escaped by the king's death, but it is still more reliable that the Duke of Norfolk only escaped capital punishment through the same cause. His son, the Earl of Surrey, had already been executed. And as to Gardiner, he had only escaped by a very narrow issue. Hence, many of those in public positions, seeing how the savage intolerance of the monarch had increased with his infirmities, and how repeatedly he had veered round from one standpoint to another, must have welcomed his death as a relief from the possibility of a sudden and sanguinary fate.

(B) EDWARD VI. (1547-1553).

The king's Council kept Henry's death secret for three days. This gave time for young Edward, who was to succeed to the throne to be brought from Hertford by his uncle, Seymour, who was to become Protector to his royal nephew. *Proceedings of the Royal Council.* The late sovereign's will, besides making this appointment, was found to have put the arrangement of affairs into the hands of the Royal Council, while excluding Gardiner from all share in the power. Seymour was created Duke of Somerset, while other partisans of that family received various titles of honour. On the other hand, from the general pardon accorded at the coronation, the Duke of Norfolk, as well as Courtenay and Cardinal Pole, was expressly excepted. Consequently, all power fell into the hands of the supporters of Protestantism, and Cranmer became their willing tool in ecclesiastical affairs. In July two publications came from the press under royal authority: the "Book of Injunctions" and the "First Book of Homilies." These were both calculated to support the doctrines of the Reformers. The Injunctions exhorted the clergy to preach against the Bishop of Rome, and to destroy all shrines and images which had been treated with religious veneration. But the inconsistencies with which the Injunctions were marked must have been rather perplexing. While priests were roundly abused, the common people were told to remember that this office was from God and hence bidden to treat those who held it with due respect. The twelve discourses in the "Book of Homilies" were issued on the sole authority of the Council, and when handed to Bonner, Bishop of London, by the royal visitors, were only received by him under protest, and "as far as the Law of God allowed," to quote his own expression. The result was that in spite of his excuses he was in September committed to the Fleet Prison, and not more than a week elapsed before he was joined there by Bishop Gardiner, who had made a similar protest, which he afterwards renewed from his captivity. Both Bonner and Gardiner contended that the Royal Supremacy was in abeyance on account of the minority, or nonage, of the king. Meanwhile, the Council despatched visitors in all

380 THE CHURCH IN ENGLAND

directions to see that the prescriptions of the "Book of Injunctions" were complied with.

When Parliament met in November, it repealed the previous Heresy Acts, as well as the famous Six Articles.

Action of Parliament. It next went on to permit the marriage of the clergy, and likewise ordained that Holy Communion should be administered under both kinds. It also passed an act confiscating to the crown all the chantries, chapels, and colleges which had hitherto escaped the rapacious appropriations under Henry VIII. Cranmer urged upon Convocation, which met at the same time, the framing of laws for the reform of the Church. Meanwhile, the Protestant preachers got tacit leave, and even encouragement, to harangue the people in favour of their new doctrines, as Latimer, for example, did at Paul's Cross in January, 1548. There followed a succession of royal proclamations, which abrogated one after the other, a number of the customary Catholic rites. There were to be no candles for Candlemas, no ashes for Lent, no palms for Palm Sunday. Though the Latin Mass was left for the time untouched, an order for giving Communion in English was prescribed. The order which prescribed the removal of all sacred images from the churches was of a bolder character, and caused a revolt in Cornwall, which led to thirty executions there. Gardiner was now liberated from prison, and given to understand that he would be expected to conform to the new order of things. But when on his return to his diocese he began to preach against the "unknown teachers of novelties," he was summoned before the Council, and required to deliver before the king a sermon to be written and approved of beforehand. He objected to the demand that his sermon should be censored, but on the other hand agreed to speak only on the subjects specified. After a long and anxious preparation, he delivered his sermon, endeavouring to teach Catholic doctrine, and yet to avoid matters of controversy. Nevertheless, his discourse gave so much dissatisfaction to the Council that on the following day he was arrested and committed to the Tower. There he had to remain untried for more than two years.

Besides the order for Communion, another means was adopted in order to break with the old Catholic rite for the Liturgy. This was the composition and the subse-

THE ROYAL SUPREMACY

quent enforcement by statute of the Book of Common Prayer. A commission was named to put this book together in 1548, and in 1549 the book appeared. It bore upon it ample marks of Cranmer's spirit, cloaking under Catholic language deeply anti-Catholic doctrine. It was, of course, distinctly meant as a compromise, and was gathered in the main in eclectic fashion from the Sarum Missal and Breviary, from the Breviary of Cardinal Quignon, from the Greek Liturgies of the East, and from the Spanish Mozarabic Ritual. Yet in spite of its obligations to these sources it retained in substance but two sacraments, Baptism and the Lord's Supper. Confirmation, Holy Order, and Matrimony remained, but were treated as rites only. Penance and Extreme Unction entirely disappeared. The sacrificial character of the Mass was ignored, and the doctrine of the Real Presence spoken of with studied ambiguity. On the other hand a " mixed chalice " was ordered, water being added to the wine, and the use of unleavened bread was prescribed. Prayers for the dead were likewise retained, as well as vestments for the Communion service, and a crosier for the bishop. An Epiclesis, or invocation of the Holy Spirit, was introduced into the Liturgy from the Greek rite, while a large number of Scriptural Post-Communions were likewise inserted. In this way a form of worship was gradually made familiar to the people, which, though capable of a Catholic interpretation on many points, prepared the path for the advance of the more drastic changes embodied in the Second Prayer Book, which appeared in 1552. This latter work carried the changes in a Protestant direction so far that any later alterations rather made for a restoration of what was then omitted than for any further obliteration of Catholic rites.

The Book of Common Prayer (1549).

In the meantime intelligence of the way in which events were moving in England had reached the Continent of Europe. The result was a veritable invasion of the country by a host of foreign reformed divines, partly at the invitation of Cranmer, who wished to use them in the propagation of the new doctrines, and partly because they hoped to secure in this country more favour and freedom than could be found elsewhere. The

Foreign Protestants swarm to England.

Austin Friars' Church in London was made over to them as a place of worship. Henceforth, there began a period full of theological disputations at the universities between these men, such as were Ochino, Peter Martyr, Bucer, with their English disciples, and the main body of the English theologians who were still Catholic, such as Dr Richard Smith, Professor of Divinity at Oxford, Dr Cox, Dean of Christchurch. But while every liberty was given to the innovators to spread abroad their teachings, both in sermons and through the unrestrained use of the printing-press, the like freedom was denied to the other side. Both Cranmer and the Protector, Somerset, were preparing their plans for still more fundamental changes, when the date arrived (9th of June, 1549) for the abolition of the old Liturgy of the Latin Mass, and the substitution by law of the new Communion service authorised in the Book of Common Prayer.

There was much distress at the time in nearly every part of the country, and even a Catholic historian, Dr Lingard, admits that this acted as a stimulus to rouse the nation into rebellion against their rulers. Yet the fact remains that the Liturgical changes were the signal for formidable outbreaks of revolt in quite a number of widely distant neighbourhoods. In fact, few counties really were exempt. Surrey, Sussex, Hants, Berks, Wilts, Kent, Gloucester, Somerset, Worcester, Leicester, Rutland, Warwick, Herts, and Essex, all are recorded as having witnessed an uprising of their inhabitants against the government. But in addition to these local risings, which were easily suppressed, a far more serious outbreak took place in Oxfordshire, where Lord Grey had to call in the aid of Italian mercenary troops to cope with the insurgent forces. In Devonshire affairs took on a yet more threatening aspect. Having compelled the celebrant at Sampford Courtenay Church to resume the ancient Liturgy on Whit Sunday, 1549, the people rose *en masse* under Humphrey Arundell, and marched on Exeter, to which they then laid siege. It was only after forty days that this city was relieved by Lord Russell, when there was a parley in order to hear the demands of the insurgents. Meanwhile, in Norfolk an equally formidable rebellion had broken out under the leadership of Ket, a tanner of Wymondham. Having collected

THE ROYAL SUPREMACY 383

some twenty thousand under his standard, Ket held almost royal state outside Norwich, and when Lord Northampton entered that city with some English troops and a body of Italian and German mercenaries under Malatesta, succeeded in driving them out again, and setting fire to the place. However, being reinforced under the Earl of Warwick, the king's forces came back, and at last having surrounded Ket's army, forced it to capitulate. It would appear that the insurrection in Norfolk was not of so purely a religious character as that in Devonshire and Cornwall, but partook also of a social character. An equally wide difference was observable in the comparative severity used in the suppression and punishment. While Ket and a dozen of his chief supporters exhausted the list of those who were executed at Norwich, wholesale slaughter followed the rising in Devonshire, Oxfordshire, and other places. It is computed by a moderate writer that during Edward VI.'s short and turbulent reign four thousand persons lost their lives in England, either by the axe of the headsman, or by the hangman's halter. This is a number which quite overshadows the executions of which have any record in either of the subsequent reigns of Mary or Elizabeth, though they do not equal the wholesale slaughter of the reign of Henry VIII.

It does not fall within the scope of this book to narrate in detail the bitter rivalry between Somerset, the Protector, and Lisle, Earl of Warwick. This had really begun when Somerset was made Protector and essayed to continue under new forms the despotism of Henry. But for a while there was the outward seeming of friendship, and it was only as the predominance of Somerset became more overwhelming that Warwick put himself openly at the head of his enemies. The Protector was at last arrested, tried on various capital charges, and being found guilty by his peers, beheaded on Tower Hill on the 22nd of January, 1551. This threw the direction of public affairs into the hands of Warwick, now become Duke of Northumberland, and his powerful family—the Greys. They retained the supremacy for the next two years until Edward's death in 1553. The Catholic party headed by the former Lord Chancellor, Wriothesley, Earl of Southampton, seem to have united with Warwick's friends in procuring the downfall of Somerset.

They hoped, no doubt, that the disappearance of one who had been so cruel an enemy to them would lead to a reaction. But it proved quite otherwise. Northumberland threw himself into the arms of the extreme Protestants, and Cranmer, under the influence of the foreign reformers, proceeded further than ever in the direction of Calvinism.

As early as 1549, Cranmer had drawn up a set of Articles of Religion, which were to be signed by every preacher before he was licensed. Two years later these articles were laid by him before the bishops when they met together. They were next sent to the Royal Council, and by their order examined by the Calvinist preacher, John Knox, and five other selected censors. They were then sent back to Cranmer for further revision. The compliant Archbishop changed and retouched them once more, and then, at last, while Parliament and Convocation were both sitting, the articles, now forty-two in number, were brought before the latter body. No formal authorisation took place in Convocation, but on the 25th of March they were approved of by Royal Letters Patent. For the time they became the official declaration of Anglican doctrine. They were, in the main, Cranmer's work conceived in a spirit of compromise to all non-Catholic opinions. Of course they were not very consistent, and in more than one place ambiguous, but it was hoped that by their means the various schools of reformers would be brought into some kind of uniformity under the authority of the crown.

Articles of Religion.

Hand in hand with these innovations went the changes in the Prayer Book. In the order for Holy Communion the alternative expression "commonly called the Mass" was struck out. The formula for giving Holy Communion was likewise changed. An explanation as to the rubric directing a kneeling posture at the time of receiving stated that no adoration, as though Christ's body were really present, was intended. The "mixed chalice," the Sign of the Cross, and the Invocation of the Blessed Virgin and of the Saints were left out. So were the Introits. Unction of the Sick, as well as Reservation for their Communion, was omitted. The Prayers for the Dead were eliminated. In lieu of the customary vest-

Second Book of Common Prayer (1552).

ments a surplice was to be worn by the officiating clergyman.

No doubt there was a double aim in these and in similar changes not mentioned above. The former of these objects was to abolish the traditional ritual as far as it was feasible. The other was to make the Church services as unlike as possible to those of Catholic times, while the framework on which these were built was retained. But, even so, the innovations were not drastic enough to satisfy the Calvinist party, and had the reign been prolonged, an effort would surely have been made to secure a fuller revision according to these views. But, as a matter of fact, the Second Prayer Book had an authoritative existence of some eight months, for when the king died in 1553 the book was abolished, and the Latin Missal and Ritual were restored throughout the land.

It had become now evident that the young king's tenure of life was most precarious. He had preserved fairly friendly relations with his half-sister, the Princess Mary. The Protestant Lords of his Council had used every effort to force her to abandon the Catholic worship, and brought her letters from Edward requiring her to conform to the ritual of the new formularies, but she must have known how little he really had to do with this. She continued to attend Mass in secret, and yet they remained friends. Northumberland now formed the audacious plan of setting aside the succession of Mary and Elizabeth as laid down in King Henry's will, and diverting the inheritance to his own family. For this end he had Lady Jane Grey, daughter of the Duke of Suffolk, married to his son, Guildford Dudley. Having won over Edward, he prevailed upon him to direct the Chief Justice, at a meeting of the Royal Council, to draw up a deed altering the succession in the way he desired. The Chief Justice demurred, protesting that this was quite illegal, but being overcome by Northumberland's threats, and after receiving a royal pardon for his breach of the law, he drew up the required document. This was produced in Council, and in an atmosphere of threatened violence was signed by all the judges and councillors, by Cranmer, and last of all by the king himself. Cranmer protested ineffectually, but signed. To Edward personally it mattered little, for he was by this time failing rapidly in health. Within a month after these events he breathed his last at Greenwich Palace on the 6th of July, 1553.

(c) RESTORATION UNDER MARY (1553-1558).

Lady Jane Grey and Queen Mary. Northumberland and those who took part with him in the "Great Conspiracy" hoped that the days which were suffered to elapse before Edward's death was announced to the public would suffice to secure the crown for Lady Jane Grey, and also to seize the person of Mary, who was at Hunsdon in Herts. Being warned of the plot, Mary fled with her suite to Kenning Hall in Norfolk. Meanwhile, Northumberland having got possession of the Tower of London, proclaimed Lady Jane in the city as Queen of England. He then left London at the head of an armed force in order to effect the capture of the Princess Mary. The latter, however, was rapidly collecting her loyal subjects around her in Norfolk. Jerninghams, Pastons, Bedingfelds, and others brought their tenants to defend her. At the same time Tresham secured for her the county of Buckingham, and Hastings held Northampton. The Duke of Northumberland strove, as soon as he realised how things stood, to beat a retreat, but it was too late, and he was made prisoner at Cambridge. The Council, which he had coerced, now deserted him, and Queen Mary was proclaimed in London on the 19th of July, just nine days after her unfortunate rival, whose brief tenure of royalty was limited to that span. Entering the city in state at the Tower Gate, Mary there met the State prisoners, Norfolk, Edward Courtenay, Bishop Gardiner, and others. She kissed them, saying: "Ye are my prisoners," and on the next day they were set at liberty. Mary had Mass sung by Gardiner for her brother's soul, but the funeral took place according to the maimed rites of the Edwardine Prayer Book. The chief conspirators in the plot to raise Lady Jane to the throne were lodged in the Tower, yet Mary spared all of them whom she could. But Northumberland with his son Guildford, as well as Sir Andrew Dudley and the

Marquess of Northampton, were condemned to death. All these suffered at the Tower on the 22nd of August, after pleading guilty, and after a formal recantation of their Protestantism and a profession of the Catholic Faith.

The bishops deprived of their sees in the last reign on account of their religion were now restored; these were Gardiner, Bonner, Tunstall, Heath, Day, and Voysey. Gardiner was made Lord Chancellor, and Lord Paget became secretary to the queen; but Mary was not at first too well provided with counsellors whom she could trust. She certainly contemplated the restoration of Catholicism even from the first, but she realised the need of proceeding gradually and cautiously. Still, the fact that Mass was sung in St Paul's and in several London churches spontaneously before any order to that purpose came from the crown showed the sentiments of the majority, and encouraged the queen to advance. Royal letters were sent to the universities requiring the restoration of the ancient worship and statutes. This measure was a signal to the foreign Protestant teachers to take flight, and most of them escaped to the Continent. Peter Martyr at first took refuge with Cranmer at Lambeth. But Cranmer could not now protect himself, much less shield others, so Peter Martyr departed without let or hindrance across the seas. Cranmer made a written protest against what was being done, but on the 13th of September he was summoned before the Council, and committed to the Tower of London.

Gradual Restoration of Catholicism.

Cardinal Pole received a papal commission to go to England with full powers as legate, but his journey was delayed, and it was determined to proceed with the restoration without waiting for him. Mary wrote to the Pope asking for his consent to her coronation even before the full reconciliation of the realm with the Holy See could take place. In consequence of this, on the 1st of October the solemn rite was performed by Bishop Gardiner, who on the occasion proclaimed in her name a general pardon for all prisoners, except those in the Tower and in the Fleet. In the Coronation Oath Mary swore to maintain the rights of the Holy See as well as the liberties of the

Mary's Coronation.

kingdom. Then Parliament met. It was opened in traditional fashion, with the Mass of the Holy Ghost and a speech from Gardiner, the chancellor. A declaration was made that the queen meant to rule her subjects with mildness, more through love than fear. All new treasons, made such since the time of Edward III., were abolished. Then an act was passed declaring the legitimacy of Mary's birth. All the anti-Catholic legislation under Edward VI. was repealed. In all thirty-one statutes were passed before Parliament was dissolved.

By this time it had leaked out that Mary had taken a private engagement to marry Philip II. of Spain, and the Commons ventured to petition her to marry an Englishman, so unpopular was the Spanish alliance, and more than one candidate was suggested, Courtenay, Earl of Devon, and Pole, not yet a priest, being the most prominent of these. But the mind of the queen was already made up. She had but few advisers whom she trusted, and in this matter acted against the views both of Gardiner and others, and the protest of Noailles, the French envoy. The prejudice against a foreign king as consort was used by the Protestant party to set on foot what Dr Gairdner calls a "religious conspiracy with a political pretext." This was the rebellion of Wyatt, which began in Kent in March, 1554, while at the same time Carew and Courtenay led a rising in Devon. Another revolt broke out in Wales about the same time, while there was a rising in the Midlands under the Duke of Suffolk. Mary, who could after all count on the loyalty of most of her subjects, behaved with great promptitude and courage. Wyatt succeeded in penetrating into London at the head of the insurgents, but he was met by the royal troops and the train bands and forced to surrender. The rising in the West had already collapsed. Wyatt, in confessing his treason, accused the Princess Elizabeth and Courtenay of complicity in the rebellion. Elizabeth's guilt or innocence is a moot point in history. Wyatt was executed, Elizabeth conveyed to the Tower, though with every external sign of respect. The sentence passed long before on Lord Thomas Grey and his niece was now carried out, and they were both beheaded at the Tower. Suffolk also suffered the extreme penalty.

The Rebellion of Wyatt.

For the rest, Mary was still ready to spare as far as she could, and the four hundred rebels who were brought before her with halters round their necks received the royal pardon.

The marriage of Philip and Mary was celebrated at Winchester Cathedral by Gardiner, bishop of that diocese, on the 25th of July, with great splendour. And the rites of the day were followed by a whole series of brilliant festivities in which the riches of Spain were exhibited before the eyes of the natives of England. {Marriage of Philip and Mary.} The culmination of these ceremonies was the investiture of Philip as Knight of the Garter at Windsor on the 18th of August. But the popular opposition was not killed, and there were signs that this political alliance did not commend itself to the country at large. Both Philip and Mary were proclaimed Sovereigns of England, France, Naples, Jerusalem, and Ireland, Princes of Spain, and Archdukes of Austria. If England was hostile the emperor felt that he had immensely strengthened his son's position. The French were naturally displeased, and no assurances of peaceful intentions could appease them.

Obstacles had been deliberately placed in the way of Cardinal Pole's arrival as legate by the imperial party until the royal marriage was an accomplished fact. But in the Parliament opened by Philip and Mary in person in November, 1554, the first business was the reversal of Pole's attainder in order to make his landing possible. {Legation of Cardinal Pole.} Pole landed at Dover, and was met there by a distinguished band including Lord Montague and the Bishop of Ely. As he rode towards London his cortege gradually swelled until it was estimated to reach one thousand eight hundred horsemen. At Gravesend he entered a State barge after receiving a copy of the Act reversing his attainder. The rest of the journey to London was made by water, the legatine cross being carried aloft in the prow of the barge. At Westminster he was received in turn by the Lord Ch⁓ncellor, the King, and the Queen. He then took up his abode in Lambeth Palace, which was already prepared for him. Four days later, Lords and Commons were summoned to the court, where Pole addressed them in a felicitous speech, returning thanks for the Act passed in his favour, at the same time exhorting them to repeal all laws against the papal authority, and promising his hearty aid to make things as easy as possible. The Houses then retired to deliberate apart, and on the morrow the motion for reunion with Rome was carried almost unanimously, and the two Houses joined in a petition to the king and queen, asking them to gain absolution from the Holy See through the cardinal legate for the schism, and promising the repeal of all laws contrary to union with the Universal Church.

On the next day, November the 30th, the Feast of St Andrew, took place the memorable scene, when, before the Queen on her throne, Philip being seated on the one side and the Legate on the other, the Lord Chancellor in the presence of the whole Parliament read the petition, and Pole, rising, delivered an address at the end of which he absolved "all present and the whole nation from all heresy and schism, and restored them to the Communion of Holy Church." King and Queen and Lords and Commons all knelt while he pronounced the formula. On the Sunday following their Majesties attended Mass in state at St Paul's, where Gardiner preached a remarkable sermon lamenting the heresies of the last twenty years, from the epistle of the day: "It is now time for us to rise from sleep." He especially expressed contrition for his own share in the schism of Henry VIII., and exhorted all who had fallen with him to rise with him and adhere to the Universal Church. He also indicated to the assembly that Henry VIII. had twice entertained thoughts of seeking reconciliation with Rome, first in 1536, and again in 1541; he, the preacher, was secretly commissioned to ask the mediation of the emperor for this purpose. He also said that the Royal Council of Edward VI. had taken steps in the same direction. Gardiner came to the end of his long and chequered career within a year (November 12th, 1555). His effigy is still to be seen in his own cathedral at Winchester, where he was buried.

Meanwhile, the legate was proceeding in his great work of reconstruction with a large-minded liberality and an enlightened statesmanship which was far in advance of his age and of most of his contemporaries. The main lines of the settlement which owes more to him than to any other were (1) that all cathedral churches, hospitals, and schools founded during the schism should be kept, (2) that all marriages within forbidden degrees should be held valid, (3) that all cases before ecclesiastical judges should be upheld, (4) all holders of Church property through the confiscations should remain undisturbed in their possessions. After the bishops who had been appointed by the Council in Edward VI.'s reign had been deposed, it was necessary to fill their places with validly consecrated prelates of staunch Catholic doctrine. Moreover, there were other vacancies in the episcopal bench to be filled. The Primate, of course, was Cardinal Pole, though he was not consecrated till 1556, and Dr Nicholas Heath was translated from Worcester to York. Gardiner and Tunstall once more took possession of Winchester and Durham respectively, and Bonner of London. Day retook Chichester, and Voysey was restored to Exeter by patent. Dr White was made Bishop of Lincoln, and Dr Bourne of Bath. Henry's sees of Gloucester and Chester were retained, Dr Brooks being named to the former, and Dr Coles to the latter. After a vacancy of three years Rochester was filled by Maurice Griffin. All these were consecrated by Bishop Bonner in St Saviour's, Southwark. Then before the year 1554 was out Richard Pate was appointed to Worcester, Ralph Baynes to Lichfield, and John Hopton to Norwich. In the following year James Turberville was made Bishop of Exeter, while Willian Glynn and Thomas Goldwell were put into Bangor and St Asaph respectively. Cuthbert Scott replaced Dr Coles at Chester when the latter died in 1556. And when Gardiner died in 1555, Bishop White was transferred to Winchester, and his place taken at Lincoln by the learned Thomas Watson, who was consecrated by Archbishop Heath in 1557, together with Oglethorpe, the new Bishop of Carlisle, and David Poole for Peterborough. The last of the Marian bishops to be consecrated was John Christopherson, who was consecrated at London House by Bonner in 1557, but who died in the following year.

Alongside of the restoration of a legitimate hierarchy went as far as it was possible a restoration of the religious houses as well. The Grey Friars were restored at Greenwich in April, 1555, and in the next year the Dominicans were installed at St Bartholomew's, Smithfield, and the Benedictines at Westminster under Feckenham once more as their abbot. Carthusians once more inherited Shene, and Brigittines, Sion House. But the ruin wrought had been so complete and vast that a long period would have been needed for a general restoration, and this long period was never to be given.

A burning question, which affected most of the new nobility who had risen to wealth in the reign of Henry VIII., as well as not a few others of lower rank, was the alienation of church lands to which they owed their wealth, their homes, and much of their position. As to this Pole took a very bold, but indeed the only practical line that was open to him, namely, to secure the possession of such property to its present holders without their being in danger of being sued in the ecclesiastical courts. Next year (1555) Pope Paul IV. published a bull laying down the general principle of the invalidity of all alienation of church property to secular uses, but Pole, foreseeing what would happen if this was applied to England, procured a second bull expressly exempting church property in England from the operation of the former bull, and on this he acted with a consistent moderation which deserved far better success than he in fact was able to attain. Meanwhile, he was accused in Rome of temporising, and thereby playing into the hands of the Protestants and other enemies of the Church. Eventually Paul IV. gave credit to these accusations, and withdrew his favour from the cardinal legate.

Alienation of Church Property.

Although by this time the policy of leaving the church property in the hands of its present holders had convinced the numerous class who, not being profoundly religious, clung above all to the temporal goods they held that they had nothing to fear from the government, it was quite otherwise with those zealous for Protestantism. The queen's government, with all its moderation, was to be a Catholic one, and they threw themselves into the ranks of the seditious and treasonable. Slowly and reluctantly the queen and her advisers embarked on the path of religious persecution. The Parliament of 1554, before it separated, passed a short bill to re-enact three old Acts for the punishment of heretics who had already amply proved themselves a great danger to the

Forcible coercion of Protestants.

THE ROYAL SUPREMACY

tranquillity of the State. A fortnight later the former Acts against the See of Rome were repealed, while the establishment of the laity in the church possessions they had acquired in the two last reigns was confirmed by the authority of Parliament. On the 16th of January the Houses were dissolved. Three of the deprived Edwardine bishops and other men of note were summoned before Gardiner, the chancellor, at St Mary Overy's on the 22nd following, and formally charged with heresy. But there was no disposition to act with any bigoted fierceness. All that was wanted was to bring them back to the Church. Gardiner cited his own case, and urged them to follow his example. Public processions of the Blessed Sacrament, in which the king, the cardinals and eight bishops took part with a multitude of the clergy, passed through the streets of London to return thanks for the reconciliation of the realm to Christendom and the Holy See. Meanwhile, the knot of prisoners in the Tower and elsewhere held firm in their refusal to recant, and a legatine commission was issued to Gardiner to try them. The trial took place a few days later, and a few recanted, but they were only a minority, and the condemnation and execution of the others began to follow. The preacher, John Rogers, was the first to suffer; he was burned at Smithfield on the 4th of February. Hooper suffered the same punishment at Gloucester, and others in turn usually in their own part of the country. Even in the midst of these dreadful scenes it is undeniable that the Protestants continued to show disgraceful violence in interfering with Catholic worship and in the spreading abroad of blasphemous and anti-Catholic teaching. The authorities felt the danger of severity. Pole, Bonner, nay, even the king and queen exhorted the bishops to use all the mildness possible, but burning was still the legal penalty for heresy, and it was put in force in the course of the next two years and a half in nearly three hundred cases. The most celebrated cases were those of Archbishop Cranmer, who after repeated retractations and tergiversations,[*] eventually held firm and was burnt at Oxford on the 21st of March, 1556. Ridley and Latimer had suffered together at the same place five months sooner.

At the death of Gardiner, Nicholas Heath, Archbishop of York, was made Lord Chancellor, and was soon called upon to consecrate Cardinal Pole as Archbishop of Canterbury. Being only a deacon hitherto, Pole was ordained priest at Grey Friars on the 20th of March, two days before his consecration. He was not, however, to reign long as Primate of England. The new Pope, Paul IV., made war upon the Spaniards in order to free the Holy See and the kingdom of Naples from their domination, and encouraged the French in their attacks upon King Philip. Pole tried his best to keep England neutral between the contending powers, but the task was an impossible one, and Pole became involved in the papal hostility for Philip and the Spaniards. His first step was to cancel the Archbishop's legatine appointment. Sir Edward Carne, the English ambassador, gave a warning that the step would cause trouble in England, but Paul IV. declined to go back on what he had done. Meanwhile, Pole had been summoned to a consultation at the royal court, and had given his consent to a declaration of war against France. Joint letters from Philip and Mary were despatched to Rome to protest against the revocation of Pole's legatine powers, but the Pontiff was not to be won over. To obviate the inconvenience of there being no legate in England, Paul named the aged Observantine, Friar Peto, to that office, and at the same time summoned Pole to Rome. However, this brief was kept back by the royal envoys from the fear lest Pole, like Cardinal Morone, might be incarcerated in St Angelo. But before anything more could be done, King Philip routed the French at St Quentin, whilst the Spanish commander, Alva, entered Rome at the head of a victorious army. Philip II. used his triumph with moderation, and peace was concluded. Yet the harm already done in England could not be repaired. Friar Peto was legate, indeed, but he was so unpopular that he scarcely dared to appear in public. On the other hand, these differences among Catholics encouraged the Protestants to take further seditious and illegal action. Some of them were apprehended, and some were burnt, but they continued to give trouble to the government. The last blow to the life of the now infirm queen was the loss of Calais, which fell to the French on the 6th of January, 1558. A fortnight later, on the 20th of January, Parliament met. It was attended not only by the Bishops, Lords, and Commons, but by the restored Abbot of West-

Death of Queen Mary and Cardinal Pole (1558).

minster and by the Grand Prior of the Knights of St John. From March 7th the Houses were prorogued until November the 5th. During the interval there were several prosecutions of Protestants for illegal assemblies and for heresy. The summer was a very unhealthy one, and Queen Mary was gradually sinking into a mortal sickness. King Philip, who was in Flanders, sent the Count of Feria to her with his greeting in a special letter, and with instructions also to visit the Princess Elizabeth, and assure her of his support for her succession. The dying queen sent her jewels to her sister with the request that she would provide for her attendants, pay her debts, and be faithful to the Catholic religion. Lady Jane Dormer, afterwards Countess of Feria, who was charged with this message, won from Elizabeth the wish that the earth might swallow her up alive if she was anything but a true Catholic. Count of Feria could report this to his master. On the 17th of November, just at the end of Mass, which was celebrated in her presence, Queen Mary died. She was buried in Westminster Abbey. Her lifelong friend and chief counsellor, Cardinal Pole, who had been for some time lying ill at Lambeth, only survived her about twelve hours, dying in the evening of the same day. The cardinal was buried in St Thomas's Chapel in the cathedral at Canterbury.

The death of Mary and of Pole extinguished the chief hopes of the Catholics for a permanent restoration. Mary had incurred unpopularity on account of her consent to the persecution of heretics, of whom two hundred and seventy-seven suffered the extreme penalty of burning during her reign. She was also unpopular with the gentry, who had been enriched with the plunder of ecclesiastical property. For, in spite of Pole's statesmanlike action in the matter, the queen refused to keep any such property herself, and the moral effect of this was that it acted like a reproach cast upon others. Pole's loss was hardly less than that caused by the death of the queen. He was a prelate of lofty character, whose morals were above suspicion, and whose moderation was a lesson to the hot-headed enthusiasts of his day. He had held aloof from the executions, and had saved several who had been already condemned to the stake. He towers high above nearly all his contemporaries in public life.

Summary.

396 THE CHURCH IN ENGLAND

The whole period from the Act of Supremacy in 1534 to the death of Mary was a space of twenty-four years, and therefore just equal to the Catholic part of the reign of Henry VIII. (1509-34) or to the whole reign of Henry VII. (1485-1509).

XXVII.

THE ELIZABETHAN SETTLEMENT.

(1558-1603.)

IN the afternoon of the day (17th of November, 1558) on which Queen Mary died the Commons were summoned to the bar of the House of Lords. Nicholas Heath, Archbishop of York, and chancellor, announced Mary's death, and at the same time the accession of Elizabeth by virtue of the statute of 1544. She was then proclaimed at Temple Bar and Westminster. A deputation went to Hatfield from the Royal Council to tell her of her accession. She had expected the news, and made a reply which was carefully prepared beforehand. She meant to make no innovations, many of the old Council she would retain, and as to the others, she said, they were only superseded to avoid delay, and not from lack of confidence in them. Her choice of new counsellors was nevertheless significant: Heath had to hand over the Great Seal to Sir Nicholas Bacon, and William Cecil was named secretary. Both these men were known to be on the side of the Reformers. What the queen's own opinions were she was slow to proclaim. She had conformed under her father's, and again under her sister's regime, and she was still at first content to go to Mass and even to Communion. She suffered Mary to be buried with Catholic rites, and ordered a Dirge and Requiem for Charles V., just then deceased. But, on Christmas Day, Bishop Oglethorpe of Carlisle, while preparing to say Mass for her in the Royal Chapel, received a message from her to omit the Elevation. This he declined to do, and Elizabeth left the chapel, like a catechumen, after

Accession of Elizabeth (1558).

the Gospel. When the news of this spread, and still more when proclamation was made that the clergy were not to preach, nor to make alterations in the Liturgy until Parliament could be consulted on the matter, the bishops took alarm. They met and resolved that they could not in conscience crown Elizabeth until she had given more indubitable proofs of her orthodoxy. The coronation was fixed for the 15th of January, 1559, but the difficulty was to find a bishop to perform the ceremony. Elizabeth was in a real strait, but at length Oglethorpe of Carlisle agreed to officiate, the queen on her part promising to take the usual Coronation Oath, to communicate under one kind and to have the full Catholic rituals. This thing was indeed carried out, but at the Mass said by Carew, one of the queen's chaplain's, there was no Elevation, whereupon all the bishops left the abbey. Their absence from the rest of the proceedings and the non-attendance of the Spanish ambassador were ominous signs of the future.

Parliament and Convocation. Parliament met ten days later after a Solemn High Mass, and the queen attended in state. Lord Keeper Bacon opened the proceedings with a speech in which, after drawing a gloomy picture of the state of England during the last reign, he explained that the queen, though in no way bound to do so, had called the members together to arrange for a settlement of religion, for the reform of abuses, and for the safety of the kingdom. The Commons, before proceeding to business, presented a petition begging the queen to marry, but she replied that she had no intention of taking a husband, but gave them credit for good intentions in their address. The first act, necessary indeed for the royal security, was that which recognised her title to the throne, without, however, reversing the attainder of Anne Boleyn. The Houses then went on to the ecclesiastical legislation which was expected of them. The statutes passed under Mary in favour of Catholicism were repealed, and most of the anti-papal Acts of Henry VIII., together with the more distinctly Protestant statutes of Edward VI., were re-enacted. Each bill as it appeared was met by a vehement resistance on the part of the clergy, especially on that of the bishops, but the opposition proved quite useless. The Convocation, which was sitting at the same time as the

Parliament, presented to the House of Lords a declaration in favour of the Real Presence, of the Mass, and of the Papal Supremacy. Moreover, in order to try and strengthen the hands of the bishops, this declaration was likewise subscribed by the Universities of Oxford and Cambridge. Emboldened by this, the bishops made a good fight in the House of Lords, but they were overweighted by the force of the various opposing influences, and the process of disestablishing the Catholic religion went on apace.

Of course it was only gradually that the various Acts of Parliament on religion were enacted, and that what is called the Elizabethan Settlement came into force. But the die was cast when the queen herself, without any very pronounced religious opinions, called to her counsel such men as Nicholas Bacon and Cecil, Lord Burghley. Parliament went on to pass once more the Act of Royal Supremacy and enforced an oath on the bishops and other officials, and after them on all the clergy and many of the laity, to the effect that the queen was "Governess" of the English Church. It then proceeded by means of the Act of Uniformity to make a new Liturgy compulsory, thereby abolishing the Mass under severe penalties to all who should celebrate it. This new Liturgy, which went back to the Second Liturgy of Edward VI., in the main was to come into force on the 24th of June, 1559. Meanwhile, convocation having reasserted the Papal Supremacy, Transubstantiation and the Sacrifice of the Mass, followed this up by rejecting the title *Gubernatrix Ecclesiæ* for the queen. Thus Parliament and Convocation appeared in full opposition to one another. The expedient adopted by Elizabeth to secure agreement was to summon a conference of eight Catholic and eight Protestant divines to meet at Westminster, with the avowed object of determining the points in dispute. But the proceedings had been arranged beforehand by Bacon, so as to give every advantage to the Protestants, and when the Catholics protested against this, the Lord Keeper summarily cut short the conference, and the bishops were at once called upon to take the Oath of Supremacy.

Legal enactments against Catholics (1559).

The bishops surviving out of the hierarchy of Queen

Mary's reign were fourteen in number, and with the solitary exception of Anthony Kitchin, Bishop of Llandaff, they all refused to take the Oath of Supremacy.

Fate of the Marian Bishops. They were then deprived of their sees, one by one, their honours and goods being at the same time taken from them. They were, moreover, all placed under various degrees of restraint, ranging from mere surveillance to hard captivity in prison. They gradually succumbed to the rigour with which they were treated, and to the effect produced upon men of advanced years by the fate which had befallen them. Goldwell, Bishop of St Asaph, escaped from England when the rest were put under restraint, and arrived at Trent in 1561. He was the only English bishop who took part in the Ecumenical Council held in that city. He never returned to England, but proceeded to Rome, where he lived at St Silvestro, which belonged to the Theatine Order, of which he was a member. He was called on to preside over several general chapters of the order, and likewise served as Vicegerent to the Cardinal-Vicar of Rome. After a life spent in good works and piety he died in 1585, having survived all the other English bishops. Cuthbert Scott, Bishop of Chester, having suffered four years' imprisonment in the Fleet, was released on bail, and effected his escape into the Low Countries, where he died in 1565. The aged Cuthbert Tunstall of Durham, who was entrusted to the keeping of Archbishop Parker at Lambeth, as well as Ralph Baynes of Lichfield, and Owen Oglethorpe of Carlisle, who were both confined in the Bishop of London's house, near St Paul's, all died before the end of 1559. John White of Winchester, imprisoned in the Tower of London, shortly before his death was sent to South Warmborough, near Farnham, where he died on the 12th of January following, and was buried in his own cathedral. David Poole of Peterborough was at last committed to the Fleet after some time spent under surveillance at the house of Bryan Fowler in Staffordshire. In the Fleet probably he died in 1568. Edmund Bonner of London was put into the Marshalsea Prison, but afterwards sent into Essex to a manor belonging to his diocese. Dying there in 1569, he was buried in Copford Parish Church in the same county. There were four other bishops who suffered imprisonment in the Tower of London besides the Archbishop of York. Of these Richard Pate of Worcester, and probably also James Turberville, died within that prison, the one in 1565, and the other in 1570. Gilbert Bourne of Bath and Wells was sent from the Tower to Silverton in Somerset, where he died in 1569, and Thomas Thirlby of Ely died at Lambeth in custody of the Primate in 1570. Nicholas Heath, Archbishop of York, survived his deprivation for nearly twenty years, as he only died in 1578. Part of this time was spent in confinement in the Tower, and another part at Chobham Park, Surrey, under strict guard. He lies buried in the ancient church at Chobham. Thomas Watson of Lincoln spent a still longer life of captivity, chiefly in Wisbech Castle, whither he was sent with some twenty other prominent Catholics, while amongst those added to this band of prisoners later on was the illustrious Feckenham, the last Abbot of Westminster. Bishop Watson died in 1584. It is true that none of these bishops had to confess their Faith on the scaffold like Bishop John Fisher, but the Elizabethan government could claim little credit for leniency, since the harsh treatment meted out to these learned and venerable men was harsh enough to win for them the title of Confessors, if not of Martyrs, for their religion.

The deprivation of the Marian bishops in 1559 made it a matter of vital importance for Elizabeth to fill up their sees with new incumbents who might become the subservient instruments of her will. There was one inglorious exception to the determined attitude taken by the existing hierarchy in the person of Kitchin, Bishop of Llandaff. He had taken the oath, and was therefore allowed to retain his diocese. The first care of the queen and of her advisers was to provide a new Primate to fill the see left vacant by the death of Pole. It was first offered to Dr Wotton, Dean of Canterbury, but he, being a Catholic in doctrine, and apprehensive of the coming storm, prudently declined the proffered dignity. The royal choice then fell upon Dr Matthew Parker, who had been a chaplain in the Boleyn family. But, of course, he had to be consecrated, and none of the Marian bishops could be counted on to perform the rite. Recourse, therefore, was had to the following expedient. Four

New Elizabethan Bishops.

Edwardine bishops who had been deprived at the revival of Catholicism under Mary were called upon to assist: these were Barlow, late of Bath and Wells, Hodgkin, formerly suffragan Bishop of Bedford, John Scory, once Bishop of Chichester, and Miles Coverdale of Exeter. The two first seem to have been consecrated according to the Catholic Pontifical, the two last according to that of Edward VI. On the 1st of August, 1559, these men met in the archiepiscopal palace at Lambeth, in the chapel of which the first-named, Barlow, assisted by the others, imposed hands on Parker, according to a rite of their own devising, studiously omitting all mention of the office of a Catholic bishop, as well as several other points deemed essential by the main body of orthodox theologians. Parker, once installed in the see of Canterbury, proceeded to consecrate those who were chosen by the crown to fill up the vacant sees. Barlow and Scory were only instituted, their previous consecration being admitted as valid. The former received the diocese of Chichester, the latter that of Hereford. Grindal, who was considered to be the best theologian of the Protestant party, was named Bishop of London. Cox, formerly preceptor to King Edward VI., was appointed to Ely. Jewell, who surpassed all the other Protestants in general scholarship, received Salisbury, while Robert Horne was named to Winchester. Sandes obtained the see of Worcester, while Richard Cheney had Gloucester bestowed upon him. The other dioceses were not immediately filled. It will thus be seen that these first appointments were all, with the exception of London, made to sees already vacant before the deprivation of the Marian prelates. But, gradually, as the years went on their dioceses were also filled up, and Protestants were in possession of all the bishoprics of the land.

The Lower Clergy. The difficulty of finding incumbents for the twelve thousand or thirteen thousand parishes into which England was divided was one that pressed on the government even more than the appointment of bishops. The Oath of Supremacy was proffered to the parochial clergy after the bishops, as well as to all holding office in the universities, the public schools and colleges, and the cathedral chapters. The records of what happened in the case of individuals are very incomplete, but historians seem justified in the conjecture that at any rate a large majority of the parish clergy took the oath. A minority refused it, and, as in the case of the bishops, were in consequence ejected from their benefices. Out of a probable total of eight thousand beneficed clergy, Dom Birt, with painstaking industry, has discovered " the names of over seven hundred holders of benefices who underwent deprivation." Adding to these the number who succeeded in leaving the country and in other ways avoiding the test, the same writer with R. Simpson and Father Pollen conjectures that about two thousand, or roughly one quarter of the whole, did not take the oath. It is also admitted even by non-Catholic writers that a large proportion took the oath, not because they believed in it, but more or less against their conscience, hoping that the recent changes in religion would not be the last. They trusted in this way to be able to keep out intruders, and then when the storm had passed to get a dispensation from the Pope for what they had done. The idea was both unworthy and unlikely to be realised. The stalwart minority who were cast out became what were called "hedge priests." But, doubtless, many parishes were thus left as they were, and it seems certain that many others, as with the bishoprics, were vacant. Yet, even so, the government was at its wits' end to find incumbents in sufficiently large numbers, with the result that the cures and parishes were bestowed upon all manner of illiterate and ill-conditioned persons. These, if they could be trusted to admit the Royal Supremacy, and to use the new Protestant service, were ordained and instituted by the bishop according to the needs of time and place. For the rest, the evidence at our disposal shows that throughout the reign there was sad confusion and a great decay of religious observances in every part of England. Many people absented themselves from church altogether, some from want of all religion, others from fidelity to the old religion, to uproot which every effort was being made.

The removal of the Catholic bishops and the consequent gradual extinction of the parochial clergy did not fail to produce their natural results. The flock, left without legitimate pastors, was **The Laity.** scattered and spiritually starved. Then there was the double attack made upon their constancy by the unceasing spread of heretical teaching, and by the sharp tooth of persecution. In estimating the number of Catholics the test of attendance at the state worship is of course a fallacious one under the circumstances. Many Catholics went to save themselves from molestation, all the more that the queen and her ministers declared all they aimed at was external conformity, while they did not require interior assent. Under these conditions it is very difficult to determine how many of the people remained true in belief to the old religion. They may be cautiously estimated at anything between ninety and fifty per cent of the total population. Yet the external collapse was very complete and very sudden. The bishops were removed, the faithful portion of the clergy were living in concealment and in disguise, the peers were subservient for the most part, the restored religious communities did their best to escape to the Continent.

The course of the Elizabethan government in religious matters in the early part of the reign was much influenced by international politics. Elizabeth found England and Spain in close alliance—Ruy Gomez, Count of Feria, the Spanish ambassador, the most powerful diplomatist at court, and his wife, the pious Lady Jane Dormer, the bosom friend of Queen Mary. It was only gradually that the queen cut herself off from the Spanish influence and proclaimed her Protestantism openly in the face of the Spanish envoy. Philip of Spain, on the other hand, was exceedingly slow to break with Elizabeth, hoping to win her over by one project of marriage after another, even when his plan of marrying her himself was proved to be hopeless. Elizabeth had everything to win by gaining time, and dallied with these proposals, deceiving not only De Feria, but his successor, De Quadra, Bishop of Aquila. It was owing to this that the excommunication, threatened in 1561, was averted for nearly nine years, for King Philip opposed the sentence as long as he thought there was any chance of winning the queen by milder means. The interval was used by Elizabeth and her ministers to strengthen their position in England. The Second Parliament, which met in 1563, passed a Bill for the Assurances of the Royal Supremacy, invoking heavier penalties on those who refused to subscribe to it, while at the same time the more violent anti-Catholics called out for the trial and execution of the deprived bishops, or "caged wolves," as they called them.

It is clear that the Sovereign Pontiffs of the period and their Roman counsellors realised even better than Philip II. and the Spaniards what a disaster was threatening Christendom in the gradual settling down of England among the enemies of the Church, and endeavours were not wanting, on their part, to avert the calamity. Two attempts were made to send a nuncio to invite the participation of the English Queen in the Council of Trent, which had resumed its sessions about this time. The later and more important of these missions, that of Mgr. Martinengo, came to an untimely end when notice was given that Elizabeth refused to receive a nuncio from the Pope. This decision was come to after much hesitation on the queen's own part, through the determined opposition shown in the Protestant interests by the royal councillors, Cecil and Bacon. When this rebuff became known at Trent there was much discussion among the assembled fathers as to whether Elizabeth ought not to be at once excommunicated by the Council itself. Under Spanish and imperial influence the negative view prevailed, based on the hope that even now all hope of final reconciliation was not lost. It was left to the next Pope, seven years after the Council was over, to carry this sentence into effect. The play of international politics could not but exercise a potent influence on the situation, and Catholics themselves, however united as to the end they aimed at, namely, the reunion of their country with Christendom, were hopelessly divided as to the means they looked to for accomplishing this. Some were looking to Philip of Spain, while others built their hopes on Mary Stuart, Queen of Scots. This princess, whose title to the English throne was thought better than Elizabeth's by all those who looked upon the latter as illegitimate, was filling an ever growing place in the minds of the English Catholics. After being reduced to helplessness after the Protestant Revolution of 1560 in Scotland, Mary had recovered a precarious tenure of power through her marriage with Lord Darnley. But the Protestant "Lords of the Congregation" rose in arms

Elizabeth and the Council of Trent.

against her, and having captured her, imprisoned her in Lochleven Castle. From this island fortress she escaped, and put herself at the head of an army. But she was easily defeated at Langside in 1568, and then fled into England. To her intense disappointment she was straightway led into captivity, being removed from Carlisle to Bolton, and thence to Tutbury and other places. Elizabeth and her advisers knew how important was the prey which had fallen into their hands, and resolved to strain every point and to scruple no deception to prevent her regaining her liberty.

Though Mary was held under guard her friends managed to communicate with her, and were exerting themselves in her favour, both at the English court and also with the Holy See. The Duke of Norfolk, leader of the Conservative party among the Catholic nobles, was credited with the design of marrying the Queen of Scots, and thus perhaps of paving his way to the crown. But he did not put himself at the head of any armed rising. Still, supported by him and informing the Holy See of their designs, the two Catholic Earls of Northumberland and Westmoreland with Lords Lumley, Dacre, Mowbray, and the Nortons and Markenfields—all leading Northern gentlemen—raised the standard of insurrection with the avowed object of restoring the ancient religion and of freeing the Queen of Scots from captivity. Durham was seized by the insurgents, the Mass once more sung in its cathedral, and the Book of Common Prayer publicly burnt. But there was dissension and lack of organisation in the army which had been collected, while the royal ministers, realising that the situation was critical, acted with energy and promptitude. The forces of the insurgents were attacked in detail and scattered, so that before long all that was left to do was to inflict punishment on those who shared in a vain rebellion. Westmoreland escaped to the Continent. Northumberland and other leaders were executed, as well as about nine hundred of the common folk. A bloody vengeance surely, if it be compared with the numbers executed after the failure of similar attempts against the actual government before and since. The Duke of Norfolk too was apprehended on a charge of treason, and executed in London. Elizabeth was now

The Rising of the North. (1569).

ELIZABETHAN SETTLEMENT

able once more to breathe freely, but she was more than ever determined that the Queen of Scots should not pass out of her hands alive.

In the early years of Elizabeth's reign the hopes of her advisers on the gradual reduction of the Catholics to conformity with the state religion were based upon the dying out of the bishops and clergy, and upon the pressure exerted by the penalties against the celebration of Catholic worship. But the contest was soon to assume a more violent and extreme character. The imperfect reports which reached Rome concerning the Rising of the North, which was certainly looked at in too rosy a light, made St Pius V. think that the opportune moment had arrived for vindicating the Catholic cause against Elizabeth by issuing the long-threatened and oft-delayed excommunication. As a matter of fact the Rising had already collapsed, and the opportunity had been lost. However, on the 5th of February, 1570, proceedings were begun in the Apostolic Chamber. Evidence was given by prominent Catholics such as Bishop Goldwell, Sir Richard Shelley, Grand Prior of the Knights of Malta, and others, and then the English queen having been found guilty as an obstinate heretic, the bull *Regnans in Excelsis* was published on the 25th of February, by which Elizabeth was not only excommunicated as an obstinate heretic, but deposed from her kingdom, her subjects being released from all allegiance to her. King Philip of Spain and the Emperor Maximilian were both unfavourable to its publication, but the French approval was unquestionable. Instead of shaking the throne of the queen, the bull had the effect of bringing a more bitter persecution on the heads of the English Catholics. But it certainly drew clearer the complete opposition between the Catholic Church and the English government, and though it may have led to the apostasy of many who in a loose and half-hearted way still clung to the Church, it showed the need of separation from the Anglican worship on the part of Catholics, and welded them into the solid though lessened body of recusants, who refused to attend the heretical worship of the Church of England. Whether it was a politic or an impolitic move, St Pius held that he was only using the authority which had been entrusted to him by God

Excommunication of Elizabeth (1570).

and the common law of mediaeval Christendom for the highest interests of souls. The reply of the Elizabethan government was an increased severity of penal legislation against Catholics.

Further penal legislation. Parliament met in 1571, and proceeded to pass bills devised for this purpose. One act which then became law made it high treason to declare that the queen was a heretic or a schismatic. Another invoked the penalties of treason against any who should introduce into England any papal bull or letter. A third act ruled that any subject of the queen who passed beyond the sees without licence and did not return within two months forfeited all the profits of his lands during his lifetime, together with all his movable goods. This last act was clearly directed against the colleges or seminaries which were in process of formation to educate English clergy on the Continent. It was not long before the fruits of this law-making appeared in the shedding of the blood of several men who now take a foremost rank among the English martyrs. It was thus that Blessed John Felton was hanged, drawn, and quartered in St Paul's Churchyard on the 8th of August, 1570, for having affixed the Bull of Excommunication to the Bishop of London's gates. It was thus that Blessed John Storey underwent the same penalties on Tower Hill on the 1st of June, 1571, for his courageous stand in the House of Commons against the anti-Catholic legislation which was being enacted. Thomas Woodhouse, who had been admitted into the Society of Jesus, suffered martyrdom in like manner on the 13th of June, 1573. There were also several executed in connection with the Rising of the North, whose claims to be considered as martyrs of the Faith have been admitted. These were Blessed Thomas Percy, Earl of Northumberland, who, refusing the offer of his life at the price of apostasy, was beheaded at York on the 22nd of August, 1572, and the secular priest, Blessed Thomas Plumtree, who was hanged at Durham in the same year.

Catholic worship never completely ceased in Protestant England, but the clergy were gradually dying out, and it seemed obvious both to friend and foe that in time it must come to an end for lack of priests unless some new source of supply could be found. It is here that the

ELIZABETHAN SETTLEMENT 409

work of Cardinal Allen and the foundation of the various seminaries on the continent of Europe come in to mark the turning point from despair to a new hope for a Catholic revival. It is very difficult to exaggerate the services rendered in this way to the Church by Allen, though it is true that he did not at first contemplate a missionary college, but one which would train clergy for the great change of fortune which he hoped would not be too long delayed. William Allen was born in 1532, his father being a native of the Rossall district in Lancashire, and his mother from Yorkshire. When he went to Oriel College, Oxford, in 1548, the Catholic unity of his boyhood had been broken, and a Protestant king was on the throne. Yet he pursued his studies as a Catholic, taking his B.A. in 1550, and his M.A. in 1554. By that time the Pope had reconciled England to the Holy See, and Allen became head of St Alban's Hall, and also Canon of York, though as yet only in Minor Orders. When Elizabeth began to enforce the Protestant settlement upon the universities, Allen's post at Oxford became no longer tenable, and he sought refuge at Louvain in 1561. He came back to England in the following year, and tried to work for Catholic interests as a layman; but his zeal attracted the attention of the persecutors, and he had once more to seek safety in flight. We have positive evidence that he received the priesthood at Malines in 1565. His first sphere of activity then was the composition of several works of a dogmatic and controversial character, which he easily got printed in the Low Countries and then shipped into England. Amongst these he wrote a book on the "*Priesthood,*" another on "*Indulgences,*" and a third on "*Purgatory,*" as well as other works. He seems to have gone to Rome with one of the Flemish bishops, and there to have conceived the plan of founding a college in some continental city to train clergy for the English mission. Having interested this Flemish prelate in his project, and having gained financial assistance from him and from other powerful friends, he was able to take a large house at Douay, and make a beginning of the English College there on the 29th of September, 1568.

Allen succeeded in gathering round him at Douay quite a circle of distinguished scholars. The first president

William Cardinal Allen (1532-1594).

was Dr Thomas Smith, and among the early professors we may refer to the dogmatic writer, Thomas Stapleton, to Richard Bristow, to Gregory Martin, and to John Reynolds. The college flourished exceedingly, so that before the lapse of very many years it was frequented by one hundred and fifty students. It has been calculated that before the end of the sixteenth century Douay had sent three hundred priests upon the English mission, while the era of persecution did not close before it had inscribed one hundred and sixty names upon its roll of martyrs. It was also the armoury where the chief controversial works were forged which kept up the battle against the calumnies and misrepresentation which the works of Protestants of the day rained upon the members of the old Church.

Foundation of Douay (1568).

The troubled condition of Douay and its neighbourhood during the wars of the period between the Spanish and the French made it necessary to transfer the college temporarily to Rheims in 1582. But when tranquillity was restored to the Low Countries the establishment was brought back to Douay, and there it continued to exist until the French Revolution in 1795. It was at Rheims and at Douay respectively that the New and Old Testaments were translated into English in a version which still remains the groundwork of all later Catholic translations of the Vulgate into English. Allen was the centre and inspiration around which the scholars who contributed to this did their work, but the actual translation was in the main the achievement of the Oxford convert, Dr Gregory Martin, one of the professors, who was distinguished for his knowledge of Hebrew and Greek. Martin had formerly been tutor to Philip, Earl of Arundel. The work was indebted for revision and other assistance to Dr Richard Bristow, and to Thomas Stapleton, the foremost Catholic controversialist of the time. The notes and finally the publication of the complete work are due to Dr Richard Worthington, the third president, in 1610, after the death of both Allen and Martin. Its primary aim was a faithful rendering of the Vulgate, but in its original form it was a noble and vigorous monument of the English of the Elizabethan period.

Rheims and Douay Testaments.

The same year—1575—which saw the papal recognition of Allen's success at Douay by the conferring of a grant upon the college, also beheld the commencement of the Venerable English College in Rome. There had been an English Hospice in the city for the entertainment of pilgrims all through the Middle Ages. The idea, the credit of which may be shared between Allen and Dr Owen Lewis, an Oxford scholar in exile from England, was to make this Hospice the nucleus of a seminary for missionary clergy. The plan had been broached as early as 1560, but at the moment it came to nothing, and there can be little doubt that the phenomenal success of Douay was the example which led to its realisation in 1575. Allen was summoned to Rome to aid in the commencement, and, Douay being then overcrowded, the first band of students was sent thence to the Roman Hospice in 1576, another party following them in the course of the next year. Gregory XIII., whose efforts to provide for the education of the clergy constitute one of his fairest titles to fame, gave a Bull of Foundation and a grant of money in 1579. By 1585 the number of students had increased to seventy. After some unseemly quarrels between Welsh and English on national grounds, the Welsh superiors, Dr Maurice Clennock and Dr Lewis, being accused of unduly favouring their compatriots, the management of the college was entrusted to the Jesuits. They were able to apply to it the carefully organised system of education which had enabled them to change the face of half Europe. Of course their system had its opponents, while the Jesuits were also accused of selecting from the students the most suitable candidates for their own order. To decide between them and their accusers, several papal visitations of the college were held by such notable visitors as the well-known Cardinal Sega, but very little substantial ground of complaint was found. It was recommended that the rector should always be an Englishman. Under a series of Jesuit rectors the House went forward and furthered the great object of its foundation. The most distinguished of its superiors was the zealous and talented Father Robert Parsons. This celebrated convert was Tutor and Fellow of Balliol College, Oxford, until, being under suspicion of Catholic sympathies, he fell into disfavour there in 1574, when he went to the Continent and

The Venerable English College and others.

was received into the Church. Next year he was admitted into the Society of Jesus. He was Campion's companion in the missionary journey to England of 1580, and, while in the country, made many converts, and set up a printing-press, whence he issued a considerable number of ably written controversial works. He travelled to Spain and afterwards resided in Rome, where his active advocacy of the armed intervention of the Spanish king in favour of the English Catholics caused him to be regarded as the leader of the "Spanish Party." His superior talents made him a formidable antagonist to those who differed from him, and later on his name was the storm centre for the disputes between seculars and regulars as to the organisation of the Church in England. He had a plan for the appointment of two bishops, each with a staff of archpriests for the government of the clergy. When this project fell through, the nomination of the archpriest Blackwell for the secular clergy, the regulars being left under their own superiors, was due to him. The secular clergy resented this arrangement, and Parsons became very unpopular. He died in Rome in 1610. His vigorous English style is praised by Swift, and in several ways he was the foremost native Catholic at the death of Queen Elizabeth. It remains to be said that through his influence, and under the protection of the Spanish monarch, colleges for the English clergy were established at Valladolid in 1589, and at Saville in 1592. Other similar houses were begun later on in Madrid, Lisbon, and in the Spanish Netherlands.

Meanwhile, using the pressure applied through the penal laws against recusants, the Elizabethan government was advancing in its attempt to secure general conformity with the settlement they had determined upon. But new opponents were starting into life to oppose the compromise between Catholicism and Calvinism. These were the Puritans. They made their influence felt in the Parliament of 1571. The Thirty-Nine

Thirty-Nine Articles. Articles of Religion, now reduced from the forty-two drawn up in a spirit of compromise under the auspices of Cranmer were accepted by convocation in 1568, but the attempt to get them also sanctioned by Parliament was defeated by the Royal Council. However, in 1571, they were approved by Parliament against the queen's wish, and any attempt to preserve Anglo-Catholicism received a powerful setback. They have remained the doctrinal constitution of the Anglican Church ever since, though innumerable efforts have been made to interpret them in a sense not inconsistent with most Catholic dogma. The Puritan bias can also be seen in urging still more stringent legislation against Catholics. The period from 1568 to 1580 was a dark and depressing one for the faithful remnant. They were divided in counsels; they were harassed by persecutors at home.

In 1577 Blessed Cuthbert Mayne, the Protomartyr of the Douay Seminary and fifteenth missionary it had sent into England, suffered the penalties of high treason at Launceston. From that time martyrdoms began to grow more and more numerous as the years went by. Blessed Edmund Campion, the ablest and most illustrious of the early martyrs from the Roman College, who was the standard-bearer of the Jesuits, suffered at Tyburn on the 1st of December, 1581. His life was written by his former companion on the mission, Father Parsons, who afterwards became the first provincial of his society. Campion's "*Ten Reasons of a Challenge to the Universities of England*" was for some time the most effective literary contribution to the defence of the Faith. After these appears a stately procession of triumphant champions who gave their blood for Catholicism, whose Acts form the most valuable part of English history for the succeeding years. They were not drawn from one class only. There were secular priests, Jesuits, Benedictines, schoolmasters, country gentlemen, simple yeomen, nay, gentlewomen and youths. Some of these went to death, others suffered imprisonment and other penalties. Under the one act of 1585 it is calculated that in all one hundred and fifty priests suffered martyrdom.

<small>Martyrs under Elizabeth.</small>

All this time the Scottish queen was in captivity, chiefly at Sheffield and Fotheringay Castle, and Elizabeth neither dared to release her nor to execute her. She is accused of suggesting private assassination to the agents who surrounded her, and in the end, after signing her death warrant, complained that means had not been found to make away with her in secret. The elaborate controversy as to the character and previous record of

<small>Mary Queen of Scots (1587).</small>

Mary can, of course, find no place here. But it is clear that Elizabeth, knowing her claims to the English throne, did not feel secure upon it as long as she lived. The discovery of the Babington plot for the deposition and even the assassination of Elizabeth brought matters to a head. An order was made for the trial of Queen Mary on the ground of complicity in this plot, as well as of wishing to subvert the succession to the crown. She consented to plead before the appointed judges, and the trial began at Fotheringay on the 14th of October, 1586. For two days she defended herself with admirable clearness of mind and great courage. She admitted that she had desired and spoken of the restoration of the Catholic religion, but denied all participation in the assassination plot. Elizabeth now revoked the case to the Star Chamber Court at Westminster, at which, in her absence, Mary was found guilty and sentenced to death. She was told that her life was incompatible with the security of the succession to the crown, and of the Protestant settlement. She eagerly embraced the admission that she was to die in order that the Catholic religion should not be restored at the expense of Protestantism, and met her fate on the scaffold at Fotheringay on the 8th of February, 1587. Whatever may be thought of her innocence or the reverse during the stormy scenes of her early life in Scotland, there had been years of wearisome and humiliating captivity before the tragedy came to a close, and she faced her doom in the spirit of a martyr. Benedict XIV. held that in her case there was nothing wanting to justify her claim to that glorious title. Her death changed the outlook of her fellow-Catholics to a considerable extent: up to then their chief hopes of liberty and restoration had rested on her. Now they were faced with the sharp alternative either to look for the triumph of their Faith through foreign intervention, which practically meant the victory of the King of Spain, or to go on hoping against hope that in some incalculable way the Providence of God would come to their aid.

Before the death of Mary, Queen of Scots, England and Spain were already at war. Philip II. always acted tardily, and was for many years most unwilling to be drawn into a conflict with Elizabeth. He had, in a manner, supported the Catholic cause, but rather than

ELIZABETHAN SETTLEMENT

break with England, had endured affronts and even hostile action in favour of his rebellious Protestant subjects in the Netherlands. Still, it was recognised that this could not go on indefinitely, and at last it was only a question of whether England or Spain would be the first to declare war. The Protestant party in England elected to be the first in the field, and in 1585 began the contest in earnest by very successful naval expeditions. Moreover, when Pope Sixtus V. came to realise how intensely anti-Catholic the English government had become, he did not indeed renew the Bull of Excommunication of St Pius, but issued a manifesto referring to it, and urging Philip II. to act on it, and carry out the sentence of deposition therein pronounced against Elizabeth. This led to the Spanish Armada, which was prepared on a large naval and military scale, and carried a banner blessed by the Pontiff, under whose approval it set out. **The Spanish Armada (1588).** But neither Pope nor king had correctly gauged the material power of England, or the state of feeling there. The Armada seemed to be doomed to failure from the outset. Under a Catholic admiral, Lord Howard of Effingham, the English fleet proved more than a match for the Spanish Armada. Then came a succession of storms which wrecked a large proportion of its vessels. Besides this, the English Catholics, who were divided in opinion and quite unorganised, gave no sign of rising in unison with the foreign invasion. Before the year had come to an end it was known both at Rome and at Madrid that the Armada had failed, and that the English queen was victorious. Spanish pride was deeply wounded, all the more that they met with little sympathy from the Catholic leaders either in France or at Rome. For a time there was talk of a second Armada, but as a matter of fact the defeat was a decisive one.

Loyal as so many of the Catholics had been, victory for England did not mean any alleviation of the harrowing persecution from which they were suffering. On the contrary, the executions became more numerous, and the prisons became crowded with recusants who had been incarcerated for their Faith. There is no year which furnished so many English martyrs known to us by name as the **Further persecution.**

year of the Armada, 1588. No fewer than eight suffered on the same day, the 28th of August, at Tyburn, Lincoln's Inn Fields, Mile End, Clerkenwell, Southwark, and Hounslow, to be followed two days later by six others. In fact we know the names of thirty-one sent to their death in that one year. But this was far from being the end: there were eight in 1589, eleven in 1590, fifteen in 1591, three in 1592, five in 1593, while the remaining ten years of Elizabeth's reign furnish us with the names of at least fifty-four others. Each one of those names is truly worthy of record, but they make a list too long for the present little book. They may be found for the most part in the inspiring narrative of the Acts of the English Martyrs, though we may reasonably believe that the full tale will not be revealed until the Judgment Day.

The government had doubtless indulged the hope that the terrible prospect of torture and death which was always hanging over the heads of all who dared to exercise the priestly office would act as a strong deterrent to hinder even the boldest from entering on the path which so often ended on the gallows. Yet we do not find that the spring of missionary vocations ran dry even to the end of the persecuting age. There is an estimate, which seems to be a careful one, that at the end of the sixteenth century there were in all about three hundred and sixty-six priests exercising their ministry in England. This number would comprise about fifty survivors of the old priests ordained in the reign of Queen Mary, about three hundred missionaries from the various seminaries on the Continent, and about sixteen fathers of the Society of Jesus. The estimates offered by various writers as to the number of the Catholic laity differ widely from one another, and are not worthy of too great credence. But we may well suppose that they were something between one hundred and twenty thousand, and, as some believe, one third of the whole population.

The foreign policy of Elizabeth came to its climax in the defeat of the Armada. In the political plots and the rivalries of the last years of her reign this history has little concern. The queen had been a Protestant chiefly for reasons of state, and she bitterly resented the growing power of the Puritans towards the end of her life. Those years were years of transition to the contest between the

ELIZABETHAN SETTLEMENT

crown and the Puritans, which was to be the main characteristic of the following reigns. Her old age was one of loneliness and depression. She had no family ties, and her ministers and favourites, Cecil, Walsingham, Leicester, and Essex, died before her. She became more and more out of touch with the nation, and her popularity waned. At last, falling into bad health, she died at Richmond on the 24th of March, 1603, and was buried in Westminster Abbey.

Death of Queen Elizabeth (1603).

XXVIII.

CATHOLICS AND PURITANS.

(A) JAMES I. (1603-1625).

James I. (1603-1625). THE King of Scots, who at Elizabeth's death became King of England by right of descent and also possibly by the will of the late queen, had been baptised a Catholic. The splendid ceremonies, attended by the Scottish bishops in full array, and by the peers in their robes, which marked his christening in 1567, formed the last solemn Catholic function held in Edinburgh. Beaton officiated, and a golden christening bowl given by Queen Elizabeth was used. But the royal infant had soon fallen into the hands of the "Lords of the Congregation," and had been educated in Protestantism. So the Faith, planted in baptism, had never grown to show any visible results, and James was fully committed to the religion of the Reformers. It is true that, seeing what a thorough Catholic his mother, Queen Mary, had been, and how his own life had begun, Catholics could never be to him as they were to those who had never been in the fold. Hence also, it was quite natural for the members of the Catholic Church to cling to the hope that his accession to the English throne would mean to them a new era of liberty and freedom from persecution. But they were doomed to disappointment. This was equally true of the Puritans, who were tempted to look for much from a prince who had been so carefully trained in Calvinistic principles. His classical education had been entrusted to George Buchanan, who was a violent enemy of his pupil's mother, and extremely anti-Catholic, but at the same time was the most polished Scottish scholar of his day. Therefore, this part of his training was very thoroughly done, and James became, if by no means the wisest,

CATHOLICS AND PURITANS 419

certainly the most learned king who had ever reigned in England or in Scotland. But he had also been indoctrinated with Calvinism, and had been kept under the control of the reformed clergy. He had often grown restive under the yoke, but was not man enough to shake himself free. In England, on the contrary, he found Episcopalian clergy pliant and even subservient, and, as a devoted believer in the Divine Right of kings, he had no further use for the Presbytery.

It was not to be expected that the Puritans would give up the contest without a struggle: they had numerous friends in England as well as in Scotland, and they followed up the new king with a petition, presented by a deputation, asking for certain changes in the Prayer Book and Ritual of the Established Church, which were designed to meet their views on doctrine and Church government. James's answer was to invite them to a conference at Hampton Court Palace in the following year, when the matters in dispute could be thrashed out. The king himself presided at the conference, and he was at the height of his glory in displaying his knowledge of theology and of Holy Scripture in such an assembly. **Hampton Court Conference (1604).** But, although a revision of the Prayer Book was readily agreed to, the Puritans could gain little else. James was manifestly on the side opposed to their ideas, and they left the conference disappointed and fearful of the future. In point of fact, when Parliament met, uniformity of ritual was insisted upon in an Act which made deprivation of benefices the penalty for non-compliance with its prescriptions. Some hundreds of ministers were actually deprived of their livings, but their friends in the House of Commons fought these proceedings, as well as any attempted extension of the royal power, with such determination, step by step, that the monarch could see from the very first that both as to Church affairs and as to his theory of regal power he had embarked in a struggle of which no man could see the end.

But there was one point on which the most subservient of Anglicans and the most rebellious of Puritans were at one, and that was hostility to Catholics, and the desire to keep in force the penal legislation of the last reign against them. Hence it came to pass that, together with enactments enforcing anew the existing laws, several new penalties were made, which drove the Catholics well-nigh to desperation. The fine of twenty pounds a month for non-attendance at the Anglican Service, which James was considered to have forgiven, was again demanded, and the king pretended that he had never really forgiven it, but merely delayed claiming it. This was enough to reduce to beggary even many in moderately affluent circumstances. James made use of the fines thus exacted as a means of rewarding his needy Scottish dependants. It need hardly be wondered at that the prospect of ruin and the failure of their long cherished hopes should have driven some of the less conscientious characters into wild and criminal plots.

The Gunpowder Plot (1605). The darkest of these was the well-known Gunpowder Plot. The chief conspirator and inventor of this sanguinary design was a member of the landed gentry in Northamptonshire, William Catesby, who, having led a wild and irregular life in his youth, became a Protestant for a while, and then, reverting to Catholicism, shared in the designs of the Spanish party among his co-religionists to impede the succession of James I. At last, becoming convinced that no help was to be expected from the Continent, and that without foreign help insurrection would be hopeless, foreseeing also that a new storm of persecution was already threatening, he conceived the desperate plan of blowing up the Houses of Parliament with gunpowder at the opening of the session, thus involving in one common destruction King, Lords, and Commons: in fact, as he imagined, all who were responsible for the laws against the Catholics. The number of the conspirators was not large, and the dangerous task of firing the mine was entrusted to a professional soldier named Guy Fawkes, while Catesby engaged to organise a simultaneous rising in Northamptonshire. However, before the date fixed for the opening of the Parliament, knowledge of what was intended came to the royal ministers through the correspondence of Francis Tresham, one of the conspirators, who wished to save the life of his relative, Lord Monteagle, from the common destruction of the peers. Hence, on the night of the 5th of November, 1605, the cellars under the Parliament were occupied by an armed force, and Guy

Fawkes was caught with the apparatus of his intended murderous project. The danger was thus averted, and efforts were made to seize the other conspirators. Catesby and three of his companions fell fighting against their capture at Holbeach House in Worcestershire, but Guy Fawkes and four others were taken to prison. Three Jesuits, Fathers Garnet, the Provincial, Greenway and Gerard, were likewise apprehended on suspicion of being implicated, and every possible effort was made to prove them guilty. Father John Gerard, after hairbreadth escapes and perilous adventures, succeeded in effecting his passage into freedom from the Tower of London. The story of his sufferings and of his dangers forms a romantic and vivid picture of the life of a missionary of those days. It fell out quite otherwise with Father Garnet, who was at the time Superior of the Jesuits on the English mission. After his arrest in the company of Father Oldcorne at Hindlip Hall in Worcestershire on the 31st of January, 1606, every effort was made by the agents of the government to incriminate him in the plot. Both he and Father Oldcorne were committed to the Tower of London, and then Father Garnet was craftily told that the cells in which he and his fellow-Jesuits were kept were so near that it was possible for them to speak to one another through a chink in the wall. Not suspecting that they were overheard, they went to confession to one another, and then went on to speak of the plot. Garnet said that there was but one man in the world who could speak against him on that matter. Both Garnet and Oldcorne were repeatedly examined, and both were tortured to induce them to confess. Garnet denied that he had favoured the plot in any way, but admitted that the one person he was speaking of to Oldcorne was Father Greenway (or Tesimond). He then confessed that he knew of the plot, and had endeavoured to dissuade the conspirators from it. However, he was condemned to death on his confession of this, which was called " misprision of treason." There was some delay between the sentence and the execution, but he was hanged in St Paul's Churchyard on the 3rd of May, 1606. Father Oldcorne had already suffered the same penalty at Red Hill, Worcester, on the 7th of April, after all efforts to connect him with the plot had failed. He suffered therefore merely for the crime of being a priest. With him was likewise executed the Venerable Ralph Ashby, who was probably a Jesuit lay brother. As for Father Greenway, or Tesimond as he is sometimes called, he effected his escape to the Continent, and died at Naples, leaving an interesting autobiographical sketch of his mission.

The immediate consequence of the Gunpowder Plot was the infliction of heavy fines on the three Catholic noblemen already imprisoned in the Tower on suspicion, Lords Stourton, Mordaunt, and Montague, but it had a more general result, which told on the whole body of the faithful in the enactment of a new Penal Code. The Parliament of 1606 had first to provide for the king's pecuniary resources, depleted by his extravagant manner of living, and by the lavish gifts made to his favourites, but it then proceeded at great length to enact a new code of Penal Laws against the Catholics. It was not that one iota of the Elizabethan enactments was repealed, but in addition to these the zeal of the Puritan bigots managed to incorporate in two bills a whole system of persecution, far more extensive than the severe laws already in force.

New Penal Code (1606).

(1) Catholics were forbidden to appear at court, or within ten miles of London, or anywhere further than five miles from their usual place of residence.
(2) They were debarred from practising or acting as physicians, surgeons, lawyers, patrons of livings, trustees or guardians.
(3) Husbands and wives could not derive any pecuniary benefit from the property of one another.
(4) Anyone sent beyonds the seas for education was disinherited until he should conform to the Established Church.
(5) Right of search was given over Catholic houses with authority to seize any property having reference to the religion of the inmate, while at an order from the magistrates a Catholic must yield up his horses and weapons.
(6) The penalties for absence from church were strengthened by the provision that the king might take at will either the existing fine or two-thirds of the personal and all the real estate.
(7) A new Oath of Allegiance was given forth with the

added penalty of perpetual imprisonment with forfeiture of much of their goods for all who should refuse to take it.

The new Oath of Allegiance was drawn up with a view to creating dissension among the Catholics themselves. Its terms required a formal renunciation of the so-called deposing power of the Roman Pontiff. This was a matter on which there was not unanimity of opinion, and fatal divisions ensued. Some held that this aspect of the temporal power of the Pope might be lawfully abjured, while others maintained that it could not in conscience be renounced in the language employed in the oath. For those taking it had to swear that it was "impious, heretical, and damnable" as a doctrine. Very likely James, who was not naturally of a severe or blood-thirsty character, meant gradually to free those who took the oath from the grevious burden of the Penal Laws. But, however this may be, Pope Paul V. sent a secret envoy to the king, expressing his abhorrence of the Gunpowder Plot, and endeavouring to negotiate for the relief of the Catholics. The envoy was received by James, but failed to come to a satisfactory understanding with him. Still, he utilised his stay in England to make inquiries concerning the Oath of Allegiance, which was defended by Blackwell, the archpriest, but vehemently attacked by the Jesuits and others, who urged the need of taking strong action, if the last remains of Catholicism were not to disappear out of the land. It was not long before Paul V. issued a brief condemning the oath, and declaring that it was unlawful for Catholics to take it. However, the controversy was far from being ended, since the defenders of the oath now contended that the brief only represented the Pontiff's private opinion, and did not bind in conscience. The archpriest, Blackwell, declined to publish the brief, and he himself made no difficulty about taking the oath when it was tendered to him. His compliance did not save him from sharing in the persecution which broke out through the resentment of the king at the papal action. He was not, indeed, called upon to suffer the extreme penalty, as was the priest, Robert Drury, who was executed at Tyburn as a traitor on the 26th of February, 1607. But he was apprehended

New Oath of Allegiance.

The Archpriest Blackwell.

and imprisoned, first in the Gatehouse, and then in the
Clink for the rest of his life. All this time he persisted
in his view, though both Bellarmin and Parsons wrote
endeavouring to persuade him that he was in error. All
this correspondence he handed to the government, and
there can be no doubt that his adherence to his opinion
was counted by King James as a victory. Yet, so great
was the prejudice of the anti-Catholic party in Parliament that the monarch was unable to give effect to his
wish that Blackwell should be liberated from prison. He
could and did hinder his being brought to trial on the
charge of having been ordained beyond the seas, but
in prison Blackwell had to remain until his life came to
an end in 1613.

Long before death came to put an end to the captivity
of Blackwell, the Holy See had taken action upon his
refusal to condemn the oath. On the 1st of February,
1608, he was superseded as archpriest by George
Birkhead, who thus became the second head
of the English mission. He was but a few
years junior to Blackwell, and had had a
somewhat similar career. He enjoyed
almost universal respect for his tact and
conciliatory disposition, and during the six years for
which he filled the office of archpriest, did his best to
try and heal the division amongst the flock, which the
action of Blackwell and the vehemence of his opponents
had provoked. Those who refused the oath were in a
majority, but, on the other hand, all the twenty Catholic
peers, with the exception of Lord Teynham, took it, as
well as others of lower degree. Birkhead died in 1614,
the year following the death of Blackwell. His assistants
then took it upon themselves to nominate the learned Dr
Anthony Champeney, who had supported Blackwell in
his controversies, but having heard the nuncios in France
and Flanders, the Holy See set this aside, and in 1615
appointed Dr William Harrison as the third archpriest
of the English mission. As the clergy had been petitioning the Pope for the re-establishment of episcopal
government in England this prolongation of rule by an
archpriest must have been a disappointment to them.
But Harrison was personally acceptable, and had already
won a high reputation both for prudence and for learning. He was able to point to intimate relations of

*The Arch-
priests Birk-
head and
Harrison.*

friendship both with Archpriest Blackwell and with the Jesuit Superior, Father Parsons. This latter friendship did not, however, prevent him from getting the Jesuit confessor removed from Douay College, or from having the students withdrawn from the Jesuit classes there. He had not been long in his office as archpriest when he became convinced that the only means of securing peace and progress for the Church in England would be the restoration of episcopal government. He, as well as Drs Bishop, Smith and Champeney, addressed memorials to the Holy See, petitioning that this boon should be granted. Eventually, the reply was a favourable one, for in 1623 Dr William Bishop was appointed to the see of Chalcedon with this object in view. Harrison seems to have made his chief place of residence at the princely mansion of Cowdray, the seat of Lord Montague. But he did not live to see the appointment of a Vicar-Apostolic, dying in 1621, when he was about to start to Rome to press still more urgently for the change which was so generally desired.

An opportunity for relieving the sufferings of the English Catholics seemed to come upon the horizon in 1616, when negotiations were seriously undertaken for a marriage between Prince Charles, the heir apparent to the English throne, and the sister of the King of Spain. **The Spanish Marriage Treaty.** There had been little shedding of the blood of Catholics for several years, but the fines and other penal exactions were so constant that King James derived from them an income of thirty-six thousand pounds a year. Moreover, the prisons were full of recusants on account of the Faith, both priests and laity. When these were liberated in 1616 as a first preliminary for a treaty with Spain, it was found that they numbered no fewer than four thousand persons. For political reasons the proposed marriage recommended itself both to the court of Spain and to that of England. But the religious question loomed large in the front rank of difficulties. However, through the assiduity of Gondomar, Spanish ambassador in England, and of Digby, the English envoy to Spain, an agreement was drawn up in twenty articles directed towards securing for the princess the free exercise of her religion. James was further induced to promise that he would grant the English Catholics every indulgence in his power, and would send no more priests to execution for the exercise of their ministry. A further difficulty arose from the necessity of obtaining a papal dispensation for the mixed marriage. The King of Spain undertook to obtain this, but James had also his secret agent in Rome in the person of John Bennett, a secular priest who was acting as the representative of the clergy in the matter of the appointment of a bishop. The Pontiff said that King James promised much, but had performed little. Let him act up to his promises, and the dispensation would be granted. James thereupon directed pardons for recusancy to be granted to all Catholics who should apply for them within five years. Prince Charles, with his favourite, the Duke of Buckingham, then proceeded to Spain, where they were received with every demonstration of joy and honour. Yet the project never became an accomplished fact. The provisions of the Marriage Treaty were discussed again, and after delay revised again and again, the Spanish minister, Olivarez, striving to take advantage of the presence of Prince Charles to win better terms for Spain and for Catholicism. But the delay was fatal to success. Charles indeed was won over, at least in appearance, but Buckingham became hostile; and then the marriage was not popular in England, partly from the very fact that it involved peace towards the co-religionists of the Spanish bride. So the arrangements were broken off at the last moment, and Charles and Buckingham returned to England. The disappointment of King James was deep. Being now forced to meet his Parliament for a vote of supplies, he put all the blame of the failure on the Spanish court, and to appease the charge of having promised indulgence to the Catholics, declared that during the whole time he had never thought or intended to dispense with any of the Penal Laws. A proclamation was now issued commanding all the missionaries to leave the country under penalty of death, while the magistrates all over the country were exhorted to put in force the Penal Laws in the accustomed fashion. In London the Lord Mayor received instructions to arrest any English Catholics who were found coming from Mass in the ambassadors' chapels, and Parliament was asked to advise as to the means of educating in the reformed religion the children of all who were proved to be recusants.

CATHOLICS AND PURITANS

Meanwhile, the first bishop appointed for the needs of the faithful had received his consecration. This was Dr William Bishop, who was henceforward known as the Bishop of Chalcedon. Born about 1553, he had been sent to Oxford for his education, though a Catholic, but found the tone and bigotry then prevailing at the University so distasteful to him that after a few years he decided to quit the hall in which he was studying, and proceeded to the English College at Rouen, where he took the mission oath in 1579. In 1581, probably after his ordination, he left Rome for the English mission with William Smith, George Haydock, and Humphrey Maxfield. He had not been long in the country before he was arrested and sent to prison. Being banished to the Continent, he lived for some years in Paris, taking his degree at the Sorbonne. He then made a second attempt to lead the missionary life, but was a second time arrested and banished. Going to Rome as representative of the secular clergy in their dispute with the Jesuits, he was shut up in the English College for three months as a promoter of faction, but after being liberated once more returned to England, where in company with twelve other priests he made a Protest of Allegiance to Queen Elizabeth. In spite of this he was a third time imprisoned, but, as soon as he was released, went to France, where he resided in a community of secular clergy at Arras. When in 1621 the repeated petitions of the secular clergy for a bishop began to bear fruit, William Bishop was looked upon as the most suitable person to fill the office, and in 1623 he was consecrated to the see of Chalcedon *in partibus infidelium*, as Ordinary Bishop for England and Scotland. On the last day of July he landed at Dover, and thence went in turn to the residences of Lady Dormer and Lord Montague. He then resided in London in the greatest retirement that was possible, taking every precaution to avoid inflaming popular passion or embarrassing the government. He did not consider himself as a Vicar-Apostolic so much as an Ordinary, pointing to the words of his brief of appointment, but this view was hardly sustained at Rome, where his successor was made unequivocally a Vicar-Apostolic. He wrote several controversial tracts, both in controversy with the Arch-

[margin: Bishop William Bishop, the Vicar-Apostolic.]

bishop of Canterbury, Dr Abbot, and in that with the
Jesuits. But his bearing was so conciliatory that he won
the respect both of seculars and regulars. He also
constituted a chapter of twenty-four canons headed by
a dean, and divided the country into archdeaconries.
But his career as bishop was an exceedingly brief one,
for on the 16th of April, 1624, he died at Bishop's Court,
the residence of Sir Basil Brooke, and the Holy See had
once more the task of filling the vacancy which was
thereby caused in the English clergy.

A second matrimonial scheme before the death of King
James once more brought the affairs of the Church into
prominence. This was the plan for a marriage between
Prince Charles and Henrietta Maria, sister of the French
king. As soon as ever the negotiations with Spain were
formally broken off, the Earl of Carlisle and Lord
Kensington opened proposals to this effect in Paris, as
ambassadors of the English king. Urban VIII. and
Philip of Spain both tried to dissuade Louis XIII.
from giving his consent to the match, but in vain. It
appeared to the French king and his advisers to offer
solid advantages to France. But the religious difficulty
rose up as imperiously as in the case of Spain, and
Richelieu, the French minister, refused to be content
with any lesser measure of concession to the Catholics
than had been promised to the Spaniards. This put
James into an unenviable position. He had but recently
agreed to the enforcement of the Penal Laws, and now
was called upon to come back upon all this again, and
guarantee indulgence and toleration. Various devices
were suggested to overcome the obstacle. At last the
French king and his ministers professed themselves contented with a public treaty arranging the terms of the
marriage, the freedom of the princess to practice her
religion, and the provision that she should have the
custody of her children until they were thirteen years
of age. But this had to be supplemented by a secret
undertaking signed by James, by Prince Charles, and by
the Secretary of State, promising the main body of
Catholics even greater concessions than they would have
gained under the terms of the Spanish match. After
King Louis had sworn to use the whole power of France
to enforce this if the English king should recede from
his engagement, the papal dispensation for the marriage

CATHOLICS AND PURITANS

was given. But James did not live to see the matter concluded, for on the 27th of March, 1625, he died after receiving Communion according to the rite of the Anglican Church.

(B) CHARLES I. AND THE COMMONWEALTH (1625-1660).

When Charles I. became king at the death of his father on the 27th of March, 1625, he found the Puritans in great strength in the House of Commons, and at least equally so in the country at large. They were grimly determined to use their power for a thorough new reformation of Church and State according to the opinions of their sect. And when they ranged themselves in hostile array against Catholic influence and life, they were reinforced by the Anglican or so-called Country Party. Hence, at the beginning of the reign, after a day of public fasting and humiliation, the Commons presented a petition to the king, praying that the Penal Laws against the Catholic recusants and their clergy might be put in force. This demand brought King Charles into an immediate difficulty. He had just married a Catholic princess, he had signed a secret treaty which covenanted to give her co-religionists an indulgence with regard to the practice of their Faith, and he was surrounded with Catholic noblemen, both from the Continent and from the different parts of his own dominions. What was he to do? He followed the path of least resistance, and ignoring the secret treaty, put the Penal Laws into execution as far as was needed to satisfy the bigots. The King of France at once protested, but in vain; the opportunist sovereign was not ashamed to declare that the treaty had only been a device to procure the consent of the Pope to his marriage.

Charles I. and the Catholics.

One result of this crooked policy was that there were quarrels between the king and his consort as early as 1627, and both religion and national feeling were combined to keep these alive. For Henrietta Maria had a practically foreign court, made up in great part of Frenchmen, who were at the same time Catholics. This provided a double grievance, one for the national patriots against the influence of foreigners, and another for the religious bigots, owing to the presence of ecclesiastics of the Church of Rome. At one time all these personages to the number of sixty were sent home to France, six English ladies, four of whom were Protestants, being named to wait upon the queen. However, the King of France expressed his resentment at the treatment thus meted out to his sister in such forcible fashion that there was talk of a possible declaration of war on his part. An envoy named Bassompierre was sent from France to discuss the position of the queen, and he very skilfully effected a reconciliation between Charles and Henrietta Maria. He also secured for the queen a more suitable establishment. It was arranged that henceforward her household should consist partly of French and partly of English attendants. A French bishop, two confessors, and ten other priests were to be admitted. In addition to the Chapel in St James's Palace, another at Somerset House was to be provided for the queen's use. The arrangement thus made, in spite of Puritan abhorrence, persisted until the year 1643. But during all this period Catholics of English birth were supposed to be rigidly excluded from the services in the Royal Chapel.

Queen Henrietta's Catholic Court.

Meanwhile, ecclesiastical government within the fold had undergone a change, which was considerable in outward seeming, but in practical operation left things much as they had been in the preceding reigns. Dr William Bishop died before King James, and it was at once determined to name a successor to carry on his work. The choice of the Holy See fell upon one of the best known of the English clergy of the day, Dr Richard Smith, who was given the same title of "Chalcedon" which his predecessor had held. Born in Lincolnshire in 1583, he left Trinity College, Oxford, for Rome, whence he proceeded to the English College at Valladolid. Here and at Seville he taught philosophy and controversy; he then distinguished himself as agent in Rome for the English clergy from 1606 to 1609. Then, after a brief period on the mission in his native land, we find him at the head of the community of English controversialists, who were housed at Arras

Bishop Richard Smith (1567-1655).

CATHOLICS AND PURITANS 431

College in the University of Paris. It was during this period that most of his works were produced. They included "*Florum Historiæ Ecclesiasticæ gentis Anglorum*," "Life of Lady Montague," "On the Distinction of Fundamental and Non-Fundamental Points of Faith," treatises on "Confession," "Confirmation," and on other matters of Christian doctrine. Coming to England after his consecration, he claimed to exercise all the powers of a bishop according to the decrees of the Council of Trent. This brought him into sharp collision with the regular clergy and their supporters, who argued that he was only a papal vicar with just the limited faculties accorded to him by the Holy See. The dispute came to the ears of the agents of the government, and the latter was urged to issue orders for the bishop's arrest in December, 1628, and March, 1629. The Pope also intervened in the controversy, and suspended several of the bishop's regulations. Dr Smith came to the conclusion that until a decision was given in his favour it was useless for him to remain in England. He therefore retired to France in 1631, and offered to resign his office. The offer was accepted, and the Holy See declined henceforth to recognise him or the chapter appointed by his predecessor. The rule of a Vicar-Apostolic was by no means welcome to the regular missioners, who feared that the extent of their ample faculties would be thereby limited. Dr Smith therefore accepted the Abbey of Charroux in France, and there seemed to be small chance of his return being feasible.

Under these circumstances the Holy See considered that the best step to take would be to send a diplomatic envoy to England, who might report both upon the unfortunate differences between the Vicar-Apostolic and the regular clergy, and also give the Pope a good general account of the state of religion in the country. The trusty agent despatched on this mission in 1632 was Gregorio Panzani, whose report, which is still extant, gives an interesting summary of the state of religious affairs in the earlier part of the reign of Charles I. Panzani estimates the total number of Catholics at one hundred and fifty thousand, which comes much nearer to our present proportion than would at first appear, for the

The Panzani Mission (1632).

total population of the country being then only about five million, Catholics would be nearly one in thirty. The priests, including both seculars and regulars, he counts at about eight hundred. He names, as amongst the most notable members of the Church, the Earls of Shrewsbury, Worcester, Rivers, and Castlehaven, Viscount Montague, and Lords Petre, Morley, Arundell, Teynham, Abergavenny, Vaux, Windsor, and Baltimore. But he hazards the guess that there are many others who endeavour to be reconciled on their death-bed, and even keep a priest in their house in order to be secure of being able to accomplish this. Queen Henrietta's chaplain or almoner, he says, is the French Bishop of Angoulême, and in the public chapel which she maintains, as well as the private one in her palace, a full round of services is kept up with splendid music and ceremonial by the French Oratorians, or at another time by the Capuchin Friars. He declares that the king and court are present on the occasions when high festival is kept. He likewise bears testimony to the gradual adoption of Catholic rites on the part of the High Church Anglican clergy, as well as of an approximation to Catholic doctrine. He laments the hostility of the Puritans, whom he estimates to be more than half of the nation. He then goes into some detail as to the difficulties, weaknesses, and manner of life of the various missionaries, and notifies the Holy See of the prevailing irregularities in administering the Sacraments and other rites of religion. On the whole he is in favour of the appointment of a bishop, and asserts that Queen Henrietta is of the same opinion, but he fears that it may not at the moment be feasible on account of the opposition of King Charles, who had been sounded on the subject through a friendly minister of state. The result was that the Holy See took no further steps in the matter. Dr Smith continued to live in France for the rest of his prolonged life, dying in the house of the English Augustinians at Paris in 1655 at the age of eighty-eight. By that time Oliver Cromwell was already in power, and for the next thirty years no appointment was made to the vacant vicariate, though during that interval several petitions were forwarded to Rome asking for the nomination of a bishop to rule the English Catholics either as Ordinary or as Vicar-Apostolic.

CATHOLICS AND PURITANS

Meanwhile, in proportion as the power of the Puritans increased and that of the king declined, the persecution became more violent. Charles I. could never have been a willing oppressor of his wife's co-religionists, but he did not, or could not, do much to mitigate the storm. The faithlessness with which he was charged in his conduct in dealing with the constitutional demands of the people may be urged with even greater truth against his treatment of his Catholic subjects. Yet in both cases he was face to face with an obstinate and fierce resistance. Sometimes it is hardly realised, especially in reading histories in sympathy with the opposition which the absolutism of Charles I. evoked in civil matters, how very anti-Catholic the movement was. Bigotry and republicanism did not always exist in equal measure in the same individual, but while some fought for civil liberty in the first place, and were only persecutors in a secondary sense, believing Catholicism to be inseparably mixed up with the royal pretensions, others were not ashamed to put their hatred of the Catholic religion in the first place. They denounced it and all toleration of it in the most violent language, and were ever on the watch for any relaxation on the part of the king or his ministers in applying any of the savage provisions of the Penal Code. The effect of this was to throw the faithful children of the Church far more generally into the king's camp in the Civil War than would otherwise have been likely. They became anxious to prove their loyalty, and had perforce to see in the overthrow of the Puritans the defeat of their bitterest enemies. On the other hand, during the early stages of the conflict, there was considerable hesitation on the part of Charles and his Cavalier supporters in availing themselves of the proffered assistance. There was bigotry, and there was hatred of Catholicism, in the royal ranks as well as among their opponents. It was only as the war proceeded, and the royal difficulties increased, that the king was only too glad to obtain support from any quarter. Under this pressure the disabilities and restrictions against them were ignored or suspended, and Charles found that he had no more faithful followers. But, considering what had gone on before, it is nothing short of marvellous how the noblemen and squires levied their dependants

Persecution through the Puritans.

and fought with obstinate valour in the armies of Prince Rupert and of the Marquess of Newcastle. Several of the most romantic episodes of the Civil War are to be found in the defences of their ancestral castles by Catholics against the besieging forces of the Parliament. It was in this way that Raglan was held by the Marquess of Worcester, and Basing Hall also, which was another of his seats. Wardour Castle, Wilts, was held for Lord Arundell, who was absent in the royal army, by the brave Lady Blanche Arundell, and though at the time surrendered, was afterwards retaken by her son, and blown up with a mine, that it might not fall as a fortress into the hands of the Parliamentary army. Such instances might be multiplied. And with the sacrifice of lives and homes went also immense gifts and loans of money to fill the depleted coffers of the king. It is sad to have to record that both in the case of Catholics, and of many other Cavaliers, these obligations were afterwards but imperfectly requited, and men who had impoverished themselves to fight for the king were allowed to ask in vain for an adequate recompense when the royal cause was again triumphant.

Catholics in the Civil War.

The earlier part of the reign of Charles I. passed with very little addition being made to the white-robed army of English martyrs. The case of Father Arrowsmith, who was a Jesuit, was exceptional. This zealous missioner, the son of a Lancashire yeoman, was born in that county in 1585, and being most piously brought up by his mother, Margaret Gerard, passed into the English College at Douay in 1605. He came upon the mission in 1613, and was sent to labour in his native county. It was only in 1624 that he entered the Society of Jesus. Owing to the troubles of the times, he made his novitiate by means of a spiritual retreat spent in retirement in Essex, and then went back to work in his former missionary field. He was apprehended at the end of the reign of King James, but was released again when so many Catholics found at least passing relief on occasion of the negotiations for the Spanish marriage of Prince Charles. However, his space of freedom was not to be of long duration, for in 1628 he was again seized, and this time the captivity ended in his glorious martyrdom. He

English martyrs of the reign.

was tried before Justice Yelverton at Lancaster. A servant of the judge, and a boy of twelve years of age, said to be the judge's son, were the witnesses against him that he had striven to persuade them to be Catholics. Two others, whose immoral lives he had denounced, deposed that he was a Jesuit. On this evidence he was condemned to death as a traitor, and went to his martyrdom rejoicing. He was hanged, drawn, and quartered on the 28th of August, 1628, and his head, fixed upon a pole, was set upon the battlements of Lancaster Castle. His hand has been preserved as a precious relic at the Catholic Church of Ashton-in-Makerfield, and many miraculous cures are attributed to its touch. On the following day at the same place suffered the stalwart layman, Richard Herst. In a scuffle which occurred at his apprehension a man named Dewhurst was accidentally killed, and hence an excuse was found to add the charge of wilful murder to the recusancy for which he was apprehended. But, though found guilty against all likelihood and justice, he was offered his life if he would forswear his religion. He stoutly refused this, saying that for his Faith he would give a thousand lives if he had them. The sentence was then allowed to stand, and he joined the white-robed army of martyrs.

Yet, in spite of these occasional martyrdoms and the constant activity of the pursuivants, who visited, and the magistrates who fined, the Catholics of England, it must be admitted that the persecution during the reign of Charles I. was less severe than under either of his two predecessors. The zeal of the missionaries was unremitting, and they were in considerable numbers. Hence it came to pass that, besides a large number of individuals in the lower ranks of life, notable men not a few were reconciled with the Church in the reign of Charles I. Among these must be noted John Sergeant, who afterwards became well known for his controversial work, Sir George Calvert, *Caroline Converts.* created Lord Baltimore, who afterwards became the founder of the Catholic American Colony of Maryland, Sir John Matthews, the celebrated scholar, who lived in retirement, but in safety, until a ripe old age, and Dom Cressy, the Benedictine, who had been chaplain to Lord Falkland, and becoming a Catholic and a priest, devoted himself to Catholic historical work.

Walter, Lord Montague, son of the Earl of Manchester, was employed on several secret embassies to France and Spain under the administration of Buckingham, and became a Catholic in 1635. He afterwards joined the Benedictines, having been a zealous supporter of the Cavalier cause in the Civil War against the Puritans. He suffered imprisonment in the Tower at the hands of the Parliament, but being liberated, retired to France, where he was made Abbot of Pontoise, and died in 1677. He is the author of the "*Shepherds' Calendar,*" a comedy, and several other works. Baron Cottington, who was in the early part of Charles I.'s reign one of his chief ministers, a supporter of the Spanish alliance against the policy of Buckingham, also became a Catholic, though he reverted to the Anglican Church for a time. He was exempted by name from the indemnity at the end of the Civil War, and followed Prince Charles abroad, where he became one of his chief advisers. He had probably been a Catholic at heart ever since 1623, but at any rate he was reconciled to the Church before he died in 1653. He was buried after the Restoration in Westminster Abbey. Alongside of these men is also to be counted the only bishop of an Anglican see who hitherto has made his submission to the Holy See. This was Dr Godfrey Goodman, Bishop of Gloucester (1583-1656), who was marked out for early preferment as nephew of the Dean of Westminster. He became chaplain to Queen Anne of Denmark, but soon became well known for his teaching on the Real Presence and other points of Catholic doctrine. Strong objection was taken to this by the Protestant leaders, and even Archbishop Laud and the High Churchmen found fault with him. He refused to sign the new canons drawn up by Convocation under Laud's direction. However, when under the pressure of deprivation and prison he did so, he fell under the displeasure of the Puritan Parliament, and was again incarcerated at their order. In 1643 he was made to retire from the see of Gloucester and became a Catholic. He was able to live in retirement at Westminster, under the spiritual direction of the Franciscan, Father Davenport. He was buried near the font in St Margaret's Parish Church in that city.

The Catholic tendencies of Goodman were not shared

to the full by the High Church divines of King Charles, and yet on the part of the majority of them there was considerable revival of Catholic doctrine and even ritual. The leader of this school of divines was William Laud (1573-1645), who first took a prominent place in the affairs of the Anglican Church at the accession of Charles I. *[margin: Caroline High Churchmen.]* He had been in conflict with the Puritan views of Abbot, Archbishop of Canterbury, for the greater part of the preceding reign, and when Abbot fell under the royal displeasure, and was practically suspended, he was one of the five commissioners who supplied his place. Then, when Abbot died, he succeeded him as archbishop. He considered the Anglican Church as part of the Catholic Church, but would not submit to the Holy See. Another of his contemporaries, Richard Montague, Bishop of Norwich, went further, and is supposed to have told Panzani that he thought reunion with Rome quite feasible. He wrote on the " Eucharistic Sacrifice." Laud was the main driving force, both in the attempt to force Episcopalian government on the Presbyterians in Scotland, and in imposing uniformity of worship upon the Puritans in England, and for these reasons incurred their undying hatred. The Long Parliament in 1643 impeached him for high treason, but though sent to the Tower, he was not tried until 1644. Naturally enough Charles I. was most averse to the trial taking place. At last, however, he was tried and condemned, and in 1645 beheaded on Tower Hill. With him must also be counted William Juxon, his successor, both at London and later on at Canterbury. He it was who attended Charles I. on the scaffold, and was made primate at the Restoration. Jeremy Taylor, though he never was promoted to an English diocese, and was in some things latitudinarian in his views, may in the main be called one of the Caroline High Churchmen. Laud was his patron, and it was through his influence that he became one of the chaplains of Charles I. Afterwards he received the see of Dromore in Ireland. He is one of the most eloquent and stately writers of prose that the English language has produced. On the one side the movement championed by these men may be looked on as an effort to counteract the effect of the papal invitations to union, suggested through the mission of Panzani, and by the numerous conversions to Catholicism which took place about that time. On the other side, it would seem to be a phase of that counter-reformation which by this time had done its work on the Continent of Europe, and could not fail to evoke sympathetic chords even in a land so cut off from the centre of Christianity as England was.

Martyrs under the Long Parliament (1640-1644).
The fresh outburst of persecution which followed the meeting of the Long Parliament in 1640 must, of course, be attributed, not to King Charles and his advisers, but to the Puritans who predominated in that assembly. It scarcely met before it gave proof of its blind hostility to the Church. It complained of the king's having shown indulgence to the recusants. It found that commissions had been given to Catholics in the army, and that Catholic soldiers had been levied in Ireland. Hence the orders issued in the king's name that all Catholics should leave the court, that the army should be purged of their presence, and that priests should go into banishment really came from the pressure exerted by the Commons. Already, in 1640, John Goodman received sentence of death for having taken orders in the Church of Rome, but in spite of petitions from both Houses for his execution, Charles refused to sign the warrant for his execution. He was willing to imprison him, but left the responsibility of his death upon the Parliament. Goodman wrote, offering his life as a peace offering to reconcile king and Commons. However, the Parliament then shrank from taking his execution upon themselves, and Goodman was incarcerated in Newgate, where he died in 1645. But as the years went on the blood of Catholics was shed without scruple. In 1641 the Venerable Edward Barlow, a Benedictine, suffered at Lancaster, while the Venerable William Ward, a Franciscan, was executed at Tyburn in the same year. Not long after, Father Bartholomew Roe, O.S.B., and Father Reynolds or Green, both mounted the gallows at Tyburn. The year 1642 was still richer in martyrs. Foremost among these may be placed the aged Yorkshire priest, John Lockwood or Lascelles, who is said to have worked on the English mission for no fewer than forty-four years before the day of his execution in company with another younger priest, John Catterick. The quarters of these brave champions were exposed, their heads being

fixed on poles at two of the bars of York city. In the same year the Franciscans had a noble martyr in the person of Father Thomas Bullaker, while the Jesuit Society contributed their share through the execution of Father Thomas Holland. Both these suffered at Tyburn. At the same place was likewise executed the secular priest, Edward Morgan. Next year also was not without its glorious example of constancy until death, for in April the Franciscan, Henry Heath, a zealous convert from Protestantism, but lately sent on the English mission, was condemned and executed as a traitor at Tyburn, and the last month of the year witnessed the martyrdom in the same place of Father Arthur Bell, likewise a son of St Francis. Then came the martyrdom of two secular priests, who were executed together on the 7th of September, 1644; these were the Venerable Ralph Corby and the Venerable John Duckett. Five months later the same Tyburn Cross was the scene of the triumph over death of the Jesuit, Venerable Henry Morse. Not one of these brave champions of the Faith should be passed over, but it is not easy to make the list complete. A priest, named Price, was shot by the Parliamentary soldiers, after the taking of Lincoln in 1644, with no form of trial on his bare confession that he was a Catholic. But besides those mentioned above, and others whose martyrdoms cannot all be told here, several others under sentence of death expired in the filthy dungeons of the prisons in which they were confined. Others again were caught by the soldiery in the open country, and in one way or another tortured to death. No doubt by this time the cause of the Church and that of the Cavaliers had become inextricably woven together in the minds of the republican Puritans, and no fewer than one hundred and seventy Catholic gentlemen were killed in the Civil War fighting for the king.

Long before Charles I. had been executed at Whitehall all real power had passed into the hands of the Parliament. In this assembly the Presbyterians at first had a majority, and used all their influence to promote uniformity of religion, based upon an abjuration of both prelacy and of Catholicism. The clergy of the Established Church were all ejected from their benefices, while Catholics were condemned to the forfeiture of two-thirds of their goods as a penalty for their recusancy. It was then with a sigh of relief that both the one and the other saw the supremacy pass into the hands of the Congregationalists or Independents. But, loudly as these latter had proclaimed themselves the champions of religious freedom, their advent to power brought no alleviation of the hard lot of the faithful. They did indeed repeal the Acts enforcing attendance at the Church, but refused toleration either to Episcopalians or to Catholics. In 1650 an Act was passed offering rewards for the seizure of priests and Jesuits equal to those for the capture of highwaymen. In consequence, Catholic houses were searched, and many priests caught and tried, and then found worthy of the death sentence. In most cases, indeed, the authorities refrained from inflicting it, but instead, exiled them from England, and trusted to the pressure of financial exactions to crush the life out of the laity. But there were exceptions. Such was not the fate of Father Peter Wright, S.J., chaplain to the Catholic Marquis of Winchester, who was sentenced to death, and suffered with heroic gladness and courage at Tyburn on the 19th of May, 1651. Neither was it the lot of the veteran missioner, John Southworth, who had earlier in life, while on the Lancashire mission, given the last absolution to the martyr, Father Arrowsmith. This good priest was apprehended in the first year of Cromwell's Protectorate, and executed at Tyburn on the 28th of June, 1654.

The general effect of the break up of the power of the Long Parliament by Oliver Cromwell and the substitution for it of the military dictatorship was anarchy in religious matters for the bulk of the nation. With the repeal of the Acts enforcing attendance at the Presbyterian worship came also the proclamation of liberty of worship, or of "prophesying," as they phrased it, which resulted in the encouragement of innumerable small conventicles led in prayer and preaching by laymen, sometimes fanatical soldiers, sometimes religious enthusiasts among the civilians. But from this freedom papists and prelatists were excluded by name. The Independents, as these sectaries who favoured the formation of free autonomous congregations under a preacher chosen by themselves were called, forbore indeed in the main to shed the blood of Catholics or of Episcopalians, but they

The Commonwealth and Catholics.

plundered and harassed them almost at will. The sequestrations carried out under the authority of military warrants were drastic enough to reduce the most opulent to poverty, and to drive the poor to actual want and beggary. Every petition for indulgence was contemptuously rejected, while, as a further means of showing hatred to all that reminded men of the Catholicity of their forefathers, the most venerable and historic buildings which England possessed were ruthlessly defaced by the Puritan soldiery. Crosses were broken up, the statues of the saints on the walls of churches and cathedrals were torn down and destroyed, many noble buildings were reduced to a state of ruin. Almost the only thing left to record the memory of the usurpation of Cromwell and his army, now that their vigorous doctrines have scarcely an apologist left, is the dark trail of ruin which their barbaric destructiveness has still left on the antiquities of the land.

To Prince Charles, who since his father's death had been regarded by all loyalists as their lawful monarch, the English Catholic continued to give proofs of their most disinterested devotion. When after the battle of Dunbar, Charles tried the fortune of war for the last time at Worcester (1651), and suffered complete defeat at Cromwell's hands, he became a fugitive from the battle-field. It was mainly through the shelter given him at the risk of their lives by Whitgrave, a Catholic gentleman with his chaplain, Father Huddleston, and above all by the loyal service of a family of Catholic yeomen named Penderel, that he was enabled to elude his pursuers and escape to France.

There can be little doubt that while Charles was in exile on the Continent his company was in very great part composed of Catholics. The Penal Laws could not touch them there, and hence both escape from persecution, and their loyalty to the royal cause combined to bring them to him whom they considered their king, and whose advent to the English throne they hoped would prove their salvation. It is quite probable that during these years Charles himself became convinced of the truth of Catholicism, but his life was not one which would lead him to sacrifice present pleasures and rosy hopes to conscience, so he did not make any public move in that direction.

XXIX.

CATHOLICS AND THE RESTORATION.

(1660-1689.)

CATHOLICS had fought and suffered as much as any of their countrymen for the royal cause in the Civil War. They had groaned under the fanatical intolerance of the Puritan army. They also bore a large share in securing the return of the Stuart monarch to the English throne.

Catholic hopes. They had every reason to cherish a hope that gratitude and policy would combine to win for them from the restored sovereign, if not full liberty, at any rate some measure of relief. King Charles II. was, even if not already a Catholic at heart, in fullest sympathy with their aspirations for freedom. But they had not rightly estimated the amount of anti-Catholic feeling which lay dormant in the country. Moreover, the rival politicians of the day vied with each other in exploiting the ignorance and the bigotry of the masses for their own purposes. Lord Clarendon, possibly out of honest prejudice, set himself at once at the head of the opposition to any general measure of relief, and Charles preferred to sacrifice the Catholics rather than lose the support of the Cavalier minister and his party. Later on, Lord Shaftesbury became the leader of the hostility to the Church, and must bear a great share of the responsibility for a persecution which even brought martyrs to the scaffold.

The case against persecution seemed at first to be greatly strengthened by the negotiations which had for object the marriage of Charles II. with a Catholic princess, Catherine of Braganza, of the royal house of Portugal. In the marriage contract every possible provision had been made to allow this lady the full exercise

THE RESTORATION

of her religion. The marriage took place at Portsmouth on the 21st of May, 1662, according to the Catholic ritual, but privately. Nor was it except privately that the ceremony was afterwards performed in the Anglican Church, and Catherine was never crowned. This did not look like very courageous facing of the difficulties, but still the queen held to her religion. At Somerset House and at Whitehall there was always a staff of priests in attendance on the queen, and forming part of her court. Louis Stuart, Count d'Aubigny, son of the Duke of Lennox, was at first chief almoner, and then, when in 1665 he left the court, the Dominican Father, Thomas Howard, brother of the Duke of Norfolk, who was already one of the chaplains, was named Lord Almoner with an allowance of one thousand pounds a year. He enjoyed considerable influence and credit at the royal court for the next ten years, and had a hand in the publication of the Declaration of Indulgence in 1672. The Portuguese confessor to the queen, Father Christopher, was also a Dominican. Moreover, in pretty constant attendance on the court were the Capuchin Friars who had been in the suite of Queen Henrietta Maria. The Benedictine, Father Huddleston, likewise enjoyed a position of privileged freedom at Whitehall as the acknowledgment of his past services to the king. These are but a few of the notable ecclesiastics, who, in one way or another, were in communication with the court of the queen consort.

The Queen Consort.

The Protestant agitation increased considerably as the reign of Charles II. advanced, being stimulated by the conversion to Catholicity of several well-known personalities, the chief of whom was the king's brother, James, Duke of York. The storm centre as far as the Catholic clergy were concerned appeared to be Father Thomas Howard, who therefore deemed it prudent to leave England and retire to the convent of his order at Bornhem in the Low Countries. Even amid the splendours of the gay court at Whitehall he had ever remained a true religious, sighing for the retirement of his priory. It had always been a great loss to his brethren to be deprived of his services as Superior. For he it was who in 1658 had been instru-

Cardinal Thomas Howard (1629-1694).

mental in founding the house at Bornhem as a means of saving the English Province of the Dominicans from extinction. During his residence at Whitehall he had remained nominally Prior of Bornhem, administering it between his annual visits through a sub-prior. But now he came into constant residence there, more than ever bent on promoting the interests of the English province, and of Catholicism in his native land. He was not, however, left long in this peaceful seclusion, for in 1675 he was named Cardinal-Priest of St Cecilia, and hence compelled to leave his beloved foundation and take up his residence at Rome. The rest of his life, which extended for nearly twenty years more, was that of a cardinal in Curia. He was usually spoken of as the Cardinal of England, and this was no mere compliment, for whenever possible he busied himself with the interests of his country, and of the order to which he belonged. Amid the hopes excited by the accession of the Catholic, James II., the plan was mooted of sending him as bishop, rather than as merely Vicar-Apostolic, somewhat as Pole had been sent in the preceding century to try and organise a restoration of the institutions of the Church in England, but other arrangements were made, and the original design came to nothing. He was strongly opposed to the imprudent policy of James II., and did all in his power to hold him back, while his position at the papal court enabled him to present matters in their true light to the Sovereign Pontiff. His health began to fail early in 1694, and on the 17th of June he died. He was buried in the Dominican Church of St Maria *Sopra Minerva*, which he had exchanged for St Cecilia as his Titular Church.

There resided in the neighbourhood of Whitehall Palace a member of the Franciscan Order who was only less celebrated than the Cardinal of Norfolk.

Father Christopher Davenport, O.S.F. (1598-1680). This was Father Christopher Davenport, sometimes called Francis a Sancta Clara. In the preceding reign he had been one of the queen's chaplains, retaining the office of guardian in one of the houses of his order, somewhat as Cardinal Howard had done in the case of Bornhem. He had managed to maintain himself at Westminster even during the Commonwealth by eluding his persecutors. Then at the Restoration he had continued his ministra-

THE RESTORATION

tions with equal prudence and zeal. He was, moreover, a prolific writer, his chief work on Church and State being an elaborate attempt to show that the Anglican Articles of Religion were capable of a Catholic interpretation. In this way he may be looked on as in some sense a forerunner of the Tractarians, who with Newman and Keble published their tracts in the days of the Oxford movement. His labours in this direction seem to have made him acceptable both to Laud and to Charles I. He was instrumental in reconciling many High Churchmen with the Holy See. There were two converts of exceptional position with whom he was in close connection. The one was Bishop Goodman of Gloucester, whose confessor and counsellor he was until the bishop died in retirement at Westminster in 1656. The other was Anne Hyde, Duchess of York, and daughter of Lord Clarendon, who after being a devout Anglican turned to Catholicism before her death, and was reconciled by Father Davenport in 1670. The zealous friar was several times provincial of his order, and died in old age in 1680. He was buried in the Savoy Chapel Royal.

Another saintly religious who made his influence felt in the royal court, especially in the latter half of the reign of Charles II., was the Jesuit father, the Venerable Claude de la Colombière. This apostolic man only came to England in 1676, having been recommended by Père la Chaise as a suitable Confessor for Princess Mary of Modena, whom the Duke of York had espoused, after the death of his first wife, Anne Hyde. He came to London at a moment when the Protestant feeling evoked by the conversion of the Duke of York was intensified by his marriage to a Catholic princess. Yet during the two years for which he remained he was able, while trying to avoid public notice, to do much good in various ways. In addition to the support he afforded to Mary of Modena in spiritual matters, he was able to receive several influential Anglicans into the fold, as well as to foster vocations to the religious state. It must not be forgotten either that by Father de la Colombière the devotion to the Sacred Heart was first introduced into England. In 1678, at the outbreak of the Titus Oates Plot, he was arrested and imprisoned for three weeks. He owed his freedom to the protests

V. Claude de la Colombière (1641-1682).

of the French ambassador, Barillon: He was then ordered to leave the kingdom, and returned regretfully to France.

A considerable part of the credit for another good work for the advantage of the English Catholics must also be given to Queen Catherine of Braganza. This was the foundation of the Convent of the Institute of Mary at Hammersmith. In 1669, at her invitation, Mother Frances Bedingfeld left the house of the Institute of Mary at Munich to establish a foundation in England. This heroic woman with her companions settled first in St Martin's Lane and then at Cupola House, Hammersmith, aided by the protection and means furnished by the good queen. Very soon a school for girls was set on foot which became a flourishing establishment. It was in this house, of which she can rightly claim to be the foundress, that Queen Catherine sought consolation amongst its devout inhabitants from the vexations of court life and her husband's infidelities; she spent much time at the Hammersmith Convent. Mother Bedingfeld was able to make a second foundation at Micklegate Bar, York, in 1686, which subsists to the present day. But, although there were several religious houses on the Continent peopled by Catholic exiles from England, Hammersmith and York remained for a century the only establishments of this kind actually on the soil of the country.

First Convents in Modern England.

During the whole of this reign the ecclesiastical government of the country remained in an abnormal and irregular state. After the death of Bishop Richard Smith in 1655, no Vicar-Apostolic was appointed for about thirty years. Consequently, the only members of the clergy in bishop's orders were the foreign ecclesiastics who either came on various embassies or were attached from time to time to the court of the queen. The jurisdiction was held to reside in the chapter as mentioned above. But, evidently, this was a somewhat irregular arrangement, and led to difficulties both with the regular clergy and with others. Presumably the Holy See supplied what was wanting to the validity of the chapter's action.

Ecclesiastical Government.

THE RESTORATION

King Charles held himself bound in honour to try and give effect to the Declaration of Breda, made before his return from exile, promising to give indulgence to all, whether Catholics or Dissenters, whose delicate conscience would not allow them to join in the worship of the Church of England. *Declaration of Indulgence.* But when he strove to act on this he found himself confronted by an opposition which included Cavaliers of the old school, the Anglican bishops, and not a few of those Presbyterians and other Dissenters who would themselves profit by general freedom of worship. They would take it for themselves, but they would be no parties to its being conceded to Catholics. As to the king's sincerity and unwillingness to persecute or ostracise any man for his religion, there can be no longer any reasonable doubt. Besides, the more the evidence at our command is investigated the stronger grows the proof that before he returned to England at the Restoration he was already a convert at heart, intellectually convinced of the truth of the Catholic religion. But he was not of the stuff of which martyrs, or even confessors, are made, and he would not sacrifice crown or even convenience to the supremacy of conscience. To make laws against the members of the Church was therefore, he felt within him, to make laws against the professors of the true religion. And these were amongst the most loyal subjects he had, only they were not strong enough to secure him against an alliance of all the anti-Catholic elements which the nation contained. He protested that his honour was involved. He openly taxed the Anglican bishops with bigotry. He quarrelled with Clarendon and the Royalist politicians. But when the battle was fought in Parliament and in the Council he had to accept the humiliation of being beaten. And so the *Corporation Act* was passed to exclude Dissenters from all public bodies, by requiring the members, when they came into office, to receive the Sacrament according to the rite of the Church of England. And the *Test Act*, imposing a solemn declaration against the doctrine of Transubstantiation, was passed to prevent Catholics from taking their seats in Parliament, or serving the crown in any public capacity.

The king's brother, James, Duke of York, was made of sterner stuff, and in 1669, in private conference with

his brother, gave him to understand that he believed in
Catholicism, and meant to act upon his belief and make
his submission to the Church. Charles,
Conversion of the Duke of York and others. with tears in his eyes, protested how hard was his own lot to be forced to a conformity with a religion he did not believe in, but all the same he left his brother to go his
way alone. Still, notwithstanding all this, the new
ministry, which in the same year replaced Clarendon and
his friends, contained at least one zealous convert to
Catholicity, and another who had at least an open mind
about the claims of any and every religion. The Catholic
was Sir William Clifford, created Lord Clifford of
Chudleigh, while Sir Henry Bennet, Lord Arlington,
had gone to Mass when in exile with the king, but
imitated, and perhaps supported his royal master in dissembling his real sentiments after the Restoration. It
was only on his death-bed that he, in this also like
Charles, was finally reconciled. These with the Duke
of Buckingham, the Earl of Lauderdale and Ashley,
later on Earl of Shaftesbury, formed the so-called Cabal
administration.

Finding that he had nothing to hope for from the
main body of his subjects, Charles formed the dangerous
plan of calling in foreign aid. Another Catholic, Lord
Arundell, was among the king's most intimate advisers.
But it is likely that this plan was suggested, or at any
rate fostered, chiefly through Lord Arlington. The
former of two secret treaties contained a
Secret Treaties of Dover (1670). proviso that at a suitable moment the king should declare himself a Catholic and grant liberty of conscience; (1670) the latter treaty only gave the conditions of a
political alliance with Louis XIV. against Holland.
Charles had already negotiated with the court of Rome,
first through Sir Richard Bellings, and then through the
eldest of his natural children, James de la Cloche. The
discovery of these secret treaties led to an outburst of
indignation and of Protestant feeling throughout the
country. It is true that they contained much that was
humiliating to England. It is also true that the
provisions contained in them were contrary to the wishes
of the majority of the people. But a great deal of the
excitement was manufactured by politicians for political

THE RESTORATION 449

ends. The outcry against taking money from the French king for supporting his policy was exaggerated: French money had been accepted for political support even in Clarendon's time. And on the religious question the king's side was that of liberty of conscience and equality against sectarian prejudice and the blindest of bigotry. But Charles saw nothing to do but to bend to the storm, and unwillingly gave his consent to the reversal in public of what had been done in private, and the shutting out of Catholics from the limited royal favour they had enjoyed. The Catholic peers were debarred from taking their seats in the House of Lords. It may be interesting to recall their names: they were the Duke of Norfolk, the Earls of Shrewsbury, Berkshire, Portland, Cardigan and Powys, Viscounts Montague and Stafford, Barons Mowbray, Audley, Stourton, Petre, Arundell, Hunsdon, Bellasis, Langdale, Teynham, Carrington, Widdrington, Gerard, and Clifford. The Marquess of Worcester conformed in order to take his seat, and in the following year his example was followed by Lord Mowbray and the Earl of Berkshire. But the chief efforts of the Protestant party, now that the Duke of York had become a Catholic, turned upon his exclusion from the succession to the throne, and these efforts Charles II. set himself to combat and defeat with all the courage he had, and with still greater dexterity. At first the prospect was by no means encouraging.

The agitation both against Catholics in general, and against the peers and the Duke of York in particular, was marvellously assisted by a false plot invented and imposed upon the popular imagination by the perjuries of an unscrupulous adventurer named Titus Oates. This notorious character, who was the son of a weaver, had been known as a Baptist preacher in the days of the Commonwealth. At the Restoration he promptly veered towards Anglicanism, was sent to Cambridge, took orders, and held curacies in several parishes in turn. He then became a chaplain in the navy. But he lost all these situations one after the other on account of misconduct, the suspicion of immorality, and repeated perjury. He was in a sad plight when he fell into the hands of a clergyman, somewhat deranged in mind, by name Dr Tonge, whose credulous imagination was ever haunted

Titus Oates' Plot (1678).

by alarms of Jesuits' plots, which he took it upon himself as a duty to reveal to his fellow-countrymen. He fastened upon Oates as a fit instrument to rouse the feelings of the nation against Catholics in general and Jesuits in particular. The first arrangement made by this worthy pair was that Oates should pretend to wish to be reconciled with the Church, so that thereby he might be able to collect information for the denunciation of those who might take him up as a genuine convert. The priest who received him after instruction was himself a person of changeable and unsound mind named Berry or Hutchinson, who had passed twice from Protestantism to Catholicity. Through the influence of this priest Oates was admitted to study at the Jesuit College, Valladolid. However, five months' experience of him was sufficient to procure his expulsion in disgrace. Still, backed up by Tonge, he professed contrition, and was at last taken back into the College of the Jesuits, but this time at St Omer. Once again he betrayed himself, and was ignominiously sent away. He now tried no more hypocritical shows of conversion, but returned to his supporter in London, Dr Tonge, to offer what material he had been able to gather on which to found the accusation of there being a great popish plot in preparation. By means of a chemist named Kirby, employed in the royal laboratory, Charles was given to understand that a plan was on foot to assassinate him. Charles brushing the idea aside as improbable, Tonge was admitted the same evening to an interview in which he detailed the supposed particulars of the plot, and was sent by the monarch to Danby, the treasurer. But though the latter proposed to lay the matter before the Council the king remained incredulous, and instructed Danby to ask for documentary evidence. There was delay about giving this, and when the papers appeared they seemed evident forgeries. Oates now made an affidavit before a magistrate to 'the truth of his statements, which he enlarged to the number of eighty-one articles. Finally, yielding to the entreaties of his brother, Charles ordered that Oates should appear before the Privy Council to tell his story. The general drift of his statement was that there was a popish plot to reduce all his Majesty's dominions to the Romanist religion and obedience. When he came to specify the means by which this was

THE RESTORATION

to be accomplished he indicated the assassination of the king, the raising of a rebellion in Ireland, the appointment of Catholics to all the chief offices in the government and in the army, and further the assassination of the Duke of York if he refused to pardon those who had killed the king and assassinated his Protestant subjects and set fire to his cities, as he said they had already done to London in 1667, and finally the entry of the French to seize the kingdom. In cross-examination Oates was caught in palpable inventions, and his credit was well-nigh gone. Fortunately for his story, among many papers which were seized at his request appeared a correspondence between one, Coleman, secretary to the Duchess of York, and the French court, which in the excited state of public feeling was made the most of to press the case for a plot, though no plot was mentioned. However, the case was taken up by Lord Shaftesbury and the leaders of the Whig party to use against the Duke of York. Coleman was committed to prison, and Oates became the hero of the mob. The perjuries of Oates were supported by those of another abandoned wretch named Bedloe, and Coleman was brought to trial. In the excited state of public opinion and with a judge and jury strongly prejudiced against him, the charges made by Oates and Bedloe were believed, and Coleman, being found guilty of high treason, suffered at Tyburn. But he was only the first of a long series of victims who were sacrificed to the false information of the two informers and the anti-Catholic prejudice of the multitude. One after another with the connivance of the "managers," as the leaders of the ultra-Protestant party were called, those whom Oates and his companions marked down were tried, found guilty, and executed. Upon the foundation of the popish plot were reared two political designs—the one to exclude James, Duke of York, from the succession to the throne, the other to overthrow, in the Whig interest, the ministry in which Danby was Lord Treasurer and the moving spirit. King Charles, to save his favourite minister, dissolved the Parliament, known as the Cavalier Parliament, which had lasted for eighteen years (1660-78), but only succeeded in this way in gaining a short breathing-space. For after the election it was evident that the new House of Commons was more anti-Catholic and anti-Royalist than its predecessor. Shaftesbury was all powerful, and the Exclusion Bill was brought up again, and quickly passed through the Commons. It was thrown out in the House of Lords in spite of the advocacy of Shaftesbury and the king's son Monmouth, mainly through the personal intervention of the king and the argumentative eloquence of Lord Halifax. Charles, keenly alive to every sign of change in public opinion, thought the tide was beginning to turn in his favour, and dissolved the Parliament (1681). He at the same time summoned a new one to meet at Oxford in two months' time. The interval was employed by him in strengthening his position by a secret treaty with the King of France, negotiated by Hyde and Barillon. Then, when Charles met the Lords and Commons at Oxford, Halifax proposed a regency in the event of the Duke of York succeeding to the crown, hoping thus to disarm the advocates of his exclusion. The violence of the Commons, supported by Shaftesbury and others, nevertheless made all compromise futile, and the king coming suddenly upon the Lords, dissolved the Houses, thus for the time putting an end to all parliamentary discussion, both on the Bills of Exclusion and of Regency. This short session, known as the Third Short Parliament of Charles II., was the last held during his reign. By this time the reaction was in full swing, and for the remaining years of his reign the "Merry Monarch" ruled without calling any Parliament together. He further proceeded to take vengeance on the leaders of the Protestant party. Lord Russell was tried and executed for high treason. So was Algernon Sydney, as well as several less prominent Whigs. Shaftesbury saved himself by flight to Holland, where he died in 1683. Monmouth owed his pardon to his father's tenderness, but only repaid this by putting himself at the head of the conspirators against the succession who were in exile on the Continent. Halifax advised the king that if he now called a Parliament he would have one of a thoroughly loyal complexion. Lawrence Hyde, now Earl of Rochester, on the other hand, succeeded in dissuading him from doing so, and his advice prevailed.

Meanwhile, in spite of the fact that political currents had gradually set strongly in the king's favour, trials and executions of those supposed to be implicated in the popish plot had gone on with unabated fury, and the

THE RESTORATION

king had not intervened to prevent them. Though Coleman alone had suffered in 1678, in the following year Father Pickering, O.S.F., Fathers Ireland, Gavan, Harcourt, Turner, Whitbread, and Fenwick, of the Society of Jesus, together with the secular priests and one layman, Richard Langhorne, all endured the extreme penalty. All these were charged with being concerned in the imaginary plot. But in the same year there also suffered simply on account of their being priests William Plessington, Philip Evans, John Lloyd, Nicholas Postgate, Charles Mahony, John Kemble, John Wall, O.S.F., and the Jesuit, Charles Baker. In 1680, besides the secular priest, Thomas Fleming, and the illustrious Catholic nobleman, William Howard, Lord Stafford was brought to the block, after being confined in the Tower on suspicion for fifteen months together with the Earl of Powys and Lords Petre, Arundell, and Bellasis. The evidence against him was quite unreliable; he firmly protested his innocence, but was condemned by a vote of his peers, and died heroically on the scaffold on the Feast of St Thomas of Canterbury, 1680. Six months later the Venerable Archbishop of Armagh, Blessed Oliver Plunket, suffered the same penalty at the same place on equally false and unworthy evidence. This holy man brought to an end the long roll of martyrs, who from the Act of Supremacy in 1535 had in their turn, during a period extending for a century and a half, given their blood for the Catholic Faith in England. Blessed Oliver Plunket was solemnly beatified by Pope Benedict XV. in the year 1920. His relics rest in the Benedictine Abbey at Downside with the exception of his head, which is in the Dominican Convent at Drogheda. [Martyrs for the Faith.]

Much as King Charles detested the injustice and bigotry of the popular outcry which had brought these sufferers for conscience to a bloody death, he had not intervened to save their lives. Perhaps he could not have effectually done so, but his conduct lay open to the suspicion of time-serving shiftiness and indolent attraction to take the path of least resistance. Yet, while they had died, he had triumphed. The Duke of York was now able to return and take up his residence at court, and the discovery of the Rye House Plot to assassinate the royal brothers only [Death of Charles II. (1685).]

served to complete the king's victory. He enjoyed henceforward about two years of reign undisturbed by any effective opposition, while his brother gradually regained all the power and influence he had ever had. But for Charles the end was nearer than he could have imagined. He had led a life of licentious dissipation, and his constitution was worn out by his excesses. On the 2nd of February, 1685, after rising as usual, he was struck down by a fit of apoplexy. In the course of the day he rallied, but suffered a relapse towards night. Once again an improvement took place, and for the next few days he lay conscious, but hovering between life and death. He remained gently passive amid the ministrations of the Archbishop of Canterbury and the other Anglican prelates who were in assiduous attendance. At length, at the suggestion of the king's mistress, the Duchess of Portsmouth, the Duke of York privately introduced the Benedictine, Father Huddleston, who enjoyed a privileged position at the court on account of his having assisted Charles's escape after the battle of Worcester. To him the dying monarch gladly made his confession, and from him received Holy Communion and Extreme Unction, being thus reconciled to the Church he had long before believed in as the Home of Truth. On the 6th of February he calmly expired.

James II.
(1685-1689).

The Duke of York seems to have anticipated that his succession to his deceased brother would not be accomplished without some trouble or breach of the peace. Nothing of the kind, however, happened. Meeting the Privy Council but a brief interval after witnessing Charles's death, he made a short speech which gave general satisfaction. He promised to preserve the government as by law established both in State and Church, engaging to keep within the limits of the royal prerogative and keeping all the just rights and liberties of the people. He was then proclaimed in absolute peace at the usual points of the city. Even when he proceeded to levy ordinary taxes in advance of parliamentary votes it was acquiesced in, so strongly did the tide run in the direction of loyalty. He chose Lords Rochester, Sunderland, and Godolphin as his chief counsellors. Halifax, though thanked for his services in defeating the Exclusion Bill, was not employed. But the religious difficulty arose at

THE RESTORATION

once. On Maundy Thursday and on Easter Sunday, within six weeks of his brother's death, James went to Mass and Communion in state in the Queen's Chapel, attended by the Knights of the Garter and a great number of lords. Four days later, on St George's Day (April 23rd), he was crowned in Westminster Abbey by Archbishop Sancroft of Canterbury, after the usual rite, but with the omission of the Communion Service. This was taken as a pledge that he meant to maintain the Church of England in its place in the country, and when Parliament met a month later he repeated his previous declaration expressed on the day his brother died. The Protestant members moved an address to the king begging that the laws against papists and dissenters might be enforced, but it met with such disfavour from the loyal sentiments of the House that it was rejected without a division. They declared they felt they could rely on the royal declaration. But on the other hand there were symptoms already well fitted to alarm the supporters of the Anglican ascendancy. The Catholic lords in the Tower were liberated from prison where Lord Petre had already died in captivity, while several thousand Catholics, who were in detention on various pretexts up and down the country, were also set at liberty. Prosecutions were begun against Oates, Dangerfield, and the dissenting preacher, Baxter. The first named was flogged and pilloried, as was also Dangerfield, while Baxter was sent to prison.

The loyalty of the body of the nation to their monarch received a stimulus in the course of the following months by the arrival of two hostile bands sent from abroad by the exiles who were in conspiracy against James, with the object of forwarding a general insurrection against his government. The former of these expeditions was under the leadership of the Earl of Argyle, and came to land in the Firth of Clyde. It did not attain any measure of success. Argyle himself was soon captured, and being conducted to Edinburgh, was executed on the 30th of June. The second attempt was made in the South by the Duke of Monmouth, the natural son of the late monarch, who had pledged himself not to assume the royal title, but was afterwards induced by some of his supporters to do so. He landed at Lyme in Dorset-

Rebellions of Argyle and Monmouth.

shire on the 11th of June, as the professed champion of the Protestant religion, and was able to make a triumphant entry into Taunton some days later. Among the ultra-Protestants of Dorsetshire and Devon he gained considerable support, but the landed gentry all held aloof from him. As soon as a force of regular troops could be gathered, it was sent against him under Lord Faversham. Monmouth attempted a surprise attack upon the royal camp at Sedgemoor, but his untrained insurgents were easily routed by the royal army, and the duke took refuge in flight. This affray under the name of the Battle of Sedgemoor is pointed to by historians as the last conflict between hostile armies which has taken place in England. It was a comparatively easy matter for the cavalry in the king's army to overtake Monmouth, whose life had been already forfeited by an Act of Attainder, and he was taken prisoner to London. He sought and obtained an interview with the king, during which he pleaded for his life with the most abject submission, even offering to become a Catholic if his execution could thereby be stayed. But James was unmoved, and Monmouth was beheaded on Tower Hill on the 15th of July. Some five hundred of the insurgents had fallen on the field of battle, but the law was to take a relatively heavier toll of their lives in what is known as the Bloody Assize conducted by Lord Chief Justice Jeffreys in the following months. In all some three hundred were executed as traitors and felons, while eight hundred were sold into slavery. The whole thing must be looked on as an untimely and cruel echo of the legal barbarities which followed the Rising of the North in Elizabeth's reign. It is hard to divide the responsibility accurately between Jeffreys and his royal master.

James had scarcely mounted the throne before he sent a confidential envoy to Pope Innocent XI. in the person of Mr Caryll, a Catholic gentleman of position. He was commissioned to ask that Reginald d'Este should be made a cardinal, and that the archpriest, Dr Leyburn, should receive the episcopal dignity. The sagacious Pontiff waived aside the petition as to D'Este, but authorised the consecration of Leyburn, to whom the king promised one thousand pounds a year with a residence at Whitehall. Monsignor Ferdinand d'Adda

THE RESTORATION

was then sent to London from the papal court with the powers, but without the status of a nuncio. All his instructions were in the direction of counselling moderation in English affairs, and of soliciting intervention in favour of the French Huguenots against whom Louis XIV. had just revoked the Edict of toleration of Nantes. But these counsels were unwelcome to the blind precipitancy of the king and the imtemperate zeal of many of his advisers. Thereupon Caryll was replaced by Lord Castlemaine as the English agent in Rome, and he was directed to cultivate the friendship of the Jesuits and of the French, and to push for a more active policy. Este was already made cardinal, and the Pope now agreed to Adda assuming the public dignity of a nuncio-apostolic, but when Castlemaine went on to ask for the cardinal's hat for Father Petre, the king's Jesuit confessor, Innocent refused, and Castlemaine left dissatisfied with the results of his mission. Adda was consecrated with much state in Whitehall Chapel by the Archbishop of Armagh on the 1st of May. As far as it was in his power, James resolved to push on with his own policy. The ambitious Lord Sunderland was reconciled with the Catholic Church by Father Petre, but Leyburn's efforts to do the same with Rochester did not meet with any success. Henceforth the influence of the more moderate party was on the wane; Father Petre was made a Privy Councillor, and shared with Sunderland and Richard Butler, Marquis of Ormonde, the direction of public affairs. It is true that James professed the noblest of aims in the policy he was pursuing, but on the other hand even the Dissenters with the exception of the Quakers would not willingly take it from his hands if Catholics were to be included. It must be remembered also that the laws of the country were of a bitterly anti-Catholic complexion, built up under a century of Puritan bigotry. It was no easy matter then for the wisest or most skilful to square toleration with the existing constitution of the country. And James was neither wise nor skilful. The means he took stirred such a storm that he was hurled from the throne, and the Church received a set-back which drove it into the background for another hundred years. The foremost cases which came up for his decision were those of

Toleration for the Catholics.

the Catholic officers who had been admitted into his service in spite of the Test Act, which required a declaration against the Catholic doctrine of the Holy Eucharist. James decided to make use of what was called the Dispensing Power of the crown, and patents were issued under the Great Seal liberating such officers from the penalties incurred under the Act of Charles II., or "any Act of Parliament whatsoever." It was in virtue of just such a dispensation that James himself had held the office of Lord High Admiral in his brother's reign. Yet the legality of it was doubted, so the opinions of the judges were sought, and four who pronounced in the negative were removed, and others put in their place. As a test case Godden, a coachman, was instructed to bring an action against Sir Edward Hales for the penalties which the latter, a colonel in the army and a Catholic, had incurred under the act of Charles II. Hales pleaded his patent. Herbert, the Lord Chief Justice since Jeffreys had become chancellor, after consulting the other judges, found that only one of indifferent fame persisted in denying the legality of the patent. He therefore gave judgment for Sir Edward Hales.

The decision, though not strictly illegal, was very unpopular, and the king considered it vital to secure the adhesion of the clergy to this exercise of his prerogative. When Compton, Bishop of London, refused to suspend Dr Sharp for preaching in a way that impugned the motives of recent converts to Catholicism, the king instituted a court of Ecclesiastical Commissioners consisting of the Lord Chancellor with the treasurer, the president of the council, and several bishops who were empowered to try Compton for his disobedience. The result was that he was suspended, and his diocese placed in the hands of administrators.

Ecclesiastical Commission (1686).

Meanwhile, considerable accessions had been made both to the number of converts, and to the religious establishments which the Catholics possessed. Most distinguished among the converts was the great poet, John Dryden, though a more influential one was Obadiah Walker, Master of University College at Oxford. Besides the chapels at St James's and Whitehall Palace, a Jesuit college was opened in the Savoy, while the Franciscans

THE RESTORATION

were installed in Lincoln's Inn, the Carmelites in the city, and the Benedictines near Whitehall. Still the opposition to Catholics was growing, and in order to be in a position to suppress any open outbreak the king formed a camp at Hounslow for the greater part of the twenty thousand men to which he had raised the standing army. In 1687 he published what was called the Declaration of Indulgence, suspending all laws against both Catholics and Dissenters equally. But though many of the latter accepted the boon, there were others who preferred to remain under disabilities themselves rather than share their freedom with Catholics. The attempt to call a Parliament which could be relied on to give legislative sanction to the Liberty of Conscience, which the king had proclaimed, was a failure. James then published a Second Declaration of Indulgence on April 22nd, 1688, stating his resolution to secure for all his subjects "freedom of conscience for ever," and abolishing all religious tests for office under the crown. This was ordered to be read in all churches and chapels, but as many of the Anglican clergy demurred seven of the bishops signed a petition to the king begging that the clergy might be excused from reading it. They delayed presenting this until the last moment, but at last faced the monarch. Taken by surprise, he gave vent to his anger and disappointment, which was only augmented when he found that but few of the clergy had read the Declaration on the appointed day. A fortnight later the bishops were summoned before the Royal Council, and, refusing compliance, were committed to the Tower. Three weeks later they were tried in Westminster Hall, there being about thirty peers besides the judges on the bench. The pleadings of the lawyers on both sides were conducted with great vehemence, and the jury were for some time divided in opinion. Next day, however, they brought in a verdict of *Not Guilty*, and the bishops were liberated amid a scene of undescribable popular enthusiasm.

The unwise prosecution of the bishops, combined with the birth of a son to Queen Mary d'Este, drove the supporters of Protestantism to desperate measures. An invitation was sent to William, Prince of Orange, to come and deliver the land from the supposed danger of

[margin: Declarations of Indulgence.]

Catholic ascendancy. Seven prominent politicians set out with the invitation on the very day of the bishop's acquittal, and by the 5th of November William was in Torbay at the head of a considerable armament of English, Swedish, Dutch, and Huguenot troops. James at first intended to oppose the invasion by force, but he soon found that he could not count on the loyalty of either the officers or the men of his army. William marched on London, and having sent his wife and son to France beforehand, James himself set sail on the 23rd of December, and was hospitably received by Louis XIV.

The landing of William of Orange (1688).

XXX.

CATHOLICS AND THE REVOLUTION.

(1689-1745.)

THE revolution, which began in 1688, and was completed by the elevation to the throne in 1689 of William, Prince of Orange, and of Mary, elder daughter of James II., was a victory for Protestantism. Not that it really strengthened the position of the Established Church, many of whose clergy refused to admit its lawfulness, and became known as the Non-Jurors. But all that was latitudinarian in doctrine together with all that was Puritan in the dissenting sects united to thrust back Catholics into that odium and social outlawry from which the later Stuarts had in vain tried to rescue them. It was not that King William III. was personally a lover of persecution, but his hand was forced by the anti-Catholic elements which had combined to set him on the throne. Hence when the Toleration Act was passed under the patronage of the Whig politicians to give relief to Dissenters, Catholics were expressly excluded from any share in it. None of the sanguinary provisions of the Penal Code were withdrawn, and though in most cases they were suffered to remain in abeyance, there was no intention thereby of permitting Catholics to remain unmolested. As a sign of this several new enactments were made to harass them with fresh disabilities and exactions, which proved in the end more dangerous than the savage legislation of Henry VIII. and Elizabeth. There was no more shedding of blood; the age of the martyrs had passed. But it was followed, not as in the days of Constantine by the peace of the Church, but by a period demanding a confessorship which made most exacting demands on the courage and constancy of those who were of the household of his Faith.

Toleration of Dissenters.

462 THE CHURCH IN ENGLAND

Further penal legislation. Some of these new Acts of Parliament must be mentioned if we are to gain a true idea of the burden which our forefathers had to carry. Perhaps some of them may have been meant as substitutes for not putting a more ancient and bloody law into execution. There was a new Act of Allegiance; it included an explicit renunciation both of the papal deposing power, and of any jurisdiction, spiritual and temporal, of the Holy See in England. There was an Act of Parliament ordering all papists to remove to a distance of ten miles from the cities of London and Westminster. There was another Act which forbade papists to possess arms or any horse above the value of five pounds, while a third Act vested in the Universities of Oxford and Cambridge the right of presentation to any benefices in the gift of Catholic patrons. All these laws were passed in the first year of the reign of William and Mary. And as the reign went on, instead of anti-Catholic feelings being satisfied with these enactments, an Act was passed ordaining that after the 25th of March, 1700, any popish bishop, priest, or Jesuit convicted of saying Mass, exercising his office or keeping school, would be subject to perpetual imprisonment; and a reward of one hundred pounds was offered to any informer who should give information leading to their conviction. Moreover, it was enacted that Catholics were incapable of possessing or buying landed property, which was to go to the next Protestant heir, until they swore allegiance and abjured Transubstantiation, the Sacrifice of the Mass, and Invocation of the Virgin Mary and the Saints. Popish parents incurred a penalty of one hundred and fifty pounds for sending their children to be educated beyond the seas. This comprehensive and oppressive law is known as that " of the eleventh and twelfth of William and Mary for further preventing the growth of popery," and it proved a more powerful engine in the hands of the government to root out the Catholic Faith than the bloody statutes of the Reformation period. It did not repeal these statutes, which were left still hanging over the heads of the devoted faithful, though not put into execution. It put the Catholic gentry at the mercy of their Protestant neighbours, and it put a premium on apostasy in the case of those who had land to inherit. It is hardly to

THE REVOLUTION 463

be wondered at that, under the dull pressure of these legal monstrosities, a certain number of Catholics gradually dropped off and gave up the struggle.

It may be well now to turn to sketch the fortunes of the four Vicars-Apostolic, amongst whom the papal brief of January, 1688, just on the eve of the Revolution, had divided the administration of the English mission. The London district was in the care of Bishop John Leyburn. *Fortunes of the Vicars-Apostolic.* The imprisonment of this worthy prelate in the Tower of London lasted for two years. He was then liberated, and allowed to live in retirement in London. He was only required to notify to the government any change of lodgings, and in other respects was unmolested. At the Revolution he was already more than seventy years of age, and, bearing, as even Macaulay testifies, the character of "a wise and honest man," survived until 1702, when he died at the age of eighty-six. Bishop Bonaventure Giffard, who was arrested in his flight with James II., as well as Dr Leyburn, remained in prison in Newgate, together with Bishop Ellis of the Western district, but after about a year he also was set at liberty, and at the death of Bishop Leyburn was transferred to the London district, which he administered in the midst of continual dangers and anxieties, harried by priest-catchers, forced to change his place of abode as often as, in one case, fourteen times in the course of six months, but ever persevering in his charge, until his holy death in 1723, at the age of ninety-one. He also had to superintend the affairs of the Western district for some time, for Bishop Ellis, when freed from Newgate, fled to the Continent, and never succeeded in returning to take charge of his district. He went to Rome, and his return to England was opposed by James II. and his son, the Old Pretender. Eventually, in 1708, he resigned his office, and in 1708 was made Bishop of Segni, where he lived as a zealous pastor for eighteen years, dying in 1726. The Revolution of 1688 found Bishop Smith at York in charge of his vicariate. He then took refuge with a Catholic gentleman, Mr Tunstall of Wycliffe, in whose house he resided, making what pastoral journeys he was able in aid of the Catholics in the Northern counties. His pastoral staff was seized by Lord Danby, the high treasurer, and sent to York Cathedral, where it still remains. It was proposed to make Bishop James Smith a cardinal (1700) and also to transfer him to London, but he energetically, though most humbly, protested against both these plans. He died in 1711, and was probably buried at Wycliffe. Bishops Leyburn and Giffard were both probably buried in St Pancras' Old Churchyard, while Bishop Ellis found his last resting-place in his cathedral at Segni.

It will be convenient here to summarise the succession of vicars in the four vicariates up to the end of the Revolution period, which we will consider as ending after the abortive rising of 1745. The first bishop consecrated after the four vicars mentioned above was Bishop George Witham, who was chosen to succeed Bonaventure Giffard in the Midlands in 1703, when that pious prelate was transferred to London. Dr Witham, who was the son of George Witham of Cliffe Hall, Darlington, four or five of whose sons became priests, was a doctor of theology, and had acted as the Roman agent of the English bishops for the eight years before his elevation to the episcopate, governed the Midland district until 1715, when he in his turn was translated. He was named to the vicariate in his native North, which he then administered until his death in 1725. He was succeeded in the Midlands by Dr John Stonor, whose long episcopate of forty years (1716-56) carried him well into the next period, and made him contemporary with the earlier days of Bishop Challoner. In the same way, when at last a coadjutor was found for the aged Bishop Giffard in the person of Benjamin Petre in 1721, the London district gained the services of a prelate who only died thirty-seven years later at the age of eighty-one, having been assisted for the latter half of his episcopate by the venerable Challoner as coadjutor. Meanwhile, Bishop Witham had been replaced in the North by the Dominican bishop, Thomas Dominic Williams, who survived until 1740. The West, however, after the retirement of Bishop Ellis, and the refusal of the vicariate by Andrew Giffard, brother of the vicar in London, had a rather long vacancy. At last the Franciscan, Matthew Pritchard, was chosen, and presided over the vicariate for five-and-twenty years. When he died in 1750, he was succeeded by Lawrence York, O.S.B. The vicars of the next generation had

Succession in the Vicariates.

best be spoken of when we are treating of Challoner and the men of his time.

The defence of the Church in England in William III.'s reign in the field of controversy was undertaken almost single-handed by John Gother. This saintly and learned priest, who was a convert from Presbyterianism, was educated at St Omer, and sent on the English mission towards the end of the reign of Charles II. **Dr John Gother (1633-1704).** He was a man of exceedingly retired and studious habits, and soon found the vocation of his life to be the defence of the Church by writing rather than by preaching and pastoral activity. He became chaplain to Lady Henrietta Stafford, daughter of the martyred Lord Stafford, and to her husband, Mr Holman, at Warkworth in Northamptonshire, and during a residence there of nearly twenty years (1685-1704) composed a series of works which were the main support of the Catholics against the attacks of the Protestant divines. These works, of which the most celebrated is "*The Papists Represented and Misrepresented*," which appeared in 1685, have been many times since reprinted. They extend in all to sixteen volumes. He was in conflict with such well-known Protestant writers as Stillingfleet, Sherlock, and Bernard, and was well able to hold his own against them all. John Dryden, his contemporary, said in his sweeping style that Gother was the only one except himself who could write pure English. And in fact his style is perhaps the best model extant of the language of the period. Yet such is the force of sectarian bias that the ordinary works on English literature of that time, while abounding in praise of Protestant divines, far his inferiors in literary English, simply ignore his books so limpid in expression, so weighty in their matter, and so historically important. It was these books which held the Catholic position not unworthily against a host of assailants. At Warkworth Dr Gother took up the boy Richard Challoner, the son of a domestic of the household, was instrumental in getting him sent to college, and thus helped to provide the Church with a doughty champion, who drew upon the stores, which Gother's works furnished, for weapons to fight the battle of the Faith in another generation. Gother was proposed as successor to Bishop Ellis in the Western district, but death prevented the carrying out of the plan. He was on a voyage to Lisbon on the affairs of the clergy when he took ill and died at sea. Out of respect for his character, his body was not buried in the waters, but conveyed to the English College at Lisbon, where he was interred with solemn rites in the church attached thereto.

The great master of English prose and verse, whose praise of John Gother is cited above, was himself a power for the true religion, scarcely less efficacious, and of course infinitely more celebrated in the history of literature. But his influence was more indirect. This was John Dryden. His conversion, not like that of so many in the ephemeral moments of James II.'s reign, was sincere and lasting, and it put the mightiest pen in England at the service of Catholicism. He had much to atone for in the licentious freedom of his earlier writings, and he seems to have done his best to make amends. In the "Hind and Panther" he had given a controversial form to one of the noblest poems in the language, but this was in the day when the star of Catholicity was in the ascendant. Still, the cold breath of the Revolution did not kill the devotion of the poet to his religion. When William III. became king Dryden was of course deprived of the office of poet, together with the salary attached to this office. He owed to the munificence of the Earl of Dorset a pension equal to that which he had lost, and extolled his benefactor in rolling verse, which is excusably obsequious and hyperbolic. He remained a firm adherent of the ancient Faith until his death. His skill was enlisted for the translation of the Latin hymns which were inserted in the primer of 1702. And it is easy to contrast the free and masterly flow of his English with the more measured and sometimes cramped versions of earlier and even of later translators. He is buried in Westminster Abbey. One of his sons became a Dominican, for all three of them were bound in close friendship with Cardinal Howard. This son finally succeeded to the baronetcy held by the poet's family, but dying of consumption at Canon's Ashby, the family seat, the title returned to a Protestant branch of the Drydens, by whom it has been enjoyed ever since.

John Dryden (1631-1700).

Somerset House, where Catherine of Braganza, who at once made her peace with William and Mary,

THE REVOLUTION

continued to live, was for some years a Catholic centre, where Mass was said for her household. But, though William treated the widowed queen considerately, unfriendly politicians always suspected her household to be a focus of intrigue against the new order of things. *Catholic Centres.* Catherine was made miserable by espionage and petty vexations, and soon expressed her wish to return to her native Portugal. This she accomplished in 1692, and Somerset House ceased to be a royal residence. Other quiet houses where Catholics cautiously gathered when they could avoid suspicion were the two convents founded by the Institute of Mary at Hammersmith and York. Every precaution was taken to hide their character as religious houses, and, in the midst of alarms and even dangers, both successfully maintained themselves all through the period. They were both zealously fostered by the Vicars-Apostolic, and the nuns conducted flourishing schools for girls. No religious house for men could possibly survive in the midst of the hostile population, ready at a moment's notice to break out into the violence of persecution. The rest of the Catholic points of influence were the country seats of the gentry who had remained faithful to the ancient religion.

The study of the general history of England shows that although William III. and Mary kept their throne till they died, they were always very far from having secured the heartfelt loyalty of the whole nation. Many of the unscrupulous politicians who had lent their aid towards establishing them in the place of the Stuarts were quite ready to veer round and assist a return of the expelled royal family if circumstances had shown they could thus serve their own interests best. A large section, especially of the upper classes, were Jacobites for long after the Revolution. A considerable proportion of the clergy of the Established Church were willing to forfeit their benefices rather than take an oath of allegiance to the new line of succession. These conscientious men were known as the Non-Jurors. And it is certain that the majority of the English Catholics remained Jacobites for fifty or sixty years after the first landing of William of Orange. The new dynasty gave them little reason for hope or for gratitude. The Revolution had been accomplished in spite of them, and its result in their regard had been a still heavier yoke of bondage, and a more grinding code of penal laws. The reign of Queen Anne (1702-14) left things pretty much as they had been, but with the advent of George I., as representing for the first time a definite abandonment of the Stuart line, came an access of petty persecution which was most galling, and calculated slowly to crush out all life and security of existence among the Catholic body.

The issue was complicated by the fact that a considerable number of them became deeply involved in the attempts which were made to overthrow the Hanoverian dynasty. The first of these enterprises was set on foot by the heir of the Stuart claims, called James III. by his supporters, and the Old Pretender by the adherents of the government in possession in 1715. A rising took place under the Earl of Mar in Scotland, which spread to the north of England. The chief leaders among the English Catholics were General Forster, the Earl of Derwentwater, and Lord Widdrington. But the attempt was doomed to failure from the outset. James was a contemptible leader, Forster an incompetent general, and at Preston the Jacobite army surrendered. The leaders were taken to the Tower or to Newgate. The Earl of Derwentwater was tried for his life and executed on Tower Hill in the February of 1716. Although he did not suffer as a martyr in a religious cause, he was given the offer of his life if he would make an acknowledgment which he considered incompatible with the Catholic religion. He then bravely went to his fate, and his estates were forfeited to Greenwich Hospital. His body lies in the chapel at Thorndon Hall, the seat of Lord Petre. Lord Widdrington was tried and sentenced also, but reprieved and eventually pardoned, but when he died the peerage became extinct. Thus the rebellion led to the extinction of two English Catholic peerages. Forster escaped from Newgate, and took refuge in France, where he died at Boulogne.

The Jacobite Rising of 1715.

But upon the Catholics of lower rank the hand of vengeance fell heavy indeed. Of all those who were concerned in the rising they were the most helpless, and advantage was taken of this to mulct them in pecuniary penalties, which were of crushing severity. In 1722 an act was passed requiring the registration of all papists who possessed any real property. And subsequently a provision was introduced that Catholics should pay double land tax. Grievous indeed was the yoke laid upon them, and great the patience which it demanded on their part. The return made in accordance with the Act of Parliament just referred to has been recently edited and published under the title of "Catholic Non-Jurors of 1715," and presents us with a fairly detailed account of the temporal condition of the children of the Church at this time. The old family names are to be found there over and over again of those who have held to the Faith of their fathers all through the years of storm and darkness, as well as of a few, alas! who in easier times let go their hold upon the treasures they were still holding firmly to in the days of the double land tax and penal oppression. Neither is this roll of honour confined to the gentry or the nobility. We find the sturdy Catholic yeoman, the tradesman, the merchant, no doubt to some extent under the protection of their more wealthy Catholic neighbours, but yet equally with them refusing the oath, and paying the penalty for their loyalty and devotion to their principles.

Walpole's penal legislation.

Henceforward the cleavage between the Catholics and the body of the nation became deeper than before. Holding firmly to their Faith under these grievous penal restrictions the body of the faithful shrank into a still more retired existence, suspected as they were of Jacobitism, and the victims of a carefully fostered Protestant tradition, which falsely accused them of holding doctrines they abhorred, and practising rules of morality which they would be the first to condemn as lax. They were more than ever excluded from the stream of national life, and they remained in the seclusion of their retired homes, or sought on the continent of Europe that religious freedom which was denied them in the land they loved so well.

The administration of Walpole had been corrupt but peaceful (1722-42), and it was not until his power came to an end that one last attempt was made by the exiled family of Stuart to recover their already forfeited inheritance. This resulted in the expedition of Prince Charles Edward and the rebellion of 1745. The French govern-

The Stuart Rising of 1745.

ment, which was at war with England, was desirous to encourage the enterprise, and as early as 1744 proposed to put a military expedition, under Marshal Saxe, at the disposal of the prince. However, nothing came of it that year, but in the next Charles Edward landed in Scotland, relying on the support he might expect from the supporters of the Stuart cause both in Scotland and England, and likewise on the landing of a French force in the South. Several thousand Highlanders rallied to his standard, and having taken Perth and Edinburgh, he was able to defeat at Prestonpans a body of troops under General Cope which had been sent against him. But he did not take immediate advantage of this victory, and several months elapsed before he began the invasion of England. Still, even then, things went well with him at first: Carlisle, Preston, and Manchester fell into his hands. At the last named place Colonel Towneley and some two hundred English recruits joined his ranks. He pushed on to Derby, but in view of the fact that three armies were in the field against him, and that the Highlanders were desirous to return to Scotland, a retreat was then commenced. There were several months of desultory fighting between the English armies which were closing in and the various bodies, chiefly of Highlanders, who were in arms for the Stuart cause. At last the disastrous battle of Culloden Moor in 1746 broke up the Highland army, and was followed by a savage pursuit of the fugitives and merciless executions. In England, Towneley with his small levy of troops was detached to hold Carlisle, and of course was quite unable to do so. The city was soon surrendered, and Towneley executed for his share in the rising. In all seventy-three persons suffered the death-penalty, and there was a certain amount of confiscation of the Jacobite estates. In Scotland both the number which suffered on the scaffold and the amount of property forfeited to the crown was far greater.

After many thrilling adventures and many narrow escapes, Prince Charles, sheltered by the heroic devotion of a Highland lady, Flora Macdonald, found his way to the Continent, and never renewed his attempt. He came once to London in peaceful guise, and that with the connivance of the government. He resided first in France, and afterwards at Florence, and finally in Rome, where his brother, Henry, Duke of York, had been made Cardinal by Benedict XIV. Hence it came to pass that in Rome, where he had been born, he also died, in 1794. The Cardinal-Duke of York survived until 1807 as Cardinal-Bishop of Frascati, and took part in the election of Pius VII. He was also archpriest of St Peter's, and a pension was conferred upon him by the British government. He sent the crown jewels, which he had inherited from his brother, to George IV. There is a family vault which contains the remains of the last legitimate descendants of the Stuart kings, under St Peter's in Rome, and a marble monument to their memory stands in the aisle above.

XXXI.

THE PRESSURE OF THE PENAL LAWS.

(1745-1778.)

Failure of the Jacobites. THE failure of the various attempts which had been made to bring about a restoration of the Stuarts, and especially the final collapse of the rising in 1745, could not but have a considerable effect upon the position of the Church in England. This effect was a somewhat complex one. On the one hand Catholics had clung more patiently than others to the hope that the cause which promised them relief and liberty might after all triumph. Their disappointment was consequently all the deeper when this was proved to be no longer within the range of practical politics. Even then the lesson was assimilated but slowly by a large proportion of them. It had been faced by some long before the rebellion of 1745, while others would not accept it as a fact until a still later date. Nevertheless, if we speak of the majority, this disastrous rising was the turning point which determined them as a body loyally to accept the Hanoverian dynasty as a permanent institution in their native land.

Catholics still under the Penal Laws. Yet, even when they were ready to fall in with the results of the Revolution, their past record must have prejudiced their position both politically and socially. Their loyalty was apt to be under suspicion, as being of the sort which sprang from necessity. Any attempt to gain a relaxation of their hard lot was hopeless. They were still made to feel that they were as outlaws in their own country, subject to all manner of legal disabilities. They were tempted to shrink back into their shell, aiming only at being forgotten and left alone. A kind of dull discouragement fell on them as a body. Hence it is easy to understand that, though there was no widespread defection, their numbers went on gradually declining for a long series of years. It was difficult to make any headway against the grinding pressure of the body of legislation which had been contrived to crush them out of existence. And, if as sometimes happened, the support of the clergy failed, whole congregations dwindled away and even died out.

It happened providentially that during the greater part of this very trying period, which marks the zero of Catholicism in England, the faithful were governed by four Vicars-Apostolic who were men of sterling worth, and, in general, of quite unusual abilities and virtues. **The Vicars-Apostolic.** These four were Bishop Richard Challoner, who practically ruled the London district from his consecration in 1741 until his death in 1781; Bishop Francis Petre, who was Vicar-Apostolic of the Northern district from 1752 to 1775; Bishop Hornyold, who succeeded Bishop Stonor in the Midlands in 1756 and died in 1778; while the Western district had the services of Bishop Charles Walmesley, O.S.B., from 1756 to 1797. These are the outstanding personalities in the Church in England during the years we are speaking of in this chapter. But it will be seen from the dates that they were only strictly contemporaries in their respective charges for the two decades from 1756 to 1775. Yet between them it was chiefly these four who gave a tone and character to the episcopal government of the epoch. They carried on faithfully the traditions of the past, and took what measures were possible against the distressing circumstances of the times.

The veneration of the Catholic faithful has gone out to Bishop Richard Challoner more than to any of the others. He was and is still recognised as the foremost champion of the children of the Church in this dark era. In fact a halo of sanctity crowns his venerable figure, which seems destined never to suffer eclipse. **Bishop Richard Challoner (1691-1781).**

The future bishop was named Richard after his father, a wine cooper, residing at Lewes in Sussex, where he was born on the 29th of September, 1691. His father, who was a Presbyterian, had him christened a Protestant, but died soon after. Thereupon his mother entered into the services of two Catholic families in succession; the

Gages of Frile, and the Holmans of Warkworth Castle. Dr Gother was chaplain in the latter establishment, and he it was who received Mrs Challoner into the Church and took charge of the early instruction of Richard. Gother then joined his recommendation to the patronage of Lady Holman, daughter of Lord Stafford, the martyr, to procure Richard Challoner's admission to Douay, where he completed his education from his entrance there in 1704 until his ordination in 1716. Challoner remained at Douay for four years as professor, and for ten more as vice-president, until 1730, and then was sent on the English mission. London was his residence for the half-century of industrious labour, which only ended when his long life of ninety years was drawing to a close. Efforts were made to win him back to Douay as president, but the Vicar-Apostolic of the district intervened, and got him appointed as his coadjutor in 1741. He was consecrated on the 29th of January of that year at Hammersmith by Bishop Benjamin Petre, who had procured his nomination. Although it was not until 1759 that the death of this prelate put the vicariate in his hands in the full sense, yet, since Bishop Petre led a very secluded life at the country seat of his family in Essex, Challoner soon found that nearly all the practical administration of the vicariate fell upon him. He it was who made the visitations all through the widely scattered missions of the district. He was the preacher whose earnest discourses were like a lamp and a centre of heat to the Catholics of London. His was the correspondence that had to be carried on concerning public affairs, both with Rome and with the other vicars. His too, especially, was the unobtrusive but edifying example shown to the world of a Catholic bishop keeping up his courage and that of his flock when progress and even freedom seemed almost hopeless, and all this time leading a life of strict asceticism and heroic constancy to the path of duty.

Bishop Challoner was likewise a very voluminous writer; in fact he seems to have attempted with his pen **Bishop Challoner's Works.** to exercise that wider apostolate which the sad circumstances of the times debarred him from in other ways. He began the publication of books at the very beginning of his career as a missionary priest, and kept it up even to a period of old age when most men would have long ceased from all active exertion. The long list of his publications begins with the short set of meditations styled, "*Think well on't*," which saw the light as early as 1728. In the course of the next ten years he followed this up by a number of lesser controversial works, the most important of which is "*The Catholic Christian Instructed*," which was a reply to the anti-Catholic assertions of Dr Conyers Middleton. The "*Garden of the Soul*" appeared in 1740, and attained a popularity as a manual of popular devotion that has never since been completely lost. The "*Memoirs of Missionary Priests*" was published in 1742 and 1743, containing a patiently compiled account of lives and deaths of the English martyrs. The counterpart to this was the "*Britannia Sancta*" of 1745, which gave the lives of English, Scottish, Irish, and British saints up to the Reformation. Some years later he made another important addition to his hagiological labours in bringing out the lives of the fathers of the desert, under the title "Wonders of God in the Wilderness." His revision of the Rheims Testament and the Douay Bible saw the light between 1738 and 1750, and as far as the ordinary use of English speaking Catholics was concerned, quite superseded the older editions. He is also responsible for an abridgment of Whitehead's "Life of St Teresa," and for translations of "The Confessions of St Augustine," "St Francis de Sales' Philothea," and Boudon's treatise on "The Presence of God," and of the "Imitation of Christ." His "*Meditations*" for every day in the year has ever since been a favourite both in the households of the laity and in the convents of religious, while we also owe to him a treatise on the "*Devotion of Catholics to the Blessed Virgin*," as well as a considerable number of tracts, pastorals, and short treatises designed to meet the passing needs of the hour. In fact Challoner ever wrote with severe attention to the practical wants of his brethren. Literary style, the display of learning, rhetoric, was as nothing in his eyes, but he undertook the labours of composition with the sole intention of providing for the needs of reading Catholics in every department to which he could reach. And it is not too much to say that he attained his aim with a success that was quite phenomenal.

476   THE CHURCH IN ENGLAND

Contemporary Prelates.

When Dr Challoner was consecrated in January, 1741, as coadjutor for the London district, that of the Midlands was in the hands of Bishop John Stonor, but in 1756 he was succeeded by the well-known Catholic writer, Dr John Hornyold, who had been made his coadjutor some four years before. He it was who ruled the Midland vicariate for the remainder of this period. He was a member of the ancient Catholic family of Hornyold of Blackmore Park in Worcestershire. His reputation, however, rests still more upon his quite indefatigable labours in the missionary field, and on his printed works. With regard to the former, he visited with the greatest assiduity the Catholic missions in the fifteen counties comprised in his vicariate, often replacing priests who were absent, even at the risk of apprehension and imprisonment, while hairbreadth escapes from his pursuers made his record of travel one of danger if not of romance. His chief works are "*The Decalogue Explained*," "*The Sacraments Explained*," and the "*True Principles of Catholics*," which last work may be considered as having been in its time a standard book of controversy. Dr Hornyold made his home at Longbirch, near Wolverhampton, the residence of the pious "Madam Giffard." Dr Edward Dicconson was consecrated for the Northern district in the same year as Challoner, but he was already an aged man, and after about eleven years was succeeded by his coadjutor, Dr Francis Petre, who then administered the Northern district for five-and-twenty years (1751-75). The vicars of the Western district were all from the ranks of the regular clergy, and Bishop Pritchard, O.S.F., survived until 1750, though a Benedictine coadjutor, Dr Lawrence York, was consecrated for his assistance in 1741. But the choice of Bishop Charles Walmesley, another Benedictine, in 1756 to assist him in turn, gave the West the services for more than forty years (1756-97) of one of the best scholars of the day. Dr Walmesley was the author of various mathematical and astronomical treatises, and in his "*General History of the Christian Church*," developed under the name of Pastorini a theory of applying the Apocalypse of St John to the history of the Church in all ages, rather than to the early ages alone, which makes this book quite a remarkable

contribution to the exegesis of St John's revelations.
It is through consecration at the hands of Bishop
Walmesley that the present English Hierarchy, as well
as the hierarchy which began with Baltimore in the
United States, traces its apostolic succession.

True as it is to say that there was no wholesale defection
from the Church in England during the period which
this chapter is concerned with, the defec-
tions which did take place were in some **Apostasy in High Places.**
cases among those whose high position
made their departure all the more disastrous. The
houses of the Catholic gentry were the chief centres
which held together nearly all the little congregations
of the faithful which were scattered up and down the
country. Hence, when one of these failed, it usually
meant the break up of at least one of these bodies, and
the scattering or perversion of those who composed it.
The most grievous loss which Catholics suffered in this
way in the period of the present chapter was the
closing of the great Catholic house at Cowdray in Sussex,
through the lapse of Lord Montague from the Faith of
his fathers. But it was not the only one. A place of
considerable splendour had ceased to be a Catholic centre
when Standon Lordship was sold in 1767 at the death of
the last Lord Aston. Moreover, though a priest was
kept at Arundel by the Duke of Norfolk, the castle was
allowed by the duke of that day to fall into a state of
decay, and the family resided elsewhere. The chapel,
which had long been a centre of religious worship for
the Lancashire Catholics at Croxteth Hall, Liverpool,
was no longer so, after the apostasy of Lord Molyneux
in 1768, though provision was made for services at a
neighbouring farmhouse. When the noble family of
Herbert became extinct, as far as its Catholic members
were concerned, Powys Castle was no longer a Catholic
home, and another gathering place for the faithful had
ceased to be such.

All honour then to the faithful remnant who
persevered while others fell away, leading for the most
part regular and edifying lives, and in
their secluded and carefully kept homes **The Faithful Remnant.**
doing what lay in their power to shelter
the priests, to find a decent place of worship for
their poorer neighbours, and to save their souls in the

midst of general distrust and a host of galling restrictions. It would not be easy to exaggerate the debt of gratitude due to those old Catholic families, whether gentry or yeomen, who have been Catholic even in the worst times, some of which survive still, for keeping the lamp of the Faith burning in many localities where otherwise it must, humanly speaking, have been totally extinguished. It is a roll of honour and of undying fidelity. Not a single name or house should be forgotten. But it is of course quite impossible to inscribe the full list here. There are some of these venerable shrines, for they are such, still in existence. Baddesley Clinton, the seat of the Ferrers, still has Mass in the secluded chapel, with its priests' hiding-place within the moated grange as in those evil days. The mission at Biddlestone, the old home of the Selbys, goes back to the thirteenth century. Oxburgh carries on the tradition of the Bedingfields' faith from the worst days of persecution. Moreover, there were smaller, but not less honourable, centres which have survived. East Hendred and the Eystons still hold the primacy among the Berkshire Catholics. And there are Langdales and Middletons and Silvertops and Vaughans and Arundells still upholding the Faith for which their fathers suffered. The names given above are but a few, chosen almost at random, out of what would be a remnant of Catholic days indeed, but a remnant each thread of which is golden with sacrifice, and quite too extensive to find mention in this short record.

While Challoner and other devoted clergy, trained at Douay, were undauntedly rowing against the stream in England, not to lose ground in the chilling atmosphere of the period, another pious and learned scholar was earning for himself a place in Catholic literature, at least as high, and possibly more permanent.

Alban Butler (1710-1773). This was Dr Alban Butler. When Challoner was a young professor in the Douay Seminary, Alban Butler was a junior student in the same institution, and they became and remained friends through life. The same zealous Mr Holman of Warkworth, who had filled so great a place in Challoner's early life, was also responsible for Butler being sent to college in 1718. He was at the early age of eight, having been born in 1710. At Douay he remained for the full course of study, there he was made a priest in 1735, there too he remained as a teacher for another ten years, professing in turn philosophy and theology. But in 1745 he accepted the position of tutor in the family of the Earl of Shrewsbury, and travelled the grand tour with the young earl and his two brothers, afterwards Bishops James and Thomas Talbot. On his return he was sent for some years in the Midland district on the English mission, serving one congregation after another with exemplary piety and zeal. His next employment was that of superintending the education of Edward Howard, nephew and heir presumptive to the Duke of Norfolk. His residence was first in the duke's palace at Norwich, and afterwards, when foreign travel came into the scheme, at Paris. Young Howard, who is called by Charles Butler "the Marcellus of the English Catholics," unfortunately died in his youth. This left Butler free to accept the office of president of the College of St Omer, which had recently been taken over by the secular clergy from the Jesuits at the time of their suppression in France. In this position he remained for seven years till his death (1766-73). This last period of his life, which he had looked forward to as affording him opportunities for deeper study, was really the busiest of his life; he was overwhelmed with public affairs, being made Vicar-General for four French dioceses, but he always returned to his books and his prayers as soon as ever the pressure from without was taken off. He was a tireless reader and author—the ecclesiastical scholar *par excellence.* His nephew, Charles Butler, gives an account of his industry: "He generally allowed himself no more than four hours' sleep, and often passed whole nights in study and prayer. All his day was spent in reading. When he was alone he read; when he was in company he read; at his meals he read; in his walks he read; when he was in a carriage he read; when he was on horseback he read; whatever he did he read." And a very rapid and cursory perusal of books enabled his extraordinary memory to retain an accurate knowledge of their contents. We have the fruit of his studies in his great work "*The Lives of the Saints,*" which was published between the years 1756 and 1763. It contains an account of some one thousand six hundred saints and holy servants of God, and is equally distinguished by its accurate learning and its earnest piety. It is still a standard work, not only in English, but in the translations made into foreign languages. Though it stands on a pinnacle by itself as admittedly the best English book on the subject, it does not exhaust the list of Alban Butler's works. He is also the author of a work on the "*Movable Feasts of the Church*," and of several volumes of sermons. Several separate biographies and a book of travels were also published by him.

Alban Butler's life was written by his accomplished nephew, the well-known Catholic lawyer, Charles Butler,

Charles Butler (1750-1832). who gained rather an equivocal fame in the following period through the prominent part he took in the opposition made by the laymen of the Catholic Committee to the Vicars-Apostolic. Much of his public action at that period can surely not be justified from a Catholic point of view. And yet we must in fairness admit that Charles Butler was a real staunch member of the old Faith, and from his attainments and general knowledge an ornament to it. His private life was devout and pious to the verge of asceticism. And whatever concerned Catholic interests as he understood them lay near to his inmost thoughts. It was his line, taken in connection with the activities of the Catholic Board and Catholic Committee, which on occasion exposed him to the merited censure of the most trustworthy leaders and to the lifelong hostility of Bishop Milner. In all the controversies connected with the Repeal of the Penal Laws he was always a foremost and arresting figure. He was learned in the law, and though debarred from practising as a barrister by those very Penal Laws against which he strove, was deep in his profession as a consulting lawyer and in other ways. His attainments were so varied that he could write with ease on such diverse subjects as law, history, music, social science, and even Sacred Scripture. In the midst of his great activity as a Catholic leader and as a professional man, it was only by the greatest industry combined with the most methodical arrangement of his hours that he was able to find time for literary composition. Yet he did manage it with some success. His best known book is the "*Historical Memoirs of English, Scottish, and Irish Catholics*," but he also published "Commentaries on Coke on Littleton," a legal work often reprinted, Lives of Alban Butler, Fénelon, Bossuet, Grotius, and Erasmus. Also he is to be credited with a continuation of Butler's " Lives of the Saints," with a work on " Church Music," and with several controversial works arising out of his disputes with his co-religionists in the matter of Catholic Emancipation, and the legal oaths required against Catholics. After Emancipation had been won independently of him in 1829, one of its consequences was his being appointed King's Counsel, when he received a message of congratulation from the king. This was the crown, as far as this world goes, of his long and laborious life of devotion to Catholic interests in the way he conceived them to be best forwarded

XXXII.

THE EARLY RELIEF ACTS.

(1778-1803.)

The Relief Act of 1778. THE situation of the faithful in England up to the end of 1777 was such that they presented the appearance of having settled down into a position of frost-like rigidity. But with the commencement of 1778 there dawned upon them a new ray of hope from the prospect of a Relief Act, whose sudden passing into law was striking rather than generous or satisfactory. The bill owed its introduction to the accident of the government of the day being in difficulties over other questions. The war with the American colonies was going on very unfavourably, and there was danger of war with France and Spain as well. Under these circumstances the royal ministers turned their attention to the Catholic Highlands of Scotland as a likely recruiting ground for the army. They sounded the Vicar-Apostolic, Dr Hay, as to what measures of relief would be needed to secure the hearty allegiance of the Highland Catholics and their support in the war. Bishop Hay suggested the repeal of all laws against the hearing and saying of Mass, as well as security for the property of Catholics, and a modification of the oath to be taken by recruits for the army. At the same time, he urged that the co-operation of the Vicar-Apostolic in London and his coadjutor should be sought for. Consequently an interview was arranged between Bishop Challoner and Sir John Dalrymple, who was acting for the government. The meeting took place in April, but does not seem to have been very successful, for on the one hand Challoner shrank from arousing anti-Catholic feeling, and on the other considered that more should be conceded than Bishop Hay asked for. Dalrymple now turned to the laity, who were more favourable to his proposals. A committee of the laity drew up an address to the king protesting their loyalty, and praying for relief from the grievous disabilities from which Catholics were suffering. The address was presented by the Earl of Surrey at a levee on the 1st of May, and was graciously received. It then appeared in the *Gazette*.

The time now seemed ripe for the introduction of a bill into Parliament, as the ministerial necessities had not diminished. Moreover, such Whigs as Edmund Burke, Sir George Savile, and Lord Rockingham wished that Catholics should be relieved of their burdens more from motives of justice than of mere expediency. Eventually it was thought best that the bill should limit itself to the repeal of the act of William III. which prevented Catholics from inheriting or buying land, and put their estates at the mercy of the next Protestant heir, while it also inflicted the punishment of lifelong imprisonment on every bishop, priest, or schoolmaster, awarding a grant of one hundred pounds to any informer who led to their conviction. It did not remove the death penalties decreed by the legislation of Elizabeth, nor did it apply to any who within six months should not have taken the Oath of Allegiance to George III. which it embodied. The bill was entrusted to Sir George Savile, who brought it in, and was supported by speeches from Lord Thurlow and Mr Dunning, and had the approval of Lord North. It was limited to England and Wales, but notice was given that a similar bill should be brought in separately for Scotland. In the House of Lords it was supported by Rockingham and Shelburne. Its various stages followed one another with little opposition and with great expedition during the last days of May, and on the 3rd of June it obtained the royal assent. *The Relief Act Passes (May, 1778).*

The effect of the Relief Act of 1778 upon the constitutional position of Catholics in England, though it was of considerable importance, was, of course, far short of what liberty and justice required, but it was all that could be obtained at the time, and it was gained with unexpected ease. It left, indeed, the sanguinary laws of Elizabeth, but they were most unlikely to be put into force. It *Effects of the Relief Act.*

did not open Parliament or the professions to Catholics, but it gave them security in their estates and their worship. It exacted an Oath of Allegiance, which involved the renouncing of the Stuart Pretender, of the temporal and civil power of the Pope in England, and of the deposing power, but it did not call on them to abjure any article of the Faith. But its effect was not only political, but social and moral as well. It broke down prejudice, it restored to them a greater share in the social life of their neighbours than they had hitherto enjoyed, and thus paved the way for the still further liberties which were gradually realised during the future years.

Still, the immediate result of the act was an outbreak of bigotry, which probably was almost foreseen by the cautious Challoner, and which culminated in the formidable Gordon Riots of 1780. Beyond the fact that the Relief Act was distasteful to all those who were hostile to the admission of Catholics to civil rights, the remote causes of the explosion are obscure. But when the more immediate agencies are sought for, we can easily find them in the establishment of the Protestant Association in 1779. Its avowed object was the defence of the Protestant religion against the encroachment of popery, but it adopted means both in public and private which were worthy of anarchists or revolutionaries. The Dissenters, notwithstanding that they to some extent still laboured under civil disabilities, were more hostile to Catholic relief than the members of the Church of England. We have unhappily to couple with the agitation the celebrated name of John Wesley, the founder of Methodism. It is painful to think that one possessed of so much zeal and religious feeling could be so led away by prejudice, and lend himself to so sinister an enterprise. The campaign began with an organised attempt to awaken alarm and dislike of the Catholics by means of sermons and pamphlets. The next step was the drawing up and signing of monster petitions to Parliament asking for the repeal of the Relief Act. The next step was to elect as president of the Protestant Association the eccentric Lord George Gordon. This strange young nobleman, a son of the Duke of Gordon, was a member of the House of Commons, whose name

The Gordon Riots (1780).

was already a by-word for extravagance and half-demented effrontery. He it was who, after fruitlessly presenting petitions to the Prime Minister, Lord North, and to George III. in person, took upon himself to carry a monster petition of the Protestant Association against popery to the House of Commons, and he promised that he would be at the head of many thousands of his supporters. The day chosen was the 2nd of June, 1780, and on that day three processions, assembled in various localities, converged upon the Houses of Parliament along appointed routes. The badge of the association was a blue cockade, and as soon as the vast assembly had gathered in front of the Parliament, those of the members who were met without it, or refused to wear it, were set upon, knocked down, and maltreated. Among those who for a time fell into the hands of the mob were Lord Mansfield, Thurlow, Bathurst, the Duke of Northumberland, the Archbishop of York, Lord Ashburnham, and others. In the midst of the confusion it was impossible to proceed to business either in the Lords or in the Commons. The crowd penetrated into the lobbies, and could scarcely be debarred from forcing their way into the very chambers of debate. The mob was repeatedly harangued in inflammatory language by Lord George Gordon, but when evening came on, the Guards having been at last brought from their barracks, the mob dispersed, and the House adjourned, having almost unanimously voted against the immediate consideration of the petition.

As the night wore on the mob, which had gone off in various directions, began to indulge in acts of violence in quarters which had evidently been deliberately designated in advance. The chapels of the Bavarian and Sardinian embassies were wrecked that night, and various private houses damaged. *Progress of the rioting.* The following day brought a lull in the storm, but this unfortunately was not taken advantage of to provide for the public tranquillity. Bishop Challoner, however, and most of the priests succeeded in leaving their lodgings and betaking themselves to places of safety. The bishop took refuge under the hospitable roof of his friend, Mr Mawhood, at Finchley. In the evening there was some renewal of the disorder, but it was not until the next morning, Sunday, that the full violence of the mob began to show itself. A great crowd bore down upon the chapel in Ropemaker's Alley, Moorfields, and burned it, as well as several adjoining houses. And all this day the magistrates of the city, overcome with fear, declined to take any steps to put down the riot. On Monday the Catholic chapels in Smithfield and Wapping were destroyed, as well as many Catholic houses. Sir George Savile's house, that of the eminent Lord Mansfield, Lord Chief Justice, as well as those of several judges and magistrates, were plundered, and there gradually came into view forces of lawlessness and anarchy which threatened far wider ruin than that of the Catholics. The highest pitch of disorder was reached on Tuesday, when Newgate prison was burst open and burnt, and some three hundred prisoners liberated. At last the government took serious steps to quell the riot. A proclamation authorising the suppression of disorder by military force was read, and all the available troops were used against the rioters. Volleys were fired and charges were made at the point of the bayonet, wherever resistance was attempted. Many of the rioters perished in this way as well as in the confusion of the destruction of so many buildings by fire. But it was Thursday before tranquillity was entirely restored. It was found that two hundred and eighty-five had been killed or mortally wounded by the soldiers, nearly as many being more slightly wounded. Twenty-one rioters were executed on the scaffold. Besides the chapels, fifty-seven Catholic houses had been destroyed, for which compensation was afterwards paid by the county, this levy in itself being a proof of the advance made in the willingness to deal fairly with the faithful as compared with the outlawry of earlier penal days. There were minor riots at certain towns in the country, the most notable being at Bath, the residence of Bishop Walmesley. The bishop's house was destroyed, and the archives of the Western district burned, but the prelate himself escaped, and remained in safe concealment until the storm was over. But nothing occurred elsewhere to equal the very formidable character of the Gordon Riots.

Bishop Challoner, who had remained in security in Mr Mawhood's house at Finchley until there was a return of tranquillity, was in extreme old age, and though he thus escaped actual violence, he seems to have been much affected by the scenes enacted in the metropolis. He soon felt that his strength was ebbing away and death approaching. He fixed his thoughts more than ever on eternal things, but otherwise pursued the even tenor of his edifying routine of life unto the end. He was struck with paralysis while at dinner with his priests on the 10th of January, and on the 12th calmly breathed his last. He was buried in the chancel of the parish church of Milton, Berkshire, at the earnest request of his friend, Mr Barrett, the squire of that village, and solemn requiems were celebrated for his soul in all the chief Catholic places of worship in London. His death meant the succession to the charge of the vicariate of his coadjutor, Bishop James Talbot, who had assisted him in the labours of his office since 1759. He was only to survive as the chief pastor of the vicariate until 1790. His brother, Thomas, had been consecrated as coadjutor to Dr Hornyold in the Midlands in 1760, and the latter dying shortly before Challoner, he was then ruling the Midland vicariate. He died in the same year as his brother. They were both brothers of Gilbert, Earl of Shrewsbury, who had succeeded to the earldom on the death of the Duke of Shrewsbury, who had received that higher title from William III. as the price of his adhesion to the Revolution, which brought with it conformity with the Established Church. Gilbert was a priest, and hence in default of issue the title passed at his death to a junior branch of the family. Both these prelates were men of conciliatory disposition, whose chief work for the Faith lay in the direction of education, for while Bishop James completed the arrangements begun by Challoner for the foundation of Old Hall, Bishop Thomas commissioned the Rev. Thomas Barr to begin the scholastic establishment which developed into Oscott College. Almost in spite of themselves, both the Talbots became involved during the last years of their lives in the disputes between the bishops and the laity arising out of the foundation of the Catholic Committee. Bishop James, hoping to control it, at first became a member, but in the end their proceedings took so high-handed a tone that both joined with their fellow Vicar-Apostolic in the condemnation which

Bishop James and Thomas Talbot (1790).

they issued. But to the end Bishop James strove to show all possible consideration to the individual leaders of the movement.

The mention of the Catholic Committee a few lines above naturally leads to the narration of the rather disedifying history of that celebrated body of Catholics. In some sense it may be said that it took its origin in the committee formed to secure the passage of the Relief Act of 1778. However, in 1782 at last practically a new start was made in the following way: What was called a " General Meeting of English Catholics " was held on the 3rd of June, 1782, at the chambers of Mr William Sheldon in Gray's Inn, with the avowed object of choosing a committee to manage the public affairs of Catholics in England. Thirty persons, each representing a family of distinction, were present, and though it was truly contended that they were too few and too exclusive in class to claim to be a general meeting of all the Catholic body, it must be admitted that they enjoyed the support of a much larger number of influential laymen than attended the meeting. Five gentlemen were chosen to form the committee: Lords Petre and Stourton, with Messrs. Hornyold, Throckmorton, and Stapleton. The well-known Catholic lawyer, Charles Butler, nephew of Alban Butler, accepted the office of secretary. The first business they undertook to accomplish was the carrying out of a plan for substituting a regular hierarchy of Ordinary bishops for Vicars-Apostolic who had hitherto guided the Catholic flock. They held that the exceptional dependence of mere vicars of the Pope on the Roman see was an obstacle to the gaining of a more complete relief from civil disabilities on the part of the Catholic community at large. But when they went on to address the bishops in the following year in favour of promoting this scheme, only two out of the four returned even a moderately favourable answer, and on account of this the committee went no further in the matter, at least at that time. In fact for the next few years, although an annual meeting was held, the state of political parties made it almost impossible to further Catholic interests by taking any action in which government would be concerned. Moreover, the marriage of the Prince of Wales with the Catholic widow, Mrs Fitz-

The Catholic Committee (1782).

THE EARLY RELIEF ACTS 489

herbert, in 1785 was thought to add a social reason to the political ones, which dissuaded the leaders of the Catholic body from taking any immediate action in any attempt of the kind.

A new impetus was given to the agitation in the year 1787, when a larger and more powerful committee was formed out of the original five at a meeting held on the 3rd of May. Besides the attempt which had been made to work for the restoration of the hierarchy, the members of the committee had already been thrown into opposition with the Vicars-Apostolic by means of a second subject which had been ventilated by some of the members. This was the establishment of a central college or high school for the upper classes of the faithful in England. One of the effects of this would have been to withdraw pupils taken from the higher classes of society from the English colleges on the continent of Europe. For this reason it attracted hostility from other quarters as well as from the Vicars-Apostolic. However, it was not until the Committee of 1787 was formed that these domestic controversies became public. But about this time the members were joined by Bishop Berington, who had been consecrated in 1786, as coadjutor to Bishop Talbot in the Midland district, and also by a well-known Benedictine, Father Wilkes. They then almost at once got into touch with the powerful Premier, William Pitt, by means of a memorial which they presented to him. The minister in an informal interview showed some disinclination to receive a formal deputation, and counselled that no attempts should be made to introduce a Relief Bill before the next year (1788), but said that they were free to take their chance if they preferred to proceed at once. Eventually, however, he did receive such a deputation, and encouraged them to draft a bill, while he suggested that Catholics should make some public declaration upon the points of the papal dispensing power, as that had been so often objected against them in discussion with Protestants. Charles Butler then proceeded carefully to draft a bill for the objects aimed at. With regard to the suggestion that some public declaration against the papal dispensing power should be made by Catholics, the committee drew up a *Protestation* without any consultation with the Vicars-Apostolic,

The Committee of 1787.

which went so far in abjuring the papal deposing power, the papal power of dispensing with the oaths, the papal infallibility and jurisdiction, and the necessity of keeping faith with heretics, that it was landed into language which was so inaccurate that a Catholic could hardly in conscience sign it. However, after drafting the Protestation the committee set themselves to get it generally subscribed both by the clergy and by influential members of the laity. By dint of persuasion and explanation and some amount of not too straightforward manipulation some one thousand five hundred signatures were obtained, of which two hundred and forty were those of priests, thus being signed by more than two-thirds of the priests in England. In the same way the Protestation was also signed by the Vicars-Apostolic with the exception of Bishop Gibson.

The drafting of the bill took Charles Butler at least four months, and he had not completed it until March, 1789. It was at first hoped that it might be brought into Parliament and passed during that year, but the illness of the king and other causes led to delay. The Lay Committee seem to have acted throughout with very little consultation with the bishops, and tried to arrange things with the government over their heads. When later on in the year the king recovered his health, thereby giving Pitt a renewal of power, the prospects of getting a Relief Act passed grew brighter, and the bill was got ready. In the process of preparing it, however, very important changes were made by the committee with whom Bishop Berington alone was acting, and the result was disastrous. A new oath was incorpor-

Condemnation of the Oath and of the Draft Bill.

ated in the bill, by which Catholics were made not only to swear allegiance to the House of Hanover, but also to abjure the deposing powers of the Pope as well as his temporal power in general. In the bill Catholics were spoken of by the new and strange title of "Protesting Catholic Dissenters," and contrasted with papists, who were forbidden to educate any child in popery. Moreover, it was to be enacted that all property dispositions heretofore treated as superstitious were to continue to be so treated. Though the bishops were not consulted, with the possible exception of Bishop James Talbot, they before long came to know what was proposed,

THE EARLY RELIEF ACTS 491

and held a meeting at Hammersmith to consider the situation. The result was a specific condemnation of the new oath, and also of the objectionable provisions in the bill, as well as the drawing up of a circular letter to the Catholic body informing them of this, which was signed by the four Vicars-Apostolic. This was communicated to the members of the committee, who replied earnestly begging that the publication of the circular might be delayed until explanations could be given. Eventually Bishops Walmesley and Gibson published the circular, but in the Midland and London districts, under the two Bishops Talbot, it was never published. However, it remained true that the oath and much of the bill had been explicitly condemned. Very soon after this Bishop James Talbot, who had been for some time in bad health, died, and the London vicariate was vacant. Bishop James Talbot was a man of blameless and edifying life, not by any means indifferent to the progress of Catholicism in his district, as witness his efforts for the firm establishment of the missions at the Spanish and Bavarian embassies, and for the building of the new church in St George's Fields, Southwark. But he was of too weak and yielding a character to take the lead in difficult public affairs.

The Catholic Committee now endeavoured to intervene in the selection of a new vicar for the London district, trying to secure the appointment of Bishop Berington. The London clergy also held a meeting, at which they somewhat informally put forward the Rev. John Douglass. The Roman authorities were informed of all this, and every effort was made on both sides to secure success. The contest was ended by the unexpected refusal of Bishop Berington to accept the office. The Rev. John Douglass was then named. While the London district was vacant, Bishop Gibson also died, but though there were signs of some similar trouble in the North, when the wishes of the late bishop became known in favour of his brother, Rev. William Gibson, president of Douay, he was appointed without much further trouble. Both Bishop Douglass and Bishop William Gibson were consecrated at Lulworth Castle, the latter on the 5th and the former on the 19th of December, 1790. A month later the new bishops joined with Bishop Walmesley in

Bishop Douglass (1790-1812).

issuing a second condemnation of the oath, though Bishop Thomas Talbot still refused to sign.

The reply of the committee was to draw up and sign a protest and appeal: the protest being against the action **The Relief Bill of 1791.** of the bishops, and the appeal to God and the Holy See. There was no time to lose, for the Relief Bill was on the eve of appearing in the House of Commons. Four days later Mr Mitford applied for leave to introduce it, and it was referred to a committee of the whole House. Knowing that it would be worse than useless with the oath and provisions as they then stood, the Vicars-Apostolic conferred, and making use of the assistance of the Rev. John Milner, also had more than one conference with the members of the Catholic Committee. Nothing in the way of a compromise could be arranged at these meetings, and much heat was displayed in discussion. Milner, who was assiduous in his attendance in the lobbies of Parliament, circulated on his own authority two hand-bills exposing the weak points in the bill. These were disavowed by the bishops, and Milner withdrew to Winchester. Meanwhile the bill was introduced with a debate in the House of Commons, Burke, Pitt, Fox, and nearly all the chief speakers being in favour of Catholic relief, but Fox being dubious as to the limitations to freedom inserted in the measure. In this way it was read for the first time on March 10th, and for the second on March 21st. It then went through committee and was read the third time. It was still unamended so far as the bishops' objections went, and Dr Walmesley declared he would rather it failed as it then stood. The only hope now was the House of Lords. The intercession of the Anglican bishops was sought with but indifferent success. However, on the second reading, on May 31st, Bishop Horsley of St Davids made a remarkable speech, which put the bishops' objections in such striking form that he carried the House with him. The oath was amended, the term Catholic Protesting Dissenters disappeared, the bill was read for the third time, and finally received the royal assent on the 10th of June. Though many restrictions remained, it became now lawful to open churches, to profess Catholicity, and to feel free from the arbitrary prosecutions to which they had hitherto been subject.

THE EARLY RELIEF ACTS

A phenomenon which was the occasion of much interest among the English Catholics, and, as time went on, became a potent agent for good, appeared in the country during the last years of the eighteenth century. This was the arrival in England of large numbers of the French clergy exiled from their native land through the irreligious policy of the leaders of the French Revolution. *French Exiled Priests from the Revolution.* The first large emigration took place in the years 1792-3, during the earlier stages of the National Assembly, and was a consequent of the law passed by that body banishing all those priests who reformed to swear to the Civil Constitution of the Clergy. The precursor who was first to establish himself in England was Monseigneur de la Marche, Bishop of St Pol de Léon, and this holy and energetic prelate remained, as long as he lived, the very soul and almost the superior, at least informally, of all the French exiles. A second stream followed the first in the year from 1794 to 1795. This seems to have been accelerated by the terrible fate of the clergy who fell into the hands of the revolutionaries at the Reign of Terror. What is looked upon as a third stream of emigration took place from 1797 to 1799, during the new persecution set on foot by the Directory. Of course by no means all the priests who escaped from France came to England: it is said, for example, that as many as twelve thousand at one time took refuge in the Papal States. Still for most of the years mentioned the number domiciled in the country was truly considerable, far outdistancing the number of native priests, and making quite a noticeable addition to the population of the district where they lived. In the year 1793 there were computed to be in London one thousand five hundred, in Winchester six hundred, in other districts of England five hundred, in the Channel Islands over two thousand. The reception they met with from the Protestant public was an astonishingly friendly and generous one. Public subscriptions were set on foot, and largely contributed to by the people of means, in such wise that every month an allowance was made ranging from ten pound to thirty shillings, which at first was organised without the assistance of the government. The first direct help given by the British government was the grant of the old palace of King Charles at Winchester, known as the

King's House, as a residence for them, and here no less than six hundred led a kind of community life, full of piety and exercises of devotion. Later on the government came to the rescue with pecuniary help to the extent of about two hundred thousand pounds a year, and the allowance first made out of individual subscriptions could thus be kept up. In the front rank of those who thus befriended the French clergy in the hour of their trial were to be found such well-known names as those of the Marquis of Buckingham, Mr John Wilmot, Edmund Burke, Pitt, Lord Fitzwilliam, all well-known in contemporary history. Among the clergy were to be found at one time no fewer than nineteen bishops, and it must be said that the conduct of all this vast body of clergy thrown out of their ordinary surroundings was most exemplary. There can be little doubt that an immense good work in the way of softening prejudice and showing the English people the Catholic clergy in an attractive light was done by these exiles or *émigrés*, as they were called, in the midst of their misfortunes.

When the concordat gave peace to the Church in France, the vast majority of these priests returned to their country, but we have a still greater debt of gratitude to the minority who remained behind, began to work for the natives as well as for the French, and became the means of establishing many new missions which since their time have grown into large and prosperous parishes. The following parishes are amongst those which in this way owe their origin to the French clergy: the French church in King Street, Portman Square, was for them the official centre of French Catholicism until our own times. The Hampstead mission owes its origin to the Abbé Morel, who attended to it for fifty-six years. The Abbé de Fanous was the founder of the mission at Cadogan Street, Chelsea. The Tottenham mission was begun by the Abbé, later on cardinal, Chéverus. The labours of the Abbé Carron in the establishment at Somers Town were still more arduous and effective, leading as they did besides this to the coming of the Faithful Companions to England in 1830. Others remained in England who did excellent work as curates or auxiliaries to the priests in charge of the various missions up and down the country.

Churches built by the French Clergy.

THE EARLY RELIEF ACTS 495

Over and above the general effect of the French Revolution in promoting the growth of liberal opinions on matters of religion and in restraining the bigotry which had hindered the relief of Catholics from their disabilities, its very violence had told in favour of the growth of the Faith in England. It had thrown upon our shores thousands of pious and zealous priests who had tried to repay the temporal favours they had received by becoming the instrument of the spiritual gift of faith coming down upon their benefactors. But it had done more than this. It had made necessary the return to their native land of those colleges and religious houses which had sheltered the Catholics in penal days. The colleges at Douay and St Omer were both seized by the Revolutionary government in the summer of 1793, and the students from Douay made their escape to England as best they could. On the 16th of November the first band of them was taken by Bishop Douglass to make a new beginning at Old Hall Green, Ware, on St Edmund's Day. In the following October another band of Douay students were installed at Crook Hall, Durham, under the presidency of Rev. William Eyre, with Rev. John Lingard as his vice-president. But there were still students from the North at Old Hall, and there was some controversy between Bishop Douglass and the Northern clergy as to whether a distinct college should be established in the North, but eventually all those from the North were recalled to Crook, and the two colleges grew side by side. Crook Hall was moved to Ushaw in 1804, and a new college was built at Old Hall in the years 1795-99. The students from the Jesuit College at St Omer had to suffer imprisonment for some time, but after the end of the " terror " they were released, and settled in a mansion given them by Mr Charles Weld at Stonyhurst, near Blackburn, in 1794. It was in 1794 and 1795 that the greater number of the English religious communities effected their **Return of the Exiles.** return. The Benedictine house at Douay had no better fate than the Seminary at the hands of the French republicans. The community, consisting of about thirty persons, suffered imprisonment repeatedly up to the year 1795, but in that year a petition for their release being granted; the monks were able to pass over into England, where they were first received by a former pupil, Sir Edward Smyth, at Acton Burnell. There they remained until in 1814 they were able to begin the monastery at Downside. Somewhat similar were the fortunes of the English Benedictines of Dieuleward. They too were obliged to flee before the Revolution, and were welcomed equally cordially at Acton Burnell. In 1802 they established themselves in their present home at Ampleforth. Meanwhile the Benedictine communities of nuns were also finding their way back to England. The Brussels foundation, which was the parent of the others, was obliged to leave that city for England in 1794, and settled at first in Winchester, whence they moved to East Bergholt in 1857. In like manner the house at Ghent was sold, and the nuns crossed over to their native land in 1794. After a period at Preston and another at Caverswall, they established the existing abbey at Oulton in 1853. St Scholastica's Abbey, Teignmouth, represents the filiation from Ghent which went to Boulogne and Dunkirk, whose first home after their return in 1795 was Cupola House, Hammersmith. In the same year (1795) the nuns of Cambray Abbey came over to Woolton, and at last, in 1838, founded their present home at Stanbrook. The English Benedictine nuns from Paris returning in the same year, have found a home at Colwich in Staffordshire. But there were other nuns besides Benedictines to return. The Austin Canonesses of St Ursula's, Louvain, left that city in 1794, and after a prolonged stay at Spettisbury in Dorset, founded the priory of St Augustine, Newton Abbot, in 1860. About the same time the Canonesses of the Holy Sepulchre left Liège, and as early as 1799 were able to take possession of their present beautiful home at New Hall, near Chelmsford. Three Carmelite houses also were transferred to English soil, the nuns of Antwerp founding the house at Lanherne, the Lierre community after some time establishing itself at Darlington, while the Hoogstraet nuns, after many wanderings, at last settled at Chichester. As soon as they could get free from their imprisonment after the fall of Robespierre, all the English Poor Clares returned; they eventually established themselves at Darlington, Baddesley Clinton, and other places. There were also English Franciscan nuns of the Third Order who came home; they have founded the house

THE EARLY RELIEF ACTS

at Taunton. The Dominicanesses likewise came about the same time, and survive at Carisbrooke in the Isle of Wight. The Brigittines of Sion House, long settled at Lisbon, are still represented by the convent at Chudleigh in Devonshire. Thus did the persecution on the continent of Europe prove indirectly an agent in the revival of the religious life in England, and gave occasion to an important movement, which has been fraught with blessings to the body of the faithful.

XXXIII.

CATHOLIC EMANCIPATION.

(1803-1829.)

A PERIOD of twenty-six years may be conveniently marked off between the two dates of 1803 and 1829, during which the question of Catholic Emancipation shared with that of Parliamentary Reform the front place in domestic politics. The advance towards a satisfactory settlement of the former subject was a very gradual and chequered process, the steps in which we must now proceed to show. The two Relief Acts, passed in 1778 and in 1791 respectively, had freed Catholics from the most onerous and most grievous burdens laid on them by the Penal Laws, but much remained to be done before they were put on a footing of equality with their Protestant fellow-countrymen. The restrictions which still bound them were so considerable that they could hardly do otherwise than strive to get them removed. Yet so many of their efforts to obtain for themselves complete liberty had so often failed that they had greatly slackened under the weight of discouragement. However, since the Act of Union of 1801, it became a question of treating the demands of Great Britain and Ireland as one whole. Now while in Great Britain the claim was that of a numerically small and insignificant minority, in Ireland the demand was that of four-fifths of the people. Consequently the main issue depended on the steps taken and the attitude adopted by the faithful in Ireland. It was this which supplied the chief driving power to force the problem upon the consideration of politicians. As early as 1805 the Catholic question, as it was called, was raised both in the House of Lords by Lord Granville, and in the

Gradual progress towards Emancipation.

CATHOLIC EMANCIPATION

Commons by Charles James Fox, but the petition for the admission of the Irish Catholics to equal rights was rejected in both assemblies by large majorities. Fox had been supported by the great man of whom we have now to speak, but in vain.

It seems likely that on many hands the part taken in the securing of Emancipation by the noble Irish orator, Henry Grattan, is almost overlooked. He was not a Catholic, but played such a part in securing the legislative independence of his country that the Parliament which met in Dublin in 1782 was popularly called Grattan's Parliament. **Henry Grattan (1746-1820).** And he never faltered in his opinions about the independence of Ireland in a legislative sense. However, after the Act of Union in 1801, he retired into private life for four years, as he looked upon his career in Ireland as over. In 1805 he was prevailed upon to enter the British Parliament, and from that time until his death in 1820 filled an honoured and honourable place on its benches. He was called forward by Fox from the back seat, where he had modestly placed himself, with courteous words of friendship. A patriot still, he yet looked on the Union as an accomplished fact, and only strove to gain from it whatever advantages he could for his native land. But the immediate point to which he devoted himself was the advancement of Catholic claims to religious equality. His first speech, made in 1806, was devoted to this subject. He brought forward the Catholic question again in 1808, stating that he was duly authorised by Milner to offer a veto on episcopal appointments. In the following year, however, Milner retracted, and when Grattan's bill was introduced in 1813 it contained a provision for this. The opposition to the veto had by this time become so strong that Grattan became unpopular with the Catholics, and though the bill passed, it was withdrawn in the face of the concessions made. Grattan died in 1820 through an illness brought on in journeying to London to speak once more in favour of the Catholic claims. He was buried in Westminster Abbey.

But a more uncompromising advocate of the Catholic claims had before this arisen amongst the English clergy in the person of Dr John Milner. This illustrious prelate, whose life history was bound up with the fortunes

Bishop Milner (1803-1826) and Bishop Poynter (1803-1827).
of his co-religionists for the next twenty-three years, was consecrated as Vicar-Apostolic of the Midland district at Winchester on the 22nd of May, 1803. He was at the time just over fifty years of age, having spent twenty-three years as priest in the important mission which that city was then considered to be. His previous life from his birth in 1772 had been equally divided between his native land and Douay College. His influence on the affairs of the Church for the preceding part of his life as a priest has been spoken of in the last chapter. At Winchester also he had written his "*History of Winchester*," and his "*Letters to a Prebendary*." Henceforward he was to be the central figure in the controversies which gathered round the Emancipation question. A week after Milner's elevation to the episcopate St Edmund's College, Old Hall, saw a similar function for the consecration of Dr William Poynter as coadjutor to Bishop Douglass in the London district. The last named prelate had wished to have as coadjutor Dr Gregory Stapleton, the first president of St Edmund's, but in 1801 this worthy man was made Vicar-Apostolic of the Midland district in succession to Bishop Berington. He only survived his appointment as bishop for one year, dying in 1802. It was then that Milner was chosen to govern the Midland district. As coadjutor in London the Holy See now fell back upon the Vice-Rector at St Edmund's, Dr Poynter, so that for the next twenty years and more Milner in the Midlands and Poynter in London became the leaders of the clergy in their public action. They were pious and learned men, but were as sharply contrasted in policy and outlook as it was possible for two men to be. Milner found himself set down in the midst of a clergy whose Cisalpine views but ill accorded with his own opinions. Yet only a limited time was needed before they learned to appreciate him, and thus established a bond of mutual trust between him and the majority of them.

Meanwhile Bishop Sharrock in the West had received as coadjutor the Franciscan father, Peter Bernardine Collingridge, who relieved him of nearly all the active work of the vicariate, and survived until the Emancipation year. Bishop William Gibson, who in 1790 followed his brother Matthew as Vicar-Apostolic in the

CATHOLIC EMANCIPATION 501

North, lived to administer that district for more than thirty years (1790-1821), and then the vicariate passed under the government of his coadjutor, Bishop Thomas Smith, who had aided him in his charge since 1810, when he was appointed for that purpose. Bishop Smith continued to rule the Northern district until his death in 1831. But however much Milner had won the respect of the great part of the clergy in his own vicariate, from the very first it became evident that he was far from seeing eye to eye with the other bishops. Unfortunately, his bearing and his brusque and uncompromising manner of pushing his own views led to friction. Often these views were the best and most correct, but these personal characteristics went far to interference with the harmony which ought to have reigned amongst the members of the episcopate. The other bishops resented the assumption on his part of a superiority which they did not consider him entitled to. They further thought themselves aggrieved by the charges he made against them of lukewarmness and want of independence. So difficult did conference between them become that between the years 1810 and 1825 there were only about two meetings of the Vicars-Apostolic held for the transaction of business.

In the year 1808 the Catholics in England who had for some years been quiescent under their remaining disabilities began once again to organise themselves with a view to their removal. The means they adopted was the formation of a society of prominent Catholic laymen, which was known as the Catholic Board. They included a very representative list of the nobility and gentry, and the chief organising spirit seems to have been Charles Butler. A public subscription to further the objects of the association was set on foot, which by the following March amounted to about one thousand five hundred pounds, and among the subscribers were all the Vicars-Apostolic and members of the clergy and of almost every well-known Catholic family. In April the Board met to take into consideration a petition they had received from the Northern Catholics, headed by Bishop Gibson, asking them to prepare an address to Parliament begging for the removal of their remaining grievances. This was done, and when ready was found to be couched in very suppliant tones, expressing gratitude for past

The Catholic Board (1808).

relief, and asking in particular for freedom to hold commissions in the army and navy, and for the right to vote at parliamentary elections. Milner was full of misgiving on account of the language used, but at last signed, as did all the Vicars-Apostolic, eight peers, three hundred priests, and eight thousand laymen. It was in consequence of this that Sir John Coxe Hippisley brought forward a scheme which he hoped would be generally acceptable. The veto was to be granted: in fact the government was to choose one out of a list of candidates submitted to them for vacant vicariates. But on the other hand it provided a State endowment, and spoke ambiguously of a government *placet* for papal letters. Nevertheless, the reception given to this plan was not so favourable as its author had hoped. It revived the agitation against the veto in Ireland, and excited considerable alarm in the north of England and elsewhere. Thereupon the Members of Parliament who were in favour of granting the Catholic demands tried to get into touch with their leaders in order to obtain from them in one form or another some tangible expression of their loyal acquiescence in the established order of things. The Board was not in a position to pledge the whole body of English and Irish Catholics to any definite proposals, but a meeting was held which the parliamentary supporters of the claims attended to draw up resolutions for submission to a more general meeting. This second meeting took place at St Alban's Tavern on the 29th and 30th of January, 1810. It was attended by three Vicars-Apostolic and by representatives from Ireland, as well as by the members of the Catholic Board. Five resolutions were drawn up and put into the form of a petition to Parliament, praying for the recognition of the full civil rights of Catholics. The fifth resolution was couched in language which seemed to many to give an opportunity for the introduction of a negative or veto on proposed episcopal appointments. It was defended by others as not intending any such thing. It was known that the government at that time was anxious to obtain such a veto, and this made its opponents suspicious of all ambiguous language on the subject. Eventually the resolutions were signed by all the English bishops with the exception of Dr Milner, who argued against signing, and further protested that he was acting as agent for the Irish bishops, who had already formally condemned the veto.

The result of the signing of the five resolutions by the Vicars-Apostolic, as well as by the Catholic Board, was on the one hand communicated to the friends of Emancipation in Parliament, and on the other hand at once became known in Ireland through the letters of Milner and in other ways. It produced a storm of angry protest. The Irish bishops met and reiterated their disapproval, and this was followed by a meeting of the laity, where the same sentiments were re-echoed with one accord. The language of the bishops was firm but measured: on the other hand irresponsible individuals assailed the English bishops and their flocks with words of unmitigated abuse, making the solitary exception of Dr Milner, to whom a vote of thanks was tendered. A lengthy and sharp correspondence ensued between members of the two episcopates, represented above all by Dr Poynter and Archbishop Troy of Dublin. Milner likewise plunged into the thick of the fight with a pamphlet styled the "Elucidation of the Veto." A champion of the veto was found in a priest named Dr O'Conor, who was acting as chaplain at Stowe, or rather as librarian in the Duke of Buckingham's house. O'Conor, however, gradually passed in the course of controversy to such heterodox and unsound views that he was suspended in 1812, both in the London district and in Dublin. Milner was now publicly disavowed by the Catholic Board, who passed a resolution that they did not consider themselves implicated or in any way responsible for his political opinions, conduct, or writings. The Vicars-Apostolic had no part in this, but later on they drew up and signed a joint letter of complaint to him, declaring that he had both misrepresented them to the Irish bishops, and injured their episcopal character before their own flocks. Milner replied at full length, in a letter to Bishop Douglass, answering the charges in detail, point by point, but finishing up with a long personal attack on the whole administration of the London vicariate under Bishop Douglass. He followed this up with somewhat similar letters to the other bishops, and thus ended the correspondence after a short note of acknowledgment from Bishop Douglass. For some years

Controversy on the Veto.

all possibility of friendly association between Milner and the other prelates was at an end.

On the 18th of May, 1810, the Catholic question was again raised by Grattan in the House of Commons. It was supported by Lord Castlereagh, Sir John Hippisley, Canning, and others. Mr Ponsonby quoted a former letter of Milner in which he professed to offer the veto on behalf of the Irish bishops. It is true that Milner and a standing committee of the bishops had accepted the veto, but when it was referred to all the Irish Hierarchy it did not gain their ratification, and Milner was disavowed. It was only afterwards that he became such a thoroughgoing opponent of the plan. Grattan's motion was defeated by a majority of one hundred and four, while a similar motion made by Lord Donoughmore in the House of Peers was negatived by a majority of ninety-six. Still the cause was gaining ground. In 1811 the same motions made by the same devoted advocates were defeated by the lessening majorities of sixty-three and fifty-nine respectively. It is true that in 1812 the same proposals encountered adverse majorities of one hundred and two and seventy-five, but later on in the year there were considerable changes in the government, Lord Liverpool becoming Premier, while Canning was introduced into the Cabinet. The latter was known to be in favour of the Catholic claims, and made use of his new position almost immediately to raise the question of removing the civil disabilities which stood in their way. Supported by Lord Castlereagh, he spoke and argued to such effect as to secure a majority in the Commons, while the motion in the Lords was only rejected by one vote. This was so encouraging that Grattan introduced and carried his annual motion by a majority of forty early in 1813, and a small committee of three, consisting of Grattan, Ponsonby, and a Mr Elliott, was appointed to prepare a Catholic Relief Bill, the drafting of which was entrusted to Charles Butler.

Catholic Question in Parliament.

As the bill left Charles Butler's hands it was quite short and simple in structure. It provided for the admission of Catholics to commissions in the army and navy, to the magistrates' bench, to sit and vote in Parliament, and to do the same in the corporations of cities

CATHOLIC EMANCIPATION

and towns. The only exclusion was from the offices of Lord Chancellor, Lord Lieutenant of Ireland, and from the right to present to livings in the Established Church. The condition exacted was the taking of a new Oath of Allegiance.

Proposed Bill of 1813.

There was no mention of any veto. The bill, however, underwent modification at the hands of Mr Canning, who introduced new clauses which enacted a veto by means of a commission, which was to advise the king on episcopal appointments, and to examine all bulls and dispensations received from Rome. Canning doubtless made these proposals in good faith, foreseeing that the Protestant feeling of Parliament would demand some definite securities, as they were called, for the loyalty of Catholics. But the effect of the additions was to alienate the support of the clergy, and to spoil the bill. Milner led the opposition at once, and the Irish bishops declared against it. Drs Poynter and Collingridge hesitated to pronounce a final verdict, and seemed to consider that the acceptance of the commission was not too high a price to pay for the concessions contained in the original draft. They protested that they did not like the proposed veto, but judged it to be the lesser of two evils. Against this view Milner argued in forcible and uncompromising language. As the event showed, there was no need for so much discussion, for the bill broke down in the committee stage of the second reading. The result of the debate on the clause admitting Catholics to Parliament was a majority of four against the clause. Mr Ponsonby then declared that without this the bill was not worth having. It was then formally withdrawn. The Catholic Board attributed its failure to Milner, who claimed to have wrecked it by his tract called a " Brief Memorial on the Catholic Bill." They showed their anger by the unjustifiable measure of expelling the bishop from the Board, which, however hostile he may have been, cannot be squared with the respect due to his position and episcopal character. The Irish bishops sent him a vote of thanks, and Daniel O'Connell thanked him in the course of a public speech.

The Catholic Board followed up their recent action by asking that the bishops would meet and discuss in common what securities could be given to the British government to ensure the passing of the Emancipation

Bill. It was in great part due to this request that the Vicars-Apostolic of England, who were joined by the two Scottish bishops, met in Durham at Bishop Gibson's house on the 25th of October. Bishop Milner was not invited, as they feared disunion and stormy scenes. Of course in this way the meeting retained an informal character, but Milner resented his being passed over, and spoke of the assembly as a " Conciliabulum." The result of the discussions at Durham was that the prelates there came to the conclusion that though certain provisions of the late bill could not be accepted, some limited form of veto might be admitted, and they composed a joint pastoral embodying the decisions at which they had arrived. An agent was then sent to Rome to represent both English and Scottish vicars before propaganda, and to endeavour to get a decision from the Holy See on the subject.

When this agent, the Rev. Mr Macpherson, arrived in the capital of Christendom he found everything in confusion. Pius VII. was absent, a prisoner in the hands of the Emperor Napoleon. Consalvi, the papal secretary, was also away, as well as Cardinal di Pietro, Prefect of Propaganda. The business of propaganda had been temporarily entrusted to the secretary, acting as a vice-prefect. This was the aged Monsignor Quarantotti. Persuaded by the representations of the Abbé Macpherson, Quarantotti took it upon himself to issue a rescript in the name of the Congregation of Propaganda, in which, while condemning certain points in the procedure ordained by the bill, he declared that a merely negative veto, which did not give the English government the positive choice of candidates for the episcopate, might be permitted. He at the same time put forth a second rescript inviting the British government to use its influence to bring about the restoration of the temporal power of the Pope and the restitution of the Holy Father's rights, which had been taken away by the usurpation of Napoleon.

The Quarantotti Rescripts.

Armed with these documents, Macpherson set off for England, where copies were circulated both among the English Vicars-Apostolic and among the Irish bishops. In England Milner and those who thought with him were dismayed, while in Ireland a storm of protest and

CATHOLIC EMANCIPATION 507

dissent was evoked. It was not long before Bishops Murray, representing the Irish point of view, and Milner, voicing the opinion of those who were dissatisfied in England, were on their way to Rome to lay their case before the Pope. Pius VII. by this time was on the way to his capital, being released from his long captivity at Fontainebleau. Meanwhile Dr Troy at Dublin, and the English bishops once more assembled at Durham, had at any rate provisionally accepted the rescript, though it was felt that the last word had not been said. Milner reached Rome on the very eve of the Pontiff's own triumphal entry, and no time was lost in laying before him the case against the rescript, both on account of its character, and on account of the subordinate position held by Monsignor Quarantotti. Pius VII. admitted in audience with Milner that Quarantotti ought not to have acted in a matter of such importance without consulting his superiors, and had a letter addressed to the bishops which was a practical revocation of the rescript. To pursue the object dealt with in the second rescript, namely the intervention of England in favour of the temporal power of the Pope, Cardinal Consalvi left Rome for London a week after the return of the Holy Father.

Not content with what had been accomplished with regard to the veto, Milner availed himself of his visit to Rome to carry the war into the enemies camp, arraigning before the Holy See the general administration of the Vicars-Apostolic, and of Bishop Poynter in particular. *The Genoese Letter and its sequel.* The latter then felt it to be his duty to proceed to Rome in person in the November of the same year, accompanied by Rev. J. Bramston, in order to answer the accusations levelled against himself, and also to speak for his brother bishops, as far as it might be necessary. He reached Rome early in January, 1815, but the course of the controversy was soon afterwards interrupted by the news that Napoleon had escaped from Elba, and that the Neapolitan army was marching on Rome. The Pontiff once more took refuge in flight, this time passing to Genoa, which had an English garrison, and was considered safe. He was accompanied by the cardinals of his court, and followed after some delay by Bishops Milner and Poynter, who travelled separately, and were not acquainted with one another's plans. They both had audiences with the Pope, and also with Cardinal Litta, who had now become Prefect of Propaganda. Divining that the presence of Milner was one of the main causes of disunion in England, the Pope and Litta endeavoured to keep him in Italy, but when it was seen how distasteful to him the plan seemed to be it was not pressed. Poynter received from Cardinal Litta the letter afterwards known as the Genoese Letter, which while refusing any kind of *exquatur* or permission for the publication of papal documents, gave permission for a negative veto. Poynter at once returned to England, and sent copies of the letter to Dr Troy and Dr Milner. None of the parties concerned, however, thought it prudent to publish the letter, and it was seven months before its contents became generally known. Rumour on the other hand had whispered what was in it, and great was the ferment which it occasioned. The Irish bishops passed resolutions condemning the veto in very decided language, and O'Connell spoke at a mass meeting of the laity in equally strong but more personally vituperative language. Milner, though disliking the veto, seems to have thought that the Genoese Letter ought to be accepted as decisive, out of respect for the Holy See. Drs Murray and Murphy were again sent to the papal court to press for the speedy withdrawal of the letter, but Pius VII. declined to do this, and wrote to the Irish bishops confirming the decision. It was the subsequent course of events in Parliament which prevented it ever having any practical application.

The Catholic question was debated both by Lords and by Commons in 1815, 1817, and 1819. But in each year there was a majority against any grant of the concessions which were hoped for. The dissensions over the veto had become more or less public, and doubtless must have prejudiced the question in the eyes of many. In 1820, after the death of Henry Grattan, the advocates of Emancipation changed their ground, and in the following year the Right Honourable William **Plunket's Emancipation Bill (1821).** Plunket, who had practically taken Grattan's place as their parliamentary leader, introduced a bill, which on the one side exacted the Oath of Supremacy with a declaration that it only applied to the civil power of the king, and on the other hand gave the right to sit in

Parliament, to follow the learned professions, while the blasphemous declarations against Transubstantiation and the Invocation of the Blessed Virgin were to be abolished. Both Milner and Poynter insisted on the amendment of the oath in order to make it clear that no spiritual right of supremacy was admitted. This, it seems, was the extent of the opposition made by Poynter, but Milner held firm in his hostility. In Ireland many of the bishops, such as Dr Doyle, the Bishop of Kildare, and Daniel O'Connell, among the laity, were in favour of accepting the bill, but neither were unanimous, and their sentiments did not influence the result. The bill passed through the Commons by a majority of eleven, but was thrown out on the second reading in the Lords by two hundred against one hundred and fifty-one. The controversy was carried on in England, and to some extent in Ireland, for some time after the bill was dead, but these disputes had little result. There supervened a period during which the whole matter fell into the background, for the most enthusiastic supporters of constitutional action could hardly fail to be disappointed at the repeated collapse of their efforts.

Milner survived into old age, but his active temperament was such that in his zeal he was hardly ever out of the fray. He ever found some new error to refute or some new adversary of the Church to attack. Still his labours and the advance of years sapped his strength, and at last he asked for the appointment of a coadjutor. Bishop Baines had already been consecrated to assist Dr Collingridge in the West, and Dr Poynter had been authorised to consecrate his constant friend, John Bramston, as coadjutor for the London district. This he did at Old Hall on the 29th of June, 1823. Next year Dr Penswick was given to Bishop Smith to aid him in the same capacity in the North. Milner's choice fell upon the Rev. Thomas Walsh to come to the aid of his failing strength. He himself summoned what remained of his old vigour to perform the ceremony of raising him to the episcopate at Wolverhampton on the 1st of May, 1825. On this occasion all the Vicars-Apostolic had been invited, no fewer than eight Catholic bishops—an unprecedented number since the Reformation—being gathered at the function. In renewed harmony they all accepted Milner's invitation to Sedgley Park after the ceremony, when great celebrations and college holidays were held in commemoration of the event. Within a year Bishop Milner had breathed his last, on the 19th of April, 1826. His contemporary, Bishop Poynter, died a year later, and was succeeded by Dr Bramston.

The main power in the final and successful effort to win Emancipation was supplied almost exclusively from Ireland. The detailed account of the stages by which it was accomplished belong rather to the religious history of that country than to that of England. Yet a short summary of what was done must be introduced here, however inadequate to the importance of the issue. Turning with disappointment from the failure of past efforts, O'Connell now looked to a popular agitation to accomplish his purpose. In 1823, in conjunction with John Keogh and Richard Lalor Sheil, he founded the Catholic Association, whose avowed object was to gain civil liberty for Catholics "by all lawful and constitutional means." By 1825 the association had spread all over Ireland, and had become so powerful that the government in alarm made an unsuccessful attempt to suppress it, but O'Connell outwitted them, and the association went on under a new name. Several Protestant supporters were returned to Parliament in 1826 and afterwards through its influence. At length, in 1828, O'Connell stood for the vacant constituency of Clare, though considered ineligible as a Catholic. The united influence of the clergy and of the association gave him an overwhelming victory by a ten to one majority. O'Connell at first meant to go to Westminster and there test the legality of his being required to take the unamended Oath of Supremacy before he could take his seat. But he later on decided on the more prudent course of watching events which were rapidly marching in the direction of Emancipation. The Clare election had raised the agitation in Ireland to the highest pitch, while the growth of liberal views in England made a majority for it almost a certainty in the House of Commons. Wellington and Peel, the two chief ministers, though personally averse to the Catholic claims, felt that their government would not be able to remain in power

Emancipation won by O'Connell.

CATHOLIC EMANCIPATION

on any other terms. They could not face at the same time the civil war in Ireland and an adverse majority in the Commons. But they had the greatest trouble to win the king's consent. For a while they believed that their threatened resignations had been accepted. But it was not so: the king yielded, and the Duke of Wellington was able to pass the Emancipation Bill through both Houses. It amended the objectionable oath, and threw open nearly all the offices of public life to Catholics. The Duke of Norfolk took his seat on the 1st of May, being the first Catholic to do so since the days of Charles II. Four days later Lord Surrey took the oath in the Commons. O'Connell tried to take his seat on the strength of the Clare election, but it was argued that the act was not retrospective, and the Oath of Supremacy was tendered to him. Of course he refused it, and though he was allowed to argue the point, the majority decided against him. Thereupon a new writ was issued for Clare; O'Connell was returned unopposed, and then took his seat in triumph.

The period embraced in this chapter was one of great literary activity on all sides, especially under the influence of the so-called Romantic movement, which was the written expression of the political liberalism of the age. England took its full share in this, as illustrious names abundantly testify, and, though but few in number, Catholics bore a part which was no unimportant one. A few of the chief writers amongst them must be mentioned. While the battle of Emancipation was being fought in Parliament under the leadership of O'Connell and other staunch champions, a retired scholar was winning for his work an unfading glory by the composition of a history which still stands in the front rank among the general accounts of the past of the land. This was Dr John Lingard, son of a carpenter of Claxby in Lincolnshire, who was born at Winchester in 1771. The child was eight years old when Milner was sent to take charge of the Catholic mission there.

Dr John Lingard (1771-1851).

In 1782 he was sent to Douay, where he went through the usual course of studies in preparation for the priesthood until the outbreak of the French Revolution. He was one of the band of students who then came back to England, and continued the work of Douay at Crook

Hall, Durham. In 1795 he was ordained at York by Bishop Gibson, and the next fifteen years of his life were devoted to the labours of professor and vice-president at Ushaw College. When he reached the exact middle of his long life in 1811 he was established in charge of Hornby, Lancashire, and there the remaining forty years of his career were almost exclusively spent. It was an ideal scholar's life, with just enough of external occupation to prevent him from becoming merely a bookman, but not enough seriously to impede him in his literary tasks. Before this he had already in 1806 published his "*History and Antiquities of the Anglo-Saxon Church*," but it was at Hornby that he patiently elaborated and successively published the ten volumes of his "*History of England.*" The first volumes were published in 1819, and the last in 1830. It remains to this day almost the only first-class and reliable history of the country up to the Revolution. It was a striking success at the time, and has been over and over again reprinted since. Lingard also published several controversial works, and a translation of the New Testament, besides contributing to periodical literature. He survived until 1851. It is thought possible that he was created a cardinal *in petto* by Leo XII., but that Pontiff died in 1829, and the secret died with him. Lingard is buried at Ushaw.

In the same year in which the great Lingard breathed his last there also departed this life a still older scholar, whose attainments in erudition, though lacking the literary and historical genius of Lingard, were extraordinarily wide and deep. This was Rev. Dr John Kirk, who at the time of his death was in his ninety-second year. Born in 1760, he passed from Sedgley Park to the English College at Rome. After a college course of eleven years he was ordained priest, and returned to the English mission in 1785. He first served the mission at Aldenham, the seat of Sir John Acton. He then passed successively to Sedgley Park and Pipe Hall. But in 1801 he was appointed to the mission at Lichfield, which continued to be his residence until his death half a century later. He was instrumental in the building of the churches at Lichfield and at Tamworth, which was also included in his charge. He was likewise responsible for the original idea of beginning a college at Oscott, and the plan which he drew out for the new establishment was in the main carried out by the Vicar-Apostolic. Dr Kirk was a widely read man of letters, but so poor a speaker that he never ventured upon other preaching than reading from a manuscript. His knowledge of Latin and Greek was thorough, while he was so devoted to Hebrew that he received special permission from the Pope to recite the Psalms of the Breviary in the original language. His share was an important one in the celebrated work, "*Faith of Catholics*," which was brought out by him in 1813, in collaboration with the Rev. Joseph Berington, and republished more than thirty years later by Rev. James Waterworth, with many corrections and additions. Dr Kirk also made extensive collections for the continuation of Dodd's Church History of England, which were never printed, but were utilised by Canon Tierney when he undertook the continuation which Dr Kirk had abandoned. Dr Kirk died at Lichfield on the 21st of December, 1851. Canon Tierney, whose career was not so very unlike Kirk's, was chaplain to the Duke of Norfolk at Arundel Castle from 1824 to 1862, and used the leisure which was thus at his disposal to pursue the antiquarian researches which were his delight. His "*Continuation of Dodd*" was published between 1839 and 1843. He also wrote on the "*Antiquities of Arundel*," as well as various controversial letters and pamphlets. In the year in which Tierney died, his contemporary, Dr George Oliver, also breathed his last at the age of eighty. He was educated by the Jesuits, and after his ordination was sent to the former Jesuit mission of Exeter, which he held as "locumtenens" for the Society from 1807 until 1851. He then resigned his charge into the hands of the Jesuit Fathers, and became provost of the new diocese of Plymouth, but he continued to reside at Exeter until his death in 1862. He is the author of invaluable "Collections" illustrating the history of the Catholic religion in the Western counties, as well as of several works on the "*Ecclesiastical Antiquities of Devon*," and of a "*History of the City of Exeter*," while his articles and other literary communications to Catholic periodicals were almost innumerable. Over two hundred of these have been collected in two large volumes. It would be easy to enlarge the list of those able men who devoted their pens to the cause of Catholic truth in the period we are dealing with, but enough has been said to indicate what solid scholars were at work in this cause, to whom the present generation owes a debt of gratitude which it can never thoroughly repay.

XXXIV.
THE RESTORATION OF THE HIERARCHY.
(1830-1865.)

(A) THE CATHOLIC REVIVAL BEFORE THE HIERARCHY
(1830-1850).

MOST of the leading personalities who were concerned in Catholic Emancipation in England had passed from the scene of their labours before or not long after the Act of Parliament came into force. In the course of the following year King George IV. died. The Conservative government of the Duke of Wellington, which had carried the act almost in spite of itself, gave way about the same time to Lord Grey and the Liberals. There was likewise a new Pope, for the aged and infirm Pius VIII. was succeeded in 1831 by Gregory XVI. Charles Butler only survived until 1833, when he died in an honoured old age. In Ireland indeed it was otherwise, for Daniel O'Connell, having secured religious freedom for English and Irish alike, proceeded to take up the agitation, which he continued for nearly twenty years, for the repeal of the Act of Union. But the general effect of Emancipation was to make English and Irish Catholics part company in their political action and in their organisation. Their ideals were not the same, outside of matters of Faith, and although powerful voices were lifted to call them together, there were still stronger voices at work in a contrary direction.

With regard to the pastors of the flock in England, Bishop Poynter died about a year before Emancipation was passed. He was succeeded in the London district by his coadjutor, the convert, Bishop Bramston. Bishop Thomas Smith of the Northern district only lived until 1831, when Bishop Penswick took up the government of that vicariate. In the Midland district there

The new Vicars-Apostolic.

was no change, for the pious and prudent Dr Walsh had still a long career before him. In the West Bishop Collingridge had died on the very eve of the passing of the Emancipation Act, rendering a new vicar necessary in the West also. The vacancy was filled by the imposing and enterprising prelate who became without doubt the most striking figure among the rulers of the Church in England for the next twelve or thirteen years.

Dr Peter Augustine Baines, O.S.B., a Lancashire man by birth, had been brought up by the Benedictine monks at Lambspring in Bavaria, and at Ample-

Bishop Baines (1787-1843). forth, being admitted to profession in the latter monastery in 1804. After many years spent in various positions at Ampleforth, he was appointed to take charge of the mission served by the fathers of his order at Bath. There he continued to reside until named coadjutor to Bishop Collingridge in 1823. He was then about thirty-six years of age, and until the death of that prelate, his energy and ability made him of the highest usefulness in the work of administering the district. As soon as he became Vicar-Apostolic himself, he fixed his residence at Bathampton. Whatever others might think, Bishop Baines was intimately convinced that a new vista of progress had at last opened out before the Church in England. He drew out bold and far-reaching plans for the development of his vicariate, and began an energetic effort to realise them. His first idea was that the whole vicariate should be administered as a district to be evangelised almost exclusively by Benedictines under a Benedictine bishop. On this principle he carried on negotiations at great length, both with Ampleforth and with Downside. Nevertheless, he was not able to achieve his purpose with either House, and in the case of Ampleforth he became involved in a long controversy which brought on an appeal to the Holy See. He tried to effect a bodily transfer of as many of the Ampleforth monks as would follow him into his own vicariate. This effort was naturally enough resisted by the authorities of that monastery, and the plan ended in failure. His next enterprise was to acquire a large property at Prior Park, near Bath, which he strove to develop into a seminary for the whole of the West of England on a scale which equalled, even if it

RESTORATION OF HIERARCHY 517

did not surpass, the three existing seminaries in the country. The expense incurred in acquiring and maintaining this establishment proved a crushing burden to Bishop Baines and his successors. But the buildings, which still remain, are conclusive evidence of the grandiose lines on which he planned, and of the determined efforts he made to realise his ambitious scheme.

The spirit of hopefulness in the future progress of the world which accompanied the political victory of the Liberals in 1830, and in the succeeding years, produced a similar frame of mind with regard to religious matters as well. There seemed to be abroad a new disposition towards toleration, which gave every form of belief credit for much that was good, and was willing to let each one of them work away as it chose, untrammelled by external coercion. *Agitation for the Hierarchy.* At any rate it is to this epoch that we must trace a rapidly growing feeling among Catholics, both clergy and laity, that the time was ripe for their being taken out of the purely missionary condition usual *in partibus infidelium*, and brought back under the government of Bishops in Ordinary. We find evidence of this in the year 1833. It did not entirely come from the longing for progress, at least as far as the clergy were concerned, but also in part from a desire to limit the power of the Vicars-Apostolic. These held the extraordinary faculties of purely missionary bishops, and were felt to be almost absolute in the matters of naming their successors and making local appointments among the priests. For some time the Vicars-Apostolic themselves kept out of the controversy, but such prominent men as the historian, Dr Lingard, and the Rev. John Jones of Warwick Street, were keen on the subject, particularly in so far as it touched the mode of action of the bishops. Valuable support for those agitating for a change was given later on by the rector of the English College at Rome, Dr Wiseman, and among the laity by the zealous Catholic nobleman, the Earl of Shrewsbury. At length, in 1836, a petition was drawn up, first circulated, as it appears, in the Northern counties, and extensively signed by the clergy. This was presented to the Holy See in the spring of 1837. The gist of it was to ask that the number of bishops should be increased, that the clergy should be given some voice in the selection of the prelates who were to rule over them, and that a chapter should be established in each district. This was not necessarily to ask for a hierarchy, since it was evident that the number of bishops could be made greater by dividing the vicariates without setting up regular residential sees. Moreover, the view that this was the better course commended itself to many. Others, on the contrary, were in favour of either creating a new hierarchy at once, or in default of this, leaving the existing vicariates unchanged for the moment. But although the Vicars-Apostolic moved so slowly in the matter that they brought upon themselves the charge of being opposed to both the suggested developments, the evidence does not show that this was really the case. The Holy See eventually took the decision into its own hands, and decided, at any rate for the time being, on the alternative of dividing the four vicariates into eight, rather than on the rival plan of the immediate erection of a new hierarchy. This decision was in part due to the great influence exerted by Monsignor Acton, who held high office in the Roman court, and whose experience and skill were highly esteemed by Pope Gregory XVI. Dr Wiseman, at the English College, was in his own way an equally strong supporter of the action which was taken.

It was in consequence of these discussions that in January, 1840, the four vicars received a letter from Monsignor Acton, informing them that the Pope had decided on the erection of four new vicariates, and asking them to make recommendations as to the best candidates to fill them. Henceforth the negotiations proceeded practically without a break during the first half of 1840, and on the 3rd of July apostolic briefs were issued for all the new vicariates. Acton, who was already a cardinal *in petto*, was proclaimed in January, 1842, but only survived until 1847, when he died at Naples. Bishop Griffiths was left undisturbed in the London vicariate, and Bishops Walsh and Baines still retained their titles, though with narrower boundaries to their respective territories. Dr Thomas Brown, the Prior of Downside, took over that part of the Western district which comprised the new Welsh district. Dr Wareing became Vicar-Apostolic of the Eastern district. With

Division into Eight Vicariates (1840).

RESTORATION OF HIERARCHY

regard to the North, the actual vicar, Dr Briggs, retained Yorkshire only, Lancashire now forming a new district under Dr George Brown. The energetic and amiable Dr Weedall, president of Oscott, was proposed as the bishop to rule the four northernmost counties, now called the Northern district, but his protests at Rome resulted in his being relieved from the burden. He was destined to spend another fifteen years at the head of Oscott College, with which he had been identified for the greater part of his life. In his stead Dr Francis Mostyn was consecrated for the Northern district. Last but not least, Dr Nicholas Wiseman was made coadjutor to Bishop Walsh in the Midland district, and at the same time president of Oscott. Another ten years and there would be a further increase in the number of bishops, together with the restoration of hierarchical sees, but for the greater part of the interval (1840-50) the personnel of the episcopate was almost unchanged, most of the surviving Vicars-Apostolic being translated to the new sees in 1850. The most notable change was caused by the sudden death of the energetic Bishop Baines in 1843, followed by the equally unexpected loss of his successor, Dr Baggs, 1845, the gap being filled by the consecration of Dr William Ullathorne, O.S.B., as Vicar-Apostolic of the West in 1846.

Meantime, outside the borders of the Catholic Church, a religious movement, hardly recognised at first at its true value, was gathering strength, and thus preparing to modify considerably the prospect of Catholicity in the land. This was the Tractarian or Oxford Movement as it is now universally called. It would appear that the High Church theory of Anglicanism held by such Caroline divines as Laud, Hooker, and Montague had never died out. It had been overlaid and crushed by the formalism and torpor of the eighteenth century. Then came the Methodist Revival under Wesley and Whitfield, the force of which in its pristine vigour can hardly be exaggerated, but which gave a rude blow to the life of the Anglican Church when the Wesleyan exodus really took place. Then came the stimulus administered by the activity of the so-called Evangelical School, amongst the noblest of whose adherents were to be found a circle of religious thinkers whose centre was or had been Oriel

The Oxford Movement (1833-1845).

College, Oxford. Many of these distinguished clergymen never became concerned in what is now known as the Oxford Movement, but some of them by preparing the way, others by opposition to what they considered dangerous in it, really fanned it into life. Almost the earliest articulate voice to give expression to the ideas of these new High Churchmen was John Keble (1792-1866), who, after carrying off the highest honours in his college and university, settled down in the rural living of Fairford. His volume of religious poems styled the "Christian Year" appeared in 1827, and became immensely popular. It gave colour to the old High Church theory of Anglicanism, while breathing a spirit of meditative and sincere piety. About the same time John Henry Newman was advancing to the same standpoint by other and more intellectual processes. Under the influence of the almost rationalistic discipline of Dr Whateley he passed from Low Church pietism to the acceptance of the so-called patristic foundation for the teaching of the Anglican Church, making the fathers the true interpreters of primitive Christian tradition, and judging of doctrines and worship by their agreement or the reverse with the Church of the Fathers. There now intervened between Keble and Newman a third earnest leader, James Hurrell Froude (1802-36), who gave out more uncompromisingly Catholic views, and yet strove to bring into harmony with each other the teaching of Keble and of Newman. The united influence of these three men worked with magical effect on the numerous scholarly and pious men who were then at Oxford. Keble's assize sermon from the University pulpit on "National Apostasy," preached in 1833, is pointed to by Newman as the beginning of the movement.

Tracts for the Times. In that same year also the publication of short essays on religious subjects under the title of "Tracts for the Times" was begun. It was from these tracts, written by Newman, Froude, Keble, and the disciples who had gathered round them, that the whole movement was properly spoken of as Tractarianism. Dr Pusey, the Regius Professor of Hebrew at Oxford, soon afterwards lent the movement the support which came from his learning and position in the University. So great indeed was the effect on the people of the country at the time of his adhesion to the party that it promptly called them after him, Puseyites. Pusey organised the publication of an edition of the High Anglican divines of the seventeenth century, such as Laud, Andrews and others.

This was followed up by a series of translations of the "Fathers of the Church" and other standard works of the early Christian ages. Newman, while continuing his trenchant controversial articles in the "Tracts for the Times," also became responsible for a set of "Lives of the English Saints," which was published gradually as the years went on, and was contributed to by himself, Church, Oakeley, Coffin, and others. As Vicar of St Mary the Virgin at Oxford, Newman likewise used his very remarkable powers of pulpit oratory to persuade his hearers to adopt the same theory of a visible Anglican Church, part of the Church Catholic, which on this theory included three branches, the Roman, the Orthodox Eastern, and the Anglican. The whole time embraced between the commencement of "Tracts for the Times," and Keble's sermon until the reception of Newman into the Catholic Church was one of twelve years (1833-45). In the earlier years the great preacher was at no pains to conceal a certain hostility to Rome, based upon the branch theory and the exclusively patristic tests he applied to doctrine. In fact he argued that Catholics in England who adhered to what he called the Roman or papal branch were really in schism. In 1836 he undertook to edit a periodical which, under the name of the *British Critic*, was to be the organ of the Tractarian party. The death of Hurrell Froude in the same year was a blow to the leaders, but it put Newman more exclusively at the head of the movement. In 1837, in his "*Lectures on the Prophetical Office of the Church*," he developed the theory of the *via media*, which explained the Anglican position as being the middle course between the two erroneous extremes of liberal rationalism on the one side, and papal authority on the other. He still spoke of the English Catholics as schismatics. The movement was still gaining impetus, and the "Memoirs of Froude," which Newman and Keble published in 1838, gave it an additional attraction. The "Tracts for the Times" were growing in bulk, and were extending their circulation, when the untoward discovery,

Newman at St Mary's, Oxford.

in the study of the history of Monophysites in 1839, that these latter, who like the Anglicans took their stand on antiquity, had had their claim disallowed by the Church in general, gave him a shock, as this case could not be made to square with the theory of the *via media*. Then, in the September of the same year, an article in the recently established *Dublin Review* by Dr Wiseman, Rector of the English College at Rome, on the Donatist controversy gave him a blow, and made an impression upon him which he says was as though he had seen a ghost. Wiseman quoted the words of St Augustine, "*Securus judicat orbis terrarum*," against the appeal to antiquity, and the words kept ringing in the ears of Newman and of other Tractarians such as W. G. Ward and Arthur Stanley, on whom the impression made seemed equally deep.

The High Church movement at Oxford, which began in 1833, had hardly got under way when there came to England the great man who was to be for nearly thirty years the foremost figure among Catholics in the land. This was Nicholas Wiseman, Rector of the English College in Rome. He was born in Seville on the 2nd of August, 1802, being the son of an Irish wine merchant residing in that city, and loving to trace his descent from the old Catholic family of Wiseman in Essex. After an early education at Waterford, his father's native city, and at Ushaw College, Nicholas Wiseman was one of the little colony sent to repeople the English College in Rome in 1818. His remarkable abilities enabled him to shine in the Roman schools, and academic distinctions came thick and fast. He was made D.D. in 1824, Vice-Rector of the English College, and finally Rector in 1828. He held this office until 1840. But being full of zeal for the interests of the Church, and keenly alive to the events passing in England, Catholic freedom from civil disabilities, and the hopes encouraged thus, and by the Oxford Movement towards Catholic doctrine, convinced him that a new period of growth and progress was opening out before the Church in England. He made a prolonged stay in England from July, 1835, to September, 1836, visiting his friends in different parts of the country, preaching a remarkable course of Lectures on the Chief Doctrines of the Catholic Church, first at

Nicholas Wiseman (1802-1865).

RESTORATION OF HIERARCHY

the Sardinian Chapel, and afterwards at Moorfields, and acquainting himself with the state of Catholic affairs in the kingdom. The lectures were later on published, and may be counted amongst the most useful of the great cardinal's works. He also took temporary charge of the Lincoln's Inn mission in the absence of its pastor, and before his return to his post in Rome had formed to himself a clear idea of the strong and weak points in the Catholic camp.

Brimful of energy and intellectual life as Wiseman then was, he was able during his stay in England to set on foot a literary enterprise, which for long after he continued to direct, and which is in full activity still. He thought that the Catholic cause needed a literary organ in the form of a quarterly review, which might champion Catholic interests and principles somewhat as the *Quarterly* and *Edinburgh* did the causes they represented, and which should do it with ability not less than theirs. He accomplished this in conjunction with the Irish patriot, Daniel O'Connell, and Dr James Quin, by the foundation of the *Dublin Review*, the first number of which appeared in May, 1836. Wiseman returned to Rome before the end of 1836 to his duties at the English College; but he continued to take a large share in the work of the *Dublin Review*. At the same time he continued to follow with, if possible, more enthusiastic hopes than ever the progress of the Catholic movement in England. This interest was repeatedly stimulated by the distinguished English visitors who came to him at the Venerabile, with many of whom he was able to discuss the future of the Church and the plans he was gradually forming for its development. Among those who came to him were Gladstone, Manning, Macaulay, and O'Connell. Meanwhile, though his own life was deepening in spirituality, and his proximate concern was with the training of the students, it is clear that from 1839 his heart was in England in the thick of the controversy for the Church. His opportunity came in 1840, when the new vicariates were made. His name was of course prominent among the suggested new bishops, and it was thought best that he should be consecrated as coadjutor to Bishop Walsh of the Midland district, and should reside at Oscott as president of the College. This seemed to him to lead to the hope that Oscott might be made the centre of the new Catholic revival on which his thoughts were fixed. He was consecrated by Cardinal Franzoni, June 8th, in the chapel of the English College, and reached Oscott on the 16th of September, after a retreat in the Passionist monastery of SS. John and Paul.

Meanwhile the Oxford Movement was taking on a development far beyond the dreams of its first founders. Among those who joined the movement about 1838 were to be counted such men as W. G. Ward and Frederic Oakeley, who made no secret of their admiration of Rome, as well as of their dissent from the anti-Roman views of more cautious leaders like Pusey and Palmer. Then there came younger and more independent adherents such as Frederic Faber and R. A. Coffin. It was into the midst of this forward impulse that the blow delivered by Wiseman's Dublin article was driven, and the hitherto main position of the Anglicans was forced. Newman had to take new ground. This he did in February, 1841, by the publication of the celebrated "Tract 90," whose main contention was that the thirty-nine articles, though often interpreted in a Protestant sense, could and ought to be explained in a Catholic one. He thought that this contention combined with the evidence of holiness of doctrine and life in the Church of England would avail to keep back those whom he thought likely to secede altogether. He little counted on the reception he met with: the tract evoked a storm of protest and a charge of equivocation on his head. Four tutors of colleges protested, bishops charged, and preachers declaimed against the tract. The Bishop of Oxford demanded the suspension of the series of tracts. Pusey was suspended, and other leading Tractarians censured. Newman retired from Oxford in April, 1842, to a set of cottages at Littlemore, where he was joined by his disciples, St John, Dalgairns, Stanton, and Bowles, and where for the next two years he led in their company a kind of semi-monastic life. But his submission to the Church was now only a question of time. The end came on the 9th of October, 1845, when he was received into the Church with his friends, Stanton and Bowles. Dalgairns and St John had been reconciled at Prior Park a week earlier, and Oakeley and Walker were received by Father Newsham at Oxford two days later. For the remaining months of that year converts from the Oxford Movement followed in quick succession at different places. Among them may be noted Fathers Faber and Coffin. Fathers Christie and Meyrick, the Jesuits, Canon Northcote, and George Ryder and David Lewis, as well as Dr W. G. Ward—all these converts belong to 1845 and 1846.

The first home of Newman and his friends after their reception was Old Oscott, the buildings of which were scarcely needed by the college since the New Oscott was opened in 1838. But in the next year, 1846, they went to Rome to study and at the same time to deliberate on their future course of life. While there they were ordained, and eventually accepted what had been Wiseman's original idea for them, the foundation of an English house of the Oratory of St Philip Neri. Some kind of a novitiate was made in Rome, and then Newman and his companions returned to take up their work at Old Oscott, or Maryvale, as they called it. Newman had published as a Catholic the "*Essay on the Development of Christian Doctrine,*" which he was writing at the time of his conversion, while Father Faber had set his companions to work with himself on an extensive series of "Lives of the Saints." But almost from the first there were two communities with somewhat differing aims and spirit. Father Faber was for some time with a number of others at Cotton Hall, Staffordshire. Wiseman wished Newman to transfer himself to London, but to this he would not consent. He agreed to the plan of sending a colony thither, and early in 1849 Newman, with many of his disciples, was established in Birmingham, while Faber, Dalgairns, and others had made a beginning of the London Oratory. Early in 1850 Newman delivered in the London Oratorian Chapel his "*Lectures on Anglican Difficulties.*" Then came the establishment of the hierarchy with the changes this brought. Ever since the two oratories have gone their way, the one at Birmingham, including a high class school, finding its prototype in the Naples community, which has included education in its scope, the one at Brompton adhering more closely to the model furnished by the Chiesa Nuova in Rome. Another institution which owed its origin to Wiseman's inspiration was that

The English Oratorians.

of the Oblates of St Charles, whose first superior was Henry Edward Manning, who after a career of many years in the Anglican Church, where he reached the dignity of Archdeacon of Chichester, was received into the Church in 1850. They sought for their model in a society of secular priests established by St Charles Borromeo at Milan, and aimed at forming a community of clergy living together without religious vows, who might hold themselves at the disposition of their bishop to undertake any diocesan work to which he might ask them to devote themselves. Both the Oratorians and the Oblates by their zeal and ability have exercised an influence over the Church in England far in advance of their numbers or resources.

A remarkable impetus had been given to the religious life, strictly so called, on the continent of Europe during the years which followed the restoration of peace at the Congress of Vienna. The eyes of many of the most zealous men engaged in fostering this were directed towards England as a promising field for their labours. On the other hand, those leaders of the English Catholics who felt convinced that a new era of progress had begun naturally were disposed to offer them a warm welcome. It appeared that through their means a new and healthy breath of life would be infused into the elements with which progress had to be made. This must be the chief explanation of the advent of so many new religious orders to the country during the epoch with which this chapter is concerned. The pioneers in this fresh departure were the Fathers of Charity, founded by Rosmini at Domodossola in 1828. The invitation to them came originally from Bishop Baines, in response to whose call Dr Gentili with two companions was sent to London in 1835, and thence proceeded to Bishop Baines' College at Prior Park. It was intended at first that the newcomers should make Trelawney Castle in Cornwall the centre of their activities: this had been the ancestral seat of the well-known convert, the Rev. Sir John Trelawney. But Bishop Baines was so taken with their zeal that he entrusted to them the chief part in the superintendence of Prior Park, where owing to his insistence Father Gentili and his companions stayed for several years. Eventually, misunderstandings arose, and Gentili was

Coming of new Religious Orders.

recalled to Italy by his superiors. In 1840, however, at the invitation of Ambrose Phillips de Lisle he returned to England, where he made this gentleman's home at Grace Dieu Manor his abode for three years, and from it evangelised the neighbouring villages with such success that he received several hundred people into the Church. From 1845 to 1848 he was employed with his companion, Father Furlong, in giving regular courses of mission exercises in the great cities of England, and also in Ireland, until he was struck down by death quite suddenly at Dublin in 1848. He may be considered the first to have devoted himself to the work of mission exercises in these countries.

It was also under the encouragement given by Mr Phillips de Lisle that the sons of St Paul of the Cross came to England in 1841. The saintly Passionist, Father Dominic of the Mother of God, left his native Italy to go on that English apostolate which his holy founder had ever prayed for, and for which he had himself longed from the years of his childhood. Father Dominic established the first retreat of his order in 1842 at Aston Hall in Staffordshire. He it was to whom John Henry Newman applied for reception into the Church in 1845, and in the following year, just as he opened the door of the Church to Newman, so did he open the door of his own order to a convert priest of an early period: this was the Rev. George Spencer, who from that day until his death in 1865 remained the indomitable apostle of prayer for the conversion of England. Father Dominic, like Father Gentili, had but a short career, dying at a wayside railway station in 1849. But other members of his institute gradually followed him into the land, and thus the Passionist congregation struck firm root in the field of labour its founder had foreseen.

The coming of the Redemptorists was due above all to the zealous enterprise of Bishop Baines, who when passing through Liège made the invitation to the Superior, Father de Held, in 1841, and who, when they arrived in 1843, gave them charge of the mission of Falmouth in Cornwall. Here they laboured until 1848, when a centre of more extended usefulness was found with the foundation of St Mary's, Clapham. Meanwhile Father Lans, C.Ss.R., under the patronage of the Hornyold family at Blackmore Park, Worcester, assisted by a small community, was able to reproduce the surprising harvest of individual conversions almost as it had been reaped by Father Gentili at Grace Dieu some years before. It remains to be mentioned that the recently founded Oblates of Mary Immaculate sent Fathers Aubert and Cooke to Grace Dieu in 1844, whence they passed into Yorkshire, finally establishing an important Catholic centre at Mount St Mary's in Leeds in 1851. The Pious Society of Missions or Pallottini despatched their future general, the celebrated Dr Faa di Bruno, to London in 1844 to attend to the spiritual wants of the Italian denizens of the capital. This work has never been abandoned since, but has rather grown into a more general missionary apostolate.

The coming of such bodies of religous as those just mentioned so nearly at the same time was no doubt something of a phenomenon, and therefore strikes the eye more than an equally important work which was going on in the revival of the more ancient orders. With regard to the friars, who had never really died out in England, the Dominicans were first in the field in effecting a vigorous renovation of what had once been a flourishing province of their order. As best they could they had kept up their foundations at Hinckley and Leicester, in the days long before the Catholic Revival, but it was with the establishment of Woodchester in Gloucestershire that a new breath of vigorous life made itself felt. The Franciscans were somewhat later in their new enterprises, being established anew from Belgium in 1858. The return of the Carmelites and the beginning of the Servite province belong to the next period.

Revival of the Older Orders.

The Jesuits and Benedictines had always between them ever since the days of the Elizabethan persecution formed the majority of the regular clergy, and both these great orders were now able to develop in prosperity the work they had never ceased to do in England in the midst of imprisonment and martyrdom. They still form more than half of the regular clergy of England. After the suppression of the Jesuits in 1773 there remained in the country a number of the former members of the society, who at the time of its restoration amounted to about forty. The foundation of Stonyhurst in 1794 gave them a considerable centre for their educational work. The remainder of the fathers remained scattered in the towns and country missions, where they had kept the Faith alive in penal days, but there were great developments to come. The Benedictines, who were second to none in the dogged perseverance with which they had clung to the post of danger in the worst days of persecution, still had forty-four fathers engaged in missionary labours in 1773. There was thus something to build upon when the return of the fathers from Douay, Dieuleward and Paris, which has been narrated above, still further strengthened their numbers. Since then they have been able to increase the importance of their monastic establishments as well as to open out new fields of missionary activity.

The long felt desire for the restoration of the government by hierarchical bishops had never died out. In 1839 a society called the Adelphi was set on foot by the clergy with the object of promoting this. The increase made in 1840 in the number of vicariates was only meant by the Holy See as a temporary measure, a sort of half-way house towards full episcopal rule, and the beneficial results which the new arrangement produced only served to accentuate the longing for the accomplishment of the full measure of restoration. The leading spirit who identified himself with the proceedings of the Adelphi and the priests banded together for this purpose was Dr Daniel Rock. He it was who eventually drew up the petition which they soon after addressed to the Holy See on the subject. This learned and skilful Dr. Daniel Rock (1799-1871). antiquarian, born in 1799, had been companion in study of Tierney, and then was one of the students first sent to re-open the English College in Rome. After his ordination in 1824 he came home to England, and after a few years on the mission at Moorfields, became chaplain to the pious Earl of Shrewsbury, whose tastes were congenial to his own. At Alton Towers he remained in closest intimacy with the earl until 1840, during which period he was able to compile and publish his classic work, "*Hierurgia or the Holy Sacrifice of the Mass*," which appeared in 1833. In 1840 he went to Buckland as chaplain to the old Catholic family of Throgmorton, and while there wrote his still more celebrated "*Church of our Fathers*" (1849-54), which led to his becoming recognised as the first English authority on the subject. When the hierarchy, which he had done so much to appeal for, became an accomplished fact, Dr Rock became one of the first Canons of Southwark. However, before very long he retired from active work, and after several changes of abode fixed his residence at Kensington, where he died in 1871.

After a few years of more or less unofficial activity on the part of the Adelphi, the case for the hierarchy had been taken up by higher authorities.

Negotiations for the Hierarchy. The Vicars-Apostolic at their annual meeting in 1845 decided upon the course of sending envoys to Rome in their name to conduct the negotiations on this matter with the Holy See. The two first sent were Bishops Wiseman and Sharples, who were coadjutors in two of the existing vicariates. Wiseman drew up a memorandum on the subject, but Cardinal Acton and others opposed themselves to the plan. The outbreak of the Revolution, which led to the absence of the Pope from Rome from November, 1848, until April, 1850, likewise proved an obstacle. Two vacancies in the episcopate which occurred through the death of Bishops Griffiths and Mostyn in 1847 caused the transference of Wiseman to London as pro-Vicar-Apostolic, though the Northern vicariate was not at once filled up. The remaining bishops decided at their meeting in 1848 to send Dr Ullathorne to Rome to carry on the negotiations as well as to arrange about the Northern vicariate. He started without delay, and reached Rome on the 25th of May, 1848. The original plan was to give territorial titles to the eight Vicars-Apostolic, and then to leave them to arrange any further subdivisions afterwards, Bishop Walsh as part of this plan being brought from the Central district to London. Circumstances, nevertheless, led to several modifications being adopted. Dr Ullathorne presented a memorial, asking for the filling-up of the vacancies, for titles in regard to the existing vicariates, and also for the creation of four or five new sees. Bishop Walsh was so infirm that he petitioned not to be moved, and although for a while it was intended to bring Wiseman to Rome as a Cardinal in Curia, the

RESTORATION OF HIERARCHY

English prelates felt that he would be badly missed in England. Hence, at last, the decision was come to that he should be the new metropolitan, and that he should be created a cardinal as well. The differences of opinion both as to the number and as to the designation of the new sees did not at once come to an end. It was decided before long to avoid all titles already held by Anglican prelates. The chief opposition to subdivision did not occur as might have been expected in the case of the less important centres, but in the two cases where Catholics were more numerous, namely, with regard to London and to Lancashire. Notwithstanding, the decision to have two dioceses in London and two in Lancashire was maintained. The five new sees were put under the administration of the eight Vicars-Apostolic until the following year. The death of Bishop Walsh in 1849 made a determination as to the position of Wiseman imperative, and thus on the 29th of September, 1850, the apostolic letters, *Universalis Ecclesiæ*, were published, and in this way the negotiations for the re-establishment of the hierarchy were crowned with success. Wiseman proclaimed the issue of the matter in his celebrated Pastoral from the " Flaminian Gate."

(B) DEVELOPMENT UNDER THE HIERARCHY (1850-1865).

The period which elapsed between the restoration of the hierarchy in 1850 and the death of Cardinal Wiseman in 1865 was on the whole one of peaceful and gradual expansion. It is true that under the influence of the prevailing liberalism in religious matters, and under the efforts made by the High Anglicans to retain their adherents, the stream of converts from the clergy grew less in volume than it had been. But on the other hand there was growth and development from within the Catholic body. It can easily be seen that there was much to be done to fill up the outline drawn out by the papal letter, *Universalis Ecclesiæ*. Through the emigration from Ireland, which was in the main due to the terrible famine of the preceding years, the number of the faithful in the large towns received an immense and sudden increase. Naturally enough there was no sufficient provision of churches, schools,

Development in Organisation.

or religious institutions of any kind to minister to the crowds which had been brought into the country. Something had to be done to meet their needs. Hence it came to pass that these years were years of strenuous enterprise in finding priests, building churches, gathering nuns and teachers to meet the new situation. The financial means available were not great, though the zeal of the flocks was great. Thus it came to pass that many years elapsed before the new dioceses were even tolerably equipped for the task before them. In some cases the work of development and organisation had to begin from the very simplest elements.

Lord John Russell in a letter to the Bishop of Durham had deeply committed the government in the direction of legislation against the Catholic hierarchy. And there were too many bigots at the back of the agitation which was going on to allow him to draw back. Consequently, when Parliament met on the 4th of February, 1851, the promise of a bill in this sense was inserted into the queen's speech. Russell redeemed the promise by introducing a bill three days later. It proposed to inflict a fine of one hundred pounds for assuming the titles of pretended sees, to make void any deeds executed by those who used these titles, to make void all endowments of such sees or gifts to such persons, and to compel those liable to this penalty to answer on oath in spite of the penalty in cases of trusts, charitable bequests, and so forth. The bill was of course strongly opposed by the Irish members, by Mr Roebuck, by Gladstone, by Henry Grattan, and Sir John Graham, while Disraeli supported it in a satirical speech which was more damaging than plain opposition. But open opposition grew, and neither Lord Aberdeen nor Graham would join Russell in his reconstructed Cabinet unless the bill was remodelled. The chief changes made were the omission of the clauses as to endowments and deeds, leaving the mere enactment of the unlawfulness of the assumption of territorial titles with the penalty. In this form it passed both Houses of Parliament, and received the royal assent on the 1st of August, 1851. It became a dead letter, and though the Catholic bishops continued to use the titles of the sees to which the Pope had appointed them, no one ever chose to put the Act into motion against them. At

Ecclesiastical Titles Act (1851).

RESTORATION OF HIERARCHY 533

last it was quietly repealed by Mr Gladstone in 1871, and its history is nothing more than a curious record of illjudged and impotent bigotry.

Some time had to elapse after the publication of the bull establishing the hierarchy before all the thirteen dioceses thus created could be provided with bishops. Cardinal Wiseman, in being made Archbishop of Westminster, was also made administrator of the see of Southwark. *Members of the New Hierarchy.* He continued to rule both dioceses until Dr Thomas Grant was made Bishop of Southwark in the course of the following year. In the same way Dr Ullathorne, the new Bishop of Birmingham, had entrusted to him the temporary administration of Nottingham as well. On the 27th of June, 1851, Bishop Hendren of Clifton was translated to Nottingham. With Clifton he had also held Plymouth as administrator, but on his transfer, Dr Burgess was appointed to Clifton, and Dr George Errington became Bishop of Plymouth. Dr Briggs for Beverley, Dr Hogarth for Hexham, Dr Wareing for Northampton, and Dr Thomas Brown, O.S.B., for Menevia and Newport only exchanged their vicariate titles of sees *in partibus infidelium* for the names of their residential sees. Bishop George Brown of Liverpool also practically kept the whole of the old Lancashire district, since he administered Salford as well until his Vicar-General, Dr William Turner, was named Bishop of Salford in 1851. The Hundred of Leyland was at the same time at Bishop Brown's request transferred from Salford to Liverpool, thus giving the latter diocese twothirds instead of one-half of Lancashire. Dr James Brown, the first bishop of Shrewsbury, was not consecrated until the 27th of July, 1851. Thus it came to pass that the year 1851 was far advanced before all the thirteen dioceses created by the Pope had been provided with pastors, and the complete organisation of a new ecclesiastical province had been added to the Universal Church. Henceforward each diocesan could proceed in his own sphere of action with the great work of reconstruction which had been entrusted to him.

Among these new bishops there stood by the side of the great cardinal a commanding personality, whose services to Catholicity have been only less than his. This was the Benedictine, William Bernard Ullathorne,

Archbishop Ullathorne (1806-1889).

now made Bishop of Birmingham. His ancestry represented the best of the faithful few who never lost the Faith, as he was a lineal descendant of Blessed Thomas More. Born at Pocklington in Yorkshire, he listened to the youthful longing for a sea-faring life, which is so often almost irresistible to an English boy, and spent more than three years before the mast in various voyages to the Baltic and Mediterranean. It was at Memel in the Baltic that he felt the call of God to devote himself to His special service, and returned to England and entered the Benedictine Novitiate at Downside in 1823. Mounting up through his novitiate and his studies to the priesthood in 1831, he soon after volunteered for the Australian mission, and spent eight years in those colonies, labouring with bold and persevering zeal, and as Vicar-General drawing out the plan for a regular Australian hierarchy. This was adopted, but he did not himself accept any place in it, but came back to England where, after taking charge of the Coventry mission, he was three years later made Vicar-Apostolic of the Western district. His experience with regard to the Australian hierarchy made him the fittest negotiator for the English one also, and he was sent to Rome in 1848 for the purpose. His efforts were crowned with success, and his own share in the new development was the government of the diocese of Birmingham for thirty-eight years. He was his colleagues' candidate for Westminster when Wiseman died, but the Holy See intervened, and he remained at Birmingham. He was able to point to steady and constant progress in his see, and was the trusted friend and counsellor of the bishops and of Cardinal Newman. Resigning through old age in 1888, he was made a titular archbishop, and died in the following year at Oscott. He was buried at Stone, the head house of those devoted Dominican Tertiary Nuns, who, beginning under his protection with the saintly Mother Margaret Mary Hallahan at Coventry in 1845, had always held the first place in his heart. His sterling, pious, straightforward character comes out in the books with which he has enriched Catholic literature. The chief of these are the "*Endowments of Man,*" the "*Groundwork of the Christian Virtues*," and "*Christian Patience.*"

RESTORATION OF HIERARCHY 535

The first Bishop of Plymouth was also a remarkable man, and was to play quite a prominent part in ecclesiastical affairs, though not in the see of Plymouth. George Errington had been Archbishop Wiseman's fellow-student at Ushaw, and lifelong friend in Rome, where he had been Vice-Rector of the English College during Wiseman's rectorate. After this the two men had lived together almost in the same relation at Oscott, until Wiseman became archbishop and Errington Bishop of Plymouth. He was a careful and legal minded scholar of strong and independent character, zealous in his own way, but an enthusiast for law and canonical procedure. In 1852 Wiseman applied for a coadjutor, and by leave of the Holy See the matter was brought before the chapter, who voted for Errington more to provide Wiseman with the man of his choice, who would supplement his activities and relieve him from business worries, than because they thought him suitable. He was accordingly translated from Plymouth to the archiepiscopal title of Trebizond with right of succession to Westminster. This was in 1855. Errington accepted the appointment with some misgiving, as he knew well how much he differed in methods and in views from the cardinal, and it was not long before occasions of difference arose. The first collision took place over the appointment by Wiseman of the celebrated lay convert, W. G. Ward, to teach theology at Old Hall. From this Errington strongly dissented, and when Wiseman held to his arrangement felt still more strongly that things would not work well. A temporary respite was obtained by his accepting the duties of administrator to the vacant diocese of Clifton, but when he returned in the following year a further cause of dispute arose in the line taken by Wiseman with regard to the Congregation of the Oblates of St Charles which he founded in 1857, putting at the head of it Henry Edward Manning, the former Archdeacon of Chichester in the Anglican Church. Errington headed the opposition which the Westminster chapter expressed through its mouthpiece, Monsignor Searle, to the rule of the Oblates which made them exempt from ordinary diocesan control. Eventually, the controversy became one with the cardinal supported by Manning against the chapter, with Dr Errington his coadjutor at

Errington (1806-1886).

their head. Personally it was a very awkward situation for all concerned. As a matter of policy it has been called the turning point between the Roman and liberal policy of Wiseman, and the older conservatism of the body of the clergy. Wiseman, with the persevering help afforded by Manning, won in the end, but only after heart-breaking anxieties and disappointments. Errington, who refused to make a voluntary resignation of his position, was deposed by the Pope after a personal interview with him in 1860. Errington, of course, like a good Catholic, accepted the papal decision and retired into private life. Ten years later he accepted the direction of the studies at Prior Park College, where he spent the years of a long, old age. He died in 1886.

With regard to the hierarchy as a whole, it was at the First Provincial Council held at Oscott that it was further gathered in solemn session round its metropolitan. This synod may in fact be looked on as the crowning event of that series of ecclesiastical events of which the Papal Bull of 1850 was the centre. It may also be considered as the fullest exercise of the varied and superlative powers of mind which Cardinal Wiseman was gifted with, for its legislation owed its inspiration, its order, and much of its expression to him. "The decrees," wrote Ullathorne, "that emanated from it were his masterpiece." At the opening session (July 7th) it was Wiseman who both sang the Mass and preached. Then on Sunday there was High Mass by the bishop of the diocese, and Manning preached. On Tuesday the 13th, when Bishop Briggs sang Mass, Newman preached the well-known sermon on the "*Second Spring*," which was the climax of his oratorical works. All the bishops except those of Liverpool and Nottingham were personally present. Moreover, nearly all the most notable ecclesiastics of the day, as far as the Church was concerned, were gathered together in that historic assembly. In addition to the eminent converts already named there were others scarcely less known. There were the future Bishops Weathers, Vaughan, Roskell, Clifford, Goss, and while Husenbeth, Newsham, Crookall, Weedall, Crook, and Maguire added weight to the representation of the secular clergy, Fathers Molyneux, O.S.B., Etheridge, S.J., Aylward, O.P., Eugene, C.P., and Pagani, I.C., attended as the provincials representing the religious

RESTORATION OF HIERARCHY

orders to which they belonged. In attendance on the cardinal were his secretary, Monsignor Searle, and Sir George Bowyer as a layman. All was done with strict adherence to the canonical and ceremonial prescriptions in which Wiseman took delight, and it was the visible fulfilment of his life's aspirations and of the work for which he had studied and fought. In 1855, when the Second Council was held in the same place, the proceedings were embittered by the steady opposition which some of the cardinal's plans encountered from his own coadjutor and some of the bishops. However, even here some useful supplementary legislation was enacted, and work of solidification done for the great outline which had been already sketched out.

Once again was Cardinal Wiseman enabled to gather the clergy of the province around him in Provincial Council. This was in 1858 when the Third Council of Westminster met at Oscott. The opposition of which the beginnings were noted above made itself felt more strongly here, and was led by the coadjutor, Dr Errington; it was successful so far as to put the government of the colleges on the same footing as that of Tridentine Seminaries, which Wiseman contended they were not. It was in consequence of this opposition that the Oblates were withdrawn from St Edmund's, Old Hall. In other respects the cardinal was able to continue his policy of large-minded development. Endeavours were made to provide for the wants of Catholic soldiers, as well as of prisoners and inhabitants of workhouses, who in a large proportion belonged to the household of the Faith. The revised Catechism, which had been undertaken at the direction of the previous council, was now promulgated. Note is taken of the fact that the religious orders were able to participate in the synod in larger measure than heretofore, at which Wiseman expresses his joy in an eloquent passage of the synodical letter. Father Faber of the Oratory also attended this council, but Newman was, of course, occupied with the University at Dublin, and hence did not attend. Hampered as he was by failing health, Wiseman succeeded in holding, in addition to these three councils, four diocesan synods at St Mary's, Moorfields, and, ever solicitous for the training and efficiency of his clergy, made great efforts

Other Councils and Synods.

to secure that the conferences held in the various deaneries should be regular and instructive.

In the year 1857, growing out of the Tractarian Movement, and out of the general wish for uniting the religious forces of Christianity against the advance, ever more threatening of rationalism and materialism, there arose a society which adopted the name of the Association for Promoting the Union of Christendom. Several prominent members of the High Church party among the Anglicans took the lead, amongst whom may be mentioned Dr Frederic George Lee, but the scheme held out so much that was attractive to zealous and charitable minds that it was not long before several well-known Catholics also enrolled themselves in the association. The Earl of Shrewsbury and Ambrose Phillips de Lisle were the chief among these, and they both became most earnest in advocating the spread of the association. The main contention of the scheme was that the corporate reunion of the separated bodies of Christians with one another was a better thing than individual conversions, and that it was a duty incumbent on those who possessed any influence to work for its attainment. It followed almost of necessity that before long the Catholic members of the association applied to the Roman authorities for sanction and support. They had secured the adhesion of the Patriarch of Constantinople and of the Russian primate, and counted their numbers at no less a figure than nine thousand. For England they quoted and relied greatly on a "Letter on Catholic Unity" addressed by Wiseman to the Earl of Shrewsbury in 1841, in which without committing himself to details he had contemplated the corporate reunion of the Anglican Church with the Holy See as a possible and highly desirable ideal. Naturally, therefore, when the Holy See was asked for its approval, the matter was referred to Wiseman to report upon. This he did in a long *Memorandum*, in which he pointed out the limitations which would have to be imposed on any such scheme. He did not think that any immediate action from Rome was either desirable or opportune. There were others, however, who looked upon the association as quite dangerous, and they pressed for its condemnation. It was in consequence of

Marginal note: Association for Promoting the Union of Christendom.

RESTORATION OF HIERARCHY

these representations that a decree was issued in 1864, pointing out the shortcomings of the view taken by its promoters, and forbidding Catholics any longer to form part of it. Mr Ambrose de Lisle, Fathers Collins and Lockhart, and other members were much disappointed at this, but like good Catholics they withdrew from the association, which henceforward subsisted as a purely non-Catholic society.

Already during the discussions which led to the retirement of Archbishop Errington, Cardinal Wiseman had had several illnesses, and showed signs of failing health; the break up did not come all at once. The year 1858 was one of great activity for him. In that year he made an extended tour in Ireland, where he was enthusiastically welcomed, and where a diversified series of sermons and addresses gave proof of his ready powers and width of outlook. These addresses were afterwards published in a collected form. In 1858 also took place the Ushaw College Jubilee, for which he wrote the sacred drama, the "*Hidden Gem.*" About the same time he also published his well-known "*Recollections of the Last Four Popes.*" But by 1860 he had become quite an invalid, and most of the administration of the diocese fell upon the shoulders of others, Manning his provost, Searle his secretary, and Maguire his Vicar-General. He spent much time at a suburban villa he had rented at Leyton, and also sought rest and renewed health at such seaside towns as Ryde, Broadstairs, and Scarborough. He had repeatedly to visit Rome on the affairs of the Church, and always did so gladly, for it was the scene of his studious and happy youth, even though the journey cost him fatigue which he was ill fitted to bear.

It was with longing memories of the Roman Academia still haunting his mind that he founded in London in 1861 the Academia of the Catholic Religion, which was to unite with the encouragement of a wide range of cultivated pursuit of science, the fostering of devotion to the papacy, and even its temporal power. Wiseman retained sufficient strength to deliver the inaugural address in June, 1861. In 1863 he journeyed to Malines as the guest of Cardinal Sterckx to be present at the Catholic Congress held in that city. He delivered an eloquent and instructive discourse on the Work

Catholic Congress of Malines.

and Progress of the Church in England, and held his audience spellbound while in easy French he recounted what had been accomplished since the date of the emancipation of Catholics until that hour. His figures were a striking evidence of progress. Whereas in 1830 there were four hundred and thirty-four priests, in 1863 there were one thousand two hundred and forty-two. The sixteen convents had become one hundred and sixty-two. There were fifty-five religious houses of men, where in 1830 there was not one. The cardinal ended with a note of unconquerable hope and confidence in the fairness of his fellow-countrymen, and in the future progress of the Church, both at home and abroad. Next year brought a more serious illness still, and was the beginning of the end for Wiseman. He spent much time in revising his sermons for publication, and in composing a "*Lecture on Shakespeare*" which he had been asked to deliver, but which was only published after his death. He faced his last illness and approaching death with the greatest calm and with childlike piety. He bore testimony to himself that he had never stood in the way of any good work which others could do, and that all his love had been for the Church, her teaching, her rites, her glories, and her hierarchy. In fact, it may be claimed for him that by his width of culture and his deeply ecclesiastical spirit he was eminently fitted to represent the Universal Church in England in all its greatness and variety as far as any one individual possibly can. This is his glory aptly expressed in the motto: *Omnia pro Christo*.

Fifteen years had passed since the hierarchy had been established, but comparatively few changes had taken place in the interval among the bishops of the province. Drs Roskell and Amherst had succeeded to Nottingham and to Northampton respectively, and in the West the sees of Plymouth and Clifton had new incumbents, both chosen from the staunchest families who had held to the Faith in penal days. These were Dr Hugh Clifford at Clifton and Bishop William Vaughan at Plymouth. With these exceptions the suffragans had either been named at the same time as Wiseman or not so very long after. But even though most of the bishops of the original hierarchy still

Marginal note: The Province at Wiseman's death.

RESTORATION OF HIERARCHY

survived, they could all of them point to changes and to developments which were encouraging signs of progress. The figures given by Wiseman at the Catholic Congress of Malines could have been expanded and carried into detail on the same lines which he there sketched out. It is true that the actual number of Catholics had not increased in proportion to the clergy, nor in direct ratio with the growth of schools and other institutions. The figures given in the census of 1851, which dealt with Sunday attendance and church accommodation, would seem to point to a Catholic population in that year of about eight hundred thousand. We have even less to guide us in 1865. Probably by that time the Catholics were slightly over a million. But with all deductions made there remains quite enough to characterise the period as one of solid and important progress. It now remained to find a leader who would continue the great work which Wiseman began, and fill in as far as in him lay the outline which that prelate had sketched with such bold and true strokes.

XXXV.

THE BATTLE FOR CATHOLIC EDUCATION.

(1865-1892.)

THE death of Cardinal Wiseman on the 15th of February, 1865, at once raised the important question, studiously left in abeyance as long as he lived, as to who was to succeed as Archbishop of Westminster. The late cardinal had filled an ever higher and higher place in the eyes of churchmen and of the world as the years rolled by. Could anyone be found to step into his position without a notable descent in influence? During the last years of his life he had relied much for support and counsel on Henry Edward Manning, Superior of the Oblates at Bayswater, whom he had raised to the dignity of Provost of the Chapter. *Archbishop Manning.* This remarkable man already enjoyed weight at Rome, and was in favour with the convert section of the clergy. On the other hand, he was disliked and to some extent distrusted by the hereditary Catholics. Consequently there was great difference of view as to who should be the new archbishop. The majority of the older clergy would appear to have thought that the moment had come for the reinstatement of Archbishop Errington, who ever since his compulsory retirement had been living in seclusion at Prior Park, but was still alive and vigorous. However, many of the bishops, conceiving Errington unsuitable for the office, and remembering the past action of the Holy See, favoured the translation of Bishop Ullathorne from Birmingham. After hearing all the arguments, and after praying earnestly for guidance, Pius IX. at last fixed his choice on Manning. It was a bold and unusual step. Manning was not a bishop, was a convert, and had been a married man. Still he was a born ruler, a skilful

CATHOLIC EDUCATION 543

diplomatist, a polished representative of Oxford culture, and an enthusiatic lover of Rome, even in such minor matters as architecture and rubrics.

In looking at events from the standpoint of the Church's general interests, the greatest event which happened in the days this chapter is concerned with was the Vatican Council. Small as was the number of English Catholics in comparison with the whole world, their share in it was no mean one. The fact that the mass of the nation did not admit the papal claims as well as the deeply religious character of large numbers of these non-Catholics made it a matter of deep interest in England. Moreover, in Archbishop Manning universal consent saw one of the most notable figures in that venerable assembly. Few of the fathers exercised a more potent influence in promoting the definition of papal infallibility, which was after all the chief battle-ground during the discussions. He spoke but twice in the council, but he had other spheres of influence. He kept in close touch with Lord Odo Russell, then British minister at the Roman court, and through him was able to counteract the efforts made by Döllinger and Lord Acton to gain over Gladstone to the policy of diplomatic interference. He was one of the chief leaders at the meetings held in the Villa Caserta to organise the voting in favour of the definition. All the English bishops except two were in favour of the doctrine being defined, but among the clergy and educated laity there was a not inconsiderable opposition. As far as this party was in any way organised they were known as inopportunists, which meant that their opposition was not directed against the truth of the doctrine, but the opportuneness of its being made an Article of Faith by the council. At the head of this band must be placed the illustrious Newman, and not far behind him the learned Lord Acton, who went much further than Newman in his opposition. There was also a knot of Oxford converts represented by Mr Richard Simpson, Mr Capes, Mr Ffoulkes, Le Page Renouf, and others. Outside the Catholic ranks the opposition in England was very general, though not intense. Unfortunately the Prime Minister, Mr Gladstone, had placed himself at the head of this adverse stream of opinion. When, at the

The Vatican Council.

beginning of 1870, the definition seemed on the point of being made, Gladstone was only prevented from joining the protests of the French and Bavarian governments by the contrary views of Lord Clarendon and the majority of his Cabinet. And when the doctrine had been proclaimed, and the wheel of time had brought Gladstone into conflict with the Irish bishops, this conflict impelled him to take his pen in hand and strive to show in his pamphlet, "*The Vatican Decrees*," that civil allegiance was incompatible with the holding of the papal infallibility. The attack was sprung upon the Catholic body at a time when the excitement which accompanied the close of the council had in great measure died down. The leaders of the opposition to the decrees, whose hearts were loyal to the Church, had already submitted, and those who were not had passed into open heresy. Hence, both from those who had said *placet*, and those who had not, there were not wanting able champions to answer the misrepresentations and sophisms to which the great Liberal statesman had committed himself. Manning considered that his position required him to reply at once, and he did so in a pamphlet, remarkable for the lucid simplicity of its exposition of the real doctrine as distinguished from the caricature of it which came forward in Mr Gladstone's pages. Newman, though unwilling to cross swords with Gladstone, did so at last in a masterpiece of argumentative and critical writing under the title of "*A Letter to the Duke of Norfolk.*" Many other replies also saw the light. Notable among them was one by Dr Ullathorne, who had been for a time an "inopportunist." In Ireland a particularly able answer appeared from the pen of the learned theologian, Dr Neville of Maynooth. Gladstone wrote again, but he had had his all sufficient and well merited castigation, and probably the controversy served the useful purpose of bringing out the limitations and the moderation of the Vatican Decrees with a clearer light before the British public than would otherwise have been possible. In fact it was easy to show that Mr Gladstone had misconceived the whole bearing of the decrees, and that civil allegiance was as secure as ever.

Whilst in this way the Catholic doctrine on the unity of the Church and on the supremacy of the Holy See was emphatically taught at Rome, and zealously

CATHOLIC EDUCATION

defended by the champions of Catholicism in England, Manning and other leaders were keenly alive to the importance of keeping in touch with the leaders of intellectual life of all schools in order that their influence might be felt directly by those whose opinions moulded those of others. A striking instance of this is to be found in the co-operation which they extended to the Metaphysical Society, which was founded in 1869 for the interchange of philosophical ideas and freedom of discussion among the leaders of different schools of thought. The list of members, especially when supplemented by the names of those who joined in the later years, includes a galaxy of talent that could hardly be matched in any intellectual region to which we might direct our gaze. There were six Catholic members: Manning, W. G. Ward, Dalgairns, St George Mivart, Gasquet, and Robert Clarke. Of these Manning was of course the most prominent on account of his position as "the distinguished head of a great Church," in Tennyson's words. In 1870 Ward was elected president of the society. It survived for ten years, but in 1880 came to an end, since there was in fact very little common ground except personal respect for one another among the remarkable men, several of whom still survive, who became members of it. Dr W. G. Ward was at that time the foremost exponent in English of the Catholic standpoint in the fundamentals of philosophy and the Metaphysical Society provided him with the widest arena for intellectual discussion that he ever enjoyed. His very striking part in the controversies of the Oxford Movement has been noted above, but as a Catholic his influence both on contemporary thought and on periodical literature ought not to be passed over. His best known book, "*The Ideal of the Christian Church*," was published in his Anglican days; but in the later period he wrote an important essay on "*Nature and Grace*," which was published in 1860. It would, nevertheless, be true to say that Dr Ward's championship of the Holy See and of the general interests of Catholicism found a more abiding field in his editorship of the *Dublin Review* during the years from 1863

Manning and the Metaphysical Society (1869-1880).

Dr Ward (1812-1882) and F. Dalgairns (1818-1876).

2M

to 1879. The periodical was published regularly every quarter for all this time, and there was scarcely a number but contained one or more articles from his pen. Dr Ward died in 1882. The philosophical discussions of the Metaphysical Society, which were so keen a delight to Ward's vigorous mind, seem to have overworked the sensitive but highly intellectual nature of Father Dalgairns, though there were few members whose association with the society impressed their fellows more. Father Dalgairns was already well-known as the author of two beautiful treatises on the "*Sacred Heart*" and on "*Holy Communion*," which are still highly valued. But as the years went on the overwrought brain refused to work, and he died before reaching old age on the 6th of April, 1876.

The contest to secure that the children of Catholic parents should be brought up in a Catholic atmosphere was brought to a head by the passing of Forster's Elementary Education Act through Parliament in 1870. This enactment established local bodies called School Boards all over the country, and for the first time made education compulsory. A large number of additional schools had to be provided to accommodate the vast proportion of the children who up to this time had not frequented any school at all. The Catholic schools were not interfered with, but as they did not provide for anything like all the children, the alternative was before the Catholic body of either building new schools sufficiently large to take in all the children, or of seeing their children forced to attend the schools known as Board schools, where the education was of a secular or non-religious type. The English Catholics rose to the emergency, and made great sacrifices of money and labour to meet the circumstances. Archbishop Manning put himself at the head of the movement, and was able to secure the unanimous support of the bishops, the clergy, and the chief members of the laity. Public meetings were held, large sums of money were subscribed, energy that would otherwise have been used for other purposes was concentrated upon this. A great era of Catholic school-building was begun. It was laid down that it was more important to build a school than a church: sometimes both purposes were accomplished by

School Board Act of 1870.

CATHOLIC EDUCATION

the erection of a so-called school chapel. The archbishop himself declared that for his part he would not consent to any money being spent upon the proposed cathedral for Westminster until every Catholic child in the diocese was provided with a place in a Catholic school. In this way the onset was met, and what at first seemed an attack proved in the end a powerful means for consolidating and strengthening the congregations of the faithful.

To compare smaller things with greater, just as the Vatican Council was the crowning event of this generation for the Universal Church, so was the Fourth Provincial Synod of Westminster for the Church in England. It was held at St Edmund's, Old Hall, from the 21st of July to the 12th of August, 1873. Fourteen years had passed since the Third Council, and the personnel of the rulers of the Church was greatly changed. Besides Westminster, five suffragan sees were filled by new incumbents, but all the living diocesan bishops were present as well as Archbishop Vaughan, coadjutor of the Archbishop of Sydney. There were six provincials of religious orders, Fathers Burchall, Gallwey, King, Coffin, O'Loughlin and Rinolfi, and two or three other religious of note took part in it as theologians: Father Emidius the Capuchin, Father Bosio the Servite, Fathers Eyre and Porter the Jesuits, and Abbot Alcock and Prior Raynal of the Benedictines. Moreover, most of the best known canons and theologians among the secular clergy took part in the deliberations, but Newman was not there, nor was there any representative of the Oratorian or Oblate congregations. The most important decrees dealt with elementary, secondary, and university education, and in these the formation of a university college and of several diocesan seminaries was foreshadowed. Warnings were given against mixed marriages, and safeguards published anew for the cases in which they had to be contracted. The faithful were exhorted to unity and to gratitude to God for the growth given to the institutions of the province during the period since the last assembly. The chief subject broached at the council about which there was nothing like unanimity shown, but rather some warm speaking and the clash of contending views, was the state of relations between the bishops and the regular clergy.

Fourth Provincial Council of Westminster (1873).

The result of this was that the council made no decree on the subject, but it was evident that further legislation would be needed. In fact, after two years of protracted appeals and discussion at Rome, in which the Jesuit fathers defended the cause of the customary privilege of the Regulars, while the Bishop of Salford appeared as the representative of Manning and the bishops, an end was put to the controversy by the now celebrated decree, *Romanos Pontifices*, which has ever since been the *norma* of procedure in England on this question. It has furthermore been applied to settle similar questions which have since arisen in other countries.

In 1875 Archbishop Manning was among the list of noteworthy champions of the papacy and of the Church whom Pius IX. raised at one and the same time to the dignity of cardinal. He had now filled the see of Westminster for ten years, and in addition to his labours at home for education and the spread of the Faith, had served the Holy See well in what concerned the Universal Church. He travelled to Rome to receive the insignia of the dignity, and the public ceremonies were brought to a climax with the solemn investiture of the new members of the Sacred College on the 29th of March, 1875. To his great joy he was given the title of St Gregory on the Cœlian, and at the reception which he held, according to custom, in the English College, he delivered an eloquent address, showing how highly he valued the honour bestowed upon him, but at the same time vindicating himself from the charge of ambition. His elevation was greeted with pleasure, not only by his fellow-Catholics, but also by many of his non-Catholic fellow-countrymen, who had learned to look upon him by this time as one of the leaders of their race. He soon came back to his sphere of labour at Westminster. He was soon deep in controversy, now on Communion under one kind, now with regard to devotion to the Sacred Heart. During the next few years he was able to publish several books, especially the "*Internal Mission of the Holy Ghost,*" "*The Glories of the Sacred Heart,*" "*The Independence of the Holy See,*" and "*The True Story of the Vatican Council.*" When he was called to Rome to assist at the conclave made necessary by the death of Pius IX. in 1878, he took a leading part in its proceed-

Manning a Cardinal (1875).

ings, and was even suggested by some of the cardinals as a possible candidate for the papacy. He certainly was one of the leaders who met together and brought forward the name of Cardinal Pecci, whose candidature they forwarded. Cardinal Pecci on the third day of the conclave became Pope Leo XIII.

As the name of Manning had not been one of the three submitted by the English bishops to the Holy See as possible successor to Wiseman, there must have been a feeling that the direct action of Pius IX. in appointing took all responsibility out of their hands. By training and antecedents he was not one of themselves, but with a noble sense of duty they had extended to him a cordial welcome on his appointment, and loyal co-operation in promoting the interests of Catholicism. Drs Clifford and Vaughan continued to occupy the sees they had filled in 1865 for all Manning's life-time. Manning gave his support to the choice of Dr Cornthwaite for Beverley and of Dr Chadwick for Hexham and Newcastle at the very beginning of his own episcopate. Both the Lancashire sees fell vacant in 1872, and while the zealous Irish pastor of St Vincent's Church was consecrated to succeed Dr Goss at Liverpool, the archbishop had to use his influence more directly to secure the appointment of Herbert Vaughan to Salford. Though later on he differed from the last named churchman on several points of public policy, they each had the most sincere admiration for one another. Another Oblate of St Charles whom his late superior recommended for the responsibility of episcopal rank was Dr O'Callaghan, who was named Bishop of Hexham and Newcastle in 1888. In another case he had found a candidate of his choice in the ranks of the London Oratorians in the person of Dr Edward Bagshawe, who became Bishop of Nottingham, and continued to rule that see until long after Manning's death. He was also in part responsible for the consecration of Dr Patterson as auxiliary to himself, and towards the end of his life for that of the veteran army chaplain, Dr Virtue, to the newly formed diocese of Portsmouth. Notwithstanding his views with regard to the religious orders, he warmly recommended the Redemptorist Provincial, Father Coffin, an Oxford pupil of Newman's, and one of Manning's own most

Contemporary Bishops.

trusted counsellors, for the vacant diocese of Southwark in 1882. But Father Coffin, being already somewhat advanced in years, and already in bad health, only survived as bishop for three years (1882-5), when the coadjutor whom he had himself selected, Dr John Butt, became bishop in his stead. The learned Prior of Belmont Benedictine House succeeded the aged Bishop Brown as Bishop of Menevia and Newport when the latter died in 1880. He had been coadjutor since 1873. Dr Ullathorne had already provided himself with a successor at Birmingham in his secretary, Dr Ilsley, who in that capacity and then as coadjutor had worked for the aged patriarch who was the sole survivor of the days of Wiseman and the vicariates. When Beverley was divided in 1878, Dr Cornthwaite had easily found a chief pastor for the new diocese of Middlesbrough in Dr Lacy, the priest who had built the principal church in that busy town.

Cardinal Manning was the leader of a determined effort made by the English Hierarchy in his day to

Diocesan Seminaries.
establish diocesan seminaries after the model indicated in the decrees of the Council of Trent. To provide for his own diocese the archbishop built a portion of a handsome Gothic college at Hammersmith, and opened it in 1884. Dr Weathers was placed at the head of it, and a staff of professors was gathered. It only just outlasted Manning's lifetime, being then sold to the Sacred Heart nuns. But the effort was not confined to Westminster. Bishop Ullathorne began a similar seminary at Olton, since sold to the Capuchins. Bishop O'Reilly built a college for Liverpool at Upholland, near Wigan. Bishop Butt founded the Southwark Seminary at Wonersh, near Guildford. Both these colleges exist as flourishing establishments. The attempts made on similar lines at Salford and Nottingham had no lengthy existence, though Leeds still has its diocesan college. It was out of the power of the smaller dioceses to do anything on similar lines, so they continued to send their students to Ushaw, Rome, Lisbon, and Valladolid, or to one of the seminaries in the larger dioceses. Bishop Baines' imposing foundation at Prior Park was carried on for many years, but it was an expensive adjunct to the Clifton diocese, and at last succumbed to the strain.

CATHOLIC EDUCATION

It may be doubted, seeing his devotion to the older Catholic colleges, whether Wiseman would have fully shared the zeal of his successor for separate diocesan seminaries, but at least one new college established during the year under review would have had his heartiest support, nay, the inspiration came through him, though he did not live to see its actual realisation. This was the Foreign Missionary College begun at Mill Hill, near Hendon, by Dr Herbert Vaughan in 1866. Wiseman had blessed the young founder's courageous begging tour, but when Herbert Vaughan came home with what seemed a sufficient sum for a commencement the cardinal had already breathed his last. Still, armed with the full approval of his superior, who was at the same time head of the Oblate Community, and Archbishop of Westminster, Father Vaughan settled down to his work. A start was made on the 1st of March, 1866, and the foundation stone of the new college laid in June, 1869. In March, 1871, it was opened, and at that time had a community of thirty-four. Its founder was soon after this made Bishop of Salford, but he had the consolation during his lifetime to see the work attain considerable development. Schools for studies preparatory to the course at Mill Hill and for students of less advanced age were opened at Rosendaal in Holland, in the Tyrol, and at Freshfield, near Liverpool. These establishments trained from schoolboy age those who seemed likely to have a missionary vocation, and thus filled up the ranks at Mill Hill.

Mill Hill Missionary College.

There was still the higher education of the laity to provide for, and opinions were not at all unanimous as to the best means to employ. Newman considered that a Catholic hall might profitably be looked for at Oxford, and his views found so much favour with many educated men among his contemporaries. Negotiations were set on foot: Newman was to fix his residence at Oxford, and young Catholics were to be attracted to go there under the ægis of his name and reputation. But Manning did not share these views. He considered that the general atmosphere of a non-Catholic centre of culture, such as Oxford then was, would be most dangerous to our young men. He felt that the Oxford of the

Protestant University training condemned.

seventies was no longer the University of Newman's day, but had gone very far in the direction of free thought and rationalism. The controversy was carried on among the intellectual leaders of Catholicism for a time with some heat and strong convictions on both sides. At last Manning resolved to appeal to the Holy See, and thus the cause was called to Rome. The result of this was that Newman was refused permission to open an educational establishment at Oxford. Furthermore, on the 6th of August, 1867, there came a rescript from the Holy See discountenancing Catholic parents from sending their sons to the universities, but leaving it to the bishops to give individual leave when in some special case there seemed to be reason for it. In this way any general frequentation of the universities by Catholic young men was for the time impossible. There were always a few both at Oxford and at Cambridge for whom some special reason existed or some special advantage could be claimed. But, in the main, they were thrown back for their higher studies upon the existing Catholic schools and colleges, of which the chief were the Jesuit College at Stonyhurst, the Benedictine House at Downside, the Oratory School at Birmingham, and the mixed clerical and lay colleges at Ushaw, Oscott, and Old Hall. A certain number of the *alumni* of such colleges as these were presented for examination for the degrees of the University of London, and in some cases with such brilliant success that much credit was reflected on the actual class-work of the establishments from which they came, but the University of London, being merely an examining body, was powerless to supply what these colleges lacked as to university associations.

Kensington University College. One effort in the campaign against secularism into which Cardinal Manning had thrown himself was not destined to be crowned with success. This was his determined attempt to begin a university college for Catholics under Catholic teachers and in a Catholic atmosphere. He had urged the issue of the papal rescript discountenancing the frequentation of the national universities as dangerous to the Faith, and it was for the Holy See and the bishops to try and find a substitute. The plan which was adopted was to start a college of higher studies at Kensington, from which students could be sent up to take their degrees at the University of London. The enterprise failed partly from its inherent difficulty and partly from the mistakes made in its administration. There were neither endowments nor collegiate buildings to put it on a plane with existing colleges, and the narrow view which decided on carrying on the work without the co-operation of the Jesuit Fathers was a heavy weight in the adverse scale. However, for a time, considerable financial help was given by wealthy Catholics, a collection was made throughout England, and a commencement was launched. The choice made of a rector was an unfortunate one, as the popular preacher, Monsignor Capel, was not qualified for the exacting duties of the office. But various scholars of reputation were engaged, who constituted a quite remarkable teaching staff. F. A. Paley, one of the earliest of the university converts, and a leading Cambridge tutor and editor, lectured in classics, the well-known Barff in chemistry, Mivart in biology, Devas in political economy, while the profound savant, Dr Robert Clarke, took the chair of modern philosophy. Gordon Thompson lectured on English literature, Croke Robinson on Church history, while Fathers Angus, MacMullen, and William Lloyd were attached to the institution in various capacities. The number of students, which never exceeded forty-five, soon began to decline, and after a few years, in spite of the cardinal's tenacity in holding to his plan, it became evident that it could never be a permanent success. There was a brief period under Dr Robert Clarke at Cromwell Road, Kensington, and then the college was closed, whatever balance of funds remained being utilised for educational purposes elsewhere.

Another of Manning's chief enterprises was in close connection with his Congregation of the Oblates of St Charles. This was the foundation of St Charles's College at Bayswater, which existed for practically the whole period of his episcopate, under the direction of the fathers of this community. Suitable scholastic buildings were erected, and then under the government, first of the cardinal's nephew, Monsignor William Manning, and after his early death in 1879 under that of Dr Butler, his trusted friend and confessor, the college attained some degree

<!-- marginalia: St Charles's College. -->

of popularity and success as a public day school for boys. Eventually, like the seminary at Hammersmith, the buildings passed into the possession of the Nuns of the Sacred Heart, who used them as a training college for schoolmistresses.

As Manning passed into old age, he saw one after the other the contemporaries of his youth fall beneath the dart of death, leaving him somewhat lonely as far as personal friendships went, but still keenly interested in the public movements of the day both in Church and State. Frederic Oakeley, who had been one of the leading figures among the Oxford Tractarians, and was somewhat older than Manning, died at the age of nearly eighty in the year 1880. He was spoken of by Newman as "an almost typical Oxford man," and was coupled by Manning with Newman and himself as one of a band of converts from Anglicanism, who had laboured during a long career for the cause of the Catholic Church in England. Oakeley's scholastic attainments were considerable, but he had humbly turned from any thought of high honours or dignities to the pastoral charge of St. John's, Islington. There he persevered in the exemplary discharge of the ordinary duties of the parochial clergy for thirty years, from 1850 to 1880. Still he continued to give proof of his abilities as a writer in a long series of publications which came to an end only with his death. We owe to him among other works "*The Priest on the Mission*," "*The Ceremonies of the Mass*," the "*Lyra Liturgica*," and "*Reminiscences of the Oxford Movement*," to mention but a few of them.

In 1890 Newman died in his ninetieth year. His long day had been brought to a close with an evening of honour and peace. For nearly twelve years he had enjoyed the lofty station of a cardinal of the Holy Roman Church, and had been regarded with an ever-growing sentiment of admiration and affection by a circle which was ever widening in its extent. These twelve years were a fitting counterpart to the twelve years at Oxford from 1833 to 1845, when he was the light and guiding star of the Tractarian Movement. During the years since he arrested the attention of the entire reading public by his masterly "*Apologia*" in 1864, he had

Death of Newman (1890).

added but few books to the long list which preceded it. There was the " *Grammar of Assent* " in 1870, and the " *Letter to the Duke of Norfolk* " in 1875, but with these exceptions his publications were small in extent, however excellent in quality. But he had utilised his old age to revise his earlier works, so that we have them now; a procession of some forty classical volumes, expressing in eloquent English, which has never been surpassed, his deep thoughts on history, philosophy, the fine arts, doctrine, and much of the inner Christian life which he ever cherished above everything. His motto, *Cor ad cor loquitur*, well expresses the spirit in which they were written, nor is there any real scepticism in those other words which he chose for his humble grave at Rednal: *Ex umbris et imaginibus in veritatem.*

As for the archbishop, with the advance of old age he retired somewhat from the burning controversies in which he had spent so much of his earlier years. But it cannot be said that his influence over the mass of his fellow-countrymen in any way declined. Rather may it be claimed that it grew greater as time went on. One notable instance of this was his intervention in the strike of the dock labourers of the Port of London, which took place in 1889. When almost all hope of an agreement between the directors and the men on strike had vanished, the patience, courage, and persuasiveness of the cardinal induced the men to listen to terms. Hence it came to pass that his influence with the working classes contributed more than any other cause to effect the settlement then reached. He had always led a most ascetic and self-denying life, setting thus in his own person the standard which in his " *Eternal Priesthood* " and other writings for the clergy he strove to inculcate upon them. Whenever he was able to issue from his seclusion he was a welcome and venerable figure at public meetings, at the highest social gatherings, and at ecclesiastical functions. But at last he was practically confined to his house. From it he continued to rule the diocese, and, feeling that his strength was gradually decaying, took advantage of the warning thus conveyed to put his papers and the affairs of his high office in order and to prepare for the end. At the beginning of 1892 the medical opinion was that he had

Death of Cardinal Manning (1892).

not long to live. After making his profession of Faith according to the ritual in the presence of the Canons of Westminster, he spent his last night in devotion under the watchful care of Bishop Herbert Vaughan, Canon Johnson, his faithful secretary, and Dr Gasquet. Early next morning, while Bishop Vaughan was saying Mass for him, Cardinal Manning breathed his last. It was the 14th of January, 1892. By a remarkable coincidence the Duke of Clarence, son and heir of Edward, Prince of Wales, afterwards King Edward VII., died on the same day, and kind messages of mutual condolence were exchanged between the royal court and archbishop's house. The funeral of the cardinal, which took place a week later, was attended by sixteen bishops, an eloquent memorial sermon being delivered by Bishop Hedley, and a solemn requiem sung at the Brompton Oratory. The popular demonstrations of respect along the route of the procession to Kensal Green Cemetery exceeded anything of the kind which had been seen since Wiseman's death. They were a striking testimony to the hold which the deceased prelate had gained over the minds and hearts of the mass of his countrymen.

XXXVI.

THE DAWN OF THE TWENTIETH CENTURY.

(1892-1919.)

IF we accept the accredited view that an error of six or seven years has been made in the chronology of the Christian era nearly all the period embraced in this chapter falls within the twentieth century. The year 1892 was not marked by an epoch-making event in secular history, but the death of Cardinal Manning and the appointment of his successor, with the changes which resulted therefore, give quite a sufficiently important turning point for the history of the Church in England. For the first decade of the period now under review the central figure in the life of the kingdom of God in our midst was Herbert Cardinal Vaughan. At the moment of Manning's death he stood out in general estimation as the most prominent figure in the episcopate, and not a few Catholics considered it as a foregone conclusion that he would be the next archbishop. He was already sixty years of age, but he was still so energetic and full of zeal that ten or eleven more years of fruitful activity were still before him in the metropolitan see. Born at Gloucester in 1832, he came of an old established Catholic family of Herefordshire, and was originally destined for the army. Yet, at the age of twenty he had abandoned all idea of a career in the world, and embraced the clerical state with all the ardour of his simple enthusiastic character. His education was completed in Rome; and he then joined that zealous band of secular clergy whom Manning had gathered at Bayswater. Here he remained as an Oblate of St Charles, at the call of his bishop. It was quite in accordance with the spirit of the institute that he was sent from Bayswater

Cardinal Vaughan (1832-1903).

to St Edmund's, Old Hall, as vice-president in 1855. There was much opposition to any share in the government of the seminary being entrusted to the Oblates, and the result was that Herbert Vaughan went back to Bayswater. Great was the zeal which prompted him in 1860 spontaneously to offer himself to Cardinal Wiseman for the great work of commencing a missionary college, a project which had been deep in the heart of the first Archbishop of Westminster. When the offer was accepted he devoted himself unreservedly to the work. He begged for it through North and South America, and then he returned provided with means; he grappled with the labours of its inception so successfully that what had seemed a dream became a reality, and in 1871 St Joseph's College, Mill Hill, was opened free of debt, with a community of thirty-four to prepare for the apostolate to the heathen. In the next year he was named as successor to Bishop Turner in the see of Salford. For twenty years he had governed this Lancashire diocese with self-sacrificing work and single-minded devotion to duty. He might, had he chosen, have pointed to a stirring record of works set on foot, and progress made before he was translated to be metropolitan. As far as figures can be trusted he had succeeded in nearly doubling the statistics of clergy, of institutions, and of schools in the diocese. He was now called to other work, different in kind, and from which in his humility he almost shrank, protesting his unsuitableness. But the call of God was clear; and so he shouldered the burden with a still lively desire to push forward the frontiers of the kingdom of God, and to show forth its glories. In the year after his translation, 1893, he was created cardinal, but this was rather a testimony to what he had already accomplished in Salford and at Mill Hill. There was no traditional right to the dignity on the part of the metropolitan see.

Cardinal Vaughan had not been long established in the see of Westminster before a scheme for a new cathedral for the diocese began to take shape in his mind. It seemed to him that such a building, if on a sufficiently grand scale, would be a powerful lever to raise the whole external position of the Church in London. No material thing seemed to him better suited to advance the spiritual

Westminster Cathedral.

he had at heart. He aimed high and planned on grandiose lines, for nothing would content him but an edifice conceived not on the scale of the modern cathedral, but on the far ampler scale of the mediaeval builders. Yet even here his practical sense came to the aid of his idealism. He realised that means could not be found to rival the magnificent Gothic edifices of the Ages of Faith. Therefore, he would have a church which would not challenge comparison with them in the same style, but which would be imposing enough to form a striking contrast in another style. He found an architect of genius combined with the most painstaking attention to detail in J. F. Bentley, already well known for excellent Gothic work. With his self-sacrificing collaboration he planned out a church in the Byzantine style, three hundred and sixty feet in length, and broad and high in proportion, with an elegant towering campanile. To obtain the necessary funds the cardinal was willing to beg and to collect, but he was not willing to go into debt. All those who contributed one thousand pounds had the honour of being reckoned as founders. The foundation stone was laid on the 29th of June, 1895, in the presence of Cardinal Logue, and a large assembly of bishops, priests, and laity. From that time the construction went on almost without interruption for the rest of Cardinal Vaughan's life-time. Generous benefactors came forward one after another, so that the noble prelate who had conceived the idea of the cathedral had the consolation of seeing at any rate the shell of what could only be decorated quite gradually, practically complete before his death. Ever since it has gone on justifying the foresight of its chief founder that it would become a growing centre of Catholic life, of liturgical services, and even of private devotion.

It is no more than the truth to affirm that the interest which Cardinal Vaughan took in the great work of education was no whit less than that which his illustrious predecessor showed. He had abundantly proved this while Manning still ruled at Westminster, and had steadfastly supported him in his enterprises in that field. No other bishop had suppassed him in the efforts he had made to meet the crisis created by the Education Act of 1870. When Manning urged that the time had come to establish Tridentine Seminaries in each diocese, Salford promptly set hands to the work. There were times when he stood almost alone at Manning's side as in the university project. But before he became archbishop he had seen the Catholic University College go down in failure, and one of his last acts in Salford was to close the Study House for Theology, which was the nearest he could approach to a diocesan seminary. Hence, his zeal for education showed itself by a somewhat marked reversal of what had previously been done. For the education of the clergy he advocated the establishment of a central seminary at any rate for all the Southern dioceses instead of a number of smaller ones, not so much to supplement or extend their course, as to take their place, providing both a more competent staff and a more profitable course of studies. He succeeded in getting such a plan adopted at Oscott in 1893. He then removed his senior students from Old Hall to Oscott, and persuaded several of the other bishops to do likewise. Unforeseen difficulties arose, and the plan did not long survive its author. He also applied to the Holy See, at the earnest request of many influential Catholics in England, asking to have the prohibition against attendance at Oxford and Cambridge removed. This was done in 1895, though the Congregation of Propaganda in reversing the previous decision made stipulations as to the religious training of Catholic students, which were readily complied with under the direction of a board appointed for the purpose. The result has been eminently satisfactory, and as the succeeding years have gone by the gradual increase of Catholic students at both these seats of learning, as well as the credit they have done themselves, argues for the wisdom of the change of policy. And, now, with the establishment of Catholic halls, and the return of the religious to the Alma Mater which once owed so much to them, whether at Oxford or Cambridge, the signs of progress are written large to anyone who visits these beautiful university towns.

Cardinal Vaughan and Education.

The fight for the elementary schools had gone on bravely during the whole of the preceding period, but it could not be said to have been won. The demands of the national education authorities, and of the local bodies were steadily growing, both as to teachers and as to buildings and equipment, while the assistance given by the government grant was insufficient to enable our schools to compete on a footing of equality with those which enjoyed the help of the local rates as well. Hence, these years were years of strain, ever increasing so threateningly that final success in the struggle seemed highly doubtful. The Act of 1870, which established the local School Boards, and which had led to a great multiplication of expensive school buildings, and a still greater increase in the average attendance of school children, had been supplemented by another Elementary Education Act in 1880, introduced by Mr Mundella, the effect of which was to make the permissive powers granted to School Boards compulsory, and thus to complete the system of universal obligatory education. Meanwhile, the additional funds which were at the disposal of the School Boards enabled them to give better remuneration to their teaching staff, as well as to furnish their buildings with better equipment. In both these matters the standard was being perseveringly raised, and the financial strain on the voluntary schools thereby made more severe. A measure introduced in 1896 by Sir John Gorst to redress the balance by means of a special aid grant from the County Councils to the voluntary schools was dropped in face of the opposition it encountered. In 1897 the Voluntary School Act was passed by way of compromise granting an aid of five shillings per head of average attendance to the voluntary schools. But these halting provisions proved quite insufficient to meet the situation. At length in 1902 a more statesmanlike effort at a final settlement was made by Mr Balfour through an act superseding the School Boards, and handing over the control of elementary education to the County Councils. Equal pay for the teachers and equal maintenance in the equipment was established for denominational and for non-denominational schools alike. The sacrifice demanded for the right of denominational teaching was the provision of the school buildings which were provided by the county in the case of non-denominational schools. Cardinal Vaughan and the bishops, as well as the Anglican authorities, were consenting parties to this arrangement, from which dates a new era of prosperity and of efficiency for the Catholic schools.

The Battle of the Schools renewed.

562   THE CHURCH IN ENGLAND

Anglican Orders.   One of the most interesting episodes of the ecclesiastical history of England in the last years of the twentieth century was the reopening of the question of the validity of Anglican Orders. Though the membership of the Society for Promoting the Reunion of Christendom had been banned for Catholics, the activities of the association still went on. And they took a new development in the year 1890 as a result of repeated conferences between a French priest—the Abbé Portal—and Lord Halifax, president of the English Church Union, at Madeira. The Abbé Portal thought there was a case for the reopening of the question of the validity of Anglican Orders, and was supported by the learned Abbé Duchesne. It was an attractive prospect. Though persecuted and condemned by their own bishops and the vast body of Protestant lay thought in the country, the result of successive cases of conflict had nearly always been a gain to the High Church party. And in their ministry one after another the various doctrines of the Catholic Church, and her rites also, had been replaced with a steady development which was to say the least a phenomenon. Encouraged by a number of influential French priests and in Rome by Monsignor Gasparri, Lord Halifax with Messrs Lacey and Puller, notable clergymen of the High Church party, determined to lay their case before the Holy See. The Abbé Portal went to Rome in 1893, and had more than one interview with Leo XIII., which seemed to him to hold out some hope of a revision of the Church's practice on the matter. The weak point was that these hopes were founded on a partial and unreal view of the true position and teaching of the Church of England. Cardinal Vaughan, Abbot Gasquet, and other Catholic leaders grew considerably alarmed lest the partial statements of the Abbé Portal and his friends should create a false impression at Rome. They determined to do their best to warn the Pope and the Roman authorities. It must be said also that the Archbishop of Canterbury, Dr Benson, took a much more general and well-informed view of the matter, and gave the propaganda of agitation for revision of the " order's " question no encouragement whatever. However, Leo XIII. was anxious to do all in his power, and in March, 1896, appointed a special commission of six members, Father de Augustinis, S.J., Monsignor Gasparri, the Abbé Duchesne, Father Fleming, O.S.F., Abbot Gasquet, O.S.B., and Canon Moyes, to whom were afterwards added Canon Scannell and the Capuchin, Father Llanaveras, to examine the whole question anew. Monsignor Merry del Val was named secretary. Cardinal Mazzella, S.J., presided at the meetings of the commission. The Rev. Messrs Lacey and Puller also came to Rome to present the views of the High Church Anglicans, and besides writing a book in Latin styled "*De Hierarchia Anglicana*," were always at hand to answer questions and discuss difficulties. Abbot Gasquet undertook a laborious search through the Vatican Archives, beginning in the spring of 1895, in order to try and discover the papal bull directing Pole how to deal with the question of the reordination of the clergy found in possession in 1555 at the Marian Restoration. After a week's painstaking inspection of the papal registers of Paul IV., the bull *Præclara Charissimi* rewarded his labours, which directed the reordination of clergy who had been ordained according to the Edwardine Ordinal. This discovery cleared the ground for the theological discussions of the commission. Henceforward its members sat twice or three times a week, threshing out the question in the fullest detail during April and May, 1896, and then transmitted the reports of their findings to the Congregation of the Holy Office. The cardinals of the Holy Office spent a month in consideration of the evidence, and then in a Plenary Session held on Thursday, 16th June, in the presence of the Holy Father himself issued their decree declaring Anglican Orders to be absolutely invalid. Leo. XIII. in the following September published the bull, *Apostolicæ Curæ*, which confirmed the decision of the Holy Office pronouncing Anglican ordinations to be null and void.

Between the termination of the labours of the commission and the authoritative pronouncement, every effort had been made by the supporters of the validity of Anglican Orders to ward off any adverse decision. Messrs Lacey and Puller argued, Mr Gladstone, and others wrote. It was urged that conditional reordination could be accepted more easily. Furthermore, that a solemn and uncalled-for condemnation could not but widen the breach

Subsequent Developments.

between Anglicans and Catholics, and set back indefinitely the cause of reunion. However, once the decision was made known it was accepted with less hostility than might have been anticipated by the country at large. Cardinal Vaughan proclaimed the authoritative character of the decree, and called men off from the false lights which might lead them away from individual submission. *The Times* newspaper found fault with him for calling null and void what the English law declared valid. But the cardinal met this objection by replying that the Holy See never meant to question the validity of the orders in English law, but only according to the standard of the Catholic Church, which required a priesthood which offered a real sacrifice and really consecrated or transubstantiated the bread and wine. With this *The Times* and the main body of opinion declared itself satisfied. Naturally the Anglican clergy were angry, and the Archbishops of Canterbury and York published a reply to the papal bull, maintaining that they held a sacrifice of thanksgiving and self-oblation. However, it was no hard matter for the English Catholic bishops in their vindication of the bull, *Apostolicæ Curæ*, to show that the Anglican Eucharist was not held to be a sacrifice of the Body and Blood of Christ, and that they did not even claim the power of consecrating these sacred elements.

From the year 1897, or at least 1898, Cardinal Vaughan's health and strength were evidently on the wane. But he was not a man to give up exertion without being forced to it, and was ever full of schemes which he pushed forward enthusiastically for the good of his flock. There was the Converts' Aid Society, there was the Catholic Social Union, there was the Society of Priests of Our Lady of Compassion, there were the Ladies of Charity. All these plans were entered into by the cardinal with a zeal equal to what he would have felt if each one of these had been the sole work which appealed to him. Only he had to husband his physical strength. At one time he plunged into the work of evangelising the country villages of his dioceses, personally passing from one small town or hamlet to another to proclaim the credentials of the Church of Christ. Meanwhile he was ever at work upon his own soul to deepen that interior spiritual life, which always

Death of Cardinal Vaughan (1903).

DAWN OF TWENTIETH CENTURY 565

for him took precedence of everything else. The Education Bill of 1902 was the last great public achievement in which he took part. His share in the settlement has been already noted above. In that year repeated heart attacks warned him that the end was drawing nigh. He first sought relief by passing intervals at various health resorts, and in the homes of one or two of his devoted friends. But he steadily grew worse, and then elected to spend his last days at the Missionary College which he had founded at Mill Hill. After making his profession of Faith before the Canons he gradually sank into death. He breathed his last on the 19th of June, 1903, with the names of Jesus, Mary, Joseph, on his lips. His body was taken to Westminster Cathedral for the requiem, but afterwards brought back for interment in the place of his predilection—the foot of the Calvary in the midst of his missionary sons.

When Cardinal Vaughan breathed his last it was known indeed that the Bishop of Southwark had been summoned to earnest conference with him shortly before, but the succession was looked upon as quite an open question. The name of Cardinal Merry del Val, and that of Abbot Gasquet were mentioned, but the doubt was not of long duration. It became known that the Holy Father had appointed Bishop Bourne, and he proceeded to take possession of the archiepiscopal see. He was succeeded in Southwark by the zealous former pastor of St Mary and St Michael's, Commericial Road, the Right Rev. Peter Amigo. Meanwhile, the new archbishop began to take up the work of administration with quiet and cautious energy. He had already been a bishop for seven years, so that he had experience in diocesan government, though still much younger than any of his predecessors at the commencement of their reign over the see. He had been first as coadjutor and then as diocesan bishop the chief champion of the Tridentine Seminary, and he soon made it clear that the same principles would be applied to Westminster. Notice was given of the withdrawal of the students of the archdiocese from Oscott, and a new wing or "divine's" house was built at St Edmund's, which henceforth began a career of wide range and with an increased staff. This was the middle course between having practically two seminaries as Manning and

Ullathorne had done, and having none at all as it had chanced in Cardinal Vaughan's day.

Deliberately, but firmly, Archbishop Bourne set himself to pick up one after the other the threads of administration left him in the archdiocese. In 1905, just as Cardinal Logue had been the chief guest at the laying of the foundation stone at Westminster, so did he cross to Armagh to be present at the consecration of the primatial church of the Irish cardinal. He expressed the deep obligation of the Church in England to the Irish Hierarchy and to their people. Passing on from this, he spared no pains to keep alive and knit closer the bonds uniting the Church in England to its brethren on the continent of Europe, visiting France to take part in the celebrations in honour of Blessed Joan of Arc, at Rheims in 1920. There was also much to do at the new cathedral, where, since the requiem for Cardinal Vaughan, services had been held without any other formal opening than the Mass, which was chanted with the building thronged and bishops and clergy present in full numbers, for him whose thought and energy had built it. In 1907 the remains of Wiseman and of Manning were transferred from their resting-place at Kensal Green to the chapel in the crypt of the cathedral, in both cases with solemn rites and every sign of respectful remembrance. Then there was the perennial education question to face once more. In 1906 a new bill was introduced into Parliament by the Minister of Education, Mr Runciman, which was in the main promoted by those who were in favour of secular or undenominational education, and considered that the Act of 1902 gave aid out of the rates for the teaching of Catholicism and Anglicanism. A movement for passive resistance to the payment of such rates had been organised. But, though individuals had carried their convictions to the pitch of braving prosecution in the courts and even imprisonment rather than pay the obnoxious rate, the agitation as a popular demonstration collapsed, and the compromise was generally accepted. The denominationalists had made their sacrifice in providing their own schools, and now they were to enjoy at least some measure of equitable treatment in return.

The happy and courageous inspiration to invite the Eucharistic Congress to meet in London in 1908 gave the occasion for the most imposing demonstration of Catholic life and piety which the capital has seen since the Reformation. Westminster Cathedral was the chief centre of the celebrations. There the papal legate was received. There the solemn High Masses were celebrated, including a most interesting Liturgical Act, namely, High Mass according to the Greek rite. There the great procession of the Blessed Sacrament took place. But there were inspiring scenes elsewhere also. Two thrilling public meetings in the Albert Hall, a touching procession of the Catholic school children through the streets, and a general procession of the chief prelates and dignitaries who were present at the congress. As a record of the distinguished character of the ecclesiastics who gathered for this congress it may not be out of place to mention that they included besides Cardinal Vincent Vannutelli, the papal legate, seven other cardinals, fifteen archbishops, seventy-five bishops, eighteen abbots; and nearly every lay Catholic of note in England seems to have made a special effort to join the imposing throng which made these days a period of almost unmixed gladness, of cordial greeting and spiritual profit to the Children of the Faith who took part in them.

The Eucharistic Congress of 1908.

With the march of events and the proofs of the vigilant guardianship of the Catholic position given by the Archbishop of Westminster, there arose in many minds a not unreasonable longing that he might be called into the ranks of the Sacred College. There was a period of waiting indeed, for Rome proverbially moves slowly in the steps she takes when these involve complicated and interlocked considerations. But in the year 1911 the moment for this appointment had arrived. On the 27th of November Archbishop Bourne was created Cardinal-Priest, receiving the same title of St Pudenziana which had been borne by Cardinal Wiseman. At the same time a further step forward in the gradual development of the English Hierarchy was taken by the division of the province of Westminster into three, the Bishops of Liverpool and Birmingham being made archbishops with metropolitan rights. In 1916, five years later, a fourth province was created for Wales, under the name of

Archbishop Bourne a Cardinal.

Cardiff, the old title of Newport, which had only been borne by itself by one bishop, the illustrious Dr Hedley, being at the same time suppressed. The only further addition which remains to be chronicled up to the present is the creation of the see of Brentwood by the cutting-off of the county of Essex from Westminster. The learned Canon Bernard Ward, long president of the college at Old Hall, became the first bishop of the new diocese. Then, when he died, after three years of strenuous episcopate, Monsignor Doubleday, Rector of the Wonersh Seminary, was appointed to rule the vacant diocese.

CONCLUSION.

CATHOLIC LIFE IN MODERN ENGLAND.

THE preceding chapter brings us down in chronological order almost to the passing day. Yet, before laying down the pen, it would seem desirable to make a few remarks on the general characteristics of Catholic life during this modern period in which we live. For what can be established with regard to this must surely have an interest even surpassing anything that can be proved concerning distant ages, however noble or venerable. It is admitted on all hands that the Catholic Church has made notable progress in many directions in the England of our days. And this advance would seem to be of a kind that can be but imperfectly measured by any numerical comparison. It means the attainment of a distinctly higher position of influence among the forces which mould the national life. The days when the Children of the Faith were an isolated and obscure remnant appear to have definitely passed away. Friends and foes alike are now brought face to face with a living and energising Catholicism which is a great and patent fact in their midst. Moreover, this fact is so obvious in its significance that it has to be reckoned with by that body of public opinion which tries to gauge all things, and can hardly be counted as warmly favourable or bitterly hostile. This is what gives the highest interest to the problem of England and Christendom at the present day. Is Catholicity to become the one great antagonist of all the gathering powers of sensuality and irreligion? Or is it to remain, as it still is, in spite of the remarkable advances it has made, the religion of a small minority of the nation, respected at last and recognised as a power for good, but not on a scale to embrace the nation as a whole, or to bring the full

Christian revelation within the reach of the thirty-six millions who now dwell in the land?

Numerical strength of Catholics. If we discuss in the first place the numerical proportion in which Catholics stand to the total population, it is to be noted that we have not quite reliable data to build upon. Numbers, at best, only form the skeleton, so to speak, of the corporate existence of the Church, but at the same time they give a more definite outline of the state of things than can be gained by mere vague generalisation. There is no official census of religion in England as there is in most civilised countries and in our own colonies, and thus we are left to make estimates based upon such things as the birth-rate, the marriage-rate, the roll of children in the Catholic schools, and the lists of known Catholics compiled locally by the priests in charge of them. Of course these necessarily precarious calculations have to be supplemented by the increase due to individual conversions, and to the excess of immigration over emigration on the part of foreign Catholics. This is no place to work out in detail the results pointed to by these things. It will be enough to name the following considerations as furnishing some of the data available for calculation:

(1) The Catholic baptisms of infants *nearly* equal one-twelfth of all the births in the country.
(2) The annual register of adult conversions counts from eight thousand to ten thousand, there being no obligation to reckon young children.
(3) There are strong evidences to indicate that not more than three-fourths of the Catholic children are in Catholic schools.
(4) For many years past the immigration from Catholic countries has far exceeded the emigration.

All the available data being balanced, the fairest estimate would seem to be that the number of Catholics in England is approximately two million two hundred thousand. This is a figure which agrees with that given in the last edition of the "Encyclopædia Britannica." It is obvious that the exclusive use of any one method out of those indicated above leads to widely different conclusions.

The division of England into dioceses made at the restoration of the hierarchy may be looked upon in the main as an extension of the division into eight vicariates in 1840. It provided for one metropolitan and twelve suffragan sees, and involved scarcely any cross-division of the limits of those districts. The additions to the number effected since then have been the subdivision of Beverley into Leeds and Middlesbrough in 1878, that of Southwark through the creation of the see of Portsmouth in 1882, and the erection of the Welsh Vicariate in 1875, which has since been made the residential see of Menevia. This last change involved the separation of the Welsh counties included in Shrewsbury and Newport from those two dioceses. Newport was suppressed in 1916 when the archiepiscopal see of Cardiff was created as the metropolitan see of a new province for Wales. In 1911 the Province of Westminster was made into three by the elevation of the sees of Liverpool and Birmingham to the rank of archbishoprics. In most cases the civil boundaries of the counties were adhered to, it being understood on the one hand that the importance of both Lancashire and Yorkshire was thought to demand two dioceses in each of these two counties, while the small number of Catholics in other counties involved the grouping of several in the same diocese. In fact the only case hitherto of the diocesan boundaries being identical with those of a single county is afforded by the recently formed diocese of Brentwood, which comprises Essex neither more nor less. We have thus for the moment seventeen dioceses in England and Wales, so that counting a few auxiliary bishops, there are rather over twenty pastors of souls in episcopal orders to shepherd the flock.

The Dioceses of the Present Day.

The number of the clergy has grown of late years much faster than that of the faithful. There are now about four thousand priests, of whom some one thousand five hundred are religious, and two thousand five hundred seculars. This relatively large proportion of religious is something of a phenomenon, for, though of course it is far smaller than what obtained in the pre-Reformation period, it is more than a third, and therefore much greater than the sixth which is to be found in Ireland or in the Universal Church, or even than the fourth, which is about

The Ranks of the Clergy.

the proportion in the United States of America. We dare not assume that this is due to any special aptitude for the religious life among the inhabitants of Great Britain. There is an explanation which seems far more likely to fit the facts, based on the circumstance that whereas in Ireland and in many Catholic countries religious priests are confined to the so-called extraordinary and supplementary labours of missions, education, and other occupations outside the ordinary care of souls; in England, both now and in the Middle Ages, a large number of them have been employed alongside the secular clergy in parochial work. Consequently, there is both occupation and maintenance for a larger number of such clergy than would otherwise find their place. At any rate it is no exaggeration to say that there is scarcely any religious order of men of any extent in the Universal Church which has not aspired to make a foundation in modern England, and that there are not many whose aspirations in this regard have not been crowned with some measure of success. The Benedictines and the Jesuits, as might have been expected from the great part they have played in the past history of the country, are in a considerable majority over all the other religious bodies of men. Several other orders hardly maintain the relative position which was once theirs in pre-Reformation days, but on the other hand new institutes have arisen unknown to our forefathers, and they each of them seem to have their work to do in the future development of Catholicity in our midst.

Religious Life among Women. A still more remarkable manifestation of the religious life amongst us is furnished by the growth in the number of convents for women. This is upon a scale which far exceeds anything that the Middle Ages can boast of, and is likewise far beyond the extent of what has been so far accomplished by the various institutes for men. At the present time there are between eight hundred and nine hundred houses of female religious of different kinds, and even though it be admitted that some of these are of very modest dimensions, others have attained almost the dimensions of miniature towns inhabited by numerous and efficient communities, organised for a very great variety of pious and charitable works. Among the most flourishing of these congregations or institutes we may mention in the work of education, the Sisters of Notre

Dame, the Ladies of the Sacred Heart, the Faithful Companions of Jesus, the Ursulines, the Daughters of the Cross, and the nuns who keep up the Convents of the Holy Child. A noble work of even more general scope is done by the Sisters of Mercy and the Sisters of Charity, who seem to possess at least sixty establishments apiece, combining the care of the poor with extensive educational work. To provide a comfortable home for the aged there is scarcely any town of great size which has not a House of the Little Sisters of the Poor, or of the equally devoted Sisters of Nazareth. The fallen are sheltered in the excellent houses of refuge which are maintained by the Sisters of the Good Shepherd. It is somewhat invidious to mention some institutes and to pass over others, but space would fail if even the names of all were given. Those that are referred to are simply selected as specimens distinguished from the rest more by the wider extent of their distribution than by superior excellence in the quality of the work they accomplish. Nor must it be forgotten that, alongside of these comparatively modern institutes, the nuns of the more ancient enclosed orders have made many flourishing foundations in England. There are the venerable Benedictine nuns so long in exile on the continent of Europe, and now once more firmly planted in their native land. There are Trappistines, Poor Clares, Carmelites, Nuns of St Dominic, Brigittines and Canonesses both of St Augustine and of the Holy Sepulchre. It must, of course, be admitted that the growth of contemplative orders will be but slow in an age like the present, while the chief opportunities for the expansion of the religious life among women arise from the fact that a very large share of the educational work for Catholic girls is in the hands of nuns. The labours these have undertaken in that sphere provide a career sanctified by all the exercises of religion to numerous devout souls who otherwise might be at a loss for an outlet for their zeal.

Outside of the priesthood, the development attained by the religious life in the strict sense among men is on quite a small scale in comparison with what has been attained by the devout female sex. Yet it would be ungrateful for a Catholic not to acknowledge the valuable work done for the education of boys by the Brothers of the Christian Schools, *Teaching Brothers.*

founded by St John Baptist de La Salle, by the Irish Christian Brothers, by the Xaverian, the Marist and the Presentation Brothers. For the care of the sick we have the Brothers of St John of God and also the Alexian Brothers. But there seems all the more reason to regret that the numbers at the disposal of the teaching orders of men are not greater on account of the development of secondary education which is going on in our midst. It seems almost certain that we are in a stronger position to deal with the question of secondary schools and colleges for girls than for boys, and almost as certain that the relatively powerful position held by the teaching orders of women is the chief reason why that side of the problem is the one which presents less difficulties for the Church.

If we turn now to the life of devotion as it is led by the best and most thorough-going of our laity, we shall find *Life of the Devout Laity.* that it has certain features about it which contrast it rather markedly from what was customary in earlier ages. Moreover, there are differences which distinguish it from what is usual among pious Catholics in the other countries of Europe. Anything like a general attendance at the daily Sacrifice of the Altar is, we may take it, out of the question for the main body of our people. To persevere in it seems almost heroic virtue considering the obstacles which here surround the faithful. They are scattered, and they are nearly all busily employed. But on Sundays the proportion who comply with the precept to hear Mass would seem to compare very favourably with places where the bulk of the population are baptised Catholics. Furthermore, there is still considerable willingness on the part of many to go beyond the strict obligation, and take part in the more lengthy and solemn service of High Mass. Nor can it be said that there is any general avoidance of sermons or even of Sunday evening services. But the character of these evening devotions has considerably changed. The share of the laity in the Divine Office or Sacrifice of Praise, while never an obligatory one, has now shrunk to very narrow limits. The piety of the faithful of our day is more stirred by such services as Benedictions, processions, popular hymns, expositions of the Blessed Sacrament, and many other forms of devotion unknown to the mediaeval Catholic. On the other hand most of the attempts to make vespers, or any other selec-

LIFE IN MODERN ENGLAND

tion from the round of the Liturgy, the staple of public devotions seem to result in either emptying the churches or at least in lessening the attendance. Visiting the Sacred Host in the Tabernacle has become a favourite devotion in our days in rather sharp contrast with the practice of earlier times. At home, also, the practice of formal meditation is a much more prominent feature in devotional life than of old, and the same thing may be asserted of systematic daily examination of conscience. The devotion to the Rosary has grown under papal approval, while the time-honoured practices of the Sign of the Cross, the Angelus and the ringing of the Angelus retain the wide extension they ever had.

A surer index of progress than any numerical calculation is afforded by the fact that there is now no department of public life to which Catholics remain strangers. For it was not always thus. Now, however, they take their place in both Houses of Parliament, and are to be found in greater or less prominence in every government that is chosen. As to the House of Lords several notable Commoners in the Catholic body have been raised to the peerage, while individual conversions have added to the ranks of ancestral noble families who have kept faithful to the religion of their forefathers all through the penal times. In the Commons, though every vestige of legal disability has gone, it is only quite recently that the last remains of bigotry seem to be vanishing from the general electorate. Besides, since success at the polls depends on a variety of personal and political considerations and on willingness to vote on party lines, a Catholic's definite stand where religious interests come in make him a less pliable joint in the organised party machine. Yet there are always prominent Catholics in the House of Commons. In the learned professions, too, they have risen to the highest levels: judges, barristers, solicitors, physicians, surgeons all count among their brightest ornaments, members of our Church. In the Army and in the Navy we have a record to which we can point with quite legitimate pride. Then, when we turn to the realms of taste and refinement, we find professions in which the Children of the Church are represented out of all proportion to their general numerical strength. This is emphatically so in architecture, in music, and in the drama. On the dramatic stage are to be found Catholic actors and actresses in numbers far beyond what our ratio to the population would lead us to expect. In painting and sculpture our co-religionists are well to the front. In literature and poetry there are names which yield to none in inspiration and celebrity. It would be quite easy to demonstrate all this by mentioning a certain number of well-known names, but there is no need, for the challenge is not likely to be lifted.

Ever since the Reformation burst upon Europe with the printing-press already in full work, Catholics have been keenly alive to the importance of utilising this engine to the highest of its power both for the defence of the Faith, and for the diffusion of the Truth.

The Catholic Press.

It may be safely asserted that their contributions to printed literature have always been from one point of view or another quite notable. It is true that their work has often had to be done under every species of difficulty, and sometimes under a censorship from English authorities far more stringent than that of the Roman Index. But these days are now long past, and the relative importance of the Catholic Press is still maintained up to the present day. Numbers do not indeed justify the publication of a Catholic daily paper, especially when we remember that all the existing powerful organs of this kind are secured by colossal interests of a financial kind in which Catholics have but a small part. But they can and do keep up several weekly journals, although here also there is great room for improvement and development. The truth is that we are so divided by local politics that no common line of policy outside of the universal interests of Catholicism seems feasible. Monthly periodicals are better able to keep aloof from what is local and momentary, and thus afford a better field for Catholic enterprises. The *Dublin Review* appears still full of life and vigour; the Jesuit Fathers have maintained the *Month* during a long and useful existence; the *Tablet*, though it appears weekly, possesses much of the character of a literary review. The *Universe* and *Catholic Times* have persevered in regular weekly publication in the midst of many vicissitudes. For strictly theological periodicals we are so far dependent upon Ireland and America, but several important series of religious and historical books have

LIFE IN MODERN ENGLAND

been brought out since the beginning of the Catholic Revival, such as the "Clifton Tracts," the "Oratorian Lives of the Saints," the "Jesuit Red Series," the "Notre Dame Lives of the Saints," the "Westminster Library," and others. If any single literary work deserves to be mentioned as rising above all passing controversy, and as grappling with a great subject on broad lines, showing an excellence of execution which makes it fit to be a classic, there can be little hesitation as to what that book is. It is the monumental "*Formation of Christendom*," by T. W. Allies (1813-1902), an Oxford scholar, who though old enough to be a contemporary of the Tractarians, survived into the present century. No English Catholic has produced anything that can be put in the same category with it unless we go far back into the distant past.

When due recognition has been given to the varied enterprises of the Catholic Press, it remains true that the most striking development of its activities in our days has been the Catholic Truth Society. This work of zeal was begun by Bishop Vaughan at Salford in 1872, but after a period of activity it gradually declined, and at last became practically extinct. A second attempt at the same work was made in 1884 by Mr James Britten with the co-operation of a band of devoted laymen in London, with the special object of spreading good and cheap Catholic literature for the edification of those within the fold and for the enlightenment of those still outside her fold. Meanwhile, Bishop Vaughan had become Archbishop of Westminster, and it is easy to imagine the enthusiasm with which he welcomed the effort to give the Society a new and extended life. The literary publications of the Society in history, biography, controversy, doctrine and devotional teaching now reach many hundreds of distinct pamphlets and books, the circulation of some of the most popular of these having mounted to hundreds of thousands of copies, while the collective output amounts to millions. The Catholic Truth Society has proved itself a most valuable auxiliary to the cause of the Church in England, and has done yeomen service in dispelling ignorance from the minds of those outside.

Catholic Truth Society.

Another work closely connected with the last named,

and one which has in a manner grown out of it, is the foundation of the Annual Catholic Conferences. The first of these was held in 1893, and since that date these gatherings have taken place in turn in nearly all the chief centres of religious life in the country. These conferences have afforded golden opportunities for the discussion of matters of general interest to the faithful members of the Church. Valuable papers have been read by leading representatives both of the clergy and of the laity, while much useful interchange of ideas by word of mouth has taken place in conversation among individuals. Moreover, both Cardinal Vaughan and his successor have chosen these assemblies as providing fitting occasions for authoritative pronouncements on great questions of the day. Finally, the conferences seem to have paved the way under the inspiration of Cardinal Bourne for the gathering of something of a still more general character, namely, the holding of an Annual Catholic Congress. The first of these latter assemblies met at Leeds in 1910, and was followed by others in Newcastle, Norwich, Plymouth, and Cardiff until the Great War of 1914-18 led almost perforce to the temporary cessation of all such peaceful celebrations.

Catholic Conference and Congress.

However great the importance of organising for the spread of Catholic Truth, this great end has not been allowed to monopolise the efforts which have been made in our midst to combine for the development of activities for the spread of the Church's ideals in the realms of practice. The *Catholic Social Guild* can justly claim to be grappling boldly and with some measure of success with that most pressing problem of our age which is often called the Social Question. The *Catholic Women's League* also has taken up work which both from its extent and its importance makes it a not unworthy compeer of the Societies already mentioned. A persevering effort is now being made to bind together all ranks of the laity in the essential duty of helping on the always increasing missionary needs of the Universal Church through the extension of the *Association of the Propagation of the Faith.* Alongside of this the *Society of St Vincent de Paul* has struck deep root in the charitable life of the country, and now comprises in England nearly four

Catholic Organisations.

hundred conferences with more than four thousand active members. There are aid societies, benefit societies, aged poor societies; there are Catholic hospitals, homes, refuges, and orphanages. Thus without scrupulously mentioning every noble and inspiring institution which is to be found in our ranks enough has been said to show that brilliant minds and energetic wills are at work with the object of equipping the Catholic body with all the apparatus of organisation needed to further her aims in the modern world.

With a hierarchy such as has been indicated in outline, with a relatively numerous body of clergy both secular and regular, with churches, convents, schools, and organisations such as those that have been pointed to above, the body of the faithful now possesses a corporate existence which is both definite and vigorous. To compare them with the days long since past, before the Reformation, they are now more numerous than those who lived in the land in the Norman period, only that then they were the whole nation, whereas now they are surrounded with thirty millions and more who neither believe the full Christian revelation, nor submit to the central authority in Christendom. There seems every reason to hope for steady and progressive growth within that limited circle which is united with the Universal Church. But there is a larger hope than that, which shines and glows before the minds of those whose highest aspirations are first for the coming of Christ's kingdom, and then for the real happiness of the island-kingdom which is their native land. This undying wish is that the England, so long the faithful servant of the Faith, of Catholic rites, and of the See of Peter, may once more become one with the undivided and indivisible Church which transcends all national boundaries.

LEADERS AND PRELATES

ENGLISH POPE
Adrian IV. Nicholas Breakspear (1154-1159)

ENGLISH CARDINALS

Robert Pulleyn, 1144-1147
Nicholas Breakspear, 1146-1154
Boso (nephew of Adrian IV.) Breakspear, 1155-1181
Stephen Langton, 1206-1228
Robert Curzon, 1212-1218
Robert Somercote, 1238-1241
John Kilwardby, O.P., 1278-1279
Thomas Joyce, O.P., 1305-1310
Walter Winterbourne, 1304-1305
Simon Langham, O.S.B., 1368-1376
Adam Easton, 1382-1397
Robert Hallam, 1411
Philip Repingdon, O.S.A., 1408-1424
Thomas Langley, 1411-1437
Henry Beaufort, 1426-1447
John Kemp, 1439-1454
Thomas Bourchier, 1473-1486
John Morton, 1493-1500

Christopher Bainbridge, 1511-.1514
Thomas Wolsey, 1515-1530
B. John Fisher, 1535
Reginald Pole, 1536-1558
William Peto, O.S.F., 1557-1558
William Allen, 1587-1594
Philip Howard, O.P., 1675-1694
Henry, Duke of York, 1747-1807
Thomas Weld, 1830-1837
Charles Acton, 1840-1847
Nicholas Wiseman, 1850-1865
Henry Edward Manning, 1875-1892
John Henry Newman, 1879-1890
Edward Howard, 1877-1892
Herbert Vaughan, 1898-1903
Francis Bourne, 1911
Francis Aidan Gasquet, O.S.B. 1914

ENGLISH ARCHBISHOPS AND BISHOPS
Canterbury

St Augustine, 597-604
St Laurence, 604-619
St Mellitus, 619-624
St Justus, 624-627
St Honorius, 627-653
St Deusdedit, 655-664
St Theodore, 668-690
St Brihtwald, 693-731
St Tatwin, 731-734
Nothelm, 735-740
Cuthbert, 741-758
Bregwin, 759-765

Jaenbert, 766-790
Ethelheard, 793-805
Wulfred, 805-832
Feologild, 832
Ceolnoth, 833-870
Ethelred, 870-889
Plegmund, 890-914
Athelm, 914-923
Wulfhelm, 923-942
St Odo, 942-959
St Dunstan, 960-988
Ethelgar, 988-989

582 LEADERS AND PRELATES

Sigric, 990-994
Alfric, 995-1005
St Elphege, 1005-1012
Lyfing, 1013-1020
St Ethelnoth, 1020-1038
St Eadsige, 1038-1050
Robert of Jumièges, 1051-1052
Stigand, 1052-1070
B. Lanfranc, 1070-1089
St Anselm, 1093-1109
Ralph d'Escures, 1114-1122
William de Corbeil, 1123-1136
Theobald, 1139-1161
St Thomas Becket, 1162-1170
Richard of Dover, 1174-1184
Baldwin, 1185-1190
Hubert Walter, 1193-1205
Stephen Langton, 1207-1228
Richard Grant, 1229-1231
St Edmund Rich, 1234-1240
B. Boniface of Savoy, 1245-1270

Robert Kilwardby, 1273-1279
John Peckham, 1279-1292
Robert Winchelsea, 1294-1313
Walter Reynolds, 1313-1327
Simon Meopham, 1328-1333
John Stratford, 1333-1348
Thomas Bradwardine, 1349
Simon Islip, 1349-1366
Simon Langham, 1366-1368
William Whittlesey, 1368-1374
Simon Sudbury, 1375-1381
William Courtenay, 1381-1396
Thomas Arundel, 1396-1414
Henry Chichele, 1414-1443
John Stafford, 1443-1452
John Kemp, 1452-1454
Thomas Bourchier, 1454-1486
John Morton, 1486-1500
Henry Dean, 1501-1503
William Warham, 1503-1532
Thomas Cranmer, 1533-1556
Reginald Pole, 1556-1558

ROCHESTER

St Justus, 604-624
Romanus, 624-627
St Paulinus, 633-644
Ithamar, 644-655
Damian, 655-664
Putta, 669-676
Chuichelm, 676-678
Gebmund, 678-693
Tobias, 693-726
Eadulf, 727
Dunno, 741
Eardulf, 747
Diora, 785-804
Weremund, 805
Beornmod, 805-842
Tatnoth, 844
Badenoth, uncertain
Weremund II., 860
Cuthwulf, 868
Swithwulf, 897
Ceolmund, 909
Kynfirth, 931
Burrhic, 946
Elfstan, 962-995
Godwin I., 995
Godwin II., 1046
Siward, 1058-1075
Ernost, 1075-1076
Gundulf, 1077-1108
Ralph d'Escures, 1108-1114
Ernulf, 1115-1124
John, 1125-1137
Ascelin, 1142-1148
Walter, 1148-1182
Waleran, 1182-1184

Gilbert Glanville, 1185-1214
Benedict de Sansetun, 1215-1226
Henry Sandford, 1227-1235
Richard Wendover, 1238-1250
Lawrence of St Martin, 1251-1274
Walter de Merton, 1274-1277
John Bradfield, 1278-1283
Thomas Ingoldsthorpe, 1283-1291
Thomas of Wouldham, 1292-1317
Haymo of Heath, 1319-1352
John Sheppey, 1353-1360
William Whittlesey, 1362-1364
Thomas Trilleck, 1364-1372
Thomas Brinton, 1373-1389
William Bottlesham, 1389-1400
John Bottlesham, 1400-1404
Richard Young, 1404-1418
John Kemp, 1419-1421
John Langton, 1422-1434
Thomas Brown, 1435-1436
William Wells, 1437-1444
John Lowe, 1444-1467
Thomas Rotherham, 1468-1472
John Alcock, 1472-1476
John Russell, 1476-1480
Edmund Audley, 1480-1492
Thomas Savage, 1493-1496
Richard Fitzjames, 1497-1503
B. John Fisher, 1504-1535
Maurice Griffin, 1554-1558

LEADERS AND PRELATES

St Mellitus, 604-619
St Cedda, 654-664
Wini, 670-675
St Erconwald, 675-693
Waldhere, 693-705
Ingwald, 705
Egwulf, 745
Ethelnoth, 811
Ceolbert, 824
Deorwulf, 860
Swithulf, 898
Elfstan I., uncertain
Theodred, uncertain
Wulstan I., 951-953
Brightelm, 953-959
St Dunstan, 959-960
Elfstan II., 961-995
Wulfstan II., 996-1003
Elfwin, 1004-1012
Elfwy, 1014-1035
Elfward, 1035-1044
Robert of Jumièges, 1044-1051
William, 1051-1075
Hugh d'Orivalle, 1075-1085
Maurice, 1086-1107
Richard de Beames, 1108-1127
Gilbert Universalis, 1128-1134
Robert de Sigillo, 1141-1151
Richard de Beames, 1152-1162
Gilbert Folliott, 1163-1187
Richard FitzNigel, 1189-1198
William de St Mere Eglise, 1199-1221
Eustace Fauconberg, 1221-1228

LONDON

Roger Niger, 1229-1241
Fulk Bassett, 1244-1259
Henry Wingham, 1260-1262
Henry Sandwich, 1263-1273
John Chishull, 1274-1280
Richard Gravesend, 1280-1303
Ralph Baldock, 1306-1313
Gilbert Segrave, 1313-1316
Richard Newport, 1317-1318
Stephen Gravesend, 1319-1338
Richard Bintworth, 1338-1339
Ralph Stratford, 1340-1354
Michael Northburgh, 1355-1361
Simon Sudbury, 1362-1375
William Courtenay, 1375-1381
Robert Braybroke, 1382-1404
Roger Walden, 1405-1406
Nicholas Bubwith, 1406-1407
Richard Clifford, 1407-1421
John Kemp, 1421-1426
William Gray, 1426-1431
Robert Fitzhugh, 1431-1436
Robert Gilbert, 1436-1448
Thomas Kemp, 1450-1489
Richard Hill, 1489-1496
Thomas Savage, 1496-1501
William Warham, 1502-1503
William Barons, 1504-1505
Richard Fitzjames, 1506-1522
Cuthbert Tunstall, 1522-1530
John Stokesley, 1530-1539
Edmund Bonner, 1540-1569

WINCHESTER

St Birinus, 634-650
Wini, 662-663
Leutherius, 670-676
St Hedda, 676-705
Daniel, 705-744
Hunfirth, 744-754
Cynehard, 754-766
Ethelheard, uncertain
Egbald, 778
Dudda, uncertain
Cynebert, 801
Ahlmund, 805
Wigfrith, 828
Herefrith, uncertain
Edmund, uncertain
Helmstan, 838
St Swithin, 852-862
Alfred, 862
Tumbert, 872
Denewulf, 879-908
St Frithstan, 909-931
St Beornstan, 931-934

St Elphege, 934-951
Elfsine, 951-959
Brighthelm, 960-963
St Ethelwold, 963-982
St Elphege II., 982-1005
Kenwulf, 1005
Ethelwold II., 1006
Alfsige II., 1014-1032
Alfwin, 1032-1047
Stigand, 1047-1070
Walkelin, 1070-1098
William Giffard, 1109-1129
Henry of Blois, 1129-1171
Richard Tocliffe, 1174-1188
Godfrey de Lucy, 1189-1204
Peter des Roches, 1205-1238
William Raleigh, 1244-1250
Aylmer de Valence, 1260
John Gervais, 1262-1268
Nicholas Ely, 1268-1280
John of Pontoise, 1282-1304
Henry Woodlock, 1305-1316

584 LEADERS AND PRELATES

John Sandale, 1316-1319
Reginald Asser, 1320-1323
John Stratford, 1323-1333
Adam Orlton, 1333-1345
William Edington, 1346-1366
William of Wykeham, 1367-1404
Henry Beaufort, 1405-1447

William of Waynflete, 1447-1486
Peter Courtenay, 1487-1492
Thomas Langton, 1493-1501
Richard Fox, 1501-1528
Thomas Wolsey, 1529-1531
Stephen Gardiner, 1531-1555
John White, 1556-1560

SALISBURY (SARUM)

St Osmund, 1078-1099
Roger the Great, 1107-1139
Jocelyn Bailleul, 1142-1184
Hubert FitzWalter, 1189-1193
Herbert Poore, 1194-1217
Richard Poore, 1217-1229
Robert Bingham, 1229-1246
William of York, 1247-1256
Giles Bridport, 1257-1262
Walter de la Wyle, 1263-1271
Robert Wickhampton, 1274-1284
Walter Scammell, 1284-1286
Henry Brandston, 1287-1288
William Corner, 1289-1291
Nicholas Longuespée, 1292-1297
Simon le Gand, 1297-1315

Roger Mortival, 1315-1330
Robert Wyvil, 1330-1375
Ralph Erghum, 1375-1388
John Waltham, 1388-1395
Richard Mitford, 1395-1407
Nicholas Bubwith, 1407
Robert Hallam, 1407-1417
John Chandler, 1417-1426
Robert Neville, 1427-1438
William Ayscough, 1438-1450
Richard Beauchamp, 1450-1481
Lionel Woodville, 1482-1484
Thomas Langton, 1485-1493
John Blyth, 1494-1499
Henry Dean, 1500-1501
Edmund Audley, 1502-1524
Lorenzo Campeggio, 1524

EXETER

Osbern, 1072-1103
William Warelwast, 1107-1136
Robert Chichester, 1138-1155
Robert Warelwast, 1155-1160
Bartholomew, 1162-1184
John FitzLuke, 1186-1191
Henry Marshall, 1194-1206
Simon of Apulia, 1214-1223
William Brewer, 1224-1244
Richard Blondy, 1245-1257
Walter Branscombe, 1258-1280
Peter Wyvil, 1280-1291
Thomas Button, 1292-1307
Walter Stapledon, 1308-1326
James Berkeley, 1327
John Grandison, 1327-1369

Thomas Brantingham, 1370-1394
Edmund Stafford, 1395-1419
John Catterick, 1419
Edmund Lacy, 1420-1455
George Neville, 1458-1464
John Booth, 1465-1478
Peter Courtenay, 1478-1487
Richard Fox, 1487-1492
Oliver King, 1493-1495
Richard Redman, 1496-1501
John Arundel, 1502-1504
Hugh Oldham, 1505-1519
John Voysey, 1519-1554
James Turberville, 1555

WELLS and then BATH AND WELLS

Athelm, 909-914
Wulfhelm, 914-923
St Elphege, 923-937
Wulfhelm, 938
Brighthelm, 956-973
Cyneward, 973-975
Siger, 975
Alfwin, 997
Lyfing, 999-1013

Ethelwin, 1013
Merewit, 1027-1033
Dudoc, 1033-1060
Giso, 1061-1088
John of Tours, 1088-1122
Godfrey, 1123-1135
Robert, 1136-1166
Reginald FitzJocelyn, 1174-1191

LEADERS AND PRELATES

Savaric, 1192-1205
Jocelyn Trotman, 1206-1242
Roger, 1244-1247
William Button, 1248-1264
Walter Giffard, 1265-1266
William Button, 1267-1274
Robert Burnell, 1275-1292
William March, 1293-1302
Walter Hasleshaw, 1302-1308
John Drokensford, 1309-1329
Ralph of Shrewsbury, 1329-1363
John Barnett, 1363-1366
John Harewell, 1366-1386

Walter Skirlaw, 1386-1388
Ralph Erghum, 1388-1400
Henry Bowett, 1401-1407
Nicholas Bubwith, 1407-1424
John Stafford, 1425-1443
Thomas Beckington, 1443-1465
Robert Stillington, 1466-1491
Richard Fox, 1492-1494
Oliver King, 1495-1503
Adrian di Castello, 1504
Thomas Wolsey, 1518
John Clerk, 1523-1541
Gilbert Bourne, 1554

HEREFORD

Putta, 669-688
Tyrtel, 693
Torthere, 710-727
Walstode, 727
Cuthbert, 736-740
Podda, 747
Hecca, 758
Ceadda, 770
Aldbert, 777
Esna, 785
Ceolmund, 788
Utel, 798
Wulfhard, 800
Beonna, 823
Eadulf, 836
Cuthwulf, 837
Mucel, 857
Deorlaf, 866
Cynemund, 888
Edgar, 901
Tidhelm, 930
Wulfhelm, 934-940
Alfric, 941
Athulf, 973
Athelstan, 1012-1056
Leofgar, 1056
Walter, 1061-1079
Robert de Losinga, 1079-1095
Gerard, 1096-1101
Reinhelm, 1107-1115
Geoffrey de Cliffe, 1115-1120
Richard, 1121-1127
Robert Bethune, 1131-1148

Gilbert Folliott, 1148-1163
Robert Maledun, 1163-1167
Robert Folliott, 1174-1186
William de Vere, 1186-1199
Giles Bruce, 1200-1215
Hugh de Mapenore, 1216-1219
Hugh Folliott, 1219-1234
Ralph Maidstone, 1234-1239
Peter d'Aquablanca, 1240-1268
John Britton, 1269-1275
St Thomas Cantelupe, 1275-1282
Richard Swinfield, 1283-1317
Adam Orlton, 1317-1327
Thomas Charlton, 1327-1344
John Trilleck, 1344-1360
Lewis Charlton, 1361-1369
William Courtenay, 1370-1375
John Gilbert, 1375-1389
John Trevenant, 1389-1404
Robert Mascall, 1404-1416
Edmund Lacy, 1417-1420
Thomas Polton, 1420-1421
Thomas Spofforth, 1422-1448
Richard Beauchamp, 1449-1450
Reginald Boulers, 1451-1453
John Stanbery, 1453-1474
Thomas Milling, 1474-1492
Edmund Audley, 1492-1502
Adrian di Castello, 1502-1504
Richard Mayew, 1504-1516
Charles Booth, 1516-1535

WORCESTER

Boisil, 680-691
Oftfor, 692-693
Egwin, 693-717
Wilfrid, 717-743
Milred, 743-775
Weremund, 775
Tilhere, 777

Theatored, 781-798
Danesert, 798-822
Edbert, 822
Aldwin, 848-872
Werefrith, 873-915
Ethelhun, 915
Wilfirth, 922

586 LEADERS AND PRELATES

Kinewold, 929-957
St Dunstan, 957-961
St Oswald, 961-992
Aldulf, 992-1002
Wolstan, 1003-1016
Leofsin, 1016-1033
Brihteag, 1033-1038
Lyfing, 1038-1044
Eldred, 1044-1061
St Wolstan, 1062-1095
Samson, 1096-1112
Theulf, 1115-1123
Simon, 1125-1150
John of Pageham, 1151-1158
Alfred, 1158-1160
Roger Fitzcount, 1164-1179
Baldwin, 1180-1185
William Northall, 1186-1190
Robert Fitzralph, 1191-1193
Henry de Soillis, 1193-1195
John of Coutances, 1196-1198
Mauger, 1200-1212
Walter Grey, 1214-1215
Sylvester of Evesham, 1216-1218
William of Blois, 1218-1236
Walter Cantelupe, 1237-1266
Nicholas Ely, 1266-1268

Godfrey Giffard, 1268-1302
William Gainsborough, 1302-1307
Walter Reynolds, 1308-1313
Walter Maidstone, 1313-1317
Thomas Cobham, 1317-1327
Adam Orlton, 1327-1333
Simon Montacute, 1334-1337
Thomas Hemenhale, 1337-1338
Wolstan Bransford, 1339-1349
John Thoresby, 1350-1352
Reginald Brian, 1352-1361
John Barnett, 1362-1363
William Whittlesey, 1364-1368
William Lynn, 1368-1373
Henry Wakefield, 1375-1395
Tideman, 1395-1401
Richard Clifford, 1401-1407
Thomas Peverel, 1407-1419
Philip Morgan, 1419-1426
Thomas Polton, 1426-1433
Thomas Bourchier, 1435-1443
John Carpenter, 1444-1476
John Alcock, 1476-1486
Robert Morton, 1487-1497
John de Gigli, 1497-1498
Sylvester de Gigli, 1498-1521
Richard Pate, 1554

LICHFIELD (CHESTER AND COVENTRY)

Diuma, 656-658
Ceollach, 658
Trumhere, 659-662
Jarman, 662-667
St Chad, 669-672
Winfrid, 672-675
Saxulf, 675-692
Hedda, 692
Aldwin, 721-737
Huitta, 737
Hemele, 752
Cuthfrith, 765
Berthun, 774
Higbert, 785-801
Aldulf, 803
Herewin, 816
Ethelwald, 818-828
Humbert, 828-870
Cynferth, uncertain
Tunbert, uncertain
Alfwin, 926
Algar, 941-948
Kinsige, 949
Winsige, 964
Elphege, 975
Godwin, 1004
Leofgar, 1020
Brithmar, 1026-1039

Wulfsy, 1039-1053
Leofwin, 1053-1067
Peter, 1072-1085
Robert, 1086-1117
Robert Peche, 1121-1127
Roger Clinton, 1129-1148
Walter Durdent, 1149-1160
Richard Peche, 1161-1182
Gerard la Pucelle, 1183-1184
Hugh Nonant, 1188-1198
Geoffrey Muschamp, 1198-1208
William Cornhill, 1215-1223
Alexander Stavenby, 1224-1238
Hugh Pateshull, 1240-1241
Roger Weseham, 1245-1256
Roger Longuespée, 1258-1295
Walter Langton, 1296-1321
Roger Northburgh, 1322-1359
Robert Stretton, 1360-1385
Walter Skirlaw, 1386
Richard Scrope, 1386-1398
John Burghill, 1398-1414
John Catterick, 1415-1419
William Hayworth, 1420-1447
William Booth, 1447-1452
Nicholas Close, 1452
Reginald Boulers, 1453-1459

LEADERS AND PRELATES 587

John Hales, 1459-1490
William Smith, 1493-1496
John Arundel, 1496-1502

Geoffrey Blyth, 1503-1533
Ralph Bayne, 1554

LINCOLN

Remigius, 1092
Robert Bloët, 1094-1123
Alexander, 1123-1148
Robert Chesney, 1148-1167
Walter de Coutances, 1183-1186
St Hugh of Avalon, 1186-1200
William of Blois, 1203-1206
Hugh Wallis, 1209-1235
Robert Grosseteste, 1235-1253
Henry Lexington, 1254-1258
Richard Gravesend, 1258-1279
Oliver Sutton, 1280-1299
John Alderby, 1300-1320
Henry Burghersh, 1320-1340
Thomas Beck, 1342-1347

John Gynwell, 1347-1362
John Buckingham, 1363-1398
Henry Beaufort, 1398-1405
Philip Repingdon, 1405-1419
Richard Fleming, 1420-1431
William Grey, 1431-1436
William Alnwick, 1436-1449
Marmaduke Lumley, 1450
John Chadworth, 1452-1471
Thomas Rotherham, 1472-1480
John Russell, 1480-1494
William Smith, 1496-1514
Thomas Wolsey, 1514
William Atwater, 1514-1521
John Longland, 1521-1547
John White, 1554-1556

NORWICH

Herbert de Losinga, 1091-1119
Everard, 1121-1145
William de Turbe, 1146-1174
John of Oxford, 1175-1200
John de Grey, 1200-1214
Pandulf, 1222-1226
Thomas Blunville, 1226-1236
William Raleigh, 1239-1244
Walter Suffield, 1245-1257
Simon de Wanton, 1258-1266
Roger Skirving, 1266-1278
William Middleton, 1278-1288
Ralph Walpole, 1289-1299
John Salmon, 1299-1325
William Ayermin, 1325-1336

Anthony Beck, 1337-1343
William Bateman, 1344-1355
Thomas Percy, 1356-1369
Henry Spenser, 1370-1406
Alexander Tottington, 1407-1413
Richard Courtenay, 1413-1415
John Wakering, 1416-1425
William Alnwick, 1426-1436
Thomas Brown, 1436-1445
Walter Hart, 1446-1472
James Goldwell, 1472-1499
Thomas Jane, 1499-1500
Richard Nykke, 1501-1536

ELY

Hervey, 1109-1131
Nigel, 1133-1169
Geoffrey Riddell, 1174-1189
William Longchamp, 1189-1197
Eustace, 1198-1215
John Pherd, 1220-1225
Geoffrey de Burgh, 1225-1228
Hugh Norwold, 1229-1254
William Kilkenny, 1255-1256
Hugh Belsham, 1257-1286
John Kirby, 1286-1290
William Louth, 1290-1298
Ralph Walpole, 1299-1302
Robert Orford, 1302-1310
John Keaton, 1310-1316
John Hotham, 1316-1337

Simon Montacute, 1337-1345
Thomas de Lisle, 1345-1361
Simon Langham, 1362-1366
John Barnett, 1366-1373
Thomas Arundel, 1374-1388
John Fordham, 1388-1425
Philip Morgan, 1426-1435
Louis of Luxemburg, 1438-1443
Thomas Bourchier, 1443-1454
William Grey, 1454-1478
John Morton, 1479-1486
John Alcock, 1486-1500
Richard Redman, 1501-1505
James Stanley, 1506-1515
Nicholas West, 1515-1533
Thomas Thirlby, 1554

588 LEADERS AND PRELATES

CHICHESTER

Stigand, 1070-1087
Gosfrid, 1087-1088
Ralph Luffa, 1091-1122
Seffrid, 1125-1145
Hilary, 1147-1169
John Greenford, 1174-1180
Seffrid II., 1180-1204
Simon de Wells, 1204-1207
Richard Poore, 1215-1217
Ralph Wareham, 1218-1222
Ralph Neville, 1224-1244
St Richard de la Wych, 1245-1253
John Bishop, of Climping, 1254-1262
Stephen Berkstead, 1262-1287
Gilbert of St Leofard, 1288-1305
John Langton, 1305-1337
Robert Stratford, 1337-1362
William Lynn, 1362-1368
William Reade, 1368-1385
Thomas Rushook, 1385-1388
Richard Mitford, 1388-1395
Robert Waldby, 1396-1397
Robert Reade, 1397-1415
Stephen Patrington, 1417
Henry de la Ware, 1418-1420
John Kemp, 1421
Thomas Polton, 1421-1426
John Rickingale, 1426-1429
Simon Sydenham, 1431-1438
Richard Pratu, 1438-1445
Adam Moleyns, 1450
Reginald Peacock, 1450-1457
John Arundel, 1459-1477
Edward Story, 1478-1503
Richard Fitzjames, 1503-1506
Robert Sherborne, 1508-1536
John Christopherson, 1557-1558

YORK

St Paulinus, 625-633
St Ceadda, 664-669
St Wilfrid, 669-692
Bosa, 692-705
St John of Beverley, 705-718
Wilfrid II., 718-732
St Egbert, 734-766
Ethelbert, 767-780
Eanbald I., 780-796
Eanbald II., 796
Wulfsy, 813
Wigmund, 837
Wulfhere, 854-900
Ethelbald, 900
Rodewald, uncertain
Wulfstan I., 931-956
Oskytel, 958-971
St Oswald, 972-992
Aldwulf, 995-1002
Wulfstan II., 1003-1023
Alfric Puttoc, 1023-1051
Kinsy, 1051-1060
Eldred, 1061-1070
Thomas of Bayeux, 1070-1100
Gerard, 1101-1108
Thomas II., 1109-1114
Thurstan, 1119-1140
St William of York, 1143-1154
Henry Murdach, 1147-1153
Roger of Pont l'Eveque, 1154-1181
Geoffrey Plantagenet, 1191-1212
Walter de Grey, 1215-1255
Sewall de Boville, 1256-1258
Geoffrey Ludham, 1258-1265
Walter Giffard, 1266-1279
William Wickwain, 1279-1285
John Romayne, 1286-1296
Henry of Newark, 1298-1299
Thomas Corbridge, 1300-1303
William Greenfield, 1306-1315
William de Melton, 1317-1340
William de la Zonch, 1342-1352
John Thoresby, 1352-1373
Alexander Neville, 1374-1388
Thomas Fitzalan of Arundel, 1388-1396
Robert Waldby, 1397-1398
Richard Scrope, 1398-1405
Henry Bowett, 1407-1423
John Kemp, 1426-1452
William Booth, 1452-1464
George Neville, 1464-1476
Laurence Booth, 1476-1480
Thomas Rotherham, 1480-1500
Thomas Savage, 1501-1507
Christopher Bainbridge, 1508-1514
Thomas Wolsey, 1514-1530
Edward Lee, 1531-1544
Nicholas Heath, 1555-1579

LEADERS AND PRELATES

DURHAM

Aldhun, 1018
Edmund, 1020-1040
Edred, 1041
Ethelric, 1042-1056
Ethelwin, 1056-1070
Walcher, 1070-1080
William of St Calais, 1081-1096
Ralph Flambard, 1099-1128
Geoffrey Rufus, 1133-1140
William of St Barbe, 1143-1152
Hugh Pudsey, 1153-1195
Philip of Poitou, 1197-1208
Richard Marsh, 1217-1226
Richard Poore, 1229-1237
Nicholas Farnham, 1241-1249
Walter Kirkham, 1249-1260
Robert Stichell, 1261-1274
Robert of Holy Island, 1274-1283

Antony Beck, 1284-1306
Richard Kellaw, 1311-1316
Louis de Beaumont, 1318-1333
Richard de Bury, 1333-1345
Thomas Hatfield, 1345-1381
John Fordham, 1382-1388
Walter Skirlaw, 1388-1405
Thomas Langley, 1406-1437
Robert Neville, 1438-1457
Laurence Booth, 1457-1476
William Dudley, 1476-1483
John Sherwood, 1484-1494
Richard Fox, 1494-1501
William Senhouse, 1502-1505
Christopher Bainbridge, 1507-1508
Thomas Ruthall, 1509-1523
Thomas Wolsey, 1523-1530
Cuthbert Tunstall, 1530

CARLISLE

Adelulf, 1133-1156
Bernard, 1203
Hugh, 1219-1223
Walter Mauclerc, 1224-1246
Sylvester Everdon, 1247-1254
Thomas Vipont, 1255-1256
Robert de Chausse, 1258-1278
Ralph Ireton, 1280-1292
John Halton, 1292-1324
John Ross, 1325-1332
John Kirkby, 1332-1352
Gilbert Welton, 1353-1362
Thomas Appleby, 1363-1395
Robert Reade, 1396-1397
Thomas Merks, 1397-1399
William Strickland, 1400-1419

Roger Whelpdale, 1420-1423
William Barrow, 1423-1429
Marmaduke Lumley, 1430-1450
Nicholas Close, 1450-1452
William Percy, 1452-1462
John Kingscote, 1462-1463
Richard Scrope, 1464-1468
Edward Story, 1468-1478
Richard Bell, 1478-1495
William Senhouse, 1496-1502
Roger Leyburn, 1503-1508
John Penny, 1509-1520
John Kite, 1521-1537
Owen Oglethorpe, 1557

VICARS APOSTOLIC OF ENGLAND (1623-1688)

William Bishop, 1623-1624
John Leyburn, 1685-1688
Richard Smith, 1625-1655

FOUR DISTRICTS (1688-1840)

LONDON

John Leyburn, 1688-1702
Bonaventure Giffard, 1703-1734
Benjamin Petre, 1734-1758
Richard Challoner, 1758-1781

James Talbot, 1781-1790
John Douglass, 1790-1812
William Poynter, 1812-1827
James Bramston, 1827-1836
Thomas Griffiths, 1836-1840

MIDLAND

Bonaventure Giffard, 1687-1703
George Witham, 1703-1715
John Stonor, 1716-1756
John Hornyold, 1756-1778

Thomas Talbot, 1778-1795
Charles Berington, 1795-1798
Gregory Stapleton, 1801-1802
John Milner, 1803-1826
Thomas Walsh, 1826-1840

NORTHERN

James Smith, 1688-1711
George Witham, 1715-1725
Thomas Williams, 1725-1740
Edward Dicconson, 1741-1752
Francis Petre, 1752-1775
William Walton, 1775-1780

Matthew Gibson, 1780-1790
William Gibson, 1790-1821
Thomas Smith, 1821-1831
Thomas Penswick, 1831-1836
John Briggs, 1836-1840

WESTERN

Philip Ellis, 1688-1708
Matthew Pritchard, 1715-1750
Lawrence York, 1750-1763
Charles Walmesley, 1768-1797

William Sharrock, 1797-1809
Peter Collingridge, 1809-1829
Peter Baines, 1829-1840

EIGHT DISTRICTS (1840-1850)

LONDON

Thomas Griffiths, 1840-1847 | Thomas Walsh, 1848-1849
Nicholas Wiseman, 1849-1850

WESTERN

Peter Baines, 1840-1843
Charles Baggs, 1843-1845

W. B. Ullathorne, 1846-1848
J. W. Hendren, 1848-1850

CENTRAL

Thomas Walsh, 1840-1848 | W. B. Ullathorne, 1848-1850

EASTERN

William Wareing, 1840-1850

WELSH

Thomas Joseph Brown, O.S.B., 1840-1850

LANCASHIRE

George Brown, 1840-1850

YORKSHIRE

John Briggs, 1840-1850

NORTHERN

Francis Mostyn, 1840-1847 | William Riddell, 1847
William Hogarth, 1848-1850

RESTORED HIERARCHY

WESTMINSTER

Nicholas Wiseman, 1850-1865
Henry Edward Manning, 1865-1892

Herbert Vaughan, 1892-1903
Francis Bourne, 1903

SOUTHWARK

Thomas Grant, 1851-1870
James Danell, 1871-1881
Robert Coffin, C.Ss.R., 1882-1885

John Butt, 1885-1897
Francis Bourne, 1897-1903
Peter Amigo, 1904

PORTSMOUTH

John Virtue, 1882-1900 | John Baptist Cahill, 1900-1910
James Cotter, 1910

PLYMOUTH

George Errington, 1851-1855
William Vaughan, 1855-1902

Richard Graham, 1902-1911
John Kiely, 1911

CLIFTON

Joseph Hendren, O.S.F., 1850-1851
Thomas Burgess, 1851-1854

William Clifford, 1857-1893
William Brownlow, 1894-1901
George Burton, 1902

NORTHAMPTON

William Wareing, 1850-1858
Francis Amherst, 1858-1879

Arthur Riddell, 1880-1907
Frederic Keating, 1908

NOTTINGHAM

Joseph Hendren, O.S.F., 1851-1853
Richard Roskell, 1853-1874

Edward Bagshawe, 1874-1901
Robert Brindle, 1901-1915
Thomas Dunn, 1916

BIRMINGHAM

W. B. Ullathorne, O.S.B., 1850-1888 | Edward Ilsley, 1888

SHREWSBURY

James Brown, 1851-1881
Edmund Knight, 1882-1895
John Carroll, 1895-1897

Samuel Allen, 1897-1908
Hugh Singleton, 1908

MENEVIA AND NEWPORT

Thomas Brown, O.S.B., 1850-1880 | John Hedley, O.S.B., 1881-1898

MENEVIA

Francis Mostyn, 1898-1921

NEWPORT

John Hedley, 1898-1915

LIVERPOOL

George Brown, 1850-1856
Alexander Goss, 1856-1872

Bernard O'Reilly, 1873-1894
Thomas Whiteside, 1894-1921

SALFORD

William Turner, 1851-1872
Herbert Vaughan, 1872-1892

John Bilsborrow, 1892-1903
L. C. Casartelli, 1903

LEADERS AND PRELATES

BEVERLEY
John Briggs, 1850-1860 | Robert Cornthwaite, 1861-1879

LEEDS
Robert Cornthwaite, 1879-1890 | William Gordon, 1890-1911
| J. R. Cowgill, 1911

MIDDLESBROUGH
Richard Lacy, 1879

HEXHAM AND NEWCASTLE
William Hogarth, 1850-1866 | Henry O'Callaghan, 1888-1889
James Chadwick, 1866-1882 | T. W. Wilkinson, 1889-1909
John Bewick, 1882-1886 | Richard Collins, 1909

CARDIFF
James Bilsborrow, 1916-1921 | Francis Mostyn, 1921

BRENTWOOD
Bernard Ward, 1917-1920 | Arthur Doubleday, 1920

CHRONOLOGICAL INDEX

A.D. 63—St Joseph of Arimathea comes to Glastonbury.
,, 170—St Eleutherius sends missionaries to Britain.
,, 304—Martyrdom of St Alban the Protomartyr of Britain.
,, 314—Three British Bishops attend the Council of Arles.
,, 347—British Bishops attend the Council of Sardica.
,, 411—Withdrawal of the Roman Legions.
,, 429-30—First mission of St Germanus and St Lupus.
,, 447—Second mission of St Germanus and St Severus.
,, 449—First landing of the Jutes under Hengist and Horsa.
,, 477—Settlement of the South Saxons.
,, 495—Settlement of the West Saxons.
,, 530—Establishment of the East Saxon Kingdom.
,, 530—East Anglia settled by the Angles.
,, 547—Settlement of the Angles in Northumbria.
,, 586—Establishment of the Kingdom of Mercia.
,, 597—Landing of St Augustine at Ebbsfleet in Kent.
,, 601—Mellitus, Justus, and Paulinus join Augustine.
,, 604—Death of St Augustine and of St Gregory the Great.
,, 625—Mission of St Paulinus to Northumbria.
,, 633—SS. Felix and Fursey preach to the East Angles.
,, 634—Mission of St Birinus to the West Saxons.
,, 635—Joint labours of St Aidan and St Oswald.
,, 664—Synod of Whitby : St Hilda.
,, 668—St Theodore sent from Rome to Canterbury.
,, 673—Council of Hertford.
,, 681—Sussex, last of the Saxon Kingdoms, converted by St Wilfrid.
,, 685-7—St Cuthbert, Bishop of Lindisfarne.
,, 709—Death of St Wilfrid.
,, 735—St Bede, the Venerable, dies at Jarrow.
,, 747—Council of Cloveshoe.
,, 754—Martyrdom of St Boniface.
,, 765—Lichfield made an archbishopric for Mercia.
,, 785—Council of Chelcuith.
,, 787—First hostile landing of the Danes.
,, 800—Accession of King Egbert.
,, 803—Lichfield again becomes suffragan to Canterbury.
,, 816—Second Council of Chelcuith.
,, 852-62—St Swithin, Bishop of Winchester.
,, 870—Martyrdom of St Edmund.
,, 871—Accession of Alfred the Great.
,, 878—Peace of Wedmore.
,, 893—New Invasion of the Danes.
,, 901—Death of King Alfred.
,, 909—Increase in the number of Bishops in the Hierarchy.
,, 924—Death of Edward the Elder, and accession of Athelstan.
,, 937—Battle of Brunanburgh.
,, 940—Death of Athelstan.
,, 942—St Odo becomes Archbishop of Canterbury.

CHRONOLOGICAL INDEX

A.D. 959—St Odo is succeeded by St Dunstan.
,, 978—St Dunstan retires on the accession of Ethelred II.
,, 988—Death of St Dunstan.
,, 1002—Massacre of St Brice.
,, 1003-7—Ravages of the Danes in revenge.
,, 1012—Martyrdom of St Elphege.
,, 1013—Sweyn conquers England.
,, 1016—Edmund Ironside.
,, 1017—Canute the Great becomes king.
,, 1020—Death of Archbishop Lyfing.
,, 1027—Canute in Rome.
,, 1036—Death of Canute.
,, 1036-40—Harold Harefoot.
,, 1040-42—Hardicanute.
,, 1042—Accession of St Edward.
,, 1050—Dispute as to see of Canterbury at Eadsige's death.
,, 1053—Death of Earl Godwin.
,, 1066—Death of St Edward: Harold seizes the throne.
,, 1066—Battle of Hastings and accession of William the Conqueror.
,, 1070—Council of Winchester: Lanfranc Archbishop.
,, 1072—Second Council of Winchester.
,, 1075—Council at St Paul's, London.
,, 1086—Completion of Domesday Book.
,, 1087—Death of William I. and accession of William II.
,, 1089—Death of Lanfranc. Vacancy in the Primacy.
,, 1093—St Anselm Archbishop.
,, 1100—Death of William II. and accession of Henry I.
,, 1109—Death of St Anselm. Diocese founded at Ely.
,, 1129—Henry of Blois made Bishop of Winchester.
,, 1135—Stephen of Blois crowned king after death of Henry I.
,, 1143—The Council of London proclaims the Truce of God.
,, 1148—St Gilbert of Sempringham founds the Gilbertines.
,, 1153—Treaty of Wallingford.
,, 1154—Death of King Stephen and accession of Henry II.
,, 1162-70—Archiepiscopate of St Thomas Becket.
,, 1174—Henry II. does penance for the death of St Thomas.
,, 1176—Assize or Council of Northampton.
,, 1184—Baldwin becomes Archbishop of Canterbury.
,, 1186—St Hugh is chosen Bishop of Lincoln.
,, 1189—Henry II. is succeeded by his son Richard I.
,, 1191-2—Richard I. in Palestine on the Crusade.
,, 1193-4—Captivity of Richard I.
,, 1199—Death of Richard I. and accession of John.
,, 1200—Death of St Hugh of Lincoln.
,, 1207—Stephen Langton consecrated as Primate.
,, 1208—England placed under Interdict.
,, 1213—John does homage to the Papal Nuncio.
,, 1215—Magna Charta.
,, 1216—Death of King John: accession of Henry III.
,, 1217—Treaty of Lambeth secures the succession.
,, 1221—Coming of the Friars to England.
,, 1222—Provincial Council of Osney.
,, 1228—Death of Stephen Langton.
,, 1233—St Edmund becomes Archbishop of Canterbury.
,, 1236—Council of Merton.
,, 1240—Death of St Edmund.
,, 1245-53—St Richard ruled the see of Chichester.

CHRONOLOGICAL INDEX 595

A.D. 1258—Provisions of Oxford.
,, 1264—Battle of Lewes.
,, 1265—Commons summoned to Parliament.
,, 1270—Prince Edward goes on the Crusade.
,, 1272—Henry III. succeeded by Edward I.
,, 1275—The First Statute of Westminster.
,, 1275-82—St Thomas, Bishop of Hereford.
,, 1279—John Peckham made Archbishop of Canterbury.
,, 1282—Conquest of Wales.
,, 1292—End of Legislation of Edward I. Death of Peckham.
,, 1301—Confirmation of Charters.
,, 1307—Edward I. dies on his way to Scotland.
,, 1308—Edward II. made to banish Gaveston.
,, 1310—The Lords Ordainers.
,, 1314—Battle of Bannockburn.
,, 1322—Death of the Earl of Lancaster.
,, 1327—Deposition and death of Edward II.
,, 1338—Beginning of the Hundred Years' War.
,, 1346—Battles of Crécy and Neville's Cross.
,, 1348-9—First appearance of the Black Death.
,, 1351—Statute of Labourers.
,, 1353—Statute of Premunire.
,, 1360—Treaty of Bretigny.
,, 1376—The Good Parliament.
,, 1377—Death of Edward III. and accession of Richard II.
,, 1381—Rising of the Commons under Wat Tyler.
,, 1384—Death of John Wycliffe.
,, 1396—Thomas Arundel becomes Primate.
,, 1399—The House of Lancaster obtains the succession.
,, 1401—Statute of Heresy.
,, 1405—Revolt and execution of Archbishop Scrope.
,, 1413—Death of Henry IV.
,, 1414—Death of Archbishop Arundel.
,, 1415—Battle of Agincourt.
,, 1420—Treaty of Troyes.
,, 1422—Death of Henry V.
,, 1428—Siege of Orleans.
,, 1431—St Joan of Arc burnt at Rouen.
,, 1450—Insurrection of Jack Cade.
,, 1454—Thomas Bourchier succeeds to Canterbury.
,, 1455—The Wars of the Roses begin.
,, 1471—Battle of Tewkesbury.
,, 1476—William Caxton settles in England.
,, 1483-5—Usurpation of Richard III.
,, 1485—Battle of Bosworth Field and accession of Henry VII.
,, 1487—Conspiracy of Lambert Simnel.
,, 1497—Perkin Warbeck heads a rebellion.
,, 1509—Henry VII. succeeded by his son Henry VIII.
,, 1513—Wolsey becomes chief Minister.
,, 1520—Field of the Cloth of Gold.
,, 1521—Henry VIII. writes against Martin Luther.
,, 1527—First divorce proceedings for the King.
,, 1529—Fall of Wolsey.
,, 1533—Marriage and Coronation of Anne Boleyn.
,, 1533—Excommunication of Henry VIII.
,, 1534—Act of Royal Supremacy.
,, 1535—Martyrdom of BB. John Fisher, Thomas More, and the monks of the Charterhouse.

CHRONOLOGICAL INDEX

A.D. 1536-40—Suppression of the monasteries.
,, 1540—Execution of Thomas Cromwell.
,, 1547—Henry VIII. dies: accession of Edward VI.
,, 1549—First Book of Common Prayer.
,, 1549—Risings in Norfolk, Devonshire, and elsewhere.
,, 1551—Death of the Protector Somerset.
,, 1552—Second Book of Common Prayer.
,, 1553—Death of Edward VI. and accession of Mary.
,, 1554—Rebellion of Wyatt. Legation of Pole.
,, 1554—Reconciliation of England with the Papacy.
,, 1555—Execution of Protestants.
,, 1556—Execution of Cranmer.
,, 1558—Death of Queen Mary: accession of Elizabeth.
,, 1559—Royal Supremacy and Deprivation of the Bishops.
,, 1563—First Penal Law against Catholics.
,, 1569—Rising of the North.
,, 1570—Excommunication of Queen Elizabeth.
,, 1571—The Thirty-Nine Articles approved by Parliament.
,, 1576—First landing of the Seminary Priests.
,, 1577—Martyrdom of Blessed Cuthbert Mayne.
,, 1587—Execution of Mary Queen of Scots.
,, 1588—The Spanish Armada.
,, 1603—Death of Elizabeth and beginning of the Stuart Dynasty.
,, 1604—Hampton Court Conference.
,, 1605—Gunpowder Plot.
,, 1606—New Penal Code.
,, 1623—William Bishop, First Vicar-Apostolic.
,, 1625—Death of James I. and accession of Charles I.
,, 1632—The Panzani Mission.
,, 1640—The Short Parliament followed by the Long Parliament.
,, 1645—Battle of Naseby.
,, 1649—Execution of Charles I.
,, 1653-8—Protectorate of Oliver Cromwell.
,, 1660—Restoration of Charles II.
,, 1665—Plague of London.
,, 1666—Great Fire of London.
,, 1670—Secret Treaties of Dover.
,, 1678—Titus Oates Plot.
,, 1680—Execution of Lord Stafford.
,, 1681—Martyrdom of Blessed Oliver Plunket.
,, 1685—Death of Charles II. Rising of Argyll and Monmouth.
,, 1687—Declaration of Indulgence.
,, 1688—Landing of William, Prince of Orange.
,, 1689—Revolution: William and Mary made King and Queen. Four vicariates established.
,, 1702—Queen Anne succeeds to the crown.
,, 1713—Treaty of Utrecht.
,, 1714—Hanoverian line begins with George I.
,, 1715—Jacobite rising under the Earl of Mar and Lord Derwentwater.
,, 1738—Rise of Methodism.
,, 1745—Rising under Prince Charles Edward.
,, 1759-81—Bishop Challoner, Vicar-Apostolic in London.
,, 1778—The First Relief Act.
,, 1780—The Gordon Riots.
,, 1782—The Catholic Committee.
,, 1791—Second Relief Act.

CHRONOLOGICAL INDEX 597

A.D. 1793—Arrival of French Clergy at the Revolution.
,, 1794—Return of the exiled Religious Communities to England.
,, 1803-26—Episcopate of Bishop John Milner.
,, 1808—The Catholic Board.
,, 1828—Election of Daniel O'Connell for Co. Clare.
,, 1829—Catholic Emancipation Act.
,, 1840—Division of England into eight vicariates.
,, 1833-45—The Oxford Movement.
,, 1845—Reception into the Church of John Henry Newman.
,, 1850—Restoration of the English Hierarchy.
,, 1851—Ecclesiastical Titles Act.
,, 1853—First Provincial Council of Westminster at Oscott.
,, 1865—Death of Cardinal Wiseman. Henry Edward Manning becomes Archbishop of Westminster.
,, 1869-70—The Ecumenical Council of the Vatican.
,, 1872—Provincial Council of Westminster at Old Hall.
,, 1875—Archbishop Manning made Cardinal.
,, 1879—Newman made Cardinal.
,, 1890—Death of Newman.
,, 1892—Death of Manning: Bishop Herbert Vaughan becomes Archbishop of Westminster.
,, 1896—Invalidity of Anglican Orders declared.
,, 1902—Settlement of the Educational Controversy as to the Elementary Schools by Act of Parliament.
,, 1903—Death of Cardinal Vaughan: Bishop Francis Bourne made Archbishop of Westminster.
,, 1908—Eucharistic Congress in London.
,, 1911—Archbishop Bourne made Cardinal: Birmingham and Liverpool made Ecclesiastical Provinces.
,, 1914—Outbreak of the Great European War.
,, 1916—Metropolitan See created at Cardiff.

GENERAL INDEX

A

Abbeys of the Middle Ages, present use of, 331
Abel, Blessed Thomas, 375
Acton, Lord, 543
Acton, Mgr., 518
Acts of Henry VIII. against Holy See, 363
Adalbert, St, 136
Adelphi, Society of the, 529
Adelphius, Bishop of Lincoln, 7
Adrian, the Abbot, 44, 53
Aelred, Abbot of Rievaulx, St, 325
Aidan, St, 33, 39, 127
Alban, England's first Martyr, St, 5
Alcuin, 59; quoted on page 124
Aldhelm, Abbot of Malmesbury, St, 53
Alexander II. befriends St Thomas à Becket, 185; canonises him, 190
Alfred the Great, 75-84; his wars against the Danes, 76, 81; his work for the Church, 78; Alfred and literature, 80; his daily life and character, 82
Alfric, Archbishop of York, 108
Alien Priories in Mediaeval England, 323
Allegiance, controversy on the Oath of: in the reign of James I., 423; in the reign of William III., 462; in the reign of George III., 483; in the Bill of 1813, 505
Alleluia, Battle of, 10
Allen, Cardinal, 409-411

Allies, T. W., 577
All Souls College, Oxford, 294
Amphibalus, companion of St Alban, 6
Ampleforth College, 496, 516
Anchorites of Mediaeval England, 326
Ancren Riwle, the, 214, 327
Anglican Orders Controversy, 562-564
Anglo-Saxons, the coming of the, 11; story of their conversion, 17-42
Anglo-Saxon Chronicle, 80
Anglo-Saxon Church life, 123-140; architecture, 130; monasticism, 126-128; dealings with Rome, 124; relations with the State, 123
Annates and Appeals to Rome, 363, 393
Anne, 468
Anselm, St, 147, 150; becomes Archbishop, 155; Anselm and the Investiture Question, 156, 159; his writings, 160, 328
Apostolicæ Curæ, bull against Anglican Orders, 563
Arimathea, legend of Joseph of, 2
Arles; Council of, 6
Arlington, a member of the Cabal, 448
Armada, the, 415
Arrowsmith, Blessed Edmund, 434, 440
Arthur, King, 16
Articles, the Thirty-nine, under Edward VI., 384; under Elizabeth, 412; as expounded in "Tract 90," 524
Articles, the Six, 373, 380

GENERAL INDEX

Arundel, Archbishop of Canterbury, 277-292; banished by Richard II., 280; returns to his see, 282; holds a famous convocation, 284; makes first official use of "Our Lady's Dowry," 284; protests against confiscation of Church property, 286; his dealings with the Lollards, 291
Arviragus, King of Britain, 2
Ashby, S.J., the Ven. Ralph, 422
Ashdown, Alfred's Battle against Danes, 68
Aske, Robert, leader of the Pilgrimage of Grace, 370
Asser, Bishop of Sherborne, 80
"Assertio Septem Sacramentorum" of Henry VIII., 352
Association for Promoting the Union of Christendom, 538
Association of the Propagation of the Faith, 578
Athelstan, King, 86
Aungerville de Bury, Bishop of Durham, 254
Augmentations, Court of, 369
Augustine, St, his landing, 18; founds the see of Canterbury, 20; letters from St Gregory, 22; his death and life work, 25
Aulus Plautius, 4
Austin Canons, 322
Austin Friars, 323
Auxiliary Bishops in Middle Ages, 321
Avalon, 2

B

BABINGTON PLOT, 414
Bagshawe, Archbishop, 549
Bainbridge, Cardinal Christopher, 341, 348
Baines, Bishop P. A., Vicar-Apostolic of Western District, 509; founds Prior Park College, 516, 518, 526
Ball, John, 273
Baltimore, Lord, 435
Bangor, Episcopal see and Monastery of, 13; slaughter of monks, 24
Bannockburn, Battle of, 248

Barff, 553
Barlow, O.S.B., the Ven. Edward, 438
Barons' War, the, 225, 230
Beaufort, Cardinal, 288-301; makes peace with France, 299
Beche, Thomas, Abbot of Colchester, 374
Beck, Anthony, Bishop of Durham, 244
Bede, the Venerable, quoted on pp. 3, 5, 20, 23, 48; his life and writings, 49, 133
Bedingfield, Mother Frances, 446
Benedictines, the: established at Christchurch, 25; at Ely, etc., 97; in the Middle Ages, 322; re-established by Mary, 392; by James II., 459; return from Douay, 495, 528; in Western District, 516; in modern times, 572
Benefices in England given to foreigners, 226, 228, 263, 279, 319, 352
Benet Biscop, St, 35, 44, 47, 127; zeal for Divine Office, 129; goes to Rome, 133, 134
Benignus, St, 2
Benson, Archbishop, 562
Bentley, J. F., 559
Berington, Bishop, 489, 513
Bertha, wife of King Ethelbert, 19
Birinus, St, 38
Birkhead, George, Archpriest, 424
Birt, Dom: quoted, 403
Bishop, Bishop William, Vicar-Apostolic under James I., 427
Bishops under Elizabeth, sufferings of, 398, 400
Black Death, the, 258, 261
Blackwell, the Archpriest, 412, 423
Boleyn, Anne, 354, 356; marries Henry VIII., 359; her execution, 361
Boniface, St, 137, *sqq.*
Boniface of Savoy, Blessed, 224
Bonner, Bishop, 360, 378, 391; Bonner and the Marian Persecution, 393; his death, 400

GENERAL INDEX

Bosworth, Battle of, 314
Bourchier, Archbishop of Canterbury, Cardinal Thomas, 307; recalls Caxton to England, 311
Bourne, Cardinal, 565, *sqq.*
Bradwardine, Thomas, 262
Bramston, Bishop, 509, 515
Branch Theory, the, 521
Briggs, Bishop, 519
Bristow, Dr Richard, 410
Brown, Bishop G., of the Lancashire District, 519, 533
Brown, J., first Bishop of Shrewsbury, 533
Brown, T., Bishop of Western District, 518, 533
Bruce, Robert, 243
Bullaker, O.S.F., Thomas, 439
Burgess, Bishop of Clifton, 533
Burke, Edmund, works for Catholic Relief Act, 483, 492, 494
Burnell, Chancellor of Edward I., 234
Bury St Edmund's, 72, 373
Butler, Alban, 478
Butler, Charles, 479; dealings with the Catholic Committee, 489; drafts a Relief Bill, 490; Butler and the Catholic Board, 501; drafts the Bill of 1813, 504; his death, 515
Butt, Bishop, 549
Byrd, William, 334

C

CABAL MINISTRY, 448
Cade's Rebellion, 303
Cædmon, 40
Caerleon-on-Usk, 4
Calcuith, enactments of the Council of, 61, 69
Callixtus II., Pope, 161, 171
Cambridge University, foundation of, 165; Cambridge in the Middle Ages, 328
Campeggio, Cardinal, 351, 355
Campion, Blessed Edmund, 412, *sqq.*
Canning, 504
Canonesses of St Augustine, 323
Canons Regular, 322

Cantelupe, Walter de, 219; defends pluralities, 221; supports the cause of the Barons, 225
Canterbury, foundation of the see, 20; of Christchurch Abbey, 25; Archbishops in the eighth century; loses part of its territory to Lichfield, 61; regains it, 63; captured by the Danes, 104; rivalry between Saxons and Normans for the primacy, 114, 115; power of the primate in Saxon times, 124; Canterbury and Rome in Saxon times, 124, 135, in Middle Ages, 316, 317; saintly primates, 139; quarrels between Canterbury and York, 142, 162, 183, 188, 247, 264; the famous election of 1205, 206; contested election under Henry III., 217; Canterbury registers taken to Rome and lost, 234; King Edward II. opposes the choice of the monks, 247; visitation of the Archbishop resisted by the Bishop of Exeter, 253; the primates and the Statute of Provisors, 263, 264
Canute, 107; his letter from Rome, 109
Capel, Mgr., 553
Capes, Mr, 543
Carlisle, foundation of the see of, 165
Carmelites, 323
Caroline Converts, 435
Caroline High Churchmen, 437
Carthusians, Order of the, introduced by Henry II., 197; foundation of the monastery at Sheen; Carthusians in the Middle Ages, 322; the Carthusian martyrs, 365; return under Mary, 392
Castelli, Bishop of Salisbury, 342, 352
Catesby, 421
Catterick, John, martyr under the Commonwealth, 438

Cathedrals of England, 331
Catherine of Aragon, 354, 360
Catherine of Braganza, 443
Catholic Board, the, founded, 501; Board and the Veto Question, 502-508; expels Bishop Milner, 505
Catholic Committee, the, 480 487; the Committee and the Vicars-Apostolic, 488; Committee's work on the Catholic Relief Bill, 492
Catholic Congresses, 578
Catholic Social Guild, 578
Catholic Social Union, 564
Catholic Truth Society, 577
Catholic Women's League, 578
Catholic Worship, in Anglo-Saxon times, 128; promulgated by Council of Calcuith, 61; in Lanfranc's time, 146; points insisted on in 1222, 216; council of St Edmund Rich, 220; Catholic rites abandoned under Edward VI., 380, 384
Caxton, 311
Cecil, Lord, 397, 405
Cedd, St, 35, 41
Celestine, Pope St, 10
Celestius, companion of Pelagius, 9
Ceolfrid, Abbot of Jarrow, 48
Ceolwulf, St, 58
Chad, St, 35, 44
Chadwick, Bishop, 549
Challoner, Bishop, 464, 473; his writings, 475; his work in London, 478; the Bishop and the Relief Act, 482; his death, 486
Charles I., 429-439
Charles II., 441-454
Charles Edward, the Young Pretender, 469
Charter of rights under Stephen, 168
Chichele, Archbishop of Canterbury, 288, 291, 293; founds colleges at Oxford, 293, 302
Christ Church College, Oxford, 354
Christian Brothers, the, 574

Church property, confiscated by Henry VIII., 369, 392; allowed to remain in owners' hands, 392
Church-shot, 131
Cistercians, Order of the, introduced into England, 172, 175, 177; in the Middle Ages, 322
Civil War, the Catholics in, 434, 441
Clare Election of Daniel O'Connell, 510
Clarendon, Constitutions of. 183; compromise between Henry II. and the Bishops, 192
Claudia, wife of Pudens, 4
Clement V., 242, 245, 247
Clement VII., 352; dealings with Henry VIII., 355; excommunicates Henry, 366
Clement, Margaret, 366
Clergy, the, legislation in Saxon times, 45, 57; legislated for by Lanfranc, 146; by St Edmund Rich, 220; by Langton, 216; they fall away under Henry VIII., 364; under Elizabeth, 402, 416; number under Charles I., 432
"*Clericis Laicos*," Bull of Boniface VIII., 240
Clifford, Hugh, Bishop of Clifton, 540
Clifford, Lord, 448
Cloth of Gold, the Field of the, 351
Cloveshoe, Council of, 57
Cluniac Benedictines, 175, 177
Coffin, Robert A., 521, 524, 547, 549
Colet, Dean of St Paul's, 329, 344
Collingridge, Peter, Vicar-Apostolic of the West District, 501, 505, 516
Colman, St., 35, 39
Colombière, the Ven. Father de la, 445
Columba, St, 33, 40
Common Prayer, Book of, the first book, 381; the second book, 384, 399
Commonwealth, the, 440
"Comperta," the, 369

GENERAL INDEX 603

Confirmation of charters under Edward I., 241
Confiscation of Chantries, 380
Constance, Council of, English Bishops at, 389
Constantine the Great, 7
Constitutions of St Edmund Rich, 220
Controversy, works of Catholic, Cardinal Allen's, 409; Campion and Parsons, 412; in the days of James I., 423, 427; Father Davenport, 445; John Gother, 465; Challoner, 475; Charles Butler, 480; Milner, 500; John Kirk, 513; Catholic Truth Society, 577
Convocation of Archbishop Arundel, the, 284
Converts' Aid Society, 564
Corby, the Ven. Ralph, 439
Cornthwaite, first Bishop of Beverley, 549
Corporation Act, the, 447
Correctorium of the Bible, Lanfranc's, 147
Courtenay, Bishop of London, 269; condemns Wycliffe, 275
Coventry and Chester Miracle Plays, 330
Cranmer, Archbishop, his election, 358; tries the Divorce Case, 360, 361; enforces the Royal Supremacy, 364; publishes Book of Common Prayer, etc., 381, 384; his death, 393
Cressy, O.S.B., 435
Cromwell, Oliver, 440
Cromwell, Thomas, 357; visits the monasteries, 368; fall and death, 376
Crusades, the, 199, 232
Customs of Henry II., the royal, 183
Cuthbert St, 41, *sqq.*

D

DALGAIRNS, FATHER, 524, 545
Danegeld, the, 102
Danelagh, the, 73
Danes, the, their first coming, 67; the Danes and Alfred, 73, 81, 85, 100

Daniel, St, 13
Davenport, Father Christopher, 444
David of Wales, St, 13
De Burgh, Hubert, 215
De Grey, Archbishop of York, 213
" *De Haeretico Comburendo* " Statute, 286, 392
De Lisle, Ambrose, 527, 538
Derwentwater, Earl of, 468
Despenser, Bishop of Norwich, 274
Despensers, the, 249
Devas, C. S., 553
Devonshire revolt under Edward VI., 383
Diocesan Seminaries, 550, 559, 565
Dioceses in England, in Saxon days, 125; new dioceses founded under Henry I., 165; in Middle Ages, 319, 321; in modern times, 531, 567
Divine office in Anglo-Saxon days, 129
Divorce case of Henry VIII., 354, 358, 360
Döllinger, Dr, 543
Domesday Book, 151, 153
Dominicans, Order of the, first coming to England, 224; settle at Blackfriars, 234; under Henry III., 244; in Middle Ages, 323; return under Mary, 391; in Stuart times, 444; in modern England, 528
Dominic, O.P., Father, 527
Dormer, Lady Jane, 395, 404
Douay, English College at, 409, 495
Douglass, Bishop, Vicar-Apostolic of London District, 491, 495, 503
Dover, the Secret Treaty of, 448
Downside Abbey, 496, 516, 522
Dowry, Our Lady's, 284
Dryden, John, 458, 465, 466
Dublin Review, 523, 545, 576
Dubritius, St, 13
Duckett, Ven. John, 439
Duns Scotus, 244
Dunstable, John, 334

GENERAL INDEX

Dunstan, St, 89-97; the saint exiled, 94; reforms Church and State, 95
Durham, burial-place of St Cuthbert, 42; under the Normans, 143; building of the Cathedral, 154; in Middle Ages, 320
Durham College, Oxford, 255

E

EADBALD, King of Kent, 27
East Anglia, conversion of, 37; reign of St Edmund, 72
Easter Controversy, the, St Augustine and the Britons, 24; St Lawrence and the Celts, 27; Pope Honorius and the Scots, 32; St Wilfrid adopts the Roman custom, 35; Roman custom adopted in Northumbria, 40; adopted by all England at Council of Hertford, 44, 54
Eborius, Bishop of York, 7
Ecclesiastical Commission court of James II., 458
Ecclesiastical courts, instituted by Lanfranc, 146; quarrel thereon between Henry II. and Becket, 181; Edward I. limits jurisdiction, 238; under Edward II., 246; their freedom upheld, 250; under Richard II., 273, 287
Ecclesiastical Titles Act, 532
Edbold, St, 73
Edgar the Peaceful, 94
Edmund I., 90
Edmund Rich, St, 218-223; his councils, 220; disputes with monks of Christchurch, 222
Edmund Ironside, 101, 106
Edmund the Martyr, St, 72
Edred and Edwy, 92
Education, battle for Catholic, Forster's Act, 546, 560; Act of 1902, 561; Mr Birrell's Act, 566
Edward I., 238-243; his laws, 237; Edward and the Church, 238
Edward II., 245-251

Edward III., 252-271; the Hundred Years' War, 256; mediation of the Holy See, 258; Edward passes Statute of Provisors, 263
Edward IV., 305, 312
Edward VI., 379-386; anti-Catholic legislation in the reign, 380, sqq.
Edward the Elder, 73, 84
Edward the Confessor, St, 111-123; quarrels between Saxon and Norman, 114; his laws, 118; founds Westminster Abbey, 120; character, 121
Edward the Martyr, St, 97
Edwin of Northumbria, 29-32
Egbert of Northumbria, St, 136
Egbert of York, St, 59, 126; his Penitentiary, 130
Egbert of Wessex, 65, 66, 71
Eldred of York, 118; crowns William I., 141, 142, 144
Elections, episcopal, in Saxon days, 124; in the Middle Ages, 318, sqq.
Eleuterius, Pope, St, 3
Elizabeth, Queen, 360-417; acts against the Faith, 398, 400, 408, 413, 415; the Queen and Trent, 405; her excommunication, 407; the Thirty-Nine Articles, 412
Ellis, Bishop, under James II., 463
Elphege, Archbishop of Canterbury, St, 97, 104
Ely, foundation of the see of, 165
Emancipation Act, its preparatory stages, 498-509; the Act, 510
Émigré Clergy, the French, 493; their work in England, 494
English College, Douay, foundation of, 409
English College, Rome, first foundation under Ine, 54, 62; Alfred protects it, 79; in Elizabethan times, 411, 412
Episcopal sees in England, in British Church, 7, 13, 14; in Saxon days, 125, 126; in Middle Ages, 319-321; Eng-

GENERAL INDEX 605

land divided into four vicariates, 463; into eight vicariates, 518; in modern times, 531, 533, 567
Erasmus, 344
Errington, Archbishop G., 533, 535, 543
Essex, conquered by the Angles, 12; brought to the Faith, 37
Ethelbert, King of Kent, 18-21
Ethelbert the Martyr, 62
Ethelfleda, Lady of Mercia, 84
Ethergar, Archbishop of Canterbury, 97, 101
Ethelnoth, Archbishop of Canterbury, under Canute, 108, 110
Ethelred I., 68
Ethelred II., the Unready, 100, *sqq.*
Etheldreda of Ely, St, 50, 127
Ethelwulf, 67; supposed to have originated tithes and Peter's Pence, 68
Eton College, 308, 329
Ettsandune, Battle of, 77
Eucharistic Congress of 1908, the, 566
Eugenius III., 175
Evangelicals, the, 519
Evesham, Battle of, 231
Exclusion Bill against James II., 452
Excommunication of Elizabeth, 407
Exeter College, Oxford, 251

F

Faber, Father, 524, 533
Faithful Companions of Jesus, Institute of the, 494
Farringdon, Abbot of Reading, 374
Fathers of Charity, 526
Feckenham, 392, 401
Felix, Apostle of Essex, St, 37, 125
Felton, Blessed John, 408
Fetherston, Blessed Richard, 375
Feudalism of the Normans, 315
Fidei Defensor, 352

Fief of the Holy See, England a, John takes oath of fealty, 207; the Pope acts on the assumption, 213, 215
Finan, St, 35, 39
Finance affairs of the Church, in Saxon times, 131; exactions of the popes in Middle Ages, 217, 221, 225, 227, 263
Fisher, Blessed John, 342; founds St John's College, 343, 352; defends Catherine of Aragon, 356, 360; refuses the Oath of Succession, 364; his death, 366
FitzWalter, Hubert, 201, 205
Flambard, Ralph, 153
"Flaminian Gate," Wiseman's Pastoral from the, 531
Folliott, Gilbert, Bishop of Hereford and London, 179, 181; opposes St Thomas à Beckett, 185, 187
Foreign Missions in Saxon times, 135
Fox, C. J., 492, 499
Fox, Bishop Richard, 337, 341
Franciscans, Order of the, 323; resist Henry VIII., 365; return under Mary, 391; under James II., 444, 458; return in nineteenth century, 528
Friars under Henry VIII., suppression of the, 372
Fursey, St, 87

G

Gairdner, Professor, quoted, 338, 351
Gallwey, S.J., Father, 547
"*Garden of the Soul*," Challoner's, 475
Gardiner, Bishop of Winchester, 355; heads the Catholic Party under Henry VIII., 378; under Edward VI., 380; his power under Mary, 386-390
Garnet, S.J., Father, 421
Gasquet, Cardinal, quoted, 344, 369, 545, 556, 562, 565
Gaveston, Piers, 245
Gaunt, John of, 268; befriends Wycliffe, 269, 272

GENERAL INDEX

Genoese Letter, the, 508
Gentili, Father, 526
Geoffrey Plantagenet, Archbishop of York, 194, 197
Gerard, S.J., Father, 421
Germanus of Auxerre, St, 10, 13
Gibson, Bishop, Vicar-Apostolic of the North, 490
Gibson, Bishop William, 491, 500
Giffard, Bishop, Vicar-Apostolic under James II., 463
Gigli, John and Sylvester de, Bishops of Worcester, 342, 350, 352
Gilbert of Sempringham, St, 120, 177, 322, sqq.
Gilbert the Universal, Bishop of London, 164
Gildas, St, 13
Gladstone, W. E., 523, 532, 543
Glastonbury Abbey, 1, 14, 53, 91, 96, 374
Godric of Finchale, St, 327
Godwin, Earl, 110, 113, 115
Goldwell, Bishop of St Asaph, 391; only English Bishop at Trent, 400
Goodman, Bishop of Worcester, convert under Charles I., 436, 445
Good Parliament of Edward III., 269
Gordon Riots, the, 484
Gother, Dr John, 465, 474
Grammar Schools, founded in the Middle Ages, 329
Grandison of Exeter, Bishop John, 252
Grant of Southwark, Bishop, 533
Grattan, 499, 504, 508
Greately in 928, Council of, 87
Greensted Church in Essex, 73
Greenway, S.J., Father, 421
Gregorian Chant in Saxon days, and in Middle Ages, 129, 334
Gregory I., Pope, St, 17; his letters to St Augustine, 22, 125
Gregory XVI Pope, 515; divides England into eight vicariates, 518

Griffiths, Bishop of the London vicariate, 518, 536
Grocyn, 344
Grosseteste, Bishop of Lincoln, 219; opposes papal exactions for money, 222, 227; his works, 226
Guilds of the Middle Ages, 330
Gundulf, 144, 155, 328
Gunpowder Plot, the, 420
Guthrun, 73

H

HALLAHAN, MOTHER MARGARET, 534
Halifax and Anglican orders, 562
Halsbury, Lord, quoted, 300
Hampton Court Conference, 419
Hardicanute, 110
Harold I., 110
Harold II., 117, 120, 122
Harrison, the Archpriest, W., 424
Hastings, Battle of, 122
Hatfield, Synod of, 47
Hay, Bishop, 482
Heath, Henry, martyr, 439
Heath, last Archbishop of York, 387, 391, 393, 397, 401
"Hedge priests," 403
Hedley, Cuthbert, Bishop of Newport, 550, 556
Helena, St, 7
Hendren, Bishop of Nottingham, 533
Henrietta Maria, Queen, 428, 432
Henry I., 158-165; quarrels with Anselm about investitures, 159, 161
Henry II., 176, 178-193; quarrels with the Church, 181-186; his laws, 193
Henry III., 212-232; is defended by the Holy See, 212, 215; quarrels with Barons, 229
Henry IV., 283-290
Henry V., 290-296; his dealings with the Lollards, 292
Henry VI., 296-305
Henry VII., 336-343

GENERAL INDEX

Henry VIII., 348-378; writes against Luther, 352; commences the divorce proceedings, 354-361; the Royal Supremacy, 363; Henry and the monasteries, 368-373; publishes the Six Articles, 373
Henry, Apostle of Finland, St, 139
Henry of Blois, Bishop of Winchester, 167, 169; made papal legate, 170, 175, 177
Heptarchy, the Saxon, 12, 37, 39
Herbert, St, 326
Herst, Richard, martyr, 435
Hertford, council under St Theodore, 44
Hierarchy, restoration of the, demanded in reign of James I., 424; by the Catholic Committee, 488; by Lingard and others, 517; by the Vicars-Apostolic, 530; the Restoration, 531, *sqq.*
High Church Party, in Caroline days, 437; in modern times, 562
Hilda of Whitby, St, 39
Hilton, Walter, author of the "Scale of Perfection," 327
"*Hind and the Panther*" of Dryden, 466
Hogarth, Bishop of Hexham, 533
Holland, S.J., Father Thomas, 439
Holywell, 15
Homelies, Cranmer's Book of, 379
Honorius III., 211
Honorius, Archbishop of Canterbury, 32
Hooper, 393
Hornyold, Vicar-Apostolic of the Midlands, 473; his travels and works, 476
Houghton, Blessed John, 365
Howard, Cardinal Thomas, 443, 466
Howard, William, 453
Huddleston, Father, 441; 443; attends Charles II. on his death-bed, 454
Hugh of Lincoln, St, 193, 197; builds Lincoln Cathedral, 198, 201, 205

Humanists, the English, 344, 351
Hundred Years' War, 256-302; the popes try to mediate, 258, 299
Hyde, Anne, 445

I

ILLUMINATION in the Middle Ages, art of, 332
Ilsley, Archbishop of Birmingham, 550
Iltyd, St, 13
Immaculate Conception, kept in the Middle Ages, 253
Ine, King of Wessex, 53; founds English hospice in Rome, 54
"Injunctions, the Book of," 379
Indulgence, Declaration of, published by Charles II., 443, 447; by James II., 459
Innocent III., Pope, 206
Innocent XI., Pope, 456
Institute of Mary, the, 440, 467
Interdict, England under, 206
Investitures, the quarrel about, 147, 158, 161
Iona, Island of, 33, 125
Ireland, coming of Irish missionaries, 33; English missionaries trained in Ireland, 136; effect of the Act of Union on English Catholic life, 498; Irish attend the Catholic Board, 502; Irish prelates and the Veto, 503, *sqq.*; Irish help to secure Emancipation, 510
Islip, Archbishop of Canterbury, 262; he amends the Statute of Provisors, 263; settles dispute between Canterbury and York, 264

J

JACOBITES, 467-472; English Catholics mostly Jacobite, 469, 472
Jaenbert, 58
James I., 418-429; formulates an Oath of Allegiance, 423; makes concessions to Spain and to Catholics, 425

James II., his conversion, 443, 445, 448; Parliament tries to exclude him from the throne, 449, 451; he ascends the throne, 454; grants toleration, 457, 459
Jane Grey, Lady, 385, *sqq.*
Jarrow, monastery of, 48
Jesuits: they are put over the English College, Rome, 411, 427; arrived in England, 413, 425; they found Stonyhurst, 528, 572
Jesus College, Cambridge, 342
Jewell, Bishop, 402
Joan of Arc, St, 297
John, 199-211; makes England a fief of the Holy See, 207; signs Magna Charta, 209
John of Beverley, St, 39, 49
John the Precentor, 47
Juliana of Norwich, 328
Julius II., Pope, 345, 348
Justus of Rochester, St, 23, 27

K

KEBLE, JOHN, 520
Kemp, Cardinal John, 302
Kenelm, St, 63
Kenilworth, the *Dictum of*, 232
Keogh, John, 510
Ket's rebellion under Edward VI., 382
Kilwardby, Cardinal, 234
King's Book, the, 377
King's College Chapel, 340
King's evil, cure for, 121
Kirk, John, 512
Kirkby, Mother Margaret, 327
Knights of St John, 323, 373
Knox, John, 384

L

LABOUR revolt under Richard II., 269, 273
Labourers, Statute of, 267
Ladies of Charity, 564
Lanfranc, 141-153; his synods, 145; as a scholar, 147, 328
Langham, Cardinal Simon, 264
Langton, 206-215; joins with the barons against John, 208; he is suspended by the legate, 210; holds a council for the reform of discipline, 216
Lateran, Second Council of, 170
Lateran, Fourth Council of, 210
Latimer, 380, 393
Laud, 437, 445
Lawrence, second Archbishop of Canterbury, St, 22, 27
Laws of Edward the Confessor, 118, 168, 173, 315
Layton and Leigh, Cromwell's visitors, 368
League, the Holy, 340, 348
Learning, state of, in Saxon times, 133; in Middle Ages, 328, *sqq.*
Leo X., 349, 352
Leo XIII., 549, 562
Leofric, 113
Letter to the Duke of Norfolk, Newman's, 544
Lewis, David, 525
Leyburn, first Vicar-Apostolic, 456, 463
Libellus Famosus of Edward III., 256
Lichfield, foundation of the see, 36; becomes an archbishopric, 61, 126; again becomes a suffragan of Canterbury, 63; cathedral built, 243
Lilly, William, 345
Linacre, Thomas, 344
Lincoln Cathedral built, 198
Lincoln, the Fair of, 213
Lindisfarne, monastery of, 33, 39, 41
Lingard, quoted, 382, 495, 511, 517
Lisbon College, 412
Lives of the Saints, Alban Butler's, 479
Llandaff, Book of, 3
Llandaff, see of, 13, *sqq.*
Llewellyn, Prince of Wales, 236, 240
Lockwood, John, martyr, 438
Lollards, the, 268, 276; condemned in council, 277. 285, 286, 299, 300; under Henry V., 291
London, 4; see founded, 23
London under Stephen, Council of, 174

GENERAL INDEX

Longchamp, Bishop of Ely, 196-199
Louis of France, St, 230
Louis, son of Philip Augustus, 211, 213
Lucius, King of Britain, 3
Lupus of Troyes, St, 10
Luther, 352
Lynwood, William, 300
Lyons, First Council of, 227

M

MACAULAY, 523; quoted, 368
Macbeth, 117
Macpherson, Rev. Mr, 506
Mad Parliament, the, 230
Madrid, English College at, 412
Magdalen College, Oxford, 308
Magna Charta, 205; obtained from John, 209; condemned by the Pope, 210; revision, 212; ordered to be hung in all churches, 239
Malcolm, 117
Malmesbury, William of, quoted, 2
Malo, St, 10
Manning, Cardinal, 523-556; becomes Archbishop, 543; holds Fourth Synod of Westminster, 547; his writings, 548; Manning and the University scheme, 551; death, 555
Manuscripts of the Middle Ages, 332
Marche, Monseigneur de la, 493
Margaret, St, 117
Margaret, Countess of Richmond, 343
Margaret of Anjou, 303
Margaret Pole, Blessed, 374, 376
Marian Bishops, their appointment, 391; refuse to crown Elizabeth, 398; their captivity and death, 400
Marian Persecution, the, 392, *sqq.*
Marsh, Adam, 227, 244
Marshall, Earl of Pembroke, 212
Martin, Dr Gregory, 410
Martyrs, the English, under Henry VIII., 365-368, 374, 375; under Elizabeth, 400, 408, 413, 415; under James I., 421; under Charles I., 434; under the Commonwealth, 438; under Charles II., 453
Mary Tudor, 385-395
Mary Queen of Scots, 405, 413
Mass, the, in Saxon times, 128; bequests for Masses, 335
Matthews, Sir John, 435
Matilda, the Empress, 164, 173, 175
Mayne, Blessed Cuthbert, 413
Meditations, Challoner's, 475
Mellitus of London, St, 23, 29, 36
Memoirs of Missionary Priests, Challoner's, 475
Meopham, Archbishop of Canterbury, 252
Mercenary soldiers first used in England, 382
Merciless Parliament, the, 279
Merry del Val, Cardinal, 563, 565
Merton College, Oxford, 234
Merton, Council of, 220
Metaphysical Society, 545
Midlands, evangelisation of the, under St Chad, 35; supremacy of Mercia, 56, 60; archbishopric for the Midlands under Offa, 60; Midlands and Wessex united, 84
Mildred, St, 51
Mill Hill College, 551, 558
Milner, Bishop, 480, 492, 499-510; Milner and Poynter, 500; Milner and the Veto Question, 502-506; he goes to Rome, 507; his death, 510
Miracle Plays, 330
Mise of Amiens under St Louis, 230
Mise of Lewes, 231
Missionary Priests, coming of the, 416
Mivart, Mr St George, 545, 553
Monasteries in British Church, 13, 14, 24; in Saxon days, 48, 126; in the Middle Ages,

2Q

321; suppressed under Henry VIII., 354, 358, 368-373
Montague, Viscount, 432, 449, 477
Montfort, Simon de, 229; convokes a model Parliament, 431
More, Blessed Thomas, 337; his humanist studies, 344, 346-352; becomes chancellor, 356; his arrest, 364, 366
Morse, S.J., Ven. Henry, 439
Mortmain, Statute of, 238
Morton, Cardinal John, 337, 341
Mostyn, Vicar-Apostolic of Northern District, Dr Francis, 519, 530
Mungo, St, 13
Music in Middle Ages, English, 334

N

NETTER, THOMAS, 288, 301
New College, Oxford, 266
Neville, Archbishop of York, George, 309
Neville, rebellion of Sir John, 375
Newman, Cardinal, at Oxford, 520-522; his conversion, 524; founds the Oratory, 525, 534, 536; Newman and the Vatican Council, 543, 544; Newman and the University, 551; made a cardinal, 554
Nicæa, Council of, 7
Nigel of Ely, 165, 167, 169, 178
Non-Jurors, the, 467
Norman Conquest, the, 140; effect, 315
Normandy, 112
Norfolk, family of, under Henry VIII., 370, 377, 378, 379; under Mary, 386; under Elizabeth, 406; under the Stuarts, 432, 443, 449, 477, 479; after the Emancipation, 511
Northallerton, Battle of, 171
North, Rising of the, 406, 408
Northampton, under Henry II., Council of, 184, 192

Northumberland, Earl of, 383, 385
Northumberland's Rising, 406
Northumbria, conversion of, 30-35; saints of, 39-43
Norwich, Cathedral, of, 165
Nunneries, in Saxon times, 39, 50, 51; in Middle Ages, 323; suppressed by Henry VIII., 372; return of the nuns, 446, 496; in modern times, 572

O

OAKLEY, CANON, 521, 524
Oates, Titus, 445; his early history and plot, 449-454
Oath of Allegiance, Controversy, under James I., 423; under William III., 462; at the time of the Relief Act, 483, 490, 505, 508
Oath of Supremacy, 363, 399, 508
Oath of Succession, 363
Oblates of St Charles, 526, 528, 535, 554
Ochino, 382
O'Connell, Daniel, 508, 510; takes up the repeal, 515, 523
Odo of Canterbury, St, 88, 90, 95
Offa of Mercia, King, 54, 60
Oftfor of Worcester, 39
Oglethorpe of Carlisle, Bishop, 398, 400
Oldcastle, Sir John, 391
Oldcorne, Father, 421
Old Hall College, 487, 495, 537, 547, 552, 566
Oliver, Dr George, 513
Oman, Professor, quoted, 341
Oratorians, the English, 525
Ordainers, the Lords, 246
Ordeal, Trial by, 131
Orleans, Battle of, 298
Orlton, Adam, 248, 250, 252
Osburga, St, 67
Oscott College, 487, 523, 533; First Provincial Synod, 536; Second Synod, 537, 552; central seminary, 560
Osmund, St, 149
Osney, Langton's synod at, 216

GENERAL INDEX

Oswald, St, Bishop of Worcester, 95
Oswald, St, King, 33, 38
Oswin, King of Northumbria, 34
Oswy, 35, 39
Otho, legate of Gregory IX., Cardinal, 220
Oxford and Wycliffe, 276
Oxford University, 294, 328
Oxford Movement, the, 519-522, 524

P

PAINTING in the Middle Ages, 332
Pallottini, the, 528
Pandulf, the legate, 207; excommunicates Langton, 210; befriends Henry III., 212
Panzani Mission and report under Charles I., 431, 437
Parish Churches of the Middle Ages, 331
Parishes in Middle Ages, 319, 320
Parker, first Protestant Archbishop, 401
Parliament and Church, dealings between, under Edward I., 238, 273; under Richard II., 275, 277, 279; under Henry IV., 283, 285, 286; under Henry V., 293; under Henry VI., 299; under Henry VIII., 363
Parsons, S.J., Father, 411, 413, 424
Passionists, congregation of, 527
Patrick, St, 2, 10
Paul IV., 392, 394
Paul V., 423
Paulinus, St, 23, 29, 32
Peacock, Bishop, 310
Peckham, Archbishop, 239
Peers, Catholic, under Charles I., 432; under Charles II., 449
Penda, King of Mercia, 32, 34
Pelagius, 9
Penal Laws, under Elizabeth, 399, 403, 408, 415; under James I., 419; James' Penal Code, 422; under Charles I., 433; under the Commonwealth, 438, 440; under Charles II., 452; James II. remits them, 457, 459; under William III., 461, 462; Walpoles' Penal Laws, 468, 472; effect of laws in eighteenth century, 477; beginning of relief, 480, 482; final relief, 492, 498, 501, 508, 510
Penitentiary of Egbert, the, 130
Penswick, Bishop, 509, 515
Percy, Blessed Thomas, 408
Perpendicular Style, 332, 340
Peterborough Abbey, 36
Peter des Roches, 208, 210, 214, 216, 219
Peter, Martyr, 382, 387
Peter's Pence, commenced by Offa, 54, 62; Ethelwulf's donation, 68; under Canute, 109, 131; the tax becomes heavy, 228, 263; Peter's Pence forbidden by Henry VIII., 363
Peto, Friar, 394
Petre, Bishop, 464
Petre, Father, 457
Petre, Francis, Bishop of Northern District, 473, 476
Pilgrimages in Anglo-Saxon days, 134
Pilgrimage of Grace, the, 370, 371
Pisa, English Bishops at Council of, 288, 301
Pitt, William, 489, 492, 494
Pius V., 407
Philip Augustus, 200, 204, 207, 211
Philip II. of Spain, 388, 394, 404, 414
Plegmund, Archbishop of Canterbury, 84
Plumtree, Blessed Thomas, 408
Plunket, Blessed Oliver, 453
Plunket's Emancipation Bill, 508
Pluralities, 96, 115, 117, 118; forbidden by Lanfranc, 146; defended by Cantelupe, 221; forbidden by Peckham, 239
Pole, Cardinal, 374, 379; legate under Mary, 387; reconciles England to the Holy See, 390, 391; death, 374

GENERAL INDEX

Poll Tax, the, 273
Pomponia, 4
Poor Clares, 496
Poore, Herbert, 214
Poore, Richard, Bishop of Salisbury, 214
Portal, the Abbé, 562
Powell, Blessed Richard, 375
Poynter, Bishop, 500; his quarrels with Milner, 503, 505, 507, 509, 515
Premonstratensians, 322
Press, the Catholic, 576
Premunire, Statute of, 263; renewed under Richard II., 279; protest of the Pope against it, 293, 299, 356
Price, martyr, Father, 439
Printing, invention of, 311
Prior Park College, 516, 526, 550
Pritchard, Bishop of Western District, 464, 476
Property of the Church, 131; confiscated under Henry IV., 286; alienated under Mary, 391, 392
Protestants from Germany, arrival of, 381
Protestation against papal dispensing power, the, 489
Provinces, division of England into, 567
Provinciale of Lynwood, the, 300
Provisions of Oxford, 230
Provisors, Statute of, 263; renewed under Richard II., 279; purpose of the law, 319
Pudens, 4
Puller, Mr, 562
Puritans, the, rise under Elizabeth, 412; their demands from James I., 419; their persecuting bigotry, 422, 429, 432, 433, 440
Pusey, Dr, 520, 524

Q

Quarantotti Rescript, the, 506
Quia Emptores statute of Edward I., 238
Quo Warranto, statute of Edward I., 238

R

Ralph d'Escures, 162
Reading Abbey, 164, 374
Redemptorists, congregation of the, 527
Redwald, 39
Regnans in Excelsis, bull of Pius V., 407
Relief Acts, Catholic, the Bill of 1778, 482; bills drafted by the Catholic Board and Committee, 488; the 1791 Bill, 492; preparatory steps to Emancipation, 498, 501; Charles Butler's Bill, 505; William Plunket's Bill, 508
Religious orders, the, in the Middle Ages, 321; in modern times, 526, 528, 571
Remnant in the Dark Days, the Catholic, 477
Renaissance in England, the, 336, 342
Restitutus, Bishop of London, 7
Restoration of the Catholic Faith under Mary, 387, 389
Revolution, effects of the French, 493
Reynolds, Archbishop of Canterbury, nominated by Edward II., 247; protests against a bishop being tried in civil courts, 250
Reynolds, Blessed Richard, 365
Reynolds, John, 410
Rheims, English College at, 410
Rhudlan, Statute of, 236
Richard I., 196-203; he taxes the clergy, 199, 201
Richard II., 271-284
Richard III., 312-314
Richard of Chichester, St, 219, 223
Richard of York, Duke, 303
Ridley, 393
Ripon, Abbey of, 35, 44, 46
Robert, Earl of Gloucester, 163, 168, 173
Robert, Duke of Normandy, 148, 152
Robert of Jumièges, 115
Rochester, see of, founded, 23; its position in the Middle Ages, 321

GENERAL INDEX

Rock, Dr Daniel, 529
Rockingham, Council of, 156
Roe, Father Bartholomew, martyr, 438
Roger, Archbishop of York, 182, 188, 194
Roger the Great, Bishop of Salisbury, 162; called to trial by Stephen, 169, 171
Rolle, Richard, 327
Roman Conquest of Britain, 4, 9
Roman Fees, English protests against, under Canute, 109, 131, 217; under Henry III., 221, 225; Bishop Grosseteste, 227, 229; under Edward III., 263
Romanos Pontifices, the Constitution, 548
Roman see, authority of, recognised in Saxon times, 124; in the Middle Ages, 316 318
Roskell, Bishop, 536, 540
Roses, the War of the, 304, *sqq.*
Rufinian, 23
Runnymede, 209

S

SACRAMENTS, Ritual of the, points insisted at the Council of Cloveshoe, 57; among the Saxons, 128-130, 150; under Lanfranc, 146; under Langton, 216; under St Edmund Rich, 220
Saints of the Anglo-Saxon Church, 139; saints of the British Church, 13, *sqq.*
Salisbury Cathedral, 214
Samson, St, 13
Sanctuary, right of, 132, 273
Sarum Rite, 150
Saville, Sir George, 483
Scandinavia evangelised, 138
Schism, the Great, 276, 287, 300
Scotch Wars of Edward I., 241, 248, 255
Scrope, Archbishop of York, 287
Sedgemoor, Battle of, 456
Selling, William, 344
Seminaries, English, 408, 410
Sergeant, John, 435

Settlement of Elizabeth, the, 398
Seven Bishops, trial of the, 459
Shaftesbury, Lord, 451
Sharples, Bishop, 530
Sheil, Richard Lalor, 510
Sicily offered to Henry III., 229
Sigebert, King of Essex, St, 36
Simnel, Lambert, 339
Simon Stock, St, 324, 326
Simony, 146
Sion Abbey, 296, 365
Siward, Earl of Northumberland, 113
Smith, Bishop of Chalcedon, Richard, 430; is opposed by the regulars, 431
Smith, Thomas, first President of Douay, 410, 382
Smith, Thomas, Vicar of the Northern District, 501, 509, 515
Social Revolution, the, 267, 273, 275
Society of St Vincent de Paul, 578
Somerset, the Lord Protector, 379-383
Soul-shot in Saxon times, 131
Southworth, John, martyr, 440
Spencer, Father Ignatius, 527
St Albans, Battle of, 305
St Charles' College, Bayswater, 553
St John, Father Ambrose, 524
St John's College, Cambridge, 343
St Omer, College at, 495
Stanbrook Abbey, 496
Standard, the Battle of the, 172
Stapleton, Bishop, 500
Statistics regarding Catholics in England, number of monasteries suppressed, 369, 372, 373; number of killed under Edward VI., 383; under Mary, 393; number of priests and laymen in Elizabeth's reign, 402, 404; number of priests in sixteenth century, 416; martyrs under Elizabeth, 413;

number of Catholics, etc., under Charles I., 431; Catholic peers under Charles II., 449; Catholics after 1745, 469, 478; at Wiseman's death, 540; in our days, 569
Statute of Labourers, 267
Statute of Westminster of Edward I., 237
Stephen, 167-177
Stephen Harding, St, 323
Stigand, 114; crowns Harold, 121, 141; he is deposed as a simoniac, 142
Stillingfleet, 465
Stonor, Dr John, Vicar-Apostolic of the Midlands, 464
Stonyhurst College, 495, 552
Storey, Blessed John, 408
Stratford, Archbishop of Canterbury, 253; his conflict with Edward III., 256
Straw, Jack, 273
Stubbs, Professor, quoted, 300
Succession, Oath of, 363
Sudbury, Archbishop, 266; tries Wycliffe, 269, 272; killed in Tyler's revolt, 273
Supremacy, the Royal, first mooted, 358; the Act, 363; refused by Fisher and More, 368; refused by Gardiner and others, 379; under Elizabeth, 399, 402, 404
Sussex, conversion of, 39
Sweyn, King of Denmark, 102
Swithin, St, 71, 80

T

TALBOT, JAMES, Bishop of the London District, 487, 490, 491
Talbot, Thomas, Bishop of the Midland District, 487, 491
Tallis, Thomas, 334
Taylor, Jeremy, 437
Taxation of the clergy forbidden by Boniface VIII., 240
Templars, the Knights, 323
Tenchebrai, Battle of, 159
Ten Reasons, Campion's, 413
Tertullian, quoted, 3
Test Act, the, 447, 458

Testament, the Douay, 410 revised by Challoner, 475
Theobald, Archbishop of Canterbury, 170, 174, 175, 178
Theodore, Archbishop of Canterbury, St, 37; visits his province, 44; deposes St Wilfrid, 46, 51; arranges episcopal sees, 125
Theodosius, 8
Thomas of Canterbury, St, 120, 175, 178-190; conflict with Henry II., 181; the Constitutions of Clarendon, 182; at Northampton, 182; he leaves England, 185; return and death, 188; plundering of the Shrine, 373
Thomas of Hereford, St, 235
Thompson, Gordon, 553
Thorpe, William, 286
Thurstan, Archbishop of York, 171
Tierney, Canon, 513, 529
Tithes, payment of, begun by Ethelwulf, 68; insisted on at the Council of Greately, 87; mentioned by Canute, 109; the obligation in Saxon Church, 131
Toleration Act, the, 460
Tonge, Dr, 450
Tostig, 122
Towneley Plays, the, 330
"Tract 90," 524
Tractarian Movement, the, 519, 554
Trent, the Council of, 405
Trinitarians, Order of the, 323
Troy, Archbishop of Dublin, 503, 507, 508
Truce of God, the, 174
Tunstall, Bishop of Durham, 353; restored by Mary, 387, 391; death, 401
Turketul, 93
Turketul, the Dane, 103, 105, 107
Turner, first Bishop of Salford, 533
Twin Statutes of Edward I., 239
Tyler's Revolt, Wat, 273

U

ULFRIC, ST, 177
Ullathorne, Archbishop, Vicar-

GENERAL INDEX 615

Apostolic, 519, 530; Bishop of Birmingham, 533, 542; answers Gladstone, 544, 550
Uniformity, Act of, first Act, 384; second Act, 399
Union, Act of, 498
Universalis Ecclesiæ, Bull of Pius IX., 531
Universities, in the Middle Ages, 328; the University question under Manning, 551; under Vaughan, 560
Urban II., 156
Ushaw College, 495, 550
Utopia, More's, 346

V

VACARIUS, ROGER, 175
Valladolid College, 412, 430
Vatican Council, the, 543, *sqq.*
Vaughan, Cardinal, Bishop of Salford, 549; founds Mill Hill, 551; becomes Archbishop, 557; fights for Catholic education, 559; on the Anglican Orders Controversy, 562; death, 564
Vaughan, Bishop William, 540, 549
"Venerabile," the, 411
Veto Controversy, the, first mooted, 499; introduced into the resolutions of the Catholic Board, 502; resisted by Milner, 503; introduced by Canning into Butler's Bill, 505; the Quarantotti Rescript, 506; admitted in Genoese letter, 508
Vicars-Apostolic, the plan of Fr. Parsons, 412; the secular clergy ask for Vicars-Apostolic, 424; a bishop appointed under James I., 427, 430; the regular object to Dr Smith, 431; bishops appointed under James II., 446; the Vicars-Apostolic at the Revolution, 463; under George II., 473; under George III., 487, 489, 491; Milner and Poynter, 500-509; agitation for the restoration of the Hierarchy, 517, 530; eight vicariates made, 518
Virgil, Polydore, 342

Virtue, Bishop, 549
Visitation of Bishops, 221, 225, 239, 253
Visitation of the clergy under Henry VIII., 365
Visitation of the monasteries, 368
Vortigern, 12

W

WALCHER of Durham, 143, 320
Waldensis, 301
Wales, the Church in, 12; its saints, 13; monasteries, 14, 236
Wallingford, the Treaty of, 176
Walmesley, Vicar-Apostolic of the Western District, 473; his writings, 476; during the Gordon Riots, 486, 491
Walsh, Bishop Thomas, 509, 516, 519
Walsingham, shrine of Our Lady of, 378
Waltham Abbey, 373
Walworth, Sir William, 272, 274
Warbeck, Perkin, 389
Ward, Mr W. G., 522; at Old Hall, 535; editor of the *Dublin*, 545
Wareing, Dr, first Bishop of Northampton, 518, 533
Warham, Thomas, Archbishop of Canterbury, 341; befriends Colet, 345, 350; upholds papal supremacy, 358
Waynflete, William, 308
Wearmouth, Abbey of, 47, 49, 127, 133
Wedmore, Peace of, 73, 77
Weedall, Dr, 519
Wesley, John, 485, 519
Wessex, its foundation, 12; evangelisation, 37; under King Ine, 53, 56; takes the lead in England, 64, 66
Westminster Abbey, 119, 331, 341
Westminster Cathedral, 559, 566
Westminster Synods, first synod, 536; second and third, 537; fourth, 547
Whitby Abbey, 39, 127
Whitby Synod, 40

White Canons, the, 322
Whiting, Blessed Richard, 374
Wight, the Isle of, 52
Wilfrid, St, 34; evangelises Sussex, 39; at the Synod of Whitby, 40; is restored to York, 44; appeals to Rome against St Theodore, 46; evangelises the Isle of Wight, 52, 126; his pilgrimages, 134; his missions, 135
William I., 121, 140-152; makes Lanfranc Archbishop, 142
William II., 148, 149-158; nominates St Anselm primate, 155
William III., 459
William of Malmesbury, quoted, 3, 101, 163
William of Norwich, the Boy Saint, 177
William of York, St, 172
Williams, Bishop of the Northern District, 464
Willibrord, St, 136
Winchelsea, Archbishop of Canterbury, 240, 245
Winchester, 4, 38, 143, 166, 300
Winchester under Lanfranc, Council of, 145
Winchester under Stephen, Council of, 169
Winchester School, 267, 329
Winifred, St, 15
Wiseman, Cardinal, 517, 519, 522-541; founds the *Dublin*, 523; Archbishop of Westminster, 531; relations with Dr Errington, 535; holds first synod, 536; his death, 540
Witan, the, 123
Witham, Vicar-Apostolic of the Midlands, 464
Wolsey, Cardinal, 349-358; papal legate, 351; statesman, 353; Wolsey and the divorce, 354; death, 357

Wolstan, St, 144, 149, 211
Woodhouse, Thomas, martyr, 408
Worthington, Dr Richard, 410
Wright, Ven. Peter, 440
Wulphere, King of Mercia, 35, 51
Wyatt's Rebellion, 388
Wycliffe, 268; teaching, 269, 273; condemned by the Church, 275; his death, 276; his works condemned at Oxford, 286
Wykeham, William of, 266; impeached by Parliament, 268; returns to favour, 272; his foundations, 329

Y

YORK, 4, 7; see founded, 23, 30; first foundation of the minster, 31; St Chad and St Wilfrid, Archbishops, 38, 44; St Egbert founds a famous school, 59, 71, 88; St Oswald, 96, 100, 108, 118, 125; metropolitan rights taken from and then restored to York, 126; York library, 133; Lanfranc and York, 142; quarrels with Canterbury, 162, 180, 182, 188, 247, 264; the Archbishop defeats the Scots, 171, 194, 213, 254, 302, 309, 346; in the Middle Ages, 317, 319; Wolsey, Archbishop, 350, 357, 364; Heath the last Archbishop, 387, 391, 397, 401
York, Lawrence, Vicar-Apostolic of the West, 464
York Plays, the, 330
Yorkshire Rising, the, 375
York, Henry, Cardinal Duke of, 471